A Practical Study
of Argument

THIRD EDITION

A Practical Study of Argument

TRUDY GOVIER
University of Calgary

WADSWORTH PUBLISHING COMPANY
Belmont, California
A Division of Wadsworth, Inc.

Philosophy Editor: *Kenneth King*
Editorial Assistant: *Cynthia Campbell*
Production Editor: *Jerilyn Emori*
Managing Designer: *Ann Butler*
Print Buyer: *Randy Hurst*
Permissions Editor: *Jeanne Bosschart*
Designer: *Wendy Calmenson*
Copy Editor: *Jennifer Gordon*
Compositor: *Weimer Typesetting Co., Inc.*
Cover: *Ann Butler*
Printer: *Malloy Lithographing, Inc.*

This book is printed on acid-free paper that meets Environmental Protection Agency standards for recycled paper.

Printed in the United States of America

1 2 3 4 5 6 7 8 9 10—96 95 94 93 92

Library of Congress Cataloging-in-Publication Data
Govier, Trudy.
  A practical study of argument / Trudy Govier.—3rd ed.
    p.   cm.
  Includes bibliographical references and index.
  ISBN 0-534-14712-7
  1. Reasoning. 2. Logic. I. Title.
BC177.G65   1991
  168—dc20   91-18111

CONTENTS

CHAPTER 3

When Is an Argument a Good One?   **61**

CHAPTER 4

Looking at Language   **87**

CHAPTER 5

Premises: What to Accept and Why   **116**

CHAPTER 6

Working on Relevance   *145*

CHAPTER 7

Those Tidy Deductions: Categorical Logic   *182*

CHAPTER 8

Those Tidy Deductions: Propositional Logic   *222*

CHAPTER 9

Analogies: Reasoning from Case to Case 267

CHAPTER 10

Conductive and Inductive Arguments 308

CHAPTER 11

Reflective Analysis of Longer Works 359

APPENDIX A

A Summary of Fallacies   **384**

APPENDIX B

Selected Essays for Analysis   **391**

 *PREFACE*

THIS BOOK IS INTENDED FOR ALL those who are interested in arguments and in arguing, and especially for university and college students taking courses designed to improve their ability to understand, construct, and criticize arguments. My goal has been to present enough theory to explain why certain kinds of arguments are good or bad and enough illustrations and examples to show how that theory can be used in practice. I present an integrated treatment of cogent argument and fallacies, of formal and informal techniques of analysis, of theory and practice. Many illustrations and exercises are given and suggestions for further practice or for examination material are made available in an Instructor's Manual.

My interest in the theory and practice of natural argumentation stems from an occasion in 1976 when someone asked me to review a text on informal fallacies. At the time, I was teaching an elementary course on formal logic to a large group of students for whom it was compulsory and—it appeared—irrelevant. The greater practicality of the informal logic fascinated me and I began to read other texts in the field and to explore some of the philosophical issues at stake. From that point my interest grew.

The first edition of this text was written between 1982 and 1984, the second in 1986, and the third in 1990. The book combines a detailed treatment of argument in natural language with a solid treatment of two central areas of formal logic: categorical logic and propositional logic. The first edition was novel in its combination of informal and formal topics and in its sustained effort to present a general theory of argument within which various types of arguments could be subsumed. This emphasis continues in subsequent editions—although because other authors subsequently moved in this direction, the combination is now less unusual than it was when the book first appeared.

Three problems commonly experienced by students of argument and critical thinking are taken very seriously in this text:

▪ *Finding and interpreting arguments*   In order to critically evaluate an argument it is necessary to have a clear sense of what that argument is. In practice, for written arguments, this means finding the conclusion and premises in a text. Students often find this matter very difficult. I spend a great deal of time on it in Chapter 2, which teaches a standardizing technique in some detail, adding treatment of implicit (or missing) conclusions and premises, subarguments, and related topics.

▪ *Having confidence in argumentative procedures*   For many students, if an issue is one of straightforward fact, it is a matter of "mere" opinion, and in the area of opinion, no distinction can be made between correct and incorrect or well supported and poorly supported. The topic of opinion is raised in the first chapter of the book, and students are advised that opinions or beliefs about controversial topics can be supported well or badly by reasons and evidence. The book offers hundred of examples, most on topics of serious concern, which illustrate this point. In the many exercises, students work on disciplined critique of a variety of arguments and have to supplement material in the book by constructing arguments of their own. The types of arguments considered are related to work in science, law, administration, ethics, and various humanities disciplines: thus, the importance of cogent argumentation is a constant theme in the book. My hope is that work in a critical thinking or informal logic course and an encounter with a book such as this one will give students a solid and enduring appreciation for the ubiquity and importance of argument and the meaningfulness of the distinction between good arguments and poor ones.

▪ *Using argument skills after the course is over*   Textbooks have to use fairly short examples, and one problem faced by many students and instructors is that of *transfer*. How can concepts and skills developed for short textbook examples be applied in further work where we are looking not just at a paragraph or two, but at a whole essay or book? New to the third edition is a chapter directly confronting this transfer problem. Detailed practical advice is given to help students write a critical analysis of an essay-length work, and one essay, given in the chapter, is analyzed according to the methods suggested. Five essays by contemporary writers are appended to the book as a convenient source of material for those who wish to do further work in this important area.

Features New to the Third Edition

▪ The writing style has been simplified in some respects; for instance, paragraphs are generally shorter than in previous editions.

▪ Examples have been updated and carefully edited to avoid excessive emphasis on nationally specific material or on particular topics that might have had more than their share of attention in previous editions. In exercises, care has been taken to include examples posing problems at various levels of difficulty, ranging from easy to intermediate to fairly hard. (In general, problems are ordered from easy to intermediate to difficult, within an exercise.) Background information is supplied where necessary. Examples are, in many cases, not only *realistic* but *real,* and they have, as before, been selected to offer material that is serious, important, and worth thinking about.

▪   There is a greater emphasis on constructing arguments—especially in the early chapters.

▪   The discussion of language, previously in Chapter 3, now appears in Chapter 4; this allows a sustained and uninterrupted introduction to argument as such in the first three chapters, which introduce the notion of argument, argument structure, and the criteria for a cogent argument. Greater effort has been made to integrate the discussion of language and definition with other material in the book, especially the discussion of the acceptability of premises in Chapter 5.

▪   The treatment of inductive reasoning has been greatly changed to offer a general, constructive account that emphasizes strong, inductive arguments rather than the mistakes in social scientific reasoning. Discussion of the philosophical problem of induction, which some instructors found to be jarring and irrelevant, has been deleted.

▪   The treatment of Venn diagrams in categorical logic is more explicit and complete than it was previously.

▪   The list of valid argument forms for propositional logic has been extended, and there are more examples of proofs.

▪   Treatments of several topics—most notably reliance on testimony, relevance, the convergent/linked distinction, and analogy—have been deepened and improved as a result of recent philosophical work on the subjects.

▪   A Chapter Summary has been included for every chapter. The summary, in conjunction with the Review of Terms Introduced (already a feature of the second edition), is a convenient and helpful study device.

There is now an Instructor's Manual, which mentions and explains many further changes. The manual was prepared by Michael Reed of Eastern Michigan University and contains overview summaries of each chapter, along with multiple-choice and discussion questions.

Acknowledgments

I have benefited from studying other texts in informal logic, from participating in many conferences at which others presented their theoretical and practical ideas, from reading papers in *Informal Logic,* and from discussions with many students over the years.

The treatment of analogies in this book derives originally from John Wisdom's lectures on "Explanation and Proof" (commonly known as the Virginia Lectures); I am grateful to Prof. Wisdom for kindly allowing me to study the manuscript for these lectures, which are not yet available in print. Carl Wellman's *Challenge and Response: Justification in Ethics* has also influenced my ideas: the term *conductive argument* is taken from his work.

Students in Philosophy 105 at Trent University, in a graduate seminar on theory of argument at the University of Amsterdam, and in adult education courses in Calgary and Vancouver have helped me a great deal—both by expressing their enthusiasm for the study of natural argumentation and by asking challenging and penetrating questions about my ideas and techniques. I have benefited over the years from being able to discuss theoretical and pedagogical points with Tony Blair, Ralph Johnson, David Hitchcock, David Gallop, John Burbidge, Bernard Hodgson, Barrie McCullough, Bela Szabados, Frans van Eemeren, and Rob Grootendorst. In their enthusiastic commitment to the development of informal logic, Tony Blair and Ralph Johnson of the University of Windsor have contributed greatly to the field—not only through their own teaching and writing, but by their editorship of *Informal Logic* and their hard work in organizing three important international conferences in 1978, 1983, and 1989. I owe them a great deal—as do many others who work in this area. Thanks also to Thomas Hurka, John McMurtry, Wendell Berry, Stephen Jay Gould, and Camille Paglia for granting permission to reprint the eloquent and interesting essays that are appended to the third edition.

Ken King's prodding and questions have been a persistent spur to action; I thank him for his ongoing concern for the future of the book. I would also like to thank the publisher's readers: Robert F. Barnes, Lehigh University; Bruce W. Brower, Tulane University; Michael Principe, Middle Tennessee State University; Michael H. Reed, Eastern Michigan University; Bea Rose, Chaffey College; and Dennis M. Weiss, University of Texas, Austin.

I owe much to Cary MacWilliams, whose critical reading and lively discussion of the entire manuscript of the third edition helped to clarify many points. Her energy and enthusiasm were tremendously helpful. Michael Reed, of Eastern Michigan University in Ypsilanti, Michigan, provided indispensable assistance in preparing the Instructor's Manual; I thank him for his cooperation, patience, insights, and hard work. For any errors remaining in the text, I am solely responsible.

As before, my greatest debt is to my husband, Anton Colijn, who, in addition to coping with the domestic stress resulting from the extra burden of a large manuscript, has been involved in the planning and writing of all three editions at more stages than he might have wished. Without his patient listening, continued enthusiasm for the subject, contribution of examples, and sustained assistance with word processing, this book would not have existed.

CHAPTER 1

What Is an Argument? (And What Is Not?)

THIS IS A BOOK ABOUT ARGUMENTS. It is about the nature of arguments—what arguments are and the different structures they have—and about the standards for judging arguments to be good or bad. It is about understanding the arguments other people give, evaluating those arguments, and constructing good arguments of your own. *Arguments* are found where there is some controversy or disagreement about a subject and people try to resolve that disagreement rationally. When they put forward arguments, they offer reasons and evidence to try to persuade others of their beliefs. Consider the following short argument:

> Eating more than one egg a day is dangerous because eggs contain cholesterol and cholesterol can cause strokes and heart attacks

Reasons are given for the claim that it is dangerous to eat more than one egg a day.

ARGUMENT AND OPINION

A natural question to ask is how argument is related to *opinion*. Many people think that if an issue is controversial, what somebody thinks about it is just a matter of opinion and that there is no point in trying to give reasons for or against opinions. They think of opinions as being a matter of individual choice, and not subject to any sort of critical evaluation. Such slogans as "everyone has a right to his opinion" and "well, that's your opinion," may suggest that, on controversial topics, people just think in whatever way they wish, and rational argument has nothing to do with the matter.

However, these ideas about opinions are oversimplified. To look at the matter carefully, we must first ask what an opinion is. An opinion is a belief, typically not fully supported by evidence, on a matter open to some dispute. For example, people have different opinions on the causes of juvenile delinquency. Some think it is due to poverty; others blame poor parenting, inadequate religious education, or lack of discipline in schools; others see drug use as a major factor; still others credit genetic theories. Evidence, though certainly relevant to the subject, does not prove which view is right and, in fact, many of the people who hold opinions on the matter, even quite strong opinions, do in a way understand that fact. Often, when we hold opinions, we are aware that they are opinions and do not hold them with the full conviction we may have for secure beliefs or as knowledge.

Opinions can be formed with or without evidence, for good reasons or poor ones. We should seek well-founded and sensible opinions, not arbitrary ones. Even concerning controversial issues there is evidence supporting various views. The evidence may be reliable or unreliable, and it may give better or worse reasons to back up our opinions. The point of arguing, and evaluating arguments, is to reach opinions based on reasoned reflection and good judgment.

Politically and legally, people are free to hold any opinion at all. From the point of view of logic and evidence, however, we cannot say that all opinions are equal. Some opinions are mere opinions, reactions based on little more than a gut response. Others are based on evidence and reasons and on careful weighing of pros and cons. Using and evaluating arguments to arrive at opinions does not turn opinion into fact, but it can help us have more reasonably based opinions. Like our beliefs and our claims to knowledge, our opinions affect our actions. It matters what we think, and we should not be content to think hastily, whether the topic is one that is a matter of opinion or not.

In this book we hope to convince you that opinions on important controversial matters can and should be defended by rational arguments, and that rational arguments can be constructed and analyzed in a careful, logical way. You can do better than say "That's just your opinion!" when someone disagrees with you; you can learn to critically assess the reasons for the view and defend your positions with solid arguments of your own. You can use rational arguments to try to discover which opinions are reasonable.

WHAT IS AN ARGUMENT?

An argument is a set of claims that a person puts forward in an attempt to show that some further claim is rationally acceptable. Typically, people present arguments to try to persuade others to accept claims. The evidence or reasons put forward in defense of a claim are called the *premises* of an argument. An argument may have several premises, or it may have only one. The claim being defended in the argument is called its *conclusion*. An argument, then, is composed of one or more premises and a conclusion.

Let us think back to the argument about eggs and cholesterol. Someone says, "You should not eat more than one egg a day, because eggs contain cholesterol and cholesterol can cause strokes and heart attacks." In saying this, he is giving you reasons, telling you why, you should not eat more than one egg a day. That is, he is stating an argument. The premises of the argument are that eggs contain cholesterol and cholesterol can cause strokes and heart attacks. Its conclusion is that you should not eat more than one egg a day. In this argument, as in others, the arguer does not merely say what he thinks or give you his opinion. He gives you a reason for this opinion, or belief. He tells you *why*.

Sometimes the word *argument* is used to mean dispute or fight as in the sentence "The parents got into so many arguments over the child's problems that finally they got a divorce." In ordinary speech, this use of the word *argument* is quite common. But this is not the way we use the word *argument* in this book. In our sense, arguments have to do not with fights but with rational persuasion. An argument is a reasoned attempt to justify a conclusion.

Both kinds of argument—rational arguments and fights—have a connection with disputes between people. When they use arguments, people respond to disputes by trying to reasonably justify their opinions or beliefs. When they fight, people obviously do not restrict themselves to these sorts of tactics. They descend to other tactics—even, sometimes, to the use of force and physical violence. It's important to keep the two senses of the word *argument* distinguished from each other; *in this book our concern is with argument as attempted or successful rational persuasion.*

In the first few chapters, we concentrate on understanding what arguments are and how they are stated. We then move on to the task of evaluating arguments—offering and explaining standards which you can use to determine how strong or weak an argument is.

Here is another example of an argument.

There are no international police. It takes police to thoroughly enforce the law. Therefore, international law cannot be thoroughly enforced.

This argument has two premises (the first two statements) and a conclusion (the third statement). We can make the structure of premises and conclusions clearer by setting the argument out as follows:

1. There are no international police.
2. It takes police to thoroughly enforce the law.
Therefore,
3. International law cannot be thoroughly enforced.

Statements (1) and (2) support statement (3), which is the conclusion of the argument. The word *therefore* here serves to introduce the conclusion.

Let us look at a somewhat more complicated example. This one is taken from a letter to the editor of a newspaper. It deals with the controversy over teaching evolutionary theory in high schools. The author of the letter is trying to respond to a claim often made by those who are against the teaching of evolution, and he refers to that claim in the opening sentence. He gives reasons—that is, offers an argument—to show that the claim he is opposed to is incorrect.

> It has been claimed that evolution is taught as dogma, when it is in fact only a theory. This confusion indicates the inadequate nature of scientific training apparently provided to some educational administrators. Evolution is a theory in exactly the same sense that gravity and magnetism are theories. No one has ever seen gravity, for example, but surely we should not stop teaching this "dogma" in our schools. The evidence for evolution is no less convincing, and evolution is called a theory rather than a law simply because the term "law" is no longer scientifically fashionable. Were Newton alive today, he would talk about the theory of gravity exactly the same way Einstein wrote of the theory of relativity and Darwin wrote of the theory of evolution.[1]

The author is trying to show that when the expression "only a theory" is used to downgrade evolutionary theory, this interpretation indicates inadequate understanding of the scientific method. He cites a comparison with other areas of science and mentions the fact that the notion of law is no longer popular in the theory of science, in order to show that evolution, as a theory, is no less scientific and no more disputable than current physical theory. Since he gives reasons to back up his difference of opinion with the critics of evolution, he has an argument.

A person who tries to persuade you by rational means offers an argument in which he or she claims that because the premises are true or acceptable, the conclusion should be accepted. The arguer is saying, in effect,

Premise 1
Premise 2
Premise 3 . . .
Premise N
Therefore,
Conclusion

Arguments may have any number of premises—from a single premise to a very large number.

In the model here, the word *therefore* indicates that the conclusion is being inferred from the premises supporting it. This word is one of a large number of words that logicians call *indicator words*. Indicator words indicate the presence of an argument. Some indicator words come before the premise or premises of an argument; others come before its conclusion. Indicator words are not part of the content either of the premises or of the conclusion. Rather, they serve to indicate which statements are premises and which are conclusions; they indicate the direction of the reasoning in the argument. Here are some of the many indicator words and phrases that come before the premises in arguments:

PREMISE INDICATORS

since	on the grounds that
because	for the reason that
for	as indicated by
follows from	may be inferred from
as shown by	may be derived from
given that	may be deduced from

Here are some of the words and phrases that come before conclusions in arguments:

CONCLUSION INDICATORS

therefore	for all these reasons we can see that
thus	on these grounds it is clear that
so	consequently
hence	proves that
then	shows that
it follows that	indicates that
in conclusion	we can conclude that
accordingly	demonstrates that

Sometimes the word *and* may precede these conclusion indicators, as in such expressions as "and therefore" or "and accordingly." In such cases, *and* itself is not an indicator word: it merely connects clauses or sentences.[2]

Both in order to understand other people's arguments and in order to construct and present clear arguments ourselves, we have to be clear about the distinction between premises and conclusion. The conclusion is the claim or statement that is in dispute and that we are trying to support with reasons. The premises are other claims, which offer evidence or reasons intended to back up the conclusion. The arguer is claiming that because the premises hold, the conclusion should be accepted.

Indicator words can help us identify which statements have which role. When a passage or speech contains these words, they give us valuable clues to show the direction of thought. For example, after words like *therefore, so, hence,* or *thus,* we will not find premises; we will find conclusions. After words like *because, for,* and *since,* we will find premises. When constructing your own arguments you can use indicator words to make the direction of your thought clear.

WHERE AND HOW DO YOU FIND ARGUMENTS?

Indicator words can often help you to find arguments, because they show that one claim is being given rational support by others. Consider the following examples:

(a) There can be no such thing as a just war in modern times, because all modern wars involve weapons and strategies that kill many thousands of innocent people, and no war in which many thousands of innocent people are killed can be a just war.

(b) Since the meaning of a word must be understood by all the people who use that word, the meaning of a word cannot be a mental image in only one person's head.

(c) There is life somewhere in the universe as well as here on earth, for the universe is infinite and it can't be that in an infinite universe only one place has the special features needed for life.

In (a) the conclusion is "there can be no such thing as a just war in modern times." The indicator word *because* introduces two premises that support the conclusion; they tell us why the conclusion should be believed. Whether a modern war can be just is something on which a person might be said to have an opinion. In (a) that opinion is backed up by reasons: modern wars kill too many innocent people, and wars that kill innocent people in this way are not just. In (b) the word *since* introduces the premise that tells you why the conclusion (that the meaning of a word can't be a mental image) is supposed to hold. In (c) the conclusion is "there is life somewhere in the universe as well as here on earth," and the word *for* introduces the reasons offered for this claim. In these simple examples the indicator words make it very easy to see that there are arguments and to see what the premises and conclusion are.

It is not always as straightforward as this to find the premises and conclusions of arguments. There are several complications. First of all, not all arguments contain indicator words. It is possible to argue without inserting any indicator words between the conclusion and premises or before the premises. You can see this by changing example (c) only slightly, in such a way that essentially the same argument is presented, but the indicator word is omitted. Consider:

(d) *John:* I think the earth is the only place in the universe where life has developed and can flourish.

Mary: I doubt it. The universe is infinite. It can't be that in an infinite universe, only one place has special features needed for life. There is life somewhere else in the universe as well as on earth.

In (d) Mary replies to John and asserts all the claims asserted in (c). We can understand which claim is her conclusion because of the conversational context that is given in the example. John makes a claim; Mary says she doubts it; she then continues on to tell John why she doubts it. That is, she gives reasons for her view, which is different from John's view. Even though she does not use the word *for* or any other logical indicator word, she is still offering an argument, and her conclusion is still the conclusion of (c). This example illustrates the fact that arguments do not necessarily contain indicator words.

Another complicating factor about arguments and indicator words is that many of the indicator words such as *so, since, because, for, thus,* and *therefore* can also occur outside arguments. The fact that we hear these words in a speech or see them in a written passage does not always mean that the speech or passage contains an argument. The words *since* and *for,* which are important and common premise indicators, can also serve other functions.

Consider, for instance, the following examples:

(e) Since Christmas John has been upset about his mother's illness.

(f) Jean bought a gift for Mary.

In example (e) the word *since* introduces a period of time; it is not a logical indicator for a premise. In example (f) the word *for* shows who received the gift Jean bought, and is not a premise indicator either. Thus, even though the words listed above as premise indicators and conclusion indicators typically have that function, they do not always have it.

You have to develop your sense of context, tone, and natural logical order in order to spot arguments. It is a matter of seeing when people are trying to justify claims rationally and which claims they are trying to justify. In practical situations, there is relatively little difficulty in determining that people are offering arguments because, as part of the situation, you know which claims are in dispute.

Suppose you are in a union and you are trying to get a raise. Whether there are indicator words used or not, you are likely to know what the conclusion of the union's argument is going to be: the workers should be given a raise. In offering arguments to management, the union tries to persuade them, on the basis of reasons, that the raise is feasible and appropriate. (Nonrational persuasion is attempted if members stop the discussion and go on strike!)

Finding conclusions and premises in written texts is often more difficult because you may know less about the situation or context of the argument. To understand whether a written passage contains an argument and what claims in the text are premises and conclusion of the argument, it is often necessary to have background knowledge about the context in which the passage was written. Indicator words can be helpful. When there are no indicator words in a text, it may still contain an argument because some statements in the text might serve as reasons or evidence for others. To see whether this is happening, we usually need some background knowledge about what is, or might be, in dispute.

If someone says, "Jane has long insisted that such and such is the case, but actually, such and such is false," it will be natural for him to follow his contention that Jane's view is false by giving reasons, and when he does this, he offers an argument. Similarly, in the example offered earlier about evolutionary theory, the author was clearly replying to a view he did not hold: the view that evolution is only a theory. In the passage, he gave reasons for thinking that that judgment of evolution is faulty.

Occasionally people construct arguments when there is little controversy about the conclusion, to see whether a good justification could be given for some belief or opinion if it were to be in dispute. For instance, philosophers have constructed complicated arguments for conclusions such as that material objects exist outside minds. Although few people would seriously doubt this claim, the claim is such a fundamental one in our picture of the world that the question as to how well it can be supported by reasons and evidence is very important. One way of exploring those foundations is to construct and examine arguments that can be put forward to support it.

If you are trying to determine whether a speech or a passage contains an argument and you are having some difficulty interpreting it, you can start by asking yourself what the conclusion would be if it were an argument. If you cannot find any stated conclusion and you do not think a conclusion is even implied by the passage, then there is definitely no argument. If you think you have found a conclusion, you then see whether other claims made seem to be put forward as evidence or reason to support that conclusion. If you can do this, and if there is some good reason to regard the writer or speaker as trying to persuade others that a claim is true, then the speech or passage contains an argument. Casual conversations about practical problems or public issues, meetings, political speeches and lectures, letters to the editor, academic books and articles, and advertisements are all natural homes for arguments.

WHAT ISN'T AN ARGUMENT?

Even the most rational speakers and writers do not offer arguments all of the time. Sometimes they raise questions, describe events and problems, explain occurrences, tell jokes, and so on. In none of these cases are they trying to justify conclusions as true on the basis of supporting reasons.

Consider:

> I can't stand broccoli!
>
> What were the causes of World War I?
>
> It was a crisp and frosty September morning, but so many problems occupied their minds that the beauty of the day went unappreciated.

None of these sentences express arguments. The first sentence does not even make a statement or claim; it expresses a feeling of distaste. The second sentence raises a question rather than stating or claiming anything. The third sentence, unlike the first two, does make a statement—but there is no argument because the statement merely describes a situation, saying how it was on that morning in September. In none of these sentences do we find an attempt to persuade people of a conclusion; therefore none of them express arguments. The sentences serve other purposes: expressing, questioning, and describing.

Let us look at several more interesting, longer passages that do not contain arguments and see just why they do not. The following excerpt is taken from a newspaper editorial.

> It's not the sort of chatter you hear at cocktail parties, but the muscle fibres of the cockroach are almost human. Really. That's why biologists at Atlanta's Emory University are teaching cockroaches to jog. They attach little weights to the roaches' legs and send them racing along the treadmill.
>
> Frankly, we're leery about doing anything that might give the insects an edge. It's hard enough trying to catch the little sprinters without having to listen to them wheezing behind the walls after a five-metre workout. But we shouldn't carp; there's always a chance the roaches will adopt not only the jogging, but the jogger's healthy lifestyle and scrupulous diet. If they start by keeping decent hours and giving up greasy foods, we'll be satisfied.[3]

This passage does not contain an argument. It first gives a humorous report of some research at Emory University and then expresses, in jocular terms, some possible risks and benefits of the research—to the insects and us! The writer obviously regarded the research as rather silly, and the style and tone of his editorial express that view. But he did not argue for it: no serious reasons are given as to why this kind of research is not worthwhile. (Probably the writer thought the point was too widely agreed-upon to bother arguing about.) Because the writer merely expressed his views in a witty and entertaining way and did not try to persuade us by reasons of the truth of any conclusion, the passage does not contain an argument.

Another example of a passage that contains no argument is taken from an essay on the German national character. The author says:

> In the united Germany that is now emerging, the special character of the East German state is historically irrelevant. It is, indeed, being sloughed off like molted skin. The character of the future Germany will be derived in its entirety from the present character of the West German state. And the most important truth about West Germany today is that it is perhaps the most complacent, satisfied *petit bourgeois* nation in Europe, if not on earth. It is the antithesis of the inflation-ravaged socially torn society of the pre-Hitler period.[4]

The author, Robert D. Kaplan, makes a strong and somewhat controversial statement in the first sentence quoted above. In the second sentence, he makes a similar claim, in slightly different words; and the third sentence again repeats the point. The fourth and fifth sentences move on to a different theme. None of these sentences make statements that seem to be evidence or reasons for the others. Kaplan, then, offers an interesting view on the significance of East and West German experience for a new Germany, but he does not argue for his position that the new Germany will take its national character solely from the West.

Arguments are fascinating, and getting the knack of identifying and criticizing other people's arguments can be entertaining and fun. In fact, it is easy to get so carried away by the feeling of intellectual power that this activity gives you that you start to see arguments everywhere—even where there aren't any! Although arguments are important and they are common in ordinary life, politics, work, and academic studies, we have to remember that much of what is written and said is not argument at all. Rather, it is description, explanation, questioning, storytelling, gentle ridicule, or any of a number of other things. Passages having these other functions can be perfectly respectable, intellectually and rationally, without containing any arguments.

You need arguments when views put forward are controversial and persuasion is attempted. The passage about German character could, perhaps, be faulted for not containing any argument. The author's claim that what were two Germanys could unite and the experience of one have no effect on the national character of the resulting state is, on the face of it, surprising and rather contrary to common sense. We might well feel as readers that we would gain more from his essay if he offered evidence or reasoning in support of such a claim. On the other hand, the passage about cockroaches jogging had no argument and that was no fault. The author of that work gave us some amusing facts and entertained us. His readers probably do not need to be persuaded that teaching cockroaches to run a treadmill has little utility. Since neither passage contains an argument, it would not be appropriate to try to find premises and conclusion in either one. Nor would it make sense to accuse either author of using a poor, or weak, argument.

If a writer or speaker does not put forward any argument, he or she obviously cannot put forward a poor argument. To critically evaluate arguments, we must first be able to find them. This means that we have to distinguish between those speeches or passages that contain argument and those that do not, and that, for those containing an argument, we have to identify the conclusion and the premises. In this book, because our special focus is on argument, we sometimes refer to speeches or texts that do not contain argument as *nonarguments*. There are many types of nonargument, including descriptions, stories, jokes, exclamations, questions, and explanations. Explanations are sometimes rather hard to distinguish from arguments, so they are discussed in more detail below.

◆———————————————————————————————

EXERCISE SET

Exercise 1: Part A

For each of the following passages, determine whether it does or does not contain an argument, and give reasons for your judgment. If the passage does contain an argument, indicate the conclusion. *Answers to exercises marked with an * are provided in the back of the book.*

1. I don't care what you say. I really think that Josie is in love with Juan. Why? Because she always wants to talk about him. And she gets very excited when he is due for a visit. She even blushes when you ask her about him.

*2. The sun was setting on the hillside when he left. The air had a peculiar smoky aroma, the leaves were beginning to fall, and he sensed all around him the faintly melancholy atmosphere that comes when summer and summer romances are about to end.

3. Many Europeans are not willing to trust a unified Germany.

*4. Any diet poses some problems. Here's why. If the diet does not work, that is a problem. If the diet does work, then the dieter's metabolism is altered. An altered metabolism as a result of dieting means a person will need less food. Needing less food, the person will gain weight more easily. Therefore, after successful dieting a person will gain weight more easily.

5. The woman who took the lead role in the film was quite beautiful, as everyone noticed right away. She was tall, with red hair and green eyes. The flowing costumes she wore were elegant and creatively styled.

*6. Hockey is an active winter game that is quite popular in northern countries such as the Soviet Union and Canada. The game requires strength, good skating, and terrific eye-hand coordination.

7. Everybody who dreams is asleep. When a person is asleep, he cannot control his mind so as to plan things. Therefore, dreams cannot be controlled by a person who is dreaming.

8. "The tradition of stand-up comics grew out of the coffeehouses of Greenwich Village in the early fifties. Now there are at least six chains in the United States, bringing laughter, of sorts, to all parts of the country."
(Toronto *Globe and Mail,* May 2, 1990)

9. *Background:* At a conference at Queen's University, Prince Philip of the United Kingdom reflected on the role of universities in solving the problems of contemporary society. The Toronto *Globe and Mail* (July 10, 1978) covered the conference and reported Prince Philip's comments as follows:

"For Prince Philip, the question facing mankind is not to find solutions to the world's problems, but to find problems that suit the solutions.

" 'The world is full of solutions, particularly in universities, but the trouble is you've got to find a problem to fit them,' he told a news conference at the close of the fifth Commonwealth study conference."

As he is quoted here, did Prince Philip offer an argument?

*10. "If all goes well, the reactor and the steam generators in a nuclear power plant of the pressurized-water variety maintain a stable, businesslike relationship such as might obtain between two complementary monopolies. The reactor can be thought of as selling heat to the steam generators."
(Daniel Ford, *Three Mile Island: Three Minutes to Meltdown* [Middlesex, England: Penquin, 1982])

11. "You not only need to control it [toxic radioactive substances] from the public, you also need to keep it away from the workers. Because the dose that federal regulations allow workers to get is sufficient to create a genetic hazard to the whole human species. You see, these workers are allowed to procreate, and if you damage their genes by radiation, and they intermarry with the rest of the population, for genetic purposes it's just the same as if you irradiate the population directly."
(Quotation from medical physicist John Gofman, cited in Leslie Freeman, *Nuclear Witnesses* [New York: Norton, 1982])

12. "If you want to be successful in business on a long-term basis, you must match your operational expertise with an ethical code of conduct practiced in every phase of your business. No exceptions! Why? Because history has proven that ethical businesses succeed in the long run and, to put it bluntly, because business ethics can be measured in dollars. Sooner or later, unethical businesses get caught."
(Jacqueline Dunckel, *Good Ethics, Good Business* [Vancouver: Self-Counsel Press, 1989], p.2)

*13. *Background:* In the face of dramatic political changes in the Soviet Union in 1989 and 1990, and ethnic and social unrest in that country, the Tokyo paper *Sankei Shimbun* commented: "The Western countries, including Japan, must carry out the major task of assisting and supporting the Soviet Union and Eastern Europe. Western support should be provided because there will be great regret later should the failure of democratization and economic reform in the Soviet Union and Eastern Europe be due to inadequate aid."
(Quoted in *World Press Review,* January 1990, p. 10)

14. "As Justice Oliver Wendell Holmes drove off after lunch with Justice Learned Hand, the latter exclaimed, 'Do justice sir, do justice.' Holmes halted his carriage and reproved Hand: 'That is not my job. It is my job to apply the law.' That story involving two of America's finest legal minds is told by a third such, Robert Bork, in his elegant and entertaining new book, *The Tempting of America.*"

(From "The Tempting of America," *Newsweek,* December 4, 1989, p. 96)

*15. "An ant is crawling on a patch of sand. As it crawls, it traces a line in the sand. By pure chance the line that it traces curves and recrosses itself in such a way that it ends up looking like a recognizable caricature of Winston Churchill. Has the ant traced a picture of Winston Churchill? A picture that depicts Churchill? Most people would say, on a little reflection, that it has not."

(Hilary Putnam, "Brains in a Vat," in *Reason, Truth, and History* [Cambridge, England: Cambridge University Press, 1981])

16. "Britain is no longer a Christian country and makes no pretence of being one. Churches are being closed throughout the nation. On Sundays in London's West End, the congregations are in the shops, some of which do booming business. There is as little attention paid to God in Britain as in Cuba. We see emerging there the grim paganism of twentieth-century life."

(Patrick O'Flaherty, in "A Growing U.K. Religion: Animal Worship," Toronto *Globe and Mail,* February 10, 1986)

17. *Background:* These comments are taken from a book review by William French. French is reviewing *The Laugh Makers: Stand-Up Comedy as Art, Business and Lifestyle,* by Robert A. Stebbins. He mentions that Stebbins's book is quite academic and not very funny, and then goes on to say:

"About the funniest thing Stebbins says on his own is this: 'Although most worthy of study, I do not delve deeply into the issue of humor and stand-up as approached, say, from the perspective of phenomenology, semiology, or critical theory.' Thank God for small mercies!"

(Toronto *Globe and Mail,* May 2, 1990)

*18. "When they took my documents away, obviously for a closer look, I almost fainted. As far as I could see, they had not done that to anyone else. But the fright passed when after a time they brought them back and resumed the questioning: 'Anything to declare? The truth! Dollars? Gold?'

"'Absolutely not! Go ahead and search.'

"They did, but cursorily. And then I was through."

(Doan Van Toai, in "Vietnam: How We Deceived Ourselves," *Commentary,* March 1986)

19. *Background:* In the summer of 1978, Andrew Young was the American ambassador to the United Nations. Young, an African-American, made the controversial statement that there are large numbers of political prisoners in the United States. In the public uproar that followed, African-American activist Jesse Jackson contended that Young's statement was quite correct:

"'Some may debate the diplomacy and timing used by Ambassador Young, but the truth and accuracy of his statement is beyond question,' Jackson told the Leavenworth prisoners.

"'Thousands are in jail because they are too poor to pay bail bond,' Jackson said. 'Thousands are in jail because of delayed trials. Thousands are in jail because they were not tried by a jury of their peers. That is political.'"

(Calgary *Herald,* July 17, 1978)

As he is quoted here, did Jackson offer an argument?

20. "We are currently overrun with reports on how the human race is destroying the very environment that it depends on for survival. There has been at least a 100-percent increase in media coverage of environmental issues in each of the past four or five years, and public interest is still rising. Practically everybody knows what the problem is, more or less, and even what sorts of changes in human behavior might make it go away. The real question is why that does not lead to instant action and prompt solutions."

(Gwynne Dyer, "The Odds of Saving the Planet," Toronto *Star;* quoted in *World Press Review,* October 1989, p. 96)

Exercise 1: Part B

In each of the minidialogues below, construct an argument for the second character, so that they give reasons for their claim. Then, indicate the conclusion and premises of the arguments you have constructed. *Note:* Of course it is better to construct good, cogent arguments than poor ones, but we have as yet said nothing at all about what makes an argument good or poor. Just construct some argument, one that seems to you to be at least superficially reasonable and sensible.

1. *John:* You should get a small car to save on gas.

    Bill: I disagree. Small cars are just not safe on the highway.

2. *Sue:* Did you see that film *The Gods Must be Crazy?* I think it is just so biased against the black liberation movements in Africa. There is a whole huge sequence about violence when some black revolutionaries try to stage a coup and take over a government. Then later these same revolutionaries take a group of schoolchildren captive and try to march them across a border. Talk about prejudice!

    Penny: That's not prejudice.

3. *Chris:* Advertising is really unethical because it is so deceptive. Ads try to mislead us and make us buy products that are shown as much better than they really are.

    Robin: That's no objection to ads.

4. *Rosita:* I am going to enroll in a course in German. I really think that German is going to become much more important as a world language, now that East and West Germany are reuniting. In a few years, Germany will be the economic powerhouse of Europe.

    Don: Well, that's interesting, but I think you are wasting your energy. There's only one international language of business, and it's English.

5. *Fred:* I just read a review of the concert our choir did last weekend. The review was pretty negative. The guy didn't like our soloist, and he said the tenors were off-key. Boy, do those critics ever make me mad! Probably none of them can sing worth a damn—or do anything else for that matter. But they can sure go all out attacking other people who try to do creative things! I don't know why newspapers hire these guys in the first place. They are completely unnecessary.

    Kathy: I disagree. Critics play a valuable role.

6. *Jim:* War will always be with us. It's just human nature.

    Jan: I don't think so. War has other causes.

7. *Melissa:* Computers in banks are so annoying. If you go in to make a deposit and the computer is down, you can't even do your business. You have to come back another day. It's so stupid! Honestly, these things are more trouble than they are worth.

    Penny: I don't think so. I think they're a terrific convenience.

ARGUMENT AND EXPLANATION: WHAT'S THE DIFFERENCE?

Some of the indicator words that may appear in arguments are also common in *explanations.* Superficially, explanations look quite a bit like arguments, but there are important differences between them.

As we have seen, in an argument, premises are put forward as grounds to justify a conclusion as true. In an explanation, on the other hand, claims are offered to make a further claim understandable—to say why it is true. Explanations are offered on the assumption that the fact, situation, or event being explained is something that does exist, and the question arising is not whether it exists, but why or how it came into existence. Much has been written about the nature of explanations. In this book we are concentrating on the logic of arguments, not on explanations. For this reason, we look at explanation only in a preliminary way, for the particular purpose of understanding the distinction between explanations and arguments.

We have seen that arguments are formed of premises and conclusions, which may naturally be arranged as:

Premise 1
Premise 2
Premise 3 . . .
Premise N
Therefore,
Conclusion

What makes it especially difficult to distinguish arguments and explanations is that explanations can be set out in a similar way. Both explanations and arguments give reasons. In explanations, these reasons are the causes or factors that show how or why a thing came to exist, whereas in arguments, they are intended to provide grounds to justify a claim, to show that it is plausible or true. Still, many of the same indicator words used in arguments are also used in explanations. Words such as *therefore, so,* and *thus,* which often precede the conclusion of an argument, may also point to a statement of something to be explained.

Consider, for example:

The window had been shut all summer and the weather was hot and damp. So the room smelled awfully musty when he returned.

Here the word *so* introduces a statement describing what is explained: the mustiness of the room. The passage does not contain an argument. Rather, it contains an explanation. The first sentence offers information that would show how the room came to be musty. The word *so* connects the reasons given for its being musty with the fact that it is musty. In this context, the mustiness of the room is taken to be an admitted fact for which the writer is stating causes. The window being shut and the hot damp weather caused the room to smell musty, according to this passage. The writer is not trying to justify or back up a claim, as he would do in an argument, but rather trying to explain how it was that a fact came to be as it is.

Sometimes, instead of offering reasons for their beliefs, people merely explain what caused them to hold these beliefs. They explain themselves but make no attempt to justify their beliefs as acceptable. You can see this in the following example:

My parents were fundamentalist Christians, and my religious education was a strong feature in my character. The church always emphasized social concern. Thus, from an early age, I accepted the Bible as a basis for action to relieve the suffering of the poor.

In this passage the word *thus,* which usually indicates the conclusion of an argument, precedes the description of a belief that is explained, not justified. Nothing in the passage would indicate that it is true that the Bible is the basis for social action. Rather, the facts that are specified show how the speaker came to believe that the Bible has that particular role. The explanation of why people hold beliefs may be very interesting in its own right, but it does not by itself constitute any argument, or justification, for those beliefs.

In an explanation, someone tries to show how something came to be. Typically, explanations are given by citing causes of the event or institution to be explained. The explanations may naturally be set out as:

Factor (1)
Factor (2)
Factor (3) . . .
Factor N
Therefore,
Fact or event (*x*) came to be.

Any number of factors may be cited in an explanation. Very often the factors cited in an explanation are causal factors; the fact or event is explained by citing causes that produce it.

Consider:

He caught AIDS because he got a transfusion of blood infected with the HIV virus.

This is a causal explanation; the transfusion led to his getting AIDS.

Not all explanations are causal. Some proceed by fitting a phenomenon into a recognizable pattern or relating it to a human purpose. Thus we might explain why a person is moving to another city by saying that she has a good job there. She is moving in order to take the job; the move is for the purpose of taking on a new job.

Another type of explanation is involved when we explain the meaning of words. These sorts of explanations are not put forward in causal terms; typically, we explain what a word means by using other words that mean the same thing. We can explain what the word *sibling* means, for instance, by saying that a sibling is a brother or a sister. This is an explanation of something—the meaning of the word *sibling*—but it has nothing to do with the causes or effects of being a sibling.

Most explanations have to do with causes: they tell how and why things came to be as they are. There are at least two additional types of explanation: explanations by purpose and the explanation of meaning. Thus, it is not accurate to say think of explanations simply as being causal. But although this view is not entirely accurate, it may be helpful to think along these lines just for a little while. A great many explanations are causal, and the ones that are hardest to distinguish from arguments are typically causal. If we think of explanations as saying what the causes of something are and think of arguments as offering reasons in an attempt to show that a claim is true or acceptable, it may be easier to sense the general difference between explanation and argument.

Here is an explanation taken from an article dealing with the politics of pro- and antiabortion movements in the United States in the early 1980s.

> The generation that crusaded for abortion rights that first time around cannot believe that it has to fight for them all over again. The younger generation takes the rights for granted and cannot believe it has to fight for them at all.
>
> To a rather astonishing degree, the feminist movement of the 1970s was carried to its zenith by a particular generation of women which came of age in the late 1960s. It was a time in their lives when freedom from forced reproduction was one of their greatest needs. These women are in their mid to late thirties today and are not as enthusiastic about leading a pro-abortion struggle. Two things stall them. First, by now many have full-time careers—feminism simply does not have the access to the volunteer womanpower that is available to the antichoice forces. Second, although they still depend on having the right to have an abortion, in personal and political terms they are now far more concerned with having children.[5]

In this passage the author offers an explanation of what she takes to be a fact—the fact that women in their thirties are not keen to lead a struggle against prolife forces on the abortion issue. She provides no rational justification for the views of these women, or for the claim that this really is a fact. Rather, she offers an explanation suggesting two causes for their unwillingness to engage in another political struggle over abortion. "Two things stall them," she says. That is, two things are causal factors holding these women back from reentering the fray of the abortion struggle: they have full-time careers, and they are currently more interested in having children. Obviously these factors are not premises the author uses to try to prove the truth of any kind of stance on abortion. She is specifying two causes of the unwillingness of these women to recommence a political battle.

Arguments offer justifications; explanations offer understanding. Even though reasoning is used both in arguments and in explanations, and even though the same indicator words may appear in both, they have different purposes.

Here are three imaginary dialogues, offered in order to bring out the different purposes of argument, explanation, and description. Suppose that two businessmen, Smith and Wilson, have a business that offers second mortgages. Wilson takes the business into a town called Slumptown, where people have little money to buy homes and where there is, as a result, a great demand for second mortgages. Wilson and Smith operate profitably in Slumptown for several years, but then the economy of Slumptown worsens, and many people are forced to default on their mortgages. The two men lose heavily. We can imagine the following dialogues between them:

DIALOGUE I

Wilson: Well, it's too bad we lost so much, but you can't win all the time. I just don't understand how it happened.

Smith: Actually, it's perfectly understandable. The causes of our good business in Slumptown were the poverty of the people and the bad job market there. Because people could not quite afford the houses they bought, the market for second mortgages was good. And yet these factors did indicate how vulnerable Slumptown's economy was. When the powerful XYZ company laid off workers, people in Slumptown were worse off than before, and they just couldn't keep up with the payments on their houses. It is easy to see what led to our losses in Slumptown.

There is no argument offered by Smith here. Smith is explaining why he and Wilson lost their money.

Now look at Dialogue II, which does contain an argument, but which contains no explanation.

DIALOGUE II

Wilson: We were unlucky in Slumptown. Perhaps we should transfer the firm to Hightown, down the road. In Hightown, there are plenty of jobs, the real estate market is booming, and people are crying out for second mortgages.

Smith: That would be a mistake, I think. Hightown is different from Slumptown in many ways, but it is similar in having a vulnerable economy. All of the economic activity in Hightown depends on one aircraft parts firm, which is expanding at the moment. If the firm loses a contract with Nigeria, it will have to lay off thousands of workers, and Hightown's economy will be severely affected. In such a situation, Hightown would become another Slumptown, and we would have the same problem with defaults all over again.

This time Smith does offer an argument. He gives reasons against taking the business to Hightown because he and Wilson do not initially agree on what should be done. In Dialogue I, both knew that they had suffered losses—there was no need to justify that proposition—and they were discussing what might have caused their losses. In Dialogue II they initially disagree. Smith then tries to persuade Wilson that moving to Hightown would be unwise, and he gives premises—reasons to support that conclusion.

Passages that do not contain arguments may contain explanations, or they may contain descriptions, suggestions, jokes, questions, illustrations, and so on. We have emphasized explanations not because all nonarguments are explanations, but rather because explanations most closely resemble arguments and are hardest to distinguish from them.

To see an illustration of a passage that is neither an argument nor an explanation, consider a third dialogue about Slumptown and Hightown.

DIALOGUE III

Wilson: I found the contrast between Slumptown and Hightown quite amazing. In Slumptown things looked so drab and messy. There were all kinds of windows boarded over, even on the main street. People looked drab too. It seemed as though the slowed-down economy even affected their clothing and the expression on their faces. Nothing much seemed to be happening, and people never seemed to have any evergy. In Hightown, on the other hand, downtown shops were busy and there were no empty retail spaces on the main street. The people seemed colorful and lively. On weekends, there were lines for movies, active bars, and even lively amateur theater and music groups.

Smith: I know what you mean. I noticed those things too. The difference was quite striking, wasn't it?

In Dialogue III, Wilson describes his perceptions and ideas of Slumptown and how they contrasted with those of Hightown. He is not trying to explain anything; nor is he trying to argue.

We have suggested, in the above discussion of the distinction between argument and explanation, that a set of claims can be either an argument or an explanation and never both at once. Unfortunately, things are not quite this simple. Two qualifications must be made. The first, which you will soon discover for yourself, is that some passages seem to be classified either as arguments or as explanations, depending on what you assume about the situation or context in which they are made.

Here is a simple example:

(a) Carol is the best math student in the class because she is the only student in the class who is going to a special program for gifted students.

Suppose that you read this passage and assume that the person making the statement is trying to persuade others that Carol is the best math student. As an arguer, that person would then be giving as evidence for his conclusion the claim that Carol goes to a special program. If you make this assumption about the context, you will see in it the following argument:

Premise: Carol is the only student in the class who is going to a special program for gifted students.
Therefore,
Conclusion: Carol is the best math student in the class.

On the other hand, you could make some different assumptions about the context in which the statement is made. Suppose that you assume that the speaker is talking to a group of people, all of whom already agree that Carol is the best math student in the class. In such a context, there would be no point in arguing for that claim, but people might be interested in a suggested explanation as to how it came to be that Carol is best. Assuming this sort of context, you would naturally interpret statement (a) as an explanation.

It would go like this:

Proposed explaining factor: Carol is the only student in the class going to a special program for gifted students.
Thus (that is, this explains or is the cause why),
Carol is the best math student in the class.

As this example illustrates, statements and short passages that are taken out of context can sometimes be interpreted either as explanation or as argument. If someone quotes such a passage and asks you whether it contains an argument, you may not know what to say. You can think about different sorts of context in which the statements might be made and try to determine what the most likely context is. You can then make an assumption that this is the context, and base your interpretation on this assumption. (When you do this, it's important to recall that you have made an assumption and what that assumption is.)

Another problem that arises is much less common, but will be mentioned here in the interests of completeness. Occasionally, the very same statement or set of statements can serve both as argument and as explanation. This happens because the same premises that constitute evidence will also, by coincidence, serve to explain why the conclusion is true.[6] Here is an illustration:

1. A constitution will be nearly impossible to amend if amendments require unanimous consent by a number of diverse regions of a federated country.
2. This tentative constitutional accord provides that all ten distinct regions of a country must consent in order for the constitution to be amended.
Therefore,
3. This tentative constitutional accord will make the constitution nearly impossible to amend.

Here, the very same things that would explain (3) will also give reasons to support (3). We could read the passage first as an argument and convince ourselves that (3) is true, and then go back and read it as an explanation, seeing statements (1) and (2) as giving us the reasons why, or causes why, (3) is true. Cases like this one, which are unusual, raise theoretical problems that are rather interesting, but too complicated to be described here.

In subsequent chapters, we try to avoid these difficult cases. In practical life, you know more of the context than you are given in a logic textbook, and it is thus easier to judge whether an explanation or an argument is being put forward. Here, you have to use your background knowledge and sense of what needs to be rationally justified to try to determine whether an argument is being offered.

EXERCISE SET

Exercise 2: Part A

For each of the following passages, state whether it does or does not contain an argument. If you think that the passage does contain an argument, briefly state why and identify its conclusion. If you think that the passage is a nonargument, say why.

1. The cause of the traffic jam was an abandoned truck in the center lane of the freeway. *N*

2. It is not essential to be tall in order to be good at basketball. This point is quite easy to prove. Just consider that basketball teams often have players of average height who make contributions to the game through fast running and expert passing. *A*

3. Good health depends on good nutrition. Good nutrition requires a budget adequate to buy some fresh fruits and vegetables. Therefore, good health requires a budget adequate to buy some fresh fruits and vegetables.

*4. *Background: Time* magazine ran an article describing a television show designed by astronomer Carl Sagan, who tries to make science accessible to the public through television shows and public appearances. The article gave rise to a number of letters, including the following one, which appeared in the November 10, 1980, issue.

"Perhaps Carl Sagan's strongest message in his efforts to bring science to the people is this: Science is the true language of the present and of the future. Only a small fraction of this planet's populace, however, can speak the language. The most significant question facing us is whether our civilization, as a whole, will learn to utilize science for the benefit of mankind. The answer will surely determine our future course: noble greatness or self-inflicted extinction."

*5. We know that males and females have different hormones. Now scientists have discovered that these hormones affect verbal and spatial abilities that are connected with different sides of the brain. Given this evidence, it is likely that men's brains are organized differently from women's.

6. The natural world is very complicated. A complicated thing could not possibly come into existence just by accident. Therefore, the natural world must have been created by an intelligent designer.

7. "The Olympics are a good way to improve relations between different countries. You don't believe me? Look, these games provide a chance for people from different countries to get together and meet each other—really know each other as individuals."

8. The human mind will always be superior to the computer, since computers are only tools for humans to use.

9. Only if they are quick and capable readers can students easily master the books required for the English courses here. But many students are poor readers. Therefore, they will have problems. Those who call our English curriculum easy are simply wrong.

*10. Because she was an only child, she did not develop the independence necessary to care for herself. Even at seven, she was unable to put on her own skates, for example.

11. "Licensing a nuclear power plant is, in my view, licensing random premeditated murder. First of all, when you license a plant, you know what you're doing—so it's premeditated. You can't say, 'I didn't know.' Second, the evidence on radiation producing cancer is beyond doubt. . . . Radiation produces cancer, and the evidence is good all the way down to the lowest doses."

(John Gofman, quoted in Leslie Freeman, *Nuclear Witnesses* [New York: Norton, 1982])

*12. If a person knows in advance that his actions risk death, then if he voluntarily takes those actions, he is accepting a risk of death. These conditions surely apply to mountain climbers, so we can see that mountain climbers accept a risk of death.

13. "The only way you could license nuclear power plants and not have murder is if you could guarantee perfect containment. But they admit they're not going to contain it perfectly." (So licensing nuclear power plants is licensing murder.)

(John Gofman, in Leslie Freeman, *Nuclear Witnesses* [New York: Norton, 1982])

*14. *Background:* The following passage is taken from Edward C. Banfield, *The Moral Basis of a Backward Society* (Chicago: The Free Press, 1958), p. 64. Banfield is describing life among peasant people in a small Italian village called Montegrano, as it was in the early 50s.

"In part the peasant's melancholy is caused by worry. Having no savings, he must always dread what is likely to happen. What for others are misfortunes are for him calamities. When their hog strangled on its tether, a laborer and his wife were desolate. The woman tore her hair and beat her head against a wall while the husband sat mute and stricken in a corner. The loss of the hog meant they would have no meat that winter, no grease to spread on bread, nothing to sell for cash to pay taxes, and no possibility of acquiring a pig the next spring. Such blows may fall at any time. Fields may be washed away in a flood. Hail may beat down the wheat. Illness may strike. To be a peasant is to stand helpless before these possibilities."

*15. *Background:* This passage is taken from the essay "On Liberty," by the nineteenth-century philosopher John Stuart Mill. Mill defends freedom of speech.

"The peculiar evil of silencing the expression of an opinion is that it is robbing the human race; posterity as well as the existing generation; those who dissent from the opinion still more than those who hold it. If the opinion is right, they are deprived of the opportunity of exchanging error for truth. If wrong, they lose, what is almost as great a benefit, the clearer perception and livelier impression of truth, produced by its collision with error."

16. "When she reached her room she found that Tom had sent the bags up, and she thought she would unpack, and lie down for a bit to get rested, and then go down and have a quiet lunch. Perhaps she would see Tom somewhere. But first she went over to the window and looked out upon the incredible radiance of blue and green and gold, and the shine of the ethereal air. She looked at the great oak trees and the graceful mimosa trees, and she thought, 'After I've tidied up and had some lunch I'll just go and sit under one of those beautiful mimosa trees and drink in this largesse of air and scent and beauty.' Mrs. Golightly had never seen anything like it. The bright air dazzled her, and made her sad and gay."

(From "Mrs. Golightly and the First Convention," in Ethel Wilson, *Mrs. Golightly and Other Stories* [Toronto: Macmillan, 1961], p. 5)

17. *Background:* In the period 1979–1982, Nestlé, a multinational corporation manufacturing chocolate, cocoa, coffee, and infant formula, was accused of overly aggressive advertising of infant formula in developing countries. Critics charged that because mothers in these countries were vulnerable to pressure to copy a western way of life, they were encouraged to switch unnecessarily to infant formula instead of breast-feeding their babies. Due to unsanitary conditions, use of formula frequently caused illness or even the death of children.

"No one questions that marketing of infant formula in the Third World can pose serious problems. Everyone, including the infant formula industry, agrees that breast-feeding provides the best and cheapest nutrition for babies. Also, mothers who are lactating are less likely to conceive. Breast-feeding also helps to space out births. Therefore, marketing practices should not induce mothers who other-wise would be willing and able to breast-feed to switch to the bottle."

(Herman Nickel, "The Corporation Haters," reprinted in Eleanor MacLean, *Between the Lines* [Montreal: Black Rose Books, 1981], p. 91)

*18. "His voice seemed suffocated and my first impulses, which had suggested to me the duty of obeying the dying request of my friend in destroying his enemy, were now suspended by a mixture of curiosity and compassion. I approached this tremendous being. I dared not again raise my eyes to his face, there was something so scaring and unearthly in his ugliness. I attempted to speak, but the words died away on my lips. The monster continued to utter wild and incoherent self reproaches."

(From Mary Wollstonecraft Shelley, *Frankenstein* [New York: Scholastic Books, 1981—first published in 1817], pp. 266–267)

*19. "The kids are rarely overpowered by life's adversities because they set up safety valves to release the mental anguish caused by their personal hang-ups. Lucy, for example, flaunts her femininity so she can cope with life more easily. Charlie Brown eats peanut butter sandwiches when he gets lonely. And Frieda wheedles compliments to restore her faith in herself and in her curly hair. Snoopy, unashamed, straps himself to his doghouse and mentally shrugs off most anything he can't handle."

(From Jeffrey H. Loria, *What's It All About, Charlie Brown?* [Greenwich, Conn.: Fawcett Publishers, 1968], p. 12)

Exercise 2: Part B

1. Think of a particular person, such as a friend, relative, or co-worker whom you know quite well, and list five claims that you might at some time wish to explain to that person. Now list five different claims that you might at some time wish to justify to that person by offering an argument.

2. Look at the two lists that you have constructed for question 1. What makes it reasonable to put a claim on one of the lists rather than the other? (That is, how do you say whether the claim would be more appropriately explained or justified, to your friend?)

WHY ARE ARGUMENTS IMPORTANT?

In general, arguments are no better or worse than other forms of communication; they are merely different, serving a different purpose. The lack of an argument is a fault in serious contexts where disputable claims are being put forward as true. For instance, if a political analyst were to claim that the next U.S. president will be African-American and offer no evidence at all, this would be a flaw in her account. The claim might be true, but it is one people would not accept as true unless they saw considerable support for it. However, many claims don't require argument; they are claims on which people agree anyway or claims for which arguments have been given in other places. It would be perfectly appropriate, for instance, for a political analyst to claim that the United States will have another presidential election in 1992 and give no supporting argument.

Since some nonarguments are perfectly acceptable and some arguments are poor arguments, we cannot in general say that one speech or text is more rational than another simply on the grounds that it contains more arguments. This leads us to the general question as to why, and in what ways, arguments are important. Why all the fuss about arguments? The general answer is that unlike descriptions, jokes, stories, exclamations, questions, and explanations, arguments are attempts to prove or justify a claim. This process of justification is important both in practical terms and in intellectual terms. When we give arguments, we try to show reasons for believing what we do. When we evaluate other people's arguments, we think critically about what they claim and about their reasons for claiming it. Arguing and evaluating arguments are indispensable parts of critical thinking—of carefully examining our beliefs and opinions and the evidence we have for them.

Careful attention to the arguments of people who disagree with us can help us understand why they think as they do. It may give us good reason to rethink our own position; by attending to the arguments of other people, we may find reason to conclude that we are wrong. Finding out that we are wrong may sound unpleasant, but it can be interesting and practically important. Holding incorrect beliefs or hastily formed opinions on subjects of importance can lead us to unwise and even dangerous actions.

Arguing back and forth is one approach to disagreement, one that is more reasonable and less dangerous than some of the common alternatives—such as shouting, threats, or physical attack. When parties disagree about a claim or theory, when they have different opinions, they can try to persuade each other by reasons. If back-and-forth argument is pursued honestly and sincerely, one or both may change their views so that the disagreement is resolved. Even if agreement is not achieved, the process will help them better understand each other.

Some people use the word *argument* as a term of praise and say, "He has not given us any argument at all" as a way of saying that someone has offered faulty arguments. We do not follow that usage in this book. In our sense of *argument,* a person has offered an argument if he has put forward premises intended to justify a conclusion. In our sense of argument, arguments may be either good or poor. Given that the premises are put forward by an arguer as backing up a conclusion, it is an open question whether they in fact do so.

When you have the ability to criticize these arguments step by step, you will have an important strategy for persuading others to come around to your point of view. You will also be far better equipped to understand their point of view and see how they are led from some beliefs to others.

In addition, arguments are significant in contexts in which knowledge is being constructed. We want to know how well justified a theory or claim is, and we can find out by assessing the arguments that are (or can be) offered in defense of the position. A careful understanding of these arguments is extremely important when we are deciding whether to accept a new position. It also helps us to better understand positions we already accept—and can sometimes lead us to revise them.

The question whether emotion, faith, authority, or beauty constitute viable alternatives to reason and rational argument has often been raised. Many people believe that in some contexts, such as religion or love, arguing is beside the point, and the careful use of reason is inappropriate. We just have the right feelings or we do not, and that is all there is to it. But even in these profoundly spiritual and emotional areas, where trust and faith are crucial to our experience, it would be going too far to say that reason and argumentation are irrelevant. Many thinkers have, for instance, tried to prove the existence of God by reason and have used reason in the process of interpreting religious texts such as the Bible, the Torah, and the Koran. And as for love, where is the lover who did not , at some time, try to weigh up evidence to determine how his loved one really feels about him?

Whether intuition or feeling are viable alternatives to reason or, on the other hand, valuable supplements to it, is a profound topic that has been explored by many people. The view taken here is that intuition and feeling are indispensable supplements to reason, but cannot replace it. Trying to justify our beliefs by reason, arguing for and against claims that are in dispute, is a central and indispensable intellectual task. Careful reasoning from acceptable premises to further conclusions is the best method of arriving at decisions and beliefs because this method is the most likely to lead to accurate beliefs and sensible decisions. Only the method of reason is based on the need to respect standards of evidence and logical principles; this method is more careful and systematic than the others and has the greatest chance of getting things right.

Our purpose here is to cultivate your ability to construct and evaluate arguments. These are not new activities, of course. You have been doing these things nearly all your life. What is new is that we are going to think reflectively about these natural activities and set out standards we can use to judge arguments as good or poor. Thus we shall be directing your attention explicitly toward things that you normally take for granted, in order to improve skills you already have.

❖ CHAPTER SUMMARY

Even though there are various opinions on controversial matters, we can seek to support our own opinions and understand other people's opinions by the process of rational argument. To argue on behalf of an opinion or belief is to put forward evidence or reasons in an attempt to show that it is true or plausible. Arguments have two basic parts: premises and conclusions. In understanding and constructing arguments it is particularly important to distinguish the conclusion from the premises. Indicator words can help us do this: words like *therefore, thus, so, because,* and *since* tell us which claims are to be justified by evidence and reasons, and which other claims are put forward as premises to support them. Indicator words are not, however, infallible signs of argument. Some arguments do not contain indicator words. And some indicator words may appear outside the context of arguments.

Speeches and texts that do not contain arguments can be regarded as nonarguments. There are many different types of nonargument—including description, exclamation, question, joke, and explanation. Explanations are sometimes easily confused with arguments because they have a somewhat similar structure and some of the major indicator words for arguments are also used in explanations. However, explanations should be distinguished from arguments because they do not attempt to justify a claim, or prove it to be true. Arguing and arguments are important as rational ways of approaching disputes and as careful critical methods of trying to arrive at the truth.

❖ REVIEW OF TERMS INTRODUCED

Argument A set of claims put forward as offering support for a further claim. The argument is composed of the supporting claims and the supported claim. A person offers an argument when he or she tries to justify a claim by offering reasons for it.

Opinion A belief typically about a matter open to dispute, where there is not full proof and others have different ideas. Often people are aware that their opinions are not fully backed up by evidence and hold less firmly to them than to other beliefs for which there is more conclusive evidence, less disagreement, or both.

Premise A supporting reason in an argument. It is put forward as being acceptable and as providing rational support for a further claim.

Conclusion In an argument, the claim for which premises are intended as support. It is this claim that the arguer tries to make credible.

Indicator words Words such as *for, since, thus, therefore,* and *because* typically used in arguments to indicate that a person is reasoning from premises to a conclusion. However, these words may also occur in explanations and elsewhere. They do not appear only in arguments.

Nonargument A passage or speech that does not contain an argument.

Explanation An account showing, or attempting to show, how it came to be that a fact or an event is the way it is. Frequently explanations are given by specifying the causes of an event. An explanation is one kind of nonargument.

Notes

1. Letter to the Toronto *Globe and Mail,* February 8, 1982.
2. For a discussion of *and* as a logical connective between statements, see Chapter 8.
3. Editorial in the Toronto *Globe and Mail,* October 23, 1980. Reprinted with the permission of the *Globe and Mail.*
4. Robert D. Kaplan, "The Character Issue: Can the Germans Get It Right This Time?" in *The Atlantic,* May 1990, p. 32.
5. Deirdre English, "The War Against Choice," *Mother Jones,* February/March 1981, pp. 16–24. Reprinted with the permission of *Mother Jones* magazine.
6. *For instructors.* I discuss the distinction between argument and explanation in a theoretical paper entitled "Why Arguments and Explanations Are Different" in Trudy Govier, *Problems in Argument Analysis and Evaluation* (Providence, R.I.: Foris, 1987). The point that the same statements can, on the same interpretation, serve both as argument and as explanation is made by S. N. Thomas in his teachers' manual for the second edition of *Practical Reasoning in Natural Language* (Englewood Cliffs, N.J.: Prentice-Hall, 1983). Thomas contends that we should dispense with the distinction between argument and explanation altogether. In the essay referred to, I offer a number of reasons for not taking this view.

CHAPTER 2

Pinning Down Argument Structure

IN MOST OF THE EXAMPLES IN the last chapter, it was easy to see which claims were conclusions and which were premises. Most examples were relatively short and worded in a straightforward way so that the line of reasoning used in the argument was easy to follow. However, things are not always quite so simple. We sometimes have to look closely at passages, and listen closely to speeches, in order to see just what the line of reasoning is. In this chapter we look at the problem of identifying the premises and conclusions of arguments and see how important it is to examine carefully the particular language in which arguments are stated. We also examine several different ways in which premises can support conclusions.

In order to evaluate an argument, we must first understand just what the argument is. That means understanding the premises and the conclusion and how the premises are supposed to support that conclusion. If we rush into the task of evaluating an argument and deciding whether we agree with the conclusion before we take the time to understand what the premises and conclusion of the argument are, we are likely to think too fast and to make mistakes.

◆ STANDARDIZING AN ARGUMENT

In order to more accurately understand an argument that someone is using, it is helpful to set out its premises and conclusion in a simple standard format such as the following:

> Premise 1
> Premise 2

Premise 3 . . .
Premise N
Therefore,
Conclusion

We'll call this *standardizing an argument*. To standardize an argument is to set out its premises and conclusion in clear, simple statements with the premises preceding the conclusion.

By numbering the premises and the conclusion, we can refer to specific statements in an efficient way. We can simply refer to (1) or premise (1) instead of copying out all the words. We can say such things as "The author uses statements (1), (2), and (3) to defend statement (4)." Standardizing arguments gives us a clear view of where they are going and forces us to look carefully at what the arguer has said. When we come to the more interesting stage of criticizing arguments, we will find standardizing extremely helpful, for it allows us to see just which stage of the argument our criticisms affect and which parts of a speech or passage are essential in the attempt to establish the conclusion.

Here is a simple example:

People are not going to be effective at an all-day and all-evening meeting where there is no scheduled recreational time. They become too tired. People who are tired become irritable, quarrelsome, and unproductive.

In this example, the conclusion is stated before the premises. It is "People are not going to be effective at an all-day and all-evening meeting where there is no scheduled recreational time." Two premises are offered as support for this conclusion: "they become too tired" and "people who are tired become irritable, quarrelsome, and unproductive."

Standardized, the argument looks like this:

1. People become tired at all day and all-evening meetings where there is no scheduled recreational time.
2. People who are tired become irritable, quarrelsome, and unproductive.
Therefore,
3. People are not going to be effective at an all-day and all-evening meeting where there is no scheduled recreational time.

We have changed the sequence of statements here. It is a convention in logic, when we set out someone's argument, to put the conclusion last. This order represents the fact that the conclusion emerges from the premises, as a claim made more reasonable by premises that have given evidence and, as it were, led us in thought to this further claim. Interestingly, though, in speech and in writing, conclusions are often stated first and then followed by supporting reasons. The reversal that we have used in setting out this standardization is often necessary.

So far we have described arguments as though each one were quite self-contained. Actually, arguments often proceed in stages in such a way that what is a premise in one argument is the conclusion in another. Premises may be defended in subarguments, so that there are really several arguments in one. A *subargument* is a subordinate argument inside a main one, in which a premise in the main argument is defended.

Consider this example:

> A computer cannot cheat in a game, because cheating means deliberately breaking rules in order to win. A computer cannot deliberately break rules because it has no freedom of action.

As in the previous example, we need reversal of order for the standardization. The argument can be set out as follows:

1. A computer has no freedom of action.
Thus,
2. A computer cannot deliberately break rules.
3. Cheating requires deliberately breaking rules.
Therefore,
4. A computer cannot cheat.

The premises supporting the claim that a computer cannot cheat are that cheating means deliberately breaking rules and a computer cannot deliberately break rules. This argument is found in the first sentence and in the first part of the second sentence. The direction of this argument is indicated by the word *because*. There is a second argument too. The premise that a computer cannot deliberately break rules is itself supported by a reason: a computer has no freedom of action. This double support process, whereby a statement that supports a conclusion in one argument is itself supported by a further statement, is a subargument structure. In the subargument, a premise in the main argument is itself given rational support; thus the premise of a main argument is the conclusion of a subargument. In the example about whether a computer can cheat, the same statement "a computer cannot deliberately break rules" serves the roles of both premise and conclusion, since it both supports and is supported.

From a practical point of view, it is easy to see why subarguments are necessary and useful. When you use an argument, you are trying to persuade someone else of your belief, trying to convince them, on the basis of evidence or reasons, that your claim is correct and should be accepted. You do this using premises. You are, in effect, asking your audience to accept your premises and to reason from them to the conclusion. If your audience doesn't accept the premises, there is little in the argument to convince them. When you need to use a premise that you do not anticipate your audience will readily accept, that is the time for a subargument. You can back up the premise so that it will be more reasonable and your whole argument will be more convincing. In the example above, for instance, many people might not find it obvious that computers cannot deliberately break rules. The subargument is an attempt to give a reason for that claim.

To speak of "the premise" or "the conclusion" or "the argument" in the above example is unclear, because there are two different arguments and thus two different conclusions and premises can be identified. The argument from (1) to (2) is one argument and the argument from (2) and (3) to (4) is another.

However, the main point of the passage is (4). We'll call (4) the *main conclusion* and the entire structure, with subargument and all the statements, the *whole argument*. In this case, the whole argument includes a subargument structure. In this book, when we standardize arguments, we generally use *therefore* as an indicator of the main conclusion and use other common indicator words, such as *thus* and *so*, before those conclusions of subargument that are, in effect, *intermediate conclusions*.

There is no theoretical limit on the number of subarguments that can be used as parts of an argument, although in practice using more than two or three is not generally advisable when you are constructing an argument. If you use too many subarguments, people will find your argument difficult to follow.

Here is another example in which there is a subargument structure. The author, Stephen Jay Gould, is a Harvard professor and science writer. He is discussing the issue of whether the human species is special, and whether it is a matter of false pride (hubris) to think of it as being unique.

> It is not mere hubris to argue that homo sapiens is special in some sense—for every species is unique in its own way. Shall we judge among the dance of the bees, the song of the humpback whale, and human intelligence?

Although this is a short passage it contains a main argument with a subargument. As in the previous example, the written order is the reversal of standard logical order. The second sentence in the passage is a rhetorical question. It is written in the form of a question, but it is a question to which the author assumes we know the answer. (Shall we judge . . . we shall not.) Rhetorical questions, which impose a particular answer on the reader or listener, are another way of making statements.

Standardized, the passage looks like this:

1. We should not judge between the dance of the bees, the song of the humpback whale, and human intelligence.

Thus,

2. Every species is unique in its own way.

Therefore,

3. It is not mere hubris to argue that homo sapiens is special in some sense.

The main conclusion is supported by a single premise, which, in turn, is an intermediate conclusion supported by a single premise.

The same premise or premises may be used to establish two distinct conclusions, so that one argument may appear to have two conclusions. Here is an example:

> Labor is the basis of all property. From this it follows that a man owns what he makes by his own hands and the man who does not labor has no rightful property.

This example is a statement of John Locke's theory of the moral basis of a right to private property. There is a single premise, which is that labor is the basis of all property. From this premise, two conclusions are drawn: one is that a man owns what he makes by his own hands, the other is that a man who does not labor has no rightful property.

There is no subargument here; the premise is not supported by any other premise, and neither of the conclusions can be used to support the other. In fact, there is *not* a main argument here; there are two arguments, each of equal weight. The wording of the two arguments is compressed; they are stated together so that the common premise is stated only once, and then two different conclusions are drawn from it.

The two arguments can be standardized as:

1. Labor is the basis of all property.
Therefore,
2. A man owns what he makes by his own hands.

and

1. Labor is the basis of all property.
Therefore,
3. A man who does not labor has no rightful property.

We can see that the passage contains two distinct arguments; there are two different conclusions drawn from the same premise.

FROM COLLOQUIAL WRITING TO STANDARDIZED FORM

Standardization is useful because it forces us to identify conclusions, premises, and subargument structures. But these are not the only benefits of standardization. A major benefit is that we isolate the premises and conclusion from surrounding text that may not contain argument at all. In addition—as we saw in the case of the rhetorical question above—we put premises and conclusions that may be expressed in indirect or unusual ways into straightforward sentences making claims.

To see the greater clarity that results when we standardize an argument, let us look at an example. The following passage is from a book about fund-raising for nonprofit groups. The author, Joyce Young, an experienced fund-raiser, wrote the book to offer advice to others.

> It may be that the general manager takes a very dim view of your group and has turned you down before. Should you try to approach head office directly? In most cases the answer is no because the people at head office are going to be very, very reluctant to go over the head of the local manager on a local matter. In fact, the head office might well send such a letter back to the general manager to draft a reply! Then the general manager will take an even dimmer view of your group.[1]

The first two sentences here set the issue that the argument is about—whether a fund-raiser who has been refused by a local manager should go over the head of a local office to approach head office directly. The beginning of the third sentence, "the answer is no," expresses the conclusion. The conclusion is that fund-raisers should not go over the head of a local manager to the head office people in a case where a local office has refused them before. There are two reasons given. The first is that the head office does not like to go over the head of a local manager on this sort of issue (this premise is stated after the logical indicator word *because* in the third sentence). The second is that the head office might send your letter back to the local manager, who would then be even less impressed by the group than he was before.

The argument can be standardized as follows:

1. Head offices do not like to go over the heads of local managers on fund-raising issues.
2. If a head office receives a request over the head of a local manager, it may well send the letter back for that local manager to compose a reply.
3. If a local manager receives a letter back from a group the manager has previously turned down, a letter that the group has sent to the head office by going over the manager's head, the manager's impression of that local group is likely to be even worse than it was before.

Therefore,

4. It is not a good idea for fund-raisers to go over the head of a local manager who previously refused them to request money directly from head office.

We can see from the standardization just which statements are used as premises and what is the conclusion. The standardization also helps to indicate how the author reasoned from the premises to the conclusion.

Here is a further example, taken from the Christian writer and religious theorist C. S. Lewis.

Creatures are not born with desires unless satisfaction for those desires exists. A baby feels hunger. Well, there is such a thing as food. A duckling wants to swim: well, there is such a thing as water. Men feel sexual desire: well, there is such a thing as sex. If I find in myself a desire which no experience in the world can satisfy, the most probable explanation is that I was made for another world. If none of my earthly pleasures satisfy it, that does not prove that the universe is a fraud.[2]

Here Lewis seems to be offering an argument. What is the point he is trying to establish? He talks about babies and ducklings and sex: this is to indicate that there are creatures on earth who are born with desires that can be satisfied on this earth. The examples seem to be Lewis's basis for saying that we do not have desires unless they can be satisfied. He goes on to consider what would be the case if people were to have desires that could not be satisfied in this world. Most likely, he says, those beings would be made for another world. The last sentence in the passage virtually repeats this point in different words. This seems to be the point Lewis is trying to establish: it is his conclusion.

The claims about the desires of babies, ducklings, and humans (sex) are used to back up his general premise about creatures being made with desires that can be satisfied, and it is from that general premise that he seeks to derive his conclusion. We should note that the conclusion is not that people are made for another world. (As a Christian, Lewis probably believed that, but he does not assert it in this passage.) Lewis asserts that if people have desires that can't be satisfied in this world, they are probably made for another world. ("If I find in myself a desire which no experience in the world can satisfy, the most probable explanation is that I was made for another world.") It's important to notice that his conclusion is qualified by the word *probably*.

In standardized form, Lewis's argument looks like this:

1. The desires of ducklings who want to swim, babies who are hungry, and men who desire sex can be satisfied in this world.
2. Creatures are not born with desires unless satisfaction for those desires exists.

So,

3. If people find in themselves desires that no experience in the world can satisfy, then the most probable explanation for this is that they were made for another world.[3]

It is worth noting what we had to do to Lewis's original paragraph in order to get this clear argument out of it. First, we had to look at the logical flow of the passage and identify that conclusion. Second, we had to decide which parts of the passage were stated as reasons intended to back up that conclusion and put these into the most natural logical order. Third, we had to abbreviate and simplify Lewis's prose, putting it into clear, complete statements that could be used as premises. These tasks are not always easy to do. People write and speak in a way that is more disorganized (and more interesting!) than the "(1) and (2), therefore (3)" format that is best for logicians to work with. They word statements in the form of questions and commands, repeat themselves, include background and aside remarks, tell jokes, wander off the topic, and so on. These elements of colloquial writing are eliminated when we put the argument in standardized form.

A passage may contain an argument even though it also contains sentences that are not premises or conclusions in that argument. Strictly speaking, background information and material inserted just for added interest or for humor are not parts of the argument because they are neither premises nor conclusions. For example, a speaker or author may take some time to introduce the topic or to explain what terms mean before offering an argument on an issue. He or she may insert personal comments such as "it has always amazed me that . . . " or "my interest is chiefly in . . . ." Such aspects of a speech or passage are not parts of an argument in the sense of being its premises or conclusion and they do not belong in the standardization.

Often passages require a great deal of shortening and editing before we can represent them as arguments in standard form. It takes practice to learn to do this, but it is an important skill that you will find helpful in many contexts. It forces you to read or listen with a view to determining the main point of a passage or speech, and it trains you to ask why the author or speaker is saying what he or she says. What are the reasons offered for this viewpoint? You may discover there are none at all, but that too is a discovery well worth making, especially if the claims made are controversial and require support.

The following is a repetitive, disorganized example that illustrates the need to standardize and the simplification you can achieve by setting out the central argument in standardized form:

In the letter "Any group could abuse children," in response to Professor Edward Shorter's column referring to the "great child abuse scam," Dr. J. Jacobs suggested: "Would it not be better to disturb the feelings of 99 families in the hope of finding one family who needed help in preventing further child abuse?"

In my "unprofessional" opinion as a mere full-time mother of three, I would say that families have been "disturbed" too much for far too long by far too many professionals and that is why incidents of child abuse have increased by 34 percent in the past year.

The professionals may not want to admit the possibility, but I believe that all the anti-parent, anti-family attitudes that gushed from the International Year of the Child campaign last year probably have a lot to do with that 34 percent increase in incidents of child abuse.

The "professional observers of human nature" don't seem to understand just how much stress and pressure you have injected into North American families, bombarding young struggling parents with one shelling of modern philosophy and psychology after another for decades now.

These "professionals" have not only brought stress, but distress into many families. Parents have been told so much that they don't know what to do any more. They have been conned into believing that their parents didn't raise them properly and they can't possibly trust their own instincts or judgments about what is right or wrong for their children.

I say to all the "professionals" who've been minding everybody's business but their own: Let parents return to being intelligent individuals who desire to make their own judgments about what is best for their own children; stop trying to "diagnose and treat" us as though we were one great massive lump; and stop making us feel like criminals for spanking a child—maybe some of them won't feel so frustrated that they end up abusing them.[4]

This is a rather rambling letter. The author does seem to be arguing. As the first paragraph tells us, she has written to oppose a suggestion made by a Dr. Jacobs, and she tries to give some basis for her stance. The conclusion may be found in her opposition to Jacobs's view: she believes that professionals should not risk disturbing 99 families in the hope of finding the one family in 100 that would need help in preventing child abuse. (Check back to the first two paragraphs.) The author contends that professionals disturb parents and that parental disturbance is probably a major cause of child abuse. These points are made in the second, third, and fourth paragraphs of the letter. The fifth and sixth paragraphs try to provide some justification for the claim that professionals have harmed parents. Parents mistrust their own judgment because of extensive professional literature, and they feel like "criminals" when they spank their children because of the attitudes professionals take.

These are the main points. If you look back at the letter, you will see that it is quite repetitive. You don't need to state the same point more than once in the premises. Nor do you need to insert such expressions as "in my 'unprofessional' opinion as a mere . . . mother" and "I say to all the 'professionals.' " In these phrases the author is adding a kind of editorial commentary to her substantive remarks. She is expressing her reaction rather than stating substantive reasons for her view. Obviously, there will be many deletions before we get a clear model with only the premises and the conclusion. This version seems reasonably accurate and tolerably short:

1. Professionals have made parents mistrust themselves and their own judgments about their own children. (fifth paragraph)
2. Professionals have brought stress and distress into many families. (fourth and sixth paragraphs)

Thus,

3. Professionals have probably brought about an increase in the incidence of child abuse. (second and third paragraphs)

Therefore,

4. Professionals should not risk disturbing 99 families in the hope of finding the one family in 100 whom they might help in preventing child abuse.

We now have a simple version of the original. Various flaws in it will more easily appear. But it is wise, in a case like this one, to look back at the original when you are about to accuse the author of a major mistake in arguing. We won't make any comment on the merits of this argument yet because in this chapter our job is to concentrate on identifying the premises and conclusions and seeing the basic structure. The evaluation of argument presumes this kind of structural understanding: you cannot accurately determine whether the premises give good reasons to support a conclusion unless you know just what the premises are and what the conclusion is.

GENERAL STRATEGIES FOR STANDARDIZING ARGUMENTS

1. Confirm that the passage you are dealing with actually contains an argument. It contains an argument if, and only if, the author is trying to support a position with claims offered in its defense.
2. Identify the main conclusion or conclusions. Indicator words should help. Often the context is helpful, particularly when one person argues against

another. Typically in that case, one person's conclusion will be the denial of the other person's position.

3. Identify those statements in the passage that are put forward as support for the main conclusion. It is helpful at this stage to look at the statements in the passage and ask yourself which ones could plausibly give support, or be thought of as giving support, to the conclusion you have identified.

4. Omit any material that serves purely as background information—for example, introductory or editorial remarks.

5. Omit material that you have already included. This instruction applies when the same premise or conclusion is stated several times in slightly different words. If this happens when the different wording indicates first a premise and then a conclusion, do put the statement twice in your standardized version. (As we will see later, this situation means there is a serious flaw in the argument.) Otherwise, don't repeat the statement.

6. Omit such personal phrases as "I have long thought," "in my humble opinion," and so on. These are not part of the content of the argument but are stylistic indicators of the author's direction.

7. Number each premise and conclusion, and write the argument in the standard form with the premises above the conclusion.

8. Check that each premise and conclusion is a self-contained complete statement. This means that premises and conclusions should not include pronouns like *he, my, it,* and *this.* Instead, the appropriate nouns should be used. Also, premises and conclusions should be in the form of statements—not questions, commands, or exclamations.

9. Check that no premise or conclusion itself expresses a whole argument. For instance, if one premise says, "John has lied before so he is unreliable," you need to break down this premise further into (1) John has lied before and (2) John is unreliable. In the structure (1) will be shown as supporting (2) in a subargument. The subargument is not shown when you write "John has lied before so he is unreliable" as a single premise.

10. Check your standardized version against the original to see whether you have left out anything essential, or included anything that, on reflection, you think should not be included.

◆————————————————————————————————————

EXERCISE SET

Exercise 1: Part A

Examine the following passages to determine whether they contain arguments. For those passages that contain arguments, represent the argument in a clear, standard form, numbering premises and conclusion(s). Remember, if a passage does not contain an argument, it does not contain premises or a conclusion either; should you find passages that are nonarguments, simply indicate that that is the case and briefly state why. For arguments, note any subarguments and indicate which is the main conclusion.

*1. If a car has reliable brakes, it has brakes that work in wet weather. The brakes on my car don't work very well in wet weather. You can see that my car does not have reliable brakes.

2. He is getting fat and the cause is not hard to see. He eats too many potato chips, drinks too much beer, and spends too much time watching television.

*3. When unemployment among youth goes up, hooliganism and gang violence go up too. So unemployment is probably a major cause of these disruptions. People who say gang violence is caused by drugs have got it all wrong.

4. Weapons tend to make people fearful and distrustful. Fear and distrust often lead to hostility. Therefore, building up weapons is likely to cause hostility between nations.

*5. Every logic book I have ever read was written by a woman. I conclude that all logicians are women.

6. A place for everything and everything in its place.

7. Either the butler committed the murder or the judge committed the murder. Since the butler was passionately in love with the victim, it was not he who committed the murder. Therefore, the judge committed the murder.

8. What is it that enables ants, bees, and other social insects to coordinate their behavior so closely?

*9. *Background:* The following passage is taken from a recent article about archaeopteryx, a type of dinosaur.

"Its [that is, the archaeopteryx's] main feathers show the asymmetric, aerodynamic form typical of modern birds. This similarity proves that the feathers of Archaeopteryx must have been used for flying."

(Peter Wellnhofer, "Archaeopteryx," *Scientific American*, May 1990, p. 70)

*10. "Science, since people must do it, is a socially embedded activity."

(Stephen Jay Gould, *The Mismeasure of Man* [New York: Norton, 1981])

11. Canada and the United States are vast countries that depend on road and air transport to a far greater extent than smaller countries in western Europe, such as France and the Netherlands. In these European countries, rail service can be more economically run than in Canada or the United States, simply because distances are shorter and populations are more concentrated. In North America, where rail systems do less business, are less modern, and are more expensive, more shipping is done by air and road. Air and road travel require extensive government support, but are necessary when vast distances are involved. Therefore, North Americans are not wasteful of money or energy for transport as compared to western Europeans.

12. "Since we are not under an obligation to give aid unless aid is likely to be effective in reducing starvation or malnutrition, we are not under an obligation to give aid to countries that make no effort to reduce the rate of population growth that will lead to catastrophe."

(Peter Singer, "Famine, Affluence, and Morality," in *World Hunger and Moral Obligation*, ed. William Aiken and Hugh LaFollette [Englewood Cliffs, N.J.: Prentice-Hall, 1977])

*13. "The source of much of California's shakiness is, as any school child knows, the San Andreas fault. On a geological map, it isn't hard to find, but in ground truth—as geologists call their legwork—the fault can be elusive. Serpentine and secretive, it lurks just below the surface along six-sevenths of California's length. A 650-mile crack in the earth, it cuts, largely unnoticed and often intentionally ignored, through almost every other geological feature of the state."

(Shannon Brownlee, "Waiting for the Big One," *Discover*, July 1986, p. 56)

14. "Of the varied forms of crime, bank robbery is the most satisfactory to both the individual and society. The individual of course gets a lot of money, that goes without saying, and he ben-

efits society by putting large amounts of cash back into circulation. The economy is stimulated, small businessmen prosper; people read about the crime with great interest, and the police have a chance to exercise their skills. Good for all."

(From Harry Harrison, *The Stainless Steel Rat Saves the World* [Lindhurst, N.J.: Putnam Press, 1972])

*15. "Apart from a few oddities such as the Venus flytrap and the mimosa, most plants do not visibly react when you touch them. Don't be deceived. If recent experiments at the Stanford University Medical Center are anything to go by, plants may even respond to physical stimuli at a genetic level. Janet Bram and Ronald W. Davis have found several genes in a common laboratory plant called arabidopsis, a member of the mustard family, that are turned on when the plant's leaves are gently touched. The response starts within 10 minutes after stimulation and lasts more than an hour."

Hint: Assume that the conclusion is expressed in the first two sentences taken together and look closely at the role of "don't be deceived."

(Biological Sciences Reports, *Scientific American,* May 1990, p. 32)

16. "No one has a right to use a relatively unreliable procedure in order to decide whether to punish another. Using such a system, he is in no position to know that the other deserves punishment: hence he has no right to punish him."

(Robert Nozick, *Anarchy, State, and Utopia* [New York: Basic Books, 1974], p. 106)

17. *Background:* The following passage is taken from a book about children's allergy problems and how they can cause behavior problems.

"It is always surprising and most gratifying to observe how the family tensions diminish after the true cause of the child's problems are recognized and resolved. Many families can cope satisfactorily once they understand why the child acts the way he does and once they know that help is available. Months to years of unacceptable behavior, however, lead to conditioned responses which are no longer acceptable after the child improves. Family counselling is often indicated, and most effective after the cause of a child's previous difficulties has been

eliminated. There is no way, for example, that a child can be evaluated fairly while he is hostile and hyperactive from eating some problem food, smelling a problem chemical or inhaling an airborne allergen."

(Doris J. Rapp, *The Impossible Child* [Tacoma, Wash.: Life Sciences Press, 1986], p. 58)

*18. *Background:* This quotation is from C. S. Peirce, a famous American philosopher. Peirce is discussing the purpose of reasoning.

"The object of reasoning is to find out, from the consideration of what we already know, something else which we do not know. Consequently, reasoning is good if it be such as to give a true conclusion from true premises, and not otherwise."

Hint: How many conclusions are drawn? Are any conclusions worded in a compressed way?

(C. S. Peirce, "The Fixation of Belief," in J. Buchler, *Philosophical Writings of Peirce* [New York: Dover Publications, 1955], p. 7)

Exercise 1: Part B

In some of the following dialogues, the main arguer could profitably use a subargument to back up a premise used in his or her main argument. Indicate for which dialogues a subargument would be useful and just which premise needs to be supported, on the basis of the dialogue given. Then try to construct a suitable subargument that will help make the arguer's case more convincing to the audience. In each case, assume that the main arguer is the first speaker and the audience is the second speaker.

1. *Mary:* I don't care what they say about freedom of religion and all that. When that school decided to let a Sikh girl wear a six-inch dagger because the Sikhs said it is part of their religion to wear a ceremonial dagger, they just made the wrong decision and that is all there is to it. There is no proper place for weapons in our schools. So kids should not be allowed to wear daggers—whether they are supposed to be part of somebody's religion or not.

Joe: I can see your point in a way, Mary, but what about kids who carry knives to protect themselves from other kids? What are you going to say about that? I don't see what basis you have for being so sure that weapons have no place in schools.

*2. *Juan:* Opinion polls have a terrible effect on the electoral process. I think they should simply be forbidden during the two or three weeks prior to an election.

Peter: Why do you think that?

Juan: The problem is, the polls get all the attention, and they take attention away from the main issues. They even take away attention from the competence and integrity of the candidates themselves. All the attention goes to what people say about the candidates, to who's leading and so on.

Peter: Isn't that just how democracy is supposed to work?

Juan: I don't think so. Democracy requires that people make an informed decision as to which candidate can best deal with the important issues and they vote according to that decision. Polls work against that kind of decision. Therefore, polls work against democracy. And for that reason, their publication should be restricted in the few weeks right before an election.

Peter: OK, I can kind of see what you are driving at. But why do you think polls work against people getting information about candidates? Don't they work to give people information?

*3. *Catherine:* Did you hear about the man in California who wants to have his brain cut out and frozen? He has a brain tumor, you see, and he wants to live forever, but he is due to die in about six months. This guy believes that someday doctors will know how to cure the tumor— they can't do it now—and he wants to have his brain frozen. Then someday, he thinks, when doctors have the cure, the head can be thawed and attached onto another body. He'll come to life again.

Nancy: You're kidding!

Catherine: No, really.

Nancy: That guy really has the courage of his convictions, doesn't he? Imagine asking people to cut your head off and freeze it. Gross!

4. *Susan:* I'm really worried about that CANDU nuclear reactor that's being built in Romania.

Jim: Why?

Susan: Didn't you hear? The Romanians bought the stuff from Canada, but then they had slave laborers working on it. These people were forced to work there, under terrible conditions. They lived in cardboard shacks with no heat or water. And besides, the Romanian leader Ceauşescu was an absolute dictator, and people were terrified of what would happen if he got mad. They just did things by the deadlines no matter how shoddy the parts were. In May 1990, the Romanian government, after the revolution, checked out the facility and decided it was very unsafe because so many things had been sloppily constructed. If that thing starts, all of Europe better watch out. It's just about sure to have an accident.

Jim: Now that you mention it, I did hear about that. It sounds pretty awful. Gosh, we all knew Ceauşescu was a terrible dictator. I wonder why Canada ever sold that thing in the first place. Aren't we supposed to have controls?

Susan: Sure, but they aren't taken very seriously.

Jim: Any dictator is going to force people to do things they don't want to do, and under forced conditions, people are not going to do careful work. Nuclear reactors require careful work. So no one should sell a nuclear reactor to any country run by a dictator. Gosh, you'd think the government would be responsible enough to think of such things!

Susan: Isn't that a bit simplistic? I think your generalization is too sweeping. Surely people sometimes do careful work in dictatorships. Do you think it's completely impossible?

*5. *Don:* Allergies are a major health problem today but my grandmother says people hardly ever heard of them when she was growing up sixty years ago.

Al: Really? I wonder why not.

Don: Maybe doctors just didn't know enough.

Al: You mean people had a lot of allergies, but doctors didn't diagnose them?

Don: Yeah. Or maybe people hadn't even heard of allergies much, so when they had problems like itchy eyes and stomach aches and sniffly noses, they just accepted it.

Al: That could be. People today may just expect a higher standard of health than they did back then.

Don: They probably do. We're all just too spoiled.

IMPORTANT DETAILS ABOUT CONCLUSIONS

Location of Conclusions

To put an argument in standardized form, you have to know what its conclusion is. Identifying the conclusion is even more basic than identifying the premises, because your sense of the point of the passage will make you decide that certain statements are merely background or "asides" and that others are intended to support the author's point. It would certainly be nice if we had some definite rules about where conclusions had to be stated—if, for instance, speakers and writers always had to state their conclusions last, or if they always had to state them first. Unfortunately there are not any rules like this, and as language works, the conclusion in a passage or a speech can come at any point. It may be first, as in the following:

> (a) The film *Blue Lagoon* was poor because its plot was thin and superficial, and it neglected some of the more frightening aspects of life on an isolated island.

The conclusion is "The film *Blue Lagoon* was poor."

Or it may be last, as in the following:

> (b) Humans were said to be the only animals that use tools. Now it has been discovered that other animals use tools as well. For instance, chimpanzees use sticks to dig for termites, which they then eat. Thus, we cannot prove that humans are unique on the basis of their use of tools.

The conclusion is "we cannot prove that humans are unique on the basis of their use of tools."

A conclusion may even be stated right in the middle of a passage, with supporting premises on either side of it. Here is a passage exemplifying that arrangement:

> (c) Rats who are only occasionally rewarded for behavior become frantically anxious to repeat the behavior to obtain a reward. We can see that inconsistent behavior toward children is likely to make them frantically anxious because it is well established that children respond to punishment in much the same way animals do.

The conclusion is "inconsistent behavior toward children is likely to make them frantically anxious." This structure, with the conclusion surrounded on either side, is fairly unusual, and rather hard to understand. Argument (c) is worth standardizing:

1.   Rats who are only occasionally rewarded for behavior become frantically anxious to repeat the behavior to obtain a reward.
2.   Young children respond to reward and punishment in much the same way animals do.
Therefore,
3.   Inconsistent behavior toward children is likely to make them frantically anxious.

The premises must be linked to offer support for the conclusion. In (c) they are stated on either side of that conclusion.

Since this kind of arrangement is often difficult to understand, we would not, in general, advise that you use it when constructing your own arguments. Putting the premise either first or last is usually clearer. In fact, conclusions may quite effectively be stated twice when an argument is substantial: they may be stated both at the beginning and at the end of a substantial speech or passage. This style is often suitable when there are subarguments or many premises. The repetition serves to emphasize the fact that the conclusion is the main point, the basic theme that the arguer wishes to communicate and on which he or she wishes to persuade the audience. When a conclusion is stated twice, it is usually worded slightly differently each time, to avoid monotonous repetition.

Varying passage (b) a little, we can see an illustration of how this technique works:

(d) Some people have claimed that human beings are different from all other species because they are the only animals that can use tools. But this isn't right. It's easy to see why: other animals use tools too. For instance, chimpanzees use sticks to dig for termites, which they then eat. Humans are not unique in their use of tools.

In (d) the phrase "but this isn't right" alludes to the first statement, because "this" refers to the claim that human beings are the only animals that use tools. Thus, "but this isn't right" says that humans are not the only species that use tools, which is the claim made in the conclusion, worded in a slightly different way.

There is no simple recipe for picking out the conclusion of an argument when you are studying speeches or writings. You have to read carefully—or listen carefully, if it is an oral argument—and try to determine what the main claim is. It is a matter of getting the primary drift of what is said. When constructing your own arguments, you can help your audience by stating conclusions clearly at either the beginning or the end of the presentation, by using clear indicator words such as *therefore, so,* or *thus,* and by repeating your conclusion (stating it both before and after the premises) when your argument is substantial and lengthy.

Scope and Certainty in Conclusions

Conclusions may be more or less sweeping in *scope,* and it is important to notice this aspect because the kind of evidence that is needed to support the conclusion will vary accordingly. It is quite easy to understand this phenomenon from a commonsense point of view. Compare the following four statements, which might be conclusions of arguments:

(a) All engineering students are adept at mathematics.

(b) Most engineering students are adept at mathematics.

(c) Many engineering students are adept at mathematics.

(d) Some engineering students are adept at mathematics.

Clearly, evidence would have to be much stronger to support (a) than to support (d). In fact, for (d), only very little evidence would be needed. When you identify the conclusion in an argument, try to determine what its scope is. The conclusion may be about one particular individual or situation, in which case the issue of scope does not apply. But often arguments are about categories or groups of things, in which case it is important to note whether the arguer is making a universal claim, about all in the group, a generalization about most or many members, a claim about some of them, or a claim about a single individual in the group.

Another crucial point about conclusions is the *degree of certainty,* or commitment, with which they are put forward. An author or speaker may state her point quite emphatically, with no qualification whatsoever. On the other hand, she may make the point more tentatively, saying only that it is probably true, or could be true. What is said matters very much for proper understanding; obviously, it will make a difference to our evaluation of the argument. For instance, much better support will be needed for a *categorical conclusion,* such as "Nationalism is definitely the main cause of wars" than for a more tentatively expressed conclusion, such as "Probably nationalism is a factor in causing wars."

When constructing arguments yourself, it is a good idea to think about how strongly you wish to state your conclusion. Do you wish to maintain that something definitely is the case? That it is very likely the case? Or merely that it might be the case? The strength of evidence you require to put forward a convincing argument will vary depending on the degree of certainty you wish to attach to your conclusion, as well as on the scope of the conclusion.

Here is an example in which it is especially important to note that the author is putting forward only a tentative or a *qualified conclusion.* We will misunderstand him if we fail to see this.

> The malaise within English studies, like the university's other complaints, has been described as a temporary crisis in the evolution of a venerable and necessary institution. Yet it should be remembered that both the university and its departments have not always existed, and that during their tenure they have not always served as indispensable channels for the flow of the cultural stream. Less than a hundred years ago, English studies hardly existed. Moreover, when they replaced classical studies, that discipline passed quietly into desuetude while hardly anyone noticed. It is not at all inconceivable, given the history of the humanities, that English studies, though at present the seemingly irreplaceable guardian of the Western cultural tradition, should decline to the current marginal status of the classics.[5]

The conclusion of this passage comes at the end: "It is not at all inconceivable . . . that English studies . . . should decline to the current marginal status of the classics." (The author is comparing the role of English to that of classics and suggesting, on the basis of this comparison, that the fate that met classics might possibly befall English studies also.) It's important to note that this author has not claimed that English studies will decline, or that they ought to decline. He merely says they might.

Sometimes people are inclined to think that arguing on behalf of claims is something we do only when we have a definite, categorical position that we want to support. This idea is not correct: it is possible, as in the preceding example, to argue for a qualified position. It may, on occasion, be important to argue for such claims as "we need to rethink our company's growth strategy" or "we have to reflect on what it means for the Cold War to end." Such claims are, in a way, modest, because they do not themselves state a clear, single position on the subject at hand. Still, there are contexts in which they would need support, and they could be conclusions in arguments. Arguments can have sweeping claims, categorically stated, as their conclusions, but they can also have conclusions that are restricted in scope or are stated as likely, probable, or possible.

It would be useful if people always used words like *certainly, definitely, probably, possibly,* or *perhaps* in front of their conclusions, and if they were also clear as to whether they were talking about all, most, many, or some of the members of a group. If we always had explicit indications of the degree of certainty and scope of the conclusions claimed, we would easily have a clearer idea of what arguers are asserting and the strength of evidence needed. Unfortunately many speeches and passages are not explicit in these ways. We often have to infer from the tone of a passage and the context in which it appears just how firmly the arguer is asserting the conclusion.

Unstated, or Missing, Conclusions

Another important point about conclusions is that sometimes they are not stated at all! This may strike you as an odd thing for us to say. After all, didn't we define an argument as a set of claims put forward to defend a conclusion? If that's what an argument is, a conclusion is by definition part of every argument. Why, then, are we not telling you that in some arguments the conclusions aren't stated? This happens not because such arguments lack conclusions but because they have *unstated conclusions.* The conclusions are suggested by the stated words as they appear in the context.

Here is an example:

Joe: Did you hear about the frozen embryo case? A couple had some of her eggs fertilized by his sperm in a test tube. Embryos started to develop and they had them frozen. The idea was to implant the embryos in her uterus so they could have a baby. So anyway, these embryos were frozen, and then the couple got divorced. They're involved in a court case, trying to determine who owns the embryos.

> *Fred:* Who owns them? That makes me sick! Embryos are developing human beings with all the genetic material necessary for human life. Nothing that has all the genetic material needed for human life is property that can be owned.

In this dialogue, Fred is shocked at the idea of a court case in which a husband and wife would dispute as to who owns frozen embryos. The idea of ownership implies that the embryos would be property. Clearly, Fred does not regard embryos as property. In fact, he gives reasons for this view, which he clearly maintains though he does not state it in just so many words. In the context of the dialogue, Fred has given an argument with an unstated conclusion. The argument is:

1. An embryo has all the genetic material necessary for human life.
2. Nothing that has all the genetic material necessary for human life is property that can be owned.

Therefore,

<u>3</u>. An embryo is not property that can be owned.

The stated premises link to support the conclusion, (3), which was unstated. We underline (3) here because it is something we have added to the argument.

Obviously we have to be sure that a person intends to argue if we are going to add a conclusion. If we were willing to do this all the time, anything could be turned into an argument! We have to be careful. When the conclusion is not stated, but is strongly suggested by the statements that are made or by the context in which the speech or passage appears, we have a missing conclusion. To standardize the argument in this case, we have to write in the conclusion.

Another example may be found in a short letter about evolutionary theory written to the popular science magazine *Discover*. The author of this letter refers to Carl Sagan, a well-known scientist and supporter of evolutionary theory. Sagan's television series "Cosmos" had occasioned a number of letters.

> Could evolution ever account for the depth of intellect that Carl Sagan possesses? Not in a billion years.[6]

The author strongly suggests here that evolutionary theory is incorrect. But he does not state this specifically. Rather, he states that there is something evolutionary theory could not account for: Carl Sagan's intellect. The tone of the passage is argumentative. (Could it? No!) The issue is one of public controversy, and the writer is suggesting that the failure of the theory to account for Sagan's intellect marks it as an inadequate theory. Given the implication, the context, and the tone, it seems appropriate to regard the letter as an argument with a missing conclusion. To regard it as an argument, we have to supply a conclusion, because there is no argument without a conclusion. The standardized version of the argument would look like this:

1. Evolution could never account for the depth of intellect that Carl Sagan possesses.

Therefore,

<u>2</u>. Evolutionary theory is incorrect.

Conclusions are unstated for various reasons. Sometimes, the point will seem too obvious to bother making, after reasons have been stated. Sometimes, the conclusion is indirectly expressed in exclamations and questions. In these cases, even though the conclusion is not explicitly stated in any direct way, it is at least partially expressed. Occasionally, the conclusion is unstated for stylistic reasons: a suggestion or an implication may be more effective than the kind of outright direct statement logicians would prefer.

There are contexts, however, where the conclusion is not directly stated because it can be more easily insinuated. That is, the person or persons writing the argument may believe that their message is more likely to be accepted if it is suggested or insinuated than if it is stated outright. There can, sometimes, be something a little sneaky about unstated conclusions. Consider, for instance, the advertisement. The conclusion or message of most advertisements is that we who hear or read the ad should buy the product mentioned. (There are, of course, variations: we may be urged to rent or lease something, or to change our lifestyle; or the ad may be an "image" ad, trying to improve the image of a company, person, or institution.) To state "you should buy product X" or "company Y is a good company" may be too blatant and obvious. For this reason advertisements are a natural home for unstated conclusions. Trying to supply them is an entertaining and valuable exercise.

Here is one well-known example:

The bigger the burger the better the burger. The burgers are bigger at Burger King.

The missing conclusion is that the burgers are better at Burger King.

When we add to the original, as we do by inserting the missing conclusion, we should make sure that we can justify the addition by checking our version against the context and wording of the original.

◆————————————————————————————————————

EXERCISE SET

Exercise 2: Part A

Assume that each of the following statements is a conclusion in an argument. Comment on the degree of certainty indicated in the statement: very tentative, somewhat tentative, quite certain, very certain.

Briefly explain your reasons for your answer by pointing out those words on which it is based and saying what you think they mean in the context of the statement given.

*1. Few teachers are likely to enjoy junior high school teaching, if the stories my daughter has to tell are anything to go by.

2. Dinosaurs are not the only animal to have become extinct.

3. Earthquakes are certain to do great damage to American and Canadian cities on the West Coast in the next two decades.

*4. Heart transplants are probably beneficial to most patients who receive them.

5. Perhaps the Soviet Union will split into five or more distinct countries.

tentative (margin note)

***6.** There's no doubt about it: abortion is murder, pure and simple.

7. I would estimate that there are few blind students who are entirely comfortable in classes designed for the sighted.

Certain (margin note)

8. Professors who enforce paper deadlines rigidly are the very same ones who have trouble meeting publication and administration deadlines themselves.

v. certain (margin note)

9. A degree in management science will get you a better job than a degree in philosophy.

v. certain (margin note)

***10.** Allergies could be aggravated by general environmental problems, especially that of air pollution.

Exercise 2: Part B

In the case of each of the following passages, state whether an argument is given. If so, identify the conclusion. Do you think any of these passages should be interpreted as expressing an argument with an unstated conclusion? If so, which ones? What is the unstated conclusion, and what are your reasons for reading it into the passage?

1. "In projecting energy consumption, let us first consider just the United States, which consumes much of the world's energy and is to some extent representative of the industrialized regions of the world. Before projecting into the future, let us look back at what has happened in the past."

N (margin note)

(John C. Fisher, *Energy Crisis in Perspective* [New York: John Wiley, 1974], p. 19)

2. *Background:* The following comments are made on the issue of how we might achieve world peace:

"Would you feel more secure now if Toronto were armed? Are you less secure now that Toronto doesn't maintain an army in case Hamilton invades? We haven't ended conflict between individuals or cities; we've just found other ways of dealing with it."

USS concl (margin note)

(J. S., Toronto, as quoted in James Freeman, *Thinking Logically* [Englewood Cliffs, N.J.: Prentice-Hall, 1988], p. 340)

***3.** *Background:* The following are comments about what is said by the use of pictures, as contrasted with statements.

"Logicians tell us . . . that the terms 'true' and 'false' can only be applied to statements, propositions. And whatever may be the usage of critical parlance, a picture is never a statement in that sense of the term. It can no more be true or false than a statement can be blue or green."

(E. H. Gombrich, in *Art and Illusion*, as quoted in Erving Goffman, *Gender Advertisements* [Harper & Row: New York, 1979], p. 14)

***4.** *Background:* This passage is taken from a letter by M. E. Surridge of the Department of French at Queen's University. The letter treats the subject of French immersion education. (In this type of education French is used as the main language of instruction for students who are not native speakers of French.) The letter appeared in the *Globe and Mail* for October 25, 1976.

"Your reporter claims that the North York experiment 'confirms the results of earlier research in St. Lambert, Que., that showed immersion programs in the early elementary grades are the most effective way of teaching a second language.' Neither experiment proves any such thing. Both tend to confirm the experience of certain other societies: that early immersion is extremely effective in some circumstances. Research has not yet isolated the required conditions for success. It also remains to be seen whether the North York youngsters continue to be bilingual, in adult life, and whether the price they pay in terms of advancement in their primary or material language is too great."

(Cited in David Hitchcock, *Critical Thinking: A Guide to Evaluating Information* [Toronto: Methuen, 1983], pp. 30–31)

***5.** *Background:* The following is a letter to *Time* magazine in the wake of an article on Gorbachev's attempts to reform the Soviet Union by introducing various democratic reforms. The issue is whether, in the chaotic situation resulting, Gorbachev can preserve his power.

"With his recent proposal to abolish the monopoly of the Communist Party in the Soviet

Union, Gorbachev should remember that for those in governing positions democracy implies permanent insecurity."

(Andrew Blum, Moroubra, Australia, in *Time*, March 12, 1990)

6. *Background:* This passage was printed in *Time* in its Letters section:

"As a German citizen born at the war's end, I agree with essayist Michael Kinsley on what America needs to do to help Eastern Europe consolidate its newborn democracies. But having lived for years in South America, I wonder why his brilliant reasoning that the U.S. is duty-bound to give financial aid has not been applied with more emphasis to neighbors in Latin America. They desperately need money and help, rather than bullets like the ones used in Panama, in order to cement progress."

(Einardo Bingemer, Rio de Janeiro, in *Time,* March 12, 1990)

*7. *Background:* The following passage is taken from an introductory philosophy book written for college and university students:

"Now consider what happens when you repeat the word 'chair' silently in your mind. Just say 'chair' to yourself over and over. Don't look at anything—close your eyes. . . . Right now, before you go on to the next paragraph, spend a few minutes repeating the word silently to yourself.

"What happens? The longer you listen to yourself repeating the word 'chair,' the more the meaning starts to dissolve. First the one mean-ing turns ambiguous—you hear the other words that compose the word 'chair,' like 'hair' and 'air.' Next, the unity of that mental sound dissolves as the end of one repetition slurs into the next. Eventually, all meaning dissolves. You hear just uninterpreted mental imagery—sounds without meaning."

(Daniel Kolak and Raymond Martin, *Wisdom without Answers* [Belmont, Calif.: Wadsworth, 1989], p. 42)

*8. *Background:* The following passage treats an aspect of the trade-off between quantity and quality in communications industries.

"There is some hope that as the structure of the mass media is altered by video cassette recorders, communication satellites, and cable television, the same media used to produce formula programming will be used to create more meaningful artistic experiences. While a number of companies were optimistic that fine arts programming was feasible, economics still guides and strangles most attempts to escape from the trap of formula. In 1981 William S. Paley, then the chairman of the board at CBS, began CBS Cable with the intention of producing high-quality cultural programming. CBS Cable went out of business in 1982 after losing more than thirty million dollars. The same fate awaited the Entertainment Channel with its BBC and Broadway productions. Tele-France USA gave up in September 1982 in its attempt to present French cultural programs."

(From Gary Gumpert, *Talking Tombstones and Other Tales of the Media Age* [Oxford and New York: Oxford University Press, 1987], p. 35)

◆
◇ ## IMPORTANT DETAILS ABOUT PREMISES

Ways Premises Support Conclusions

The subargument structures illustrated above were based on a simple argument structure where a single premise supports each conclusion. Obviously, many arguments have more than one premise. Where this is the case, it is important to understand how the premises combine to support the conclusion. They may either *link* or *converge* to support it. In either case, it is important to think of premises together when trying to understand and evaluate the argument. A mistake that is quite common when people begin to analyze arguments is to consider premise support for the conclusion by looking only at one premise at a time. This approach is not correct because it ignores the fact that when an argument has several premises, its premises combine, in various ways, in the arguer's attempt to support the conclusion.

This working together is especially easy to see when the premises are linked. Linked premises can only support the conclusion in the argument when they are taken together. In a linked argument, no single premise will give any support to the conclusion without the others. To see how this works, consider the following example:

1. Obesity is either genetic or environmental.
2. Obesity is not genetic.
Therefore,
3. Obesity is environmental.

We can reason from the combination of (1) and (2) to get the conclusion, (3). But if we were to argue either from (1) alone or from (2) alone, the argument would not make much sense. To support (3), (1) and (2) must be linked.

It is common for premises to work together by linking. Before leaving the topic, let us look at one further example:

1. A country in troubled times is like a ship in a storm.
2. A ship in a storm needs a strong, capable captain.
Therefore,
3. A country in troubled times needs a strong, capable leader.

Here again, premises must link if they are to support the conclusion. Without (2), (1) would have nothing to do with the conclusion and without (1), (2) would have nothing to do with it. To understand how the argument works, you have to see that both premises are needed. When you come to evaluate the argument this will be very important; if you evaluate without appreciating the way the premises are interdependent in their support, you will really miss the point.

Linked support contrasts with *convergent* support. Here too, we have to consider premises together to understand the argument. But with *convergent* support, the relationship between the premises is less tight. A conclusion is to be supported by several different premises, each of which states a separate reason, or separate piece of evidence that the arguer thinks is relevant to his or her case. In a convergent structure, the premises are not so interdependent that one would be unrelated to the conclusion without the others. We could take away a premise or two and still have some argument left, although the resulting argument would be weakened and less rich in detail.

Consider the following example:

1. Setting aside apartments for adults and keeping out children discriminates against people with children.
2. Setting aside apartments for adults and keeping out children encourages single childless people to pursue a hedonistic, irresponsible, and overly selfish lifestyle.

Therefore,
3.   Apartments should not keep children out.

Here, either (1) or (2) could provide some reason for the conclusion just by itself. Having both reasons together does, however, strengthen the argument.

There are, then, two basic facts to understand right now about the way in which premises support conclusions. First, premises should be considered together in their support. Second, they may be linked or convergent. In the latter case, it would be possible to see each premise as providing a separate reason or separate bit of evidence, in support of the conclusion, but the whole argument requires us to think of these separate strands together, as the weight of support accumulates. Convergent support is discussed further in Chapter 10, and various types of linked support are treated in detail in Chapters 7, 8, 9, 10, and 11.

◆────────────────────────────────────

EXERCISE SET

Exercise 3

Assume that each of the following passages represents an argument. Identify the premises and conclusion. For all cases where there is more than one premise, indicate whether you think the premises would link, or converge, to support the conclusion.

1.   People can't be taught how to be independent businesspeople by going to a free government program, because the very act of having a free program implies that you can get something worthwhile for nothing, and this is just the contrary of the attitude you need to be a successful independent businessperson.

*2.   Individuals are not reliable in their judgments, and groups are made of individuals, so probably groups are not reliable in their judgments either.

3.   Virtue is something that is valued because of the kinds of comparisons we make between people. If all people shared all good qualities equally, there would be no such thing as virtue.
(Adapted from philosopher Thomas Hobbes)

*4.   The black hole is a key scientific concept that is virtually impossible for nonexperts to comprehend. The notion of antimatter, required to account for what happens in nuclear explosions, is a real metaphysical paradox. And there is no understanding of what causation means when we come to the context of elementary physical particles. Thus we can see that modern physics is a mysterious subject indeed.

5.   There must be a devil because there is so much evil in the world, and the only way to explain it is by the existence of a supreme evil power.

6.   Language is necessary for communication and communication is necessary for advancement. Therefore, language is necessary for advancement. Any attempt to censor language could restrict advancement. This is why the censorship of books is always wrong.

*7.   "There are two methods of fighting, the one by law, the other by force. The first method is that of men, the second of beasts; but as the first method is often insufficient, one must have recourse to the second."
(Niccolo Machiavelli, *The Prince*, Chapter 18, quoted in John Hoaglund, *Critical Thinking* [Newport News, Va.: Vale Press, 1984], p. 126)

8.   "Have the notions of woman as earth mother, seductress, and paragon of virtue really

disappeared? Not entirely. . . . They are reflected in the lingering double standard about sexuality, in the popular view of rape, and in the tendency to condone wife beating. They are expressed—albeit in modified form—in the current stereotypes of femininity and masculinity."

(Joanne Rohrbaugh, *Women: Psychology's Puzzle* [New York: Basic Books, 1974])

9. "The motions of the stars proceed in a fixed order. The succession of the seasons also proceeds according to fixed laws. The change from day to night takes place without variation. We can see from these facts that nothing is better organized than the universe."

(Adapted from the Roman writer Cicero in *De Inventione;* cited in F. H. van Eemeren, R. Grootendorst, and T. Kruiger, *The Study of Argumentation* [New York: Irvington Press, 1984], p. 76)

*10. If a word could mean just anything, or could be used in any old way, there would in fact be no meaning at all. So language requires rules. To have a rule, we have to have more than one person following a rule. That's because a single person could make anything he wanted be right, and his so-called rule would not really be a rule at all. Thus private language is impossible.

(Adapted from philosopher Ludwig Wittgenstein)

The Problem of Missing Premises

Sometimes we may have the impression that the author of an argument has left out something important that he must have been implicitly claiming in order to support his case. It seems as though there is an additional premise—or even several additional premises—but these are unstated. Arguments can have *missing premises,* just as they can have missing conclusions. However, there are some differences, and unfortunately, the matter of missing premises is more complex and controversial than that of missing conclusions.

What makes an argument appear to have a missing premise? It is that, as stated, the argument strikes us as having a kind of hole or gap—a hole that we could fill in quite naturally if we added another premise to those the arguer has already stated. For example, many children argue that dads know more than moms because they are taller than moms. That is, they infer greater knowledge from greater height. This strikes most adults as quite an unreasonable jump in logic! You can fill it in if you realize that these children are relying on a premise that they haven't stated: namely, taller people know more than shorter people. When you hear or read an argument and think that it has one or more missing premises, you are perceiving a kind of logical gap that you would like to fill in.

What makes the problem of missing premises tricky is that we can't go around filling in every gap we perceive in other people's arguments just so that we can build up those arguments into something we find clear. We want to find missing premises when there really are some, but we don't want to rewrite other people's arguments just to suit our own sense of how things should hang together. When we see a gap in an argument, how do we know that the author was omitting exactly the premise that we would want to use to fill in that gap? The difficulty is to balance our own sense of logical direction with due respect for what other arguers actually said and meant.

It is hard to strike just the right balance here, and this makes the problem of missing premises one of the most difficult in the theory of argument. In fact, even trained philosophers and logicians disagree quite vehemently about it. In this book we take a very cautious approach to the problem, because we think it is too easy for people to read into arguments things that they for whatever reason want to find there and, as a result, to misinterpret what others have to say. We urge that you add missing premises quite sparingly, paying careful attention to what arguers really said or wrote, and being sure to justify any additions by reference to the material that is present.

The question of whether to add missing premises arises when you see a gap in an argument as stated. You will then see that this gap could be filled in, making the flow of the argument much more natural and clear, if a particular missing premise were written in. When this arises, write down what you think is a missing premise and then look carefully at what the author has actually said. Make sure that you can justify the addition of the premise with reference to the wording and context that are actually there. This will prevent you from wandering too far from the stated text and turning other people's arguments into your own.

Of course, you have a different situation if you are listening to someone present an argument and you think that she is relying on unstated premises. This is an easier case because you can simply ask her whether she is using the premises you see as missing as part of her argument. If she is, she can say so; if she is not, you can point out what you think is a logical gap in her argument. In the case of written arguments, even when you think that by adding premises you can improve an argument, you should not do this unless you can justify it with reference to the stated text and any background knowledge you may have about what the author would accept.

Our policy amounts to this: no supplementation without justification. The reason for this restriction is that we appraise other people's arguments in order to find out how strong their reasons are for their particular conclusions. If we start adding extra premises whenever we don't find the logical flow of an argument natural, we will end up wandering away from the arguments we started with and working on new arguments, which we have invented ourselves. In doing this, we will risk reading our own minds into other people's reasoning and, possibly, failing to understand what those others really have to say. We will look at several examples so that you can get a sense of how this policy is applied.

Here is an argument that can be considerably clarified by the addition of a missing premise. As we shall see, in this case, there is sufficient basis in the stated material for adding that premise.

> DON'T TAKE THE ADVICE OF THE NUCLEAR ESTABLISHMENT ON THE IS-SUE OF NUCLEAR SAFETY. The people that make and run nuclear power plants have assured us that there will never be a major catastrophe. But manufacturers of nuclear reactors also make toasters, dryers, washers, and television sets, and other household appliances. These simple appliances are not completely reliable and there is much less reason to believe that complex nuclear reactors are completely dependable.
>
> Remember: We're talking about millions of lives and billions of dollars in property damage.[7]

The stated premises and the conclusion are as follows:

1. Manufacturers of nuclear reactors make toasters, dryers, washers, and other simple household appliances.
2. Toasters, dryers, washers, and other simple household appliances made by the manufacturers who also make nuclear reactors are not completely reliable.

So,

3. Complex nuclear reactors are very unlikely to be completely reliable.
4. Unreliable nuclear reactors could cause millions of lives to be lost and billions of dollars to be lost in property damage.

Therefore,

5. We should not take the advice of the nuclear establishment when it assures us that nuclear energy is safe.

You can see that there is a subargument here. (1) and (2) link to support (3); then (3) and (4) link to support (5).

In this case we'll concentrate only on the subargument, since that is where the problem of a missing premise arises. In (1) the author deals with appliances like toasters, which he says are "simple." In (2) he states that these simple appliances are unreliable. From these statements, he concludes in (3) that nuclear reactors, which are complex, are less likely to be reliable than the simple appliances made by the same companies. What is missing here is an explicit assertion that complex items are less likely to be reliable than simple items made by the same company. This claim is never overtly made, but it is strongly suggested in the author's wording when he says, "These simple appliances are not completely reliable and there is even less reason to believe that complex nuclear reactors are reliable." "Even less reason," in this context, suggests:

6. Companies are less likely to make complex items that are reliable than they are to make simple items that are reliable.

The subargument may be regarded as having (6) as a missing premise. It moves from (1), (2), and (6) to (3), instead of from (1) and (2) to (3). By adding (6) as a missing premise, we make the structure of the original argument clearer, for we can see just how the fallibility of toasters is supposed to be related to the fallibility of nuclear reactors. The added statement is underlined to indicate that it is something we have placed in the argument in the process of analyzing it.

Another example with a missing premise is the following argument put forward by C. S. Lewis:

And immortality makes this other difference, which by the by, has a connection with the difference between totalitarianism and democracy. If individuals live only seventy years, then a state or nation, or a civilization, which may last for a thousand years, is more important than an individual. But if Christianity is true, then the individual is not only more important but incomparably more important, for he is everlasting and the life of the state or a mere civilization, compared with his, is only a moment.[8]

If we used the stated material only, the argument would look like this:

1.   If Christianity is true, then the individual is everlasting.
2.   States and civilizations are not everlasting.
Therefore,
3.   If Christianity is true, the individual is incomparably more important than the state or civilization.

Let us check back to the original passage to see whether this standardized version is accurate. The first sentence of the paragraph introduces the topic, and in it Lewis adds an "aside" ("which by the by"), which is not part of the argument. The second sentence states what Lewis regards as a consequence of non-Christian views: what would follow if individuals lived only seventy years. But Lewis's main concern is with the consequences of the Christian view; the alternative view is included as part of the background and is not really a premise or conclusion. The word *but* indicates a return to his main line of thinking: he spells out the consequence of Christianity for the importance of the individual. This is his main point and his conclusion.

Lewis's conclusion is qualified in an important way. He does not state here that Christianity *is* true, but that *if* it is true, the individual is incomparably more important than the state or civilization. The word *for* (an indicator word) in that sentence introduces the reasons for the conclusion: the individual would be everlasting and the state or civilization would not. Our standardization omits the background and the aside, and contains only the premises and conclusion.

In this passage Lewis reasoned from the longer life of an individual, under the Christian hypothesis, to the greater importance of that individual. In reasoning this way, he seems to be committed to the belief that longer life makes for greater importance. We can see this commitment because longer life is the only feature of the individual referred to, and it is said to make him or her "incomparably more important" than states or civilizations, which last for less time than all eternity. We might consider adding as a missing premise:

<u>4</u>.   Of different entities, the one that lasts for the longest time is the most important.

We have seen that Lewis is committed to (<u>4</u>) by other things he says and by the direction of his argument; adding (<u>4</u>) will make the argument much clearer. It will then look like this:

1.   If Christianity is true, then the individual is everlasting.
2.   States and civilizations are not everlasting.
<u>4</u>.   Of different entities, the one that lasts for the longest time is the more important.
Therefore,
3.   If Christianity is true, the individual is incomparably more important than the state or the civilization.

Statement (<u>4</u>), which has been added, should be underlined. Premises (1), (2), and (<u>4</u>) link to support (3).

This standardization of the argument will be helpful when we come to evaluate Lewis's reasoning, because having that missing premise written out clearly will bring it to our attention. (The missing premise seems rather disputable, but here we'll continue to concentrate our energies on standardizing, not on appraisal. In later chapters, when we study the evaluation of arguments, we will see how important missing premises can be in evaluation.)

Often missing premises are quite debatable, and when you write them in, you immediately see a basis for criticizing the argument. If you go on to make a criticism disputing a premise you have written in yourself, make sure that you have good reasons for interpreting the argument as you have.

A final example of an argument with a missing premise is the following:

> In fact, the ordinary orange is a miniature chemical factory. And the good old potato contains arsenic among its more than 150 ingredients. This doesn't mean natural foods are dangerous. If they were, they wouldn't be on the market.[9]

This argument was part of an advertisement put out by a food processing company. The overall thrust of the advertisement was that there is no general difference, so far as safety is concerned, between naturally grown and artificially manufactured foods. What we have shown here is a subargument used on the way to establishing that more general conclusion.

The advertisement stated (first quoted sentence) that natural foods like oranges and potatoes contain chemicals; this is said in order to associate these foods with processed foods. But many of us now think that foods containing chemicals are dangerous, and the ad wishes to assure us that they are not. This is the conclusion: "This doesn't mean natural foods are dangerous." The reason in support of this conclusion is offered in the final sentence. The first two sentences have to do with the larger argument of the ad; the last two contain the subarguments, which we will concentrate on here.

1. If natural foods such as potatoes and oranges were dangerous, they would not be on the market.

So,

2. Natural foods such as potatoes and oranges are not dangerous.

Now if you look at the reasoning from (1) to (2), you will see the ad depends on an obvious fact: such natural foods as potatoes and oranges are on the market. Consider the following as a missing premise:

<u>3</u>. Natural foods such as potatoes and oranges are on the market.

The addition of this premise makes the structure of the reasoning very clear indeed. Since (<u>3</u>) is a matter of common knowledge, which the advertiser certainly would have accepted, there is no danger of writing in something that he or she didn't believe.

This is a case in which the unstated premise is something so well known both to the arguer and to the intended audience that it does not even seem worth saying. In fact, the obviousness of a given claim is often a reason for not bothering to say it or write it in just so many words. The argument as stated here had (3) as a missing premise, and the supplemented argument has two premises, (1) and (3), which link to support the conclusion, (2).

In this example about potatoes and oranges, the missing premise was not exactly suggested by the wording used in the original. It was added on the grounds that it is such an obvious matter of fact that the arguer would have been sure to accept it. It is legitimate to add a missing premise if the wording of the text or speech provides good reasons for doing so or if that premise is required to make the argument fit together and it is something that the arguer would accept.

In some other kinds of examples, we have a choice between seeing a gap in reasoning and adding something that is not specifically suggested by actual wording or a matter of common knowledge. We sense a gap, sense that the arguer's reasoning cannot be followed through as it is stated, and sense that there must be a missing premise. Here is a simple example:

1. John is a short, slim, unathletic man.
Therefore,
2. John probably has an inferiority complex.

If anyone were to argue this way, he would effectively be assuming a connection between a man's being short, slim, and unathletic and having an inferiority complex. We can make the argument logically clear by spelling out this connection. The arguer would not need to assume that all such men have this problem, because the conclusion includes the word *probably*. Because of the direction of the reasoning and because of this qualifying word, we can justifiably add a missing premise to the effect that most short, slim, unathletic men have an inferiority complex. The resulting argument will then be:

1. John is a short, slim, unathletic man.
3. Most short, slim, unathletic men have an inferiority complex.
Therefore,
2. John probably has an inferiority complex.

Criticism of the argument would no doubt be directed to this missing premise, which is not terribly plausible. Even so, the missing premise is somewhat more plausible than another we could have added, which would also have served to link the stated premise with the stated conclusion. Consider:

4. Most short, slim, unathletic people have an inferiority complex.

This statement is less plausible than (3) because it makes a more sweeping claim and, given our background knowledge about the different expectations people still have of men and women, (4) is not nearly so likely to be true as (3). We have to be careful when adding premises not to make the original argument worse than it is. (If we do this, we commit something called the *straw man fallacy*, which is discussed in Chapter 6.) We should add the most plausible premise that will link the stated premises to the stated conclusion and that we can reasonably insist the arguer would accept or is committed to.

In short, missing premises should be added under the following conditions:

1. There is a logical gap in the argument as stated.

2. This logical gap could be filled by inserting an additional premise.

3. This additional premise is either something that the arguer accepts or something to which he or she is committed. Evidence that an arguer accepts a claim can either be found in the wording of the surrounding text or be based on the fact that the claim is a matter of common knowledge or belief— something that nearly everybody would accept. Or it can be based on the direction of the reasoning, which shows that the arguer is committed to the claim because only by such a commitment can he or she move from the stated premises to the stated conclusion.

4. Statements inserted as missing premises should be as plausible as possible, consistent with the previous conditions.[10]

In general, you should be cautious about adding missing premises. If you add more than two or three missing premises to a short passage, you are beginning to construct your own argument rather than standardizing that of the arguer.

EXERCISE SET

Exercise 4

Assume that each of the following passages states an argument in which the final sentence is the conclusion. In each case, determine what the premises of the argument are. Are there any unstated premises? If so, what are they?

1. If pollution could kill, we'd have been dead long ago. Alarmists are exaggerating the seriousness of pollution.

*2. Butterflies need warm air and sunlight to breed. So the conservatory at the zoo is just a perfect place for them.

3. Either many species of animals are going to become extinct in the near future or zoos are going to become ever more active in breeding programs for species preservation. We've got to give up our selfishness and do what's right for nature. Breeding programs are a must for zoos on an endangered planet.

4. Bicycles are the most efficient form of transport known. A bicycle uses human energy, not gas, oil, or coal. Cyclists don't contribute at all to either resource depletion or the greenhouse effect. In addition, they get good exercise and keep themselves in shape without resorting to expensive health clubs or dangerous sports like mountaineering. The bike is the most environmentally suitable vehicle for the future.

*5. If God had meant us to fly through the air, we would have been born with wings. People aren't meant to fly.

6. "I found out she's a librarian. So she's highly intelligent."
(From a cartoon)

7. Eternity is forever and forever is a long time. What would there be to do in heaven? It would be drastically boring. No one who really thought about it would want to live for all eternity.

*8. Efficiency is necessary for competition, and our industries must compete. Privatization of government-owned industry is the wave of the future; that's the route we have to go.

9. Photos of the town showed a murky yellow haze extending over the whole area. The air in the place is a danger to health.

*10. Understanding another person's ideas requires really listening to her and trying to experience the world as she experiences it. If we can't do this, we're never going to resolve conflicts and get rid of social problems. The prospects of really working out conflicts, for a full resolution, are quite gloomy.

Exercise 5

For each of the following examples, decide whether the passage contains an argument. If it does, represent the argument in a standardized form with the premises preceding the conclusion. Check carefully to see whether any passage requires either a missing conclusion or a missing premise, and indicate any subarguments. If you add material that is not explicitly stated by the author, give interpretive reasons for doing so.

*1. If you've eaten a banana, you've eaten everything in Nutrasweet.

2. High blood pressure is a real health hazard. Therefore, anyone who is overweight should get to work and reduce.

3. Anyone who has the capacity to kill should avoid keeping guns around the house. So no one should keep guns around the house.

*4. The crime rate among teenagers is going up. Can we believe that drug use is declining if teenage theft is on the rise?

5. If people were truly unselfish, they would give as much to worthy charities as they save for their old age. Do they?

6. Chicken pox is a common childhood disease that can be unpleasant but that never leads to dangerous complications.

*7. Secondhand smoke can cause minor health problems to nonsmokers, because some non-smokers suffer from headaches, runny noses, and itchy eyes as a result of exposure to smoke. I can tell you, it is downright irritating to suffer a headache for a day just because some inconsiderate person has smoked away at you in an elevator! Besides, secondhand smoke can cause lung cancer even in nonsmokers who are regularly exposed to smoke. We have good reason to ban smoking in public places.

8. It is only because we are lazy parents that we permit our children to watch television instead of pursuing healthy or creative activities. Such parental laziness has high social costs, which we can expect to feel more acutely as the television generation comes of age.

*9. "Dr. Joyce Brothers visited Weight Loss Clinic and went home impressed. It's one thing for us to tell you that we offer a superb weight loss program. But it's even more impressive when Dr. Joyce Brothers does the talking:

  " 'One of the problems I'm asked about most often is overweight. If I could put together the best possible weight loss program, I'd make sure it was run by trained professionals . . . counsellors and nurses, who were not only dedicated . . . but enthusiastic about helping each individual client achieve success. A program like the one at Weight Loss Clinic.'

  "Dr. Joyce Brothers was impressed. There's no reason why you shouldn't be."

(Advertisement, Toronto *Star,* February 25, 1981)

*10. *Background:* In 1978, Russian dissident novelist Alexander Solzhenitsyn made a widely publicized speech criticizing the materialism of western societies. He said:

  "If humanism were right in declaring that man is born to be happy, he would not be born to die. Since his body is doomed to die, his task on earth evidently must be of a more spiritual nature."

(As quoted in the Calgary *Herald,* July 6, 1978)

11. The *Challenger* shuttle explosion could not have been caused by a leaky valve. If the valve had leaked, the instrument panel would have registered it. Since the only other possibility is an expanded, overheated O-ring, that must have triggered the explosion.

*12. "Dictionaries cannot settle all questions about how words are to be used, nor are they intended to. If they were, then such a heated debate as the current one about abortion could be settled by looking up definitions for 'human being' or 'person.' "

(John Hoaglund, *Critical Thinking* [Newport News, Va.: Vale Press, 1984], pp. 45–46)

13. "The application of the physical and biological sciences alone will not solve our problems because the solutions lie in another field. Better contraceptives will control population only if people use them. New weapons may offset new defenses and vice versa, but a nuclear holocaust can be prevented only if the conditions under which nations make war can be changed. New methods of agriculture and medicine will not help if they are not practiced, and housing is a matter not only of buildings and cities but of how people live. Overcrowding can be corrected only by inducing people not to crowd, and the environment will continue to deteriorate until polluting practices are abandoned. In short, we need to make vast changes in human behavior, and we cannot make them with the help of nothing more than physics or biology, no matter how hard we try."

(B. F. Skinner, *Beyond Freedom and Dignity* [New York: Bantam Books, 1971], p. 2)

14. "Everyone who exercises to improve his muscles knows that what is physical can be altered by behavior. The brain is a physical organ; as such, we have every reason to expect that it can be altered by behavior and cultural patterns. Work with retarded infants, in which great strides have been made by the technique of extra stimulation to 'exercise' the brain, is an illustration of the truth of this claim."

(Rose Kemp, "Sexy? Or Sexist?" unpublished essay)

*15. "It is important that we understand how profoundly we all feel the needs that religion, down the ages, has satisfied. I would suggest that these needs are of three types: firstly, the need to be given an articulation of our half-glimpsed knowledge of exaltation, of awe, of wonder; life is an awesome experience, and religion helps us understand why life so often makes us feel small, by telling us what we are smaller than . . . Secondly, we need answers to the unanswerable: how did we get here? How did 'here' get here in the first place? Is this, this brief life, all there is? How can it be? What would be the point of that? And, thirdly, we need codes to live by, 'rules for every damn thing.' The idea of god is at once a repository for our awestruck wonderment at life and answer to the great questions of existence, and a rulebook too. The soul needs all these explanations—not simply rational explanations, but explanations of the heart."

(Salman Rushdie, "Is Nothing Sacred?" in *GRANTA* 31 [Spring 1990]: 104)

16. "As a torch sends rays of light out into dark places, so America should send out messages that will, if heeded, eventually improve life in other parts of the world."

(Garret Hardin, "A Lamp, not a Breadbasket," advertisement in *Harper's,* May 1981)

17. The following dialogue is taken from a cartoon:

"Did you ask Kelsey out for a date?"

"Nope. I found out she's a librarian, which means she's highly intelligent. Therefore, I'm sure she's only interested in highly intelligent guys. That rules me out!"

"No it doesn't!"

"It doesn't? Gee, thanks, Patrick!"

"They say opposites attract! Maybe she goes for simpletons."

(How many main arguments can you find here? Are there any subarguments? Set out all main arguments in standardized form.)

❖   CHAPTER SUMMARY

Understanding the structure of an argument is fundamental if we are to evaluate it correctly. A good awareness of argument structure is also useful when we construct arguments, because knowing what the structures are helps us to make our own arguments clearer.

When we consider a speech or a written passage, there are a number of distinct stages in identifying an argument it may contain. First we have to make sure that there is an argument—that is, that the speech or text is one in which the author is trying to support a claim or claims by putting forward others as evidence for it. Then, we have to identify the conclusion and listen or look carefully to determine just what scope and degree of certainty is being claimed.

Even when a passage is basically argumentative, there may be parts that are not argumentative; examples would be background information, remarks that are "asides," explanations, and jokes. In identifying premises, we have to omit these aspects and restrict ourselves to claims that seem to be put forward as supporting the conclusion. Some premises may, in turn, be supported, in which case there is a subargument structure.

When there are several premises, they support the conclusion together and will have to be considered together when we come to appraise the argument. In a linked kind of support, the premises are interdependent in the way they support the conclusion; if we did not consider them together, there would be no support at all. In convergent support, on the other hand, one premise alone would give some support to the conclusion, but the various premises, together, cumulate so that there is more support. Linked and convergent support can be found in main arguments or in subarguments.

Either conclusions or premises may, on some occasions, be unstated. Sometimes, then, when we write a standardized version of an argument, we will include statements that are not in an original text, at least not in so many words. Whether we add conclusions or premises, we should be careful to find justification for what we are doing in the stated text. We should underline any such added statements to remind ourselves that they were not strictly present in the original.

The standardized argument, with premises, any missing premises, conclusion, and any missing conclusion, should be arranged in logical order. That is, the premises should precede the conclusion. If there are subarguments, the premises of the subargument should precede that conclusion too.

Putting it all together, we can see that really grasping the structure of an argument can be a complex process. It may involve some deletion (of material that is not argument), some addition (of unstated premises and conclusion), some rewording (so that premises and conclusions are stated in clear language), and some rearranging (so that premises are stated leading to the conclusion, with subarguments fitting in appropriately along the way).

❖   **REVIEW OF TERMS INTRODUCED**

Standardizing (an argument) Picking the conclusion and premises of an argument from a passage and setting them up in a standard simple format with the conclusion at the end.

Subargument A smaller argument within a larger one, in which a premise of a main argument is itself defended.

Main conclusion The main claim defended in an argument.

Whole argument Argument for a main conclusion, including all subarguments used to support any premises.

Intermediate conclusion A premise in an argument, used to defend a main claim, but one that is itself defended in a subargument. The intermediate conclusion can be thought of as a conclusion that is reached along the way to the main conclusion.

Scope (of conclusion) Quantity of members of a group or category the conclusion is about. Scope is indicated by such words as *all, most, many,* and *some.*

Degree of certainty (of conclusion) Level of certainty or tentativeness indicated for the conclusion. The arguer may claim that something is certainly or definitely the case, that it is probably the case, that it is perhaps the case, or that it might be the case.

Categorically stated conclusion Conclusion stated in such a way that it is reasonable to attribute a high degree of certainty to the arguer.

Qualified conclusion Conclusion stated in such a way that it is reasonable to attribute less than a high degree of certainty to the arguer.

Unstated, or missing, conclusion A conclusion not put into words but suggested by the context, wording, and natural logical order of a passage. *Note:* Unstated conclusions should be added only when there is a clear interpretive justification for doing so.

Linked support A kind of support where premises are interdependent in their support for a conclusion; when premises are linked, the removal of one would affect the bearing of the others upon the conclusion.

Convergent support A kind of support where premises work together in a cumulative way to support the conclusion, but are not linked. The bearing of one premise on the conclusion would be unaffected if the other premises were removed; however, the argument is strengthened when the premises are considered together, since more evidence is then offered.

Missing, or unstated, premise A premise not stated in just so many words but suggested by the context, wording, and natural logical order of a passage and needed to fill a gap in the reasoning. *Note:* Missing premises should be supplied only when there is a clear interpretive justification for doing so.

Notes

1. Joyce Young, *Fundraising for Non-Profit Groups* (N. Vancouver, B.C.: Self-Counsel Press, 1978), p. 112.
2. C. S. Lewis, *Mere Christianity* (New York: Macmillan, 1953), p. 106.
3. The argument can be regarded as having an additional implied conclusion that there is life after death; the topic of missing, or implied, conclusions is addressed below. In the interests of having a simple exposition, it is not raised here.
4. Letter to the Toronto *Star,* October 25, 1980.
5. Peter Shaw, "Degenerate Criticism," *Harper's,* October 1979, pp. 93–99.
6. Letter to *Discover,* November 1980.
7. *Informal Logic Newsletter,* Examples Supplement for 1980.
8. C. S. Lewis, *Mere Christianity,* p. 100.
9. Advertisement by the Monsanto Chemical company, *Harper's,* October 1980, p. 25. This argument can be regarded, in addition, as implying the further conclusion that having chemicals in it does not make a food dangerous. In order not to unduly complicate the particular topic of missing premises, I have deliberately omitted discussing this further implication in the text.
10. I am grateful to Allan Spangler for suggestions about this discussion of missing premises. The problem is so difficult and yet so basic that it poses real problems for textbooks. It is a challenge to say something that is complex enough to be accurate and yet simple enough to be comprehensible at an early stage in a course. I discuss the problem at length in *Problems in Argument Analysis and Evaluation* (Dordrecht, Holland, and Providence, R.I.: Foris, 1987). See especially Chapters 5, 6, and 7.

CHAPTER 3

When Is an Argument a Good One?

WE ARE NOW READY TO PROCEED to the stage of evaluating arguments—reaching informed judgments as to how good or poor they are. Of course many different issues bear on the evaluation of arguments. We can't study them all simultaneously. The approach we have chosen in this book is to introduce the basic conditions of good argument first in a fairly simple way, and then move to more fully explain related details later. In this chapter we work at a simple level. As you use the conditions developed here, you will come to appreciate the need for the more detailed and more complete explanations that are given in subsequent chapters.

THE CHALLENGE OF ARGUMENT

Someone arguing for a conclusion on the basis of premises is trying to make a reasonable case for something she believes. She thinks there are good reasons for the claim she is defending in her conclusion, and she is trying to persuade others of this claim by giving evidence and reasons for it in her premise. She tries to use premises the audience will believe and reasoning that will lead the audience from those premises to the conclusion.

In effect, an arguer putting forward an argument does these three things:

(1) She asserts the premises.

(2) She asserts that *if* the premises are true (or acceptable) the conclusion is true (or acceptable).

(3) She asserts the conclusion.

In the ideal case, the audience accepts the premises, understands and accepts the accuracy of the reasoning from the premises to the conclusion, and is led to accept the conclusion. If the audience does not accept the conclusion, it finds some error either in the premises or in the reasoning.

What we call the challenge of argument is to construct and respond to arguments in ways that are appropriate to this basic structure. We must think through the premises and reasoning given and base our acceptance or rejection of the conclusion on this reflection. Arguing on the basis of premises to a conclusion is a natural and common human activity. Nevertheless, there are some responses to it that fail to take the basic nature of argument into account.

The most common mistake people make when others offer arguments is to ignore the premises and the reasoning and evaluate the conclusion directly. They listen or read only partially; when they come to a claim they disagree with, they simply reject it without checking to see whether the speaker or arguer has given reasons for it, reasons that should be taken into account before the claim is just rejected. Or, alternately, they hastily judge that an entire speech or passage is sensible and well-reasoned, just because they agree with the conclusion. They fail to check whether the premises used are plausible and whether the reasoning is good or poor.

It is extremely important to separate your evaluation of the argument from your prior belief about its conclusion. Someone who offers you an argument is giving you reasons or evidence to accept a claim. If you look directly at the conclusion and just accept or reject it wholly on its own, you are, in effect, ignoring the argument.

Consider the following dialogue as an example:

DIALOGUE I

Peter: Mountain climbing is a terrific sport. It gives people a chance to get out in beautiful country, it gives them good exercise, it builds really strong arm and leg muscles, and it requires great team work.

Susan: A great sport? Isn't it kind of dangerous?

Peter: More than any other sport I know it builds both health and team work.

Susan: I don't know. I've heard about a lot of accidents mountain climbing.

Peter: Furthermore, you aren't going to find a better sport for aerobic strength and arm and leg muscle development.

Susan: Mountain climbing is really risky. I just can't see the point. And besides, why should the public have to pay when these mountain climbers get into trouble? The forest rangers are in there with helicopters and heaven knows what else, and it all costs taxpayers' money.

Peter: Come on, don't be such a nervous Nellie. We're going out next weekend and I was going to ask you to come. But I guess I won't. Obviously, you're not the type.

Here Peter and Susan ignore each other's arguments to the point where they seem about to lapse into a quarrel.

Peter puts forward four reasons why he thinks mountain climbing is a terrific sport: it gets people out in beautiful country, it provides good exercise, it builds strong arm and leg muscles, and it requires great team work. Susan obviously doesn't agree with Peter's claim; and she states another view, also based on an argument: mountain climbing isn't a good sport because it is too unsafe. But what is notable is that Susan does not respond at all to Peter's argument. It is as though he did not use premises at all; she disagrees with his claim about mountain climbing, and she reacts to his argument by disagreeing with the conclusion instead of by considering his reasons and how they might support what he has to say. Peter responds in kind and ignores Susan's argument.

The dialogue thus shows the two characters talking at cross-purposes. Each is trying to defend a point of view with reasons but ignoring the reasons put forward by the other. It does not seem likely that either will convince the other or that they will resolve the dispute by coming to a third view. This reaction is a common way of avoiding the challenge of argument.

What could Susan and Peter have done to better meet the challenge of argument? Compare Dialogue II with Dialogue I to get some idea.

DIALOGUE II

Peter: Mountain climbing is a terrific sport because it's so good for muscle development and team work. Also, you see wonderful scenery when you're mountain climbing.

Susan: I doubt that mountain climbing is better for developing muscles than some other sports like soccer and tennis. Is it better for developing team work than football or baseball or basketball? I can see why mountain climbing attracts people, in a way, but I think it's too risky to be a good sport to take up.

Peter: I'm not saying it's the only way to develop muscles and good team work. You could do this through other sports, of course. But mountain climbing is such a challenge and it's so much fun and gives you such a sense of achievement. When you put these together with the good exercise and teamwork, you've really got something. As for risk, why do you think mountain climbing is so risky?

Susan: It's those stories you see in the paper every summer about how the forest rangers have to go out and use helicopters to rescue these mountain climbers who go out on ledges and so on.

This time Susan considers Peter's argument and asks him just how several of his premises are supposed to support his conclusion. She mentions her own view that mountain climbing isn't such a great sport because it is too risky. And Peter responds to her argument by asking her why she thinks it is risky. He is, in effect, questioning her premise (politely) and asking for a subargument. Whether or not Peter convinces Susan in the end, we can see that much more information is being exchanged, and the situation seems less likely to degenerate into a quarrel—an argument in the sense of a fight instead of a reasoned attempt to justify a point of view.

We are sometimes tempted to react to argument as though all we had to do was evaluate the conclusion. We are tempted to respond positively whenever we agree with the conclusion and negatively whenever we disagree with it. We behave like Susan and Peter in Dialogue I: we just don't want to follow the thinking through. We are tempted by the short cuts of dogmatic rejection or hasty agreement.

The temptation to evaluate arguments by focusing solely on their conclusion should be resisted because it deprives us of any opportunity to change our mind on the basis of an argument. This opportunity is a valuable one, one that can genuinely open our minds and give us new information.

How can another person's argument lead you to change your mind? Suppose you are inclined to disagree with, or feel some doubt about, the conclusion, but you identify premises put forward to support it and you find that you do accept those premises. You then think the argument through, from premises to conclusion, and try to see how the arguer has reasoned from the premises to the conclusion. If the premises logically support the conclusion, and they seem to be true or acceptable, then you have rational support for a conclusion with which you did not previously agree. You have good reason to change your mind—or at least to begin thinking about the issue and examining the argument to see whether you can identify the point where it has gone wrong.

In real life there are some arguments that we do not have the time and energy to respond to. If the issue is relatively insignificant it may be all right to ignore an argument; we cannot argue over everything in every detail all the time. In this book, since our goal is to practice constructing, understanding, and evaluating arguments, we try to meet the challenge of argument whenever it arises.

It is probably more common to reject or ignore arguments when we disagree with the claim defended than when we agree with it. But in fact, having a true or acceptable conclusion is not enough to make an argument a good one. A good argument must have true or acceptable premises and correct reasoning from those premises to the conclusion. The challenge of argument is to reason through, to appraise the premises and the accuracy of the reasoning from those premises as a basis for forming our judgment about the conclusion. A convincing argument may give us good reason to change our mind, and for clear, fair, and open-minded thinking, we must be alert to this possibility.

Suppose that you are absolutely convinced by common experience that the conclusion of someone's argument should not be accepted. In such a case, you will be inclined to say that there must be something wrong with the argument. But then your task is to find out what that is. It is not enough to reject the argument because you do not like its conclusion: you must find something wrong either with its premises or with its reasoning—or both.

There are two basic ways the argument can go wrong: the premises may be incorrect, or the way they are used to support the conclusion may be incorrect. To truly meet the challenge of argument, you should respond to arguments as attempts to give reasoned support for conclusions. This means doing your own reasoning to determine whether you dissent from the premises, or the reasoning, or both—that is, to determine just why you disagree. If you do not want to accept someone's conclusion on the basis of his argument, you should have reason to reject the premises, or the reasoning from the premises to the conclusion, or both. To criticize an argument merely on the grounds that you do not agree with its conclusion is not an adequate response.

EXERCISE SET

Exercise 1: Part A

Read the following dialogues. In each one, the first character gives an argument and the second character responds to it. Find those cases in which the second character's response meets the challenge of argument and indicate that it does. Find those cases in which the second character's response does not meet this challenge and indicate that they do not. In each case, explain the basis for your answer.

*1. *Caroline:* Mathematics is the most important subject you can study at a university. First, it is completely precise. There is always just one right answer to every question, and you can prove beyond any doubt that that answer is the right one. Second, by doing proofs in mathematics you learn standards of rigor and exactness. Third, mathematics is the basis of all the sciences—physics, geology, chemistry, engineering, even biology. You can't do these if you don't understand mathematics. It is surely unfortunate that mathematics is so badly taught and that many people don't like it.

Bob: I hate math and I always will. Boy, my math teacher in elementary school was the crabbiest teacher I ever had. She could never explain anything, and the whole class was lost. I never caught up. Make everyone take math and you'll soon see colleges and universities empty of students.

2. *Alan:* Animals think and feel. I would defend this conclusion by analogy. We know that other humans think and feel only because of inferences we make from what they do. Well, animals exhibit intelligent behavior and sensitive behavior just as humans do. So animals think and feel too.

David: I disagree. The premise you use ignores the very important role language plays in our understanding of other people. We can't talk to dogs and lions, so any basis we would have for attributing thoughts to them just has to be less adequate than our evidence for the existence of thoughts in other people.

*3. *Linda:* A broadly based military operation is possible only when a society has an army that genuinely represents the various distinct classes in that society. We need the best army we can get, to protect our interests abroad. A volunteer army does not represent the population at large because it is chiefly the poor and less educated who volunteer. The middle and upper classes have other opportunities for jobs. Therefore, conscription is the answer. And furthermore, conscription should not be for men only. Women have to bear their share of the responsibility. I conclude that the draft should be reinstituted, and that it should be for all men and women within the required age range.

Jan: I'm horrified at the militaristic position you have taken. You are proposing that the whole society should be drained to support the military. This is a simply scandalous suggestion. As a feminist, you should be ashamed of yourself for supporting the militarism that has so long been a central aspect of male power in the world.

4. *Jim:* A mediator should be completely neutral between the two parties in a dispute. If he is on the side of either party, the process will be

unfair to the other party. In addition, the disadvantaged party will probably detect the lack of neutrality and then the mediation won't work. Neutrality is probably the most essential of all qualities for a mediator to have.

Roger: You're wrong. Sympathy is much more important. And concern that the conflict be resolved.

*5. *Angelita:* It's quite exciting to think that a branch of McDonald's has opened up in Moscow. You know, it's only a few blocks from the Kremlin. I think it's good to have these joint economic ventures between western companies and the Soviet Union, because it builds ties that bring countries together. Countries with such close economic relations aren't so likely to get into a war.

Sam: Obviously you've got nice idealistic intentions, but I wonder. Sometimes economic ties don't do very much to prevent war. In fact countries that are potential enemies sometimes even sell each other weapons, the way the United States and Britain did to Hitler in the 30s. I'm not so excited about a McDonald's in Moscow. Gosh, I think it's nice to have some parts of the world that are really different and distinct.

6. *Steve:* I would never let myself be hypnotized by anyone, for any reason.

Peter: Why not?

Steve: Too much is at stake. I just don't trust anyone that much. When you let somebody hypnotize you, they are getting right inside your mind, and they have a lot of potential to control you. Hypnosis is dangerous because it opens your mind to too much outside influence.

Peter: I can see what you mean but I don't know; hypnosis helped me a lot when I was quitting smoking. I used it once for dental work too and it was great.

*7. *Alexander:* The European Community is integrating considerably so far as currency arrangement, trade, border crossings, and employment standards are concerned. All this is just in the interests of large capitalist companies, though. They want to be able to do business efficiently and effectively and not to be hassled by problems in currency and differing national regulations. Sure, it's a great thing for them. But for the working people of Europe, the EC is on the whole a negative development, because it makes large companies more powerful. Anything that is good for large companies just can't be good for their workers.

Sheila: I don't know, Alexander. I think your model is too simplistic. You are assuming that whatever is good for the companies is bound to be bad for the workers. That's a pretty sweeping claim. There must be exceptions. If a company expands and gets more business, its employees often have more opportunities for advancement. So in that case, the interests of the company and those of the employees coincide.

8. *Rosita:* The weather has been unusually turbulent lately. Scientists say that's just what we should expect if the globe really is warming up. You know, the greenhouse effect and all that. I'm worried. Since just the things the greenhouse effect predicts are actually happening, the greenhouse effect is probably real. Our earth is going to get too hot to live on.

Alan: Come on, don't be an alarmist. The strange weather doesn't mean anything really. It doesn't prove the greenhouse effect, that's for sure. There's been strange weather off and on for hundreds and thousands of years. So what?

9. *James:* The earth is very much affected by all the creatures that live on it—man is only one. Animals and plants affect the earth's atmosphere. Water, too, is affected by what all the creatures do, and the earth adapts. The earth can adapt to changes all these creatures make in it. It is as though the earth and all the living creatures on it constitute a single vast organism.

Richard: I disagree. In an organism the parts more or less adapt to the needs of the whole. But plants and animals do not adapt to the needs of the earth. Quite the contrary, in fact. They can reproduce until their numbers are disproportionate and harmful.

(Adapted from "Gaia: The Smile Remains But the Lady Vanishes," *Scientific American,* December 1989, p. 34)

10. *Susan:* There is still a need for reverse discrimination. After all the civil rights action and all the nice talk about how African-Americans

and women should be more represented in high positions in business, government, and university, we still have not reached a fair percentage. A fair percentage would be 50 percent women and 20 percent African-Americans (of course some of the women would be African-Americans) because those are the figures for the population at large. Just look at the major corporations, the universities, the Senate, or the House of Representatives! Can you tell me there are 20 percent African-Americans and 50 percent women? Of course not. Reverse discrimination is the only route to go.

Bruce: Not on your life. This just replaces one sort of injustice with another. Do you want government interference all the time? And what if women and African-Americans don't even want these sorts of positions? I mean, maybe women aren't interested in being professors of engineering. Until we know whether they do, why on earth should we accept all sorts of interference to make the engineering faculty 50 percent female?

Exercise 1: Part B

For those examples in which the second character did not respond to argument in Part A, attempt to construct a response that would properly recognize the challenge of argument.

WHAT IS A GOOD ARGUMENT? THE ARG CONDITIONS

As we have seen, there are basically two aspects of argument evaluation: the evaluation of the premises and the evaluation of the reasoning from premises to the conclusion. Arguments that are deemed to be satisfactory in both regards may be called *good, strong, compelling, convincing, sound,* or *cogent.*

Among logicians, the term *sound* is perhaps the most common one to use. In this book, we generally use *cogent* as opposed to *sound.* To understand the reasons for this, we should begin by understanding what *sound* typically means in logic. As logicians define the term, a *sound argument* is one in which all the premises are true and they provide logically conclusive support for the conclusion.

Logically conclusive support, or deductive entailment, will be explained in more detail below. For now, let's just say that if the premises of an argument deductively entail its conclusion, then it is impossible, as a matter of logic, for the premises to be true and the conclusion false. Such an argument is known as deductively valid, or sometimes simply as valid. Here is a simple example of a deductively valid argument.

    1.   Either interest rates will go down or inflation will go up.
    2.   Interest rates will not go down.
    Therefore,
    3.   Inflation will go up.

In this argument, *if* the premises are true, it is logically impossible for the conclusion to be false. Thus the premises, if true, provide complete support for the conclusion. If true, they *prove* the conclusion true. In a situation where the premises were true, the argument would be *sound* in the traditional sense of the term. Any sound argument is a good argument.

There are several basic reasons why we do not use *sound* in this book as the most general term for evaluating arguments. One is that there are a number of ways premises can support a conclusion: deductive entailment, as we shall soon see, is not the only one. If we said that to be a good argument, an argument must be sound in the traditional sense, we would require all good arguments to be deductively valid. This means that we would have to say that arguments based on experience, which is a relevant and important basis for most of our beliefs, were not good arguments. This consequence does not seem to be sensible or practical.[1]

In addition, the concept of truth in the traditional account of soundness poses problems. In arguments, what is really important is not so much that the premises be true but that we know them to be true or, if knowledge is not obtainable, that we have good reasons to believe them. Many important arguments have premises that are plausible and accepted by the arguer and the audience but that we would hesitate to say are true in an absolute sense.

It would be confusing to define *sound* in a new sense, for we would then be giving a definition that was at odds with common practice and that would make this book hard to study in conjunction with some other texts and major works. Thus we use *cogent* as the most general term for argument evaluation. In this book good arguments are called *cogent arguments;* poor arguments are not cogent. Arguments that are sound in the traditional sense are generally cogent in the sense defined here. However, there are many arguments that pass our standards for cogency that are not sound in the sense of having true premises and being deductively valid. These include arguments in which the reasoning from the premises to the conclusion is legitimate and sensible, but not deductively valid and arguments in which the premises are acceptable claims for which we have reasonable evidence, but which we do not know to be true.

The basic elements of a cogent argument (*ARG conditions*) are as follows:

1. Its premises are all *acceptable*. That is to say, it is reasonable for those to whom the argument is addressed to believe these premises. There is good reason to accept the premises—even if they are not known for certain to be true. And there is no good evidence known to those to whom the argument is addressed that would indicate either that the premises are false or that they are doubtful. (General points about acceptability—and some common pitfalls in this area—are treated in Chapter 5.)

2. Its premises are properly connected to its conclusion. Traditional logicians have spent most of their time and energy on this condition. The condition may be usefully subdivided into two parts:
   a. The premises are genuinely *relevant* to the conclusion; that is, they give at least some evidence in favor of the conclusion's being true. They specify factors, evidence, or reasons that do count toward establishing the conclusion. They do not merely describe distracting aspects that lead you away from the real topic with which the argument is supposed to be dealing or that do not tend to support the conclusion. (The concept of relevance,

and some common fallacies of relevance, are explored in greater depth in Chapter 6.)

b. The premises provide sufficient or *good grounds* for the conclusion. In other words, considered together, the premises give sufficient reason to make it rational to accept the conclusion. This statement means more than that the premises are relevant. Not only do they count as evidence for the conclusion, they provide enough evidence, or enough reasons, taken together, to make it reasonable to accept the conclusion. (We delve further into various sorts of good grounds in Chapters 7 through 10.)

The subdivision in (2) above is given because it is a useful tool in criticizing arguments. It can happen that a premise is relevant to the truth of a conclusion but not sufficient to provide good grounds for it. For example, if a person cites her own two children as evidence for a general claim about all children, as in "My girl is more patient than my boy, so I think girls are more patient than boys," she has given evidence in her premises that is relevant to her conclusion. It does count in a small way toward showing that the conclusion is true. Two children are a small subset of children. But the premise is obviously not sufficient to show that the conclusion is true. There are hundreds of millions of boys and girls in the world, and the son and daughter of the person arguing represent just a tiny percentage of them. They may not be typical.

We distinguish the relevance of premises from the sufficiency of grounds because it is quite possible for a premise to be relevant to the conclusion without providing good grounds—as is illustrated in the preceding case.

On the other hand, if the premises provide good grounds, or sufficient evidence or reasons to make it rational to believe the conclusion, they will be relevant as well. Obviously, if they give enough evidence (sufficient grounds) to make the conclusion rationally acceptable, they will clearly at least give some evidence (be relevant) in support of that conclusion.

If its premises are relevant to its conclusion but are not sufficient to render it acceptable, an argument could be strengthened by adding more information similar in type to that offered in the premises. For instance, if the mother arguing that boys are less patient than girls had done a survey of hundreds of children, she might have found more evidence similar to her first bits of evidence, and she might eventually have found sufficient grounds for her conclusion. If the premises are not relevant at all, more information of a similar type wouldn't improve the argument.

Argument cogency requires:

A. *acceptability*—(1)
R. *relevance*—(2a)
G. *adequacy of grounds*—(2b)

You can keep these basic conditions of argument cogency firmly fixed in your mind by noting that the first letters, when combined, are "ARG"—the first three letters of the word *argument*.

REASONING FROM PREMISES TO CONCLUSIONS: MORE ON THE (R) AND (G) CONDITIONS

Deductive Entailment

Deductive entailment is a relationship between statements, such that one provides conclusive, logically sufficient support for the other.

For simplicity, let us first consider only two statements, one of which entails the other. Statement (1) entails statement (2) if and only if it is absolutely impossible for (2) to be false, given that (1) is true. When statement (1) entails statement (2), it logically guarantees the truth of statement (2).

Here are some examples. In each of the following pairs, statement (1) entails statement (2).

(a) 1. Five is not divisible without remainder by any integer number.
   2. Five is a prime number.

(b) 1. All refugees are persons fleeing their homelands due to fear of persecution.
   2. If there were no fear of persecution, there would be no refugees.

(c) 1. Lottery winners are always people who have bought tickets.
   2. You won't win a lottery unless you have bought a ticket on it.

In each case, (1) entails (2) because it would be impossible for (2) to be false and for (1) to be true. This does not say that (1) is true in any given case; it says only that *if* (1) is true, then (2) is also true.

Any argument in which the premises, taken together, entail the conclusion is a deductively *valid* argument and satisfies conditions (2a) and (2b). That is, if the *conjunction* of the premises deductively entails the conclusion, the argument satisfies (R) and (G) because it is valid. Valid reasoning is correct reasoning, so the premises of the argument do support the conclusion. They support it in the sense that *if* they are true, the conclusion must be true as well. And *if* they are reasonable to accept, they will render the conclusion reasonable to accept. Thus, provided that an argument is valid, to determine whether it is cogent, you only have to determine whether its premises are acceptable.

A conjunction is one statement connected to another using *and*—or another word meaning *and*, such as *but* or *yet* or *also*. Suppose that an argument has two premises, as in the following case:

1.   A mathematical proof is an intellectual exercise.
2.   Some computers can do mathematical proofs.

The conjunction of these two premises is: a mathematical proof is an intellectual exercise *and* some computers can do mathematical proofs.

Now suppose we had an argument from these two premises to a conclusion:

3.   Some computers can do an intellectual exercise.

This argument is deductively valid because the conjunction of its premises deductively entails its conclusion. It is impossible for the premises to be true and the conclusion false. Thus, granting the premises, the conclusion must be true. More generally, if the premises are acceptable, then, since they provide logically conclusive grounds for the conclusion, this makes the conclusion acceptable as well.

In any argument in which the premises deductively entail the conclusion, the (R) and (G) conditions are satisfied. The only condition left to assess is the (A) condition: if it is also satisfied, the argument is cogent. (Deductive entailment is discussed again, in considerably more detail, in Chapters 7 and 8.)

Deductive entailment is so tidy and complete a connection that when we have it there is no need to consider separately the relevance of premises and the issue of whether they provide good grounds for the conclusion. It is an all or nothing thing; the premises either entail the conclusion or they do not. If they entail it, the argument is valid and the premises give relevant grounds that are also sufficient. If they do not entail it, the argument is not valid and its premises are irrelevant from the point of view of validity, so any support they give would have to be of some other type.

The life of logicians would be simpler if deductive entailment were the only way of satisfying the (R) and (G) conditions. But it is not. Claims can be supported in argument by means other than logical entailment. We could not give a general theory about arguments if we limited ourselves to those involving the deductive entailment of the conclusion by the premises. There are at least three other ways in which premises may be properly connected to a conclusion. These are *inductive support through empirical generalization, analogy,* and *conductive support.*

Inductive Support Through Empirical Generalization

Suppose that you have seen 1000 students who have graduated from a particular high school with about 1500 students, and every single one has been blind. You infer that the school is a school for the blind. When you make this inference, you use premises about past experience to get a conclusion about all experience pertaining to the students from the school. Such arguments are usually called *inductive.* The connection between the cases you have observed and other cases is based on the presumption that your experience is likely to be fairly uniform. You also use an inductive argument if you reason that because the 1000 students you have met from the school have been blind, the next one (1001) you meet will be blind also.

Life depends on such inductive reasoning. The connection between what we have experienced and what we expect to experience is, of course, not that of deductive entailment. There would be no logical impossibility in the 1001st graduate being sighted; it could happen. The point is, though, that if 1000 known cases are blind, that fact gives us good reason to suppose that the next one will be too. Inductive support is discussed in greater detail in Chapter 10.

Analogy

Suppose you want to know whether a once-a-month birth control shot is safe (you have just invented it!), but for moral reasons you cannot test it on people. You get some rats and do an experiment. As things turn out, 50 of your 200 rats develop breast cancers. You conclude that the birth control shot is not safe for humans. Your premises are that it wasn't safe for rats, and humans are similar to rats; you are reasoning from one species to another that is compared with it. Provided that the cases you compare are relevantly similar, the link between premises and conclusion is a proper one. Analogy is examined in Chapter 9.

Conductive Support

Suppose you are considering a decision about suitable office space for an activist group. You want to decide what the ideal space would be. You think about the group's needs, which are many and varied, and start listing desirable features: centrality, low cost, acceptable decor, comfort, adequacy of heating and cooling, proximity to related groups, and so on. Then you find a space. To argue that it is suitable, you point out which of the relevant features it has. If it has several, you may wish to conclude that it is a suitable place. In these arguments we often have to deal with pros and cons. The premises support the conclusion convergently, rather than in a linked way. Arguments of this type are sometimes called *conductive* and are treated in more detail in Chapter 10.

   As this discussion shows, the (R) and (G) conditions, which have to do with the reasoning from the premises to the conclusion, may be satisfied in a variety of ways. The traditional account of argument soundness required that an argument have true premises and a deductively valid inference from its premises to its conclusion. This traditional account, while valuable for arguments in mathematics and logic, is too narrow to apply plausibly to a wide variety of arguments used in science, law, humanities, and everyday life. In these areas, there are many important and rationally persuasive arguments in which premises are not known for certain to be true and in which the connection between premises and conclusions is something other than deductive entailment.

USING THE ARG CONDITIONS TO EVALUATE ARGUMENTS

By using the ARG conditions, you can assess the cogency of an argument. That is, you can determine, on the basis of a reasonable, stage-by-stage evaluation, how good the argument is—how strong is the support that it gives to its conclusion. You first put the argument into a standard form so that you can see exactly what its premises and conclusion are. Then you determine whether the premises are acceptable.

Suppose that the audience to whom the argument is addressed is you, and you ask yourself whether you have good reason to accept the premises on which the argument is based. If you do not, the argument cannot possibly provide you with a good basis for accepting its conclusion. An argument moves from its premises to its conclusion, and you will not get anywhere without a starting point.

If the premises are acceptable on the (A) condition, you move on to (R). Ask yourself whether the premises are relevant to the conclusion. How, if at all, do they bear on it? If the premises have nothing to do with the conclusion, they can't be properly connected to it, and (even if acceptable) they can't give you any reason to think that the conclusion is true. An argument with irrelevant premises is a poor argument; it fails on (R) and cannot be cogent.

If (A) and (R) are satisfied, you move on to (G). Ask yourself whether the premises, taken together, provide good enough grounds for the conclusion. Premises that are acceptable and relevant may fail to provide sufficient grounds for the conclusion; they may offer an appropriate sort of evidence but fail to give enough of it. If this is a problem, then (G) is not satisfied and the argument is not cogent.

A cogent argument passes all three conditions of ARG. All its premises must be acceptable; they must be relevant to its conclusion; taken together they must provide adequate grounds for that conclusion. If any *one* of these conditions is not satisfied, the argument is not cogent. It does not offer strong support to the conclusion.

We shall now look at some real examples and see how the ARG conditions can be used to evaluate them. We will look at examples of arguments that fail each of the ARG conditions, one at a time, and see how this failure makes the argument unsuccessful in giving rational support to its conclusion. This procedure is used for the sake of simplicity. In fact, real arguments do not have to fail on just one of the ARG conditions. They may fail with respect to more than one condition at once. For example, the premises of an argument might be both unacceptable in their own right and logically irrelevant to the conclusion, in which case the argument would have failed on conditions (A) and (R) at once. On the other hand, the argument may meet all the conditions and be cogent.

Failing on the (A) Condition

Consider this argument, taken from a letter to *Time* magazine:

> There can be no meaningful reconciliation of science and religion. Their methods are diametrically opposed. Science admits it has no final answers, while religion claims to have them. Science, despite its excesses, has gone far to liberate the human spirit; religion would stifle it.[2]

Before evaluating this argument, we have to identify its conclusion and premises. The conclusion is the rather controversial claim announced in the first sentence. The second and third sentences are related to each other, since the third sentence gives a reason for the second sentence—that methods are opposed. There is, then, a subargument in these two sentences, both of which deal with the methods of science and religion. The final sentence specifies a quite different contrast between science and religion with regard to their effects (liberation) and intentions (to stifle the human spirit). The writer argued for the conclusion that science and religion are not reconcilable by contrasting them in two ways—with regard to method and to intended effect. His point about method is defended in a subargument.

The argument would look like this in standardized form:

1. Science admits to having no final answers while religion claims to have final answers.

So,

2. The methods of science and religion are diametrically opposed.
3. Science has helped to liberate humans, whereas religion seeks to stifle them.

Therefore,

4. There can be no meaningful reconciliation of religion and science.

Given this argument, should we be convinced of the author's conclusion? Has he shown that there can be no meaningful reconciliation between science and religion? Note that the conclusion is stated in strong terms, with no qualifications. To evaluate, or appraise, the argument, we seek to determine whether or not it is cogent. We do this by working through the ARG conditions stage by stage.

First, consider the acceptability of the premises. Premises (1) and (3) are undefended premises, and they must be acceptable as stated if the argument is to work. There is certainly a problem about (1), which seems to be false as stated. Premise (1) is categorical in its tone and sweeping in scope. It draws a very sharp contrast between science and religion. When we think about it, we can see that this contrast is exaggerated and is not borne out by a careful consideration of various religions and scientific theories. Some scientific theorists (for example, Isaac Newton, author of gravitational theory) have claimed to have the final answers to the questions they asked. On the other hand, some religious thinkers have made no such claim. Buddhist thinkers, for instance, characteristically see religion as the cultivation of individual peace of mind and harmony with the natural universe. They do not see it as a body of doctrines giving definitive answers to a set of specific questions. Thus (1) is not acceptable. For this reason, (2) is not adequately defended since it is supposed to get its support from (1).

Now look at (3). Here the author used more qualified terms. He says science "has gone far" to liberate the human spirit and that religion "would stifle" it. But even when these qualifications are considered, the author is overstating the contrast between science and religion. Like (1), (3) is untrue to the facts. There are scientists who seek to use scientific knowledge to control human beings, and there are religious workers who have labored long and hard under the inspiration of religious ideals to improve the dehumanizing material conditions of their fellow human beings. Thus premise (3) is also unacceptable.

The argument, then, fails miserably on the (A) condition. All premises are disputable in the face of common knowledge about the role that science and religion have played in human history. The author has overdrawn his contrasts and has been insensitive to the concrete detail that, if recalled, would force dramatic qualification of his claims. The argument is not a cogent argument because it fails on the (A) condition. All three conditions must be met if the argument is to be cogent.

Failing on the (R) Condition

We shall now move on to consider an argument that fails in another way—by missing on the (R) condition.

The following passage was printed as a letter to the editor of *World Press Review*. The author discusses articles the magazine had previously printed, from publications outside the United States, which had criticized the withholding by the United States of its United Nations dues. (These were withheld because the United States did not approve of some policies of the United Nations and its agencies.) The author is arguing that the United States was justified in what it did and that the foreign publications were too critical of U.S. policy.

> Some foreign publications are unduly critical of my country. I believe the U.S. was justified in withholding its U.N. dues. At least twice, the Soviets have withheld theirs when they did not approve of U.N. policies (peace actions in Korea and what is now called Zaire). The foreign press did not get very worked up about it. U.N. members have constantly found fault with the U.S. They abuse us on the one hand and expect hand-outs on the other. Parents of adolescents face similar problems.
>
> I personally never insist on respect from anybody, but those who do not give it to me need not bother asking me for any financial help.[3]

The arguments in this passage can be standardized as follows:

1. The Soviets have twice withheld U.N. dues when they did not approve of U.N. policies.
2. U.N. members have constantly found fault with the United States.
3. U.N. members who abuse the United States and then expect handouts are like adolescents.

Thus,

4. The United States was justified in withholding its U.N. dues.
5. When the Soviet Union withheld U.N. dues the foreign press did not get very worked up about it.

Therefore,

6. Foreign publications criticizing the United States for withholding U.N. dues are being overly critical.

There are two arguments for the two conclusions: first the argument from (1), (2), and (3) to (4) and then the argument from (4) and (5) to (6). We shall discuss only the first argument here.

If we try to evaluate the premises for acceptability, problems arise because we would need to do historical research to determine whether they are true, or probably true. Without checking, we may not know whether, as the author claims, the Soviet Union did withhold U.N. dues. This claim would be relatively easy to check. But in fact, the argument has such serious problems of relevance that it is not necessary to do this checking.

To see the problems of relevance in this example, we need to look at some of the language used. Let us consider the meaning of the conclusion the arguer is trying to defend. He is trying to show that the United States was *justified* in withholding its U.N. *dues*. Dues are not charity; they are costs of membership, imposed according to an agreed-upon formula.

Premise (1), about the Soviets, is strictly speaking irrelevant to the conclusion because it contains no information about the United States that could bear on the conclusion. If we knew that the Soviets had been in similar circumstances to the United States and that they had been right to withhold their dues, this premise would be relevant—but we know no such thing and it is unlikely that the author believes this! His tone, and the way Soviet behavior was usually referred to in Cold War discussions, makes it more likely he thought the Soviets were quite wrong. And if premise (1) says that the Soviets were wrong in withholding dues, this point cannot show, or give any evidence at all, that the Americans were right to withhold them. Nor is premise (2) strictly relevant to the conclusion. Dues have been agreed upon and are owed; the fact that others criticize a country is not relevant to the existence of this obligation.

In the third premise, the first thing to look at is the word *handout*. This word is emotionally quite negative. A handout is something the recipient does not deserve and, by implication, should not receive. No evidence has been given that the money the United States was to have given the United Nations was charity in any sense, much less a negative sense. There is an important and crucial distinction between a handout and dues owed, and when we appreciate this distinction, we can see that the third premise too is irrelevant to the argument.

In this argument, the premises are not relevant to the conclusion. Thus the argument is not cogent, whether its premises are acceptable or not. Similarly, we need not consider the (G) condition. If premises are not even relevant to the conclusion, they cannot possibly provide good grounds for it.

Failing on the (G) Condition

We now move to another example—this time one that satisfies (A) and (R) but fails on (G). It goes as follows:

> We arrived at the park gate at 7:25 P.M. at which time the cashier gleefully took money for admission. Upon entering the zoo and walking across the bridge, the loudspeaker was stating that the zoo buildings were closing at 8:00 P.M. We asked if we would not get a pass for the following day. The answer was no.
>
> In summary, it is easy to see that Calgary is anything but a friendly city, but rather out to rake off the tourist for all they can.[4]

The writer of this letter received shabby treatment at the Calgary zoo and is inferring, or drawing the conclusion, from this fact that Calgary is an unfriendly city that is out to exploit tourists. His argument is very simple:

1. Some tourists were given unfriendly treatment at the Calgary zoo.
Therefore,
2. Calgary is an unfriendly city, out to exploit tourists.

Whether the premise is true we cannot know for sure; the writer is describing his personal experiences. But there is no good reason to think that he is either lying or deceiving himself, so we may accept the premise on his word.[5] Thus the (A) condition will be granted. The premise is clearly relevant to the conclusion; if one person (a cashier) in one Calgary institution (the zoo) is unfriendly to tourists, this is some evidence for the general conclusion that the whole city is unfriendly. It does count toward establishing that conclusion. Hence the (R) condition is satisfied. But when we come to the (G) condition and ask how good the grounds are for the conclusion, the argument obviously breaks down. The unfriendliness of a single individual in a single institution is not adequate evidence to establish the unfriendliness of a city as a whole. The argument passes on (A) and (R) but fails on (G). It is not a cogent argument.

Satisfying All Three Conditions

We now move on to look at an argument that is cogent and that passes all three conditions. This example comes from an essay on education written by the British philosopher Bertrand Russell.

> Freedom, in education as in other things, must be a matter of degree. Some freedoms cannot be tolerated. I met a lady once who maintained that no child should ever be forbidden to do anything, because a child ought to develop its nature from within. "How about if its nature leads it to swallow pins?" I asked; but I regret to say the answer was mere vituperation. And yet every child, left to itself, will sooner or later swallow pins, or drink poison out of medicine bottles, or fall out of an upper window, or otherwise bring itself to a bad end. At a slightly later age, boys, when they have the opportunity, will go unwashed, overeat, smoke till they are sick, catch chills from sitting in wet feet, and so on—let alone the fact that they will amuse themselves by plaguing elderly gentlemen, who may not all have Elisha's powers of repartee. Therefore, one who advocates freedom in education cannot mean the children should do exactly as they please all day long. An element of discipline and authority must exist.[6]

Russell is arguing that some element of discipline and authority must exist in education. (Another way of stating this point is that freedom must be a matter of degree, rather than being absolute.) He states this point several times in the first two sentences and in the final two sentences. The incident about the woman Russell met is not really a premise; it is a story about someone who held a view that Russell himself disagreed with. He describes the episode as a way of explaining the view he doesn't hold and (by contrast) his own view. The vivid and various ways boys can come to harm need not all be mentioned in the standardization of Russell's argument, for his point is simply that they can easily come to harm— whether this is by overeating, or catching chills, or whatever won't really matter so far as the fundamental point of the argument is concerned.

The argument can be standardized as follows:

1. Both younger and older children, left to themselves, can easily come to physical harm.
2. Older children, left to themselves, often are very annoying to adults.

So,

3. Children simply cannot be left to do as they please all day long.

Therefore,

4. There must be some element of discipline and authority in education.

There is a subargument structure here: the first two premises are intended to support the third one, and that is intended to support the conclusion of the main argument. The undefended premises, then, are (1) and (2). Both are clearly acceptable; these are matters of common knowledge. And they are clearly relevant to (3): that unsupervised children will naturally harm themselves and others are two good reasons for not just leaving them to do as they please all day.

Furthermore, the (G) condition is also satisfied in this subargument. These are compelling reasons. The subargument passes all of the ARG conditions and is cogent; thus (3) is acceptable since it is defended by a cogent argument. The final assessment will depend on whether (3) is properly connected to (4). Does it provide relevant and adequate grounds for (4)? To fully explain the relevance of (3) to (4), it helps to recall that children in western European societies (about whom we can presume Russell would have been writing) spend a very substantial portion of their time in the educational system. To have no discipline and authority in education would in effect leave these children to their own devices for a considerable portion of their time—contrary to what we accepted in (3). Thus (3) is not only acceptable but is properly connected to (4), because it is relevant to it and provides adequate grounds for it. Since the subargument is cogent and the main argument is cogent, the entire argument is cogent.

It is important to note just what you have shown when you show that an argument is not a cogent one. You have shown that the author of the argument failed to support his or her conclusion with adequate reasons. The conclusion is not justified by the reasoning the author put forward. To evaluate an argument as not cogent is to object to it, to object to the argument as a whole, not just to the conclusion. If you show that an argument is not cogent you show that its premises do not provide rationally adequate grounds for its conclusion. However, this process of evaluation does not show that the conclusion itself is false or unacceptable. The conclusion might be true, and there might be other evidence showing it to be true, even though the argument you considered did not.

Suppose you were to argue this way:

1. Jones offered a poor argument for the conclusion that French should be a compulsory subject in universities and colleges.

Therefore,
2. There is no good reason for having French as a compulsory subject in universities and colleges.

Your own argument would be faulty in such a case. It would fail on the (G) condition; the grounds offered are not adequate. If you were to argue in such a way, you would have only the flimsiest of evidence for your conclusion. After all, Jones is only one person among many. The fact that he happened to come up with a poor argument on a topic does not show that there are no good arguments for the conclusion he sought to reach on that topic.

To show that a person's argument is faulty is to show that his or her conclusion is not well supported by the evidence put forward. That is all. It is important to remember that you have not refuted a claim or a theory by showing that one or more of the supporting arguments for it is faulty. To refute it, you would have to come up with an independent argument in which the conclusion was the denial of the original conclusion. Often this is much harder than simply finding faults in the argument for the original conclusion.

◆ ──

EXERCISE SET

Exercise 2

Assess the following arguments using the ARG conditions as you are able to understand them at this point. There may be several arguments in combination; if so, specify your comments accordingly, noting each subargument and then pulling together your remarks to appraise the combined structure. The first arguments are prestandardized to make your work easier. In the case of arguments that are not standardized, carefully standardize them before applying ARG. For the purposes of this exercise, do not add missing premises or conclusions.

If you feel that you do not have enough background knowledge to determine whether premises are acceptable, omit the (A) condition and concentrate on (R) and (G).

1. *The Sibling Rivalry Case*
(1) People who have a brother or sister are in a different family situation from those who do not have a brother or sister.

(2) People who have a brother or sister have to compete with their sibling for the parents' attention, whereas those who are only children do not have to compete with a sibling for this attention.

(3) Competing for a parent's attention is a phenomenon that can bring out emotions of jealousy, anger, and inadequacy.
Therefore,
(4) Jealousy, anger, and inadequacy can arise in people with brothers and sisters more readily than in people who are only children.

2. *The Animal Rights Case*
(1) Animals are not human beings.
(2) Animals do not speak the same language as human beings.
(3) Animals do not have the same advanced cultures and technologies as human beings.
Therefore,
(4) Animals are of no moral significance and do not have any moral rights.

3. *The Aggression Case*
(1) People have given their children war-related toys for many centuries.

(2) Children have often enjoyed playing cowboys and Indians, and using toy soldiers and related playthings.

(3) Not every child who plays with war toys becomes a soldier.
Therefore,

(4) War toys have no tendency whatsoever to make children less sensitive to violence.

*4. *The History Instructor Case*

(1) The textbooks selected for the history course were hard to read.

(2) The assignments for the history course were difficult to complete.

(3) Many students do not enjoy studying history.
Therefore,

(4) The instructor in the history course was not competent in her knowledge of history.

5. *The Recycling Case*

(1) Recycling of newspapers and bottles will not alter the basic facts of overconsumption and overpopulation.

(2) The basic facts of overconsumption and overpopulation are fundamental causes of the global environmental crisis.
Therefore,

(3) Recycling of newspapers and bottles, though valuable in its own right, will not suffice to solve the global environmental crisis.

*6. *The Success of Technology Case*

(1) People thought an atomic bomb was impossible, and we made atomic bombs.

(2) People thought flying machines were impossible, and we made airplanes.

(3) People thought that landing a man on the moon was impossible, and we landed a man on the moon.

(4) People think getting an adequate vaccine against AIDS is impossible.
Therefore,

(5) We will discover an adequate vaccine against AIDS.

7. *The Academic Cheating Case*

(1) Plagiarism is the representation of another person's work as one's own and cheating is not.
So,

(2) Cheating on an examination is a lesser offense than plagiarism.

And,

(3) The penalty for plagiarism is failure in the course.

(4) There is no suitable penalty for cheating on an examination that is both less than failure in a course and enough to mean something to the student penalized.
Therefore,

(5) There should be no penalty imposed on students for cheating on an examination.

8. *A Professor Generalizes about Logic Students*

(1) Students in my present logic class do not work as hard as students in my logic class last year.
Therefore,

(2) Students at the university in general are not working as hard this year as they did last year.
And,

(3) Affluence and low standards in the high schools produce poor work habits in students.

*9. *Polls on a Doctors' Strike*

(1) In a poll, 75 percent of the people questioned said that they think people who perform essential services do not have a right to strike.

(2) Doctors perform essential services.
So,

(3) Polls indicate that 75 percent of people think doctors do not have a right to strike.

*10. There are only two kinds of thinkers. There are those who analyze, who like to pull problems apart and reduce them to basic simple units. Then there are those who synthesize, pulling together all sorts of different materials to bring about novel results. Therefore, all thinking is about how wholes result from parts.

*11. In schools in Cuba, girls far outstrip boys in their achievements. Cuba is a socialist state in which equality of the sexes is a matter of law. In Cuba it is even a legal requirement for men to do their share of the housework! Therefore, we can see that under socialism and true equal opportunity, women show up as superior to men.

12. It is unlikely that scientists will ever be fully satisfied with their understanding of matter. Whatever small particle they have most recently discovered, they will seek to understand further, and when they do this, they are very likely eventually to achieve the splitting of such a particle into several smaller ones. This pattern does not show that the explanation for the world is to be found outside science—in theology, art, or mysticism, for instance. But it does indicate that a scientific explanation will not likely be complete.

13. Children should not have the right to vote because children are not fully mature people, and only fully mature people should have the right to vote.

14. Intelligence tests have often been misused. Several famous psychologists who developed the tests have been widely discredited. For instance, Sir Cyril Burt, an eminent British psychologist who greatly influenced the testing of students in Britain, was found to have used fraudulent data in several of his studies. For these reasons, attempts to measure human intelligence should be completely abandoned.

*15. Competition results in the best system for all. We can easily see why this is the case if we consider how small businesses operate. If a town has only one bakery, the baker can make buns, pies, and muffins just as he wishes and charge the highest price customers will tolerate. But if there are two or three bakeries, customers can select the best products at the lowest prices. With competition, there is pressure to bring quality up and prices down, which benefits consumers. Therefore, competitiveness is a force for good and should not be eliminated.

16. If Hitler had died at the age of ten, Nazism would not have developed in Germany in the way it did. If Woodrow Wilson had never existed, there would be no League of Nations. And without Mao Tse-Tung, who knows what would have come of the revolutionary movement in China during the 30s and 40s? From these facts, we can prove that it is special individuals who determine world history.

17. *Background:* The following excerpt is from a letter written to Dr. Joyce Brothers:

"The problem is that my husband does not want to have children because I underwent therapy before we were married and my husband is afraid that my emotional troubles will be passed on to our child."

To this inquiry, Brothers responded: "When is society going to come out of the dark ages and recognize that mental or emotional problems should be no more stigmatizing to an individual than a case of German measles or pneumonia? We do not shun those who have suffered and been cured of tuberculosis, polio, or other diseases, do we?"

(Cited in the *Informal Logic Newsletter,* Examples Supplement for 1979)

EVALUATING ARGUMENTS AND CONSTRUCTING YOUR OWN ARGUMENTS

When you decide that someone else has offered a poor argument and you give an appraisal of the argument to show which of the ARG conditions are not satisfied, you are actually offering an argument yourself. If you are really meeting the challenge of argument, the response to an argument is either agreement with its conclusion or—as in this case—another argument, contending that the first argument goes wrong in some way. Unless you fully agree with everything others are telling you, it is impossible to really respond to the challenge of argument without constructing arguments yourself. Even if you do agree, it is worth thinking the argument through to understand just why you agree.

In our explanation of what makes for a good argument, we have tended to emphasize critically responding to other people's arguments. You can see that, if you use the ARG conditions to do this, you will end up constructing arguments yourself, because you will be giving reasons for your conclusion that the argument is or is not cogent. When you determine that another's argument is not cogent, you are using the ARG conditions as tools of criticism. The critique that you work out can itself be put forward as an argument. Consider the following general example:

1. The arguer used an unacceptable premise.
2. The arguer's second premise is irrelevant to the conclusion.
So,
3. The argument given fails on the (A) condition and on the (R) condition.
Therefore,
4. The argument offered is not a cogent argument.

Here you yourself need to defend (1) and (2) in subarguments, because it is up to you to show why the premise is false, or irrelevant. (Presumably the arguer thought the premises were acceptable and relevant; otherwise, it is unlikely that he or she would have used them.)

When you offer your own argument, you are working constructively. Your argument, in order to be a good one, will itself have to satisfy the ARG conditions. Make sure that what you say about the argument is acceptable and relevant and that it provides adequate grounds for your judgment that the original argument is not cogent. This practice of reasonableness is not as common as it should be. But it is worth cultivating, both in the interest of truth and in the interest of resolving disputes in a sensible fashion.

Textbooks on argument, such as this one, include many examples of short arguments written by a wide variety of people. Students working through the textbook are asked to analyze these examples. This process of analysis and criticism is very useful, but it can lead us to forget that there are two sides to the skills pertaining to argument. There is the matter of evaluating other people's arguments, and there is also the matter of becoming good at constructing arguments yourself. The most natural way to construct cogent arguments is to concentrate on the ARG conditions and the other things you work on in a logic course when you are writing or speaking on other subjects. Try to use premises that are acceptable—both to you and to those who will be hearing or reading your argument. Have a keen sense of which conclusions you are trying to defend, and make sure that what you have to say is either relevant to those conclusions or else clearly stands out as a background, or an "aside" comment. Make sure there are enough relevant premises to provide adequate grounds for your conclusions.

You have no doubt noticed that many of the arguments invented here to illustrate various themes in this book are much easier to follow than the real arguments quoted from letters to the editor and from nonfiction works. With the real arguments, sometimes it seems as though most of your work comes in standardizing, rather than in appraisal. You cannot apply the ARG conditions until you have a clear argument to apply them to. If you find this matter difficult, it might be worthwhile to spend some time reviewing Chapter 2.

The difficulties we may experience in standardizing can teach us something. We must try to make ourselves clear when we are constructing our own arguments. Obviously, when we compose a public speech or an essay, we will not tend to number our premises and conclusions, but we can introduce important conclusions with useful phrases such as "I wish to argue that" or "What I am trying to prove is," and we can state conclusions clearly either at the beginning or at the end of what we have to say. We can clarify terms that could be misinterpreted by the audience whom we are addressing, and so on.

Simply put, the various things that cause problems of interpretation or weak arguments when they appear in other people's writing also can appear in our own work, and we should try hard to eliminate them. Becoming a competent critic of other people's arguments and gaining the ability to argue clearly yourself are opposite sides of the same coin.

◆───────────────────────────────────────

EXERCISE SET

Exercise 3: Part A

Construct your own arguments in response to two of the following questions after critical examination and reflection:

(a) Does football encourage harmful aggressive tendencies in players?
(b) Would gun control mean that only criminals had guns?
(c) Should a tourist to a foreign country make some effort to learn the language of that country?
(d) Is a college education more than a means to a job?
(e) Should women keep their maiden names after marriage if they wish to do so?

Strategy for doing this exercise: First, think about the question you have selected to discuss, and think about your tentative response to it. Next, think about your reasons for wanting to answer in this way. Write them down. Now, look at what you have written and organize it into a clear argument.

Think about the question again, and think about how other people might answer it. Think of a response different from your own that strikes you as quite plausible. What reasons could be given for that response? How good an argument could be constructed for it? After developing the alternative response, look back at your original response. Revise your original

argument if thinking through an alternative position has led you to change or moderate your first one.

Example: Question: Is nuclear energy necessary?
First response: Nuclear energy is necessary.
Reasons: Nuclear energy would not have been developed unless experts thought it was necessary and, by and large, energy experts know what is likely to be needed; oil, gas, and coal are alternative sources of energy, and they are not going to last forever; growth in manufacturing, which is important to give people jobs, will require more energy; we can get virtually unlimited amounts of energy from small amounts of uranium, so nuclear energy has virtually unlimited potential and can meet these needs.
Alternative response: Nuclear energy may not be necessary under some conditions.
Reasons: We could change our habits so that we do not consume so much energy (much is wasted); solar and wind energy may be viable alternatives to oil, gas, coal, and nuclear energy; perhaps if we put massive resources into researching solar and wind energy, we would find vast potential there too; solar and wind energy do not pose the safety hazards nuclear energy does.
Resulting argument: (*Note:* This argument is an amended version of the first argument; amendments are based on considerations as to how

premises and conclusion should be clarified and qualified due to factors in the alternative response.)

1. Energy experts used to think nuclear energy was needed and they were probably right in the judgments they made, considering the time at which these were made.

2. Coal, oil, and gas are the major alternatives to nuclear energy, and they will not last forever.

3. Probably solar and wind energy will not have the same potential for expansion as nuclear energy.

4. We need vast amounts of energy to keep economies going and give people jobs.

So, probably,

5. Nuclear energy is necessary unless there is successful research on how to develop solar and wind energy.

Note any subarguments and clearly mark the premises and conclusions in your final argument. Then rewrite your argument in more natural language as though it were a letter to the editor of your local newspaper.

Exercise 3: Part B

Show that the arguments you constructed in response to Part A satisfy the ARG conditions of argument cogency.

Exercise 3: Part C

Ask a friend in the course to evaluate your argument. Note disputed points, if any, and either revise your position to accommodate these or defend your position with subarguments.

 CHAPTER SUMMARY

The challenge of argument is to meet an argument on its own terms; that is, to meet it as an argument. What this means is avoiding the temptation to judge arguments only in terms of whether we previously agreed or disagreed with their conclusions. Someone who offers an argument is offering reasons to support a case, and we should respond on that basis. If we do not wish to accept the conclusion, we should nevertheless work through the argument to find out where and why we disagree with it. Are the premises wrong? Is the reasoning unacceptable?

Traditionally logicians have tended to define good arguments as sound, where *sound* means having true premises that deductively entail the conclusion. We do not use the term *sound* in this sense to explain what a good argument is, because we think the traditional account is too narrow. It does not apply plausibly to many arguments in which the premises appear to support the conclusion by some logical relationship other than deductive entailment. In addition, requiring premises to be true is probably too strict. What is more reasonable in a practical sense is to require that they be rationally acceptable; that is, that we have a good basis for believing them.

Our general term for argument evaluation is *cogent*. A cogent argument is one in which the premises are acceptable (A), are relevant to the conclusion (R), and, considered together, provide good grounds for the conclusion (G). These three conditions of cogency are called the ARG conditions. They are readily remembered since ARG are the first three letters of the word *argument*. According to the theory of argument adopted in this book, a cogent argument, one in which all three of the ARG conditions are satisfied, is a good argument. An argument that fails to be cogent is poor, or weak.

The (R) and (G) conditions can be satisfied in various ways that are discussed in later chapters of this book. These are: deductive entailment, inductive support, analogy, and conductive support.

If an argument fails to satisfy the ARG conditions, then it is not cogent and it fails to rationally support its conclusion. It is important to note that this is not to say that its conclusion is unacceptable, just that this particular argument does not support it. The conclusion might be shown acceptable by some different argument. If you evaluate an argument using ARG and it is not adequate, then you know only that this one argument has failed to support the conclusion; you don't know whether the conclusion is false or unacceptable.

Using the ARG conditions gives you a basis for your own critical arguments. In fact, to evaluate an argument using ARG is to implicitly argue yourself: you are finding reasons to support an evaluation of the argument you are considering.

The ARG conditions are, in addition, valuable tools to use when you are constructing your own arguments. You can use them to check up on yourself. Try to make sure that your premises are rationally acceptable, are relevant to the conclusions you are trying to support, and combine together to give good grounds for those conclusions.

❖   REVIEW OF TERMS INTRODUCED

Sound argument   An argument in which the premises are true and the premises deductively entail the conclusion.

Cogent argument   An argument in which the premises are rationally acceptable and also properly connected to the conclusion. This means they are relevant to the conclusion and, considered together, provide good grounds for it.

ARG conditions   The conditions of a cogent argument. The premises must be: (1) *acceptable,* (2a) *relevant* to the conclusion, and (2b) when considered together, provide sufficient *grounds* for the conclusion. For an argument to be cogent, all ARG conditions must be satisfied.

Acceptability of premises   Premises of an argument are acceptable provided there is appropriate evidence, or reasons, to believe them.

Relevance of premises   Premises of an argument are relevant to its conclusion provided they give at least some evidence, or reasons, in favor of that conclusion.

Goodness of grounds   Sufficiency of premises to provide good reasons or full evidence for the conclusion. Premises offer sufficient grounds if, assuming that they are accepted, it would be reasonable to accept the conclusion. Taken together, the premises present enough reasons or evidence to make the conclusion something it would be rational to believe.

Deductive entailment   Most complete relationship of logical support. If and only if one statement entails another, then, given the truth of the first statement, it is impossible that the other should be false. In an argument, the premises deductively entail the conclusion if, and only if, given the truth of the conjunction of the premises, it would be logically impossible for the conclusion to be false.

Validity   Connection between premises of an argument and its conclusion in the case where the premises deductively entail the conclusion. Any argument in which the premises deductively entail the conclusion is deductively valid. The terms *deductively valid* and *valid* are used as equivalent in meaning within logic, although outside logic *valid* is sometimes used with other meanings.

Conjunction   Connection of two or more statements using the word *and* or another word or symbol equivalent in meaning.

Empirical generalization   When premises are connected to a conclusion on the basis of an empirical generalization, the premises describe observations about some cases, and the conclusion, which is more general, attributes the same features reported in the premises to a broader range of cases.

Analogy   Comparison based on resemblances. When the premises are connected to the conclusion on the basis of an analogy, the premises describe similarities between two things and state or assume that those two things will be similar in further ways not described. The claim is made that one of the things has a further property, and the inference is drawn that the other thing will have the same further property.

Conductive argument   An argument in which premises (nearly always several in number) describe factors that are supposed to count separately in favor of a conclusion because each is relevant to it. Typically, in conductive arguments we deal with matters on which there are pros and cons.

Notes

1. My views on these matters are developed in more detail and with more extensive supporting argument in *Problems in Argument Analysis and Evaluation* (Providence, R.I.: Foris, 1987).
2. *Time* magazine, February 26, 1979.
3. *World Press Review,* December 1988.
4. Letter to the Calgary *Herald,* July 5, 1978.
5. This topic is discussed in more detail in Chapter 5 in the sections dealing with testimony.
6. Bertrand Russell, "Freedom Versus Authority in Education," in *Sceptical Essays* (London: George Allen & Unwin, 1953), p. 184.

CHAPTER 4

Looking at Language

LANGUAGE IS AN ESSENTIAL TOOL OF thought, one whose effects go very deep. In understanding, constructing, and evaluating arguments, language is important at every stage. Words can be used to help understanding or they may obscure issues and contribute to careless thinking. A good sense of the meanings of words used and their role in persuasion is extremely valuable.

It is in some ways difficult to think about language, partly because it is so much a part of us that we are accustomed to using it unreflectively. Generally it is far easier to use language than to think about it. Yet it is important to reflect on language and gain some basic tools to analyze its use, because language plays an absolutely central role in shaping our thought. Our choice of terms affects which aspects of reality we attend to and which we ignore. It shapes our attention and helps us construct our picture of the world. Language does far more than describe reality; it shapes and expresses our interpretations and attitudes.

We can see this phenomenon easily in the language of politics. To call a change of government a "coup," for instance, is quite different from saying it is due to an "intervention." The first term implies that an internal group took over the government in a sudden bid for power; the second implies that outside forces had a role. An argument about a coup in Panama would set the stage for one sort of political discussion, one about an intervention for quite another.

Some environmentalists have criticized such terms as "resource" and "wealth of the earth" for their implication that such things as fish, minerals, and soil are commodities to be used and owned by people, as opposed to interdependent parts of biological systems. Whether we think of something as a resource or as a natural organism may make a considerable difference in how we treat it. Similarly, some management theorists are skeptical of the term "human resources" as used for employees. Employees, they would say, are people with dignity and rights, not commodities to be exploited for other people's purposes.

Responding to such disputes, we may feel impatient and wish to say, Get on with it. What's in a word? The answer to this last question, unfortunately, is more than you would think. In fact, sometimes almost everything.

Often language plays so many roles at once that a whole political theory or ideology seems to be captured in a single term. Here is an important illustration. The official Chinese press termed the massive student demonstrations it violently suppressed in Tiananmen Square in June 1989 the work of rebels and counter-revolutionaries. The term "counter-revolutionary" here presupposes the context of Marxist-Leninist theory, wherein the original communist revolution (culminating in victory in 1949) is seen as an uprising by working and peasant classes that is in the true interests of the people, and is understood as being for the good of the people. Given this idea of what revolution is, counter-revolutionaries are seen as wicked reactionaries working against progress for the people. Argument will hardly be necessary to prove that counter-revolutionaries are wrong; the term itself will carry the point to those trained in Marxist-Leninist theory. In fact, the evolution of the government's reaction to the student movement can be traced in shifts in the words used to describe it. First it was a "movement," then a "disturbance," then "turmoil," and finally, "counter-revolution."[1] The term "movement" is quite neutral; the others express growing degrees of disapproval culminating, just before the violent government reaction, in "counter-revolution."

Even terms that might seem at first glance to be devoid of such profound political implications can shape and express deep attitudes on matters of considerable social importance. An example is *he* used as an indefinite pronoun; another is *man* used to represent human beings in general. According to standard old-fashioned grammar, *he* and *man* can properly be used to represent human beings of either sex. However, since these words are also used to represent male human beings specifically, there is a permanent possibility of ambiguity, one that strongly encourages us to think of the human being in general as one who is a male. The male-specific meaning for *man* in *mankind* is always a possible one.

The problem can easily be seen in the following story:

(a) Dr. Blake, a dentist, had taken his son out bike riding. They narrowly avoided a large moving van, and in doing so, fell off their bikes into the ditch. Fearing that the boy was seriously injured, Dr. Blake rushed him to the hospital for emergency treatment. But then a new problem arose. The only doctor on duty was unable to treat the boy. A doctor cannot treat his own son.

The story may be puzzling at first; the suggestion from the last two sentences appears to be that the doctor is the boy's father, but this introduces an apparent inconsistency, because we have already been told that the father is a dentist. The problem is easily solved: children have two parents and his mother is a doctor. To say "a doctor cannot treat his own son" suggests that doctors are male, due to "his"; yet the statement is the very sort of general statement in which "his" is supposed to be gender-neutral. Words that have a role referring to males cannot easily shake off all the associations and interpretations that accompany that role.

The idea that *man* and related words can be used in a way that is truly gender-neutral is not plausible.[2]

The role language plays in directing our attention and in framing issues and problems is a large and fascinating topic that we cannot treat in full detail here. Our purpose is to explain some basic points about language with a special emphasis on those most pertinent to argument.

DEFINITIONS

When we think of clarifying the meaning of terms, what first comes to mind, probably, is the matter of definitions. The demand "define your terms" is often heard. Some disputes seem impossible to resolve just because people mean different things by words or cannot agree on meaning. Words like *democracy, justice, freedom, imperial,* and *colonial* have powerful emotional associations and are defined in different ways by people of differing political beliefs. In liberal democratic societies such as the United States and Canada, *democracy* is defined in terms of free elections in which every adult citizen has one vote. In orthodox Marxist-Leninist societies, it was defined in terms of the rule of the Communist Party, regarded as democratic because (according to official theory at least) it represented the interests of the people.

Many people find it annoying and picky to argue over definitions, but in fact, they can be very important. In recent decades, advances in medical technology have made it necessary to redefine *death* in terms of absence of brain activity rather than the cessation of heartbeat or respiration, as was used in an older definition. The new definition is very important. Without it, doctors who remove a heart from a traffic victim could be charged with murder! (If the heart is still beating, the person from whom the heart is removed would still be alive in the old sense. Provided the brain is no longer functioning, the person would be dead in the new sense, though his or her heart was still beating and still suitable for use in a transplant.)

The modern definition of *death* is the result of more than a mere decision that the word will begin to mean something different from what it meant before. It is not just a matter of people standing up and saying, "Well, *death* used to be defined as the stopping of the heartbeat; now we are going to define it in terms of stopping or drastic slowing of brain activity." The new definition of *death* is not arbitrary; it has important practical and theoretical functions. It was made necessary by the technology of life-support systems that can keep some human bodies breathing and operating for a long time when there is too little brain activity for consciousness. The new definition is based on the belief that consciousness is more definitive of human life than are breath and pulse—as well as an interest in legally and morally obtaining viable organs for transplants.

It is not necessary to define every term, of course. Many words are commonly used in various ways and understood by everybody. If you tell someone to shut the door, you do not normally need to define *door* in order to get him to shut it! It will be perfectly clear, when these simple words are used in an ordinary situation, what is meant.

Even when words have several different meanings, the context of a conversation will usually make it quite clear which meaning is the right one. The word *bank* has several different meanings, which you can see easily by looking at the following three sentences:

(b) They had a picnic on the banks of the Mississippi and then walked through the gardens.

(c) He got a lot of cash from the sales and took it right to the bank, because he didn't want to risk loss or robbery.

(d) Some people think corrupt politicians will be weeded out by the electoral process but I don't know, I wouldn't bank on it.

In (b) a *bank* is the side of a river; in (c) it is a financial institution. In (d) the word *bank* is used colloquially to mean count on. (This third use may derive from the second one.)

We are all of us quite capable of using and understanding words that have multiple meanings. We can do it without defining them, without even thinking about it, because very often the context, or situation, in which the word is used makes its meaning clear.

Trying to define all our terms would be a hopeless task in any case because we need some words just to define others. We look for a definition when we see a claim or argument that is hard to understand or seems very unreasonable as we would naturally be inclined to interpret it, or when there is a practical problem whose solution depends on our having an explicit definition.

As an example of a case where a definition would help to clarify a statement, consider the following. Suppose a person from England tells you that in England only the children of the upper classes go to public schools. This is an amazing statement from the point of view of North Americans. In North America, *public school* means school supported by taxpayers and open to all children without special handicaps. In some areas, parents are dissatisfied with public schools and select private schools for which they must pay tuition fees (usually at least several thousand dollars annually). Such parents are nearly always comparatively wealthy. The statement about England is very surprising against this background; it would surely be odd if only well-off people sent their children to public schools. We may suspect that the expression "public school" is used differently in England. And, indeed, this is true. In England, public schools are "endowed grammar schools—usually boarding schools—preparing students for university" (*Oxford English Dictionary,* concise version, 1951). The claim that seemed so peculiar makes perfect sense given this different definition.

When evaluating claims and arguments, we may seek definitions for key terms when we find them unclear or suspect that there is some confusion about meaning, or a misunderstanding. Various kinds of definitions can be given, and it is useful to distinguish the different types.

Reportive Definitions

A *reportive definition* is one that has the goal of accurately describing how a word is used. Its purpose is to state in a clear way the meaning of the word as people do use it and to do this by referring to the essential properties of the thing—those it must have in order to be what it is.

For example, a reportive definition of the word *chair* as used to refer to furniture is "a piece of furniture that is to seat one person; it typically has a straight back and is raised from the floor by legs." Such a definition is supposed to describe how people use the word *chair* to refer to pieces of furniture. The definition makes being a piece of furniture and being used to seat one person essential features of chairs, and suggests that having a straight back and being raised by legs are not strictly speaking essential, though they are typical.

We don't call stools chairs because stools don't have backs. We don't call sofas chairs because sofas seat more than one person. We do call large bags filled with small pellets "bean bag chairs," because they shape into a kind of back and seat and hold one person, even though they are not raised from the floor by legs. As used for a piece of furniture, the word *chair* poses few problems. It seems relatively easy to give a descriptive (reportive) definition.

However, even a simple word like *chair* has other meanings, as we can see from the following examples:

(e) The chair called the meeting to order.

(f) The college established a chair in Roman history.

In (e) a chair is a person in charge of a meeting. In (f) it is an endowed professorial position. As noted with the word *bank* earlier, the context makes clear which of these meanings is intended.

For reportive definitions, a dictionary is a good place to start. A dictionary seeks to describe how a word is actually used and uses other words to sum up that pattern of usage briefly. We must remember, however, than even dictionaries sometimes offer imperfect definitions. Because they have to be quite brief, they may leave out features that are important to understanding normal usage. Also, dictionaries may not reflect variation in use in different places and times. For words such as *justice, freedom, democracy, socialism,* and so on—words that represent abstract and profound ideas about which there are different philosophical and political theories—dictionaries are rarely helpful. In the short space they are able to allot to a single word, they cannot say enough about the issues and principles involved in these ideas to give a reliable account.

A reportive definition is open to correction against facts of usage even when it comes from a dictionary. It may be too broad (implying that the word can apply to more things than it really does) or too narrow (implying that it applies to fewer things than it really does). For instance, the *Abridged Oxford English*

Dictionary, fourth edition (1951), defines *chair* (in the context of furniture) as "separate seat for one, of various forms." This definition may be criticized as too broad, because it allows a stool to count as a chair. The case of a stool provides a counterexample to the definition; according to the definition, a stool would be a chair, but in ordinary usage, we do not call a stool a chair. A reference to a back is needed to make the definition describe common usage more closely. On the other hand, we have too narrow a definition if we define *chair* as "separate seat for one having a back and four legs" because many chairs have only three legs, and bean bag chairs have none.

In addition to being too broad or too narrow, reportive definitions may be inadequate in two other basic ways. They may use terms that are too obscure and, therefore, are not helpful in explaining the meaning of a word. For instance, a definition of *eating* as "successive performance of masticating, humectating, and deglutinating" would be open to this objection! Anyone who needed a definition of a simple English term like *eating* would not understand such uncommon words.

Reportive definitions may also be inadequate because the word to be defined occurs again in the definition. For instance, if we define *drug* as "substance commonly used to drug someone" we have a circular definition. The word *drug* is used again in the definition, so no progress in explanation can be made. Circularity is a problem because when the definition uses the term being defined, or one very closely related to it in meaning, the definition cannot possibly explain the term to someone who does not already know its meaning. When you try to understand the definition you are led right back to where you started, to the term you did not originally understand. Circularity is also found in such proposed definitions as "poets are literary artists who compose poetic works" or "philosophers are those intellectuals who study problems that are peculiarly philosophical."

Ultimately, obscurity and circularity in definitions depend on the audience for whom those definitions are intended. The examples of obscurity and circularity just mentioned here are so extreme that virtually anybody who needed such a definition would find that it didn't help to explain the meaning of the term. Other examples might be obscure to some audiences but all right for others, or they might be circular in some contexts but legitimate in others. For instance, one dictionary defines *hocus pocus* as "jugglery, deception, or a typical conjuring formula." Though the words used in the definition are quite advanced, to many people they would be better known than the expression *hocus pocus* itself. Thus, this definition can probably be helpful for many people. If *scholar* is defined as "one devoting his or her life to school and its disciplines," the circularity in the close relationship between *school* and *scholar* may well be harmless—nearly everyone knows what schools are.

Suppose that the letter *x* represents a word that is being defined. A good reportive definition of *x* has the following features:

1. It defines *x* in terms of the essential features that a thing must have in order to be *x*.

2. It is not too broad. That is, all things that the definition would have us call *x* are called *x* in ordinary usage.

3. It is not too narrow. That is, all things that are called *x* in ordinary usage are *x* according to the definition.

4. It is not too obscure. That is, for the audience to whom the definition is directed, the terms used to define *x* are not more difficult to understand than is *x* itself.

5. It is not circular. That is, for the audience to whom the definition is directed, the terms used to define *x* are not so closely related to *x* that that definition fails to explain anything.

People who know and use a language are usually in a position to check reportive definitions of basic terms in that language for themselves. You can use the above points to do this for yourself.

One interesting thing is that a definition can fail in several different ways at once. For instance, it can be both too broad and too narrow! Suppose we were given, as a reportive definition of the term *swimming pool*, the following: "A swimming pool is an enclosed, artificially constructed area of water intended for public use." This definition would be too broad because it allows wading pools with only 6 inches of water to count as swimming pools. It would be too narrow because it requires that swimming pools be intended for public use. (Many people have private swimming pools.)

Ostensive Definitions

It can in some cases be difficult to accurately describe the use of words. Sometimes it is hard to "catch" the sense of a word, in other words. We would like, if we could, to get outside language and explain a word by pointing to the world itself. *Ostensive definition* is one way in which we try to do this. In an ostensive definition of *x*, we explain what *x* is by pointing to an example of *x*, to something that is *x*—either a real thing, or a representation of *x*. For instance, instead of using words to say what a chair is, we might just point to a chair and say "that's a chair."

As children we learn language by participating in social life and by copying things others say and do. Children are taught many words by having objects pointed out to them. The same method is often used for those learning a second language. Ostensive definition is easy and useful for those who don't have a large vocabulary. It means they do not have to know thousands of words in order to come to understand others. The procedure of ostensive definition appears to tie language to the world, letting us escape from what we may feel are "words, words, and more words." It has seemed to some theorists to be the essential core of language learning for this reason.

However, ostensive definition is not as simple as it might first seem to be. It does not avoid all possibilities of misunderstanding, because when one person defines a term ostensively for another, the person to whom the definition is given will come to a proper understanding only if he knows which features he is supposed to attend to. Suppose that Mary tries to teach Bill what a window is by pointing to a window and saying "that's a window." Bill may spot something outside the window, such as a dog or a car, and think that Mary is pointing to that instead. If he misunderstands in this way, he will not go on to use the word correctly on the basis of the definition.

Ostensive definitions are especially useful for sensory qualities that are impossible to capture, or even suggest in words. To tell someone in words what pineapple tastes like, how a trumpet sounds, or what periwinkle blue is, is virtually impossible. It is so much easier and simpler if you can produce an example and say "it's like this." When the context makes it relatively easy to understand just what it is that is being pointed to, ostensive definitions may be appropriate.

Stipulative Definitions

A *stipulative definition* is one in which someone creates or restricts word usage rather than describing it. She stipulates, or lays down, a meaning for a term. This may be done when the meaning of a word that is in common use is restricted for a special purpose, such as in the context of a technical development of a subject. Also, stipulative definitions are used by those who are inventing new words and giving them meanings.

An example of a stipulative definition is "For the purposes of this scholarship award, 'full-time student' shall mean any student enrolled in eight or more semester-length courses in a given calendar year." Such a definition might be stated in the context of a description of a scholarship in order to explain eligibility conditions. It stipulates, or sets out, how the expression "full-time student" is to be used in the competition for the scholarship. Its purpose is practical—to make applicants and administrators understand who is and who is not eligible for the award. A stipulative definition like this applies only in a limited context. Legal contracts and specific legislation may include stipulative definitions of similar kinds.

Definitions constructed in technical areas may become standard in those fields and may eventually extend to common usage. The American mathematician Edward Kasner defined an expression for the number "10 raised to the 100th power." He called it a "googol." The word is now found in some contemporary dictionaries. Robert E. Kelley of Carnegie-Mellon University coined a term "gold-collar worker," which he defined as "an employee in a brain-intensive business who regards his or her intellect, experience, and inventiveness as monetary assets to be leveraged with respect to relationships with current or potential employers."[3] The distinction between blue-collar (factory) and white-collar (office) workers is often supplemented by "pink-collar workers," a term already in some popular use to refer to women workers who occupy secretarial positions with relatively little independent decision-making power. Kelley has coined the further term "gold-collar worker," presumably because he thinks the creative intellectual worker in a certain business has a distinct economic and social role that makes him or her importantly different from other white-collar workers. Perhaps the term will come into common usage.

We might think that stipulative definitions cannot really be criticized. It seems natural to suppose that if a person is laying down a meaning for a term, that person has the final say on what the meaning is going to be. This is not quite correct, though. Usually, stipulative definitions are made for some particular purpose, and they can be assessed on the basis of how well they serve that purpose. A scholarship eligibility condition requiring an eligible person to be a full-time student and defining a *full-time student* as a "student who is enrolled in at least fifteen semester courses in a calendar year and does no nonacademic work for pay" could be criticized as too narrow to be fair.

In the case of words that have important social, moral, or emotional content, stipulations that go too far from ordinary usage can be misleading. Stipulative definitions are open to criticism on such grounds if the stipulated meaning is intended for public use. For instance, if a university defined *science* as "the quantifiable study of the nonhuman physical world" and then insisted, on the basis of this definition, that psychology (about human beings) and mathematics (not about the physical world) were not sciences, it would be open to criticism. Such a stipulation would be unreasonably narrow and, because of its unusual departure from standard usage of a common term, apt to mislead students, prospective employers, and the public at large.

People may seek to win arguments merely by stipulating definitions, but this strategy is not a good one when the acceptability of the conclusion depends solely on the stipulation. It seeks to substitute a new definition for evidence and reasons. To see this, suppose we stipulate that *resource* means "any valuable substance in the earth owned jointly by all the world's people." We might think "Well, if we are going to stipulate, we can stipulate any way we want, so let's stipulate that resources are valuable substances owned by everybody." This is all right as far as it goes—we can use the word *resources* in this way if we want to. But we cannot on the basis of this stipulated definition alone contend that everybody owns all the world's resources. Suppose that we were to propose the definition and then go on to argue that since oil is a resource, all the world's people jointly own all the world's oil. The move would achieve nothing of substance, because oil is not agreed to be a resource in the sense of *resource* we have defined.

The game "Propaganda," which gives examples of various faulty forms of argument, calls such a move "victory by definition." The victory is not a real one. The stipulation will only hide and confuse the issue of who does own the world's valuable substances. Anyone who believes that separate nations separately own valuable materials within their own territory would not be willing to call these "resources" in the stipulated sense. The proposed stipulation departs too much from ordinary usage and seeks to avoid the important substantive question of just who does own the world's resources.

If a stipulated definition becomes popular, the word defined in its new sense then becomes part of public language, and it is open to changes and variations in use just as other words are. The word will appear in dictionaries, and can be given reportive definitions, which can be checked for their reliability. Its original author loses his authority as the only person who can say for certain what the word means. For example, if Kelley's term "gold-collar worker" becomes part of our language, it will not be up to just him to say, for instance, whether computer programmers are or are not gold-collar workers. This decision will depend both on facts about the creativity and ambitions of computer programmers and on how the expression "gold-collar worker" comes to be used by the general public.

Persuasive Definitions

A fourth type of definition is rather like a stipulative definition, but it is disguised. The fact that a meaning is being stipulated is not obvious, because claims are worded as though they described matters of fact or as though the definition was reportive. We often do not notice that a stipulation is being made, and we all too willingly transfer emotions and attitudes on the basis of the stipulation alone. In a *persuasive definition,* there is an attempt to alter beliefs and attitudes by redefining a term. Often words like *true, real,* and *genuine* are used in stating these definitions.

Suppose we were told that a real democracy is one in which every citizen has an equal opportunity to make his or her opinion heard. From this we could easily argue that the United States and Canada are not real democracies. People have demonstrably different opportunities to publish and broadcast their ideas in the mass media.

An argument could be set out as follows:

1. In a real democracy every citizen has an equal opportunity to have his or her opinion heard by others.
2. In Canada and the United States people have very different opportunities to have their views published in the press or broadcast on radio or television.

So,

3. In Canada and the United States it is not true that every citizen has an equal opportunity to have his or her opinion heard by others.

Therefore,

4. Canada and the United States are not real democracies.

Here, there is a subargument from (2) to (3); (3) and (1) then link to support (4), the conclusion. The argument seems entirely convincing and premise (3) is surely true. Yet the conclusion is paradoxical and at odds with ordinary usage; many of us would hesitate to accept this conclusion. What has gone wrong?

A reportive definition of *democracy* that did not allow us to call Canada and the United States democracies could be rejected as too narrow. What is wrong is that premise (1) is, in effect, a stipulation as to how the term *democracy* should be used. Most people have favorable attitudes toward democracy. By imposing a new condition for real democracy, a person would be trying to transfer those attitudes to a different kind of state and society and deny them to the United States and Canada. Premise (1) offers, in effect, a persuasive definition—a stipulative definition masquerading as a simple statement. The use of *real* in the conclusion is a clue to what has happened.

The issue raised in the argument, that of how citizens can be heard in a society where mass media institutions radically affect the construction and dissemination of information and opinion, is an extremely important one. But this issue is not going to be better understood just because someone proposes a new definition of *democracy,* especially not when the definition is a disguised stipulation.

Terms such as *real, true,* and *genuine* are often elements in stating persuasive definitions. If someone tells you that modern abstract art is not real art because real art must depict objects naturalistically, he is relying on a persuasive definition of *art* as something that must be naturalistic. The term *art* tends to be one of praise: to deny that modern abstract art should count as art is to imply, among other things, that it has no proper place in museums, art history courses, or expensive art auctions. Someone who has this attitude can express it by denying that abstract art is real art, but such a statement is only a disguised stipulative definition. It is not a good argument.

The concept of persuasive definition was first put forward by philosopher Charles L. Stevenson more than forty years ago. Stevenson was interested in ethics and, in particular, in the way in which attitudes and beliefs about facts are involved in moral judgments. He emphasized that some words have a strong emotional component and that people may wish to preserve the attitudes accompanying them while changing the factual basis for applying the words. Terms like *democracy, art, justice, freedom, socialism,* and *security* are particularly common objects of this technique.

Stevenson quoted an example from a novel by Aldous Huxley:

> But if you want to be free, you've got to be a prisoner. It's the condition of freedom —true freedom.
>
> "True freedom!" Anthony repeated in the parody of a clerical voice. "I always love that kind of argument. The contrary of a thing isn't the contrary; oh, dear me, no! It's the thing itself, but as it truly is. Ask any die-hard what conservatism is; he'll tell you it's true socialism. And the brewer's trade papers: they're full of articles about the beauty of true temperance. Ordinary temperance is just gross refusal to drink; but true temperance, true temperance is something much more refined. True temperance is a bottle of claret with each meal and three double whiskies after dinner. . . ."
>
> "What's in a name?" Anthony went on. "The answer is, practically everything, if the name's a good one. Freedom's a marvelous name. That's why you're so anxious to make use of it. You think that, if you call imprisonment true freedom, people will be attracted to the prison. And the worst of it is, you're quite right."[4]

The important thing about persuasive definitions is to notice them and not be tricked into transferring favorable or unfavorable attitudes on the basis of someone else's idea of the real, true meaning of a word. Like stipulative definitions, persuasive definitions can have their point, but they should never be a substitute for substantive argument.

EXERCISE SET

Exercise 1

1. Consult a recent dictionary for reportive definitions of the following words. Are the dictionary definitions open to any criticisms such as being too broad, too narrow, circular, or obscure? If so, explain the problem and fix the definition so that it is more accurate.

   a. geography
   b. mountain
   c. articulate (adjective)
   d. meander (verb)
   e. gentle

2. Construct your own reportive definitions for the following terms and, if possible, have a friend check their accuracy and usefulness.

   a. triangle
   b. judge (noun, as court official)
   c. lazy
   d. efficient
   e. jogging

3. Assume that you have a visitor about your own age, from Poland, and you are trying to teach English to this person, who knows only a few words. Of the following words, which do you think you could define by ostensive definition? Which do you think would not be possible to define in this way? Give reasons for your answers.

   a. bed
   b. cheese
   c. jump (verb)
  *d. wisdom
   e. cable television
   f. purple
  *g. freckles
   h. hooliganism
   i. surgery
  *j. exercise (verb)

4. Assume that the following statements are put forward as reportive definitions. Test their adequacy according to the criteria previously discussed.

  *a. "Money is a medium of exchange."
   b. "Health is the absence of disease."

   c. "Dentistry is the profession of caring for teeth and gums."
   d. "A hawk is a bird of prey used in falconry, with rounded wings shorter than a falcon's."
  *e. "To study is to concentrate very hard with the goal of remembering what you are concentrating on."

5. Specify appropriate stipulative definitions for the following situations:

   a. You are making a legal agreement to rent a small building. After discussion, you and the landlord have agreed that you will, on the terms of the lease, be able to use the building either as a private residence or as the site of a small family business. You want to be able to live there with three friends, not related to you, and he agrees to this. Also, you want to conduct either a modest secretarial business, taking in papers to type, or a small daycare center, admitting five to ten children. He agrees to this, but he does not want you to have any business that will bring a lot of traffic or noisy machinery to the neighborhood. Construct suitable stipulative definitions for *private residence* and *small family business* that will serve your purposes and those of the landlord.

   b. Your English teacher has asked you to write an essay comparing the novels of two great twentieth-century English novelists. You wish to write an introduction to your essay, explaining why you have chosen Theodore Dreiser (American) and Margaret Atwood (Canadian). Give a stipulative definition of great twentieth-century English novelists that will serve your purposes without deviating too far from standard usage.

Hint: Concentrate on the terms *great* and *English.*

  *c. You are moderating a panel on terrorism. The other members of the panel include an American-Irish sympathizer of the Irish Republican Army (a violent group active in Northern Ireland and Great Britain) and a spokesperson for the U.S. administration, which is greatly concerned about violence by anti-Israeli groups against civilians, particularly American citizens on airplanes in Europe and the Middle East. You wish to stipulate a definition of *terrorism* that the other panel members will agree to and that will help the discussion be as reasonable as possible.

d. You are a civil servant working for the income tax department. Tax credits are allowed for donations to charitable institutions or groups, but there are groups whose status in this regard is in question. These groups include antinuclear groups offering films about the risk of nuclear reactor accidents for use in schools; right-to-life groups offering counseling to women with unwanted pregnancies and seeking laws to make abortion strictly illegal; 4-H clubs; and the United Nations Association, an educational and fund-raising group seeking to further the goals of the United Nations. Suggest a stipulative definition of *charitable institutions or groups* that would help the tax department make efficient and reasonable decisions.

*e. You own a small orchard and have been experimenting with cross-pollination. By clever experimentation, you have produced a fruit that is a cross between an apple and a pear. Coin a word for your new fruit, and stipulate a definition for it.

6. Which of the following are persuasive definitions? How can you tell that the definition is persuasive, and what attitudes is the speaker trying to change?

a. "Reform means having me as your new leader."

(Comment by a candidate for the leadership of the Social Credit party in British Columbia, quoted on CBC television, July 7, 1986)

b. "With our earth shoes and the lowered heel, you can do pure walking."

(Adapted from an ad popular in the 70s)

*c. Tea is a beverage consumed widely in England, particularly in the afternoon.

d. "A real woman is one who knows how to please and keep a man."

(Adapted from the politics of Real Women, an anti-feminist group)

*e. A policeman is a criminal with a special license from the government to assault or even kill people whose activities he disapproves of.

f. Ah, music! The voice of the heart and language of the soul! How could I live without it?

g. The people out at these demonstrations cannot be true students, because students have to spend their time studying and attending classes and preparing for exams. True students do not put their energy into politics.

*h. Photography is not art. Authentic art requires artificial reproduction of reality, and photography is a natural reproduction that does not select among those aspects of reality to be presented.

Hint: Authentic means real.

i. I shall mean by *total institution* an institution such as an asylum or prison in which there are physical barriers preventing the free departure of inmates and free entry of visitors.

(Adapted from sociologist Erving Goffman)

j. An obituary is a brief notice of death including a shortened biography of the deceased person, customarily published in a newspaper.

k. An argument is an attempt to rationally justify a statement or claim by putting forward reasons or evidence on its behalf.

*l. "Insanity is the product of an accurate mind over-taxed."

(Adapted from Oliver Wendall Holmes)

m. "Men who have fathered children during brief sexual encounters do not have a right to be consulted if the mothers of those children decide to give them up for adoption. For the purpose of adoption law, these men are not parents. They are casual fornicators."

(Judges in an Ontario Supreme Court case, reported in the Toronto *Globe and Mail*, March 11, 1990)

FURTHER FEATURES OF LANGUAGE

When we come to evaluate arguments and to construct our own arguments, clarity is important. Language, which does so much to direct our attention and express and shape our attitudes, can sometimes be unclear in ways that affect the precision and accuracy of statements or arguments. Two important types of unclarity are ambiguity and vagueness.

Ambiguity

A simple example of *ambiguity* can be seen in the newspaper headline "Home Delivery Sought." As it stands, this headline might refer either to a desire for babies to be born at home rather than in hospitals or to a desire for mail to be delivered to private homes rather than to group mailboxes. In such a case, the ambiguity is easily resolved when we read the accompanying story. Other ambiguities can be more significant and harder to detect. A word or phrase may have several meanings, any of which could fit naturally in the context in which it is used. It is important to watch for this; if you miss it, you may not understand what is said. Arguments and claims often gain a spurious plausibility because of hidden ambiguities.

The phrase "home delivery sought" illustrates *structural ambiguity*. That is, the ambiguity arises because the headline, which is compressed, could naturally be interpreted as standing for two quite distinct grammatical structures. Structural ambiguity is sometimes called *syntactic ambiguity,* indicating that it arises from syntax or grammar. The phrase "home delivery sought" might mean either:

(a) People seek that babies should be delivered at home.

or

(b) People seek that their mail should be delivered at home.

The word *home* has the same meaning in (a) and (b), though *delivery* differs in meaning. The sense in which babies are delivered is not quite that in which mail is delivered! But the ambiguity of the headline is due to the fact that the compressed phrase could quite naturally be taken to represent either (a) or (b). Background knowledge is unlikely to clarify the situation if we read only the headline. The ambiguity is not serious, though, because the story will certainly indicate whether (a) or (b)—or something else—is correct.

Another type of ambiguity is *semantic ambiguity*. Semantic ambiguity is found when a word, in the context of its use, could naturally be taken as having more than one distinct meaning. Consider, in this connection, the very common claim that "Evolution is only a theory." The word *theory* has at least two different meanings:

Meaning (1)   *Theory:* A theory is a mere speculation that is not fully supported by any firm facts.

Meaning (2)   *Theory:* A theory is a body of scientific principles that are intended to explain observed phenomena.

When people insist that evolutionary theory is "only" a theory and go on to criticize the educational system for concentrating on it, they must be using *theory* to express meaning (1). But in this sense of *theory,* it is by no means obviously true that evolutionary theory is a theory. In the second sense of *theory*, it is true that evolutionary theory is a theory, but there is no reason not to teach theories in science classes.

The comment that evolution is only a theory may sound as though it both is plausible and has the implication that things other than evolution should be taught. This superficial plausibility arises because we tend to blur together meaning (1) and meaning (2) of *theory*. The first meaning would allow the inference that the evolutionary view isn't the only one that should be taught; the second makes it obviously true that evolutionary doctrine is theory.

It is generally important to be sensitive to ambiguity and to get meanings clear. Sometimes people try to exploit an ambiguity, for a particular purpose, as when they incorporate it into a title to suggest several dimensions of a problem in a single word, or put it into the wording of an agreement between contending parties in order to gloss over an area of unresolved disagreement. This sort of ambiguity can be harmless—as it usually is in titles, where the ambiguity is a kind of pun or catchiness. But usually we benefit by being sensitive to ambiguity.

Sometimes in arguments words are used in such a way that several different meanings are involved. The ARG conditions may seem to be satisfied, but only because we do not detect ambiguity. No analysis of an argument that ignores this factor can be complete or correct. In fact, there is a special *fallacy*, or mistake, of argument based on problems of ambiguity. It is the *fallacy of equivocation*.

A fallacy is an argument that is based on a common mistake in reasoning, a sort of mistake that people tend not to notice. Fallacies tend to be deceptive. That is to say, although they are not cogent arguments, they often strike people as being cogent, or good. People may be persuaded by fallacious arguments if they do not notice the mistakes.

The fallacy of equivocation is committed when a key word in an argument is used in two or more senses and the premises of the argument appear to support its conclusion only because these senses are not distinguished from each other.[5] The argument may seem to be cogent because the ambiguity is unnoticed. Presumably, the person who invented the argument did not notice the different meanings. However, the person hearing or reading the argument can avoid being taken in by the fallacy by noticing the different meanings and understanding that the argument depends on blurring these together. When the premises and conclusion are clearly understood, the ambiguity is apparent and the argument no longer seems cogent. We can see that the ARG conditions are not satisfied.

Here is an example of a kind of pun, indicating awareness of ambiguity:

> Terminal cancer is cancer that is going to be fatal, cancer that is going to kill. Not a pleasant thing to think about. Guess what—near the bus depot there is Terminal Barber Shop. I ask you, what kind of name is that? You think of going there, you think you're going to get your throat cut and die. Talk about a name that's bad for business!

These comments show awareness of the ambiguity in *terminal*, which may mean either fatal, as it does in the expression "terminal cancer," or end point, as it does in the expression "bus terminal." There is no fallacy committed in the comments;

rather, the suggestion (tongue in cheek) is that people might associate death with *terminal* and that for this reason using that word in the name of a barber shop is not such a smart idea.

Here is another example. In this case the key ambiguity is in *theory:* whether *theory* is used to mean unsubstantiated speculation, or scientific theory. The argument as stated does not indicate awareness of this ambiguity. Rather, it trades on it, exemplifying the fallacy of equivocation, because it is one sense that makes premise (1) acceptable and another that makes premise (2) acceptable.

1. Theory is speculation, not fact.
2. Evolution is only a theory.
3. Schools should not teach ideas that are mere speculation.
Therefore,
4. Schools should not teach evolutionary theory.

In this argument, premises (1), (2), and (3) are supposed to link to support (4). The argument, to be cogent, must pass the ARG conditions. To pass the (A) condition it must have acceptable premises. In this case, the premises may all strike you, at first glance, as quite plausible. However, in order for these premises to be plausible, in premise (1) *theory* must have the meaning identified as meaning (1) above, and in premise (2), it must have meaning (2). Thus, the apparent cogency of the argument depends on our giving the word *theory* two quite different meanings but failing to notice that we have done so. If we noted the distinction, the argument would not pass the (R) and (G) conditions, because the premises would not connect properly to support the conclusion. The argument depends on this ambiguity and exemplifies the fallacy of equivocation. (It tempts us to be equivocal about two different meanings—to move back and forth between them without making a distinction. If we do so, we will be persuaded by an argument based on the fallacy of equivocation.)

Ambiguity occurs when a word or phrase, as it is used in a context, could naturally be interpreted as having any one of several different meanings. We don't know just which one is appropriate. Or, as in the last case, the very same word is used with several distinct meanings in the same context, and these meanings seem not to be distinguished from each other, leading to confusion and flaws in argument.

If you are constructing your own argument, you should make your structures and terms as unambiguous as possible. If you use a term that has several distinct meanings, you should get clear in your own mind just which sense of the term you intend, and do your best to make your meaning clear to your audience.

Vagueness

Vagueness is another kind of unclarity in meaning. To say that words or statements are vague is to say that their meaning is unclear in the sense that it is too imprecise to give information needed in the context where the words are used. Vagueness is a lack of distinctness of meaning. Whereas with ambiguous words or phrases, there are several distinct meanings, with vagueness the problem is that, in the particular context where the word is used, it fails to have any distinct meaning. Here language is used with insufficient precision, so that we cannot really tell what is being asserted.

Sometimes vagueness is used as a kind of evasive technique, in order to avoid saying anything definite. Imagine that a factory manager is asked what he is going to do to improve productivity, which has been decreasing, and he replies by saying "things are being worked out so that something can be brought into effect at the appropriate moment." He has spoken but has managed to avoid the issue by not really saying anything! Words are strung together but nothing of substance is communicated. Identifying this kind of vagueness is important because it can help you understand that you have not really been given any information and can press for more genuine information if you need it. Vagueness of this sort is a technique for avoiding issues.[6]

We speak sometimes of words being vague. This is slightly misleading, for vagueness arises from the way a word or phrase is used in a particular context. If the context is one requiring that we be able to determine when the word applies to a thing, and we cannot determine that due to insufficient precision in the word, the word is used vaguely in that context. Such vagueness will pose a practical problem. However, the very same word might be used in another context in such a way that there is no problem of vagueness.

For example, if a buyer tells a real estate agent that she needs a big house for her family and fails to specify how many bedrooms, bathrooms, and so on she needs, or what kind of square footage she has in mind, she has used *big* vaguely. The agent needs guidance as to how many bedrooms, bathrooms, and so on she has in mind. What one means by "a big house" can vary a great deal. If the agent is going to search for houses, he needs more precise guidance than he will get from the unclarified expression "we need a big house." On the other hand, if someone comments that size 16 is a big size in women's dresses, it is probably not necessary to have further clarification of what is meant by *big*. The point is that the size is larger than average. It is of no great practical importance to attach a precise meaning to *big* in this context.

The problem of *ambiguity* arises when a word, as used, could have several distinct meanings, and we are unable to tell which of these it has. The problem of *vagueness* arises when a word, as used, has a meaning that is insufficiently clear to convey the necessary information in that context of use. To contrast vagueness and ambiguity, you might think of words as being used to mark out boundaries. When a word is used vaguely, the boundaries are fuzzy so that we cannot see just which area is marked out. When a word is used ambiguously, there are several different bounded areas, and we won't know which of these the word is pointing to.

Sometimes we don't know whether statements are acceptable because we don't know the relevant facts. For instance, we might not know how many people in New York City are malnourished because we lacked factual information about the availability and distribution of food. On the other hand, even if we knew many statistics about food distribution and availability, we might still be unable to determine how many people were malnourished because of not knowing just how severe the deprivation has to be before we should call them "malnourished." In this case, our lack of knowledge would be due to unclarity of language—indecision as to our criteria for using the term *malnourished*, with resulting vagueness.

In arguments, it is essential for the premises and conclusions to have meanings that are sufficiently precise that we can decide whether or not they are acceptable. If vagueness is so serious that we cannot give a reasonably distinct meaning to a premise or conclusion statement, this is an important criticism of an argument.

Vagueness can be dangerous in legal or administrative contexts because it permits authorities to apply rules selectively. For instance, if it is illegal to loiter, and if there is no clarification in law or custom as to what loitering is, police can, with no basis, charge innocent teenagers or members of racial minorities with loitering and choose to ignore white middle-aged citizens who stand around on street corners.

A currently significant term that is vague in a rather dangerous way is *sexual harassment*. The problem of sexual harassment is an important one for which administrative and legal policies have to be devised. Unfortunately it is difficult to specify in general just what should count as sexual harassment. A 1989 case in Toronto involved a claim by a woman that a man was staring at her while she swam in a university swimming pool. She found his staring so prolonged and offensive that she charged him with sexual harassment. Eventually she won her case. Commentary on the case was mixed, however, because many people found the idea that staring could constitute sexual harassment rather implausible. The case highlighted a certain amount of public confusion about just what constitutes sexual harassment.

An indication of the wide range of meanings people attach to the term can be found in the following passage, based on a 1981 survey by the women's magazine *Glamour:*

> How do you define sexual harassment? Fifty percent say that even sexual comments, innuendoes, and jokes constitute sexual harassment, while at the other end of the spectrum, 8 percent regard only an explicit sexual invitation as harassment. "My boss harassed me to the point of pulling down his pants and showing me pictures of himself nude. But even a meaningful stare can be harassing."
>
> What do you [readers of the magazine] consider sexual harassment? Fifty percent say sexual comments, innuendoes, or jokes; 33 percent say touching, or unnecessary closeness; 6 percent say suggestions for outside meetings; 8 percent say explicit sexual invitation; 2 percent say other.[7]

The vagueness of *harassment* in this context is indicated by the vast range of behavior people would count as harassment—everything from comments to explicit requests for sex. Elimination of this kind of vagueness will be necessary for any organization seeking a viable policy about sexual harassment.

Just as arguments can get their persuasiveness from ambiguity, some can trade on vagueness. An arguer may begin with a vague term and proceed through his argument applying the term to anything and everything, getting away with it because the term is so vague that it's not easy to say he's wrong. Here is an example:

> There are two types of abuse of children. The first is described as extreme and includes such elements as murder, rape and incest, multiple bruises, broken bones, gross neglect, and starvation. In many instances such abuse is fatal. The second form of abuse is more general and more moderate in that while it neither kills nor fatally wounds, it may do considerable psychological harm. Included in this abuse are parental and professional neglect through ignoring parents, inattentive teachers, and incompetent professionals. In addition, hundreds of children are abused because they are unwanted, poor, or are victims of the undue expectations of adults, or are subjected to authoritarianism in the name of religion, tradition and discipline, to physical punishment at home and at school, to name calling, to judgmental comparison, to the achievement syndrome, to pornography and violence, and to unnecessary labeling that proves to be detrimental.
>
> Children suffer abuse as well, I think, when budgetary restraints limit daycare or render it of poor quality, deny needed services for the handicapped, close school libraries, and force children to be bussed hundreds of miles a week in unsafe vehicles.[8]

At the beginning of this passage, the author seems to be using *abuse* as it is normally used in "child abuse": child abuse is deliberate assault against children, or gross neglect of them, resulting in physical harm. But then he starts to speak of moderate abuse, which sounds like a contradiction in terms. It turns out that inattentive teachers and insufficiently funded daycare systems also abuse children, according to this author. By *abuse* now, he must simply mean harm; note that this is a much less precise meaning than he started out with and that it gives a much broader meaning to *abuse* than the word usually has in contexts where people speak of child abuse. The stretching of language is virtually absurd when the author comes to the point of calling the unnecessary labeling of children abuse. Labeling may not be a good thing, but to use the same term for it and for gross physical beating is to stretch language too much. The differences between gross physical brutality and inappropriate funding for schools are more significant than the similarity the author wants us to attend to.

This author makes the word *abuse* so vague that it virtually loses its meaning. He is trying to show that children should be properly cared for, schools and daycare centers should be properly funded, and so on. By saying that children are abused when we do not do this, he tries, in effect, to carry over the negative feelings we hold toward abuse in the narrower sense to all these activities.

Before leaving the topic of vagueness, we should note that vagueness and ambiguity can occur together, in the same context and with respect to the same words. To see this, consider the example of a patient seeking to be released from a hospital. She might say to the nurse, "The doctor said I could go home if I showed some improvement." For a nurse faced with making a decision on the matter, such a promise will seem intolerably vague, because there is no guidance at all on what the doctor would have regarded as "some improvement." If the patient were to go on and argue that because her attitude is now changed and is improved, she has shown some improvement, she would compound the problem by adding ambiguity to vagueness. Improvement in attitude is quite a different thing from improvement in physical health, which presumably was what the doctor had in mind. In this exchange, "some improvement" is used both vaguely and ambiguously.

Emotionally Charged Language

As has already been illustrated, language can become a substitute for rational argument and can work to disguise the fact that important and contested claims have not been supported by reason or evidence.

Think back to the example about child abuse in the previous section. Whatever child abuse is, we are bound to be opposed to it, because *abuse* is an emotionally negative term. You can see the negative emotional charge in the word *abuse* if you imagine that a friend tells you his dentist abuses him. Most people's dentists hurt them to a degree, at least when the needle goes in. We don't normally call this abuse, however, because the hurting is done for a beneficial purpose, not to bring harm to the patient. In saying his dentist abuses him, your friend would be making a very critical remark.

Some poor arguments trade on *emotionally charged language*. The substitution of emotionally charged language for argument is also quite common. If situations are described in emotionally negative language, we tend to assume that something is wrong, whereas if they are described in emotionally positive language, we tend to think everything is fine. A mood and attitude can be set without any evidence or consideration of alternate possibilities. Think of what is implied, for instance, in the term *joystick*, to be used with computer games. You are to take up a happy attitude just because of the name of the thing, before you even start to play the game!

One way to understand the effect of positive and negative emotional language is to apply each type of the same phenomenon. Consider the difference, for instance, between calling a change a "deterioration" and calling it a "reform." The introduction of Vietnamese or Spanish language classes might be regarded as a deterioration in curriculum by some and as a reform by others. Statements about school policy referring to "this recent deterioration" or "this recent reform" could describe the same facts with a different emotional flavor. The negative term *deterioration* would tend to make us oppose the introductions; the positive term *reform* would encourage us to favor them. To work out a considered position on such an issue, we have to frame it in more neutral terms and try to objectively consider factors for and against the proposed changes.

It would be unrealistic to insist on universally *neutral language*. This pervasive neutrality may not be possible, and even if it were, it would make writing and speaking terribly boring. What we should be on the watch for is emotionally charged language that conveys a view on a controversial point where there is no supporting evidence.

To see how this works, take a look at the following two brief letters, both of which were sent to *Time* magazine shortly after the Reagan election in 1980.

> (a) Reagan is our clown prince, and we are his foolish subjects. Don't look now, America, but the whole world is laughing. Maybe he deserved an Academy Award for his startling performance, but he certainly didn't deserve to be President.[9]
>
> (b) Laurence Barret's pre-election piece on Candidate Ronald Reagan was a slick hatchet job, and you know it. You ought to be ashamed of yourselves for printing it disguised as an objective look at the man.[10]

Clearly the author of (a) believes Reagan is not qualified to be president. The author of (b) seems to support Reagan in that he expresses hostility to a critical piece *Time* ran on him, calling it "a slick hatchet job." Neither (a) nor (b) contains any argument or evidence. In (a) the author gives absolutely no basis for thinking Reagan is not qualified to be president; nor does he give any reason for his view that Americans who voted for Reagan in 1980 made a silly mistake. In (b) the author gives no basis for calling the piece slick, cites no errors in it, and gives no reason to back up his judgment that the piece was only disguised as objective. Both passages use emotionally charged language instead of argument. Emotionally charged language becomes a substitute for evidence and reasons about Reagan's experience and abilities.[11]

Passages like these do not contain any failings in argument, because they don't express arguments at all. We can evaluate them as not having a cogent argument, but that is because they have no argument! We should notice, in such cases, that a controversial viewpoint is expressed with no supporting argument, and note the emotional tone of the language used. You do not want to let the language carry you into the author's viewpoint for no good reason.

Euphemism

Euphemism is, in a way, the opposite of emotionally charged language. With emotionally charged language, terms are more emotional than appropriate. Euphemism, on the other hand, involves a kind of whitewashing effect of language. Bland, abstract, polite language is used to refer to things that, in a more concrete description, would be found appalling, horrible, or embarrassing. Language can function to dull our awareness of such things.

In 1946 George Orwell wrote an essay in which he attacked the use of euphemism in political speech. Orwell is well known for his discussion of political language in the book *1984*. That book envisages a totalitarian order in which a language called Newspeak has been especially designed in order to make unorthodox thoughts impossible to express. In his essay "Politics and the English Language," Orwell pointed out the importance of language in framing political issues and helping to determine political attitudes. He argued that people are led to condone political horror partly because of the use of euphemism. If thousands of peasants are evicted from their villages and have to flee on foot, there will be great suffering, but if the whole horrible procedure is called "the rectifying of the frontier," we are encouraged to overlook these painful human consequences.

Many appalling examples of the sort of thing Orwell was talking about can be found in officially authorized materials in communist countries. In 1974, a writer for the prominent Soviet literary magazine *Literaturnaya Gazeta* used euphemistic language to refer to the millions of people killed by Stalin in purges in the 20s and 30s. Discussing the book *Gulag Archipelago,* in which dissident author Solzhenitsyn had detailed thousands of stories of suffering and murders in Stalinist prison camps, the commentator branded the author a traitor, acknowledging only that there had been some "violations of Soviet legality" during the period.[12] Millions of false arrests, false trials, interrogations, tortures, and years of desperate suffering were blurred over in an abstract and euphemistic phrase.

When the nuclear reactor at Three Mile Island was close to a dangerous meltdown in 1979, many commentators were still following the nuclear industry in calling the crisis an "incident." This expression is euphemistic in functioning to minimize the seriousness of the situation. In the face of criticism of American nuclear policy from the nuclear freeze movement in 1982, President Reagan called the controversial MX missile system the "Peacekeeper." This name was criticized by opponents of the system, who argued that it was euphemistic and misleading. To think of a missile as a peacekeeper is to direct our attention away from the fact that if it were ever used, millions of deaths would result. The term also encourages people to assume uncritically that the missile can prevent a Russian nuclear attack—avoiding such basic questions as whether such an attack is at all likely in the first place and whether, if it were likely, the deployment of missiles would be the way to prevent it. An equally bizarre example, again from military thinking, is the expression "violent peace," used by Pentagon analysts to describe a doctrine of "low-intensity conflict" (still another euphemism) throughout the Third World.[13]

The following letter to the editor criticizes euphemisms in another area of policy, that concerning the treatment of institutionalized retarded children.

> Your editorial on behavior modification is ethically indefensible.
>
> Behavior modification procedures—such as aversion therapy, including electroshock and electric cattle-prod shocks inflicted on institutionalized retarded children—are unethical. They are forms of cruel and unusual punishment, not treatment. They all should be immediately abolished in Ontario and everywhere else in Canada.
>
> Yet they are still legal, and Canadian psychiatrists are still inflicting these tortures masquerading as treatment on many mentally ill and retarded children and adults.
>
> Incredibly, the *Globe and Mail* believes that such torture is perfectly all right, as long as it's "clearly appropriate and . . . closely monitored." Torture, whether labeled "treatment" or "behavior modification," is never appropriate, as its victims know all too well.[14]

This writer objects to a euphemistic use of language in which the use of an electric cattle-prod on a retarded child can be called "appropriate treatment" or "behavior modification" or "aversion therapy"—in addition to rejecting the practices themselves.

Like ambiguity, vagueness, and emotionally charged language, euphemisms sometimes pose no problem. They are harmless and not misleading when the aspects of reality blurred over are things that it is not really important for us to think about. For instance, if garbage men are called "sanitary engineers," the euphemism may be pretentious but it is probably harmless. The usage may slightly increase the self-respect of garbage men, and probably does not limit our understanding of what these workers do. Similarly, the custom of saying "I need to use the bathroom" instead of "I need to go to the toilet" or (still more frankly) "I need to urinate" or "I need to pee" likely does no harm and is considered to be good manners.

Euphemistic language is dangerous to our understanding when the aspects of reality blurred over are aspects that we need to think about. Imprisonment, torture, false arrests, war, nuclear reactor accidents, nuclear weapons policy, and therapy techniques are aspects of life that can bring great suffering or great benefits. These matters are profoundly important. If euphemistic phrases such as "violations of Soviet legality" and "Peacekeeper" missile blanket over serious harms and risks and discourage us from thinking about them, they are dangerous—just as Orwell maintained.

◆────────────────────────────

EXERCISE SET

Exercise 2: Part A

Check the following statements and arguments to see whether they contain examples of ambiguity, vagueness, or emotionally charged language. If you find an example of ambiguity, explain which words give rise to this ambiguity and state what the possible different meanings are. In the case of vagueness, explain where vagueness arises and see whether there is a more precise expression that you can substitute to make the meaning more clear. If you find emotionally charged language, note the emotionally charged terms. *Note:* Some passages contain no flaws in language; if this is the case, say so.

1. If you want to know what is good for you, in terms of food and exercise, just listen to your body. Your body knows and it will tell you.

2. *Background:* The following is excerpted from an ad that appeared in *Harper's Magazine* in October 1989.

"The wailing of quawwali, roller skaters, meta-decibel machine music. Live chickens . . . and let us not forget the goat. THIS IS ART? You betcha! This is the Next Wave Festival. The next frontier of the visual and performing arts. This is a window to Tomorrow. Dazzling. Exhilarating. Controversial. Perhaps even incendiary. (Has there ever been a significant new movement in the arts that hasn't driven traditionalists stark, staring mad?) It happens at the

Brooklyn Academy of Music from October 3 through December 3."

*3. *Background:* The following is taken from an ad placed by Amoco Chemical Company in *Harper's Magazine* for October 1989. The ad defends plastic products against the charge that they are a major contributor to waste and pollution.

"In addition to environmentally secure land-fills and more state of the art waste to energy incinerators, we believe that a significant answer to America's waste problem lies in recycling. Everything recyclable should be recycled. Yard waste. Paper. Metal cans. Glass bottles. And plastics. Although plastics recycling is in its infancy, plastics are potentially more recyclable than alternative packaging materials."

*4. *Background:* Carl Sagan produced a popular science presentation for television, called "Cosmos." *Time* magazine printed an extensive article covering the series. The following letter appeared in the wake of *Time*'s story:

"Sagan promotes Sagan and 'Cosmos' promotes Sagan. As he postures before lingering cameras and delivers overdramatic monologues from *Star Wars*, he skillfully blends fact with fiction, leaving viewers perplexed. By adding gimmicks and schmaltz to fascinating scientific subjects, Sagan cheapens them. This type of presentation imbues science with the razzle-dazzle of show biz and reduces it to bubble gum mentality. Fortunately a flick of the TV dial can leave Sagan out in space."
(Letter to the editor, *Time*, November 24, 1980)

*5. People are not all the same. Isn't that obvious? I mean, they look different, they have different tastes, different interests, different values, different experiences. This idea that people are just people is silly because it blurs over all the fascinating and wonderful idiosyncrasies that make individuals what they are. Equality means being the same, and there's nothing good about it. So there's no point in equality before the law either.

*6. Homosexuality must be natural because it appears in the animal kingdom in a variety of species and under a variety of circumstances. People have said that because homosexuality is unnatural, it's wrong. But this view is just mistaken. Homosexuality is natural and, therefore, it is good.

*7. Putting people in prison without trial is oppression. Making people fearful of the government is oppression. Taxing people is oppression. Making children go to school is oppression. Having parents care for children is oppression. Every human society is based on some or all of these practices. Therefore, every human society is based on oppression.

8. *Background:* The following comments are taken from a letter to a magazine, referring to an article it had published about alternate headache and pain pills.

"Using the term 'creative advertising' in the subhead of that article implies that some talent is involved in selling a dubious remedy to an uninformed public. No talent is involved here, just greed."

9. *Background:* We have seen part of this advertisement already. In this case, concentrate on the use of language, and see whether you think the ad is exploiting ambiguity, vagueness, or loaded language in order to get a point across. The ad appeared in *Harper's Magazine* in October 1980:

"Mother Nature is lucky her products don't need labels. All foods, even natural ones, are made up of chemicals. But natural foods don't have to list their ingredients. So it's often assumed they're chemical-free. In fact, the ordinary orange is a miniature chemical factory. And the good old potato contains arsenic among its more than 150 ingredients. This doesn't mean natural foods are dangerous. If they were, they wouldn't be on the market. All man-made foods are tested for safety. And they often provide more nutrition, at a lower cost, than natural foods. They even use many of the same chemical ingredients. So you see, there really isn't much difference between foods made by Mother Nature and those made by man. What's artificial is the line drawn between them."

10. "Art is energy. It is a privileged communication that passes between something and the spirit of a human."

(R. Pannell, "Arts Criticism: How Valid Is It?" Toronto *Globe and Mail,* March 3, 1979)

11. "Physicians in general do not seem to commit suicide at a rate significantly different from that of their nonmedical peers, although, perhaps because of their knowledge of drugs and access to them, their methods of choice are characteristically nonviolent: doctors poison themselves more than twice as often as the lay public, and shoot themselves less often. Psychiatrists, however, show a markedly greater tendency to commit suicide than the population at large or their medical peers."

(Thomas Maeder, "Wounded Healers," *Atlantic,* January 1989, p. 38)

*12. *Background.* In the spring of 1990 there were many discussions in Canada about the possibility of the province of Quebec leaving the country because of the difficulties in reaching a version of the Constitution satisfactory to all regions of the country. Some people speculated that if Quebec separated, the rest of the country would break up and some provinces might seek to join the United States. As a response to this debate, *Wall Street Journal* columnist David Frum wrote an article entitled "Canada? Who'd Want It?" which was reprinted widely and appeared in the Calgary *Herald* on May 18, 1990. The following letter was a response to Frum's article.

"Apparently Frum assumes that there is consensus among Canadians that our country is up for grabs. What right does he have to make such a misguided assumption? What a ludicrous idea to think that he has the audacity to take it on himself to assess what parts of Canada would be useful to the U.S. A further assumption that Alberta and B.C. 'believe they could do pretty well on their own or as American states' is not only arrogant and outrageous but absolutely disgusting. . . . I found it even more deplorable in that Frum is a native of Canada . . . And if he has chosen to depart, what right does he have to attempt to influence the destiny of the rest of us?"

13. *Jones:* Pesticides are safe because they have been used for a long time, and there is only a small chance that they will cause cancer or widespread environmental damage.
White: This is an outrageous position you are putting forward! Pesticides cannot be safe. They are chemical agents introduced unnaturally into the environment. There is some risk that they will harm the water, air, plants, fish, animals, and humans. Whenever there is some risk of damage, a product is not safe.

Hint: What does "safe" mean?

*14. There's no reason for professors and teachers to try to cultivate independent thinking in their students. Independent thinkers would have to start human knowledge again from scratch, and what would be the point of doing that? There's no point. Students should forget about independence and learn from their masters.

15. *Background:* In October 1989 *The Atlantic* printed an article on personal development seminars by David Owen. Owen satirized the seminars. The following passage is taken from a letter commenting on Owen's article.

"Apparently the success of the seminar industry is due to the addiction of many Americans to stress, which is packaged and sold. When put to use, the skills that people acquire through seminars, tapes, and books like those that Owen mentions allow them to trade their insecurity and meekness for a higher stress level and the ability to manipulate, even jab, others more expertly. As we crawl toward becoming civilized, perhaps we will overcome the need for such training."

16. *Background:* On April 15, 1986, the United States bombed the Libyan capital of Tripoli. The Reagan administration said the action was taken in response to Libyan leader Gaddafi's support of terrorism. But some critics of the administration said that the U.S. government was itself guilty of terrorism in this action. The following excerpt from a letter to *Time* magazine appeared in this context.

"The U.S., aided by Britain, acted to protect all of us from the nightmarish insanity of terrorism. This [the attack on Tripoli] is survival, not terrorism."

Exercise 2: Part B

Of the following descriptions, which would you say contain euphemisms? Emotionally charged language? Give reasons for your answers. *Note:* Not all examples contain euphemisms or emotionally charged language.

1. The dietary habits of the French are different from those of the Dutch; there is more emphasis on fish and cheese in Dutch meals than in French ones.

2. The new tax is a device for poverty amelioration.

*3. These illiterate peewee critics have no right to pick away at the trimmings; let's get on to the meat of the matter.

4. The probation officer told her client that if he was not able to keep appointments it would be necessary to consider a reinstatement of his previous situation with reference to penal institutions. The client asked whether he would have to go back to jail. The answer was yes.

5. Commenting on the Soviet invasion of Afghanistan in December 1979, the Indian Foreign Ministry said:

"The Soviet Union has given Afghanistan military assistance in order to help it organize resistance to outside aggression and interference in Afghanistan's internal affairs. True to the principles of nonalignment, the Indian government supports the sovereign right of the people of Afghanistan to determine their own fate without any foreign interference. If the Soviet Union takes certain steps in accord with the Afghan leaders' request, this is no violation of the principles of nonalignment."

(Indian commentary, reported in *Pravda* for December 30, 1979; as translated and published in the *Current Digest of the Soviet Press*, American Association of Slavic Studies Vol. XXXI, No. 52)

*6. "A great deal of the universe does not need any explanation. Elephants, for instance. Once molecules have learnt to compete and to create other molecules in their own image, elephants and things resembling elephants, will in due course be found roaming through the countryside."

(Peter Atkins, as quoted by Richard Dawkins, in *The Blind Watchmaker* [London: Penguin, 1988], p. 14)

*7. A man might need to purchase a casket if his loved one had passed away.

8. Commenting on the Nixon resignation in 1974, the British paper *Sunday Express* wrote:

"Richard Nixon had to go. He involved himself in a criminal lunatic escapade. Then by a mixture of subterfuge and deceit, he sought to evade the consequences, to place himself above the law."

(As quoted in the *Atlas World Press Review*, September 1974)

9. "Children who are unable to move on to the next grade do not fail. They are retained."
(Teacher)

10. "We do not know for certain why we sleep or why we dream, but we do know that our dreams are embedded in our sleep. So let's consider where we are and what we are like while asleep."

(Montague Ullman and Nan Zimmerman, *Working with Dreams* [Boston: Houghton Mifflin, 1979], p. 64)

Exercise 2: Part C

Consider the following situation: a school has 500 children enrolled in six grades. The working language of the school is English. However, 100 of the students do not have English as their first language and many of them do not know it when they first enter the school at the age of five or six years. Their native languages are mainly Chinese, Spanish, and Vietnamese. Teachers complain that it is hard to teach reading and writing under these circumstances. Also, they experience problems when they try to communicate with the parents of these English-as-a-second-language students, because the parents speak broken English or none at all. After several years of teacher complaints, the school board decides to hire three extra teachers to teach English as a second language for students in early grades and, in special night classes, for their parents. To pay for the extra language classes, programs in art, music, and physical education are cut back, and school field trips are eliminated.

a. Describe this situation from the point of view of someone favoring the change, using emotionally charged language and (if appropriate), euphemism in order to do so. Circle each emotionally charged word in your account.

b. As in (a), but now describe the situation from the point of view of someone opposed to the change.

❖   # CHAPTER SUMMARY

Language helps to direct attention and interpret reality, as well as describing how things are. Attention to language is important in many areas, including that of argument.

Definitions are not necessary for all terms, but they are useful when there is disagreement centering on words or when the meaning of a claim is unclear. Four types of definition may be distinguished: reportive, stipulative, ostensive, and persuasive. A reportive definition seeks to describe accurately how a word is used. It can be evaluated for its adequacy by general criteria. A good reportive definition must mention features essential to whatever is being defined. In addition, it must be neither too broad nor too narrow, and must avoid both obscurity and circularity.

Ostensive definitions seek to connect language directly to the world by pointing to examples of things. For instance, one might seek to ostensively define *lemon* by pointing to a lemon and saying "there, that's a lemon." Ostensive definitions can fail in their purpose if those to whom they are addressed attend to inessential or irrelevant features of the things being defined. They are most appropriate for terms whose meaning is difficult to convey in other words, where pointing to appropriate situations or pictures is possible.

Stipulative definitions are different in function from reportive ones because they say how a person or group is proposing to use a word. Stipulative definitions are often useful and practically important. They must be appraised according to how well they serve the practical task for which they are designed. Generally, stipulative definitions of words that have ordinary uses are misleading and can cause confusion when they give the words defined meanings that are radically different from those they ordinarily have. Stipulative definitions should not provide the major basis for an argument; issues are never solved merely by proposals to use words in new ways.

Persuasive definitions are stipulative definitions masquerading as either reportive definitions or factual statements. They are often characterized by the presence of such words as *true, real,* and *genuine.* Persuasive definitions can be deceptive in encouraging us to use words in new ways without being aware that we are doing so.

Ambiguity, where words or phrases have more than one distinct, plausible interpretation, and vagueness, where words or phrases are so imprecise as to convey practically nothing at all, are often problems in language and thought. In understanding, evaluating, and constructing arguments, it is important to check for ambiguity and vagueness and to assign a clear, consistent meaning to the terms used. The fallacy of equivocation is a mistake in argument that is committed when a key term is used in several incompatible ways, which are required in order to make its premises or conclusion seem plausible—more plausible than they would be with an accurate, consistent interpretation.

Emotionally charged language shapes and expresses positive or negative feelings toward what is being described. Such language is by no means always objectionable; without it, speech and writing would be boring and dull. It is, however, important to note the emotional "charge" in words used, especially when controversial issues are being discussed. It is all too easy to substitute emotionally charged language for evidence and reason and to prejudge issues simply on the basis of terms used. Euphemistic language can be seen as the opposite of emotionally charged language; euphemisms seek to whitewash, or cover up, objectionable or embarrassing aspects of situations and events. Sometimes it is important for us to consider these aspects and in such cases euphemisms present an obstacle to careful thought and analysis.

❖   REVIEW OF TERMS INTRODUCED

Reportive definition   A definition seeking to describe how a word is actually used.

Ostensive definition   A kind of definition in which the meaning of a word is indicated by pointing at a thing the word applies to.

Stipulative definition   A definition specifying a new or special use for a word.

Persuasive definition   A definition, usually implicit, in which there is an attempt to give a new factual content to a word while preserving its previous emotional associations.

Ambiguity   Language is used ambiguously if, in the context in which a word appears, it could have any one of several distinct meanings.

Structural ambiguity   Ambiguity due to the grammar or syntax of a phrase, which can naturally be interpreted as expressing more than one distinct meaning. (Sometimes called *syntactic ambiguity*.)

Semantic ambiguity   Ambiguity due to the fact that a single word may naturally be interpreted as having more than one distinct meaning.

Fallacy   Argument based on a common mistake in reasoning, a sort of mistake that people tend not to notice. Fallacies are poor arguments but often strike people as being cogent.

Fallacy of equivocation   Fallacy committed when a key word in an argument is used in two or more senses and the premises appear to support the conclusion only because the senses are not distinguished. The argument is likely to seem cogent if the ambiguity is unnoticed.

Vagueness   A word is used vaguely if, in the context in which it appears, we cannot determine what things or what sorts of things the word would apply to.

Emotionally charged language   Language with strong emotional tone, whether negative or positive.

Neutral language   Language with little or no emotional tone.

Euphemism   Bland, polite, usually abstract language used to refer to things that are embarrassing, terrible, or in some other way appalling. Euphemisms disguise these undesirable features.

Notes

1. R. W., Chinese journalist. Obviously, the terms were translated into English. The journalist is not named for political reasons.
2. Compare Janice Moulton, "The Myth of the Neutral Man," in Mary Vetterling-Braggin, Frederick A. Elliston, and Jane English (eds.), *Feminism and Philosophy* (Totowa, N.J.: Littlefield Adams and Co., 1977). J. J. Macintosh includes a discussion of sexist language in his "Nuclear War and Other Euphemisms," in Trudy Govier (ed.), *Selected Issues in Logic and Communication* (Belmont, Calif.: Wadsworth, 1988). The story about the dentist, the doctor, and their injured son is an adaptation of a story in Moulton's essay.
3. Quoted in *The Atlantic*, July 1986.
4. Aldous Huxley, *Eyeless in Gaza*, as quoted by C. L. Stevenson in "Persuasive Definitions," *Mind*, 1938.
5. I have benefitted from discussing this topic with Cary MacWilliams, several of whose suggestions have been incorporated here.
6. A good discussion of this sort of vagueness can be found in Zachary Seech, *Logic in Everyday Life* (Belmont, Calif.: Wadsworth, 1988), pp. 159–160.
7. "This Is What You Thought about Sexual Harassment," *Glamour*, January 1981, p. 31.
8. Laurier LaPierre, *To Herald a Child* (Toronto: Ontario Public School Men Teachers Association, 1981), p. 47.
9. Letter to *Time*, November 24, 1980.
10. Ibid.
11. What appears to be a strong claim made without argument may be the result of editing by papers or magazines, rather than a feature of the thought and argument of the writer. If such is the case, it is the editors rather than the arguer who is responsible for what appears as a cavalier treatment of an issue. However, readers can only speculate about such matters. Whatever the cause may be, the effect is a short passage with emotionally charged language and no evidence or argument.
12. *Literaturnaya Gazeta*, February 8, 1974, as translated and reproduced in the *Current Digest of the Soviet Press* for February 1974. Translation and publication by the American Association of Slavic Studies.
13. Described at length in the Calgary *Herald*, October 14, 1986.
14. Toronto *Globe and Mail*, July 7, 1986.

CHAPTER 5

Premises:
What to Accept and Why

AN ARGUMENT STARTS FROM PREMISES AND uses them to support one or more conclusions. If these premises are not rationally acceptable, then even the most elegant reasoning will not render the conclusion acceptable. When appraising an argument, we have to ask ourselves whether there is a reasonable basis for accepting the premises on which the argument is based.

THE DILEMMA OF PREMISES

When we say that the premises of an argument are rationally *acceptable*, we mean that it would be reasonable for the person to whom the argument is addressed to accept them. If you are appraising the argument, then, for the moment at least, that person is you. Of course, the argument might have been intended originally for an audience that was quite different from you in various ways, and premises that would have been acceptable for that audience may not be acceptable to you, since that audience might have had different background knowledge and a different perspective. But for our present purposes, we'll ignore this complication and attend to the acceptability of premises from the perspective of you, the reader, as the audience for the argument. This is the most practical point of view in any case.

If you can accept—that is, *believe*—the premises of an argument without violating any standard of evidence or certainty, then you find its premises rationally acceptable. But what are the standards of evidence and certainty? And how can you use them, generally, to evaluate premises on arguments that might be about any topics at all?

Arriving at general standards that will give complete and detailed guidelines for determining the rational acceptability of premises is not possible because premises, like the arguments they are parts of, can be about absolutely anything—from deserts in Africa to higher mathematics to the warming of the planet, or any topic you can think of. In fact, you may have already noticed this feature when considering the many illustrations and exercises used so far in this book. To say, in an absolutely general way and in complete detail, what makes premises on all these topics rationally acceptable is not possible. Some of the knowledge we need to appraise them will be highly specific.

For these sorts of reasons, it has until recently been traditional for textbooks on logic and argument to omit the topic of rational appraisal of premises, saying that it is a task that falls outside the area of logic. Appraising premises seems to be a topic that could lead the author and readers off into digressions on every subject from mountains to mermaids.

Let us think for a moment about premises. Premises are statements claimed to be true or rationally acceptable. Premises are like other statements; the only difference is that they are used to support a conclusion. Basically, assessing premises is no different from assessing statements that appear in descriptions, reports, or explanations.[1] We have to think about the sort of evidence that we have in favor of them and, in the light of this evidence, how likely they are to be true. But how do we do this—in general? It is a tall order.

Despite the challenge of this task, we discuss premise acceptability here because the topic is too basic to ignore. In fact, there are a number of general points that can be made about what makes premises acceptable and unacceptable. Pulling these points together, we can arrive at a useful approach to determining whether the (A) condition of argument cogency is met. If we did not consider premise acceptability and unacceptability, we would have to ignore the (A) condition entirely, leaving us with only (R) and (G), and an incomplete study of argument.

Any argument has to start somewhere. In the context of a given argument, the premises may need defending, and when this is the case, a subargument can be constructed. The subargument will also have premises. If its premises need defending, they too can be defended, in a sub-subargument. But at some point, this process has to stop: not every statement can be defended by appealing to further statements. Some statements must be acceptable without further support.

Claims about an enormous variety of topics are put before most of us every day. We read various books, papers, and magazines; we converse with other people who tell us about all kinds of situations and problems and give us their interpretations and opinions about what is going on. Some of these claims just have to be accepted. We learn language and basic facts from parents and teachers, and we build up a picture of parts of the world beyond our own experience from conversation, books, the press, television, and radio. Without relying on these other people and sources of information, we could have no intellectual competence at all.

Yet obviously we cannot simply accept everything we hear and read from every source. Some of the claims we encounter are false, implausible, or inconsistent; some sources are notoriously unreliable. Wholesale acceptance of claims is no closer to being a viable intellectual strategy than wholesale rejection of them.

The problem of when and why we should accept what other people tell us is a perfectly general one that arises not only in the context of argument but also in all of practical and scholarly life and thought. Since this is a book about argument, we address the problem in one special context: that of the acceptability and unacceptability of premises in arguments.

WHEN PREMISES ARE ACCEPTABLE

Our first approach will be to set forward and discuss some general conditions in virtue of which claims are acceptable as premises. All comments here apply to stated premises and to missing premises that have been added to an argument for the sorts of reasons discussed in Chapter 2.

Premises Defended in a Cogent Subargument

Clearly, a premise in an argument is acceptable if the arguer has already shown it to be acceptable by a cogent subargument. That means he or she has supplied evidence or reasons that make it rational to accept that conclusion. A subargument has been given, one that passes the ARG conditions and is therefore cogent. The premise has been given rational support; hence it is rationally acceptable. Although, as we have seen, we cannot always demand that this condition be met, when it is met, the premise is acceptable. In fact, the argument from Russell, quoted at the end of Chapter 3, illustrates this point. Russell used two premises—that children left alone can easily come to physical harm and that children left to themselves can be very annoying to adults—to support the intermediate conclusion that children simply cannot be left to do as they please all day long.

Premises Defended Elsewhere

An arguer may indicate that a premise is defended elsewhere, even though he or she does not supply a subargument for it in the argument being discussed. Perhaps the arguer has given good evidence for the claim on another occasion and indicates that. Alternately, the arguer may refer to someone else who has shown the premise to be reasonable.

A common way of doing this, in academic writing, is by footnotes. Claims about specific details such as statistics or particular historical or technical points are often backed up with a reference to a source in which these claims are spelled out and defended. The arguer is, in effect, relying on the authoritativeness of his or her source to back up such claims. If the authority is a proper one, the claim is acceptable. (Conditions of proper authority are described below.)

Premises Known a Priori to Be True

So far we have considered claims for which evidence is given, either in a subargument or in some independent argument. But as we have already seen, it is not possible for every claim to be supported by argument. Some claims must simply be acceptable in their own right if arguments are to get off the ground. Among these are claims that can be known *a priori* to be true.

The term *a priori* is a technical one. The words *a priori* are Latin and mean "from the first." Claims that are a priori are knowable "from the first" in the sense that they are knowable before experience, or independently of experience. (The contrasting term *a posteriori* means "from something that is posterior, or afterward" and refers to claims that are knowable only after, or on the basis of, experience.) Claims that are a priori are knowable to be true or false on the basis of reasoning and the analysis of meaning. If we can know a priori that a claim is true, then that claim is rationally acceptable. For instance, we can know a priori that a man cannot steal his own property. We do not need experience to prove this claim: in fact, there is no experience we could have, of someone stealing his own property. It can be proven by logic that it's impossible for anyone to steal his own property—just because of what stealing is. To steal is to take something that does not belong to you; a man's own property does belong to him; hence he cannot steal it.

To see the contrast between a priori and a posteriori claims more clearly, consider the contrast between these two statements:

(a) No one can steal his own property.
(b) No one can steal President Gorbachev's property.

As we have seen, claim (a) can be proven true by logic alone. It is a priori. We can know, on the basis of reasoning from the concepts of stealing and property, that (a) is true; independently of evidence and experience, we see that (a) is acceptable. The case of (b), however, is quite different. To know whether (b) is acceptable, we would have to know what sort of property President Gorbachev has and what sorts of safeguards there are for it. Statement (b) is a posteriori; it requires evidence from experience—our own or somebody else's.

If a premise in an argument seems to be a matter of definition or of the relations of concepts, or if it deals with a general issue of mathematics or logic, whether it is rationally acceptable may be determinable a priori, independently of experience. If it can be determined a priori to be true, then it is acceptable. The following claims, for instance, are a priori and would, as such, be immediately acceptable as premises in any argument in which they were to occur:

Science and religion have different purposes.

Abortion involves the premature termination of pregnancy.

Five is a prime number.

On the other hand, consider the following statement:

Playing the music of Bach and Beethoven in a park will drive out drug dealers.

This claim—taken, incidentally, from a news story about an Edmonton park—is definitely not a priori. Whether it is acceptable will have to be determined on the basis of evidence from experience.

Common Knowledge

A premise in an argument is acceptable if it is a matter of *common knowledge*. That is, if the premise states something that is known by virtually everyone, it should be allowed as an acceptable premise. Or, if a premise is very widely believed, and there is no widely known evidence against it, it is often appropriate to allow it as acceptable. Society operates on the basis of many statements that people know or believe as a common basis for communication and cooperation. From a priori claims and claims provable elsewhere, we would have only a very slender basis for communicating and justifying our beliefs; the basis of argumentation has to be extended and one of the main ways of doing that is to rely on common knowledge.

A simple example of a statement that is common knowledge is "Human beings have hearts." The claim that human beings have hearts, while very obvious, is not a priori. It is not from logic and concepts alone that we know human beings have hearts; experience is required. We can feel our own pulse and, in a sense, know from personal experience that we ourselves have a heart, but most of us learn that humans have hearts from other people—from parents and teachers, from books on health and biology, and from the mass media, which is full of advice as to means that can be taken to improve the health of our hearts. That humans have hearts is an elementary fact about the human physical structure, one known by virtually all human adults in our culture.

Here are some other examples of claims that would count as common knowledge:

Many millions of civilians have been killed in twentieth-century wars.

Slavery existed in the United States in the eighteenth and nineteenth centuries.

Japan is an economically powerful country.

Mountain climbing is a sport requiring good health and strong muscles.

Such claims as this can be deemed rationally acceptable because they constitute common knowledge. They are not a priori, but they are sufficiently widely known that they have become common knowledge and, as such, are rationally acceptable as starting points in an argument.

What counts as common knowledge is to some extent dependent on audience and context. What is *true* does not vary depending on what time people live in and what they believe, but what is *known* does. In fact, this point may occur to the critical reader, even with respect to the simple examples given above. In certain isolated nonscientific cultures, even the claim that human beings have hearts might not be common knowledge and might need considerable argumentation.

For those who follow international politics, it is common knowledge that the Berlin Wall, which had separated East and West Germany since 1961, was opened up and ceased to function as a political barrier on November 9, 1989. Someone giving an argument about German unification would not need to support the claim that the Wall was opened in 1989. The opening of the Berlin Wall was such a dramatic historical event that most adult citizens in the industrialized world know of its occurrence. The claim that it was opened would count, for most of us, as common knowledge.

Clearly, what is common knowledge at one time and place may not be common knowledge at another time and place. Thirty years from now it will still be true that the Berlin Wall opened on November 9, 1989—but this will probably no longer be common knowledge. At that time, many people may not know in just which month and year the opening occurred, and those with little interest in politics or history may not recall the event at all. Realistically, we have to allow that common knowledge varies with time, place, interests, educational level, and culture. This means that the (A) condition, and argument cogency generally, are considered with some reference to the context in which arguments appear.

We cannot realistically dispense with common knowledge as a condition of premise acceptability. Typically people argue back and forth with others with whom they share a culture and a broad background of beliefs and commitments. Arguments go on within this shared context and could not proceed without it. As we have seen, arguments have to start from premises, and not every premise can be defended in a further argument. Looking at the a priori true statements illustrated above, we can see that these alone would not give the basis for arguments about many topics. They only relate concepts to each other; they do not state facts about the world.

In order to engage in argument and discussion, people must have some common understanding of issues and problems. They must share beliefs and assumptions. The common knowledge condition for acceptability reflects these basic facts about argument and social context. Many arguments proceed from premises taken as common knowledge and move on to new conclusions. Even though the common knowledge premises are not as obvious and certain as the necessary truths, they should be accepted in virtue of the required social context for arguments.

Here is an example that starts from points of common knowledge and reaches a rather surprising conclusion:

1.   There are vast numbers of trees in Brazil.
2.   If anyone tried to count all the trees in Brazil, it would be a very long time after he started until he reached the last tree.
3.   Before a tree counter finished his counting task, some trees already counted would have died due to fire or animal destruction and new trees would be sprouting.
4.   Having a number of people count these trees would not avoid these problems of destruction and growth.

So,

5.   It is practically impossible to determine by counting just exactly how many trees there are in Brazil.

Therefore,

6.   The question "How many trees are there in Brazil?" is a question that has no practically determinable answer.

In this argument, premises (1), (2), and (3) are matters of common knowledge. To deem the argument inadequate by questioning one of these premises would be quite unreasonable. The fourth premise, however, is a different matter. It is not, as such, a matter of common knowledge and does need further defense. But to insist on proof or further evidence for something like "there are vast numbers of trees in Brazil" is going too far. Someone who takes this kind of stance on the acceptability of premises will soon find that he has no one to argue with and nothing to say.

Testimony

Under some conditions, a claim is acceptable on the basis of a person's *testimony*. That is to say, a person testifies as to, or tells about, something he or she has experienced, and, given certain conditions, we accept the claim about that experience as described. Our personal experience is limited with respect to both place and time. Others, in conversation, in writing, and through media such as television, film, and video, communicate a broader experience to us. They tell us of sights, sounds, places, and personal encounters to which we have no independent access. Life would be short and knowledge limited if human beings could not extend their knowledge by relying on the experiences of others.

Typically, if other people tell us they have experienced something, we are inclined to take their word for it. We trust their word unless we have some specific reason not to do so. Due to our reliance on others to broaden our picture of the world, this approach of initial trust makes sense.

There are several factors that rationally undermine this initial tendency to trust a person's testimony. Three main factors are involved: the plausibility of the claim asserted, the reputation of the person or source making the claim, and the degree to which the claim is about personal experience.

Plausibility of Claims   If a person claims, as a matter of personal experience, to have witnessed something that is, according to common knowledge or to our own personal related beliefs, extremely implausible, we may doubt his or her testimony merely because of the implausibility of the claim. Even if we know the person asserting the claim and that person is usually honest, accurate, and reliable, if the claim is bizarre or crazy enough, the nature of the claim will make us question the testimony.

If someone tells you a four-door 1990 Chevrolet is on sale for a thousand dollars, you are not likely to accept the claim. It is too unlikely that anyone would sell such a car for such a low price. You will assume that the person who tells you such a thing is joking, or is mistaken, or is trying to deceive you. The claim asserted is too implausible to be taken at face value; there is too much independent evidence against it for a single person's testimony to make it believable.

Unreliability of Source   People can be unreliable in various ways, obviously. The most blatant is lying or deliberate deception. If a person has been known to lie or deliberately deceive others, then it is imprudent to simply take his or her word for something. Lying and deception, especially about matters of importance, undermine a person's credibility. When people lack credibility, their testimony cannot, in general, be taken to make claims rationally acceptable. Their word has lost its force.

Another possibility is that people may be flawed observers of certain sorts of phenomena; we may know that they are, in relevant ways, handicapped or biased in some way that makes their observations nonstandard and their testimony questionable. For instance, if a person who has poor hearing attends a concert and later argues that the choir was not good because its enunciation of words was unclear, we should not accept his testimony on the point. With poor hearing, he is not a reliable observer.

Similar points can be made about a person who has such a vested interest in establishing one particular point of view that we lose confidence in the accuracy of his observations. When this happens, we will not wish to accept claims merely on his testimony, even when those claims concern only his experience: we will suspect that he is selecting and interpreting evidence in a one-sided way. An example might be a sports fan observing the home team play against its rival. He could be so attached to his own team that his observations about the competence and skill of the players on that team, as compared to the other, would not be reliable; unconsciously, even, he may select the better performances of those on the home team and compare these with the more flawed performances of players on the rival team. Selective attention can lead, in such a case, to biased observations that cannot be the basis for reliable testimony.

Such is our dependence on other people as sources of knowledge and belief that most of us tend, in general, to give a fair amount of credence to the printed word and to media in general. However, the same qualifications applied to individuals should be applied here too. If a source has printed lies and falsehoods repeatedly in the past, or is strongly biased, these features make it unreliable and inadequate as a source of testimony about other people's experience. A reputable newspaper account of an event such as a traffic accident, change of government, or earthquake is typically accepted as true. Consider, for instance, the following claim, which introduced a story in the Toronto *Globe and Mail:*

> *Budapest (Associated Press)*
>
> Scores of Albanian dissidents scaled embassy walls and rammed the gates with trucks in Tirana [Albania] in a desperate bid for asylum and escape from Eastern Europe's last hard-line Communist government, officials said yesterday. Diplomats said as many as 200 people were given refuge in various embassies, but other would-be refugees who went to the embassies of Bulgaria, Cuba, and Egypt were handed over to the Albanian authorities.[2]

The paper is reliable; the press agency, Associated Press, is a major international wire service with a good reputation; the claims are attributed to officials and diplomats whose testimony, in this context, we have no particular reason to disbelieve; the story is datelined Budapest, a location relatively close to that in which the events occurred. We are dependent on the media for knowledge of the occurrence of such events as this one and, other things being equal, we tend to believe what we read in such reports.

On the other hand, accounts from notoriously unreliable sources are not accepted in this way, especially when the claims made are themselves extremely implausible. Consider, for instance, the following claims:

> Donald Zenert was viciously gored by a 300-pound buck deer but he survived with only his wits and a penknife by grabbing the animal's antlers and holding on for a wild 90 minute ride. The 33 year old construction worker was attacked this past February 4 while videotaping deer in Alberta, Canada.[3]

These claims introduced a story in the *National Enquirer,* a tabloid-style paper full of exotic and bizarre stories and widely regarded as unreliable. Though the story was written in the first person and purported to describe Zenert's personal experiences, such testimony, reprinted in such a source, does not render these implausible claims acceptable.

Restriction of Claim to Personal Experience A person can testify, on the basis of personal experience, as to what he or she did experience, but testimony cannot render acceptable claims that go beyond personal experience to interpretation and judgment. Broadly speaking, experience includes observations, feelings, and memories.

If someone tells you that she often felt angry while attending a particular class, that is a matter of her reaction, something she knows better than anyone else, and something you should generally believe. If she is a reliable, honest person, the claim is acceptable, just because she sincerely asserts it. Similarly, if she tells you that a particular professor has a soft voice, that he is strict on deadlines, that he was late on Tuesday, or that he has been discussing classical economic theory for three weeks, you would accept such statements on the basis of testimony from a reliable person.

But if, on the other hand, she tells you that this professor is the most dynamic lecturer on campus, or that his analysis of Japanese business practice is extremely sophisticated, her comments are going beyond the nature of her own experience to areas of interpretation and judgment. These interpretive and evaluative claims cannot be rendered acceptable merely by testimony, because they depend upon a broader basis of evidence and the discretion, common sense, and background knowledge, of the person making the judgment.

Several examples from a recent book on Africa serve to illustrate this contrast between experiential claims and broader commentary. The author, David Lamb, is an American journalist who spent four years in Africa as bureau chief for the *Los Angeles Times,* traveled widely, and did some independent research. In the following passage, Lamb describes an interview with Daniel Mwangi, a blind man whom he met in Kenya. He says:

> His problem started when he was six or seven years old—itchy eyelids, blurred vision, headaches. His father thought the boy had been cursed and took him to his friend, a witch doctor. But the practitioner's herbs and chants did not help, and by the time Daniel was thirteen he was totally blind . . .[4]

Readers of Lamb's book are, in this passage, getting Lamb's testimony about an interview with Mwangi. Testimony is involved twice: Lamb is telling his readers what Mwangi told him, and Mwangi is telling Lamb how he became blind. In the absence of any special reason to regard either Lamb or Mwangi as unreliable, we would simply accept the story as told. The principles of testimony we have discussed here would recommend accepting the story on the double testimony of the author and the man interviewed.

This passage can be contrasted with others that go beyond testimony to offer commentary and predictions with regard to social and political problems in Africa. Consider, for instance, the following passage:

> However valuable the church has been in assisting Africa's five million refugees, in helping during times of drought, famine and sickness, it traditionally has acted as a tool of the white establishment. The church did not play an active role in supporting the African's struggle for independence, largely because white clergy in Africa were racist in attitude and approach.[5]

These statements may be correct, but they are not the sorts of claims we could accept on the basis of testimony because their content goes beyond what the author could experience himself. They state a generalization about the connection between the church and the white establishment and posit an explanation (racism in the church) to explain that connection.

In general, claims are acceptable on the word, or testimony, of the person asserting them, provided that the claims are not in themselves improbable, the persons claiming them are honest and reliable observers, and the claims are restricted in content to what a person could experience.

Proper Authority

Sometimes arguments are put forward by people who possess specialized knowledge about the subject they are talking about. For instance, an African historian might have made the claim about the white church and racism in Africa on the basis of a specialized study of this aspect of African history. Such a person would be an expert, or *authority,* in this area. If he made the claim as an authority, we might, under specific conditions, accept it on his authority.

When people are experts or authorities in some area of knowledge, they are said to "speak with authority." An expert has a special role in the construction and communication of knowledge because he or she has more evidence, a more sophisticated understanding of related concepts and theories, greater relevant background knowledge and—as a result—more reliable judgment in the particular area of expertise than the nonexpert. Under certain conditions, statements or claims are acceptable because they are asserted by reliable authorities or experts.

Accepting a premise on authority is similar to accepting a premise on testimony in one respect: it involves accepting claims because other people have sincerely asserted them. However, there is an important difference between authority and testimony. Authority requires specialized knowledge in a field where there are recognized standards of expertise. Recognized standards include degrees or professional certificates authorized by licensed and qualified institutions. To be an authority or expert, however, it is not enough just to have one of these degrees, such as a Ph.D. or an M.D. One must also have accomplishments in the area of study—published research or other professional attainment—and one's accomplishments must be recognized as such by other qualified people in that field of study or work. Testimony does not require specialized knowledge: we can all testify about our own experience. Whatever undermines testimony (dishonesty, incapacity to make accurate observations, bias, vested interest, and so on) would also undermine authority. But because authority must be based on expert knowledge, there are further conditions for the proper use of authority to justify claims.

If we are to accept a claim just because an expert asserts it, that claim must lie within a specific field of knowledge. The person who asserts the claim must be recognized as an expert within that field of knowledge. For example, African history, microphysics, race relations, plant genetics, and child development are specific areas of knowledge. Some endeavors, while worthwhile and fascinating in their own right, cannot exactly be termed areas of knowledge, because there are no methods and principles that are a common basis for all exploring the area to use to build up accurate beliefs, from which different interested people can come to the same conclusion. Consider, for instance, such questions as the nature of life (if there is any life) in other galaxies, or the issue of what the meaning of life is, or whether there is free will. These are fascinating topics, and it is worthwhile to think about them. But these topics do not lie within any field of knowledge; there is no systematic body of beliefs about them. Because this is the case, we cannot render a claim about one of these subjects acceptable by appealing to an expert or authority who has asserted it to be true. There are no experts in the area.

Another important point is that even when there is a systematic body of knowledge, and qualified experts study an area using common methods and on a basis of some consensus, experts in the area may have different beliefs about particular issues. Consider, for instance, the area of child development. Some experts believe that children do not acquire abstract logical concepts until their early teens while others think that they acquire them as early as six or eight years of age. In the face of such disagreement you could not hope to show that either one of these views is acceptable by citing an expert. The experts disagree, so anyone who disputed your claim could just find another expert and argue against you by citing him or her. Defending a claim on the basis of authority is appropriate only if experts in the area agree.

In addition, the expert cited must be reliable and credible. The expert or authority must not have had his or her credibility undermined by dishonest or unreliable claims in the past or by vested interest such as would result from being paid by one party to a dispute, by having lied in the past about related matters, and so on.

An especially careful appeal to authority can render a claim acceptable. Such an appeal may be set out as follows:

1. Expert *X* has asserted claim *P.*
2. *P* falls within area of specialization *K.*
3. *K* is a genuine area of knowledge.
4. The experts in *K* agree about *P.*
5. *X* is an expert, or authority, in *K.*
6. *X* is honest and reliable.
Therefore,
7 *P* is acceptable.

If we reason to ourselves as in the preceding argument, we have, in effect, constructed our own subargument on behalf of a claim asserted by an expert; and if that claim is a premise in an argument, such a subargument will render it acceptable. We have determined that we should accept the premise because an expert, or authority, has endorsed it.

Condition (6) concerns the expert's credibility, or worthiness to be believed, and the issues involved are the same as those discussed above under the topic of testimony.

We should note, of course, that there are many *faulty appeals to authority,* as well as some legitimate ones. To be cogent, an appeal to authority must meet all the conditions listed here: recognized expertise in an area with proper credentials and consensus, agreement of experts on the topic at issue, and reliability of the expert cited.

Often people who are authorities in one area make pronouncements in another area in which they are not authorities, in the hope that their expertise will transfer from one area to another. Or others seek to use their expertise in that way, thinking that their name and reputation will carry a claim in an area other than the one where their reputation was established. When this happens, the people cited have as much claim to be taken seriously as anyone else, but no more. An authoritative scientist is not, by virtue of his position in the scientific establishment, an authority about the future of mankind or the question of when human life begins. Such issues are broadly philosophical as opposed to scientific, and although philosophers are well qualified to consider these questions, they do not agree among themselves about them. Thus such questions cannot be resolved by appeals to authority.

The dilemma of different parties to a dispute citing their own experts is often seen in the courts. Each side in a dispute engages an expert, who comes to court to testify in a way that will suit the case of the side paying him.[6] In this event, the lawyers for each side will cross-examine each expert witness and the judge and jury have to try to determine which aspects of the contending expert accounts are correct. They cannot accept *all* that is said on the basis of authority because to do this would lead to contradictions. Judges have to do their best to really sift through the evidence and expert testimony. Obviously when several experts brought to the court disagree, the judge and jury cannot resolve a case by merely appealing to the authority of any one of them.

Accepting Premises Provisionally

The conditions given so far certainly do not cover all the premises people use in their arguments. As we shall soon see, there are features premises can have that make them definitely unacceptable, and we will list these. But suppose the following situation occurs: you come to study an argument, and you cannot judge the premises acceptable on any of the grounds mentioned here, but, on the other hand, neither do you have a definite basis for deeming them unacceptable, according to conditions about to be explained in the next section of this book. What do you say then, about the (A) condition of argument cogency?

We recommend deeming the premises *provisionally acceptable* and going on to evaluate the argument on (R) and (G). If the argument passes on (R) and (G), then, on the basis of a provisional acceptance of the premises, you can also *provisionally accept the conclusion.*

Sometimes premises are explicitly provisional. We may want to consider particular theories or hypotheses as a basis for reasoning, just to develop some ideas as to what consequences would follow from them. In such cases, we may speak of granting claims "for the sake of argument." For instance, someone might say

> Suppose that the birth rate in the European Community continues to be 1.4 per adult woman, whereas the birth rate required for a population to replace itself is 2.1 per adult woman. Then there will be a labor shortage in the European Community within ten years. If this is to be avoided, measures will have to be taken to ensure that immigrants come to the European Community and are well integrated into its economic and social life.

Here the initial premise about population growth is not exactly accepted; it is put forward as a supposition and basis for further reasoning. We can, in this way, grant such a supposition for the sake of argument, reasoning forward on this basis to see what conclusions might emerge.

It is important when we do this that we realize that the conclusion we reach is entirely conditional upon our provisional acceptance of the premises. The above argument would show that *if* the birth rate in the European Community continues to be below replacement level, *then* immigrants will be needed. In contexts like these the word *if* is very important and should not be forgotten. The conclusion is acceptable *if* the premises are, and we have provisionally accepted the premises because we have found no specific reason to reject them.

◆ SUMMARY OF ACCEPTABILITY CONDITIONS

A premise in an argument is *acceptable* if *any one* of the following conditions is satisfied:

1. It is defended in a subargument that is cogent.
2. It is defended elsewhere by the arguer or another person.
3. It is known a priori to be true.
4. It is a matter of common knowledge.
5. It is supported by testimony from a reliable person and its content is such that testimony is, in principle, an appropriate backup. (The claim is not wildly implausible and it is restricted in content to experience.)
6. It is backed by an appropriate appeal to authority.
*7. It is not known to be unacceptable, as such, and can serve provisionally as the basis for argument.

The last case is specially marked to remind us that a conclusion supported by provisionally accepted premises is rendered provisionally acceptable—acceptable *if* those premises are acceptable.

◆ EXERCISE SET

Exercise 1: Part A

For each of the following statements, determine whether or not it is known a priori to be true and explain the basis for your answer.

1. Every rectangle has four straight sides. A

2. Every parent is the relative of someone who A is younger than himself.

3. There is a great problem with acid rain in the lakes and forests of northeastern North America. *factual?* *claim*

*4. Everyone who is a parent is legally responsible for the well-being of at least one child.

5. "I know of no studies that adequately describe what long-range effects slavery had on Africa, a continent where up to 50 million people, mostly males between the ages of fifteen and thirty-five, were forced to migrate to other worlds."

(David Lamb, *The Africans* [New York: Random House, 1987], p.149)

6. A number is an expression of quantity.

*7. Either a person is happy or he isn't.

8. "In the summer of 1978, when crowds of demonstrators boiled onto the streets of his cities chanting 'Dorud bar Khomeini!'—Long live Khomeini!—in obedience to the commands issued by the Ayatollah in Najaf, the Shah asked President Saddam Hussein of Iraq to expel the Ayatollah; and Saddam Hussein, anxious to keep on good terms with the Shah, agreed."

(John Simpson, *Behind Iranian Lines* [London: Fontana, 1989], p. 17)

9. There is a distinction to be made between sexual reproduction and asexual reproduction.

*10. All is fair in love and war.

*11. Any action that is caused must result from something that has preceded it.

12. Playing with guns is likely to make young children see violence as something natural and approved by adults.

13. If a tribe has members who fight with each other over titles and lands to the point of causing each other severe physical injury, then that tribe is not one where expressions of jealousy and aggression are absent.

*14. Girls brought up by their mothers are brought up by a parent of their own sex.

*15. "Harry Houdini used his consummate skill as a conjurer to unmask legions of lesser magicians who masqueraded as psychics with direct access to an independent world of pure spirit."

(Stephen Jay Gould, *The Flamingo's Smile* [New York: Norton, 1985], p. 392)

Exercise 1: Part B

For each of the following claims, try to reach a decision as to whether it is acceptable. State why you think it is acceptable referring to the conditions of acceptability explained in this chapter.

*1. Every living creature has some kind of reproductive system.

*2. Having a previous life would require surviving as a soul during the time interval between several different bodily existences.

3. No mental desire is in any way a physical thing.

*4. Everyone alive today has experienced innumerable past lives.

5. If exercise leads to a feeling of well-being and a greater zest for life, then exercise is good for you.

*6. Siamese twins have difficulty leading a normal human life if they are not separated.

7. Football is an important sport in North American colleges and universities.

8. As the impoverished father of three sons, I can say that it is hard not to buy expensive sports equipment for children when there are a lot of pressures for such purchases from schools.

9. As a professional therapist, I would say that a primary cause of divorce today is problems with money.

10. An AIDS vaccine is likely to be discovered before the year 2000, it was agreed by scientists at the VIth International AIDS Conference, which met in San Francisco in June 1990.

WHEN PREMISES ARE UNACCEPTABLE

Now that we have described some general conditions that make premises acceptable, we will go on to deal with some of the things that make them unacceptable.

Easy Refutability

Some premises can easily be *refuted*, or shown false, because they are contradicted by experience, testimony, authority, or common knowledge. This is especially common when premises are sweeping in scope. Consider, for instance,

(a) Slavery has been completely abolished all over the globe.

(b) Nuclear weapons make war impossible and obsolete.

(c) If women were political leaders, a nonaggressive style of conducting political business would automatically result.

These statements, all worded in universal and categorical terms, are easily refuted. Consider (a): if slavery were abolished everywhere on earth, there would be no slavery left, but there is some slavery in parts of Africa and the Middle East. To anyone knowing this, statement (a) is easily refutable. Even those who do not know specifically about residual slavery in Africa and the Middle East should raise their critical eyebrows at statement (a) because the words "completely abolished" are so sweeping and categorical. As for statement (b), since the invention of nuclear weapons in 1945, there have been many wars; hence it cannot be true in an unqualified sense that nuclear weapons have made war obsolete. As for (c), there have been women leaders, such as Britain's Margaret Thatcher and Israel's Golda Meir, who have been very hard-line and aggressive in their approach to politics; this statement, too, would have to be qualified in order to be acceptable. As it stands, it is easily refuted.

Here is an example of an argument with an easily refutable premise. The example is taken from a discussion of the acceptance of refugees by the United States:

A century ago an open-ended invitation may have been safe enough. America was a new country then, unfilled. The supply of possible immigrants wasn't so great. Now the huddled masses of the wretchedly poor amount to 800 million. More than three times the U.S. population. It would be insane to invite them all in. Even one percent would be too many.

Variety in a nation is good. So also is unity. But when variety (of which we've always had plenty) overwhelms unity, how are we to keep a complex society like ours running?

When newcomers arrive too fast, they gather into enclaves and resist learning the national language. Immigrants then become the new isolationists. Tribalism becomes a reality: Goodbye, unity![7]

One premise in this argument against admitting refugees to the United States is the following:

When newcomers arrive too fast, they gather into enclaves, resist learning the national language, and become isolationists.

This premise is rather vague since it is not clear how fast "too fast" is. But when refugees have come in large numbers to Canada and the United States in the past, they have not, in fact, refused to learn the language and adapt to a new life. Many Hungarians came to Canada and the United States in the 1950s and learned

English, assimilating into the mainstream of life. Many Italians and Germans did the same thing after World War II. Unless he has a very strict meaning for "arriving too fast," the author has simply asserted a premise that is not acceptable because we can refute it on the basis of common knowledge.

Claim Known a Priori to Be False

We saw that some claims can be known a priori to be true. In an analogous way, some claims can be known a priori to be false. Any such claim is unacceptable and cannot serve as a premise in a cogent argument. Here is an example:

(i) The man's headache did not hurt him at all.

Claim (i) must be false, and we can see this by reasoning alone. A headache is something that aches, something that hurts a person; it is impossible, by definition, to have a headache that does not hurt at all. A person might have something wrong with his brain, something that did not hurt even though it was an injury or disease, but if it didn't hurt, it couldn't be a headache. There is an inconsistency within (i) between being a headache and not hurting, and because of this inconsistency, we can know a priori that (i) is false.

Another example of a claim known a priori to be false is:

(ii) There are things outside the universe.

The term *universe* refers to everything that exists, so it is impossible for things to be outside the universe. If (ii) were a premise in an argument, it would be unacceptable because we can determine a priori that it is false.

Inconsistency Between Premises

Sometimes an argument will contain a number of premises, and several of these premises will *explicitly* or *implicitly contradict* each other. They explicitly contradict each other if one premise asserts what another premise denies. For example, if one premise asserts, "All men are emotionally tough" and another asserts, "Some men are emotionally vulnerable," the argument in which both premises occur has premises explicitly contradicting each other.

As you can imagine, this mistake is too obvious to occur very frequently. It is more common for premises to contradict each other implicitly. This means that when we think about what the premises say and make some simple deductive inferences, we can arrive at an explicit contradiction from the premises. If there is either an explicit or an implicit contradiction in the premises of an argument, they are *inconsistent* and we know they cannot all be true; hence they are, as a set, unacceptable.

Here is an example of an implicit contradiction:

1. Some women have taken jobs away from men in cases where the men in question have more appropriate qualifications.

2. Hiring should be solely on the basis of having appropriate qualifications for the job.
3. Until now, hiring has been solely on the basis of having appropriate qualifications for the job.
4. To prefer women to men of more appropriate qualifications for a job would be wrong.

Therefore,

5. Women should never be hired over men who have more appropriate job qualifications.

Looking closely at this argument, you will see an inconsistency between (1) and (3). The author states in (1) that women have taken jobs away from men of more appropriate qualifications. Yet he insists, in (3), that hiring has always been on the basis of the most appropriate qualifications. Both these statements cannot be true. The author is, in fact, contradicting himself in his premises. Even without knowing anything about the hiring of women and men, you can know that this argument has faulty premises. The premises are inconsistent and cannot all be true. When premises are explicitly or implicitly contradictory, they are inconsistent and therefore unacceptable.

A contradiction could not possibly be true; we can determine, a priori, that it is false. In the preceding example, the premises commit us to the contradiction:

Hiring has sometimes deviated from the principle of hiring according to appropriate qualifications, and hiring has never deviated from the principle of hiring according to appropriate qualifications.

This statement is a priori false due to what is meant by "sometimes" and "never." No matter what the facts are about the job qualifications of women and men, they couldn't make this statement true because, by reasoning alone, we can establish that it is false. Since the premises commit us to this contradiction, they are unacceptable. At least one premise used in the argument must be false, for no set of true statements can entail a contradiction—and we can know this a priori.

Vagueness or Ambiguity

In order to rationally accept premises, we must know what they mean and know what sort of evidence would establish them as true. For this reason, problems in language can sometimes render premises unacceptable. If a premise is stated in language that is vague or ambiguous to the point where we cannot determine what sort of evidence would establish it, then it is unacceptable as stated. Either its meaning will have to be clarified, or the argument in which it appears will have to be rejected as not cogent.

Dependence on Faulty Assumptions

Sometimes problems with false premises are more obvious when we see the *assumptions* underlying those premises. We may find an argument and suspect that there is something wrong with the premises, but we may see this only when we stop to ask why these premises are stated as they are. When we do this, we can see that what the arguer says makes sense only if we grant her a particular assumption or set of assumptions.

Assumptions are not stated premises, nor are they missing premises: they are *presupposed by the argument* and we can see that this is the case by studying the premises.[8] The language of the premises is particularly helpful in this regard. As we have seen in Chapter 4, language articulates a framework for classifying and evaluating events. An argument will appear in some such framework, and the wording of its premises will indicate the framework. A word such as *resource,* for instance, indicates that material is to be used and exploited. To refer to employees as human resources is to assume that they are there to be used and developed by managers, in the ways that will suit the purposes of managers. Such an assumption would be most objectionable in the context of a labor negotiation in which managers and employees were participating as equal parties. If it were to be made, premises on which it was based would be unacceptable.

Assumptions are in the background, in a way, and we may have to think for a while to notice them. When we do, it can be very important. Sometimes the assumptions are controversial or even wrong; they should be rejected. Then, since the premises depend on them, the whole argument will be rejected.

It is worthwhile studying the premises of an argument carefully to try to determine whether they rest upon an unacceptable assumption. Often background assumptions on which an argument is based are false or highly questionable. When they are, it is worth finding them and discovering this, because the argument will be faulty as a result. If premises depend on an assumption that is questionable in the context in which the argument is offered, then they themselves are questionable.

You can see how this business of assumptions works by looking at this advertisement:

> If you think advertising is a bunch of baloney, why are you reading this ad? You read to learn. Reading brings new ideas and thoughts into your life. It opens up a whole new world. That's what advertising does. It communicates information from one source to another. Advertising gives you the opportunity to make up your own mind by familiarizing you with a product. That's why advertising is a freedom. The freedom to know quality and what is available. You read and listen to advertising to obtain information. Information on just about anything. Including the price of baloney.[9]

This passage is rather repetitive; its basic point seems to be that advertising is good and useful because it gives us knowledge and information. The premises, then, are based on the assumption that advertisements consist largely of accurate statements. This assumption is clearly necessary because both information and knowledge can be obtained only if the statements made in advertisements are accurate. The premises assume that advertisements are primarily composed of accurate statements.

Let us spell out that assumption and take a close look at it:

Advertisements are composed primarily of true statements.

There is much evidence against this assumption; in fact, it is easily refuted. Common knowledge is enough to indicate this. Many advertisements contain no statements at all but consist merely of questions, suggestions, pictures, jokes, and so on. Others contain exaggerated or misleading statements, and some even contain statements that are downright false. If the author had tried to prove, or justify, his underlying assumption, he would have faced an impossible task. Instead, the assumption is unstated in the hope that readers won't notice it. It is smuggled in through words like *knowledge, learn, information,* and so on. You have only to spot this assumption to see that the argument breaks down.

If you can see that the premises of an argument depend on an assumption that is readily refutable or highly controversial, then you know that the argument has unacceptable premises. Looking for background assumptions, which you can then criticize, is a very powerful technique for finding flaws in premises. But it should be used with some care. It is easy to "see" assumptions that are not really there! If you think you have spotted a faulty assumption, you should stop to make sure that the premises really do require it. If they do, then they are unacceptable.

Premises Not More Certain Than Conclusion

The purpose of an argument is to lead an audience from the premises to a rational acceptance of a conclusion. For this purpose to be achieved, the premises of an argument should be more certain than its conclusion. That is, they should be more readily acceptable by the audience to whom the argument is addressed than is the conclusion that they are used to support.[10] In the context of a particular argument, premises may be unacceptable because they fail to be more certain than the conclusion that they are used to support.

Let us suppose that someone were to argue as follows:

1. The pyramids of ancient Egypt were built with the assistance of creatures from outer space.
Therefore,
2. There has been at least one extraterrestrial civilization that was advanced enough to send some of its members to visit our earth.

This argument is extremely unconvincing because the premise is so improbable. It states a bold claim about a very specific question of history (How were the Egyptian pyramids built?), one which goes against common knowledge and established authority. This premise is even less probable than the very controversial conclusion it is used to defend. If anyone were to use such an argument, its premise would be unacceptable.

G. E. Moore, an influential philosopher who taught at Cambridge University during the first half of this century, was famous for attacking the arguments of philosophers on grounds similar to these. He saw that philosophers invented special theories of their own about how the mind acquires knowledge, or what objects are made of, or whatever, and then used their own theories to argue against the beliefs of common sense. Moore maintained that this strategy of argument could not work because the commonsense claims that such philosophers attacked were always more certain than the philosophical theories that they used to dispute them. The philosophical theories, he maintained, did not have enough strength on their own to serve as a basis for undercutting common sense.

Moore was concerned about the special case in which philosophers tried to undercut commonsense beliefs about such things as the existence of hands and pencils by using philosophical theories about the nature of the mind and knowledge. This is just one kind of case where the argument can go wrong because the premises are not more certain than the conclusion.

A more specific sort of case in which an argument can go wrong because the premise is not more certain is the fallacy of *begging the question.* An argument begs the question if one or more of its premises asserts the conclusion (in slightly different words) or presupposes that the conclusion is true. Sometimes when this fallacy is committed, a person is trying to prove a conclusion, C, and chooses premises that are so logically close to C that they make the same claim in other words. For instance, he might use a premise stating, "Smoking is unhealthy" in trying to establish the conclusion "Smoking is bad for you." Since the premise really just asserts the conclusion in slightly different words, the argument is faulty. It begs, or avoids, the question: the issue of whether smoking is unhealthy is not really addressed. Anyone who disputed the conclusion in this case would also dispute the premise.

It may seem amazing that anyone would ever use or be fooled by a question-begging argument. Yet this often happens. It happens sometimes because people are not looking closely, do not have the concept of argument with its premises and conclusion very clearly in their minds, or are misled by complicated, ponderous language. In fact, it is quite easy to use a question-begging argument yourself without intending to, especially if you are trying to set out reasons for one of your fundamental and most cherished beliefs. Trying to find premises that will support that belief, you may easily—and quite unwittingly—come up with claims that would be acceptable only to people who already agree with the conclusion you are trying to prove. If this happens, you will have begged the question.

Here is another simple example. Let us suppose that you smoke cigarettes and you are feeling rather defensive about it, given all the objections nonsmokers are making these days about polluted air and the effects of second-hand smoke on the health of nonsmokers. You would really like to be able to smoke in public places like stores and airport departure lounges without feeling guilty. You try to prove to a friend of yours that when you smoke, you are doing something entirely legitimate and within your rights. You come up with the following argument:

1.   People have a right to smoke in public places.
So,
2.   I am perfectly entitled to smoke in public places if I wish to do so.

The trouble with this argument is that you assume in the premise everything you are trying to prove in your conclusion. This problem can be seen when we think about the expressions "have a right to" and "am perfectly entitled to." These expressions mean just the same thing in this context. You have stated as your premise that people in general are entitled to smoke to prove in your conclusion that you personally are entitled to smoke. This argument would work if your friend and others who object to people smoking in public places had already conceded in advance that people do generally have this right. But, of course, it is just this right that they deny. They think people don't have any such right because smoking results in polluted air and in health damage to nonsmokers. You have, in this context, given an argument that begs the question.

Sometimes, when we are trying to construct arguments for our most basic beliefs, we cannot find any premises that do not already require acceptance of the conclusion. When this happens, it is better to admit that we have no argument to prove our fundamental principles than to use arguments that look rational but beg the question. We can simply admit that we are operating under an assumption that seems reasonable and effective but cannot be fully defended by arguments.

A problem that is not exactly that of begging the question but is closely related to it arises when you have a controversial premise used to support a conclusion, which is, in fact, less controversial than that premise. Here you may not have to believe the premise in order to believe the conclusion. But, nevertheless, the premise may be too controversial to be of any use in the context of the argument.

This problem arises in the following argument, which was used in a report on childhood education. The author is considering the issue of whether languages other than French and English should be taught in public schools in Canada. (Both French and English are official languages in Canada, although there are other native and immigrant groups whose mother tongues are different: Cree, Ojibway, Greek, Italian, Japanese, Chinese, and so on.) When you read this argument, keep in mind that the author is trying to answer an objection to having third languages taught in public schools:

> It will not surprise anyone that I reject these arguments. A child has the inalienable right to his mother tongue and to his cultural heritage, which not only determines who he is, but also who he will be. No school system, therefore, must be allowed to interfere with that right. The opposite is also true; everything must be done to encourage the child's awareness of his heritage and to develop the language skills of his mother tongue. Without these provisions we will merely be paying lip service to the multicultural reality of Canada.[11]

The author's whole case here rests on the following premise:

> A child has the inalienable right to his mother tongue and to his cultural heritage, which not only determines who he is, but also who he will be.[12]

If we knew that every child had an inalienable right to his mother tongue and cultural heritage, we would indeed know that schools should teach all mother languages. The problem is that this starting premise is so controversial—more controversial, even, than the question it is used to resolve. Obviously, if all children had an inalienable right to their mother tongue, and a right that had to be supported at all costs, then schools would have the obligation to teach all mother tongues. But perhaps it is not true that all children have such a right; no independent argument was given for this sweeping premise. Obvious reasons against this premise exist in terms of costs and the need to maintain a society with a common culture and efficient communications.

As the premise stands, it is unacceptable, and even though the conclusion can be derived from it, it doesn't give the conclusion any real support. To show that a conclusion follows from a sweeping and unsubstantiated supposition is not to prove that conclusion acceptable.

A number of different conditions, then, will show that the premises of an argument are unacceptable.

SUMMARY OF UNACCEPTABILITY CONDITIONS

1. One or more premises is refutable on the basis of common knowledge, a priori knowledge, or reliable knowledge from testimony or authority.

2. One or more premises is a priori false.

3. Several premises, taken together, produce a contradiction, so that the premises are inconsistent.

4. One or more premises is vague or ambiguous to such an extent that it is not possible to determine what sort of evidence would establish them as acceptable or unacceptable.

5. One or more premises depends on an assumption that is either refutable or highly controversial.

6. One or more premises would not be rationally acceptable to someone who did not already accept the conclusion.

7. For the audience to whom the argument is addressed, the premises are less certain than the conclusion.

EXERCISE SET

Exercise 2: Part A

Inconsistencies. Can you detect an inconsistency in any of the following sets of statements? If so, which ones? Explain your judgment.

*1. The people of Samoa value virginity in young women very highly. However, they do not care how many sexual encounters young women have before they are married.

2. Squares are rectangles, but rectangles are not squares.

3. Most boys have a tendency to shoving behavior at age two. Few girls have a tendency to shoving behavior at age two unless they are the regular playmates of pushy little boys. A degree of aggression is probably innate in the human species, particularly in the male.

*4. The economic situation of African-Americans in the United States has not improved as much as we might think since the bad old days before the civil rights movement. Even though some African-Americans are in successful and conspicuous positions in politics, law, and medicine, it is still true that unemployment affects blacks far more than whites.

5. Either the doctor deliberately murdered his own patient, or the doctor made a mistake in his diagnosis. Mistakes in diagnosis are quite common. The doctor might have made a mistake in diagnosis. Deliberate murder is a terrible crime.

6. If a person gives birth to a child, she is responsible for taking care of it. Responsibilities are something we acquire voluntarily. Of course, some children are born as a result of accidents with birth control or even as a result of rape or incest, sexual attacks to which women are involuntarily subjected.

*7. All goodness derives from God and would not exist without Him. God is good. God created all the goodness in the world. No act can create value. Of many values, goodness is the primary one.

8. All human beings are carnivorous. Carnivorous beings eat meat. Some human beings are vegetarians.

*9. All knowledge depends on proof by argument. Proof by argument requires premises. Those premises must be known to provide the basis for that proof.

*10. An extraterrestrial civilization that was both technically and morally more advanced than we are would have some reasons to come to earth and other reasons not to come. Presumably such a civilization would wish to exhibit its technological innovations to others, and it might wish to communicate its advanced moral standards to others. On the other hand, earth is a pretty repellent place from a moral point of view—full of war, torture, murder,

greed, robbery, and hypocrisy. A morally advanced civilization might be too disgusted to wish to visit.

11. Babies cannot focus well in the first weeks of life. However, they can see colors. A baby's favorite color is red.

*12. Canadian foreign policy is often vacillating and hesitant. Sometimes it is independent of American foreign policy and sometimes it is not.

*13. The value of life is absolute. Life has a sanctity that people are not entitled to violate. We can never justify deliberately taking a life. However, capital punishment is morally permissible, and wars in self-defense are sometimes necessary.

Exercise 2: Part B

Evaluate the premises of the following arguments for acceptability using the criteria explained in this chapter and explain your answers with reference to these criteria. Also, say whether you think the assumptions are faulty. If there is any passage that does not express an argument and therefore contains no premises, say so.

1. Anyone who has the capacity to kill should avoid keeping guns around the house. Actually, when you think about it, we all have the capacity to kill. So no one should keep a gun around the house.

2. Nobody should undertake college education without at least some idea of what he or she wants to do and where he or she wants to go in life. But our world is so full of change that we cannot predict which fields will provide job openings in the future. Given this, we can't form any reasonable life plans. So nobody should go to college.

*3. Withholding information is just the same as lying and lying is wrong, so withholding information is wrong.

4. Nuclear energy has a potential to cause environmental damage that will last for many thousands of years. It is unique in this regard; damage from coal, water, and other electric sources can be serious but will be much shorter

in duration. Therefore, nuclear energy should be approached with extreme caution.

5. If a law is so vague that it is difficult to know what counts as a violation of it, and if there is really no distinct and clear harm that that law could prevent, then the law should be abolished. Laws that prohibit obscenity have both of these defects. The conclusion to which we are driven is obvious: laws against obscenity should be abolished.

6. Every even number larger than 2 can be divided by 2, with no remainder. No prime number, other than 2, can be divided by 2 with no remainder. Therefore, no even number larger than 2 is a prime number.

7. A great leader is infallible and can never be wrong. Hitler was clearly a great leader. Yet anyone advocating genocide was clearly wrong, and Hitler did advocate genocide. Therefore, Hitler was not infallible.

*8. Sex is private and intimate. AIDS has to do with sex. Nothing that is private and intimate should be discussed publicly. So AIDS should not be discussed publicly.

9. Tennis is a much more demanding game than basketball because it is played either singly or in pairs, which means that a person is moving nearly all the time. Basketball is a team sport, and you can sometimes relax and leave things up to the other members. Also, tennis calls for much more arm strength than basketball.

10. Either the western world will have to take over energy production and marketing to bring about gasoline rationing or the Arabs are going to control everything. It would not be good for the Arabs to take over, obviously, so we are going to live with state control of energy industries.

*11. *Background:* The following letter was written in response to a newspaper article dealing with problems of addiction among doctors:

"When doctors become addicts it is because of 'pressures' of their job and the 'lack of family life.' Yet when illiterate employables become addicts, it is because society has failed to train them for a job. If the housewife becomes ad-

dicted, it is because she is not appreciated by her family. Or if it is addicted youth, their problem is lack of parental understanding. That is, no matter what segment of society is addicted, another segment can be blamed, with rationalized plausibility.

"This circular slipping away from personal responsibility is clever, but it is fundamentally unjust. Obviously no one knows why some persons of all strata of society, including the clergy, become addicts. Why cannot the experts admit their problem—the problem of not knowing final causes—instead of producing plausible but innocent scapegoats?"

(Letter to the editor, Toronto *Globe and Mail*, October 8, 1980)

*12. A hunger strike to try to influence policy is immoral in a democracy because, in a democracy, an individual already has all the means he needs to influence policy. When Canadian Liberal Senator Jacques Hebert went on a hunger strike to try to save a youth employment program (winter 1986), he exhibited undignified, presumptuous, and morally outrageous conduct.

13. An introduction should convey the importance of the discussion that will follow. As a matter of fact, it is often easier to write a clear introduction after, rather than before, you have finished an essay.

*14. Swimming is the safest form of exercise for the many people who have problems with their joints, such as arthritis, because the water supports the swimmer, and there is no stress on such problem joints as the knee and the ankle.

Exercise 2: Part C

For any two of the following claims, imagine that you have to construct an argument in defense. Specify for each case one or more premises that would be acceptable and one or more that would not be acceptable for this purpose, according to the conditions developed in this chapter. Say which conditions make your premises acceptable or unacceptable in each case.

1. The United States is going to win out in the economic competition with Japan.

2. The Cold War is definitely over.

3. Change is not always the same thing as progress.

4. Having a college degree is absolutely necessary for having a successful and financially secure life.

5. A holy book such as the Bible, the Talmud, or the Koran provides a good guide to moral behavior in the modern world.

6. Writing poetry is more difficult than writing term papers.

7. The ability to evaluate arguments is an important practical skill.

❖   ## CHAPTER SUMMARY

Because no account of argument cogency is complete without saying something about which premises to accept and why, we set out some general principles about this matter. These principles apply as well to the acceptability of claims outside argument, with the sole exception of those that relate premises explicitly to the argument's conclusion. Using the principles, we chart a cautious path between wholesale acceptance of claims and wholesale rejection: neither of these policies is realistic.

There are conditions under which the premises of arguments are acceptable, and there are conditions under which they are unacceptable. These have been stated above, but are repeated here for ease of reference.

ACCEPTABILITY OF PREMISES

A premise in an argument is acceptable if any *one* of the following conditions is met.

1. It is defended in a subargument that is cogent.

2. It is cogently defended elsewhere by the arguer or another person.

3. It is known a priori to be true.

4. It is a matter of common knowledge—a statement that is known by most people or is believed by most people, and against which there is no known evidence.

5. It is supported by testimony from a reliable person and its content is such that testimony is, in principle, an appropriate backup. The claim is not wildly implausible, and it is restricted in content to experience.

6. It is backed up by an appropriate appeal to authority.

*7. It is not known to be unacceptable, as such, and can serve provisionally as the basis for argument.

UNACCEPTABILITY OF PREMISES

Premises in an argument are unacceptable if any *one* of the following conditions is met.

1. One or more premises is refutable on the basis of common knowledge, a priori knowledge, or reliable knowledge from testimony or authority.

2. One or more premises is known, a priori, to be false.

3. Several premises, taken together, can be shown to produce a contradiction, so that the premises are inconsistent.

4. One or more premises is vague or ambiguous to such an extent that it is not possible to determine what sort of evidence would establish them as acceptable or unacceptable.

5. One or more premises depends on an assumption that is either refutable or highly controversial.

6. One or more premises could not be rationally accepted by someone who does not already accept the conclusion, so the argument begs the question.

7. For the audience to whom the argument is addressed, the premises are not more certain than the conclusion.

Referring to these conditions, as explained here, you can often decide whether to accept the premises of various arguments. If any one of the conditions of acceptability is met, the premises are acceptable; if any one of the conditions of unacceptability is met, they are unacceptable. It is important to recall that provisional premises give you a provisional conclusion, one that is shown acceptable *if* the premises are accepted.

❖   **REVIEW OF TERMS INTRODUCED**

A priori statement   A statement that can be known to be true or false on the basis of logic and reasoning alone, prior to experience. If a claim is known a priori to be true, it is acceptable as a premise in an argument. If it is known a priori to be false, it is unacceptable.

Common knowledge   A statement that is known by most people or is widely believed by most people and against which there is no known evidence. What is a matter of common knowledge will vary with time and place, but if, in a given context, a certain claim is a matter of common knowledge, then it is acceptable in that context as the premise of an argument.

Testimony   Typically, statements based on personal experience or personal knowledge. A statement is accepted on the basis of a person's testimony if his or her telling of the statement and certifying it as acceptable is the basis for us to believe it. To rationally accept a claim on someone's testimony, we must believe that: he or she is reliable; he or she observes and remembers things accurately; he or she is not lying; the claim is one that is not implausible; and the claim is restricted in content to the experience of the person whose testimony is put forward in its support.

Authority One who has specialized knowledge of a subject and is recognized to be an expert on that subject. Appeals to authority are legitimate provided: the claim supported is in an area that is genuinely an area of knowledge; the person cited is recognized as an expert within that field; the experts in the field agree; and the person cited is reliable.

Faulty appeal to authority Argument based on authority in which one or more of the conditions of proper appeal to authority is not met.

Provisional acceptance of premises Tentative supposition of premises in a context where there is no special basis for regarding them as unacceptable.

Provisional acceptance of conclusion Acceptance of conclusion because it is related, by proper reasoning, to premises that have been provisionally accepted. In such a case, the conclusion can be said to be provisionally established: if the premises are acceptable, the conclusion is acceptable too.

Refutability A statement is refutable if and only if it can be shown, on the basis of acceptable evidence, to be false. Statements that are completely universal in nature, that are categorical in tone, or both, are often easily refutable.

Inconsistency When and only when one statement asserts what another denies, the two are inconsistent. Putting them together, we would then have a contradiction—a statement of the type P and not-P, which can be known a priori to be false. Explicit inconsistency occurs when the contradiction is apparent right on the surface, in the way the statements are worded. Implicit inconsistency occurs when the meaning of the statements allows us to infer, by valid deduction, a further statement that is a contradiction. In practice, a single statement is rarely explicitly inconsistent, but may be implicitly inconsistent.

Assumption A claim, typically of a fairly general nature, that is taken for granted and is presupposed by the premises of an argument to be true. A premise in an argument depends on an assumption if the denial of that assumption would mean that the premise was pointless or could not possibly be true. The assumption is a background belief, usually more fundamental and general than the premise itself.

Begging the question A fallacy that occurs when one or more premises either states the conclusion (usually in slightly different words) or presupposes that the conclusion is true. Arguments that beg the question are also sometimes called circular arguments.

Notes

1. *For instructors:* The points made in this chapter about accepting and not accepting premises can be applied directly to the more general subject of accepting and not accepting claims. The sole exception concerns the discussion of premises that are unacceptable as a basis for argument because they are less certain than, or too logically close to, the particular conclusion they are intended to support.
2. Toronto *Globe and Mail,* July 4, 1990.
3. *National Enquirer,* July 3, 1990.
4. David Lamb, *The Africans* (New York: Random House, 1987), p. 261.
5. Ibid., p. 145.

6. There are many complicated problems underlying this dilemma, which tends both to discredit experts in general and to confuse juries and judges. The problem is by no means handled by the preliminary remarks made here; it is mentioned merely as a specific illustration of the general point that when experts disagree we cannot prove our point merely by citing an expert who is on our side.

7. Garret Hardin, "A Lamp Not a Breadbasket," *Harper's Magazine,* May 1981, p. 85.

8. The topic of assumptions is a difficult and complex one that is handled only in a preliminary way here. A complete treatment of assumptions would include not only assumptions that pertain to premises but also those underlying the identification of the subject of the argument as an issue and those underlying the reasoning used in an argument. Here, since our topic is premises, we discuss only those assumptions that are required in order for the premises to be acceptable.

9. *The Peterborough Examiner,* April 16, 1981. Reprinted with permission of the *Examiner.*

10. This is the aspect of premise acceptability that does not apply to claims in general, because of the specific comparison between the content and certainty of the premises to that of the conclusion.

11. Laurier LaPierre, *To Herald a Child* (Toronto: Ontario Public School Men Teachers Association, 1981), p. 36. LaPierre is considering the argument that students would not have time, in Canadian schools, to learn languages other than Canada's two official languages: French and English.

12. Note that even if children did have this inalienable right to learn their mother tongue, it would not follow that it was the duty of the schools (as opposed to their parents) to teach it to them.

CHAPTER 6

Working on Relevance

WE NOW PROCEED TO DISCUSS THE second condition of an argument's cogency: relevance. The concept of relevance is so basic to thought and the development of knowledge that it is difficult to define and explain. But no matter how adequate the premises of an argument are, they cannot possibly support its conclusion unless they are relevant to it. Thus we have to try to improve our grasp of this fundamental, but elusive, concept.

CHARACTERISTICS OF RELEVANCE

In this section there are three basic ideas we wish to explain: *positive relevance, negative relevance,* and *irrelevance.* First we will explain these ideas in a general way and then we will offer more precise definitions. Positive and negative relevance are relationships between statements that exist when one statement has a bearing on the truth or falsity (and therefore also on the acceptability or unacceptability) of the other. To say that a statement is positively relevant to another is to say that it counts in favor of it. It constitutes evidence or reason for it, or makes it more likely to be true. To say that a statement is negatively relevant to another is to say that it counts against it, is reason or evidence that it is false, or makes it less likely to be true. In the case where a statement is neither positively relevant nor negatively relevant to another, then it is irrelevant. It counts neither for nor against the truth of the other statement; it has no bearing on the matter.

Suppose that B is the statement that plump people are as healthy as thin people. Now let A be the statement that most plump people's hearts are as healthy as the hearts of thin people. Here we can see that A is positively relevant to B; A counts in favor of B's being true. That plump people's hearts are as healthy as thin people's hearts would be some reason to think that the plump are as healthy as the thin. It is relevant because it is evidence for the claim, even though it is not sufficient evidence to establish it as true.

Contrast this situation with another one in which we consider another statement, C, instead of statement A. Let us suppose that C is the statement that plump people have a greater incidence of diabetes than thin people do. If C is true, that would be reason to think that B is not true. Again it would not be complete proof. But C is negatively relevant to B; C counts against B being true.

A third considered statement, Z, might have nothing at all to do with B. Let's suppose, for instance, that Z is the statement that Albany is the capital of New York. Z, in this case, makes no difference at all to the truth or falsity of B. As far as B is concerned, Z is irrelevant.

Relevance of a premise to a conclusion is not just a matter of the premise having something to do with the conclusion. That is too vague. If we consider the idea of going to Europe, well that has something to do with the idea of going to Africa, because both involve travel and expense, but whether we should go to Europe is irrelevant to whether we should go to Africa; our going to Europe is generally neither a reason for nor a reason against our going to Africa, even though there may be, in some loose sense, a relationship between these two things.

Relevance is such a basic concept in thinking that it is hard to pin it down with an exact definition.[1] For our purposes, the following definitions are adequate:

POSITIVE RELEVANCE

Statement A is positively relevant to statement B if and only if the truth of A counts in favor of the truth of B.

NEGATIVE RELEVANCE

Statement A is negatively relevant to statement B if and only if the truth of A counts against the truth of B.

IRRELEVANCE

Statement A is irrelevant to statement B if and only if the truth of A counts neither for nor against the truth of B.

When there is positive relevance, one statement supports another; when there is negative relevance, it undermines it; when there is irrelevance, there is no relation of logical support or logical undermining between the two statements.

The ARG conditions require positive relevance. If the premises in an argument are to support the conclusion, then they must count in favor of that conclusion—they must give some evidence for it, some reason to think that it is true. If the premises are negatively relevant to the conclusion—that is, actually give reason to suppose the conclusion is incorrect—or if they have nothing to do with it, there is a fault in the argument.

Let us look at some simple examples of positive relevance. In each of the following cases, the first statement is positively relevant to the second:

(a) 1. Jones has appendicitis, gout, and cancer of the bladder.
    2. Jones is not healthy enough to run the 26-mile Boston Marathon.

(b) 1. Basketball is a game in which height is a great advantage.
    2. Basketball is a game for which physical characteristics of players make a substantial difference in people's ability.

(c) 1. In May 1981, the interest rate in the United States was more than 18 percent.
    2. Banks in the United States in May 1981 were earning a good return on the money they loaned.

In each pair the first statement, if true, would provide some reason to suppose that the second statement is true. In each case, to say that (1) is positively relevant to (2) means that if (1) were true, it would constitute evidence in favor of (2). This claim does not say that (1) is true; nor does it say that (1) is complete proof of (2). It merely says that *if* true, it is *some* evidence, at least.

Negative relevance is quite different from positive relevance. A positively relevant statement supports a statement to which it is positively relevant, whereas a negatively relevant statement counts against, or is an objection to, a statement to which it is negatively relevant. Consider the following examples of negative relevance:

(d) 1. Jogging often results in knee injuries.
    2. Jogging improves a person's general health.

(e) 1. Between 10,000 and 100,000 deaths are predicted, by doctors and scientists, to result from the Chernobyl nuclear reactor accident in 1986.
    2. Nuclear reactors are a safe form of energy.

In both these examples, statement (1) is negatively relevant to statement (2). That is, if the first statement is true, that is some reason to think the second one is unacceptable.

Now let's examine some simple examples of irrelevance. A statement is irrelevant to the truth of another statement if it has no bearing on that further statement. That is to say, whether it is true or false makes no difference at all as far as our beliefs about the second statement are concerned:

(f) 1. Smith is old and fat.
    2. Smith's views on Chinese politics are unacceptable.

(g) 1. Women give birth to babies and men do not.
    2. Women are sensitive to people's needs and men are not.

(h) 1. Natural catastrophes such as earthquakes and tidal waves are beyond human control.
    2. Human beings have no freedom of choice concerning their actions.

In all these cases, the first claim provides no evidence either for or against the second one: it is completely irrelevant to it. In the flow of natural arguments, irrelevance can easily escape our attention. In (h), for instance, the fact that we cannot control natural catastrophes has no bearing on the question of whether we have freedom of choice regarding our own actions. But because they both refer to the topic of human control, we may fail to see that (1) is irrelevant to (2).

As we have seen in Chapter 3, when we discussed the cogency of arguments, the failure of premises to be positively relevant to the conclusion constitutes a serious flaw in an argument. If its premises, considered together, are irrelevant to its conclusion, or are negatively relevant, the argument is not cogent and is without merit because no evidence to support the conclusion has been given.

SOME WAYS OF BEING RELEVANT

Relevance can take many forms, as should be obvious from the very general way in which we have had to define it. Premises are positively relevant to the conclusion when, if true, they constitute some reason to believe the conclusion is true. The problem is that "constitute some reason" is awfully vague. There are many ways in which the truth of one statement can provide us with reason to believe another.

Relevance and Complete Support: Deductive Entailment and Validity

Obviously if the premises of an argument deductively entail the conclusion, they are relevant to the conclusion. In such a case, as we have seen already, the premises when taken together give full logical support to the conclusion. If true, they logically guarantee that the conclusion is true also. If true, they prove the conclusion, and therefore they obviously provide reason to believe the conclusion. Deductive entailment, then, is one sure way of getting relevance. Here is an example in which the premises are relevant to the conclusion because the premises together deductively entail it:

> Unilateral disarmament would not work unless all grievances, or hostile emotions, of the neighbors of the unilateral disarmer were zero. Since this is not the case, unilateral disarmament will not work.[2]

The conclusion here is "unilateral disarmament will not work." The reasons given are that for unilateral disarmament to work, there must be no grievances in neighboring countries and this just doesn't happen.

The argument is very clear as stated, but it can be clarified further if we set it out in standard form as the following:

1.   Unilateral disarmament will not work unless the unilateral disarmer has no neighbors with grievances or hostile emotions.

2. Countries for which unilateral disarmament might be proposed do have neighbors with grievances and hostile emotions.
Therefore,
3. Unilateral disarmament will not work.

Since (1) and (2), taken together, deductively entail (3), they provide conclusive reasons for believing (3). Since that is so, they obviously provide some reason to believe (3). They are relevant—and also provide full grounds, in this case. We might say these premises are relevant, and more: they are also sufficient. By providing at least some evidence for the conclusion, they are relevant to it and, in this case, since they also provide sufficient grounds, they go beyond merely being relevant: they provide not only good, but complete, reasons for the conclusion. That means that the adequacy of the argument will depend on the (A) condition. If the premises are acceptable, the argument is cogent.

Relevance and Similarity: Analogy

Deductive entailment is not the only way in which the relevance condition can be met. There are various ways in which statements can support each other, as we have seen earlier in Chapter 3. One is by an analogy between things described in the statements. The basis of arguments by analogy is that when two things are known to be similar in a number of respects, we have some basis for inferring that they may well be similar in further respects also. For instance, if rats and human beings were shown to have similar enzymes and hormones, this would give some reason to suspect a further similarity as to the way the two species digest sugar. We would be arguing on the basis of an analogy between rats and humans if we experimented with doses of sugar on rats and drew a conclusion about the effects of similar doses on humans. No argument by analogy can conclusively prove its conclusion, but when an analogy holds, information about one case is relevant to another. Analogies may be used for many different reasons; usually a prime reason is that one case is better known and more familiar than another. In the case of rats and people, often experiments done on rats would be quite immoral if done on people. (In fact, many critics argue they are even immoral when done on rats, but that's another problem.)

Relevance can be established on the basis of a comparison between one area of experience and another (for example, between living together before and after marriage) or between one case and another (U.S. intervention in Grenada and in Panama). When we argue on the basis of analogy, the similarities between the two things compared make points about one relevant to our consideration of the other. These basic similarities establish relevance. Arguments based on analogies are not as logically tight as deductive arguments, but their premises are often genuinely relevant to their conclusions because of the close similarities between the things compared.

Relevance and Experience: Inductive Reasoning

In more inductive reasoning, extrapolations are made from the past to the future. Events that have been experienced are described, and an inference is drawn that future or yet-to-be experienced events will be similar to those already encountered. In inductive arguments of this type, relevance comes from the basic assumption that regularities that have been encountered already will persist; on this assumption, past cases are relevant to future ones. Like most analogies, and unlike deductively valid arguments, inductive arguments cannot absolutely prove their conclusions to be true. But they make them likely or probable—at least in the case of good inductive arguments. The experienced events are relevant to those not experienced, for the inductive assumption is basically sound. (Without it, we could not function in the world at all.)

Here is an example of an inductive argument:

> Nearly every arms race that has occurred in human history has led to a war between the countries that were involved in that arms race. The current arms race between India and Pakistan is similar to the others in involving a basis of ethnic and religious hostility, growing enmity expressed in the press, and increasing expenditures on arms. So the arms race between India and Pakistan will probably lead to a war.

A person who used such an argument would be reasoning as follows:

1. Most previous arms races have led to wars.
2. The current arms race between India and Pakistan is similar to previous arms races in three significant respects.
Therefore,
3. The current arms race between India and Pakistan will probably lead to a war.

This argument is inductive. The data about past arms races is relevant to the conclusion about the India-Pakistan arms race because it is basically reasonable to assume that various arms races throughout human history are similar. We expect many aspects of experience to persist over time. The inductive assumption that is behind such arguments makes the data in the premise relevant to the conclusion, though the premise is about past experience and the conclusion is about the future. Of course, in such a case, relevance will not amount to full proof. What has happened in most past arms races gives us some reason to think that the India-Pakistan arms race will lead to war, but not conclusive reason. This particular arms race just might be different from most of the others.

Relevance and Reasons

When premises of an argument support the conclusion convergently, or separately, each premise is put forward as, itself, constituting a reason that the conclusion should be accepted. In such a case, the relevance of each premise has to be assessed separately, because the premises are not linked in the way that they support the conclusion. Such support is distinct from deductive validity, analogy, and experiential induction.

The following letter to the editor provides an example. The writer is trying to show why a particular concert hall should be preserved.

> As a person who, in the past, enjoyed many concerts in the Eaton Auditorium, I am deeply concerned that this fine concert hall may be destroyed. Apart from the historical significance is a need for a hall of its size and fine acoustical properties. It is also in a central location with public transportation available. This is often forgotten when locating cultural and recreation facilities but will become an increasingly important factor. Toronto has become a city of ever-increasing cultural activity and facilities are needed for these diverse interests. Many of us who are concerned sincerely trust that this much-needed facility will be retained.[3]

The author offered a number of separately relevant premises to support her view: (1) the hall is historically significant; (2) the hall is of a suitable size and has good acoustic properties; (3) the hall has a convenient location; and (4) there is a need for cultural facilities of its type in the city where the hall is located. Each of these four factors is relevant to the author's conclusion because each specifies a feature of the hall that would make it serve the purposes a concert hall should serve. The author points to these features to establish the value of the hall as a concert hall and to support her conclusion that the auditorium should be preserved.

In this argument, the premises are relevant to the conclusion because the conclusion is about something that should be done, and the premises each give some reason to do it. Each premise states a reason relevant to establishing that the hall deserves to be preserved. In this example, unlike the others we have looked at, each premise is separately relevant to the conclusion. In the other examples, premises have to be linked together to be relevant to the conclusion.

We have explained relevance by looking more closely at some of the ways in which premises can be relevant to a conclusion: by deductive entailment, by analogy (based on similarity of cases), by inductive relationships (based on experience), and as converging reasons. Usually it is easy to tell in which of these ways relevant premises bear on the conclusion. But even if you cannot tell, the most important thing is to make sure that the premises are relevant somehow. To do this, you have to ask yourself how, and to what extent, the premise would count in favor of the conclusion. To meet the (R) condition in ARG, the premises must be positively relevant to the conclusion. If they are negatively relevant, or irrelevant, the (R) condition is not satisfied. As we shall see, irrelevance is a fatal—and surprisingly common—flaw in an argument.

IRRELEVANCE: SOME GENERAL COMMENTS

If a premise used in an argument is irrelevant to its conclusion, it does not matter one bit whether that premise is true or acceptable; it cannot provide any basis for the conclusion. Obviously, in this case, it cannot possibly provide good grounds for the conclusion. Thus an argument that fails on the (R) condition will necessarily fail on (G), and whether it passes on (A) won't matter. From this you can see that irrelevance is a fatal flaw in an argument. If you can show that someone else's argument is based on irrelevant premises, you have given a conclusive refutation of it. An argument in which the premise or premises are irrelevant is often called a *non sequitur.* The Latin words *non sequitur* mean "it does not follow"; the premises won't lead you to the conclusion.

Another term sometimes used to refer to irrelevance is "red herring." A *red herring* is a distracting remark that has no bearing on the topic of discussion and that tends to lead people away from the point at issue and distract attention from the fact that the conclusion is not being properly supported.

It might seem amazing that non sequiturs and red herrings exist. Yet they are relatively common, and unwary audiences are often deceived by them. One explanation for this phenomenon may be found in the character of the irrelevant premises. Often they are clearly true or are points of clear agreement between an arguer and the audience. In contexts of controversy, such agreement can seem so important that an audience may forget to ask just how the uncontroversial points are really related to the topic at hand. Another factor, sometimes, is that of emotion. Premises that are, in fact, irrelevant, may arouse in us such emotions as pity, fear, or anger, and our emotions may distract us from the point at issue. In addition, irrelevant premises may be interesting in themselves, or they may be easier or more entertaining to think about than the problem under discussion.

All these factors are compounded by the fact that we often do not stop to analyze arguments. We simply listen or read and do not bother to spell out the premises carefully (as in a standardization) and to reflect on just how they are related to the conclusion. But for our purposes it does not matter so much what causes people to use or accept arguments containing irrelevance. Rather, our main interest is in understanding what irrelevance is and in learning to recognize some of the common fallacies of relevance.

Logicians have labels for kinds of irrelevance that are especially common and interesting. In this chapter we shall study a number of these, but we shall not try to learn all of them. This itself can become an irrelevant distraction if the basic goal is to learn to understand and evaluate various types of arguments! You can sometimes sound especially knowledgeable by talking about non sequiturs or red herrings, and it is fun to use special fallacy labels, such as "ad hominem," "straw man," "guilt by association," and "argument from ignorance." Understanding these common types of irrelevance is useful, because studying them makes you better able to spot them. However, our main goal is to recognize irrelevance when we see it. Provided that you spot irrelevance, it does not matter so very much whether you say "that's a red herring" or "you've committed the ad hominem fallacy." The important thing is to understand that one or more premises is irrelevant, and understand why.

Criticizing an argument on grounds of relevance is a strong line of criticism. But you have to back up your criticism by saying why you think the premises used are irrelevant to the conclusion. Presumably the person who used the argument thought her premises were relevant. If you just say "non sequitur" or "that's irrelevant," it does not put discussion on a very high level. You should explain why you believe that the truth or falsity of these premises will make no real difference to the conclusion. You have to show how and why such a label applies to the argument you are talking about. All of this serves to emphasize a point we have previously made: criticizing an argument requires that you yourself argue. This point is as true for analyses of relevance as it is for any other aspect of argument evaluation.

EXERCISE SET

Exercise 1: Part A

For each of the following pairs of statements, comment as to whether the first statement is relevant to the second. If you think it is irrelevant, briefly state why.

*1. (a) Elephants have been known to cover the corpses of other dead elephants with leaves and branches, whereas they do not so cover sleeping elephants.

(b) Elephants have a concept of death.

2. (a) In many Third World countries the governments are run by ill-educated dictators and there is no freedom of the press.

(b) The United States has an admirable and perfectly acceptable system of government.

3. (a) There are tribes in which it is normal and economically useful for two brothers to be married to the same woman.

(b) Marriage as we know it in western cultures is not a universal human custom.

4. (a) When prices go up, people have to pay more for food, housing, and clothing.

(b) When prices go up, poor people have more financial problems than they had before the increase.

*5. (a) The chemical names of some ingredients of children's snack foods are completely impossible to pronounce.

(b) Some children's snack foods contain dangerous artificial chemicals.

*6. (a) Some French historians dispute whether large numbers of Jews were killed in World War II.

(b) The large number of Jews killed in World War II would have been larger still had it not been for the protective activities of some outstandingly courageous citizens in Holland, France, and Sweden.

7. (a) In virtue of the fact that it is still mothers who do most of the childrearing, girls are typically brought up by a parent of the same sex, whereas boys are typically brought up by a parent of a different sex.

(b) Girls, in growing up, have more difficult problems in establishing identity apart from the main child-rearing parent than boys do.

8. (a) Swimming uses more muscles of the body than nearly any other sport.

(b) Swimming can provide a good form of balanced physical exercise.

*9. (a) Agriculture is a key to the well-being of a country.

(b) The inefficient agricultural system of the Soviet Union is an important obstacle to efforts to raise its standard of living.

10. (a) Children who have a long bus ride to school often arrive at school rather tired and restless.

(b) Children who have a long bus ride to school will achieve lower grades than children who are able to walk to a neighborhood school.

Exercise 1: Part B

For each of the following passages, do you find any cases where an irrelevant premise is used in an attempt to support a conclusion? Determine the conclusion (if any) in each passage, and then indicate any premise that you consider irrelevant to the support of that conclusion. State why you think the premise is irrelevant, if you do. *Note:* Not all examples involve irrelevance.

*1. A number of different religious denominations are represented within the public school system. It is for this reason that the system must be secular, not religious.

2. People diving into unknown waters have sometimes hit their heads hard on the bottom, with resulting injuries that are very serious. In fact, such injuries often damage the spinal cord, turning the injured person into a paraplegic. Diving is dangerous if one does not take proper precautions.

3. *Background:* In 1984, the former prime minister of Jamaica, Michael Manley, published an essay on poverty and underdevelopment in *Harper's Magazine*. Manley claimed that poverty in the Third World was a result of imperialism in the colonizing of many countries during the nineteenth century. Thomas Sowell, of the Hoover Institution, wrote objecting to Manley's theory. He said:

"The notion that either the capital or the standard of living in the West depends upon the Third World will not stand the slightest contact with evidence. When the British Empire was at its zenith [peak], around the First World War, more British capital was invested in the United States than in all of Africa or all of Asia outside Australia. The French had more trade with little Belgium than with all its farflung African empire. Germany's trade with its colonies was less than 1 percent of its exports."

(Quoted in "Just What Was Said," Toronto *Globe and Mail,* January 7, 1984)

4. *Background:* The following report, describing an incident in Falls Church, Virginia, appeared in the Toronto *Globe and Mail,* July 20, 1985.

"A pregnant woman who says she was accused of hiding a basketball under her dress has filed a 600,000 dollar suit against the store that alleged she was shoplifting. A cashier had told her supervisor Ms. Nelson had stolen a basketball and put it under her dress, said Stephen McCarron, Ms. Nelson's lawyer. The lawsuit says Ms. Nelson was given the option of opening her dress or going to the police station. 'I had to disrobe in front of six male security guards and police officers in the store,' said Ms. Nelson. She went into labor shortly after the incident and gave birth to a healthy baby boy, Darius."

Hint: Does this report contain an argument?

*5. "There is no single source or reason that can explain all intractable conflicts. Rigid and/or mutually exclusive values lead to some, as perhaps, may be the case with the Lake Tahoe conflict or the Arab/Israeli confrontation over the West Bank. In other instances, disagreements stem from different perceptions of the facts, as in the long-standing US/Canada dispute over acid rain. Different perceptions of risk, of causal connections, and even of the motives or strategies of one's opponents can [also] lead to conflict."

(Susan Hunter, "The Roots of Environmental Conflict in the Tahoe Basin," in Louis Kriesberg, Terrell A. Northrup, and Stuart J. Thorson (eds.), *Intractable Conflicts and Their Transformation* [Syracuse, N.Y.: Syracuse University Press, 1989], p. 25)

6. Children are unique and sensitive creatures. They are very imaginative, and they are different from adults. Therefore, every child has an absolute right to state-supported education.

*7. Nations such as France, the United States, Canada, and the United Kingdom support systems of nuclear weapons that they say are intended for their defense. Such systems require a threat to use terrible violence against enemies: if there were no threat to use the nuclear weapons, there would be no point in having them. These same states criticize those South African blacks who have announced their willingness to use violence against an apartheid state. Obviously, the nuclear states are using a double standard when they assume their own threat of violence in self-defense is right and that of South African blacks in self-defense is wrong. Given this kind of hypocritical inconsistency, we can see that South African blacks have every entitlement to threaten violence when seeking change in the system of apartheid.

8. *Background:* In 1983, a scandal emerged when it became known that a high school social studies teacher, James Keegstra, was teaching that the murder of 6 million Jews during World War II did not occur. Keegstra lost his position as teacher. The following was a contribution to the controversy. (Assume that the implied conclusion is that the murder of Jews during World War II did occur.)

"I recall one Sunday afternoon I was visiting my uncle, who lived on the outskirts of the city [Udine, Italy]. My cousin noticed a train that was not moving, so we decided to investigate. When we got to within 50 metres, we were told to halt by a German soldier. We were close enough to realize what it was.

"It was a train (boxcars only) loaded with Jews on their way into Austria, 90 kilometres to the north. The screaming that was coming from these cars was unbelievable. Babies were being held on the upper ventilation openings, perhaps for fresh air. How many died before reaching their destination in concentration camps?

"How do I know they were Jews? Almost all of the cars had in bold letters written on the side, JUDEN. These were Italian Jews going to their final destination. Does Keegstra think I can ever forget? Why did I talk to my children about my youth? Because I don't want it to happen again."

(Vic Gomirato, letter to the Calgary *Herald*, October 3, 1983)

*9. Multicolored fish are more restricted to particular territories than fish of less dramatic coloration. The bright colors serve to warn other fish that they are there. The sense of territory has an important survival function for these fish, and it is indicated by the colors that have evolved. We can see that a sense of territory is basic in the evolution and nature of higher primates such as humans.

(Adapted from Konrad Lorenz's work on aggression in humans and animals)

*10. *Background:* The following passage is taken from a philosophical book on justifying beliefs in God's existence.

"Suppose religion could be provided with a method of proof. Suppose, for example, that the divine omnipotence was so manifest that whenever anyone denied a Christian doctrine he was at once struck dead by a thunderbolt. No doubt the conversion of England would ensue with a rapidity undreamt of by the Anglican bishops. But since the Christian faith sees true religion only in a free decision made in faith and love, the religion would by this vindication be destroyed. For all the possibility of free choice would have been done away."

(Alastair MacIntyre, *Metaphysical Beliefs* [London: SCM Press, 1957])

11. *Background:* In the late 70s university professors in France were accused of incompetence on the basis that students graduating were not well trained. A spokesperson, François Chatelet, sought to defend them against this charge. (*Note:* Assume that there is a missing conclusion, which is that professors should not be criticized for giving credits to students who are weak—"idiots.")

"Our degree is not recognized but we have more students than ever. They come because they think they might learn something. Sure there are idiots. And I have given them credits. There are bigger idiots in the Government. Is it up to me to be more rigorous than the electorate?"

(As quoted in the *Canadian Association of University Teachers Bulletin*, September 1978)

12. *Background:* The following was written in response to a proposal to license cats.

"Cats are free spirits, the last really independent creatures around. You can no more license cats than you can license the wind. Dogs may submit to bureaucracy. Cats won't. The same spirit tends to rub off on cat owners. They have enough trouble being pushed around by their cats without being asked to submit to man-made laws. Besides, there's an economic factor. They've never had to buy licenses, so why start? No, it just won't work."

(Quoted by Ralph Johnson in "Charity Begins at

Home," *Informal Logic Newsletter* Vol. iii, no. 3 [June 1981], pp. 4–9)

13. *Background:* The following letter concerns the issue of what is the appropriate response by the Catholic Church to Catholic public officials in the United States who support abortion rights.

"Both France and Italy, which are overwhelmingly Roman Catholic countries, allow legal abortion. In addition, West Germany and the Netherlands, both roughly half-Catholic, also allow legal abortion. In none of these countries has the national Catholic Church excommunicated or threatened to excommunicate Catholic public officials who are supportive of abortion rights. Charles W. Colson should take note of these facts when he vigorously defends Cardinal John O'Connor's threat to excommunicate American Catholic public officials who support abortion rights. Both he and Cardinal O'Connor must answer the question why Catholic public officials in the United States should be uniquely punished when the Catholic officials of other nations are not similarly threat-

ened. If the Catholic Church is truly universal, shouldn't the hierarchy in the United States practice the tolerance exercised by the Catholic Church in Europe?"

(Letter to the *New York Times,* July 16, 1990)

***14.** *Background:* The following question and reply are taken from an interview with President Ronald Reagan. Assume that President Reagan is offering an argument for the claim that the Bible is of divine origin.

"*Mr. Otis:* We would like to know . . . what the Bible really means to you.

"*President Reagan:* I have never had any doubt about it being of divine origin. And to those who . . . doubt it, I would like to have them point out to me any similar collection of writings that have lasted for as many thousands of years and is still the best-seller worldwide. It had to be of divine origin."

(The interview, which appeared in the *New York Review of Books,* is cited by Howard Kahane in *Logic and Philosophy: A Modern Introduction,* 6th ed.; Belmont, Calif.: Wadsworth, 1990], p. 313)

◆ *FALLACIES INVOLVING IRRELEVANCE*

A fallacy is a common mistake in arguing, a mistake in the reasoning that underlies an argument. Some fallacious arguments are hard to spot; we may think they are cogent, satisfying the ARG conditions, even though they are not. Fallacies of relevance are mistakes in argument, mistakes that involve irrelevance. There are many different ways of being irrelevant. The specific fallacies of relevance discussed here have been given special names because they are quite common and can be deceptive.

Not all fallacies involve irrelevance. Some have to do with the acceptability of premises of certain types or with the sufficiency of the premises to establish the conclusion. In this chapter, however, we are concentrating particularly on relevance and irrelevance, so we shall discuss only fallacies in which the mistake in reasoning is due to mistaking an irrelevant premise for a relevant one.

The Straw Man Fallacy

In Chapter 2 we discussed the interpretation of passages—whether they contain arguments, how you identify the premises and conclusions, and how to decide whether to add missing premises or conclusions. You were advised not to read in extra premises or conclusions without good evidence that the author of the argument would have accepted them. If you read in something that is not there, you mistake the author's position. If you criticize a weak position that an author did not really hold and infer from your criticism that his real position is flawed, you have committed the *straw man fallacy*. This fallacy is committed whenever someone distorts a position, criticizes the distorted version of a theory or claim, which is weaker than the genuine position, and then takes his criticism to refute the real position.

If someone claims that X is true, and you represent him as having claimed Y (a weaker theory than X) and then attack Y and understand or represent yourself as having refuted his real position, you have committed the straw man fallacy. Instead of refuting a real man, you have refuted a "man of straw." A man of straw is easier to knock over than a real man. You have committed an error in thinking, a mistake about relevance, in believing that your attack is relevant to the real position when it is not.

THE STRAW MAN FALLACY

The straw man fallacy is committed when a person misrepresents an argument, theory, or claim, and then, on the basis of that misrepresentation, claims to have refuted the position that he has misrepresented.

To avoid the straw man fallacy, then, you have to interpret other people's arguments and positions patiently, accurately, and fairly. You have to base your criticisms on the position someone actually holds, not on some other position that (in your mind) is somehow related to it. The best way to avoid the straw man fallacy is to make sure that you direct your comments and criticisms to the actual position held. The actual position held may be quoted, in which case it is put forward in exactly the same words as those used by the person who originally expressed it. Clearly you cannot misrepresent people by quoting their exact words—though you still need to interpret the quoted material carefully, to avoid error. In addition to being committed to what they say, exactly, people are committed to any claim that is deductively entailed by what they seriously say or write, and also to claims that are strongly suggested by what they say or write. Obviously it is easiest to go wrong when you are working with what is strongly suggested. You have to make sure that the suggestions are not just in your own mind but are interpretations people would typically make, in the context in which the argument or position was stated.

These remarks will be more clear if we see how they apply to a specific example. In an issue of the *Nation* that appeared in the fall of 1982, when the Cold War was in a particularly negative phase, writer Sidney Lens made the following statement:

It is mere cliché to say we cannot trust the Russians.[4]

This comment was the theme for a short essay in which Lens went on to argue that no government should be trusted, and that disarmament and foreign policy arrangements had to be made in such a way that international verification agreements and a strong basis in national interests would supplement trust as the grounds for lasting agreements. But the comment is just the sort of thing that could easily be misinterpreted.

Obviously, if you wished to discuss Lens's remark, one way to avoid the straw man fallacy would be to quote him directly. If you wish to reword the comment, you must ensure that what you attribute to Lens is deductively entailed by what he actually said.

Suppose, for instance, you attributed view (i) to Lens:

(i) It is a mere common saying that the Russians are not trustworthy.

This rephrasing would be quite all right because (i) is merely a verbal variation on the original claim; you get (i) by replacing "cliché" with "common saying" and replacing "we cannot trust the Russians" with "the Russians are not trustworthy." The original claim deductively entails (i); in saying it, Lens clearly meant (i). Putting the view as (i) rather than as the original statement would be proper interpretation. You wouldn't commit the straw man fallacy by doing that.

You would venture further in interpretation if you said that Lens had asserted (ii):

(ii) It is false to say that the Russians are not trustworthy.

This remark, (ii), is not deductively entailed by Lens's original comment. It is perhaps suggested by his expression "mere cliché." A statement that is merely a cliché is one that is only a cliché; that is, it is nothing more than a cliché. One way of interpreting this would be to say that the statement is not true. (Being true could be one way of being something more than a cliché.) Whether Lens meant to assert (ii) is a debatable point if you have only this single comment to go by.

If we represented Lens as having asserted (iii), we would clearly be misinterpreting his comment:

(iii) The Russians are just as reliable as the British.

No such comparison as this was stated, entailed, or even suggested by the original remark about trusting the Russians.

It is easiest to avoid misrepresenting a theory or position when you have a specific version of it to deal with—as in our example here. You then simply check to see that your interpretation has a firm basis in what was actually said. You do not add premises or conclusions inappropriately, and you proceed with great care in reading into the position anything that is not either explicitly said or deductively entailed by what is said. By taking care in this way, you can avoid committing the straw man fallacy yourself. On those occasions when you are able to compare the author's representation of another position with the original statement of that position, this strategy will help you spot instances of the straw man fallacy.

Let us consider a specific passage and see how easy it can be to commit this fallacy. The following paragraph is taken from a book on building stable, effective relationships:

> But it would be a mistake to define a good relationship as one in which we agree easily, just as it would be a mistake to define a good road as one that is easy to build. While it is easier to build a good road across a prairie than through mountains, a good road through mountains may be more valuable than one across a prairie. Similarly, a good relationship among parties with sharp differences may be more valuable than one among parties who find it easy to agree.[5]

There are a number of ways this passage might be misinterpreted. The authors might be represented as arguing from an analogy between roads and relationships. It would then be possible to say that mountain and prairie roads have nothing to do with relationships and that the authors are arguing irrelevantly. However, looking carefully, we can see that the passage does not contain an argument. (The words *while* and *similarly* are not logical indicator words here.) The example of prairie and mountain roads serves to vividly illustrate the point that the authors are making about relationships; it is not supposed to support that point.

It is important, too, to understand just what the authors are saying about relationships. They are saying that a good relationship between parties with differences *may* be more valuable than one between parties who easily agree. This is a qualified claim; we would be misinterpreting if we read them as saying that difficult relationships are always more valuable than the easier ones. Another misinterpretation we might fall into would be to read the passage as saying that relationships where agreement comes easily are of no value. The authors do not say this; they say, rather, that such relationships are sometimes of less value than the other sort.

If we were to interpret this passage as an argument based on an analogy between roads and relationships, or as making a categorical claim about all difficult relationships as compared to all easy ones, or as dismissing the value of relationships where agreement is easy, we could then easily dismiss the authors' ideas as silly. But our criticisms would be misplaced—directed against straw men, not real ones.

The straw man fallacy is more difficult to detect when the views being criticized are not quoted explicitly. This happens when the positions discussed are general ones, not identified with the stated ideas of any single specific person, such as the environmentalist position on DNA research, feminism, evolutionary theory, the capitalist position on free markets, the belief in free will, and so on. In these contexts, you have to depend on your own background knowledge to determine the real content of the position. In this case straw man is less clear-cut than it was in the previous example. But often distortions are quite blatant, and you can detect them even in the absence of explicit quotations.

Consider, for instance, the following example of an advertisement written to criticize the "soft energy" option. Soft energy advocates urge that solar and wind power be developed as environmentally sound alternatives to nuclear power and oil and gas. The advertisement assumed that soft energy advocates wanted everyone to adopt a rural lifestyle and attacked their view on the basis of this erroneous assumption.

Wrong for many. That's the reality of "soft energy"—massive, often unsightly projects. But the dream is appealing partly because it seems small-scale and spread out, like another fantasy of the back-to-nature movement—do-it-yourself farming for everybody. Yet to give every American family of four a 40 acre farm would take more land—including deserts and mountains—than there is in all of the lower 48 mainland states. And such a program would surely mean good-bye wilderness. Besides, what about people who like cities, or suburbs—rather than . . . the "constant ruralism" in between? There may be a lot of good in soft energy to supplement conventional power. But we're uneasy with people who insist it will do the whole job and who then insist on foisting their dreams on the rest of us. Especially when their dreams can't stand up to reality.[6]

To detect the straw man fallacy being committed here, you merely ask yourself just what it is that advocates of soft energy are recommending. Their position is that energy sources like the sun and wind are better, environmentally and politically, than nuclear power or oil and gas. Whether their position is correct is a biological and policy issue about the quantities, costs, and production effects of these various sources of energy.

Soft energy advocates have a position about how energy should be produced. Their position on energy is not a position about farming or lifestyle. The possibility that there is not enough land on the U.S. mainland states for all families of four to have their own farms is completely irrelevant to the merits of the various sources of energy! The advertisement misrepresents the soft energy advocates, changing their position from one about the economics and biology of energy to one about farms and getting back to nature. The misrepresented position then becomes vulnerable to attack. As far as the real soft energy position is concerned, the comments in the advertisement are completely irrelevant. So no relevant evaluation of the soft energy position is offered in the passage.

In summary, the way to avoid committing straw man yourself is to make sure that you do not misrepresent another person's position. The way to detect straw man in other people's arguments is to check to see that positions criticized are properly represented and that criticism focuses on the points central to, and actually contained in, the position that is being criticized. In these ways you can avoid the kind of irrelevance that results from the straw man fallacy.

The Ad Hominem Fallacy

Another kind of irrelevance deserving special attention is the *ad hominem fallacy*. The words *ad hominem*, in Latin, mean "against the man" and the ad hominem fallacy is one in which a critic mistakenly attacks a man or person instead of arguing against the claims, arguments, or theories that the person has put forward. In ad hominem reasoning, people try to prove a point by attacking a person who holds the opposite view. Or they criticize a person's personality, background, actions, or situation and from that they conclude that his or her position is faulty. These debating tactics are almost always mistaken as far as logic is concerned. Yet they are often practically and rhetorically very effective.

Many a proposal has been defeated because the person putting it forward was not the "right" age, sex, race, nationality, or social class or had some personality trait taken to be undesirable. Such arguments are called *abusive* ad hominems. The premises abuse a person by attacking him or her on the basis of some characteristic, and the conclusion states that the person's claims or arguments are not acceptable or not true—on the basis of the personal attack. Such arguments commit a fallacy of relevance; their premises are not relevant to their conclusion.

Implicitly we reason ad hominem if we reject a presentation because the person making it does not look presentable and middle class, or when we are skeptical of a view simply because all those who support it are young and haven't held responsible jobs. Far too often we connect the merits of theories with the personal qualities of the people who support those theories. These are abusive ad hominems.

In other ad hominem arguments, people are attacked not so much because of their personal traits but because of their actions or circumstances. These arguments are called *circumstantial* ad hominems. An example would be rejecting a doctor's argument against smoking because the doctor herself was a smoker, or rejecting the idea that wages should be kept low because the politician who is supporting this idea has a high income himself.

The following is an example of a circumstantial ad hominem argument. The author, Gordon Lowe, is reviewing a book by Thomas Szasz. Thomas Szasz is an outspoken critic of psychiatry who has for several decades argued in the most categorical terms that mental illness does not exist. Szasz uses the phrase "the myth of mental illness" and argues that no one is really mentally ill. Lowe picks up on this by titling his review "The Myth of Szasz." He makes a number of points against Szasz, the last of which is that Szasz does not live up to his own principles.

> He launches his attack of psychiatry from a unique and special position. He is an M.D., Professor of Psychiatry . . . He is on the editorial board of at least four medical and psychiatric journals and on the board of consultants of a psychoanalytic journal. That is, he is not only a practising psychiatrist and a teacher of psychiatry, but a veritable pillar of the psychiatric community. What on earth can he tell his students? . . . How can Szasz reconcile what he professes with a professorship? He sees the whole psychiatric subculture as a "medical tragedy" and a "moral challenge," insists that it must be improved, then adds "but we cannot do this so long as we remain psychiatrists." Why then is Szasz still a psychiatrist? . . . His logic is relentless only when he applies it to his colleagues. He appears to regard himself as exempt from his own criticism merely because he is critical.[7]

If Lowe were to go on to conclude that Szasz's theory about psychiatry is incorrect, on the grounds that Szasz himself is inconsistent in his support for this theory, he would have committed a circumstantial ad hominem: inferring the incorrectness of a claim or position from the personal inconsistency in the person putting forward that claim or position.

Some other ad hominem arguments are less obvious and direct. It is easy to see that a substantive issue has been sidetracked into a discussion of personalities. But it may be hard to see that there is an explicit argument with premises containing personal information and a conclusion about some substantive point. For instance, seldom would you find in print an argument so blatant as this one:

1. The men who support liberal abortion laws are cowards intimidated by feminists.

So,

2. Liberal abortion laws are faulty laws.

Here, the ad hominem element is so blatant that the argument would not convince anyone. The premise is too obviously irrelevant to the conclusion.

It is more common for ad hominem remarks to be inserted more subtly. One tactic is to leave the conclusion unstated. The writer or speaker inserts the personal charges and suggests that the position held by the "disreputable" people is false. How this works can be seen from the following example, which appeared in a magazine article dealing with abortion:

> Women's Lib is chic and news, and the men who praise it become chic and newsworthy. To this group belong the sycophant, the male camp-follower, the half-sexed male who allows his woman to have him gelded and then hits the media trail to brag about it. They are the male counterparts of women who allow their lovers to force them onto the Pill or into an abortion, or who wrote idiot books about male supremacy or sexual surrender.[8]

The article, entitled "On Killing Inconvenient People," took a position strongly opposed to abortion under any circumstances.

The question arises as to how these strongly negative comments about the men who support a liberal position on abortion are related to the author's opposition to liberal abortion laws. The passage is a strident attack on these men: notice the negative emotional language in such terms as *half-sexed, gelded,* and *brag.* Obviously, the author thought that these men were pretty terrible characters. But we should ask ourselves just what the negative characteristics of these people (if they really have them) have to do with the moral correctness of liberal abortion laws. They are irrelevant to issues about the morality and legality of abortion. If male feminists were all saints, it would not make abortions morally good; and if they were all devils, that would not make abortion morally evil!

The author was not straightforward enough to reason directly from these insults to her moral stance on abortion law. If she had, the irrelevance of the comments would have been all too obvious. It does seem, however, that she was trying to get support for her antiabortion position from the hostile remarks she makes about men who favor liberal laws.

In view of these facts, we could regard the passage as an argument with a missing conclusion. Then we would see the negative comments as part of an argument. If there is an argument, it is certainly an example of the ad hominem fallacy. It would go like this:

1. The men who support women's liberation are weak attention-seekers.
2. The men who support women's liberation are less than fully male.
3. The men who support women's liberation are intimidated by the fact that feminism is fashionable.
4. The men who support women's liberation support a liberal policy on abortion.

Therefore,

5. A liberal policy on abortion is wrong.

You may not know whether it is appropriate to read a passage as having a missing conclusion. However, it is certainly important to note that discussions of personalities typically do not contribute to discussions of substance. If you did not regard the passage about half-gelded men as part of an argument, you would still have to note that this discussion is irrelevant to the abortion issue. Either the author uses an argument (with a missing conclusion) and her argument is a fallacious ad hominem one, or she has included some insulting remarks that are not relevant to the abortion issue. In neither case can we get substantive support for a view on abortion from the insults addressed to men who support feminism. Whether or not the allegations were intended to support the conclusion, they simply don't.

We have said that typically premises about personalities do not lend support to conclusions about matters of substance. Now it is time to explain why we have used the word *typically:* by this usage we suggest that there are some cases in which personality and character considerations really are relevant to the logical assessment of theories, positions, and arguments—and indeed there are such cases.

First, sometimes an argument or stance is actually about a person. For instance, a man may contend that he is a suitable candidate to be mayor. Here he is the issue: so, obviously, someone who brings aspects of the candidate's character into the debate is not committing any fallacy of relevance. Suppose someone were to argue the following:

1. Jones was convicted on a charge of using cocaine.

So,

2. Jones is not wholeheartedly against cocaine use.

Therefore,

3. Jones is not a suitable mayor to head up an urban project against cocaine use.

Such an argument would not be ad hominem. Ad hominem is a fallacy occurring when premises about personal characteristics are used in an attempt to support refutations of claims and positions to which they are not relevant. Here the conclusion is also about Jones himself and premise (2), defended in a subargument, is relevant to it. There is no fallacy of relevance and no ad hominem.

The second category of exception is rather more complicated. Think back to our discussions of authority and testimony in Chapter 5. Ad hominem, authority, and testimony have a certain inverse logical relationship: ad hominem has to do with the improper use of personal traits to criticize claims, whereas authority and testimony concern the proper use of persons' credible expertise and experience to support views. If you are deciding whether to accept the claim on someone's authority, then aspects of her background (her qualifications and experience as a scientist) and character (her honesty, accuracy of observations, and independence) are relevant to this decision. Some of these aspects are relevant to the question of whether she is an authority, and whether this question is one we should be willing to accept on her authority.

Consider the following example: Rosalie Berthell is a biologist and statistician who has emphasized that damage to sperm and other human tissue can occur due to radiation, even when radiation is at very low levels.[9] Now there is considerable disagreement among biostatisticians and biophysicists as to how the data on low-level radiation effects should be interpreted.

Suppose we were to argue as follows:

1. Berthell is a figure whose findings have been disputed by other people in her field.
So,
2. We cannot simply accept Berthell's claims on the basis of her authority as an expert.

We would not be arguing ad hominem. Why not? It is because the information in (1) is relevant to (2), as is obvious when we recall our discussion in Chapter 5 about proper appeals to authority. The information that Berthell is someone whose claims have been disputed does not constitute a personal attack, and it bears directly on the issue of whether appeal to authority is appropriate in this case. We should note that the conclusion in the above argument is not about low-level radiation as such. It is about whether Berthell's claims about low-level radiation can be accepted solely on her authority.

Reasoning from character and background never establishes points of substance about other topics, but it may be relevant to our decision about how seriously a person's testimony or authority should be taken. It would be ad hominem and fallacious to argue as follows:

1. Berthell is a Catholic sister.
Therefore,
2. Berthell is not an authority on low-level radiation effects.

It is true that Berthell is a Catholic sister, but this fact does not mean that she does not have knowledge of nonreligious subjects, and it is entirely irrelevant to the issue of whether she is an expert as to the harmfulness of low-level radiation.

The same sorts of points can be made for testimony. Suppose you must depend on personal testimony in order to accept a claim. In such a case you won't be committing a fallacy if you reason that because the person testifying is unreliable as to honesty, accuracy of observation, or independence, the claim cannot be accepted solely on the basis of his or her testimony. Here information about character (past dishonesty, for instance) is relevant to your decision to accept testimony or suspend judgment. Such reasoning is used frequently in courts of law. If a person known to have lied about important matters were to testify in a criminal trial, the defense lawyer would try to bring out his past dishonesty and it would be sufficient reason not to accept key statements solely on the basis of his testimony.

We can sum up these exceptions and our account of the ad hominem fallacy as follows:

THE AD HOMINEM FALLACY

A premise about the background, personality, character, or circumstances of a person is irrelevant to the merits of his or her theories and arguments, except in the very special case in which those theories and arguments happen to be about the person.

Specific points about a person's background may bear on the reliability of testimony or the legitimacy of authority. That means that they are relevant to our decision whether to accept his or her claims on testimony or authority even though they are not directly relevant to the question of whether these claims are true or false.

To reason from premises about the backgrounds, personalities, or characters or circumstances of people to substantive conclusions about their arguments or theories is to commit the ad hominem fallacy unless the premises are relevant to the conclusion in one of the ways described earlier.

Generally, points about personality and character are irrelevant to the substance of a case. Only in quite special circumstances are they more than rhetorical distractions from the main point.

The Guilt-by-Association Fallacy

We have seen that in the ad hominem fallacy, an argument or theory is attacked through attacks on the person who holds it. The fallacy of *guilt by association* is rather similar, except that in this case the attack on the person is indirect. In this fallacy, comments are made linking a person with a group or movement that is commonly believed to be bad. The implication is that the person himself is also in some sense bad and —usually—that his opinions are incorrect.

Frequently references to Hitler and the Nazis are used in fallacies of guilt by association—probably because the Nazi movement is one that nearly everyone agrees was terrible. For instance, many who argue against legalizing voluntary euthanasia (merciful early death) contend that it is morally evil because it was practiced in Hitler's Germany. This is a guilt-by-association criticism. The fact that something once happened in a terrible context does not show that the thing itself is bad or that it would be bad in all other contexts. To associate advocates of voluntary euthanasia with the Nazis is slander pure and simple; here guilt by association has become vicious.

In the example of defenders of voluntary euthanasia and Hitler's Germany, the connection alleged is wholly fictitious; these people are not fascists and never supported Hitler. But sometimes, even when a connection is a real one, it does not give a basis for any criticism. When discussing the ad hominem fallacy, we saw that it is only in rare cases that personal characteristics are relevant to the substantive issues under discussion. What we have in guilt-by-association fallacies is a charge against the person on the basis of an association, real or imagined, with a group or movement thought to be disreputable. Such associations are irrelevant to the merits of people's arguments or opinions. Even if someone really is a member of a group that really is disreputable, it is still likely that he has some opinions not held by the group as a whole—and also that the group as a whole has some correct opinions. Given these possibilities, you obviously cannot get very far by arguing from his associated "guilt" to the conclusion that his opinion or argument is wrong.

Here is a case of guilt by association, found in a report describing the responses of Canadian doctors to a study of medical insurance. The study was done by Emmett Hall. Canada has state-supported universal medical insurance, but at the time this argument was written, many doctors had been expressing dissatisfaction with the level of payment they receive from the scheme. They had begun to practice "extra-billing," charging patients more than the state-supported scheme would pay, and having patients make up the difference between the two amounts. Hall's report on medical insurance recommended that extra-billing be disallowed for doctors receiving payment from the scheme: doctors would have to bill entirely within the scheme or opt out of it altogether. To this suggestion, the following response was made:

> Of Mr. Hall's fear that extra-billing will destroy the health care systems and discriminate between rich and poor, Dr. Mandeville said that this is "a socialist concept that comes through in a socialist report. Hospitals treat people equally more than any other segment of society. Just look at the hospital. We have the low class people who aren't taking care of themselves."[10]

If Dr. Mandeville is correctly quoted here, then he certainly seems to have committed the fallacy of guilt by association. It comes when he terms the resistance to extra-billing "a socialist concept" and says it is part of "a socialist report."

For free enterprise-type doctors, socialism may appear to be a rather terrible thing, and many of the public in North America have been encouraged to link socialism with communism—and communism with prison camps and secret police. (This link is also guilt by association.) Since it is believed in many circles in North America that socialism is pretty awful, Mandeville tried to dispute Hall's view by linking it with socialism. Linking a person's argument to something undesirable is the classic device of guilt by association.

The argument implied would be a fallacy because the connection with socialism—real or imagined—does not show that Hall's view was incorrect. It is irrelevant to that issue. Socialism concerns the ownership and control of resources and the distribution of income, whereas Hall was concerned about equality of access to health care. (We might make a number of criticisms of Mandeville's argument, but we concentrate here solely on his appeal to the "evils" of socialism, which amounts to the guilt-by-association fallacy.) It's a mistake because there is no real connection between Hall's proposal and socialism. If there were a real connection, it would not show that there is anything wrong with Hall's proposal anyway.

To sum up, we can define the fallacy of guilt by association as follows:

THE GUILT-BY-ASSOCIATION FALLACY

The fallacy of guilt by association is committed when a person or his or her views are criticized on the basis of a supposed link between that person and a group or movement believed to be disreputable. The poor reputation of any group is irrelevant to the substantive correctness of its own views, or of the views of any member of the group, or of the views held by people or groups that may be loosely connected with it.

Guilt by association is not usually real guilt or real association. Even when the association is real and the guilt of the associated group is real, it does not transfer logically to every opinion held by the associated person.

It is possible to define a fallacy of *virtue by association* analogous to that of guilt by association. Just as it is irrelevant to criticize a claim or theory on the basis of an alleged link with a negatively regarded group, it would be irrelevant to try to buttress a claim or theory on the basis of its link with some positively regarded group. Even if the very "best" people believe something, that something may be incorrect! Trying to infer virtue by association would be a fallacy, just as guilt by association is. But virtue by association is not usually mentioned as a distinctive argumentative type—perhaps because it is relatively rare.

Fallacious Appeals to Ignorance

There are many things people do not know, or have not been able to prove. Sometimes fallacious arguments are based on this ignorance, in which case the fallacy of *appeals to ignorance* occurs. If we do not know something, then that point is often an important one to observe. The problem comes with attempts to infer from the fact that we do not know claims, the conclusion that they are either true or false. An argument of the type

1. We do not know that statement S is true.
Therefore,
2. Statement S is false.

is a fallacious argument. The premise is irrelevant to the conclusion because the premise is about what we do not presently know regarding S and the conclusion is about S itself. Similarly, to argue

1. We do not know that statement S is false.
Therefore,
2. Statement S is true.

would also be a fallacy. If there are discoveries we have not been able to make, this fact shows something only about the limits of our knowledge. It does not show how things are in the world, distinct from our beliefs or knowledge about them. It would also be fallacious to argue that since we have no grounds to accept not-S, we should accept S, or that since we have no grounds to accept S, we should accept not-S.

Slightly more subtle forms of the argument from ignorance occur when people argue from our failure to know the truth or falsity of some claim, S, to the conclusion that some further claim, R, should be accepted. Obviously, in such a case, the premise is irrelevant to the conclusion; the fact that we do not know one particular claim is generally not a reason for accepting some different claim.

Many phenomena exist where it is hard to get compelling evidence either way. Think, for instance, of questions about the existence of ghosts, life on other planets, and UFOs, or of the reality of telepathic communication. Because of the nature of these things, it is hard to prove either that they exist or that they do not exist. With ghosts, for instance, people seem to see and hear them, and some events that people want to explain by hypothesizing ghosts as the cause have occurred. However, we cannot get conclusive evidence that ghosts are present on any given occasion, no matter how fervent people may be in their testimony. A ghost is supposed to be an immaterial spirit, representing the soul of someone who has died. Representations such as voices and apparitions that have no known natural cause are often thought to be ghosts. But the problem is that you cannot be sure that they are. (Here too we often have an appeal to ignorance. People too easily conclude that because they do not know the natural cause of a sound or an apparition, it has a supernatural cause.)

In some New Age religions, it is fashionable to believe in reincarnation. People practice something they call "channeling," and think that they are connected with spirits informing them of lives of past selves. To critics they may reply "you can't prove I'm wrong; prove that I didn't have past lives as a Mongol warrior and a Greek slave maiden." But the fact—if it is a fact—that a conclusive disproof is unavailable is no reason to believe the claim true. Ignorance as to disproof is not proof; it is just lack of knowledge.

If arguing from ignorance were a sound way to argue, we could both prove and disprove the existence of ghosts! First, we could argue that since we have not been able to prove that ghosts do exist, ghosts do not exist. Then, we could turn around and argue that since we have not been able to prove that ghosts don't exist, they do exist. That is, we could argue from ignorance in two directions and thus arrive at inconsistent conclusions. Obviously something has gone wrong. The mistake is in thinking that from our inability to definitely confirm or definitely disconfirm the existence of ghosts, we can reach a conclusion about their existence or nonexistence. From our ignorance, we can only infer our own lack of knowledge—nothing more.

To argue that a new product is safe because it has not been proven to be dangerous is to fallaciously appeal to ignorance. This fallacious line of argument has been of great public importance in some policy issues. An important concept in these disputes is that of the *burden of proof*. (*Note:* Burden of proof is not a fallacy; it is a concept related to fallacious appeals to ignorance.) The notion of the burden of proof is that of the obligation, or duty, to support one's claims.

Where does the burden of proof lie—with those who seek to restrict a product, or with those who seek to market it? Until quite recently it has generally been thought that those who would restrict or ban a new product have the burden of proof: it is they who must provide studies to indicate that the product they seek to restrict is harmful.[11] Behind this particular allocation of the burden of proof is probably the assumption that, other things being equal, markets should be free.

In the past few years, public thinking on this matter has changed, partly due, no doubt, to well-publicized cases of drugs and other products with unforeseen harmful effects. We may see a shift to the idea that those who wish to market new products should first prove, to a rigorous degree, that these products are safe. The burden of proof, with a stringent standard of proof, would shift to those who would introduce a new product rather than to those who would restrict it.

Issues in this area are quite complicated, but however the burden of proof is allocated, it is clear that a mere appeal to the failure to demonstrate either harmfulness or safety will not prove the opposite. Ignorance as to the effects of a proposed product cannot, by itself, provide a basis for policy decisions as to whether it should be marketed. Such ignorance as to the existence of bad effects is irrelevant to the question of whether these products are really safe.

Many appeals to ignorance are rather tricky to detect. Because of the way they are worded and the context in which they appear, they may escape our attention. Consider, for instance, the following example, taken from a book about bringing up children. The author, A. S. Neill, is trying to show that punishment should never be used:

> To say that punishment does not always cause psychic damage is to evade the issue, for we do not know what reaction the punishment will cause in the individual in later years.[12]

Neill suggests that punishment may cause psychic damage in children. His reason is that we do not know what their reaction to punishment received now will be in later years. This appeal is to ignorance and it is fallacious. Neill does at least qualify his conclusion, admitting that he knows that our ignorance does not prove that there may be damage. His argument is of the type:

1. We do not know that not-S.
Therefore,
2. S may be true.

If all that is meant in (2) is that, for all we know, S may be true, that conclusion does follow. But if what is meant is that there is a significant likelihood of S being true (a probability worth paying attention to in practical decision making), that conclusion would not follow. Since Neill is giving a practical argument about how children should be treated, he clearly needs a likelihood that has some practical significance, so (2) must be interpreted as asserting more than an abstract possibility. In that sense, (2) is not supported by (1) which is, in fact, irrelevant to (2).

Another example of a faulty appeal to ignorance—one that is still heard quite frequently in discussions of the difficult public health problem of AIDS—is the following:

> We do not know whether the AIDS virus can be transmitted by mosquitoes who bite one person and then fly off to another person, still carrying the blood of the first. For this reason, spraying against mosquitoes should be resumed.

The problem here is just the same as it is in the previous argument. There might be some possibility that AIDS could be transmitted by mosquitoes or other insects; that possibility is logically consistent with what we know so far about AIDS. However, the practical recommendation made in the conclusion requires that any such logical possibility be regarded as something significantly probable; yet this significant probability cannot be inferred from our ignorance regarding AIDS.

To spot fallacious appeals to ignorance, use the following procedure:

1. Look for premises with phrases like "we do not know," "no one has been able to prove," "is not yet confirmed," "has never been discovered," and "has not been shown."

2. Check whether the conclusion asserts that the statement not known is false or that it is true or that it is quite probable or that it is quite improbable.

3. Check to see whether a further, logically distinct statement is inferred from our ignorance of the initial statement.

If you find ignorance described in a premise and then it is used in an attempt to support a conclusion alleging the truth, falsity, probability, or improbability of the claim we do not know *or* in an attempt to support a further distinct statement, you have found a fallacious appeal to ignorance.

To sum up, the fallacy of appealing to ignorance may be described as follows:

FALLACIOUS APPEALS TO IGNORANCE

An argument exemplifies a fallacious appeal to ignorance if and only if the premises describe ignorance, lack of confirmation, lack of proof, or uncertainty regarding a statement S and a conclusion about the truth or falsity or probability or improbability of S, or a further statement is inferred simply on the basis of this ignorance. From ignorance we can infer only lack of knowledge. We cannot infer truth or falsity or objective probability or improbability.

Fallacious Appeals to Popularity

Many arguments are based on popularity. Someone tries to show that a product is good because many people select it or that a belief is correct because many people hold it. Such arguments are extremely flawed because the merits of something are one matter and its popularity another. The problem is that things can be popular for many reasons, and only one of these is their good quality.[13] It would be different if people selected products for only one reason—quality—and if they held their beliefs as a result of only one kind of cause—careful, deliberate evaluation of pertinent evidence. In an ideally rational world, perhaps these factors might determine human choice and belief. In our world, however, they do not.

People may choose products because those products are cheap, because they have been well advertised, because they are for sale at a convenient store, because their friends have bought them (another *appeal to popularity*), or for many other reasons having little to do with the quality of the product. Similarly, they may believe things that are attributed to a product because they have heard them somewhere, read them in the paper, or picked them up during childhood. A claim may be widely believed only because it is a common prejudice. Thus the fact that it is widely believed is irrelevant to its rational acceptability.[14]

Arguments in which there is a fallacious appeal to popularity are based on premises that describe the popularity of a thing ("everybody's doing it," "everybody's buying it," "everybody believes it"), and the conclusion asserts that the thing is good or sensible. The arguments are fallacious because the popularity of a product or a belief is in itself irrelevant to the question of its real merits. Here is an example of a fallacious appeal to popularity:

> The perfume of the nineties. Women of the nineties choose a subtle feminine fragrance. Carfoor is the most popular choice of today's new woman. Career women say, "It's feminine, but discreet enough for the office and those important business lunches." Today's woman can work and be a real woman. Today's woman chooses Carfoor.

Such an ad contains a number of appeals in emotionally charged language ("subtle," "feminine," "discreet") and a persuasive definition (real women are "feminine" enough to wear perfume). It also gives some relevant reasons for Carfoor's attractiveness to career women: it will do for business purposes but is subtly feminine. A major aspect of such an ad, however, is an appeal to popularity. Potential consumers are urged to jump on the bandwagon, do what other real women are doing, and buy Carfoor. The point is that this perfume is one a woman should buy; one reason she should buy it is that other women are buying it. Another implicit appeal to popularity exists in the idea that "today's woman" works (presumably outside the home) and is yet aware of the need to be feminine. An unwritten message underlying the ad is that this lifestyle is the one women should choose because it is the most popular today. (Working outside the home is what today's woman does.)

Another example, this time referring to a belief rather than a product, is the following:

> A majority of the American people now (1974) believed that the American participation in the Vietnam War was wrong. All Americans who resisted such

participation were therefore patriotic and serving the American government, and all those who cooperated were unpatriotic and disserving the American government.[15]

The writer of this letter clearly wishes to infer from the fact that a majority of people believed (in 1974) that participation in the Vietnam War was wrong that such participation was in fact wrong. This implicit conclusion emerges from his first statement. There are two explicit conclusions derived from this intermediate step: resistance was patriotic and cooperation was not. The crucial step is the claim about the wrongness of participating in the war. There is only one piece of evidence for this claim, and it is the statement that a majority of the American people believed it. That belief, however, does not show that participation was wrong. However popular it might be, it could still be in error. If we use popularity as a guide to truth, we shall have to change our minds whenever public opinion shifts.

Needless to say, it is equally fallacious to infer that a belief, or a product, is flawed just because it is unpopular. A child who argues that he shouldn't have to go to bed at 7 o'clock because the other kids don't is making such an irrelevant use of unpopularity.[16] Similarly, an argument that disco music isn't any good because nobody listens to it anymore would be a fallacious appeal to unpopularity.

FALLACIOUS APPEALS TO POPULARITY

The fallacious appeal to popularity is a fallacy that occurs when people seek to infer merit or truth from popularity. It is also known as the fallacy of *jumping on a bandwagon* or, from the Latin, the *ad populam.*

The premise or premises of such an argument indicate that a product or belief is popular. It is endorsed by most people or by almost everybody. The conclusion of the argument is that you should get the product or that you should accept the belief because it is popular. Appeals to popularity (or unpopularity) are fallacious because the popularity of a thing is irrelevant to its real merits. Too many other reasons for selecting products or beliefs exist for the fact of their selection to count as good evidence of quality, truth, or rational acceptability.

Other Fallacies Involving Relevance

Sometimes an argument of a type that is basically legitimate can be grossly flawed, to such an extent that its premises have no bearing on its conclusion. They are then irrelevant to the conclusion. Thus examples of what are generally correct types of argument can contain irrelevant premises. Since this is the case, some examples of irrelevance will also be discussed in later chapters of this book. It would be futile to try to describe every possible kind of irrelevance. There are just too many: it is a little like the number of ways of getting lost in a forest!

Analogies can, when seriously flawed, contain premises that are irrelevant to their conclusion. Here is an example that illustrates just how far this can go. In

1986 a South African government representative in North America argued against economic sanctions against South Africa by using an analogy between the South African economy and a zebra. He said:

> There is no point in western countries applying economic sanctions to South Africa in an attempt to help the black people there. Sure, sanctions will hurt the economy, but they will hurt everybody. You can see this when you think of killing a zebra. If you shoot him in a white stripe he will die and if you shoot him in a black stripe he will still die. The whole animal goes down. And so it will be with the South African economy. The whole country will suffer from sanctions—not just the white part of it.[17]

There are many problems with this argument. For one thing, it involves the straw man fallacy. Many advocates of western economic sanctions against South Africa understood that South African blacks would suffer from them in the short term but believed that sanctions could, in the long term, work to the benefit of blacks by destabilizing and eventually defeating a racist government.

In addition, however, the argument is based on an analogy, one that is so grossly flawed that it cannot support the conclusion. There is little real similarity between a zebra and a complex modern economy such as that of South Africa! While the conclusion that blacks and whites are interdependent in this economy is probably correct, the analogy gives no evidence to support it. Zebras and modern economies are just too different. The speaker was trying to reason by analogy, but the two things he compared—an animal and a complex modern economic system—are so different that his premises are irrelevant to his conclusion. The example is to vivid and entertaining that we may miss this point.

The same kind of point can be made with appeals to authority; when things go badly wrong, the premises can be irrelevant to the conclusion. As we noted in Chapter 5, appealing to the proper kind of authority, in the proper circumstances, can be a good defense of a claim. But often entirely inappropriate authorities are cited. On occasion a person will try to defend a claim by appealing to someone who is an authority in some area entirely unrelated to the matter. Sometimes scientists are referred to as sources of expertise on topics other than science, such as peace and war or the future of mankind. In such cases, appeals to authority are totally flawed, for the expertise of the authorities is in areas that are irrelevant to the question at hand.

It is interesting to know the beliefs of famous people, and their opinions are certainly worth listening to. However, an argument of this type

1. S is a statement in area K.
2. X is an expert in area L (and not in area K).
3. X asserts S.
Therefore,
4. S is acceptable.

gives no support for S when K and L are two distinct areas of knowledge. In such cases, appeals to authority amount to fallacies involving irrelevance.

EXERCISE SET

Exercise 2

For the following examples, determine whether the passage contains an argument. If it does, assess whether the premises are relevant to the conclusion. If you find any premises to be irrelevant, say why you think they are irrelevant and—if appropriate—label the argument as containing *straw man, ad hominem, guilt by association, appeal to ignorance, appeal to popularity, improper analogy,* or *misuse of authority. Note:* Not all passages contain arguments, and not all arguments cited contain mistakes.

1. Background: In a letter to a Toronto paper, a writer commented on a favorable review of a feminist book. She took the occasion to give her own reasons for rejecting the feminist view of relations between the sexes, saying:

"I will not subscribe to a philosophy that purports to represent some sort of vague liberation from alleged wrongs while at the same time advocating to destroy traditions and democracy. . . . Let me just say that I vigorously oppose any ideology that arrogantly proposes to reduce my husband, my children, and myself (a traditional family) to superfluity simply because we don't fit into some sort of elitist, sexist new order."

(Assume for the purposes of this example that feminist philosophy is a general view of society according to which men have tended to dominate women, that women are entitled to legal and political rights fully equal to those of men, and that women are entitled to equal pay for work of equal value.)

(Letter to the editor, Toronto *Globe and Mail,* March 6, 1976)

2. *Background:* A museum has just fired four people from its board of directors. Jones criticizes the firing, whereas Smith defends it.

Jones: You know, the board of directors has behaved quite badly in firing four new directors. The people who were fired were all conscientious individuals who could have done a good job of administering the museum if they had been given a chance.

Smith: Really, you should not be so sentimental and emotional. Jobs come and go, and people in a competitive field have to be prepared to take some risks. You only reveal your own lack of understanding of the real problems of museum management when you pretend to criticize a public administrative body like the museum board.

3. Background: Smith and Jones are discussing moral vegetarianism. Moral vegetarianism is the theory and practice of not eating meat for the moral reason that the killing of animals is considered wrong, much in the way we consider the killing of people wrong. Jones defends the idea; Smith attacks it:

Jones: People should not kill animals for food. Animals can feel and be harmed just as humans can. Those being raised for food are often raised in inhumane conditions before they are killed. And, more often than not, they are killed in brutal ways and feel a lot of pain. Besides, people do not need meat in order to maintain their health. Vegetable proteins, such as the ones in peas, beans, and lentils, will do just as well.

Smith: This idea is ridiculous. Carnivorous animals kill other animals for food. Humans are more than carnivorous; they are omnivorous. It is natural for them to eat both plant and animal foods. We do not know what animal consciousness is like, so we must assume that they do not feel pain. Anyway, since animals kill each other, there is nothing wrong with us killing them.

4. In a poll, 75 percent of people interviewed said that they thought most other people would not be honest enough to return a lost wallet with $50 in it. You can see from this that most people are natural thieves.

5. Nature looks fantastic without clothes. Nobody thinks that seals, penguins, elephants, and

birds should be covered in the latest fashion. So why should people wear clothing? Nudity is great!

*6. *Background:* Journalist Peter Marin wrote an article in *Harper's Magazine* (1981) in which he claimed that Americans had not yet come to terms with the moral questions arising from their participation in the Vietnam War, and that veterans of that war were suffering from their incommunicable questions and feelings of guilt. A critic wrote to say that the article did not discuss any failings of anti-Vietnam spokespersons, such as actress Jane Fonda:

> "Jane Fonda and her pro-totalitarian pals are not only without guilt concerning the boat people, the poison-gassed Laotians, and the Cambodian victims of the Khmer Rouge genocide, they are avid apologists for such practices."

7. "A major cross-cultural difference in the way people approach problems is the speed at which they act and expect others to act. Americans, particularly in an East Coast business environment, often move at a hectic pace; appointments and travel plans are tightly scheduled. Among other peoples and in other parts of the world, life proceeds more leisurely."

(Roger Fisher and Scott Brown, *Getting Together: Building a Relationship That Gets to Yes* [Boston: Houghton Mifflin, 1988], p. 176)

*8. *Background:* In January 1984, an outspoken critic of pornography, Maude Barlow, published an essay against free distribution of pornography. She claimed that Playboy bunnies teach us that women have no proper place next to men. An objection to Barlow's views follows:

> "Why is it that Maude Barlow and others of her ilk feel compelled to argue their point by portraying the male half of society as a slobbering congregation of dimwits whose poorly formed collective intelligence lies putty-like waiting to be molded by Hugh Hefner and Bob Guccione? This attitude not only constitutes an insult to all men, but, ironically, betrays tremendous contempt for the real (not fantasy) women who actually shape our view of the world.
>
> "Inasmuch as Maude Barlow, like Mr. Hefner and Mr. Guccione, resorts to stereotypes to

sell her product, she should be classed with these other purveyors of drivel, and universally ignored."

(Letter to the Toronto *Globe and Mail,* January 27, 1984)

9. "More than 250,000 hairdressers the world over believe in what L'Oreal Hair Colouring can do for you. What more can we say?"

(Ad cited by R. H. Johnson and J. A. Blair in *Logical Self-Defense* [Toronto: McGraw-Hill-Ryerson, 1983], p. 160)

10. "As a child I accepted evolution until I saw the illogic of it. If life originated from non-life, how come our present superscientists can't even define it, let alone reproduce it? Where is the so-called missing link between animal and man? There is just no such thing. Certainly there is no evidence the animal pelvis rotated 90 degrees to produce the upright man, nor can any animal reason or think."

(Letter to the Calgary *Herald,* January 3, 1983)

11. Highly ambitious scientific projects have, for several decades, made attempts to communicate by radio wave with intelligent beings from planets other than earth. No response has been made. So probably there is no intelligent life elsewhere in the universe.

12. *Background:* A proposal was made to eliminate a tax deduction for a spouse who is financially dependent on a wage earner. The cabinet minister suggesting this elimination was Judy Erola:

> "Judy Erola's intent to deprive the family of spousal income tax deduction benefits is a clear indication to me of socialist-communist trends. Erola relegates women to the status of a brood sow. Let women produce and the state will take care of the offspring. It puts human reproduction ahead of the sanctity of the home and the quality of family life.
>
> "If a married woman wishes to make her home her castle, and the rearing of their children the most important goal of that period of her life, Erola should not intervene."

Hint: You should find more than one fallacy in this passage.

(Letter to the Calgary *Herald,* January 3, 1983)

*13. An art college should be administered by a professor or instructor of art, for only someone who knows art can understand art students, art standards, and the special problems an art college has.

14. *Background:* The following appeared as an advertisement in the magazine *Miss Chatelaine* in February 1976. The advertisement was accompanied by a large photograph of Wolfman Jack, a popular rock disc jockey:

"When those pimples pop up, you should break out the Clearasil Ointment. Listen—if you use a cleanser, that's fine. But I know how you feel when those pimples pop up. So lay out some acne medication on those pimples. Break out the Clearasil Ointment. Clearasil goes right after those acne pimples. Dries 'em up, helps heal 'em up, and that's just for starters.

"Clearasil hangs right in there . . . for hours . . . just soppin' up that extra oil you usually get with pimples. It's Canada's number-one selling acne medication.

"Take it from the Wolfman. Pimples . . . I've been there. I know."

*15. *Background:* A judge stated that the herbicides 2,4-D and 2,4,5-T were safe when he issued a judgment in favor of a corporation and against property owners who sought to prevent spraying near their homes. In the wake of this judgment, the following letter to the Toronto *Globe and Mail* appeared on October 31, 1983:

"It is obvious that most reporters and editorial and letter writers either have not read Judge Merlin Nunn's decision or their reading comprehension scores are abysmally low. He was unequivocal in clearly stating the herbicides 2,4-D and 2,4,5-T were safe for proper use. This legal case exposed the views of many well-known people and scientists testifying for both parties, and the decision was clearly in accord with independent, open scientific reviews held in many countries over the past 15 years. We should all be pleased that one perceived problem has been proved false, so we can concentrate on solving Canada's real ones."

16. *Background:* The following question and proposed answer are taken from a book on dream interpretation. Assume that the question posed in the first sentence is one that the authors are trying to answer in the rest of the passage and determine whether what they say is positively relevant, negatively relevant, or irrelevant as an answer to the question.

"Can we use dreams to enhance our creativity and inventiveness? I generally respond to this question by pointing out what a remarkably creative and inventive occurrence the dream itself is. Every dream is unique. The dreamer is expressing what has never been expressed before. He is effortlessly but nevertheless creatively, transforming something vaguely felt into a visual display which both captures and radiates the feelings involved. Everyone has a touch of the poet in him, even if it only comes out in a dream."

(Montague Ullman and Nan Zimmerman, *Working with Dreams* [Boston: Houghton Mifflin, 1979], p. 23)

◆ ## IRRELEVANCE, MISSING PREMISES, AND ARGUMENT CRITICISM

Criticizing an argument on grounds of relevance is a strong line of criticism, as we have seen. But you have to back up your criticism by saying why you think the premises are irrelevant to the conclusion. If you just say, "That's irrelevant," it does not put debate on a very high level. You should explain why you believe that premises are irrelevant. It is not enough, either, to just say, "that's ad hominem," or "you're using a straw man argument." The person whose argument you are criticizing may not understand these labels. Even if she does, you have to show why they apply to the particular case you are looking at.

In fact, logicians themselves disagree about relevance, but along somewhat different lines. Some claim that when arguments appear to have irrelevant premises, the problem is really that the arguments have missing premises. When these missing premises are added, they will link together with the stated premises, and the stated premises will then become relevant to the conclusion after all. This approach to irrelevance can make even the most blatant cases of irrelevance turn into something else.

For instance, consider our early example of irrelevance:

1. Smith is old and fat.

So,

2. Smith's views on Chinese politics are unacceptable.

We claimed earlier that in this argument the premise was completely irrelevant to the conclusion. But some logicians would claim that it is quite relevant to that conclusion, once the appropriate missing premises are written in. They find a basis for this approach by claiming that the arguer must have thought there was some kind of connection between being old and fat and having incorrect opinions about Chinese politics, so we should insert premises that will state the arguer's beliefs.

Here is one possible account:

1. Smith is old and fat.
3. People who are old tend to become senile and careless about the assessment of evidence.
4. People who are fat are often fat because they are emotionally disturbed, and being emotionally disturbed makes them unreliable interpreters of social affairs.

Therefore,

2. Smith's views on Chinese politics are unacceptable.

Let us call this a *reconstructed argument*. Logicians who use the missing premises approach to relevance and irrelevance would claim that this reconstructed argument is a better one than the original, for it contains no flaw of relevance. It is true, indeed, that the reconstructed argument contains no flaw of relevance. But whether it is a better argument is a debatable point, because the premises we added to avoid irrelevance are not acceptable. Also, the revised argument has the word *tend* in the premises; even if acceptable, the premises would not necessarily include Smith as an individual who shares these flaws. For that reason, it may be claimed that the revised argument fails on the (G) condition, unless the conclusion is moderated by adding a word such as *likely* or *probably*. What we have done is move the flaw in the original argument from one place (relevance) to others (acceptability of premises and adequacy of grounds for the stated conclusion).

The problem is not the only one. We have changed the original quite a lot by these additions. How did we know that (3) and (4) were the right premises to add? There are always a number of different possibilities as far as adding premises is concerned. For instance, here are two other quite different reconstructions of the argument about Smith and Chinese politics:

❖ ALTERNATIVE RECONSTRUCTION (a)

1.   Smith is old and fat.
5.   All views on politics held by people who are old and fat are false.
6.   Whatever views Smith holds on Chinese politics, these are views held by someone who is old and fat.
So,
2.   Smith's views on Chinese politics are unacceptable.

ALTERNATIVE RECONSTRUCTION (b)

1.   Smith is old and fat.
7.   The Chinese flatter the old out of respect for wisdom and the fat due to their assumption that to get fat you have to be rich.
8.   A person cannot adequately appraise the society of a country in which he and his kind are flattered.
So,
2.   Smith's views on Chinese politics are unacceptable.

A major difficulty with reconstructing arguments with the generous addition of missing premises is that there are usually a number of different, equally plausible, reconstructions that you can make up. In addition, this approach to analyzing arguments is long and cumbersome. It requires the critic to do so much writing that it almost seems as though she has been given the responsibility of writing the argument herself! If such controversial and sweeping premises were really missing from an argument, that gap would be the mistake of the person who put the argument forward. It is not really the responsibility of a critic to rectify such errors. Furthermore, generous argument reconstruction to avoid problems of relevance by including so-called missing premises can take you very far from the original in such cases as this one.

If an argument has a flaw of relevance, the extra premises that you would add in order to reconstruct it without irrelevance will be unacceptable in any case. For practical purposes, our approach and the reconstructing approach do not give such very different results. They are, however, quite different from a theoretical perspective.

❖   CHAPTER SUMMARY

We begin to explain relevance by distinguishing between positive relevance, negative relevance, and irrelevance. For the ARG conditions, positive relevance is required: in a cogent argument, the premises must be positively relevant to the conclusion. That means that they must count in favor of the conclusion; if true, they must provide evidence or reason that the conclusion is true or acceptable. If the premises are negatively relevant to the conclusion, that is, if they count against it, they obviously cannot support it in a cogent argument. In addition, premises must not be irrelevant to the conclusion; if they do not bear on its truth or falsity at all, the argument is seriously flawed. For argument cogency it is positive relevance that is required.

Ways in which the premises of an argument can be positively relevant to its conclusion include *deductive entailment, analogy* (similarity of cases), *inductive support* (presumption that examined cases provide a basis for expectations about unexamined ones), and *providing reasons* (factors that are reasons to think a claim true).

The irrelevance of premises to the conclusion constitutes a serious flaw in argument. Allegations of irrelevance should be supported and explained. It is not a good criticism of an argument to simply say that the premises are irrelevant and leave it at that.

There are a number of important and interesting fallacies involving irrelevance. These include *straw man, ad hominem, guilt by association, fallacious appeal to ignorance,* and *fallacious appeal to popularity.* In addition, arguments of types that are, in general, quite legitimate can involve irrelevance in some extreme cases. For instance, in seriously flawed appeal to authority or arguments by analogy, the premises may be irrelevant to the conclusion.

When irrelevance occurs, it can be mended or remedied by a reconstruction of the argument using one or more additional premises that link the premise with the conclusion. However, such a procedure is of little real use, because the added premises are virtually always unacceptable.

❖ ## REVIEW OF TERMS INTRODUCED

Positive relevance A statement is positively relevant to the truth of another statement if and only if its truth would give some evidence or reason to support the truth of that other statement. That is, if the first statement were true, that would count in favor of the second one being true.

Negative relevance A statement is negatively relevant to the truth of another statement if and only if its truth would give some reason or evidence for the falsity of that other statement. That is, if the first statement were true, that would count in favor of the second one being false.

Irrelevance A statement is irrelevant to the truth of another statement if and only if its truth or falsity neither counts in favor of the truth of that other statement nor counts toward that other statement's being false. If the truth of one statement is irrelevant to the truth of another, it is neither positively relevant to it nor negatively relevant to it.

Non sequitur An argument in which the premise has no bearing on the conclusion. *Non sequitur* is a Latin phrase used to refer to irrelevance; it means "it does not follow."

Red herring A premise or remark that is irrelevant to the conclusion or issue being discussed, so that it tends to distract people and lead them away from the topic at issue.

Straw man fallacy A fallacy committed when a person misrepresents an argument, theory, or claim, and then, on the basis of that misrepresentation, claims to have refuted the position the person has misrepresented.

Ad hominem fallacy A fallacy committed when an irrelevant premise about the background, personality, or character of a person is given in an attempt to show that the person's theories or arguments are false or unacceptable. Such premises about personality and background are relevant only if the person himself or herself is the issue in question (as in an election) or if the reliability of his or her testimony or authority is at stake.

Guilt-by-association fallacy A fallacy committed when a person or a person's views are criticized on the basis of a supposed link between them and a person or movement believed to be disreputable.

Fallacious appeals to ignorance Arguments in which there is either an appeal to our ignorance about S in an attempt to show that not-S is true or probable, or an appeal to our ignorance about not-S in an attempt to show that S is true or probable.

Burden of proof Obligation, or duty, to support one's claims by argument and evidence. The burden of proof is usually said to rest on the party introducing a claim that needs proof. Various different principles can be proposed as to which sorts of claims need proof, and these will give different ideas of where the "burden of proof lies," as we put it colloquially.

Fallacious appeals to popularity A fallacy in which one reasons from the popularity of a product or belief to a conclusion about its actual merits. Also called the popularity fallacy, the bandwagon fallacy, or "ad populam."

Reconstructed argument An argument in which the inferences (or steps) have been made more orderly, logical, and sensible by the addition of extra premises. Where the unreconstructed, or original, argument had a fallacy of relevance, the reconstructed argument will not. Typically, however, premises added to produce such a reconstruction are unacceptable.

Notes

1. *For instructors:* Relevance here is defined using the notion of truth. There is no contradiction between this definition and the replacement of truth by acceptability in the ARG conditions. To say that acceptability is to replace truth in conditions of an argument's cogency is not to say that truth is to be eliminated as a central epistemic and logical concept. I have benefitted from the discussion of relevance in James Freeman's text, *Thinking Logically: Basic Concepts for Reasoning* (Englewood Cliffs, N.J.: Prentice-Hall, 1988) and from discussions with Tony Blair and David Hitchcock.

There are, however, complex technical problems about defining relevance that are not dealt with here because to consider them would take us too far away from the level suitable for a textbook account. I owe my understanding of these problems to John Woods, whose deep worries about how relevance can be formally defined are only partially addressed here. Some improvement on the definition offered in the chapter can be made by the following amendments:

(i) *S* is positively relevant to *X* if and only if either the truth of *S* counts in favor of the truth of *X,* or the falsity of *S* counts in favor of the falsity of *X,* or both.

(ii) *S* is negatively relevant to *X* if and only if either the truth of *S* counts in favor of the falsity of *X,* or the falsity of *S* counts in favor of the truth of *X,* or both.

(iii) *S* is irrelevant to *X* if and only if *S* is neither positively relevant to *X* nor negatively relevant to *X.*

In this account, "counts in favor of" is taken as an undefined term and is understood as a connection logically weaker than that of material implication. For the purposes of argument analysis, the simpler definition offered in the chapter is adequate, since premises are put forward as true or acceptable, not as false.

2. Adapted from a letter to the Toronto *Globe and Mail,* February 8, 1982.

3. Letter to the Toronto *Star,* April 8, 1981.

4. Sidney Lens, "The Most Dangerous Cliché," *Nation,* September 11, 1982, p. 210.

5. Roger Fisher and Scott Brown, *Getting Together* (Boston: Houghton Mifflin, 1988), p. 5.

6. Advertisement cited by *Harrowsmith,* September 1980.

7. I owe this example to Douglas Walton, who cited it in his *The Arguer's Position: A Pragmatic Study of Ad Hominem Attack, Criticism, Refutation, and Fallacy* (Westport, Conn.: Greenwood Press, 1985), p. 284.

8. Anne Roche, "On Killing Inconvenient People," *Saturday Night,* September 1973, pp. 29–31.

9. Leslie Freeman, *Nuclear Witnesses* (New York: Norton, 1981) contains fascinating background material on this case.

10. Toronto *Globe and Mail,* September 4, 1980, p. 1.

11. It would be an exaggeration to say that the burden of proof has rested entirely on those who would object to a product as harmful; there are legal requirements for potential products, especially those involving chemicals and pharmaceuticals, to undergo tests. However, the tests do not include long-term effects and have been criticized on various grounds for their unreliability and lack of stringency.

12. A. S. Neill, cited by Richard Robinson in "Arguing from Ignorance," *Philosophical Quarterly,* Vol. 21, No. 3; pp. 97–107; see p. 97.

13. It can happen that things are popular because they are, in some respect, good. But this is not always the case and, in any event, the point at issue here is whether things can be shown to be good because they are popular.

14. Appeals to the popularity of beliefs should not be confused with the notion of common knowledge developed in Chapter 5. The difference is that the belief whose popularity is appealed to is not universal in a culture, nor is it basic and elementary. Typically, its content is somewhat controversial, speculative, or normative, but it is claimed to be popular.

15. Cited by R. H. Johnson and J. A. Blair in *Logical Self-Defense* (Toronto: McGraw-Hill-Ryerson, 1983), p. 167.

16. I owe this point to Cary MacWilliams.

17. Glenn Babb, interviewed on CBC Television on July 13, 1986, used the zebra argument to object to economic sanctions against the government of South Africa. The same argument was used a week later by U.S. President Ronald Reagan, who attributed it to a South African official.

CHAPTER 7

Those Tidy Deductions: Categorical Logic

WE HAVE DISCUSSED TWO OF THE conditions of an argument's adequacy: acceptability and relevance. We now move on to the (G) condition to see various ways in which premises may work together to provide good and sufficient grounds for the conclusion. In this chapter and the next one, our project is to become more clear about deductively valid arguments by learning about some simple forms of arguments in which the premises deductively entail the conclusion.

DEDUCTIVE RELATIONS

One statement deductively entails another if and only if it is impossible for the second one to be false, given that the first one is true. That is, the state of affairs in which statement (1) is true and statement (2) is false is logically impossible. That a person is a mother deductively entails that she is female, for it is a logical impossibility for a person to be a mother and not be female. A logical impossibility is a state of affairs that just could not exist.

When an argument is deductively valid, it is impossible for all the premises to be true and the conclusion false. An argument like this is entirely adequate as far as the (R) and (G) conditions are concerned, so any question about its cogency must have to do with the acceptability of its premises.

Many arguments that are deductively valid owe their validity to their logical form. The validity of such arguments comes from a general structural property—their logical form—and all other arguments of that form are also deductively valid. Here are several simple examples of formally valid arguments.

EXAMPLE 1

This example is deductively valid by virtue of its *categorical* form. That is, the deductive connection depends on the way in which the categories of things are related to each other in the premises and in the conclusion.

1. All consistent opponents of killing are opponents of capital punishment.
2. No opponents of capital punishment are orthodox traditional Catholics.
So,
3. No consistent opponents of killing are orthodox traditional Catholics.

Leaving out some words, we could rewrite this argument as:

All . . . are . . .
No . . . are . . .
Therefore,
No . . . are . . .

Now we will replace the words that have been left out with letters. Let C = consistent opponents of killing; let O = opponents of capital punishment; let T = orthodox traditional Catholics. These letters represent categories of things. It is a good idea to keep a kind of record or dictionary reminding ourselves which letter represents which category. The argument can be written as follows:

All C are O.
No O are T.
Therefore,
No C are T.

The connection between the premises and the conclusion depends on the way "all" and "no" and the categories are related. Any argument with the same logical form would be deductively valid as well. Consider the following.

1. All politicians are lovers of power.
2. No lovers of power are entirely trustworthy people.
Therefore,
3. No politicians are entirely trustworthy people.

This second argument has the same logical form as the original example and is also deductively valid.

EXAMPLE 2

The following example is a deductively valid argument that is also valid in virtue of its categorical form.

1. No illiterate people are able to manage tax returns.
2. Some business persons are able to manage tax returns.
Therefore,
3. Some business persons are not illiterate people.

Leaving out the details of which categories are involved, we can see that the argument has the following form:

No . . . are . . .
Some . . . are . . .
Therefore,
Some . . . are not . . .

Putting in letters to represent the categories of illiterate people (L), people able to manage tax returns (M), and business persons (B), we have the following version of the argument:

No L are M
Some B are M
Therefore,
Some B are not L

The following argument has a different content, but the same categorical form, as Example 2:

No mathematicians are frivolous characters.
Some actors are frivolous characters.
Therefore,
Some actors are not mathematicians.

You may have been puzzled to read that the arguments in Examples 1 and 2 were deductively valid when you were perhaps skeptical about whether their premises were acceptable. Deductive validity has to do with the (R) and (G) conditions, not with the (A) condition. If an argument is deductively valid, then if its premises are true, its conclusion is true also. (Of course this is not to say that its premises are true, or are acceptable.)

It is important, then, not to confuse the matter of deductive validity with the issue of how acceptable the premises are. These are quite distinct issues. Just to emphasize the point, take a look at the following argument. The premises are demonstrably false, but the argument is deductively valid.

1. All politicians are warm-hearted mothers.
2. No warm-hearted mothers are people who would do anything to increase the likelihood of war.
Therefore,
3. No politicians are people who would do anything to increase the likelihood of war.

In this example, both premises are easily refutable, so they are not acceptable. In fact, the conclusion is also refutable; we know that it is false. However, the argument is deductively valid by virtue of its form. It has the same form, in fact, as Example 1 earlier. If both premises were true, the conclusion would be true. The premises are connected to the conclusion because of the connections between the categories of things referred to.

A deductively valid argument with false or unacceptable premises gives no real support to its conclusion, even though such an argument has a certain logical elegance and very cleanly and neatly satisfies the (R) and (G) conditions: *the formal validity of an argument is distinct from the truth, or acceptability, of its premises.* A good argument must satisfy all three of the ARG conditions. Deductively valid arguments satisfy (R) and (G) but may fail to satisfy (A).

One further thing to note is that it is not always by virtue of logical form that deductive relations hold. Sometimes one statement deductively entails another by virtue of its meaning. For instance, the statement "John is a father" entails "John is male" because of what it means to be a father.[1] It is logically impossible for anyone to be a father and not be male. The meanings of the terms *father* and *male* are what make the inference from the first statement to the second one a deductively valid inference.

Simple deductive relationships based on form and meaning are essential in our understanding of written and spoken language. Indeed, we have been presupposing these relationships all along in this text—just as we presuppose them in all understanding of language. Whenever we scrutinize a passage to see whether it contains an argument, or ask how to best represent its premises and conclusions in clear simple language, we are—in effect—asking what is and what is not deductively entailed by what was said.

Probably you can intuitively grasp the fact that:

1. All *S* are *M*.
2. No *M* are *P*.
Therefore,
3. No *S* are *P*.

is a form representing a deductively valid argument. If most people could not, in some sense, understand this sort of fact, formal systems would not have developed at all. Nonetheless, the logical intuitions people have can be usefully systematized, explained, and developed by the articulation of formal systems in logic. Formal logic develops and systematizes our intuitive understanding. When arguments depend on their form for deductive validity, we can represent them in a symbolic way that will reveal that form without representing the specific content of the argument. Then, using rules dealing only with formal relationships, we can determine the deductive validity of the symbolized arguments. Often this technique can be very helpful and enlightening because the content of an argument may distract us from formal relationships.

Formal logic is a highly developed and intricate subject, and there are many excellent texts in the field. Our book does not treat formal logic in great detail. In our treatment we concentrate on those aspects of the subject most pertinent to ordinary speech and writing, and we emphasize the application of formal techniques to arguments you may find in ordinary speech, in everyday life, and in the study of a variety of subjects. Our treatment of formal logic will cover two areas: categorical logic (this chapter) and propositional logic (Chapter 8).

FOUR CATEGORICAL FORMS

Categorical logic uses *all, some, are,* and *not* as its basic logical terms. There terms are used to tell, in a general way, how many members of one category are included in, or excluded from, another category. Categorical logic is the oldest branch of formal logic. It was for many centuries thought to comprise all of formal logic. (As we shall see later, this belief is no longer held: it is now known that categorical logic is an important *part* of formal logic.)

In our simple example we considered the following argument:

1. All consistent opponents of killing are opponents of capital punishment.
2. No opponents of capital punishment are orthodox traditional Catholics.
So,
3. No consistent opponents of killing are orthodox traditional Catholics.

In this argument both premises and conclusion are in categorical form. That is, they are statements in which a subject category is connected to a predicate category. The first statement makes a universal affirmation, whereas the second two state universal negations:

UNIVERSAL AFFIRMATION

All *S* are *P.* (Says all the members of the *S* category are included within the *P* category. Example: All sisters are female persons.)

UNIVERSAL NEGATION

No *S* are *P.* (Says all members of the *S* category are excluded from the *P* category. Example: No sisters are male persons.)

For convenient reference, logicians call the universal affirmation an "*A* statement" and the universal negation an "*E* statement." Not all statements in categorical form are universal. There are two further categorical forms:

PARTICULAR AFFIRMATION

Some *S* are *P.* (Says some members of the *S* category are included in the *P* category. Example: Some sisters are pianists.)

PARTICULAR NEGATION

Some *S* are not *P.* (Says some members of the *S* category are excluded from the *P* category. Example: Some sisters are not pianists.)

The particular affirmative is referred to as the "*I* statement" and the particular negation as the "*O* statement." These shorthand ways of referring to the categorical forms come from two Latin words: *affirmo* and *nego. Affirmo* means "I affirm" and *nego* means "I deny."

The four categorical forms are arranged in a square called the *Square of Opposition.* It looks like this:

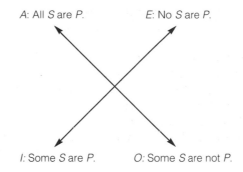

A: All *S* are *P*.   *E*: No *S* are *P*.

I: Some *S* are *P*.   *O*: Some *S* are not *P*.

The opposition is apparent when we look at the diagonals on the square. Each proposition is the contradictory of the one diagonally opposed to it: if all *S* are *P*, then it must be false that some *S* are not *P;* and if no *S* are *P*, then it must be false that some *S* are *P*. When one statement is the contradictory of another the two always have opposite truth values; if one is true the other is false, and vice versa.

The *A* and *E* statements are fully universal. They are true only under the condition that every single member of the subject class is included in the predicate class (*A*) or excluded from the predicate class (*E*). That is, an *A* statement states that every member of the subject category is included in the predicate category, and an *E* statement states that everything in the subject category is excluded from the predicate category. A technical way of putting this is to say that in both *A* and *E*, the subject term is *distributed.* A term is said to be distributed, in a categorical statement, if the statement says something about every item falling under that term. In an *A* statement, the predicate term is not distributed, although in an *E* statement, it is. Compare, for instance, the *A* statement "all sisters are female persons" with the *E* statement "no sisters are male persons." In the *A* statement, "female persons" is not distributed, because the statement is about all sisters, but it is *not* about all female persons. It does not say that all female persons are sisters. However, in the *E* statement, "no sisters are male persons," the predicate term, "male persons," is distributed. All the sisters are excluded from the entire male category; if no sisters are male persons, then no male persons are sisters.

The *I* and *O* statements do not include or exclude the whole subject category, only part of it. But *part* is rather vague. The word *some* is taken to mean "at least one" for the purposes of categorical logic. Thus, the *I* statement that some men are fathers says that at least one man is a father. The statement "some men are fathers" does not make an assertion about all men. Similarly, the statement that some men are not fathers (an *O* statement) does not make a statement about all men. In the *I* and *O* statements, the subject term (*S*) is not distributed because the statements are not about all the items within the subject category. In the *I* statement, the predicate term is not distributed either. For instance, "some men are fathers" says that the classes of men and fathers overlap; there are some men in the father category. This tells us something about part of the father category but not about all of it. However, in the O statement, the predicate term is distributed, because the subject items are, in effect, excluded from the entire predicate category.

NATURAL LANGUAGE AND CATEGORICAL FORM

A number of useful formal rules of inference can be applied to statements in categorical form. These rules can be extremely helpful in getting deductive relationships straight. But in order to use them, we have to be working with statements that really are in categorical form. The rules don't necessarily apply to other statements. Few statements in English or other natural languages, however, are spoken or written in perfect categorical form. Many statements in natural languages are basically of the subject-predicate type, and these statements can be put into categorical form. Because our purpose in this text is practical, we shall emphasize the relation between natural wording and categorical form.

The Universal Affirmative: A

The *A* statement (universal affirmative) in categorical form begins with the word *all*. The word *all* is followed by a noun or noun phrase specifying a category of things; the category is followed by the word *are* or another form of the verb "to be," which in turn is followed by another noun or noun phrase specifying a category of things. Strictly speaking, the sentence "All mothers are human" is not in categorical form, because the predicate is only an adjective. To put that sentence in categorical form, we would have to rewrite it as "All mothers are human beings." In a somewhat similar way, many sentences in English can be put into the form of *A* statements with slight linguistic alterations. (You must be careful, however, that the statement as reworded captures the meaning of the original one.)

Consider, for instance, these statements, which are all verbal variations of "All *S* are *P*."

> Any *S* is *P.*
> Every single *S* is *P.*
> The *S*'s are all *P*'s.
> Whatever *S* you look at, it is bound to be a *P.*
> Each *S* is a *P.*
> *S*'s are *P*'s.
> An *S* is a *P.*
> If it's an *S*, it's a *P.*

All can be translated into *A* statements as "All *S* are *P*."

Very often statements are made in such a way that it is not explicitly said whether the statement is universal or particular. Look at these statements, for instance:

A monkey has a tail.
A bachelor is an unmarried man.
A bank is in a good position when interest rates are high.
Wars lead to pillage and rape.
Politicians are overworked.

All these sentences are of the subject-predicate type. But as they stand, none are in categorical form. To put them in categorical form, we would have to determine whether the intent is to make a universal or particular statement, we would have to make sure we have two categories of things—not just an adjective in the predicate. The results for these statements would look like this:

All monkeys are creatures with tails.
All bachelors are unmarried men.
All banks are things that are in a good position when interest rates are high.
All(?) wars are things that lead to pillage and rape.
All(?) politicians are overworked people.

Sometimes, as in the last two cases here, merely asking whether the statement is universal or particular can be an important critical step. Often people make unqualified statements without making it clear whether they really wish to make an assertion about all of the category or part of it. The indeterminacy, or ambiguity, as to how many entities are being discussed can be exploited. A statement about all members of a category is, in general, more interesting than one about some. However, as we have seen already when discussing the scope of statements in Chapter 2 and acceptability in Chapter 5, restricted statements are generally more likely to be acceptable than universal ones.

You can be led into accepting stereotypes by an uncritical response to unqualified statements. For instance, if you hear that homeless people are alcoholics you may naturally accept the statement because it is borne out by some encounters you have had with homeless people who smell of liquor or who have bottles of wine. Strictly speaking, these cases show that an *I* statement that some homeless people are alcoholics is true. But the *A* statement (All homeless people are alcoholics), which is how "homeless people are alcoholics" would be interpreted by many people, is quite certainly false. People may come to be homeless for many reasons: premature release from mental hospitals, severe unanticipated financial problems leading to the loss of a house, prolonged unemployment, and other causes. Stereotyping people—putting them into categories and making universal judgments about all members of the category—is generally to be avoided. It is intellectually careless and, all too often, ethically and politically dangerous as well.[2]

Statements in which the word *only* is used are implicitly universal. Consider this example:

Only students fluent in English are permitted to enroll in the University of California.

Let us allow *F* to represent "students fluent in English" and *U* to represent "people allowed to enroll in the University of California." The statement may be written in simpler form as:

Only *F* are *U*.

We have to rewrite this as an *A* statement because the four categorical forms do not let us use the word *only*. The right way to do it is as follows:

Only *F* are *U* = All *U* are *F*.

That is, if only students fluent in English are allowed to enroll, then we know that all students allowed to enroll will be fluent in English.

Think about this example carefully. Statements like this can easily confuse people. They may want to interpret them as saying:

Only *F* are *U* = (?) All *F* are *U* (*Wrong!*)

Reading this over, you can see how absurd it is. It says that everyone fluent in English can enroll! Clearly this is not what the original statement asserted. Rather, it asserted that all admitted will be fluent, since the others will have been disqualified.

The Universal Negative: E

There are also many different ways of expressing *E* statements (*universal negative*) in English. Consider the following:

Not a single whale can fly.
Whales can't fly.
None of the beings who are whales can fly.
There never was a whale that could fly.
No whale can fly.
Whales are not able to fly.

All of these sentences are variations of the following:

No whales are creatures that can fly.

This statement is in proper categorical form; it has two categories of things plus *no* and *are*.

There are some other cases that people occasionally find tricky. For instance:

Not all doctors are rich. (not an *E* statement)

Here, "not all" does not mean "none." The statement that not all doctors are rich is the denial of an *A* statement (all doctors are rich); as such it is the assertion of the *O* statement, not *E*. The words *not all* before the subject should not be translated as "none."

One type of statement that is easy to confuse with the "not all" statement is "All so-and-so are not such-and-such." Statements of this type are quite ambiguous and can be very confusing in some contexts. Consider the following:

All women aren't aggressive.

This statement could be read as being of the *A* type and would then appear in categorical form with the *not* taken as part of the predicate: "All women are nonaggressive." With this reading, the statement attributes a property to all women, and the property just happens to be a negative one—negatively defined, that is. However, it can also be read as an *O* statement. On this interpretation, *not* really applies to the whole sentence, which is equivalent to "Not all women are aggressive," which is to say that (*O*) some women are not aggressive. If you come across such statements, you have to estimate whether an *A* statement (with a negated predicate) or an *O* statement (with the original predicate) is being asserted. The *A* statement and the *O* statement are *not* logically equivalent; it is important to determine which is being meant.

The Particular Affirmative: I

The *I* statement (*particular affirmative*) asserts that some in the subject category are also in the predicate category. *Some* can mean just one, several, or very many—anything greater than none and less than all. One trick about *I* statements is to be aware of what they are *not* saying! Typically, when we use them, we suggest more than we actually assert. For instance, imagine a student who remarks that some professors are competent. People who hear the comment are likely to think, "Well, if he thought that all professors were competent, he would tell us; so if he thinks only *some* are, that must be because he thinks there are others who are not." But strictly speaking this is not what the student says, nor is it deductively entailed by what he says. According to strict categorical logic, he says only that there is at least one competent professor.

When an indefinite article such as *a* or *an* precedes the subject, the statement made can be either universal or particular. We already saw some examples in which there is a universal intent, as in "A monkey has a tail." In contexts in which the statement clearly refers to some one indefinitely specified individual, as in

A women came to the door canvassing for Greenpeace.

the sentence should be put into categorical form as *I:*

Some women are persons who came to the door trying to raise funds for Greenpeace.

Categorical logic allows us to speak of all, some, or none of the items in a category. It does not allow us to speak of individuals as such. Note how tense is handled in this example. The categorical forms are indifferent to tense and must express it by specifications within the predicate category: here it appears in the framing of the predicate category as "persons who came to the door canvassing for Greenpeace."

The Particular Negative: O

We have seen that *not all* before the subject is a way of denying the universal affirmation, and thus a way of asserting the *particular negation: O*. Thus:

> Not all mammals live on land.

goes into categorical form as:

> Some mammals are not creatures that live on land.

Just as *I* often suggests *O,* but does not assert it, *O* often suggests—but does not assert—*I*. A person who says, for instance, that some patrons of health food stores are not fanatics is likely to be interpreted as saying, in addition, that some of their patrons are fanatics. This claim, however, is only suggested by his comment: it is not said and not deductively entailed. (In deductive logic, we do not take what is merely suggested to be part of the content of people's remarks.)

In *O* statements, the word *not* must perform the function of excluding some items in the subject category from the predicate category. The word *not* should not be replaced by a negative particle within the predicate category. The statement:

> Some teachers are persons who are not happy with their work.

is not a statement of the *O* form. It is an *I* statement that happens to have a predicate category (persons who are not happy with their work) with a negative particle inside it.

◆──

EXERCISE SET

Exercise 1

Translate the following sentences into categorical form and state which of the four forms—*A, E, I, O*—you have used. Be prepared to defend your answer. If you think that any sentence is ambiguous as to which of the categorical forms it exemplifies, say so and explain why. *Note:* You are not intended to discuss whether the statements are true or false, acceptable or unacceptable, but merely to write them in categorical form as *A, E, I,* or *O*.

1. Every nuclear installation is at risk of being attacked by terrorists.

*2. A student came to the office asking to be excused from the final examination.

3. No journalists are careful scholars.

4. The early bird gets the worm.

*5. Only the rich can afford to stay at London's prestigious hotels.

*6. Some evangelists are not poets.

7. Spare the rod and spoil the child.

Hint: Think of this as being shorthand for a statement about people who spare the rod.

8. At least one winning athlete was from Peterborough, Ontario.

9. No lakes near Kelowna are seriously polluted.

*****10.** Not all textbooks are boring.

11. Some cabinet ministers do not speak German.

*****12.** Mathematicians love abstraction.

13. Some confrontations lead to violence.

14. A place for everything, and everything in its place.

Hint: Use two statements.

*****15.** A woman with a job outside the home and no assistance with household work is burdened with at least two jobs.

*****16.** My enemy's enemy is my friend.

17. No mother of infant triplets could possibly have any time to relax!

18. A stitch in time saves nine.

*****19.** A rose by any other name would be as sweet.

Hint: Complete the predicate term.

*****20.** No communist country has a consumer-oriented economy.

VENN DIAGRAMS

The meanings of the *A, E, I,* and *O* statements can be shown on diagrams in which circles represent the categories of things. These diagrams are called *Venn diagrams,* after the nineteenth-century English philosopher and logician John Venn. Many people find Venn diagrams helpful because they enable us to show the meanings of the *A, E, I, O* statements visually and to understand the logical relationships between them in terms of simple pictures.

Venn diagrams offer a system for representing whether there is something or nothing in an area of logical space. Logical space is represented in circles and parts of circles. To indicate that there is nothing in an area of logical space, we shade in the area. To indicate that there is something, we put an *x* in the space.

Look at the following two overlapping circles. We call the circle on the left the *S* circle because it represents the subject category and that on the right the *P* circle because it represents the predicate category. When we make the circles overlap we have three areas for the categories *S* and *P.* There is area (1) for those things that are *S* and are not *P,* area (2) for those things that are both *S* and *P,* and area (3) for those things that are *P* and are not *S.* Things that are not *S* and not *P* would be outside the circles entirely.

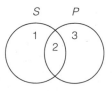

To show an *A* statement we have to indicate its meaning by marking the relevant areas of logical space. The *A* statement says "All *S* are *P.*" If all *S* are *P,*

then there are no *S* outside the *P* category. To indicate this relationship on a Venn diagram, we shade in area (1), as follows:

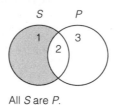

All *S* are *P*.

For instance, if *S* were the category of sisters and *P* were the category of female persons, the (true) claim that all sisters are female persons would be represented on this diagram of the *A* statement. The area of sisters who are not female is shaded in to represent the fact that nothing is in it.

For the *E* statement, we need to indicate that No *S* are *P*. That is, there is no overlap between the categories. On the Venn diagram, area (2) represents the overlap; the space in area (2) is part of both the *S* circle and the *P* circle. The *E* statement says that there is nothing in it; to represent this, we shade in area (2). For example, suppose that *S* were the category of women and *P* were the category of men. Then consider the *E* statement "No women are men." Area (2) represents those women that are men; there are none; area (2) is shaded in to indicate that this logical space is empty.

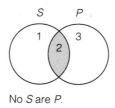

No *S* are *P*.

The *I* statement, "Some *S* are *P*," says that there is at least one thing that is both *S* and *P*. That is to say, the overlap area, area (2), does have something in it. We represent this by putting an *x* in area (2). If *S* is the category of men and *P* is the category of fathers, then the *I* statement says "Some men are fathers." There is something in area (2); the *x* placed there indicates the fact that there are men who are fathers.

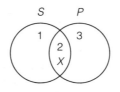

Some *S* are *P*.

The O statement, "Some S are not P," says that there is at least one thing in the S category that is not in the P category. To indicate this, we put an x in area (1), which is the space for things that are S but are not P. If S is the category of men and P is the category of athletes, then the O statement relating these categories is "Some men are not athletes." That is, there are men outside the athlete category, as is indicated by the x in area (1) of the diagram.

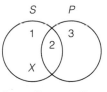

Some S are not P.

As we shall see, Venn diagrams are useful in showing logical relationships between categorical statements, and in determining the validity of some arguments that can be expressed in categorical form.

RULES OF IMMEDIATE INFERENCE

We are now in a position to see some of the formal rules of categorical logic. First we will look at rules for *immediate inference*. If you have two statements, and the first deductively entails the second, then you can immediately (that is, without intermediate steps) infer the second from the first. There are a number of operations involving the A, E, I, and O statements. These are common and important, and some will give us valid immediate inferences.

Conversion

The *converse* of a statement in categorical form is constructed by reversing its subject and predicate. Thus:

STATEMENT	CONVERSE OF STATEMENT
A: All S are P.	All P are S.
E: No S are P.	No P are S.
I: Some S are P.	Some P are S.
O: Some S are not P.	Some P are not S.

For the E and I statements, the original statement and its converse are logically equivalent. For instance, if no men are women, then no women are men; this illustrates the relationship of *logical equivalence* between an E statement and its converse. If some sisters are women, that is to say that some women are sisters; this illustrates the relationship of logical equivalence between an I statement and its converse. Logically equivalent statements deductively entail each other. When two statements are logically equivalent, either they are both true or they are both false. It is impossible for one to be false given that the other is true. You can see that the converse is logically equivalent here, in all likelihood, but in any case the logical facts can be represented neatly on Venn diagrams. The *E* statement and its converse look like this:

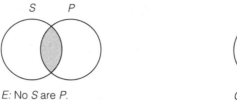

E: No S are P.   *Converse of E: No P are S.*

The *I* statement and its converse look like this:

I: Some S are P.   *Converse of I: Some P are S.*

The conversion of *A* and *O* statements does not result in statements logically equivalent to the originals. By looking at these diagrams, you will be able to see why.

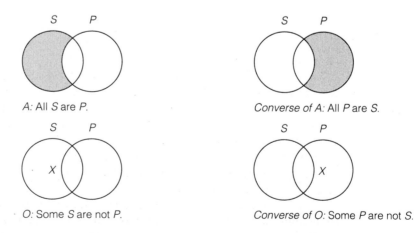

A: All S are P.   *Converse of A: All P are S.*

O: Some S are not P.   *Converse of O: Some P are not S.*

Many people mistakenly believe that there is a logical equivalence between an *A* statement and its converse. This is a common source of errors in reasoning. Consider the *A* statement "All communists are socialists." This is a true statement. But the converse, "All socialists are communists," is not true, and it does not follow from the statement "All communists are socialists." Political history in Canada and the United States might be quite different if the confusion between this statement and its converse were less common.

Contraposition

To contrapose a statement in categorical form, you first convert it and then attach a *non* to each category. It works like this:

STATEMENT	CONTRAPOSITIVE OF STATEMENT
A: All *S* are *P.*	All non-*P* are non-*S.*
E: No *S* are *P.*	No non-*P* are non-*S.*
I: Some *S* are *P.*	Some non-*P* are non-*S.*
O: Some *S* are not *P.*	Some non-*P* are not non-*S.*

For *A* and *O* statements the original and the *contrapositive* are logically equivalent. An *A* statement says that all *S* are *P.* Its contrapositive says that all non-*P* are non-*S.* Given the *A* statement, the contrapositive must be true because if it were not true, there would be a non-*P* that was an *S,* which would be contrary to what the *A* statement asserts. Consider the *A* statement "all doctors are educated"; its contrapositive, "all non-educated persons are non-doctors," is logically equivalent to it.

An *O* statement is also logically equivalent to its contrapositive. Consider, for instance, the *O* statement "some musicians are not dentists." Its contrapositive is "some non-dentists are not non-musicians." "Some non-dentists are not non-musicians" would be an odd thing to say, to be sure; the wording is clumsy because not being a non-musician is the same thing as being a musician. Nevertheless, "some non-dentists are not non-musicians" is true whenever "some musicians are not dentists" is true, and false whenever it is false. An *O* statement is logically equivalent to its contrapositive.

The contrapositives of *E* and *I* statements are not logically equivalent to these statements. The *E* statement, no *S* are *P,* has as its contrapositive, no non-*P* are non-*S.* These statements say quite different things. The first says that the two categories *S* and *P* do not intersect at all; there are no items in both at once. The second says that what is outside the *S* category does not intersect at all with what is outside the *P* category—a quite different thing. (Compare "no cats are dogs" with "no non-dogs are non-cats." The first is obviously true and the second is obviously false. A piece of cheese, for instance, is both a non-dog and a non-cat!) If one of the statements is true and the other is false, they can't possibly be equivalent to each other.

The *I* statement, some *S* are *P,* has as its contrapositive the statement that some non-*P* are non-*S.* These statements are not logically equivalent. The *I* statement asserts that there is at least one thing that is in both the *S* and *P* categories. Its contrapositive, on the other hand, asserts that there is at least one thing that is outside both categories. Compare the *I* statement "some cats are fluffy creatures" with its contrapositive "some non-fluffy creatures are non-cats." In this instance, both happen to be true. You can no doubt think of at least one fluffy cat, so you can see that the *I* statement is true. As for a non-fluffy non-cat, well many things fit this rather strange description—from swimming pools to loaves of bread! Even though in this case the *I* and its contrapositive are both true, they are not logically equivalent. They do not entail each other.

Obversion

Obversion is an operation that can be performed on all four kinds of categorical statements to produce a logically equivalent statement. To obvert a statement in categorical form, you do two things: first you add a *non* to the predicate category; then you change the statement from negative to affirmative, or vice versa. This means you change the quality of the statement (whether it is negative or affirmative).

The obverse of "all fathers are men" is "no fathers are non-men":

STATEMENT	OBVERSE OF STATEMENT
A: All *S* are *P.*	No *S* are non-*P.*
E: No *S* are *P.*	All *S* are non-*P.*
I: Some *S* are *P.*	Some *S* are not non-*P.*
O: Some *S* are not *P.*	Some *S* are non-*P.*

Contradictories

You will have noticed, perhaps, that *A* and *O* work in the same way: for *A* and *O* statements, conversion does not produce a logically equivalent statement, whereas contraposition does. Also, *E* and *I* work in the same way: for *E* and *I* statements, conversion does produce a logically equivalent statement, whereas contraposition does not. These relations exist because the *O* statement is the denial of the *A* statement, and the *I* statement is the denial of the *E* statement. *A* and *O* are *contradictory* to each other; so are *E* and *I*. The truth of one of these statements entails the falsehood of the other. If it is true that all swans are white, it must be false that some swans are not white. And if it is true that no tennis players are joggers, it must be false that some tennis players are joggers.

These relationships of contradiction are extremely important and useful. The *A* and *E* statements, being universal, are open to refutation by counterexample. We have already discussed this kind of refutation in Chapter 5. Often you find people making unguarded and cavalier generalizations, such as "no people with Ph.D. degrees are unemployed." To refute such a statement, you have only to find one person—just one—who has a Ph.D. and is unemployed. If you do, the *I* statement, "some people who have Ph.D.'s are unemployed," is true, and the *E* statement, "no people who have Ph.D.'s are unemployed"—which is its contradictory—is false. People who categorically assert *A* and *E* statements make themselves vulnerable to such refutation. More qualified statements, such as "few people who have Ph.D.'s are unemployed," are not so vulnerable.

Summary of Rules of Immediate Inference

1. *Conversion.* (To create the converse of a statement, reverse its subject and predicate.) All *E* and *I* statements are logically equivalent to their converse. No *A* or *O* statements are logically equivalent to their converse.

2. *Contraposition.* (To create the contrapositive of a statement, reverse its subject and predicate and negate both.) All *A* and *O* statements are logically equivalent to their contrapositive. No *E* or *I* statements are logically equivalent to their contrapositive.

3. *Obversion.* (To create the obverse of a statement, change its quality—positive to negative or negative to positive—and negate its predicate.) All statements in categorical form are logically equivalent to their obverse.

4. *Contradiction.* If *A* is true, then *O* is false, and vice versa. If *E* is true, then *I* is false, and vice versa.

RULES OF IMMEDIATE INFERENCE

Statement Form	*Operation*			
	Conversion	*Contraposition*	*Obversion*	*Contradiction*
A	NLE	LE	LE	NLE
E	LE	NLE	LE	NLE
I	LE	NLE	LE	NLE
O	NLE	LE	LE	NLE

Note: LE indicates that the statement formed by the operation is logically equivalent to the original statement.

NLE indicates that the statement formed by the logical operation is not logically equivalent to the original statement.

EXERCISE SET

Exercise 2: Part A

For each of the following statements, put it into proper categorical form and then form the obverse.

*1. The pilgrims who came to Massachusetts left England of their own free will.

2. "A robot would behave like a robot."

(Paul Ziff, "The Feelings of Robots," in *Minds and Machines,* ed. Alan R. Anderson [Englewood Cliffs, N.J.: Prentice-Hall, 1964], p. 1)

*3. Some technological innovations are not needed.

4. No historians are frivolous people.

*5. Not all professors are impractical.

6. Any practical skill is developed to obtain a definite result.

*7. Art is the pursuit of beauty and truth.

*8. "Nationalism is an extreme example of fervent belief concerning doubtful matters."

Hint: You need not try to represent "is an extreme example of" in categorical form.

(Bertrand Russell, *Sceptical Essays* [London: Unwin Books, 1935], p. 12)

9. Some treaties should not be respected.

*10. Not all feminists are in favor of free choice regarding abortion.

11. No multiple choice exam tests understanding of fundamental relationships.

12. Some films with subtitles are difficult to follow.

Exercise 2: Part B

Put each of the following statements into categorical form. Then form the converse and the contrapositive. State whether the converse and the contrapositive are logically equivalent to the original in each case. (Use the *A, E, I, O* labels, and use letters for the formal representation of categories. For instance, "All humans have backbones" would be "All *H* are *B*," where *H* represents the category of humans and *B* represents the category of creatures with backbones. The converse would be "All creatures with backbones are humans"—a statement of the *A* form. The contrapositive would be "All non-creatures with backbones are non-humans"—also of the *A* form. The converse is not logically equivalent to the original statement, but the contrapositive is logically equivalent to it.)

*1. Only experts understand the new technology.

2. All lonely people are prone to exploitation by others.

3. Some advisors think the policy should be changed.

*4. Whales are in danger of extinction.

5. Spring is the season of rains.

*6. Some court procedures are so complicated as to be very inefficient.

*7. Some students are not competitive.

*8. No Russian authors are insensitive to nature.

9. Every dog has its day.

10. The ozone layer about the earth could be damaged by frequent use of aerosol spray cans.

Exercise 2: Part C

For each of the following statements, put the statement into categorical form and then form the contradictory.

*1. The advice given to young parents by so-called experts is unreliable.

2. No one knows what life means.

*3. Some crops are best grown on land that has been left fallow for one season.

4. Some conflicts are not resolvable by negotiation.

*5. The only productive and innovative scientist is the one who enjoys freedom of thought and is not afraid to risk pursuing a new idea.

CONTRARY AND CONTRADICTORY PREDICATES AND FALSE DICHOTOMIES

The results of obversion often sound very unnatural to the sensitive English ear because the *non* attached to the predicate category is not so very common in natural English. No doubt you noticed this when working through Part A of the preceding exercise. Because *non* so often has an unnatural ring, people are often inclined to alter it and substitute ordinary words that seem to be equivalent to it in meaning.

For instance, given:

(1) All bankrupt persons are non-happy persons.

they would be inclined to substitute:

(2) All bankrupt persons are unhappy persons.

However, statements (1) and (2) here are *not* logically equivalent, and (2) is not a version of (1). The reason is that the category of unhappy things is a narrower one than the category of non-happy things. The non-happy include all who just fail to be happy—whether they are in a neutral (neither happy nor unhappy) state, or whether they are the kinds of things that just couldn't be either happy or unhappy at all because the very idea wouldn't make sense. (A non-person, such as a carrot, could not be unhappy, though it could be non-happy.) We can see that *non-happy* and *unhappy* do not mean the same thing.

For any predicate, *P*, we can construct a corresponding predicate, non-*P*, such that these two predicates are the basis of contradictory statements. Two statements are *contradictory* if and only if the truth of one entails the falsity of the other and one of them must be true. For example, let the predicate be *beautiful*. We can construct the predicate *non-beautiful*, and this is the contradictory of the first predicate in the sense that any item in the universe must necessarily be either beautiful or non-beautiful. For every entity it will be true that it is either beautiful or non-beautiful. But notice that *non-beautiful* does not mean the same as *ugly*. It is not true that every item in the universe is either beautiful or ugly. The terms *beautiful* and *ugly* are opposites, but they are not *contradictory predicates*. They are merely *contraries*.

Using *contrary predicates*, we can construct contrary statements, such as "Joan is beautiful" and "Joan is ugly." These statements are contrary; that is to say, they cannot both be true, but they can both be false. Supposing that Joan is moderately attractive, then it is false that she is beautiful and false that she is ugly.

The reason that obversion will always give you a logically equivalent statement is that you are always forming a contradictory predicate by using *non*. You will rarely get a contradictory predicate if you substitute more colloquial terms, such as *unhappy* for *non-happy*, or *ugly* for *non-beautiful*. Mistaking contraries for contradictories is the source of many mistakes. Compare the following lists to see how such mistakes can arise:

CONTRADICTORY PREDICATES, *P* AND NON-*P*	CONTRARY PREDICATES, *P* AND *P'*
happy, non-happy	happy, unhappy
pleasant, non-pleasant	pleasant, unpleasant
healthy, non-healthy	healthy, unhealthy
friend, non-friend	friend, enemy
fat, non-fat	fat, slim
good, non-good	good, evil
white, non-white	white, black
divine, non-divine	divine, satanic

One common result of not being clear about contraries and contradictories is the belief in *false dichotomies*. We classify ideas and situations in terms of an either-or. What makes such thinking tempting is its simplicity. Underlying it, too, however, is a tendency not to distinguish contraries from contradictories. It is not true, a priori, that everything in the universe is either good or non-good and that everyone in the universe is either our friend or our non-friend. If we confuse non-good (the contradictory) with evil (the contrary), the dichotomy "good or evil" will be the result. Thinking that everything is either good or evil is a false dichotomy; it polarizes our thinking by leading us to a false division of the world, one that ignores complexities, neutral situations, and situations not open to evaluation at all.

Evil and *non-good* are not the same. Similarly, it would be a false dichotomy to think that everyone is either your friend or your enemy. A person who believes that everyone is either his friend or his non-friend would be believing in an a priori truth, because *friend* and *non-friend* are contradictory predicates. But one who believes (as Richard Nixon was said to do during the troubled days preceding his resignation from the American presidency) that everyone is either his friend or his enemy has fallen into paranoid thinking. The terms *friend* and *enemy* are contrary predicates, not contradictories.

In fact, this kind of false dichotomizing is so common that logicians have been led to invent a special label for it. Using or accepting false dichotomies is known as *black-and-white thinking* and is a well-known mistake in thought.

CATEGORICAL LOGIC: SOME PHILOSOPHICAL BACKGROUND

Categorical logic was first discovered by Aristotle more than two thousand years ago. Seeing the formal relationships between the Greek equivalents of *all are, none are, some are,* and *some are not,* Aristotle formulated rules of inference for simple arguments in which the premises and conclusions were all in categorical form. So impressive was his achievement that for a very long time most logicians believed that categorical logic was the whole of logic. An important aspect of this theory was the belief that all statements—whatever their surface grammatical features—were really of the subject-predicate form and that all deductively valid relationships depended on the aspects of logical form that the *A, E, I,* and *O* statements express.

At the end of the eighteenth century, the famous German philosopher Immanuel Kant still clung to this belief in the Aristotelian tradition of logic. In fact, it persisted until nearly the end of the nineteenth century. However, most modern logicians do not subscribe to this theory: they see categorical relations as *some* of the important logical relations, not *all* of them.

Such statements as "If inflation continues, strikes will increase" and "Either it will be cloudy or it will rain" are not basically subject-predicate statements.

They cannot at all naturally be expressed in categorical form. (Try it for yourself and see. You have to do a lot of fiddling, and the results are not very close to the original in meaning.) There are more useful logical symbolisms to represent these statements, and these form part of modern systems of propositional logic, which are introduced in Chapter 8.

In our discussion of categorical form we did not consider any statements about particular individuals. These statements can be put in categorical form, but only in a rather unnatural way.

Consider the following:

Philosopher Bertrand Russell was a prominent pacifist in World War I.

We can't talk about Russell as an individual, so we get around the problem by inventing a class—the class of things identical with Russell. (This is all right, because there's only one thing in the class: only Russell is identical with Russell.) This statement is not about a category of things: it is about one individual, Bertrand Russell. To put it into categorical form, we have to regard that individual as a member of a group—that is, make him one of a kind. Thus:

All things identical with the philosopher Bertrand Russell are things that were prominent pacifists during World War I.

To ancient philosophers, this kind of adaptation of the particular into the universal seemed quite natural. They valued universal knowledge above all else, and they regarded individuals as such as comparatively uninteresting. But to modern philosophers, such recasting seems unnatural and unsatisfactory. In modern systems of logic, statements about individuals can be symbolized using letters that represent one individual—not a group.

These points illustrate the fact that modern logicians do not regard categorical form as the "be-all-and-end-all" of logical form. They would agree with the ancient philosophers, and with the treatment so far in this book, that many statements can be cast into categorical form. But categorical form is not the only way to appreciate logical form, nor is it always appropriate. Categorical form is a natural representation for some statements in English and other languages, but not for all.

Another interesting difference between ancient and modern theorists of logic concerns the matter of making statements about things that do not exist. Like other Greek philosophers of his time, Aristotle regarded the notion of speaking and reasoning about nonexistent things as irrational and paradoxical. He developed categorical logic on the assumption that its subjects are always things that exist. Aristotle believed that we make assertions only about those things that are real. This view of categorical logic is called the *existential* view.

Modern logicians (most of them, anyway) do not share this existential view. They point out that we often make statements about things that might or might not exist, and we want our rules of logic to apply to these statements, just as they apply to others. Scientists reasoned about genes, electrons, and black holes before they were sure that such things exist. A scientist who said, "Black holes are invisible" before he knew for sure that there is such a thing as a black hole, meant in effect "If anything is a black hole, then that thing is invisible." The *if* makes the statement *hypothetical;* the scientist did not commit himself to the claim that there are black holes.

Whereas ancient logicians always interpreted *A* and *E* statements as entailing the existence of things in the subject and predicate categories, modern logicians prefer a hypothetical interpretation in which the nonexistence of things in those categories is left open as a possibility. For the ancient logicians, "All humans are mortal" carried with it a firm presumption that humans exist. This is the existential interpretation.[3] For modern logicians, "All humans are mortal" says only that *if* anyone is a human, that person is mortal.

In modern logic *A* and *E* statements can be true, even when there are no members of the subject category. A statement such as "All students who cheat are liable to penalties imposed by the dean" can be true even if there are no students who cheat. We can make statements about electrons, black holes, mermaids, or unicorns without committing ourselves to the assumption that these things exist. That is, we can do this provided the statements are universal. Modern and ancient logic share the view that the particular statements assert existence. To say that some black holes are invisible is to say that there is at least one black hole that is invisible, and this, of course, commits you to the existence of at least one black hole.

Who is right in this dispute between ancient and modern logicians? Can we speak and reason about what does not exist? Do we need to? These are large metaphysical questions that we cannot try to answer here. By and large this book follows the modern view, since this is one you are likely to encounter in further courses on mathematics and formal logic.

In some practical contexts, however, the modern view yields strange results. One thing it does, which seems very odd, is to prevent us from deductively inferring that some (that is, at least one) lawyers are rich (*I*) from the claim that all lawyers are rich (*A*). Surely, you would think, if all lawyers are rich, then some are! But on the hypothetical interpretation of the *A* statement, we cannot validly infer the *I* statement from it because the *A* statement is interpreted as saying that *if* anyone is a lawyer, she or he is rich. And the *I* statement says *there is* at least one lawyer. We cannot validly deduce the actual from the hypothetical, so in the modern view there will be no valid immediate inference of *I* from *A*. The same point holds with *E* and *O*. But in the case of rich lawyers the results seem simply bizarre. Aren't some lawyers rich if all are? The reason the results seem bizarre is that in ordinary life we usually restrict ourselves, just as Aristotle did; we talk about things that exist. Everyone knows there are lawyers, and when we talk about lawyers, we aren't speculating about mythical entities!

We can represent the difference between the ancient view and the modern view with regard to lawyers being rich on a Venn diagram. Diagram A represents the ancient interpretation of "all lawyers are rich" and diagram B represents its modern interpretation.

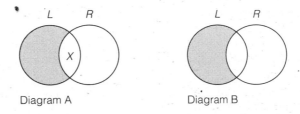

Diagram A   Diagram B

In diagram A there is an *x* in the part of the *L* circle (for lawyers) that is not shaded out; the *x* indicates that *there are* lawyers, which the ancients presumed to be part of the meaning of "All lawyers are rich." In diagram B *there is no* such *x* because, on the modern interpretation, the existence of lawyers is not presumed by "All lawyers are rich."

The solution to this problem is to step back and ask yourself whether the existence of the subject class should be assumed in the context you are dealing with. If it should, you write that assumption into the universal statement. In the case of the lawyers, you would then understand "All lawyers are rich" as presuming that there are lawyers and saying that all those lawyers are rich. On this understanding of the *A* statement, you can validly infer the *I* statement from it. In contexts like these, where it is a matter of common knowledge that the subject category is a category of existing things, we recommend *reading in* an existence assumption and reverting—in a sense—to the ancient view of things. But on the whole, we will work with the hypothetical interpretation, since it is standard in modern logic.

THE CATEGORICAL SYLLOGISM

A *categorical syllogism* is an argument with two premises and a conclusion, in which the premises and the conclusion are statements in categorical form, and there are three different categories of things involved in the argument. Each of the categories is mentioned in two different statements. The example used early in this chapter to exemplify categorical form is a valid syllogism. Here it is again:

1. All consistent opponents of killing are opponents of capital punishment.
2. No opponents of capital punishment are orthodox traditional Catholics. Therefore,
3. No consistent opponents of killing are orthodox traditional Catholics.

If *C* represents the category of consistent opponents of killing, and *T* represents the category of orthodox traditional Catholics, and *O* represents the category of opponents of capital punishment, then the argument may be formally represented as:

1. All C are O.
2. No O are T.
Therefore,
3. No C are T.

Here T is the *major term;* a major term is the one that is the predicate in the conclusion. C is the *minor term;* it is the subject in the conclusion. And O, which appears in both premises but not in the conclusion, is the *middle term*. This example is a valid syllogism because the premises, taken together, deductively entail the conclusion.

In fact, Venn diagrams can be used to represent syllogisms, and by this method of representation we can even check the validity of the syllogism on the basis of a picture. To represent a syllogism in a Venn diagram, you need three circles, one for the major term (S), one for the minor term (P), and one for the middle term (M). You draw the circles as follows:

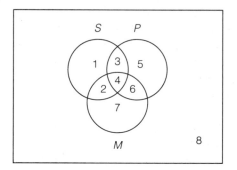

Note that S should be drawn on the top toward the left, P on the top toward the right, and M below, between S and P. (This makes sense, since M is the middle term.) A Venn diagram with three circles is more complex than one with only two. There are eight distinct areas, as numbered above.

area (1)—S, not-P, not-M
area (2)—S, not-P, M
area (3)—S, P, not-M
area (4)—S, P, M
area (5)—not-S, P, not-M
area (6)—not-S, P, M
area (7)—not-S, not-P, M
area (8)—not-S, not-P, not-M

The Venn diagram has been enclosed in a box so as to make area (8) a definite space; strictly speaking, such diagrams should always be enclosed in this way, although as a matter of practice, the boxes are often omitted for convenience.

To represent a syllogism on a Venn diagram, we first draw three circles so that the major term is on the left, the minor term on the right, and the middle term below. We mark each circle with a letter representing the category. (For example, we might mark it L for lawyers, R for rich people, and so on; try to designate circles in such a way that it is easy to remember what they stand for.)

We represent the information stated in the premises of the argument on the diagram. Premises that are universal in quantity (*A* and *E* statements) should be represented first because, as we shall soon see, their representation sometimes affects how we represent particular premises. Note that we have to shade in several areas to do this. For instance, to represent "All *S* are *P*," we have to shade in area (1) and area (2); these both contain *S*'s that are not *P*. To represent "All *S* are *M*," we would have to shade in areas (1) and (3), which contain *S*'s that are not *M*. To represent "No *S* are *P*," we have to shade in both area (3) and area (4); these both contain things that are *S* and *P*; if no *S* are *P*, there is nothing in either of these areas. To represent "No *M* are *P*," we have to shade in both area (4) and area (6).

After universal premises have been represented, particular premises (*I* and *O*) should be represented. This is sometimes more tricky. To see why, consider the statement "Some *P* are not *M*"; this statement tells you that there are *P*'s outside the *M* circle, but it does not indicate whether they should be in area (3) or in area (5). Either one would be all right; it would represent the information that there is at least one *P* that is not an *M*. If one of the areas has been shaded out in the process of representing a universal premise, then the answer is clear: put the *x* in the other. If this is not the case, the *x* should be placed on the line between the two areas, to indicate that you do not have enough information to know in which of the areas, (3) or (5), it belongs.

Once you have represented the information from the premises of a syllogism in a Venn diagram, you can use the diagram to tell whether the syllogism is a valid argument. You look at your diagram to see whether the conclusion statement is represented. (In a valid syllogism, the combined information from both premises includes everything that is stated in the conclusion.) You only have to look at the upper circles on your diagram because the middle term (by definition) is not used in the conclusion.

Here is a Venn diagram representation of the argument about Catholics, abortion, and capital punishment, which was cited earlier. As you recall, we had put the argument into categorical form as:

1. All *C* are *O*.
2. No *O* are *T*.
Therefore,
3. No *C* are *T*.

On a Venn diagram, the premises would be represented as:

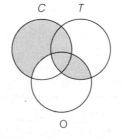

All *C* are *O*, and no *O* are *T*.

If we were to represent it separately, the conclusion would look like this:

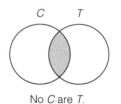

No *C* are *T*.

This model shades out all the *C* that are not *O* because of the information in the first premise, and all the *O* that are *T* because of the information in the second premise. To determine whether the syllogism is valid, we represent the premises on a Venn diagram and then look to see whether the information we have pictured includes what is expressed in the conclusion. Here the conclusion states that there should be nothing in the area that is both *C* and *T*. If the conclusion were entailed by the premises, then the model of the premises would shade out the entire *C–T* overlap. It does. Thus the Venn diagram reveals that the argument is a deductively valid syllogism.

Venn diagrams vividly illustrate something that philosophers and logicians love to say about deductively valid arguments. In a deductively valid argument, the conclusion is "already contained" in the premises. An argument is deductively valid whenever the premises assert everything needed for the conclusion to be true. In this way the truth of the premises makes it impossible for the conclusion to be false. The Venn diagram for a valid syllogism shows just how this happens. For a valid syllogism, once you have drawn the premises, you need no more drawing to represent the conclusion: it will already be pictured on your circles.

Let's look at another syllogism:

1. Some socialists are communists.
2. Some communists are docile puppets of totalitarian regimes.
    Therefore,
3. Some socialists are docile puppets of totalitarian regimes.

Here the major term, *D*, represents the category of docile puppets of totalitarian regimes; the minor term, *R*, represents the category of socialists, and the middle term, *C*, represents the category of communists. Formalized, the argument is:

1. Some *R* are *C*.
2. Some *C* are *D*.
    Therefore,
3. Some *R* are *D*.

To test the validity of this syllogism using Venn diagrams, we first diagram the premises. Both premises here are of the *I* form, and this makes our diagram more complicated than before.

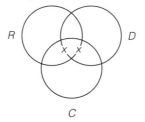

Some *R* are *C* and some *C* are *D*.

Some *C* are *D*. (The area that is the overlap between *C* and *D* is subdivided
into those *CD*s that are also *R* and those that are not *R*.)

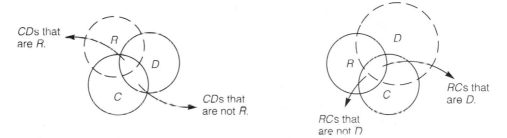

Some *R* are *C*. (The area that is the overlap between *R* and *C* is subdivided
into those *RC*s that are also inside *D* and those *RC*s that are outside *D*.)

To use Venn diagrams effectively, you have to be careful not to represent on
your diagram more information than the premises state. In this example the
premises do not indicate whether those *R*'s that are *C* are also *D*; thus the *x* that
designates that there is something in the area appears on the line. (We cannot
avoid the problem by diagramming universal premises first, because there are no
universal premises.) A similar technique must be used for the second premise.
The diagram of these two *I* statements taken together reflects ambiguities that
the information in the two premises does not resolve. The premises do not say
whether those socialists who are communists are, or are not, among those of the
communists who are docile puppets of totalitarian regimes. They assert that some
communists are docile puppets, but they make no commitment as to whether
these are the very same communists who are also socialists. By placing the *x* on
the line in these cases, we indicate that there is something in either one of the
areas that the line separates, but we do not know which.

To see whether this syllogism about the communists and socialists is valid,
we look at our diagram to see whether the premises provide the information in
the conclusion. The conclusion was "Some *R* are *D*." We look, then, at the R–D
intersection in the diagram representing both premises. We check whether the
diagram guarantees that there will be something in this area. *It does not.* There

is no guarantee that an x will be in this area, because the x's are on lines, and might both land up in the adjoining areas. Thus the argument is not valid.

To check an argument for validity using these Venn diagrams, you first make sure that it is a syllogism. Then you draw three overlapping circles to represent the three categories on which the argument depends. You represent the two premises on the diagram. Then you check to see whether that diagram expresses the information stated in the conclusion. If it does, the argument is deductively valid. The premises contain enough information to guarantee the conclusion logically. If it does not, the argument is not deductively valid. The conclusion has information that goes beyond what is stated in the premises.

We'll do one more example:

1. No lawyers are illiterate.
2. All lawyers are educated.
So,
3. Some educated persons are not illiterate.

Diagramming both premises, we get:

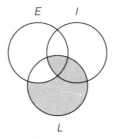

(I represents the category of illiterate persons; E represents the category of educated persons; L represents the category of lawyers.) But the conclusion would have to contain an x in the intersection area of the E that is outside the I; the conclusion says there is at least one person who is in E and not in I. The premises don't guarantee this, obviously, for there is no x in the model of the premises.

What we encounter here is the consequence of the hypothetical interpretation of the E and A statements. These drawings are based on the hypothetical interpretation. If we were to change this to the existential interpretation, on the grounds that it is common knowledge that things exist in all these categories, the premises would then contain more knowledge, as:

1. No L are I (and there are L).
2. All L are E (and there are L).
Therefore,
3. Some E are not I.

With these existential assumptions added, there is more information to be represented on our Venn diagram. We first shade in the areas indicated by the premises; both sub-areas of the intersection between L and I, and both sub-areas of the *L* category that are outside *E*. We then represent the information that there are *L;* since two of the three sub-areas into which the *L* circle has been divided have now been shaded, there is only one place for the *x* to go.

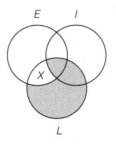

We can see that the argument is valid on the existential interpretation. The *x* we have placed on the diagram is in an area of the *E* circle that is outside the *I* circle. Thus the diagram indicates that some *E* are not *I*, which is the conclusion.

◆ ——————————————————————————————————

EXERCISE SET

Exercise 3

For each of the following arguments, put the premises and conclusion into categorical form. Check to see whether the argument is a syllogism. (Remember, in a syllogism, there are two premises and one conclusion. All are in categorical form, and there are exactly three categories in the statements.) Test all syllogisms for validity using the Venn diagram technique. Adopt the hypothetical interpretation. Does this give you paradoxical results in any case? Discuss.

1. Herpes is a viral infection. Antibiotics are an effective drug only against nonviral infections. Therefore, antibiotics are not effective against herpes.

*2. I don't know why it is, but some mothers find small children extremely irritating. And some people who find small children extremely irritating just cannot control themselves and suppress their rage. For these reasons, some mothers cannot control themselves and suppress their rage.

3. Some anarchists are pacifists. But no consistent anarchist is a pacifist. The inevitable conclusion is that some anarchists are not consistent anarchists.

4. All foods that can be kept on the shelf for several weeks without rotting are foods containing additives. But all foods that contain additives are hazardous to health. Thus, foods with a shelf-life of several weeks are hazardous to health.

5. No monkeys are swimmers, and some swimmers are amphibious. Therefore, no monkeys are amphibious.

6. Some children are hyperactive because all hyperactive persons are difficult to handle, and all children are difficult to handle.

*7. Because all well-educated persons can read and all persons who can read have heard of Hitler, there are some well-educated persons who have heard of Hitler.

8. All zoos are places in which animals are kept in captivity for display, and no places in which animals are kept in captivity to be displayed are humane environments. Thus, no zoo is a humane environment.

*9. All sunbathing carries with it some risk of skin cancer. Anything that carries with it a risk of skin cancer is dangerous. Therefore, all sunbathing is dangerous.

10. No test of honesty that can be affected by subjects' control of responses is reliable. Some lie detector tests are tests of honesty that can be affected by subjects' control of responses. Therefore, some lie detector tests are not reliable.

11. Only children who have at least one blue-eyed parent have blue eyes. Joan has blue eyes. Therefore, Joan has at least one blue-eyed parent.

*12. Some doctors are unhappy. No unhappy people find it easy to express sympathy for others. Therefore, some doctors do not find it easy to express sympathy for others.

13. Only children who have at least one blue-eyed parent have blue eyes. Bob has brown eyes, not blue eyes. Thus, Bob does not have at least one blue-eyed parent.

14. The skeptic is not afraid to admit his own ignorance. He knows that full knowledge is impossible, and all of us who know that complete knowledge is impossible can certainly admit to our own ignorance without shame.

15. No American-made car can rival the Toyota.

*16. Any position in local government that involves power and influence should be allotted on the basis of a municipal election. The position of spouse of the mayor involves power and influence, so it should be allotted on the basis of municipal election.

Question: Presuming that the mayor sought to avoid this conclusion, which premise of the syllogism should he seek to dispute if he wishes to remain consistent? Or is he compelled by categorical logic, to admit that his spouse should be selected for him by the voters?

(Used by a critic of a mayor who had said that his spouse was an important person to the local government and that for this reason she deserved to use city-paid cars to do her shopping.)

*17. Some religious people believe that morality depends on religion. No people who believe that morality depends on religion have a correct understanding of morality. Therefore, some religious people do not have a correct understanding of morality.

THE RULES OF THE CATEGORICAL SYLLOGISM

Modeling categorical syllogisms on Venn diagrams gives us a system for checking their deductive validity. However, some people find this technique clumsy and awkward—especially when it comes to representing *I* and *O* statements in cases where the *x*'s have to go on the line. Another way of checking the validity of syllogisms involves the use of rules. There are five rules, and if none are broken, the syllogism is a valid deductive argument.

In order to use the rules for the syllogism, you need a good understanding of two technical terms: *distribution* and *middle term*. Whether a term in a categorical statement is distributed or not depends on whether that statement makes a comment about every item in the category specified by that term.

Distribution of Terms

A: All *S* are *P.* The subject term, *S,* is distributed, and the predicate term, *P,* is not.

E: No *S* are *P.* Both the subject term, *S,* and the predicate term, *P,* are distributed.
I: Some *S* are *P.* Neither the subject term, *S,* nor the predicate term, *P,* is distributed.
O: Some *S* are not *P.* The subject term, *S,* is not distributed. However, the predicate term, *P,* is distributed.

As we explained earlier, the reason that the predicate term is distributed in *O* statements is that the subject category is excluded from the whole predicate category. To say that some men are not fathers, for example, is to say of the whole category of fathers that some men are not in it.

As for the middle term, this is the term that occurs in both premises of a syllogism, but not in its conclusion. It is the middle term that enables us to link the premises together to logically deduce the conclusion.

The Fallacy of the Undistributed Middle

The middle term must be distributed in at least one premise for the syllogism to be valid. If the middle term is not distributed in either premise, then both premises give information about only some of this category. This means that the predicate term and the subject term cannot be securely related to each other. Consider the following example:

1. All barbers are businessmen.
2. Some businessmen are people in debt.
So,
3. Some barbers are people in debt.

We cannot validly connect being a barber with being in debt because the middle term "businessmen" is not distributed in this argument. The first premise only alludes to some businessmen, and so does the second premise. There is no guarantee that the businessmen referred to are the same ones in each case.

The middle term is crucial in any syllogism. The *fallacy of the undistributed middle* is famous in the history of logic. The preceding argument about barbers and businessmen illustrates this fallacy.

The fallacy of the undistributed middle is committed whenever a syllogistic argument is used and the middle term is not distributed in at least one premise. Given an understanding of what distribution is, and what the middle term is, it is easy to understand the rules of the categorical syllogism.

Rules of the Categorical Syllogism

1. For a syllogism to be valid, the middle term must be distributed in at least one premise.
2. For a syllogism to be valid, no term is distributed in the conclusion unless it is also distributed in at least one premise.
3. For a syllogism to be valid, at least one premise is affirmative; that is, a valid syllogism cannot have two negative premises.

4. For a syllogism to be valid, if it has a negative conclusion, it must also have a negative premise. And if it has one negative premise, it must also have a negative conclusion.

*5. If a syllogism has two universal premises, it cannot have a particular conclusion and be valid.

It should be obvious why the fifth rule is marked with an asterisk. This rule makes explicit the hypothetical interpretation of universal statements. If you are going to use the existential interpretation, then you should drop the fifth rule. To be deductively valid arguments, syllogisms must satisfy the conditions of *all* the rules. If even one is broken, the syllogism is not valid. It is a worthwhile exercise to do one example from the preceding exercise using these rules instead of Venn diagrams. Your answer should be the same as it was when you used Venn diagrams.

APPLYING CATEGORICAL LOGIC

If an argument is deductively valid, then the (R) and (G) conditions of argument cogency are perfectly and entirely satisfied; no doubt can be raised on these. It makes no sense to grant that an argument is deductively valid and then go on to complain that the premises are irrelevant to the conclusion or do not provide adequate grounds to support the conclusion. If anything is wrong with a deductively valid argument, then it must be in the premises themselves.

Many of the immediate inferences we study in this chapter are important for the correct interpretation of statements and claims. For instance, a proper understanding of obversion helps us to see why a person saying that some children are not happy may not mean that these children are unhappy. Understanding conversion prevents us inferring that all who support disarmament are communists from the quite different claim that all who are communists support disarmament.

When you read newspapers, magazines, and scholarly articles, it is not likely that you will be struck by a conspicuous number of categorical syllogisms. Syllogisms worded as straightforwardly as those we have studied so far in this chapter are comparatively rare in natural discourse. Nevertheless, there are some clear syllogisms around, and there are also some arguments that are implicitly syllogistic, though their syllogistic form does not stand out as clearly as you might wish. In such arguments, Venn diagram techniques and rules for the syllogism will tell you whether the argument is deductively valid. But you may have to do some careful interpreting in order to apply these techniques. Remember that all the rules in this chapter apply only to those statements that are in proper categorical form. A syllogism must have two premises and a conclusion, all in categorical form, and it must involve three distinct categories of things.

To see what may be involved in the application of syllogistic rules to ordinary prose, we shall work through an example. This is an argument that the philosopher John Locke used in his defense of religious toleration:

> Speculative opinions and articles of faith which are required only to be be-
> lieved cannot be imposed on any church by the law of the land. For it is ab-
> surd that things should be enjoined by laws which are not in men's power
> to perform. And to believe this or that to be true does not depend upon
> our will.[4]

This argument is a valid syllogism, but we have to do some recasting before we
can demonstrate this fact.

Locke's conclusion is in the first sentence: "<u>Speculative opinions and articles
of faith</u> are <u>things which should not be imposed by law</u>." The premises are in the
next two sentences: "<u>things enjoined by law</u> are <u>things which it is in men's power
to perform</u>" and "<u>beliefs</u> are not <u>things which depend upon our will</u>." Here, as
indicated by underlining, we have six categories. Unless we can regard some of
these categories as reducible to others, we cannot regard Locke's argument as a
syllogism. A syllogism, by definition, is based on exactly three distinct categories
of things. We have to look at the differences in wording to see whether we really
have the same category described in different words. This does happen in the
argument. In this context, "speculative opinions and articles of faith" and "beliefs" mean the same thing. Also, "things which it is in men's power to perform"
and "things which depend upon our will" are the same. Now the only remaining
problem concerns the *should* in the first premise. Statements in categorical form
must use *are*; therefore, *should* will have to be moved from the linking position
to the internal specification of a category.

Once we grasp the necessary variations in wording, the argument may be
represented as follows:

1. All things which should be imposed by law are things which depend upon
   our will.
2. No beliefs are things which depend upon our will.
So,
3. No beliefs are things which should be imposed by law.

Allowing *B* to stand for beliefs, *I* to stand for things that should be imposed by
law, and *W* to stand for things that depend upon our will, the argument becomes:

1. All *I* are *W*.
2. No *B* are *W*.
So,
3. No *B* are *I*.

As you can see (check it using the rules for categorical syllogisms) this argument is valid. But it is quite difficult to get Locke's original passage into this form.
The passage illustrates some of the problems that arise when we try to transpose
the clear, straightforward rules of a part of deductive logic onto natural speaking
and writing in English. We have to look for verbally different ways of specifying
the same category and rewrite to represent statements in categorical form. If we
succeed in doing so, we may produce a model that says the same thing as the
original, but says it much more clearly. Our reworded argument is less eloquent
than Locke's original, but it is much easier to understand. We can show that the

argument is deductively valid, and we therefore know that any doubt about its cogency must concern the acceptability of the premises.

Another matter that often arises when we try to spot syllogistic reasoning in ordinary speech and writing is the problem of elliptical syllogisms. Elliptical syllogisms are implicitly syllogistic arguments in which either one premise or the conclusion is not explicitly stated by the arguer. Here is an example that may have a familiar ring to it:

> The bigger the burger, the better the burger.
> The burgers are bigger at Burger King.

The point of this advertisement is obviously to convince you that the burgers are better at Burger King. This claim is entailed by the two stated claims. The ad is really a syllogism with a missing conclusion:

1.   All bigger burgers are better burgers.
2.   All burgers at Burger King are bigger burgers.
So,
3.   All burgers at Burger King are better burgers.

Now if K represents the category of burgers at Burger King, and B represents the category of burgers that are better, and I represents the category of burgers that are bigger, we get the following:

1.   All I are B.
2.   All K are I.
So,
3.   All K are B.

This is a valid syllogism. The question of when you should supply a missing conclusion is not different for syllogisms than it is for other arguments. You have to have reason to believe that the author meant to assert the claim you add. If that claim is, in fact, deductively entailed by what is stated, the author of the argument was clearly logically committed to it, and you are not misinterpreting him or her by adding the conclusion.

Even more common than the missing conclusion in a syllogism is the missing premise. Consider the following case:

> A hundred years from now, should mankind survive that long, Doug Casey may well be remembered as one of the great prophets of our time, for he has displayed in Crisis Investing a keen insight into the workings of government and human nature.[5]

Here the conclusion is that Doug Casey may be remembered as a great prophet a hundred years from now. The premise is that he has displayed a keen insight into the workings of government and human nature. Both these claims can be put into categorical form as follows:

1.   All things that are Doug Casey are things that have displayed a keen insight into the workings of government and human nature.

So,
Conclusion: All things that are Doug Casey are things that may be remembered as great prophets a hundred years from now.

Now if we let *C* stand for the category of things that are Casey, *R* stand for the category of things that may be remembered in a hundred years, and *W* represent the category of things that have displayed keen insight into the workings of government, we get a stated premise and conclusion as follows:

1. All *C* are *W*.
So,
3. All *C* are *R*.

What is missing to make the argument deductively valid is a statement "All *W* are *R*"; we need a premise linking a middle term to the predicate of the conclusion. If we were to add this as a missing premise, the argument would be a valid syllogism:

1. All *C* are *W*.
2. All *W* are *R*.
So,
3. All *C* are *R*.

This addition seems appropriate, because the original argument does seem to proceed by relations of category inclusion. The arguer has asserted that Casey may be remembered because he understood government. But if this is what will make Casey one who may be remembered, and there are no qualifying comments made or suggested, it would appear that the arguer is using the claim that all who understand government may be remembered. (All *M* are *P*.) When we write this in, the argument can be represented as a valid syllogism.

It is not appropriate to regard an argument as an elliptical syllogism unless the premise you are going to add is one that will make the argument valid; the very things that make you justified in reading it in will relate it to stated material in a valid pattern. Also, not all elliptical arguments are elliptical *syllogisms*. To represent an argument as a syllogism, and not some other type, you should have a sense that the argument depends on category inclusion or exclusion in order to relate the premises to the conclusion.

◆————————————————————————————————————

EXERCISE SET

Exercise 4

For the following arguments, identify the premises and conclusions and (if necessary) put them into proper categorical form. If necessary, supply a missing premise or missing conclusion. Then test the arguments for validity using either Venn diagrams or the rules of the syllogism.

*1. Some problems experienced by human beings in developing countries are the result of climate. No problem that is the result of climate is the result of abuses of human rights. Therefore, some problems experienced by humans in developing countries are not the result of abuses of human rights.

*2. "Other men die. I am not another. Therefore I shall not die."

(V. Nabokov, *The Pale Fire* [New York: Putnam, 1962])

3. A completely unprejudiced observation is an observation that is made with no goal in mind. But no observation is made with no goal in mind. Therefore, no observation is completely unprejudiced.

4. Some sports are fiercely competitive and no activity that is fiercely competitive is unaggressive. Therefore, no sports are unaggressive.

5. Nothing that contains all the genetic information necessary to form a complete human being is mere property. A fertilized egg growing into an embryo contains all the genetic information necessary to form a complete human being. Therefore, a fertilized egg growing into an embryo is not—not by any means—mere property.

*6. "Among the vowels there are no double letters; but one of the double letters (*w*) is compounded of two vowels. Hence a letter compounded of two vowels is not necessarily itself a vowel."

(C. S. Peirce, "Some Consequences of Four Incapacities," in *Philosophical Writings of C. S. Peirce*, ed. Justus Buchler [New York: Dover Publications, 1955])

*7. "The leaders of our country have not told us, the citizens, where they want to lead us. This must mean that they are totally confused themselves."

(Duff Cornbush in the *Canadian*, quoted by Douglas Roche in *Justice Not Charity* [Toronto: McLelland and Stewart, 1970])

8. "If a much praised government dam was worth the trouble of building, someone would have been able to build it for a profit. Since it's unprofitable, it must be financed at least in part by taxes."

(From Doug Casey, *Crisis Investing* [New York: Stratford Press, 1980])

9. Despite what industry spokespersons may say, no advertising is entirely honest. Since no advertising is entirely honest and every entirely honest practice is worth emulating, it must follow that some advertising is not worth emulating.

10. "Every well-founded inference to an infinite cause is based upon the observation of an infinite effect. But no inference to God's existence from the design in nature is based upon the observation of an infinite effect. Thus, no inference to God's existence from the design in nature is a well-founded inference."

(Adapted from David Hume, "Dialogues Concerning Natural Religion," in *The Empiricists* [New York: Anchor Press, 1974])

11. Any item marked down 30 percent is a real bargain these days, you can be sure of that. Now I checked this morning, and the local store has a number of items marked down 30 percent. Thus the local store has some real bargains.

*12. Only people from expensive private schools will make it to the top of public life in Britain, for only those schools provide the sort of education that is essential for such a role.

*13. *Background:* This passage is part of a letter written to oppose the censorship of pornography in Canada:

"A nation that permits, night after night, year in and year out, the showing on TV and in cinemas of murders by the hundreds and thousands, and yet can't show one love-making scene without having it labelled obscenity—that nation is guilty of practicing gross obscenity and hypocrisy, and is consequently without redeeming social value."

Hint: You can find two syllogisms here if you add two extra premises—one for each of them.

(Toronto *Globe and Mail*, April 21, 1984)

❖   CHAPTER SUMMARY

Some valid deductive arguments owe their validity to the way in which the key logical terms *all, none, some,* and *not* are used. The relations between these terms are studied in the branch of formal logic known as categorical logic. Categorical logic was first formalized by Aristotle. Relations in categorical logic can be represented on Venn diagrams in which overlapping circles represent various relations between classes of things. Modern logicians differ from Aristotle on the issue of whether the subject terms in the universal statements of categorical logic presuppose existence; Aristotle believed that they do, whereas modern logicians believe they do not. Particular statements do assert existence, according to both ancient and modern logicians. Rules of immediate inference tell us which statements in categorical logic can be directly inferred from which others.

Syllogisms are arguments with two premises and a conclusion, based on three distinct categories, where premises and conclusion are all in categorical form. Syllogisms can be tested for their validity by Venn diagrams and also by applying the rules of the syllogism. To apply categorical logic to the sorts of statements and arguments you would find in magazines, newspapers, and books other than logic textbooks, you often have to look closely to see that statements, though not obviously categorical in form, can be rewritten in categorical form. If you can recast statements in this form, categorical logic can be helpful in enabling you to understand logical relationships and to evaluate syllogistic arguments.

❖   REVIEW OF TERMS INTRODUCED

Categorical logic   A branch of formal logic in which the basic logical terms are *all, some, are,* and *not.*

Square of Opposition   An arrangement of the four categorical forms. The opposition is apparent from the diagonals on the square.

Universal affirmative (*A*)   Statement of the form "all *S* are *P*."

Universal negative (*E*)   Statement of the form "no *S* are *P*."

Particular affirmative (*I*)   Statement of the form "some *S* are *P*."

Particular negative (*O*)   Statement of the form "some *S* are not *P*."

Venn diagram   Diagram in which circles are used to represent categorical relationships.

Immediate inference   Inference of one statement directly from another, with no intermediate logical steps.

Conversion   A logical operation on a statement in categorical form, in which the order of the terms is reversed. For example, the converse of "all *S* are *P*" is "all *P* are *S*." For *E* and *I* statements, conversion produces logically equivalent statements. For *A* and *O* statements, it does not.

Logical equivalence   Logical relation between two statements that must necessarily have the same truth value. For instance, "not all *S* are *P*" and "some *S* are not *P*" are logically equivalent.

Contraposition   A logical operation on a statement in categorical form, in which the statement is converted, and then *non* is attached to each category. For example, the contrapositive of "no *S* are *P*" is "no non-*P* are non-*S*." For *A* and *O* statements, contraposition produces a logically equivalent statement. For *E* and *I* statements, it does not.

Obversion   A logical operation on a statement in categorical form, in which the prefix *non* is added to the predicate. Then, if the original statement was affirmative, it is made negative. If the original statement was negative, it is made affirmative. Obversion always produces a statement that is logically equivalent to the original one.

Contradictory (of a given statement)   That statement that must always be opposite to the original statement in truth value. If the statement is *X*, its contradictory statement is not-*X*. When *X* is true, not-*X* is false, and vice versa. For example, the contradictory statement of "all *S* are *P*" is "some *S* are not *P*."

Contrary (of a given statement)   A logically related statement that can never be true when the given statement is true, although it can be false when the statement is false. For example, "all *S* are *P*" and "no *S* are *P*" are contraries. They cannot both be true, but they can both be false.

Contradictory predicates   Predicates logically related so that it is a matter of logical necessity that a thing possess one or another. For instance, "happy" and "non-happy" are contradictory predicates. By necessity, if a thing is not happy, it is non-happy.

Contrary predicates   Predicates logically related so that nothing can possess both, though things may possess neither. For example, "happy" and "unhappy" are contrary predicates. It is not possible for a thing to be both happy and unhappy, but it is possible for it to be neither happy nor unhappy.

Categorical syllogism   Argument with two premises and a conclusion, in which the premises and the conclusion are statements in categorical form and there are three different categories of things involved in the argument.

Major term   Term that appears in the predicate position in the conclusion of a syllogism.

Minor term   Term that appears in the subject position in the conclusion of a syllogism.

Middle term   Term that occurs in both premises of a syllogism but not in the conclusion.

Distribution   When the categorical statement in which the term appears is about all the things within the category that term designates. The subject (*S*) term is distributed in *A* and *E* statements. The predicate (*P*) term is distributed in *E* and *O* statements.

Fallacy of the undistributed middle Fallacy committed when a syllogism is put forward and it is invalid because the middle term is not distributed in either one of the premises.

Notes

1. *For instructors:* One may, of course, insist that such inferences presume that all fathers are male and that when properly understood they depend on form, not meaning.

2. See Sam Keen, *Faces of the Enemy* (San Francisco: Harper & Row, 1986) for compelling illustrations of the dangers of stereotyping.

3. "Existential" in this sense should not be confused with "existentialist" or "existentialism." Existentialism is a school of philosophy, associated largely with movements in France in the 40s and 50s, which is based on the idea that human beings have no fixed human nature and that they define what they are by the way they exist. Jean Paul Sartre, a leading existentialist thinker, is famous for his statement that existence precedes essence, which emphasized that human beings create or define their own essential nature. Aristotle, in contrast to Sartre, believed in fixed essences. Aristotle was definitely not an existentialist in the sense in which Sartre was an existentialist.

4. John Locke, "A Letter Concerning Toleration." Quoted in S. F. Barker, *The Elements of Logic*. 3rd ed. (New York: McGraw-Hill, 1980).

5. Robert J. Ringer, Preface to Doug Casey, *Crisis Investing* (New York: Stratford Press, 1980).

CHAPTER 8

Those Tidy Deductions: Propositional Logic

ALTHOUGH CATEGORICAL LOGIC IS THE OLDEST developed logic in the western philosophical tradition, it is not now believed to be the most basic part of logic. That role is reserved for *propositional logic*, which deals with the relationships holding between simple propositions or statements and their compounds. In propositional logic the basic logical terms are *not, or, and* and *if then*. These terms are used to relate statements and their compounds. The following is a simple example of an argument that is easily formalized in propositional logic:

1. If inflation continues, social discontent will increase.
2. Inflation will continue.

Therefore,

3. Social discontent will increase.

This argument is deductively valid, but not by virtue of any relations between subjects and predicates. Rather, it is the conditional relationship between statements that makes it valid. In propositional logic we use letters to represent simple statements. Symbols represent the basic logical connecting words: *not, and, or,* and *if then*. Allowing *I* to represent "inflation continues" and *S* to represent "social discontent will increase," the preceding argument can be represented in propositional logic as:

I ⊃ *S*
I
Therefore,
S

The symbol "⊃" is used to represent "if then." Provided that an argument can be accurately formalized in the symbols of propositional logic, we can test its deductive validity by a device called a *truth table*.

DEFINITION OF THE BASIC SYMBOLS
USED IN PROPOSITIONAL LOGIC

In Chapter 7 we noted that in a system of formal logic, we have to define terms more precisely than we would in ordinary natural language. This factor must be remembered when we are working with propositional logic. The symbols −, ·, ∨, and ⊃ stand for *not, and, or,* and *if then.* But they do not coincide perfectly with all the shades of meaning that these English words have. Rather, they represent a kind of logical core.

Consider the word *not.* Suppose that the letter W is used to represent a simple statement, such as "A war was being fought in Europe in 1915." *Denying the statement* that a war was being fought in Europe in 1915 amounts to asserting its contradictory—namely, "A war was not being fought in Europe in 1915." When a statement is represented by single letter (in this case, W), its contradictory is symbolized by a hyphen preceding that letter, as in − W. When W is true, − W is false; when − W is true, W is false. (You read − W as "not W.")

We can represent the simple relationship between any statement and its denial on a truth table, as follows:

P	−P
T	F
F	T

This is a simple truth table that defines the operator for *not.* P represents any statement that has only two possible truth values. P can be either true or false, as shown in the column on the left. Its denial, − P, also has two possible truth values. The truth of P and that of − P are related, as we can see by reading across the rows. When P is true, − P is false, and vice versa.

Now we move on to *and.* Frequently the word *and* is used to join together two statements, as in the sentence, "A war was being fought in Europe in 1915, and Britain was a major protagonist in that war." As we have seen already in Chapter 2, logicians call a combination of statements based on *and* a *conjunction.* A conjunction of two statements is true if and only if both these statements (called *conjuncts*) are true. That is, our statement about Europe in 1915 will be true if and only if it is true that there was a war then and it is also true that Britain was a major protagonist in that war. If either one of these conjuncts is false, the whole conjunction will be false, because the conjunction asserts both conjuncts. Conjunction is represented in propositional logic by "·". This symbol is defined by the following truth table:

P	Q	P·Q
T	T	T
T	F	F
F	T	F
F	F	F

The truth table for "·" is larger than the truth table for "−" because we are now working with two different statements, *P* and *Q*. Each may have two truth values, so there are four possible combinations of truth values (2 times 2). The truth table must represent all the possible combinations: *P* and *Q* both true; *P* and *Q* both false; *P* true and *Q* false; *Q* true and *P* false. That is why it has four rows.

We now move on to *or*. With *and* we conjoin statements. With *or* we disjoin them. That is, we relate them as alternatives: one or the other is true. In a statement like "Either obesity is inherited or obesity is environmentally caused," two simpler statements are disjoined, and the resulting compound statement is called a *disjunction*. The symbol used in propositional logic for the *or* of disjunction is "∨". The symbol "∨" is defined by this truth table:

P	Q	P∨Q
T	T	T
T	F	T
F	T	T
F	F	F

The disjunction "*P* ∨ *Q*" is true when either one of the *disjuncts* (*P, Q*) is true. It is also true when both are true. The only case in which the disjunction is false is when both disjuncts are false. You can see this by looking at the bottom row. *P* is false, *Q* is false, and *P* ∨ *Q* is false. (For example, the disjunction "Iraq is in Africa or India is in Europe" is false because both disjuncts are false; it is false that Iraq is in Africa and false that India is in Europe; hence it is false that either Iraq is in Africa or India is in Europe.) In all other rows the disjunction is true because at least one disjunct is true.

Now for the *conditional*. A conditional statement is one that asserts a relationship between two other statements. Its form is basically "if such-and-such, then so-and-so." The part of the statement that is hypothesized (that is, which immediately follows *if*) is the *antecedent* of the conditional. That which follows upon it (coming after *then*) is the *consequent*. A conditional statement asserts neither its antecedent nor its consequent. Rather, it expresses a link between the two, claiming that *if* the antecedent is true, then so is the consequent.

For instance, consider the conditional statement *"If Joe runs every day, he will become fit."* In this conditional statement the antecedent is "Joe runs every day" and the consequent is "Joe will become fit." The conditional says that *if* the antecedent is true, the consequent will be true also. It says neither that Joe runs every day nor that he'll become fit, but rather that these two things are connected. It asserts a conditional relationship between running every day and fitness; the second will follow on the first. An understanding of conditionals is very important in logic.

In propositional logic a symbol called the *horseshoe* (⊃) is used to express a minimal, but basic, meaning common to all conditionals. There are various sorts of conditionals. Consider:

(a) If a person has a mortgage on his house, he has borrowed money to buy the house. (Conditional based on definition of what a mortgage on a house is.)

(b) If a person has trouble paying a heavy mortgage, he is likely to be under stress. (Conditional based on a causal relationship between two states of mind.)

(c) If a person cannot pay his mortgage, he is open to having his house taken over by the bank or person to whom the mortgage is owed. (Conditional based on a legal situation of liability when one fails to repay debts.)

(d) If a person has incurred a debt by taking out a mortgage, he should make every reasonable effort to repay that debt. (Conditional based on the moral principle that one ought to pay one's debts.)

(e) Finally his banker made a threat, saying "If you don't get that next payment in, we're going to have the locks changed." (Banker's statement is a threat, stated in a conditional.)

(f) If you can manage to pay a thousand a month on that mortgage, I'll eat my hat! (Conditional used to assert disbelief, which is indicated by promising bizarre behavior if the disbelieved claim should turn out to be true.)

All these statements are conditionals but as we can see, they differ in significant respects. What they have in common is the relationship between the antecedent and the consequent. Every conditional asserts that *given* the antecedent, the consequent will hold as well. This connection of truth values between the antecedent and the consequent is the logical core of the conditional relationship. It is this logical core that the horseshoe is intended to capture. Because it is supposed to represent the truth functional antecedent-consequent connection in all the different sorts of conditionals, it may fail to capture certain other aspects of some particular conditionals.

It is probably easiest, for the moment at least, to regard the horseshoe as a technical symbol invented by logicians and learn it in terms of its truth table. When we come to discuss the relation between English meanings and the propositional symbols in more detail, we'll explain why it is that the horseshoe, which is different in important ways from *if then* and related terms, can nevertheless be successfully used to symbolize many arguments.

Here is how the horseshoe is technically defined:

P	Q	$P{\supset}Q$
T	T	T
T	F	F
F	T	T
F	F	T

Be sure to learn this truth table. Since the horseshoe does not in all cases correspond to most people's intuitive sense of what is logically correct, you may not understand this connective as easily as the others.

Using the logical symbols just defined and using capital letters to represent simple statements, we can represent many arguments in an elegant and compact way. Here is an example:

ARGUMENT IN ENGLISH

Either the interest rates will fall or the unemployment rate will rise. If the interest rates fall, the value of the dollar will increase. If the unemployment rate rises, there will probably be a change of government at the next election. .So either the value of the dollar will increase or there will probably be a change of government at the next election.

FORMALIZATION OF ARGUMENT

Let *I* represent "The interest rates fall." Let *U* represent "The unemployment rate will rise." Let *V* represent "The value of the dollar will increase." Let *G* represent "There will probably be a change of government at the next election."

The statements in the English argument can now all be represented using these letters and the symbols of propositional logic. The symbolized argument will be:

$I \lor U$
$I \supset V$
$U \supset G$
Therefore,
$V \lor G$

This symbolization is a compact version of the original argument. Once the argument is formalized in this way, we can use a technique involving truth tables to test its deductive validity.

An important matter pertaining to formalization is the matter of brackets. You are familiar with this, no doubt, from algebra and arithmetic. There is a great difference between the quantity $(30 + 21) \div 3$, and $(30) + (21 \div 3)$. The first quantity is 17; the second is 37. Brackets make an important difference in symbolic logic too. They function much the way punctuation marks do in English—serving to indicate how things are grouped together.

Suppose we wish to express in propositional logic the idea that a person may have either jello or ice cream, but not both, for dessert. We need to use the symbol for *not* so that it applies to the conjunction. We can do this as follows: "You may have jello or ice cream, and not both" is rewritten as "You may have jello or you may have ice cream, and it is not the case both that you may have jello and that you may have ice cream," and that is symbolized as:

$(J \vee I) \cdot - (J \cdot I)$

Look at the second set of brackets in this example. The symbol for *not* is placed outside the bracket because this symbol has the scope of applying to the entire expression within the brackets; it denies the entire conjunction. If we had simply written:

Wrong: $(J \vee I) \cdot - J \cdot I$

the symbol $-$ would deny only that we can have jello. What we wish to deny is that we can have both at once. We need the brackets to indicate the scope (extent) of the negation. Similarly, we need brackets around the disjunction to indicate that the disjunction is simply between J and I, not between J and a longer formula.

Here are some further examples where bracketing is necessary:

(a) If she is rich or intelligent, she has a good chance of getting the Liberal nomination in the electoral district.
   $(R \vee I) \supset G$
The antecedent of the condition is the entire disjunction.
(b) If the Republicans are anxious and the Democrats lack funds, then no one is ready for the next election.
   $(R \cdot D) \supset - S$
(Here S represents "Somebody is ready for the next election.") The antecedent of the conditional is the entire conjunction.

Bracketing serves to group things just the way punctuation marks do in English. It is very important to get brackets right. Look at the English sentence to see the scope of negations and other relationships. An obvious but handy rule about brackets is that if you have an odd number of them, something has definitely gone wrong.

TESTING FOR VALIDITY
BY THE TRUTH TABLE TECHNIQUE

Let's begin by looking at a logically dubious argument. It goes like this:

> If defense spending is cut, social service spending will increase. Defense spending is not going to be cut, so social service spending is not going to increase.

This argument is formally represented as:

$D \supset S$
$-D$
Therefore,
$-S$

In the symbolized version, D represents "Defense spending is going to be cut" and S represents "Social service spending will increase." The argument does seem to be a little strange. Is it deductively valid or not? Our logical intuition does not always tell us these things as clearly as we might like! We can represent the argument on a truth table and use a truth table technique to show conclusively that it is not a valid argument in propositional logic.

The argument contains two distinct statement letters, so our truth table will have to have four rows. How many columns it has will depend on the number of distinct statements, and component statements, in the premises and conclusion. We represent the premises and the conclusion on our table. We calculate truth values for these for all the possible combinations of truth values in the component statements, D and S. Then we check the argument for deductive validity. We have to make sure that in every row of the truth table in which all the premises come out as true, the conclusion comes out as true also. If there is any case where the premises are all true and the conclusion is false, the argument is not deductively valid in propositional logic. If we find even one case where the conclusion comes out false and the premises are all true, the argument is invalid in propositional logic.

Here is what the truth table looks like:

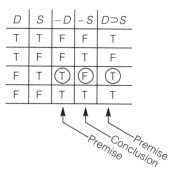

The premises are represented in the rightmost column and in the third column from the left.[1] The conclusion is represented in the fourth column from the left. We check to see where the conclusion turns out to be false. This happens in the first row and in the third row. In the first row one of the premises is false, so the fact that the conclusion is false does not show that the argument is invalid. But in the third row, the conclusion is false and both premises (circled) are true. Thus there is a case in which the premises are true and the conclusion is false. The argument is not deductively valid.

The truth table test for deductive validity works for any argument that can correctly be expressed in the symbols of simple propositional logic. If you can do this, you construct a truth table showing all the premises and the conclusion. You then check to see whether there is any row in the truth table where all the premises are true and the conclusion is false. If there is, the argument is not valid. If there isn't, the argument is valid.

There are some convenient rules for constructing these truth tables. First, you need to know how many rows to have. If n represents the number of distinct statement letters in the argument, then you need 2 to the nth power rows. For two distinct statements, you need 2 times 2 rows; for three distinct statements you need 2 times 2 times 2 rows; for four distinct statements you need 2 times 2 times 2 times 2 rows, and so on. You do not consider a statement and its denial to be distinct statements for the purposes of this calculation because the denial is, technically speaking, a compound statement formed from the original statement. What matters are distinct statement letters.

Second, in order for the truth table technique to work properly, you must represent on it all the possible combinations of truth values for the statements you are working with. The T's and F's in your columns have to be systematically set out in such a way that this requirement is met. Start in the leftmost column and fill half the rows with T's. (That is, if the truth table has eight rows, fill the first four with T's.) Then fill the other half with F's. In the next column, fill one-quarter of the rows with T's, followed by one-quarter F's, and repeat. In the third column (if there is one) it will be one-eighth T's, F's, T's, and so on. This procedure is a standard one, which ensures that the truth tables will represent all the possibilities.

To illustrate the construction of truth tables, suppose that you are setting up a truth table to represent an argument in which the premises and conclusion require four distinct statement letters: *S, C, H,* and *G.* The first four columns of your truth table would look like the one at the top of the next page.

S	C	H	G
T	T	T	T
T	T	T	F
T	T	F	T
T	T	F	F
T	F	T	T
T	F	T	F
T	F	F	T
T	F	F	F
F	T	T	T
F	T	T	F
F	T	F	T
F	T	F	F
F	F	T	T
F	F	T	F
F	F	F	T
F	F	F	F

The next matter is how many columns your truth table needs. It needs at least one for each distinct statement letter, one for each premise, and one for the conclusion. In many cases inserting additional columns is helpful—for clarity and to avoid mistakes. For instance, if you have a premise of the form "$(P \cdot Q) \supset R$," you should have a separate column for "$P \cdot Q$" even if this is neither a premise nor a conclusion in the argument. The reason is that it is a significant component (antecedent of a conditional), and if you enter it separately in its own column, you are less likely to go wrong calculating the truth value of that conditional. (Note, however, that if antecedent is not, itself, a premise in the argument, it should not be regarded as such when you are checking as to whether there is a row on which all premises are true and the conclusion false.)

Here is a more complex example so that we can study the truth table technique further:

ARGUMENT IN ENGLISH

The Iranian revolution will continue as a fundamentalist Muslim movement if there is not a surge of protest from the educated middle classes in Iran. If there is a surge of protest from the middle classes, then the security of the mullahs will be threatened and turbulence in Iran may grow to unprecedented extremes. We don't really expect further turbulence in Iran so it's reasonable to conclude that there will be no strong expression of discontent from the middle classes, and the fundamentalist governing faction will remain secure.

FORMALIZATION OF ARGUMENT

Let *S* represent "There is a surge of protest from the educated middle classes in Iran"; let *C* represent "The Iranian revolution will continue as a fundamentalist Muslim movement"; let *H* represent "The security of the mullahs will be threatened"; let *G* represent "The turbulence in Iran may grow to unprecedented extremes."

The argument may then be formally represented as:

$$-S \supset C$$
$$S \supset (H \cdot G)$$
$$-G$$

Therefore,

$$-S \cdot C$$

The number of distinct statement letters here is four. Thus we will need 2^4, or 16, rows in the truth table. We have to represent each premise and the conclusion. To avoid calculating errors, we will add columns for $(H \cdot G)$ and $-S$, which are components of premises.

The resulting truth table will look like this:

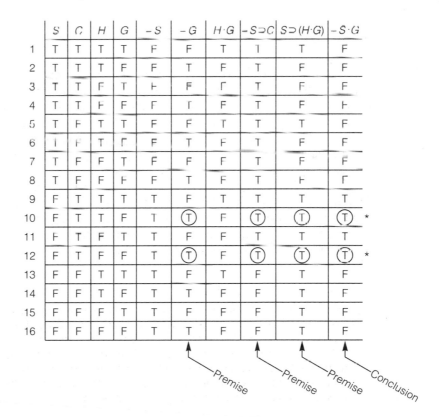

	S	C	H	G	−S	−G	H·G	−S⊃C	S⊃(H·G)	−S·G
1	T	T	T	T	F	F	T	T	T	F
2	T	T	T	F	F	T	F	T	F	F
3	T	T	F	T	F	F	F	T	F	F
4	T	T	F	F	F	T	F	T	F	F
5	T	F	T	T	F	F	T	T	T	F
6	T	F	T	F	F	T	F	T	F	F
7	T	F	F	T	F	F	F	T	F	F
8	T	F	F	F	F	T	F	T	F	F
9	F	T	T	T	T	F	T	T	T	T
10	F	T	T	F	T	T	F	T	T	T	*
11	F	T	F	T	T	F	F	T	T	T
12	F	T	F	F	T	T	F	T	T	T	*
13	F	F	T	T	T	F	T	F	T	F
14	F	F	T	F	T	T	F	F	T	F
15	F	F	F	T	T	F	F	F	T	F
16	F	F	F	F	T	T	F	F	T	F

Premise · Premise · Premise · Conclusion

The columns for the premises and the conclusion are marked with arrows. There are twelve different rows in which the conclusion is false, but in none of these rows are all the premises true. This means that there is no case in which the premises are all true and the conclusion is false. In fact, the only rows in which all the premises are true are the twelfth and tenth rows. There the conclusion is true. The truth table shows that it is not possible for the premises to come out true and the conclusion false; that is, the argument is deductively valid. Whether the argument is cogent will depend, then, solely, on the acceptability of these premises.

The truth table technique can be quite cumbersome for arguments with more than three distinct statement letters. But it is completely effective: it shows you reliably which arguments are deductively valid in simple propositional logic and which are not.

THE SHORTER TRUTH TABLE TECHNIQUE

Because the truth table technique can be so lengthy and cumbersome when there are more than two or three distinct statement letters, it is convenient to have a shorthand version. The shorter technique is based on the fact that when an argument is invalid, there is a row on the truth table representing it on which the conclusion of the argument is false while all its premises are true. If there is no such a row, the argument is valid.

To use the shorter technique, we set values of the component statements in such a way as to guarantee that the conclusion will be false. We then see whether we can consistently set values of the premise statements so that the premises turn out to be true. If so, the argument is invalid.

Suppose, for example, that we have the following representation of an argument:

A ∨ B
B⊃C
C
Therefore,
−A

The conclusion is *−A*. For this conclusion to be false, *A* will have to be true. If *A* is true, the first premise, *A ∨ B,* is true regardless of the truth value of *B*. Making *C* true makes the third premise true. Given that *C* is true, the second premise is true. All these stipulations are consistent with each other. They show that the conclusion could be false while all the premises are true. Hence the argument is invalid.

Here is another example:

$B \supset D$
$D \supset E$
$B \cdot A$
Therefore,
$D \cdot E$

For the conclusion to be false, at least one of D and E will have to be false. Let us suppose that D is false and E is true. Then, for the first premise to be true, B has to be false. The second premise will be true given that E is true and D is false. The third premise, however, cannot be true, because we have already stipulated that B is false. So this possibility is ruled out. Another way of making the conclusion false is to make D true and E false, but to do so will immediately make the second premise false, so it does not give us a way of finding the conclusion false while all the premises are true.

Alternately, we might stipulate both D and E to be false. But if we do so, we again find that B has to be false for the first premise to be true, and then B cannot be true for the third premise to be true. There is no possible way of making the conclusion false and the premises true. Hence, this argument is valid.

The shorter truth table technique can be very useful. The technique is based on the fact that when an argument is valid, there is no possible way that its conclusion can be false when its premises are true. In using this technique you try to stipulate truth values that will make the conclusion false when the premises are true. If you succeed in doing this, you have shown that the argument is invalid. You have to make sure that you check all the ways in which the conclusion can be false, as we did in the last example. Also, it is of course necessary to assign truth values accurately and consistently to all the component statements for the technique to work as it should.

◆———————————————————————

EXERCISE SET

Exercise 1: Part A

Symbolize each of the following passages, using statement letters and the symbols $-$, $\vee$, $\cdot$, and $\supset$. Be sure to state which letters represent which English sentences. Example: "Joe skates and Susan swims" is symbolized as "$J \cdot S$," where J represents "Joe skates" and S represents "Susan swims."

1. Either Fred will make the basketball team or Joe will make the basketball team. If Joe does not make the basketball team, he will be upset. However, if Fred does not make the team, he won't care much.

2. Joan is worried, Fred is upset, and Susan feels ill.

3. If it is sunny tomorrow, the mountain hiking will be pleasant. If the hiking is pleasant, it will be a good time to take some souvenir photos. If we do not take souvenir photos tomorrow, we are not going to get any. So if it is not sunny tomorrow, we will have no photos.

Hint: Use the same statement letter to represent "we are not going to get any photos" and "we will have no photos."

*4. Either Fred will come or Susan will come. If Fred comes, the outing will be a success, and if Susan comes, Joe will enjoy himself.

5. It is not true that human rights are widely respected in El Salvador. If human rights are respected in El Salvador, there are no tortures and disappearances in El Salvador of people who criticize government policy. But in El Salvador, these things are routine.

Hint: Use the same statement letter to represent "there are tortures and disappearances in El Salvador of people who criticize government policy" and "in El Salvador these things are routine."

6. If the president is not reelected and the administration changes, or if the president is reelected with a small majority, the national policy on hospital care may change.

7. If the use of refrigerators increases in the Third World and there is no global ban on CFC's in standard refrigerators, then damage to the ozone layer will be extreme. If damage to the ozone layer is extreme, all people with outdoor occupations will succumb to skin cancer. So either people in the Third World will go on doing without refrigerators or we'll get a global ban on CFC's or we'll have a lot of skin cancer in outdoor workers.

*8. Both these things are true: extensive public relations efforts are being made on behalf of the nuclear industry, and these efforts are not convincing the public. And if either one of them is true, it's an indication the nuclear industry is in trouble. So the nuclear industry is in trouble.

9. If the teacher is ill and her substitute is also ill, then school will be canceled. If school is canceled, and the school does not make alternate care arrangements, then either children

with working parents will be left at home alone or working parents will be scrambling at the last minute for babysitters. The teacher is ill, and we do not want either children of working parents left at home or working parents scrambling at the last minute for babysitters. So if the substitute is ill, the school should make alternate arrangements for care of the children.

Hint: For the purpose of this example, represent "we do not want" simply as "not."

10. If interest rates go up, investment goes up, and if investment goes up, new businesses are created. Given that new businesses are created, new jobs are created, and people benefit. Therefore, if interest rates go up, people benefit.

Exercise 1: Part B

Symbolize each of the following simple arguments and test them for deductive validity using the longer truth table technique. Be sure to stipulate what your statement letters represent.

1. Either the behaviorists are right or the liberal humanists are right. Since it's been conclusively demonstrated that the behaviorists aren't right, it is the liberal humanists who must be right.

*2. Provided that you master calculus, you will have no difficulty with the mathematical aspects of first-year university physics. But really, you know, you have mastered calculus successfully. Thus, the mathematical part of the physics course should go smoothly for you.

3. If the mind is entirely distinct from the body, there is no lessening of concentration due to fatigue. And yet fatigue does lessen concentration. We can infer from this fact that the mind is not entirely distinct from the body.

4. If oil prices increase, the western provinces will improve their economic situation, and if the western provinces improve their economic situation, easterners will move west for better jobs. Thus, if oil prices increase, easterners will move west for better jobs.

5. An owl is reputed to be wise. If an owl is reputed to be wise, this belief shows that people

use the word *wise* in a nonliteral way. Therefore, people use the word *wise* in a nonliteral way.

6. Either the murder was voluntarily committed or it was a compulsive action. If the murder was voluntarily committed, the murderer should be sent to jail. If the murder was a compulsive action, the murderer should be sent to a psychiatric institution. So the murderer should be sent either to jail or to a psychiatric institution.

7. Either the Soviet Union is a superpower or it is not a superpower. If the Soviet Union is a superpower, it can hold its various republics together and it can feed its peoples. The Soviet Union cannot hold its various republics together and it cannot feed its peoples. Therefore, the Soviet Union is not a superpower.

*8. If you are a suitable student of philosophy of science, you know either philosophy or science. You do not know philosophy and you do not know science. Therefore, you are not a suitable student of philosophy of science.

*9. If John exercises, he is in good shape. John is in good shape. So John exercises.

*10. Either the negotiations will be successful, the problem will continue to be unresolved with the situation at a standoff, or the situation will escalate into violence. The negotiations will be successful, so the problem will be resolved.

Exercise 1: Part C

Represent the following arguments in letters and propositional symbols and test them for validity using the shorter truth table technique.

*1. If the United States subsidizes grain sales to the Soviet Union, then Canadian farmers will receive less for their grain. If Canadian farmers receive less for their grain, then some Canadian farmers will go bankrupt, and if this happens, Canadian taxpayers will be called upon to help support farmers. The United States is going to subsidize grain sales to the Soviet Union. So we can expect that Canadian taxpayers will be called upon to help support Canadian farmers.

Hint: Symbolize "this happens" with the same statement letter you use for "Some Canadian farmers will go bankrupt."

2. Well-educated people should either know science or know literature. Since well-educated people should know science, they should not know literature.

*3. Both these things cannot be true: that nuclear weapons free zones are meaningless symbolic gestures and that nuclear weapons free zones hinder important alliances. Therefore, either these zones are not meaningful or they do not hinder alliances.

4. If the zoo is well administered, the animals are well cared for. If the animals are well cared for, some animals will reproduce in captivity. If some animals reproduce in captivity, we can expect that there will be baby animals at the zoo. There are some baby animals at the zoo. Therefore, the zoo is well administered.

*5. Either the murderer used a kitchen knife or the murderer carried an unusually large pocket knife, then either he was wearing loose clothing or he would have been noticed by the neighboring observers. The murderer was not noticed by the neighboring observers. If he was wearing loose clothing, either he was very thin or he was not wearing the clothing that was found at the scene of the crime. We know that the murderer was not wearing loose clothing and that he did not use a kitchen knife. Therefore, he was not wearing the clothing that was found at the scene of the crime.

TRANSLATING FROM ENGLISH INTO PROPOSITIONAL LOGIC

So far we have used examples that are relatively easy to put into the symbols of propositional logic. But there are sometimes difficulties in expressing English statements in the symbols of propositional logic. We'll work through some of the common problems that arise in connection with the basic connecting symbols.

Just to illustrate the kind of nuance in ordinary language that is not represented in propositional logic, consider the story of two drugstores that were located side by side on a Winnipeg street some years ago.[2] Each had a sign advertising its services to customers. One sign said "If you need it, we have it." The other said "If we don't have it, you don't need it." The stores apparently had quite different attitudes to the needs of their customers!

Both slogans can be represented in propositional logic. Let N represent "you need it" and H represent "we have it." The first sign is represented as "$N \supset H$" and the second as "$-H \supset -N$." It turns out that these two statements are logically equivalent. You can check this yourself by making truth tables; truth tables show them true and false in just the same circumstances. But in terms of public relations and suggestions as to the stores' willingness to serve customers, there is a big difference between the signs. The first sign, "If you need it, we have it," suggests that the store caters to customers and will have whatever they need. The second, "If we don't have it, you don't need it," suggests that customers should fit their requests to the inventory of the store.

How important are these suggested meanings? The answer has to be "it depends." If you are working for an advertising agency, they are very important; if you are doing proofs in propositional logic, they are irrelevant. Generally, however, to understand what is said, it is important both to grasp the truth functional relations dealt with in propositional logic and to appreciate these additional suggested nuances that cannot be formalized.

Not

Let us suppose that you have decided to represent a particular English statement in an argument with the letter P. If you represent another English statement in that same argument as $-P$, the second statement must be the contradictory of the first. That is, it must always have the opposite truth value. It cannot merely be the contrary of the first statement. If a statement is true, its contrary must be false. However, it is possible for both a statement and its contrary to be false. Thus a contrary is quite different from a contradictory, which must have the opposite value. For instance, if P represents "Joe is strong," then $-P$ cannot be used to represent "Joe is weak." "Joe is strong" and "Joe is weak" are not contradictory statements; they are contraries. They need not have opposite truth values; they can both be false in the case that Joe is a person of quite average strength.

A statement and its contradictory must have opposite truth values and one or the other must be true. If you wish to symbolize one statement as $-P$ when another has been symbolized as P, you must make sure that the two are genuine contradictories and not just contraries.

And

As it is represented and defined on the truth table, the symbol "·" carries no implication that the two statements that it conjoins have any real relationship to each other. That is, if *C* is "Colds frequently occur in winter" and *W* is "The Falklands War was very expensive," there is nothing wrong with "*C·W*" from a formal point of view. The conjunction just asserts both the separate statements and is not supposed to suggest that there is any kind of connection between them. But in natural speech and writing we do not usually conjoin entirely unrelated statements. Usually we assert two statements together when we believe that they are related in some way. It is important to understand that this aspect of ordinary language is not reflected in propositional logic. Relatively few arguments turn on this particular feature of *and* in English.

Another interesting point about *and* is that occasionally in English and other natural languages the order of the components in a conjunction has significance. One conjunct will be stated first to imply a sequence in time. In such contexts, the word *and* is used in English to suggest "and then." For instance, if we say "They declared war and sent out the fleet," this way of speaking suggests that war was declared *before* the fleet was sent out. To say "They sent out the fleet and declared war" suggests that the fleet was sent out before war was declared. In diplomatic contexts, the difference between these two ways of expressing the conjunctions could be extremely important. Similarly, "The doctor operated and she recovered" suggests that the operation came before the recovery and led to it, whereas, "She recovered and the doctor operated" could provide grounds for a malpractice suit! But these differences would not show up at all on a truth table. In both cases, the statements would be represented as the same conjunction, and they would come out as true or false regardless of the order of the events.

We have to recognize, then, that "·" and the English *and* differ. The former never states a temporal relationship, and the latter sometimes strongly suggests one. In any argument or context where the suggested time sequence is important, "·" would not fully represent the sense of *and* in that context.

Another point to be noted is that "·" must be used to conjoin two or more *statements*. In English, the word *and* is often used this way. But it may also appear between two subjects or between two predicates, as in these examples:

1.   Joe and Fred passed the final examination in university algebra.
2.   Mary mowed the lawn and weeded the garden.

To symbolize these statements, you have to move *and* out of the subject or predicate and construct two simple statements, which you can then link with "·." Thus:

1.   Joe passed the final examination in university algebra and Fred passed the final examination in university algebra. (*J·F*)
2.   Mary mowed the lawn and Mary weeded the garden. (*M·W*)

Sometimes this simple strategy is not appropriate because it may be an important part of the meaning of the statement, in its context, that the subjects performed the activity together. For instance, when we assert that May and Fred got married, we are not simply asserting that May got married and Fred got married; we are asserting that they married each other. This fact will not be represented if we let *M* represent "May got married." There are other contexts, too, where the togetherness implied by *and* in English will be important to the force of an argument and cannot properly be omitted in the symbolization.

Here is a simple example:

3. I know that Joe and Fred are good friends. Last week they went swimming together, played tennis with each other, and shared in the work on Fred's father's garden.

To establish that these two are friends, it will be important to assert not just that they both played tennis, went swimming, and worked in the garden, but that they did these things together. Thus we cannot appropriately represent the argument by conjoining simple propositions in which the subjects have been separated. We would have to do it like this:

3. I know that Joe and Fred are good friends. Joe and Fred went swimming together. Joe and Fred played tennis with each other. Joe and Fred shared in the work on Fred's father's garden. Let *S* represent "Joe and Fred went swimming together"; let *L* represent "Joe and Fred played tennis with each other"; let *G* represent "Joe and Fred shared in the work on Fred's father's garden." We have to keep the subjects together because the togetherness suggested by *and* in this context is important to the argument. The statements are represented as *S·L·G*.

Suppose you try to translate into the symbols of propositional logic a statement that uses *but* or *although*. These words are frequently used to introduce counterconsiderations in an argument. In a statement like:

4. No North American peace group has ever advocated unilateral disarmament although peace groups are constantly criticized for advocating unilateral disarmament. (*C* although *A*) there is a conjunction asserted (*C* and *A*), but more is suggested as well because the *although* requires a contrast between the two facts. It says that the first is surprising in view of the second. To say "*C* although *A*" is to say "*C* and *A*, and given *A* one would not expect *C*." That is, *C* and *A* are both true but their conjunction is not what one would have expected.

This element of surprise or contrast expressed by *although* or *but* is not represented by the "·" of the truth table. The same point can be made about such words as *even though, in spite of the fact that, despite, yet*, and a number of other terms that suggest contrast. The truth table and the conjunction symbol in propositional logic represent only conjunction—pure and simple. Any element of contrast is omitted. This omission means that in any context where the element of contrast is crucial to establishing a point, the symbols of propositional logic do not adequately represent the claim. Often, however, this contrastive element is not essential, so that statements in which such words as *although* and *but* are used for conjunction can be represented in propositional logic with the symbol "·".

Or

The notable thing about "∨" defined in the truth table is that it specifies what logicians call *inclusive disjunction*. An inclusive disjunction is one that is true when both disjuncts are true, as well as when either one of them is true. If you look at the truth table for "∨," you will notice that on the first row, where *P* and *Q* are both true, the compound "*P* ∨ *Q*" is also true. In this inclusive sense of *or,* a statement like:

    5.   Either the negotiations will be successful or the situation will escalate to the point of violence.

is true when *both* disjuncts are true. Suppose that the negotiations are successful, but that later the situation escalates to violence for other reasons. Statement (5) would be regarded as *true* in such a case, given the way "∨" is defined in the truth table.

However, in English and other natural languages, it is quite common to use and understand *or* and related words in an *exclusive* sense. We would in all likelihood take statement (5) to mean:

Either the negotiations will be successful or the situation will escalate to the point of violence, and not both.

The exclusive use of *or* implies that one and only one of the alternatives will hold. The inclusive *or* implies merely that at least one will hold. A restaurant menu telling you that:

    6.   Jello or ice cream may be taken as a free dessert with your meal.

is not usually telling you that you are allowed to have both. Here *or* is used exclusively. You would not be likely to be successful if you drew a truth table for the restaurant manager and insisted on having both items for dessert! You can express *exclusive disjunction* perfectly well using the symbols of propositional logic. Let's see how this works for the jello and ice cream case:

Let *J* represent "Jello will be provided as a free desert with your meal."
Let *I* represent "Ice cream will be provided as a free dessert with your meal."
The menu is stating:
    $(J \lor I) \cdot -(J \cdot I)$
That is, it allows one or the other, not both.

The inclusive disjunction defined on the truth table for "∨" is standard in propositional logic. When you are symbolizing sentences in which *or* is the connective, use "∨"—that is, inclusive disjunction—unless you are sure that an exclusive disjunction is implied. In that case, you have to add *and not both* to capture the meaning.

The other point about "∨" is rather like our point about subjects and predicates linked by *and*. In ordinary speech and writing you often find *or* between subjects or predicates, as in the following:

7.   John or Sue will help with the gardening.

and

8.   Sue will either work in the garden or swim.

But just as "·" must link statements in propositional logic, so must "∨." Thus we have to rearrange the preceding examples, as:

7.   John will help with the gardening or Sue will help with the gardening.
      J ∨ *S*
8.   Sue will work in the garden or Sue will swim.
      G ∨ *W*

If Then

With regard to the relation between English and symbols, the *if-then* symbol is the one that raises fascinating and controversial issues. Let us look again at the truth table that defines the horseshoe connective.

P	*Q*	*P*⊃*Q*
T	T	T
T	F	F
F	T	T
F	F	T

We said that "⊃", as defined on this truth table, was a minimal conditional. To see what this means, the first step is to recall that the *P* and *Q* on the truth table can represent any two statements at all. Let us stipulate that *A* represents "Argentina invaded the Falkland Islands in 1982" and *B* represents "Stephen Jay Gould is the author of a book entitled *The Mismeasure of Man*." As a matter of fact, these two statements are both true. Obviously they are quite unconnected with each other. There is no relation by definition, causation, law, morality, threat, or custom between the Argentinean invasion and Gould's authorship. (His book was about problems in measuring human intelligence, not about war or peace.)

Nevertheless, using the horseshoe to connect *A* and *B*, we will get the surprising result that the compound statement "*A*⊃*B*" is true. If this is hard to believe, just look back at the truth table. On the row where *A* is true and *B* is also true, *A*⊃*B* is true; this is just how "⊃" is defined. It would surely be most eccentric to assert:

9.   If Argentina invaded the Falkland Islands in 1982, then Stephen Jay Gould
is the author of a book entitled *The Mismeasure of Man*.

Statement (9) here is not the sort of thing anyone would assert because none of
the normal sorts of connections (definition, causation, law, and so forth) hold
between the invasion and the author. Yet if we represent the statement in symbolic logic as "$A \supset B$," it comes out as true, according to the truth table for the
horseshoe. How can this be?

The answer is that the horseshoe represents a minimum truth value connection between an antecedent and a consequent. This minimum is: provided the
antecedent is true, the consequent must be true. The only case when the minimum
conditional is false is the case when the antecedent is true and the consequent is
false. For this *minimum conditional*, there is no requirement that the antecedent
and the consequent have any other relationship to each other.

In ordinary life, we are usually concerned with conditionals where there are
further relationships between the statements. Because the horseshoe abstracts
from these features, it can mislead us. We have to remember that it is the basic
conditionality that the horseshoe represents—not anything more. The horseshoe
is important in propositional reasoning because it mirrors a core of conditionality
that can be precisely defined on a truth table and conveniently related to the other
propositional connectives.

To see puzzling aspects of the horseshoe, look at the two rows of the truth
table where P is false. Remember again that P and Q can represent any two
statements. This time let's allow P to represent the statement that Argentina
invaded Russia in 1981 and Q to represent the statement that Russia invaded
China in 1989. Since both statements are in fact false, the combination "$P \supset Q$"
turns out to be true. (Check the last row of the truth table to see that this occurs.)
But we would never assert—much less believe—that:

10. If Argentina invaded Russia in 1981, then Russia invaded China in 1989.

is true! Statement (10) is entirely contrary to common sense. There is no connection of the sort anyone is interested in for any practical purpose.

If you look at your truth table, you will see that because of the way the
horseshoe is defined, a statement of the form "$P \supset Q$" will be true whenever its
antecedent is false. The reason is that, given the falsity of P, a statement of the
form "$P \supset Q$" is true when the statement Q represents is true and also true when
the statement Q represents is false. This means, in effect, that when P is false,
the conditional "$P \supset Q$" is true regardless of the content of P and of Q. In some
ways this situation is paradoxical—at least it is contrary to common sense, if we
think of the horseshoe as expressing *if then* in English.

There is a special technical term for conditional statements in which the
antecedent is known to be false. They are called *counterfactuals*. The antecedent,
being false, is contrary-to-fact. Note, however, that this is not to say that the
whole statement is false or contrary-to-fact. As we shall see, many counterfac-

tuals are plausibly regarded as being true. In fact, counterfactuals are extremely important both in science and in ordinary life. It is often important to make claims about what would have happened or what would happen if conditions were different from what they are. The problem, when we consider representing counterfactuals using the horseshoe, is that in science and in ordinary life we usually distinguish between counterfactuals, thinking that some are true or plausible and others are false or implausible. We don't regard all counterfactuals as equally true.

Consider:

11. If Hitler had died in childhood, the Jewish population of Poland would be larger today than it is.
12. If Hitler had died in childhood, there would be no threat to the ozone layer today.

We know, of course, that Hitler did not die in childhood. Both (11) and (12) are conditionals with an antecedent known to be false: both are counterfactuals. Most of us would find (11) to be quite plausible, given Hitler's central role in the anti-Semitic campaigns of the 1930s and in the mass killings of Jews. On the other hand, we would find (12) to be entirely implausible. As represented in propositional logic, both (11) and (12) will come out to be true. What has gone wrong?

The problem is that counterfactuals are used to assert connections stronger than that of material implication, which is conveyed by the horseshoe. Counterfactuals are backed up by general lawlike connections, typically causal in nature. Statement (11) is plausible because Hitler's policies and actions were a necessary cause of the killings. Statement (12) is implausible because there is little reason to believe in any connection between Hitler's policies and actions and the current threat to the earth's ozone layer.

How counterfactual statements should be understood and what logical apparatus should be used to formally represent them are complex and controversial issues in logic. There is agreement, however, that the horseshoe is not well suited to convey the meaning of counterfactuals. This problem is quite an advanced one that we cannot treat further here. We mention it to indicate one area where there are recognized limitations to the horseshoe as the symbol for *if then*.

The core of conditionality represented by the horseshoe can best be understood by looking back at the truth table for "⊃" and focusing your attention on the second line. This line says that for any two propositions P and Q, when P is true and Q is false, the horseshoe conditional "$P \supset Q$" is false. This relationship *always* holds for conditionals in natural language. For instance, suppose someone tells you, "If you go to China you will see people wearing Mao suits." Suppose that you do go to China, and you don't see any people wearing Mao suits. That will show that his conditional assertion was false, which is just what would be indicated if you represent it on the truth table. If the antecedent is true and the consequent is false, the conditional statement is false.

It is just this minimal element of conditionals that is most basic for arguments because if we put the horseshoe between the premises and conclusion of an argument—as in "Premise and Premise⊃Conclusion"—we will not be able to move from true premises to a false conclusion. This is what we are trying to avoid when we argue and infer—we don't want to proceed from truth to falsehood. Many arguments in which *if then* and related terms play the crucial role are set up in such a way that only this minimal core of the conditional is required for the argument to proceed. In these cases you can use the horseshoe to represent *if then,* and it will give you the right results when you test the argument for deductive validity. However, this result cannot be guaranteed for counterfactuals and, generally, it is not advisable to represent them using the horseshoe.

◆———————————————————————————————

EXERCISE SET

Exercise 2: Part A

Using ·, ∨, −, and ⊃ and using capital letters to represent component statements, represent the following arguments in the terms of propositional logic.

1. If elephants are domesticated animals and domesticated animals tend to be inbred, then elephants will tend to be inbred if there is not something exceptional about the way they are raised. There is nothing exceptional about the way elephants are raised. We can conclude that elephants tend to be inbred.

2. Only if richer nations come to understand the world food problem can we hope to eliminate famine. If there is no improvement in university education about development issues, the richer nations will not come to understand the world food problem. Thus, if there is not an improvement in university education about world food problems, there is no hope of eliminating famine.

3. Juan or Paulo will come with the message, if Bill does not bring it. If Juan comes, that means that Paulo is at work and Bill is away on vacation. If Paulo comes, that means that Juan is either in class or out of town with his family. Bill did not come with the message. Therefore, either Paulo is at work or Juan is out of town with his family.

4. Either Susan and John are still quarreling or they have resolved their dispute about the broken lawnmower. If the lawnmower is not fixed, they have not resolved their dispute about it. So either the lawnmower is fixed or they are still quarreling.

*5. It is not possible to take both French and German in the last year of high school if you take both physics and chemistry, or both chemistry and biology, or both biology and physics. If you take any two of chemistry, physics, and biology, you must take either French or German and not both.

6. If Joe is healthy, he will be able to climb that hill effortlessly. If he has lung problems from smoking too much, Joe is not healthy. Smoking has given Joe quite serious lung problems. So he will not be able to climb the hill effortlessly.

7. Choral singing works well only when singers all cooperate and no one tries to be a star and steal the show. If there is a star, that person's voice stands out and spoils the united effect sought by a choir.

*8. If the land claims disputes are not resolved and the native leaders continue to distrust the government, then either there will be continued nonviolent blockades or there will be an escalation of the problem into terrorist action. If there are continued nonviolent blockades, antagonism between whites and natives will increase, and if there is an escalation of the problem into terrorist action, the whole country will be seriously affected in a most adverse way. Unless the government can inspire more confidence from native leaders, there will be either increased antagonism between natives and whites or even adverse effects on the whole country. Somehow, even if land claims disputes are not resolved, native leaders must come to trust the government.

Hint: Assume that the same statement letter can be used to represent "it is not the case that native leaders continue to distrust the government" and "native leaders must come to trust the government."

Exercise 2: Part B

Symbolize the following passages, as in Part A, and test arguments for validity using the truth table technique or the shorter truth table technique, as you prefer.

1. If French philosophy continues to flourish in universities, there will be a pull away from formal logic and philosophy of science among graduate students in philosophy. If there is such a pull, traditional teaching patterns will be upset. And yet, you know, it is quite likely that the attraction of French philosophy will persist. I conclude that we've got to expect some disturbance in traditional teaching patterns.

2. My brother is not a bald man, so my brother is a hairy man.

*3. The operation was not painful. Either the operation was painful or it was pleasant. So it must have been pleasant.

4. If July is rainy, there is really no summer. This year July was rainy, so there was no summer worth mentioning.

5. If science is entirely objective, then the emotions and ambitions of scientists have nothing to do with their pursuit of research. But the emotions and ambitions of scientists do have something to do with their pursuit of research. Therefore, science is not entirely objective.

6. If Joe makes the team, Fred will make the team. And if Fred makes the team, the team is sure to win. So if Joe makes the team, the team is sure to win.

7. Either it will snow or it will rain. If it snows, the roads will be slippery, and if it rains, the roads will still be slippery. So the roads are going to be slippery.

*8. International politics is either a difficult academic subject or it is such a mishmash that nobody can understand it at all. If respected academics study international politics, then it is not just a mishmash no one understands. Respected academics do study international politics. So it is not a mishmash. It is a difficult academic subject.

9. The textbook is either accurate and boring or inaccurate and interesting. If the textbook is accurate, it will be widely used. And if it is interesting, it will be widely used. Thus, however things turn out, the textbook is bound to be widely used.

10. If women are drafted, wars will have to provide maternity leaves. If wars have to provide maternity leaves, war will become impossible. Therefore, if women are drafted, war will become impossible, and if war is possible, women are not going to be drafted.

11. Either the United Nations will continue to function as it presently does, with its present financial and political problems, or the United States will agree to virtually subsidize the United Nations, despite having limited control over U.N. activities, or there will have to be a renegotiated basis for funding the United Nations. The United States will not agree to virtually subsidize the United Nations. The United Nations cannot just go on with the financial and political problems that presently exist. Thus there will have to be a renegotiated basis for U.N. funding.

12. If sex education is successful, children learn a lot about sex, and if they learn a lot about sex, they will know enough to protect themselves from abuse. So either sex education will be successful or children will not know enough to protect themselves from abuse.

13. If morality is entirely relative, torture is as virtuous as charity. But torture is not as virtuous as charity. Therefore, morality is not entirely relative.

14. If learning languages is recognized as important, students will work hard to learn French, Spanish, and Chinese. Students are working hard to learn French, Spanish, and Chinese. Thus, learning languages is of recognized importance.

*15. If Socrates influenced Plato, and Plato influenced Aristotle, then Socrates influenced Aristotle. Socrates did influence Plato, and Plato obviously influenced Aristotle as well, so we can see that Socrates influenced Aristotle.

16. If women are equal to men, then women are as strong as men. But women are not as strong as men. Therefore, women are not equal to men. If women are not equal to men, they have no proper claim to receive salaries as high as men's. But women should receive salaries as high as men's. So women must be equal to men. I conclude that women are both equal and not equal to men.

*17. If Iraq wins its war against Iran, the balance of power in the Persian Gulf area will be upset. If the balance of power in the Persian Gulf area is upset, then the United States will be progressively more tempted to accelerate the development of its Rapid Deployment Force. But if the development of the Rapid Deployment Force proceeds at an even faster pace than presently, world tensions will be aggravated. Thus, if Iraq wins its war against Iran, world tensions will be aggravated.

18. If the superpowers are going to bargain successfully about arms limitations, negotiators will have to communicate in a straightforward fashion. If negotiators take every statement as a political gesture, they do not communicate in a straightforward fashion. Thus if negotiators take every statement as a political gesture, the superpowers will not bargain successfully about arms limitations.

*19. If you go on a diet for more than two months, your metabolism will slow down. If your metabolism slows down, you will need less food than you do now. If you need less food than you do now, you will gain weight on what you eat now. Therefore, if you go on a diet for more than two months, eventually the result will be that you will gain weight on what you eat now. If dieting has the result of making you gain weight, dieting is futile. Thus, dieting is futile.

20. Either the economy will improve or there will be millions of unemployed young people. The economy will not improve, so there will be millions of unemployed young people. If there are millions of unemployed young people, there is bound to be social unrest. So if the economy does not improve, we can expect social unrest.

FURTHER POINTS ABOUT TRANSLATION

Let's take another look at the first example from the Part B exercises:

> If French philosophy continues to flourish in universities, there will be a pull away from formal logic and philosophy of science among graduate students in philosophy. If there is such a pull, traditional teaching patterns will be upset. And yet, you know, it is quite likely that the attraction of French philosophy will persist. I conclude that we've got to expect some disturbance in traditional teaching patterns.

This argument is a simple deductively valid one, and it can be shown valid on a truth table. But to represent the argument in the symbols of propositional logic in such a way that its deductive validity is apparent, we need to gloss over certain verbal and stylistic aspects. The correct representation of this argument in the symbols of propositional logic is:

$C \supset A$
$A \supset D$
C
Therefore,
D

Here C represents "French philosophy will continue to flourish in universities," A represents "There will be a pull away from logic and philosophy of science among graduate students in philosophy," and D represents "There will be some disturbance in traditional teaching patterns." Notice that C is expressed in slightly different ways in the antecedent of the first and second sentences. Also, D is expressed in slightly different ways in the conclusion and in the consequent of the conditional in the second sentence. In formalizing this argument we have made decisions that slightly different English words are equivalent in meaning in this context.

This example illustrates the fact that when you are formalizing, you make decisions about what you think English sentences mean. You use the same letter to represent two verbally different expressions only when you think that these expressions are functioning to say the same thing. Determining whether these expressions are or are not equivalent can be difficult. But even learning to raise the question is an important step in getting meanings clear. You have to develop your senses for the nuances of language. Also, if your formalization results in some slurring over of slight differences in meaning, you should check back to see that the omitted aspects do not affect the merits of the argument you are dealing with.

Both . . . And . . .

A statement of the type "both P and Q" is easily represented in propositional logic as a conjunction. Here is an example:

(i) Both France and Britain are concerned about the growth of German power in central Europe. Statement (i) is a conjunction of "France is concerned about the growth of German power in central Europe" (R) and "Britain is concerned about the growth of German power in central Europe" (B). To represent (i) in the apparatus of propositional logic, we simply write:
$R \cdot B$

The same schema for representation can be used for more complex variations of "*both . . . and . . . .*" Consider:

(ii) Both of these things are true: a high degree of scientific education is needed for a nation to be competitive on the international scene and scientific education in North America is relatively weak.

If we allow D to represent "a high degree of scientific education is needed for a nation to be competitive on the international scene" and W to represent "scientific education in North America is relatively weak," then (ii) is formally represented as:

$D \cdot W$

Neither . . . Nor . . .

Consider the following statement:

(i) Neither John nor Susan is able to attend the lecture.

Statement (i) is a compound statement in which the linking words are *neither . . . nor*. In effect, *nor* means "not either . . . or . . . ." If we represent "John is able to attend" by J and "Susan is able to attend" by S, we can represent (i) as:

$-(J \vee S)$

The same method of representation can be used even when the English does not include *neither* and uses *nor* at the beginning of the second statement, as in (ii):

(ii) The Prime Minister did not accept responsibility for the problem. Nor did he issue any official statement on the matter.

In (ii) we have two negations; two possibilities are described and it is said that neither of them happened; not this or that. Let R represent "the Prime Minister accepted responsibility for the problem" and I represent "the Prime Minister issued an official statement on the matter." Then, to represent (ii), we write:

$-(R \vee I)$

The fact that the formalization here is the same, structurally, as for the *neither . . . nor . . .* statement in (i) makes sense if we reflect on how easy it would be to express statement (ii) in English using *neither . . . nor. . . .* We would say "The Prime Minister neither accepted responsibility for the problem nor issued any official statement on the matter."

. . . Implies That . . .

Often we speak of statements implying each other. In propositional logic, implication of one statement by another is represented using the horseshoe. The statement that implies is the antecedent and the one that is implied is the consequent. Here is an example:

(i) That the United States was unwilling to accept the jurisdiction of the International Court of Justice in its dispute with Nicaragua implies that the United States does not respect international law.

To represent this implication statement in terms of propositional logic, let U represent "The United States is unwilling to accept the jurisdiction of the International Court of Justice in its dispute with Nicaragua" and let *R* represent "The United States respects international law." Statement (i) can then be written as a conditional with *U* as its antecedent and − *R* as its consequent.

$U \supset - R$

Sometimes *implies* is used with grammatical constructions that are not in the form of complete statements, as in the following example.

(ii) Human free will implies the ability to choose what we do.

Here "human free will" and "the ability to choose what we do" are not complete statements, and only complete statements can be represented by statement letters in propositional logic. We can, however, see (ii) as expressing an implication relation between statements. In effect, (ii) is saying:

(ii′) That human beings have free will implies that human beings have the ability to choose what they do.

Now (ii′) can be represented. Let *H* represent "human beings have free will" and let *C* represent "human beings have the ability to choose what they do." Statement (ii′), and, accordingly, (ii), which is equivalent to it, can be formally represented as:

$H \supset C$

Sometimes we negate statements of implication. When formally representing such negations, you have to be careful to put the negation outside brackets that surround the conditional. Consider the following example:

(iii) The fact that Albania is a communist country does not imply that all Albanians are miserably unhappy.

Statement (iii) is denying an implication between "Albania is a communist country" (*A*) and "All Albanians are miserably unhappy" (*M*). It is represented as:

$- (C \supset M)$

. . . Provided That . . .

We often speak of certain things being the case provided that something else is the case. These kinds of statements are conditionals and can be represented as such in propositional logic. Consider the following:

(i) Freedom of religion is conducive to political harmony, provided that religious groups pay due consideration to those dissenting from their beliefs.

Statement (i) is asserting that freedom of religion makes for political harmony under a certain condition, or, as it is sometimes called, "proviso." To represent a statement like this using the horseshoe we make the proviso the antecedent of the conditional. Statement (i) says that *if* religious groups pay due consideration to the rights of those dissenting from their beliefs (*D*), then freedom of religion is conducive to political harmony (*C*). It is represented as:

$D \supset C$

Here is another example:

(ii) Mary can sing soprano parts provided that they do not go higher than A.

The proviso here is negative. Let *H* represent "soprano parts go higher than A" and *M* represent "Mary can sing soprano parts." Statement (ii) then becomes:

$-H \supset M$

Only If

Consider a sentence like this:

(i) Peter is eligible for medical school only if he has studied biology.

Let us allow *S* to represent "Peter is eligible for medical school" and *B* to represent "Peter has studied biology." Then the sentence as a whole can be represented, using the horseshoe, as follows:

$S \supset B$

Many people want to turn examples like this around:

$B \supset S$: *Wrong*

This turnaround is wrong because the original sentence states that studying biology is necessary for Peter to be eligible. This sentence means that given that he is eligible, it will be true that he has studied biology; otherwise, he would not be eligible. The turnaround representation, which is wrong, makes a necessary condition of eligibility into a sufficient one. It says that given that he has studied biology, he'll be eligible, which isn't right. (If you think about how hard it is to get into medical school, this point will probably be very obvious!)

When you think about it, people are perfectly good at understanding the *only if* relationship in practical contexts. Consider the following familiar instruction:

(ii) Pass only from the center lane.

Such an instruction, on a busy highway, appears to be routinely understood and obeyed by drivers.[3] It is an *only if* instruction; you should pass (*S*) only if your car is in the center lane (*C*). The formal representation would be:

$S \supset C$

Necessary Condition

A *necessary condition* is one that is needed or required. A sufficient condition is one that is enough to ensure a result. For instance, having oxygen is a necessary condition for human life, but it is not sufficient. On the other hand, having 3000 calories per day is a sufficient condition for adequate human nutrition, but it is not a necessary condition. (Less will suffice.) We often find claims about conditions that are necessary for various states of affairs. Consider, for instance:

(i) For human beings, having oxygen is a necessary condition of being alive.

This claim can be symbolized using the horseshoe. Let H represent "Human beings are alive" and O represent "Human beings have oxygen." Then the relationship of necessary condition can be represented as:

$H \supset O$

To say that having oxygen is a necessary condition of being alive is to say that human beings are alive only if they have oxygen. Life requires oxygen. Thus, from the fact that humans are alive, we can infer they have oxygen. (If H and $H \supset O$, then O.)

Sufficient Condition

Sufficient conditions are not the same as necessary conditions. Sufficient conditions for a state of affairs will guarantee that a state of affairs exists. For example:

(i) Striking a match in a room full of gasoline is a sufficient condition for igniting a fire.

Let S represent "Someone strikes a match in a room full of gasoline" and let L represent "A fire is ignited in a room full of gasoline." To say that S is a sufficient condition for L is to say that if S, then L, which, of course, is represented as:

$S \supset L$

in propositional logic. Given that the match is lit, conditions are sufficient for a fire, and there will be a fire. We should note that sufficient conditions may not be necessary. Lighting a match in a room full of gasoline is not a necessary condition for having a fire in that room, because we could get a fire in other ways—by leaving a lighted candle near a newspaper, for instance.

Necessary and Sufficient Conditions

Some conditions are both necessary and sufficient for a given result. For instance, being a male parent is a necessary condition for being a father, and it is also a sufficient condition for being a father. Consider:

(i) Joe's being a male parent is both necessary and sufficient for his being a father.

If we let J represent "Joe is a male parent" and B represent "Joe is a father," then we can represent this relationship as:

$(B \supset J) \cdot (J \supset B)$

Necessary and sufficient conditions are represented in a conjunction, as this example illustrates.

Unless

Consider the statement "We will go on a picnic unless it rains." Clearly this statement is a compound one in which two simpler statements are connected. There is no symbol for *unless* in propositional logic. However, *unless* can be represented perfectly well by combining symbols for *if then* and *not*. The simplest way to do this is to begin by rewriting the sentence in English, substituting the words *if not* for *unless*. Thus for:

(i) We will go on a picnic unless it rains.

we write:

(i') We will go on a picnic if it does not rain.

And we can represent (i') using the horseshoe, as:

$-R \supset G$

where *R* represents "It rains" and *G* represents "We will go on a picnic."

The standard way of representing *unless* in propositional logic, then, is to replace it with *if not* and then use the horseshoe. The antecedent of the resulting conditional statement will be the denial of the statement that came after *unless* in the first place. Let us use this technique on another example:

(ii) You will not pass the course unless you work very hard and attend all classes regularly.
(ii') You will not pass the course if you do not work very hard and attend all classes regularly.
Let *W* represent "You will pass the course"; *V* represent "You will work very hard"; and *A* represent "You will attend all classes regularly." What comes after *unless* in (ii) is a conjunction, and this whole conjunction has to be negated in (ii'). The resulting symbolization is as follows:
$-(V \cdot A) \supset -W$

This system for understanding *unless* in the symbols of propositional logic can be mastered quite easily. Usually this method is adequate. A statement written "*P* unless *Q*" *always* asserts at least that *P* if not *Q*, which is reordered as "if not *Q*, then *P*," and can readily be symbolized.

Sometimes *unless* appears to express more than "if not." Here is an example.

(iii) Don will go to the concert unless he is broke.

According to the standard scheme wherein *unless* is understood as expressing "if not" we would understand (iii) as follows:

(iii') Don will go to the concert if he is not broke.
Let *D* represent "Don will go to the concert" and *B* represent "Don is broke." Then (iii') is formally represented as follows:
$-B \supset D$

However, this formalization strikes some people as puzzling. They think that (iii) also asserts that if he is broke, Don will not go to the concert. To say that he will go *unless* he is broke, seems to be saying that being broke is what will keep him from going; if he is not broke, he will go, and if he is broke he will not go. This second claim is:

(iii″) If Don is broke, Don will not go to the concert.

And (iii″) is formally represented as:

B⊃ – D

Statement (iii) seems to express (iii″) as well as (iii′); yet only (iii′) is represented when we translate *unless* as "if not."

The question is: do some uses of *unless* connote a double conditional? It seems to many native speakers of English that such a statement as "Don will go to the concert unless he is broke" says *both* that if Don is not broke he will go to the concert (iii′) and that if Don is broke, he will not go to the concert (iii″). If *unless* is understood as having this stronger meaning, then (iii) would be symbolically represented as a conjunction of two conditionals:

(– B⊃D)·(B⊃ – D)

Is the double conditional expressed when *unless* is used? Or is "if not" all that is expressed? This is a tricky question; "if not" is always implied, but sometimes, more certainly seems to be stated, or at least strongly suggested. In deductive logic we formalize only those aspects of meaning that are clearly asserted. We omit aspects that are suggested. Our aim is to see what is and what is not deductively entailed by what is asserted. The word *unless* is one of many that can be puzzling in this connection, though, because it is hard to draw an absolutely firm line between what is stated and what is suggested. Not surprisingly, this is one of those things philosophers and logicians sometimes dispute.

We have mentioned this problem about *unless* because in our experience many people sense this additional suggested (or asserted?) meaning and feel confused and uneasy about the standard way of representing *unless*. Using "if not" will always give you the core meaning of *unless*. If, in a given context, you are absolutely convinced that the additional meaning is there as well, you can represent *unless* using a double conditional, as illustrated here.

◆──

EXERCISE SET

Exercise 3

Represent the following passages in the formal apparatus of propositional logic, and test arguments using the longer or shorter truth table technique. *Note:* if a passage does not contain an argument it need not be symbolized. Just indicate that it does not contain an argument.

*1. Elephants have been known to bury their dead. But elephants bury their dead only if they have a concept of their own species and understand what death means. If elephants understand what death means, they have a substantial capacity for abstraction. Therefore, elephants have a substantial capacity for abstraction.

2. Swimming is an excellent form of exercise provided it neither injures joints nor stresses the heart. These conditions are met: it is both true that swimming does not injure joints and true that it does not stress the heart. If swimming is an excellent form of exercise, then swimming regularly will improve a person's general health. We can conclude that swimming regularly will improve health.

*3. If Joe becomes more fit, Joe will become more physically attractive to women. Actually, Joe has become not more fit, but less fit. Therefore, Joe has become less physically attractive to women.

4. Peter cannot graduate in psychology unless he takes either developmental psychology or experimental design. If he does not take a course in experimental design, Peter will take developmental psychology. So if he does not graduate, Peter will take neither developmental psychology nor a course in experimental design.

*5. Unless there is real snow, the Winter Olympics will not be a success. If there is no real snow, artificial snow will be produced. But if there is artificial snow, athletes will not be performing in good conditions. Therefore, if there is no real snow, athletes will not be performing in good conditions.

6. Either there is no greenhouse effect problem, or, if there is a greenhouse effect problem, it is too late to solve the problem of global warming. If there is no greenhouse effect problem, there is no point in worrying about that problem. And if it is too late to solve the greenhouse effect problem, there is also no point in worrying about it. Thus there is no point in worrying about the greenhouse effect problem.

*7. Unless workers agree not to strike within the next decade, prospects for the recovery of the plant are dim. But unless management agrees to forego special parking and washroom privileges, workers will not agree not to strike. So there can be a recovery in the plant only if management does its part.

8. The French Canadian folk dance tradition includes many elements of traditional Irish dancing. If a tradition includes Irish elements, then either it will include a significant role for the jig step or it will include a great deal of solo dancing. French Canadian folk dancing does not have much solo dancing. So it must have considerable use of the jig step.

9. Only if there is a good real estate market can Smith hope to sell his house at a reasonable price. If he gets no suitable deal on the house, Smith will either rent it at some loss or declare personal bankruptcy. Declaring bankruptcy is pretty unacceptable for someone in Smith's position: Smith won't do it. The real estate market is terrible. Thus we can infer that Smith will rent his house at some loss.

10. Children will be interested in reading, provided schools supply them with interesting books. The books supplied in our schools are both deplorably boring and simple-minded, which implies that they are not interesting. We can expect that our children won't like reading.

Hint: Assume that "children will be interested in reading" and "children will like reading" can be represented by the same statement letter.

11. Unless he is a saint, the preacher cannot spend all his time tending to the affairs of others. Unless he is a hypocrite, he cannot both advise others to devote themselves to the affairs of other people and fail to do this himself. The preacher is not a saint. But he does tell others that they should consume their entire lives in devotion to other people, which implies that he is a hypocrite.

*12. Morality has a basis only if there is a god. There is a god only if the world makes sense and is ordered. The world is ordered, so there is a basis for morality.

*13. Either television programs will improve in quality and appeal or the large networks will lose their markets to videos. Television programs can improve in quality only if programming budgeting increases, and program budgeting will not increase unless advertisers are willing to pay more. Advertisers are not willing to pay more, and this implies that budgets will not increase. Nor will television programs improve in quality. Thus we can expect the large networks to experience losses.

14. The German Green Party must either broaden its platform or sacrifice voter appeal. If the party is to maintain its environmental orientation, it cannot broaden its platform. But if it sacrifices voter appeal by failing to broaden its platform, it will lose some of its influence in German politics. The choice, then, is between some relinquishing of the environmental orientation of the party and some loss of influence in German politics.

*15. If the comedian is funny, people laugh. If he's not funny, they don't laugh. But whether he is funny or not, and whether people laugh or not, the comedian gets paid. That's one thing we know for certain: he gets paid. Provided that he gets paid, he'll be happy. Therefore, even if people don't laugh, the comedian will be happy.

Hint: "That's one thing we know for certain" does not have to be symbolized.

16. If the problems in the North American economy are due to the demands of workers, then Japanese firms operating in North America will not be able to run profitably. But Japanese firms operating in North America do run profitably. Therefore, the problems are not due to the demands of workers. Problems of firms must be due either to workers or to management. So it is the fault of management.

17. Both having liability insurance and having a valid driver's license are necessary conditions of being legally entitled to drive a car. Unless a person is legally entitled to drive a car, driving is both wrong and dangerous. So not having a valid driver's license implies being unsafe when driving.

*18. Having a good technical education is necessary in order to be a good engineer, but it is by no means sufficient. Unless a person is good at teamwork and communication, he cannot be a good engineer. Provided that a person is technically good, cooperatively disposed, and a good communicator, he will be a good engineer. In fact, these three conditions are both necessary and sufficient for being a good engineer.

SIMPLE PROOFS IN PROPOSITIONAL LOGIC

Working out validity in propositional logic does not have to be done by truth tables—long or short. You can learn to recognize some basic simple valid argument forms, and you can then show that the arguments that you have formalized are valid or invalid by referring to particular forms.

Valid Argument Forms

Here are some of the simple valid argument forms with their standard names:

P; therefore −(−P). Double negation. Also, −(−P); therefore P.

P ∨ P; therefore P. Tautology

P; Q; therefore P·Q. Conjunction

P·Q; therefore P. Simplification

P·Q; therefore Q. Simplification. (Either of the conjoined statements can be validly inferred from the conjunction.)

P⊃Q; P; therefore Q. Modus ponens

P⊃Q; −Q; therefore −P. Modus tollens

P⊃Q; therefore −Q⊃−P. Transposition. Also, −Q⊃−P; therefore P⊃Q.

P⊃Q; Q⊃R; therefore P⊃R. Hypothetical syllogism

P ∨ Q; −P; therefore Q. Disjunctive syllogism. Also, P ∨ Q; −Q; therefore P.

P; therefore P ∨ Q. Addition. Also, P; therefore Q ∨ P. (To see that this rule makes sense, look back at the truth table for "∨" and note that only one of the disjuncts has to be true for the disjunction to be true.)

−(P ∨ Q); therefore −P·−Q. De Morgan's rule (a). Also, −P·−Q; therefore −(P ∨ Q).

−(P·Q); therefore −P ∨ −Q. De Morgan's rule (b). Also, −P ∨ −Q; therefore −(P·Q).

P⊃Q; therefore −P ∨ Q. Implication. Also, −P ∨ Q; therefore P⊃Q.

P⊃Q; R⊃S; P ∨ R; therefore Q ∨ S. Constructive Dilemma

P⊃Q; R⊃S; −Q ∨ −S; therefore −P ∨ −R. Destructive Dilemma

It will be well worth your while to learn these simple valid argument forms. An easy way to begin is to test each one for validity by the truth table technique. This way you can prove to yourself that they are valid. In addition, a useful exercise is to invent arguments that exemplify each form. By learning the valid forms, you avoid the need to construct truth tables. You can simply recognize many ordinary arguments as deductively valid because they are instances of *modus ponens, modus tollens*, disjunctive syllogism, constructive dilemma, or whatever the case may be.

Examples of Simple Proofs

Sometimes we find deductively valid arguments that proceed by making several valid moves in sequence. We can see that they are valid by seeing that, for example, if we first do *modus ponens* and then disjunctive syllogism, using the premises, we will arrive at the conclusion. This shows us that the conclusion can be validly derived from the premises by a series of steps, each of which is individually valid. This strategy is the basis of proof techniques in more advanced formal logic.

Here is an example:

If Japan makes its airports more convenient for the Japanese public, Japanese tourism in Europe will increase. If Japanese tourism in Europe increases, then either European facilities in key centers will be enlarged or crowding in key centers will occur. Japan is making its airports more convenient for the Japanese public, but European centers are not expanding their tourist facilities. So we can expect crowding in main European tourist centers.

Let *M* represent "Japan makes its airports more convenient for the Japanese public," *E* represent "Japanese tourism in Europe will increase," *L* represent

"European facilities in key centers will be enlarged," and *C* represent "there will be crowding in key European centers." We can then formally represent the above argument as:

$M \supset E$ (premise)
$E \supset (L \lor C)$ (premise)
$M \cdot -L$ (premise)
Therefore,
C

The conclusion follows from the premises, and this can be proven, with appeals to some of the valid argument forms:

1. $M \supset E$ Premise
2. $E \supset (L \lor C)$ Premise
3. $M \cdot -L$ Premise
4. M from (3), Simplification
5. E from (1) and (4), *Modus Ponens*
6. $L \lor C$ from (2) and (5), *Modus Ponens*
7. $-L$ from (3), Simplification
8. C from (6) and (7), Disjunctive Syllogism

We have validly derived the conclusion from the premises, by using valid forms of argument. Since we have constructed a valid proof for the conclusion, based on the premises and valid forms of inference, the argument is valid in propositional logic. If the premises are true (or acceptable), the conclusion will be true (or acceptable) as well.

For another example of how these proofs work, consider the following:

Either he will complete his new play or he will achieve success as a political activist. But there is just no way that he can accomplish both. If he completes his play, it will surely be produced, and if he achieves success as a political activist, he will be known across the country. Since the production of the play will also bring fame, he is bound to be known across the country.

C = He completes his new play.
W = He will achieve success as a political activist.
R = His play will be produced.
K = He will be known across the country.

(We assume that "The production of a play also brings fame" may be represented as "$R \supset K$" in this context.)

The argument may be formally represented as:

1. $(C \lor W) \cdot$
2. $-(C \cdot W)$
3. $C \supset R$
4. $W \supset K$
5. $R \supset K$
Therefore,
K

The argument is deductively valid, and this may be shown without a truth table. We show how we can get to the conclusion from the premises, using deductively valid moves:

6. $C \supset K$ from (3) and (5) by Hypothetical Syllogism
7. $K \vee K$ from (4) and (1) and (6) by Constructive Dilemma
8. K from (7), Tautology

Thus we see how an argument can be shown to be deductively valid by proving the conclusion from the premises in a series of steps. At each step we appeal to a deductively valid argument form. This procedure is usually more efficient and more intellectually stimulating than writing truth tables. But it does have one deficiency: what if you cannot construct a proof?

When You Cannot Construct a Proof

You don't know the argument is invalid just because you fail to derive the conclusion. You could fail either because you lack sufficient ingenuity or because the argument is invalid. Consider the following example:

> If the newspaper comes late, he will not have time to read it before his speech and the speech will not be based on the most recent information. He did not have time to read the paper, and the speech was not based on the most recent information. So the newspaper was late.

This argument can be readily formalized. Let L represent "the newspaper comes late," R represent "he will have time to read the newspaper before his speech," and B represent "the speech will be based on the most recent information." The argument is then:

$L \supset (-R \quad B)$ Premise
$-R$ Premise
$-B$ Premise
Therefore,
L Conclusion

Try as you will, you are not going to prove this argument valid by using the valid argument forms. There is no series of valid steps that will take you from the premises to the conclusion, because the argument is not valid. (Try to construct a proof and see what sorts of problems you encounter.) When you try to construct a proof and fail to do so, you may suspect that the argument is invalid, but you do not know this for sure. The argument might be valid and your failure to find a proof might be due merely to the fact that you have not hit upon the right proof strategy.

For arguments expressible in basic propositional logic, a truth table test for validity will always show you whether the argument is valid or invalid. It is very important to note the difference between proving an argument valid and failing to do so. If you succeed in constructing a proof in which the conclusion is derived by a series of individually valid steps, then the argument is deductively valid. But if you can't find such a proof, this failure doesn't mean the argument is invalid. Either the argument is invalid or you have not found the right proof strategy: you don't know which is the case.

Thus the truth table technique has an important advantage: it will always show you whether the argument is valid or not. The only problem is that it can be rather cumbersome and involved.

Conditional Proof

An additional valid argument form not yet listed and of special importance in logic is that of *conditional proof*. In a conditional proof, a further line is introduced as an assumption. This additional claim is then used in just about the way a premise would be, in working through the proof; it gives extra material to manipulate. Anything derived from the premises and the added line introduced as an assumption follows from the premises provided that we allow, in a proper way, for the fact that we have used the assumption.

Here is an example.

1. $B \lor C$
2. $R \supset -C$
(To prove: $R \supset B$)
3. R Assumption
4. $-C$ from (2) and (3), *Modus Ponens*
5. B from (4) and (1), *Disjunctive Syllogism*
6. $R \supset B$ steps (3)–(5), *Conditional Proof*

The added premise, R, is introduced into the proof using an assumption; then we get rid of the assumption by making it the antecedent of a conditional statement in the conclusion. What can be derived from the initial premises, in this event, is if R then B:$(R \supset B)$. Conditional proof is an indispensable strategy in constructing proofs, as you will discover if you go on to do more advanced logic. It is needed because it gives us extra information to manipulate.

You might compare the technique of conditional proof with the discussion of provisional acceptance of premises in Chapter 5. There we indicated that when premises are provisionally accepted and a conclusion is seen to be justified on the basis of those premises, what we have really shown is that *if* those premises are acceptable, *then* the conclusion is acceptable too. Conditional proof involves similar reasoning: if from stated premises and an assumption, we can derive X, then from the stated premises, we know that *if* the assumption holds, then X.

The inference rule for conditional proof should be added to the elementary valid argument forms listed earlier. It is written as follows:

P(Assume); . . . . . Q; therefore $P \supset Q$ (Conditional Proof)

The dots represent the intermediate steps that would, using P and any other information provided in the premises or previous proof steps, be used to derive Q. Q itself cannot be derived, because it was only derivable on the assumption that *P*. However, the conditional statement *P⊃Q* does really follow. In more advanced formal logic the technique of conditional proof is indispensable. You can use it to derive conditional statements useful in longer proofs. Or the conditional statement itself may be the conclusion you are seeking.

A form related to that of conditional proof is the *reductio ad absurdum*. The name is taken from the Latin and means "reduction to absurdity." In this kind of argument the premises are "reduced to absurdity" because it is shown that they lead to a contradiction. They entail some proposition of the form of "*P· − P*," and no such proposition can be true. (If you don't believe this, construct a truth table for yourself, and you'll see how it works out.) If the conjunction of the premises of an argument entails a contradiction, then those premises contain an inconsistency. One or more of the premises must be false. You can use a *reductio ad absurdum* argument to prove a proposition if you start by denying that proposition and then manage to show that its denial leads to a contradiction. (If its denial leads to a contradiction, the denial of its denial must be true; that is, the statement itself must be true.) Such a method of proof is often called *indirect proof.*

We have noted *modus tollens* and *modus ponens* as two valid argument forms in propositional logic. Both are basic in human thinking. There are two invalid kinds of arguments that are relatively common and are deceptive because they are so easily confused with *modus ponens* and *modus tollens*. These are:

> (1) Invalid move: *affirming the consequent*
> *P⊃Q*
> *Q*
> Therefore,
> *P*
> (2) Invalid move: *denying the antecedent*
> *P⊃Q*
> *− P*
> Therefore,
> *− Q*

Actually, in previous exercises, you have already tested examples that had these forms. Both formal fallacies are relatively common: it is worth learning the names and checking these out for yourself on a truth table so that you see that they are, indeed, invalid argument forms. Other invalid moves have no special names, probably because they are not quite so common as these two.

◆───

EXERCISE SET

Exercise 4: Part A

Prove the conclusion on the basis of the premises, using the valid argument forms. In any case where you are not able to derive the con- clusion from the premises, use the shorter or longer truth table technique to determine whether the argument is valid.

Hint: Three of the following sequences do not represent a valid argument.

1. $A \supset (B \lor C)$; $B \supset D$; $D \supset G$; $A \cdot - C$; therefore G.

*2. $- A \cdot - B$; $- B \supset C$; therefore C.

3. $- (C \lor D)$; $- D \supset - (H \cdot G)$; $(Q \supset G) \cdot H$; therefore $- Q$.

4. $(A \lor B) \lor (C \lor D)$; $- B \supset - A$; $C \cdot (C \supset - B)$; therefore $- D$.

*5. $(A \lor B) \supset D$; $- D$; $- B \supset (A \supset X)$; $(A \cdot B) \lor X$; therefore X.

6. $A \lor B$; $- B$; $- C \supset - A$; therefore C.

*7. $(D \cdot E) \supset (F \lor G)$; $- D \supset F$; $- (D \lor E)$; therefore $F \lor G$.

8. $- A \supset (B \lor - C)$; $A \supset (C \lor D)$; $A \lor - A$; therefore B.

*9. $A \supset B$; $C \supset D$; $(B \lor D) \supset E$; $- E$; therefore $- A \lor C$.

10. $S \lor - (R \cdot A)$; $- S$; therefore $- A$.

Exercise 4: Part B

Represent each of the following arguments in the symbols of propositional logic. In any example where you believe that the propositional symbols would not capture aspects of meaning crucial to the way the argument works, say why not, and proceed no further. Test symbolized arguments for deductive validity, using either valid inference patterns and a simple proof procedure or the longer or shorter truth table technique.

1. If complex technology leads to occasional bizarre accidents, then complex technology sometimes has unpredictable effects. Complex technology does lead sometimes to bizarre accidents. Therefore, it sometimes has unpredictable effects.

2. Mankind could not understand the natural world unless human beings were equipped with an efficient set of categories in the brain. Mankind does understand the natural world. So we must be equipped with an efficient set of categories in the brain.

3. If the winter is snowy, the city will have to spend heavily on snow clearing, and if it is rainy, the streets will be slippery and there will be more accidents than usual and a higher bill for police costs. The winter will be either snowy or rainy, so the city will experience either high costs for snow clearing or a high bill for police costs.

*4. Understanding is impossible if words refer only to private sensations in the minds of speakers. Since we clearly do understand each other, words are not just references to private sensations.

5. If the media are genuinely democratic, then all citizens have equal access to the media and the media cover all publicly sensitive issues in a fair way. But the media will cover all publicly sensitive issues in a fair way only if reporters represent all races, classes, and sexes. This is manifestly not the case: the media do not fairly represent all races; nor do they represent all economic classes; nor do they even fairly represent women as well as men. So the media are not genuinely democratic.

*6. If the world food crisis is solved then either rich nations will voluntarily share their food with poor nations or poor nations will force the world economy to provide them with more. Rich nations will not voluntarily share their food with poor nations. Thus, if the world food crisis is solved, the poor nations will force the world economy to provide them with more.

7. If people could reason only after someone taught them the logic of the syllogism, then there would have been nobody reasoning before Aristotle discovered the logic of the syllogism. There were people reasoning before Aristotle discovered syllogistic logic. Therefore, it is not the case that people can reason only after someone has taught them syllogistic logic.

(Adapted from John Locke's "Essay Concerning the Human Understanding" [New York: Meridian, 1964])

*8. "I do know this pencil exists, but I could not know this if Hume's principles were true. Therefore Hume's principles are false."

(G. E. Moore, "Hume's Theory Examined," in *Some*

Main Problems of Philosophy [New York: Collier Books, 1953])

9. If perfect ideal communism exists anywhere, then there is complete equality of resources among persons in that society and there is no such thing as envy. But perfect ideal communism does not exist anywhere. Therefore there is no complete equality of resources among persons in a society and envy is all too real.

Hint: Assume that "there is no such thing as envy" and "envy is all too real" are contradictory statements.

10. If tax laws in Arkansas are reformed, then home buyers will not have to pay tax. And charges will not be levied for those starting new businesses. If home buyers have to pay tax, then, given that tax laws in Arkansas are not reformed, charges will also be levied for those starting new businesses. So charges are not going to be levied on those starting new businesses.

11. If astral projection is possible, then people can project themselves up to a book on a very high shelf and read the title. If astral projection is reliably verified, then people can project themselves up to read in this way and have the

event verified by a friend. But people cannot read titles in this way with friends there to verify the event. Therefore astral projection is not possible.

*12. The group will be successful only if all members participate willingly. Members will participate willingly only if they have a say in top-level decision making. Members do have a say in top-level decision making, so the group will be a success.

13. If children are well trained before the age of five, they seldom lapse into delinquency after the age of five. If women work outside the home, then children will be well trained before the age of five only if daycare centers and kindergartens are extremely well run. Women do work outside the home. Thus either we have extremely well-run childcare facilities or we risk delinquency in our children.

*14. She can become a good mathematician only if she studies hard. But she will study hard only if her family life is happy and her general health is good. Good health requires exercise and decent food, neither of which she has. So she won't become a good mathematician.

PROPOSITIONAL LOGIC AND COGENT ARGUMENTS

Formal logic is a highly developed technical discipline that we have introduced only schematically in this book. Because our emphasis is on developing practical skills, we stressed issues of translation and application while at the same time developing simple formal techniques.

As we noted a number of times, the deductive validity of an argument says nothing about the truth or acceptability of its premises. If an argument is deductively valid, then the (R) and (G) conditions of argument adequacy are fully met. But the (A) condition may or may not be satisfied. It's useful to remember this simple point, because a clearly worded deductively valid argument has a kind of logical flow to it that makes it seem cogent and sometimes distracts our attention from the fact that the elegant reasoning used is based on false or dubious premises. For mental exercise and in the course of speculation, it is often interesting to see that from some statements, *P* and *Q*, we can deductively derive a further consequence, *R*. But usually this relationship is of little interest in establishing the conclusion unless *P* and *Q* are premises we are willing to accept.

The flaw of a dubious premise serving as the basis for impeccably accurate deductive reasoning, seems to be particularly prevalent in *dilemma arguments*. These arguments (which, as you will recall, open with a disjunctive premise) are common in debate and in ordinary life. They often appear irrefutable. But the valid form of a dilemma too often serves only to mask the fact that the disjunctive premise on which it is based is false or unacceptable.

Here is an example of a deductively valid dilemma, which is nevertheless not a sound argument because of a flawed premise:

> Either the interest rates will come down or there will be a world disaster. In either case I won't have to worry about selling my house. If there is a world disaster, the social fiber of life will be destroyed and selling the house will be no problem. And if there is a fall in interest rates it will be easier for people to buy houses, and selling my house won't be a problem. Although the house isn't selling at the moment, I really have nothing to worry about.

The argument begins with a premise that states a *false dichotomy*. A false dichotomy is a disjunction between two things that are falsely thought to exhaust the possibilities. For instance, "John is handsome or he is ugly" is a false dichotomy, since there are other alternatives—looking moderately attractive, slightly unattractive, and so on. For the disjunctive premise of the argument to be true, there would have to be only two possible courses for world history: that in which there is a world disaster and that in which interest rates come down. If there is even one other possibility, the premise cannot be rationally accepted. (Check back to the truth table for disjunction if you don't understand why.) If you bear this in mind and look closely at the premise, you will see that it is questionable. No one has good reason to believe that interest rates coming down and there being a world disaster are the only two possible futures for our world.

Criticizing dilemma arguments in this way is such a common move that it has a special name. The critic is said to have *escaped through the horns of a dilemma*. She does this by showing a third alternative—by showing that the opening disjunction was not exhaustive, so that the argument was based on a false dichotomy. This sort of problem, which frequently arises with dilemmas, is a nice illustration of the general point that arguments can be "perfectly logical" in the formal sense, exemplifying valid forms, and yet may nevertheless be flawed because they have unacceptable premises.

A further basic point about propositional logic is that it is not always the appropriate tool to use in appraising an argument. It is the appropriate tool only when the connection between the premises and conclusion depends on the way in which statements are combined using the basic propositional terms: *or, and, not,* and *if then.* If the force of an argument depends on deductive relations between other terms, or on an analogy, or on empirical evidence for a broader empirical hypothesis, then the argument cannot be properly evaluated by applying the tools of propositional logic. When you represent these other sorts of arguments in propositional logic, you will no doubt find that they are not valid. However, since your symbolization in such cases will not properly reflect the meaning and direction of the original natural argument, this discovery will be of little importance. Propositional and categorical logic are very basic and important parts of deductive logic. But they do not apply to all arguments. Perhaps you will have discovered this fact already in some of the exercises for this chapter.

Arguments that are valid according to the rules of categorical or propositional logic fully satisfy the (R) and (G) conditions. They are cogent provided that their premises are acceptable. Arguments that are not valid according to categorical or propositional logic may be valid within some further formal logic system or they may be other types of argument—for instance analogies—to which the standards of deductive validity do not properly apply.

❖   ## CHAPTER SUMMARY

Propositional logic is a basic branch of formal logic in which symbols are used to represent *and, or, not,* and *if then* and letters are used to represent statements. Many arguments depend for their force on relations and connections between these terms. Arguments that can be formally represented in the terms of propositional logic can be tested in various ways for deductive validity.

Three ways of testing propositional arguments for validity are discussed in this chapter: the full truth table technique, the shorter truth table technique, and proof construction. The truth table techniques can be used to show either validity or invalidity. The technique of proof construction does not show invalidity; it can, however, show validity.

In the full truth table technique, arguments are tested on the basis of a full representation on a truth table that has 2 to the power *n* rows, where *n* represents the number of distinct statement variables. The full truth table shows all of the possible combinations of truth and falsity for every statement in the argument. To say that the argument is valid is to say that there is no way that its conclusion can be false given that all of its premises are true. When an argument is valid, there is no row of the truth table showing true premises and a false conclusion.

The full truth table technique is a completely effective one. That is, for any argument that is properly represented in propositional logic, a correctly constructed full truth table will show that it is valid or that it is invalid. The only problem with the full truth table technique is that it can become rather cumbersome when there are more than two or three distinct statement letters. For instance, if the argument requires four distinct statement letters for its symbolic representation, its full truth table will have 2^4, or 16, rows. If it has five distinct letters (which is not, in fact, uncommon) the truth table will have to have 2^5, or 32, distinct rows. Setting out such a truth table takes quite a lot of time, and with this much information to represent, it is all too easy to make a careless technical mistake.

The other techniques described are not completely effective in the sense that full truth tables are. The shorter truth table technique requires some ingenuity.

To use this technique, you try to set values of true and false for the premises and conclusion so as to make the argument invalid. That is, you try to set things up in such a way that all the premises turn out to be true and the conclusion turns out to be false, and to do this consistently—giving each distinct statement the same truth value each time it appears in the argument. If there is an assignment in which the premises are all true and the conclusion is false, the argument is invalid. If not, it is valid.

A more elegant technique is that of constructing a valid proof of the conclusion from the premises, using elementary valid argument forms. When you construct a proof, you use a list of elementary forms that you are entitled to appeal to because they are recognized as valid. You move in steps from the given premises toward the conclusion, justifying each move by an appeal to a valid argument form. If you can reach the conclusion in this way, you know that it follows validly from the premises. Proof construction requires insight and ingenuity and is interesting and challenging. You do have a problem, however, if you set to construct a proof for an invalid argument. You will never succeed and you won't know whether you have failed due to lack of ingenuity or because the argument is invalid. To find out, you have to use a truth table or other method of showing invalidity.

Deductive validity according to propositional logic shows that the argument meets the (R) and (G) conditions of argument cogency. It does not guarantee that the argument passes on the (A) condition, which has to be determined in another way.

❖ REVIEW OF TERMS INTRODUCED

Propositional logic   That part of logic that deals with the relationships holding between simple propositions or statements and their compounds. In propositional logic, the basic logical terms are *not, or, and,* and *if then.*

Denial (of a statement)   A statement's contradictory or negation. It must have the opposite truth value to the statement. The denial of a statement S is symbolized as $-S$ (not S).

Conjunction (of statements)   A compound statement in which all the statements are asserted, linked by *and* or an equivalent term. For the conjunction to be true, each component statement or conjunct must be true. The conjunction of statements P and Q is written as $P{\cdot}Q$.

Disjunction (of statements)   A compound statement in which the statements are asserted as alternatives; the connective is *or.* For the disjunction to be true, at least one of the disjoined statements must be true. The disjunction of statement P and statement Q is written as $P \vee Q$.

Conditional statement   A statement of the form "if P, then Q." As such it does not assert either P or Q. Rather, it asserts a connection between them in the sense that provided P is the case, Q will be the case also. Example: "If Quebec separates from the rest of Canada, the Maritime provinces will be physically isolated" is a conditional statement asserting a relationship between Quebec's leaving Canada and the Maritimes being isolated. It does not assert either that Quebec will leave or that the Maritimes will be isolated, but only that *if* Quebec leaves, the Maritimes will be isolated. In propositional logic, the conditional is symbolized as $P \supset Q$.

Antecedent (of a conditional)   Statement that follows *if* in a conditional of the form "if P then Q." For example, in "if Quebec leaves, then the Maritimes will be isolated," the antecedent is "Quebec leaves."

Consequent (of a conditional)   Statement that follows *then* in a conditional of the form "if P then Q." For example, in "if Quebec leaves, then the Maritimes will be isolated," the consequent is "the Maritimes will be isolated."

Horseshoe   A connective written as "$\supset$", used in propositional logic to represent basic conditional relationships. A statement of the form "$P \supset Q$" is defined as false if P is true and Q false, and true otherwise.

Inclusive disjunction   A disjunction that is true if and only if one or both of the disjoined statements is true. The symbol "$\vee$" in propositional logic is used to represent inclusive disjunction.

Exclusive disjunction   A disjunction that is true if and only if one and only one of the disjuncts is true. An exclusive disjunction of statements P and Q is represented $(P \vee Q) \cdot - (P \cdot Q)$.

Counterfactual   A conditional statement in which the antecedent is known to be false. Example: If Hitler had been murdered when he was twenty, World War II would not have occurred. (*Note:* Do not be misled by the term *counterfactual* into thinking that all counterfactuals are false. All have antecedents that are false; however, many counterfactuals themselves are plausibly regarded as true statements.)

Necessary condition   A condition that is required for another statement to be true. Using the horseshoe, if Q is a necessary condition of P, we symbolize as "$P \supset Q$." To say that Q is a necessary condition of P is to say that P will be true only if Q is true.

Sufficient condition   A condition that is enough to establish a further statement as true. Using the horseshoe, if Q is a sufficient condition for P, we would symbolize it as "$Q \supset P$." To say that Q is sufficient for P is to say that, given Q, P will be true as well.

Modus ponens   A valid argument form, in which from "$P \supset Q$" and P, we may infer Q.

Modus tollens   A valid argument form, in which from "$P \supset Q$" and $-Q$, we may infer $-P$.

Conditional proof   Proof incorporating an assumption explicitly introduced into the argument and then, in effect, canceled by being represented as the antecedent of a conditional of which the consequent is the conclusion derived from the given premises and the assumption introduced.

Indirect proof Proof of a conclusion by introducing its denial, on the rule of conditional proof, and then deriving a contradiction. Using *modus tollens,* we infer from the contradiction (which must be false) the negation of the statement introduced. That is, the denial of the denial of what we set out to prove. This (by double negation) is what we set out to prove.

Affirming the consequent An invalid form of inference of the type "$P \supset Q$; Q; therefore, P."

Denying the antecedent An invalid form of inference of the type "$P \supset Q$; $-P$; therefore, $-Q$."

Dilemma argument Both constructive and destructive dilemmas constitute valid forms of argument. A constructive dilemma has the form $P \supset Q$; $R \supset S$; $P \vee R$; therefore, $Q \vee S$. A destructive dilemma has the form $P \supset Q$; $R \supset S$; $-Q \vee -S$; therefore, $-P \vee -R$. However, the disjunctive premises of arguments such as this should be carefully scrutinized for acceptability.

False dichotomy Statement of the form $P \vee Q$, which is false because P and Q are not the only alternatives. Example: May is beautiful or May is ugly. This is a false dichotomy because being beautiful and being ugly are not the only possibilities; May could be reasonably attractive as opposed to beautiful and still not be ugly.

Escaping through the horns of a dilemma Showing that a dilemma argument, though valid, is not cogent because it is based on a false dichotomy. This expression is also used when a person shows a dichotomous statement to be false because there is a third alternative; the person is said to have escaped through the horns of a dilemma.

Notes

1. Strictly speaking, letters that represent particular statements should not appear at the top of columns on truth tables because the truth table allows for two different truth values for every statement letter. To avoid two levels of symbolization, this matter is ignored here, as it is in many other texts.
2. The story of the drugstores was provided by Dr. W. A. McMullen, who saw the signs when he was teaching a junior logic course at the University of Winnipeg in the early 60s.
3. The example of the center lane comes from Professor Robert Martin of the Philosophy Department, Dalhousie University, Halifax, Nova Scotia.

CHAPTER 9

Analogies: Reasoning from Case to Case

IN THIS CHAPTER WE SHALL STUDY various ways in which analogies are used in arguments and in the more general pursuit of knowledge. Also we offer some strategies for grasping the basic structure of an analogy and arriving at a sound critical assessment. We emphasize the important role analogies often play in the reasoning within law and administration and their role in providing grounds for beliefs about phenomena that cannot be studied directly. As well as good arguments from analogy, there are also many arguments from loose and irrelevant analogies that provide only the shakiest base for conclusions. In this chapter we work on understanding two different kinds of cogent analogies, and then we go on to examine some fallacies based on misusing analogies.

THE NATURE AND FUNCTIONS OF ANALOGY

As we have seen earlier (Chapters 3 and 6), arguments by *analogy* draw a conclusion about one thing by comparing it closely with another. It is convenient to call the central topic—the one dealt with in the conclusion—the *primary subject,* and the case with which it is compared the *analogue.* In the following unforgettable analogy by C. S. Lewis, the primary subject is the striptease, as it exists in our culture, and the analogue is the unveiling of a mutton chop, as this might exist in an imagined alternative culture:

> You can get a large audience together for a strip-tease act—that is, to watch a girl undress on the stage. Now suppose you came to a country where you could fill a theatre simply by bringing a covered plate onto the stage and then slowly lifting the cover so as to let everyone see, just before the lights went out, that it contained a mutton chop or a bit of bacon, would you not think that in that country something had gone wrong with the appetite for food?[1]

Lewis uses our reaction to the analogue to develop a reaction to the primary subject. In the analogous case, we would certainly think that the natural human desire for food had been warped in some way. By drawing an analogy between this case and the case of striptease, which actually exists, he urges us to conclude that our sexual desires in this culture are somehow warped. The answer to the rhetorical question at the end of the passage (would you now think . . . something had gone wrong with the appetite for food?) is clearly supposed to be yes. The implied conclusion is that in our culture, where the striptease is a form of entertainment, something has gone wrong with the desire for sex. Many arguments from analogy are similar to this one in having implied, or missing, conclusions.

An argument from analogy begins by using one case (usually agreed-upon, and relatively easy to understand) to illuminate or clarify another (usually less clear). It then seeks to justify a conclusion about the first case on the basis of considerations about the second. The basis for drawing the conclusion is the relevant similarity between the cases, which is regarded as showing a commonality of structure between the two cases compared.

In this book we concentrate on analogy as a device in argument, but analogies have many other functions as well. They are of great use in teaching—an analogue may be familiar whereas the primary subject is unfamiliar, so explanations based on analogies are often quite effective. Analogies also are used to illustrate points, or even simply to make a speech or an essay more interesting.

Albert Einstein used an analogy to explain how the enormous energy that is inherent in mass could have gone undetected by physicists until the twentieth century. He said:

> It is as though a man who is fabulously rich should never spend or give away a cent; no one could tell how rich he was.[2]

Here the primary subject is the energy within matter, and the analogue is the unspent money of the rich man. Einstein is not trying to demonstrate any conclusion about the energy in matter by this analogy; he is trying, rather, to make the notion of trapped energy intelligible to people who may not be familiar with it but would certainly understand the analogue. Einstein's analogy, then, is explanatory, not argumentative.

There are many different uses for analogies. They may be used to vividly illustrate points, to enhance descriptions, or in explanations or arguments. Because this is a book about argument, we concentrate here on the argumentative uses of analogy. However, many of the comments here are applicable also to illustrative or explanatory analogies.

◆ ANALOGY AND CONSISTENCY

Treating similar cases similarly is a fundamental aspect of rationality. It is by drawing analogies—seeing important similarities and differences—that we determine which are similar cases and which are not. Any application of a general principle or rule—whether in logic, morality, law, or administration—requires that we determine which cases are relevantly similar and merit similar treatment. This is one way that we can see just how fundamental reasoning with analogies is.

We can prove, in logic, that a contradiction, a statement of the type "P and not $-P$," is never true.[3] Such a statement both asserts and denies the same thing (for example, "Hitler is dead and Hitler is not dead"); it is inconsistent and impossible. If we are going to make sense, such inconsistency has to be avoided: one who asserts and denies the very same thing has, in effect, said nothing at all. Assertions should be consistent.

However this is not the only sort of consistency that is essential to the rational life. There is another kind of consistency—that which is involved in treating similar cases similarly. We can be inconsistent by treating similar cases differently—that is, by criticizing in one person behavior we approve in someone else, or by demanding a stiff sentence for one first-time offender while urging probation for another in similar circumstances. If a particular case merits a particular treatment, then consistency demands that relevantly similar cases receive the same treatment.

Often agreed-upon cases are used as the basis for arguments to conclusions about disputed cases. The agreed-upon cases serve as the analogues, and on the basis of similarities, one can defend conclusions about the disputed cases. Such arguments *appeal to consistency:* similar cases should be treated similarly.

In fact, this form of argument is common in logic itself. Occasions may arise when we wish to evaluate an argument and we are not certain what to say about it. One technique that may be used is to find a relevantly similar argument on which the verdict is clear and reason from the clear case to the disputed case. The technique of refutation by logical analogy is based on this procedure.

Refutation by Logical Analogy

You can sometimes show an argument to be a poor one by comparing it with another argument that is obviously poor. If the two arguments are relevantly similar, then the logical analogy between them will show that the argument in question is poor. It is relevantly similar to another that is obviously poor, so it is poor. In such a procedure the first argument is *refuted* by the use of a *logical analogy* or, as it is sometimes called, a parallel case.

To see how this works, consider this simple example:

FIRST ARGUMENT

1. If Jane Fonda exercises, she is fit.
2. Jane Fonda is fit.
So,
3. Jane Fonda exercises.

There are various ways of showing this argument to be invalid: one is the truth table technique discussed in Chapter 8. But a nonformal technique may be used too: that of constructing a logical analogy with an argument that is obviously invalid.

PARALLEL TO FIRST ARGUMENT

1. If Mother Teresa is the richest woman in the world, then Mother Teresa is a woman.
2. Mother Teresa is a woman.

So,

3. Mother Teresa is the richest woman in the world.

We know that this parallel argument is invalid because both its premises are true and its conclusion is false. (Mother Teresa is a nun who lives in humble circumstances in Calcutta, helping the poorest of India's poor.) We can use this fact to show that the first argument is invalid, arguing as follows:

1. The primary argument is like the analogue argument in the basic structure that connects its premises to its conclusion.
2. The analogue argument has true premises and a false conclusion.

So,

3. The analogue argument is an invalid argument.

Therefore,

4. The primary argument is an invalid argument.

Provided that we have correctly identified the structure shared by the arguments, this reasoning about the two arguments conclusively shows that the first argument is invalid. The first argument is structurally just like another argument that is invalid; therefore, it is invalid.

If we know propositional logic, we do not need the logical analogy technique to find out whether the argument about Jane Fonda is valid. The argument exemplifies the formal fallacy of affirming the consequent, and we could easily prove it invalid by using the truth table technique. But the logical analogy technique is extremely valuable in other cases. It is sometimes called the technique of drawing a logical parallel, or finding a parallel case. Many arguments do not depend on basic logical terms such as *and, or, not,* and *if then* in order to draw the connection between premises and conclusion. They may depend on other terms that do not appear in formal systems, such as *cause, property, important, parent, deter,* and so on.

Here is an example in which this technique was used to good effect by a newspaper columnist. The columnist was criticizing a comment by Alberta's energy minister, who had said that since Alberta possessed valuable hydrocarbon resources, it would be silly for the province to develop solar or wind energy. The columnist imagined an ancient character objecting to the development of oil and gas resources in 1914:

Puffing reflectively on his pipe, he said, "Mark my words. No good will come of this." He said it quite a lot, leaning back in a chair on the front porch of his livery stable.

Of course, anyone who paused to listen stayed to mock, but Max stuck to his guns. "Oil?" he'd say. "What for? We'd look pretty stupid if we came up with anything that reduced the value of our horse resources."

"Alberta is the horse capital of Canada," he'd continue. "Are we supposed to dig up gasoline for the Easterners so they can tell us what we can do with our horses? They'd like that, all right, but why should we oblige them?"[4]

Here the parallel focuses our attention on the basic structure of the minister's argument. The minister was saying, in effect, that if something is useful and profitable now, and if some other prospective development could replace that thing, then the prospective development should be abandoned. The columnist's entertaining parallel points out just how silly the original argument is by showing that it is essentially the same argument as one that could have been used to prevent the development of the very hydrocarbon resources the minister was trying to protect.

Many people who have never studied formal logic have the ability to construct logical analogy or parallel arguments revealing the logical flaw in a primary argument. This technique of logical analogy brings out the essential reasoning, or structure, of the primary argument and shows that, in the analogue argument, the connection does not hold—thereby showing that the structure is flawed in the primary argument. Refutation of an argument by logical analogy is based on our ability to understand that the analogue and the primary argument have the same structure and thus must be judged similarly with respect to their logical merit. If two arguments are similar in all logically relevant respects and one is fallacious, weak, or silly, then the other is fallacious, weak, or silly too. To be consistent, we must judge the structure of two arguments in the same way.

The connection on which an argument is based must hold up for all parallel cases if that argument is to be a good one. If there is a parallel case in which the connection does not work, then it is not a reliable connection, and the original argument fails.

The whole trick here, obviously, is to get the parallel just right. If the two arguments are relevantly similar, and the second is poor, the first is poor. The real question is just when they are relevantly similar and when they are not. To construct a refutation by logical analogy, we need to distinguish between those features of an argument that are merely incidental to its working and those that are central and crucial. This is something many people—including even small children—can do quite naturally. But it is not a skill that can be mechanically developed the way formal procedures in logic can be.

Ethics, Law, and Treating Similar Cases Similarly

The demand for consistency is the basis of many forceful and important moral arguments. These arguments work by bringing an undisputed case to bear on a disputed or problematic case. The cases are considered to be relevantly similar. For example, if an analogue is known to be evil, and a primary subject is relevantly similar to it, then the primary subject can be known to be evil too. What matters are relevant similarities.

Jesus used the technique of analogy, implicitly, when he said that a man who lusts after a married woman has "already committed adultery with her in his heart." In this comment, Jesus was drawing an analogy between lustful desire and actual adultery in an attempt to get his followers to extend the disapproval they already felt for adultery to lustful thoughts as well.

A similar technique was used by Dr. Joyce Brothers when she replied to an anxious reader who said, "My problem is that my husband doesn't want to have children because I underwent therapy before we were married and my husband is afraid that my emotional troubles will be passed on to my child." Brothers replied with an analogy:

> When is society going to come out of the dark ages and recognize that mental or emotional problems should be no more stigmatizing to an individual than a case of German measles or pneumonia? We do not shun those who have suffered and been cured of tuberculosis, polio, or other diseases, do we?[5]

Brothers is contending that emotional problems are relevantly similar to physical diseases and should be treated in the same way. She relies on our acceptance of the belief that people should not be shunned after they have been cured of physical diseases. She draws an (undeveloped) analogy between emotional and mental problems and these physical diseases and urges that we "come out of the dark ages" to make our attitudes consistent.

The analogy on which the argument depends may be set out as follows:

ANALOGUE

People with such physical problems as German measles or polio
    suffer
    can recover
    are not shunned by others after they recover

PRIMARY SUBJECT

People with emotional or mental problems
    suffer
    can recover

CONCLUSION

People with emotional or mental problems should not be shunned by others after they recover.

Is Brothers's argument a good one? The assessment will depend on the closeness of her analogy; how similar are physical and emotional diseases with respect to extent of recovery after treatment and possible transferred effect on children? The technique Brothers uses, appealing to consistency of treatment between similar cases, leaves her audience with a choice. It can (1) change its attitude to the primary subject; (2) find a relevant difference between the primary subject and the analogue; (3) change its attitude to the analogue; or (4) admit that it is inconsistent in its treatment of the analogue and the primary subject. Brothers is counting on people not to opt for (3) or (4) and not to be able to do (2). She presumes that people are committed to rationality so far as being consistent in the treatment of cases is concerned.

In law, the obligation to treat similar cases similarly is the essence of formal justice. Suppose two people in two separate cases are charged with the same crime. Let us say, for instance, that Jones robbed a bank on Monday and Smith robbed another bank on Tuesday. Suppose that Jones is convicted and Smith is not. If there is not some relevant difference between the two cases, this situation gives an example of formal injustice. Regardless of the contents of a law, it should be applied consistently. No two accused people are identical; nor will their circumstances be identical. But if they are relevantly similar, they should be treated similarly. If they are not treated similarly, the judge or judges should specify the relevant differences between them.

This sort of reasoning is the basis of the *precedent* system of law: to preserve formal justice, cases must be resolved as similar cases have been resolved in the past, or a differentiating point must be specified. You can see, then, that picking out central similarities and differences is an extremely important aspect of legal reasoning. Much of legal reasoning is, in effect, reasoning by analogy. The case under discussion is the primary subject, which is resolved by reference to past cases (analogues, or legal precedents).

The same kind of point applies in administrative contexts. Here the context is seldom as structured as requirements for formal justice. Nevertheless, anyone administering a policy seeks to avoid unfairness and the criticism and confusion that will follow if the policy is applied inconsistently. Administrators will seek to treat similar cases similarly and will sometimes argue against a specific decision on the grounds that it will set a bad precedent. For instance, if the chairperson of a meeting accepts a last-minute addition to its agenda by one committee member on the grounds that it strikes him as important, she may feel compelled to accept many more last-minute additions from others; presumably everyone who sought a last-minute addition would believe the addition was important. (As we shall see toward the end of this chapter, this kind of appeal to precedent is open to subtle areas that lead to fallacious argument.)

Case-by-Case Reasoning and Issues of Classification

Are the economies of western nations currently in a recession or in a depression? The most straightforward way of resolving this issue of classification is to see how similar and how different our current situation is to that of the 1930s—a classic economic case of a depression. Is a virus an animal? Are Polynesians a distinct race? All these questions have moral, legal, political, or scientific significance, and they call for correct decisions about the application of important concepts ("depression," "person," "distinct race," and so on). The issues at stake are *conceptual*. Some people regard conceptual issues as unimportant, thinking that they have to do only with words and nothing more, and that they cannot be resolved in any reasonable way. However, as we have seen already in Chapter 4, reasons can be given to back up these classifications. Often such reasons are based on analogies.

If we ask whether a questionable act counts as an act of negligence, for instance, we are raising a conceptual issue, one that often has considerable legal or moral significance. (It might make the difference of several years in jail, or thousands of dollars in fines, for some individual.) One way of resolving such an issue is to compare the act with another that is agreed to be a case of negligence. We then ask how much our problem case is like the standard case, and to what extent it is unlike the standard case. To use this technique is to approach conceptual issues by reasoning from analogies.

Consider a dispute that actually arose regarding some books written about the extermination of Jews during World War II. Some French historians wrote works alleging that 6 million Jews had not been killed in Nazi death camps and that there had been a conspiracy to fabricate evidence on this matter. Jewish students at the University of Toronto, understandably enraged at the allegation, urged library officials to *reclassify* the French historians' books, terming them fiction instead of nonfiction. They believed that the historical claims made in the works were so outrageous that they did not properly qualify as nonfiction. B'nai B'rith officials defended the students' request but were very anxious that their position not be identified as one of advocating censorship. They insisted that reclassifying books was not the same thing as having them unavailable, and therefore reclassification did not amount to censorship.[6]

In this case, both the Jewish students and the B'nai B'rith officials raised questions that were, in effect, about the application of concepts. The Jewish students raised the question of whether books that are about such world events as World War II, but that make outlandish claims about them, are to be regarded as nonfiction (history in this case) or as fiction. What makes a book count as nonfiction? Is it solely the intent of the author to describe the world as it was or is? Or is a certain minimum level of accuracy required? This question could be resolved by looking at clear cases of fiction and nonfiction and reasoning by analogy, or by looking at other borderline cases that have been resolved and using them as precedents, again reasoning by analogy. (The library didn't do this, apparently; it simply refused to consider the matter, saying too much public pressure could result.)

B'nai B'rith officials were concerned to defend what the Jewish students were proposing, but they did not want to allow that it would be censorship. They asserted that reclassification would not be censorship or book banning. There does seem, in fact, to be a clear difference between banning or censoring all or part of a book, and putting it on the library shelf in one classification rather than another. In the latter case, the book is still available to readers, and it is this availability that censors wish to prevent.

This example illustrates issues of conceptualization that we might seek to resolve by arguing from agreed-upon cases. The pattern of such reasoning, for conceptual issues, is something like this:

1. The analogue has features *a, b,* and *c.*
2. The primary subject has features *a, b,* and *c.*
3. It is by virtue of features *a, b,* and *c* that the analogue is properly classified as a *W.*

So,
4.   The primary subject ought to be classified as a *W*.[7]

Sometimes the comparison of cases omits any specification of the similar features, and merely sets the cases side by side—the idea being that similarities will be obvious. Thus:

1.   The analogue is a clear case of *W*.
2.   The primary subject is similar to the analogue.
So,
3.   The primary subject is a case of *W*.

A philosophical argument combining conceptual issues with moral ones was offered by Robert Nozick. He was trying to persuade readers that they are far too complacent in accepting the government's policy of redistributing wealth by income taxation. Nozick put his point provocatively by using the following analogy:

> Taxation of earnings from labor is on a par with forced labor. Some persons find this claim obviously true; taking the earnings of n hours of labor is like taking n hours from the person; it is like forcing the person to work n hours for another's purpose. Others find the claim absurd. But even these, if they object to forced labor, would oppose forcing unemployed hippies to work for the benefit of the needy.
> . . . The man who chooses to work longer to gain an income more than sufficient for his basic needs prefers some extra goods or services to the leisure and activities he could perform during the possible nonworking hours; whereas the man who chooses not to work the extra time prefers the leisure activities to the extra goods or services he could acquire by working more. Given this, if it would be illegitimate for a tax system to seize some of a man's leisure (forced labor) for the purpose of serving the needy, how can it be legitimate for a tax system to seize some of a man's goods for that purpose?[8]

Nozick's analogy can be set out as follows:

ANALOGUE

The government might force a person to work for some number of hours in order to support the needy.
Point (1): In such a case a person would labor for some number of hours.
Point (2): The laboring person would not receive the payment for those hours of work; he would receiving nothing for himself.
Point (3): The laboring person would be forced by the government to spend his time laboring for others.
Point (4): It would obviously be wrong for the government to put people into forced labor to serve the needy, and the wrongness of this act would be, and is, acknowledged by everybody.

PRIMARY SUBJECT

The government takes the earnings from some number of hours of work to support the needy.
Point (1): A person labors for some number of hours.

Point (2): The laboring person does not receive the payment for those hours of work.

Point (3): ? (How does the analogy hold up here?)

CONCLUSION

Taxing earned income to support the needy is morally wrong.

This argument of Nozick's may strike you as shocking. After all, we typically accept income tax, which is used (in part) to support such social programs as welfare and medical assistance, and we typically *oppose* forced labor, which we are likely to associate with the concentration camps of totalitarian regimes. Are we being inconsistent in these common attitudes? Nozick is maintaining that we are—that, in fact, labor for which one is not paid due to the income tax is just like forced labor and deserves the same bad moral reputation. This is certainly a provocative analogy! To resist it, we must find a relevant dissimilarity between forced labor as in concentration camps and labor that is 100 percent taxed and thus, in effect, unpaid.

Look at the third point in the structures set out here for a clue. People do largely *choose* to work at those jobs for which they are taxed, so their actual labor is not forced in the same sense that concentration camp labor is forced. This difference between the primary subject and the analogue is significant; taxed labor is not *forced* forced labor, because people choose their jobs. The analogy is undermined by this difference: since working at your job during hours when you do not receive pay is something you (typically) choose to do and may enjoy for various reasons, it is not strictly comparable to forced labor. What is forced is not the labor, but the payment of tax. Thus Nozick's analogy is not fully convincing: we are not inconsistent if we approve of income tax used for redistributive purposes but disapprove of forced labor.

Some arguments make a rather implicit appeal for consistent treatment of cases. Here we often find such phrases as "that's just like saying," "you might as well say," "by the same reasoning," or "according to those standards." Here is an example, wherein the writer of a letter to *Time* magazine urges that appeals by the chairman of Eastern Airlines for protection from creditors should be rejected.

> In seeking protection from Eastern's creditors in bankruptcy court, Lorenzo [Chairman of Eastern Airlines] is like the young man who killed his parents and then begged the judge for mercy because he was an orphan. During the last three years, Lorenzo has stripped Eastern of its most valuable assets and then pleaded poverty because the shrunken structure was losing money.[9]

The analogue is the case of a young man who killed his parents and then begged for mercy from the court, saying he is an orphan. This analogue forcefully brings out the general point that one who has caused his own bad situation deserves little mercy or protection from others. The Eastern Airlines case is claimed to be relevantly similar. If it is, clearly Lorenzo would not deserve protection from the court for the bankruptcy caused by his own actions.

Some Points of Method and Critical Strategy

We have now considered a number of examples of analogies in which a decision about one case is rejected or defended on the basis of consistency considerations. The analogy may be between two real cases or between a real case and a purely hypothetical case. The examples of people being shunned for physical diseases and of unemployed hippies being forced to work for the needy are hypothetical examples; these things never need to have happened, and yet the analogy can work anyway. Similarly, for the force of the argument about Lorenzo and Eastern Airlines, it does not matter whether, in fact, there ever was a young man who killed his parents and then sought mercy from the court on the grounds that he was an orphan. The analogue may be a real case or an imaginary case: what matters is that the point must be clear, the reasoning about the analogue correct, and the analogue relevantly similar to the primary case.

The imaginary, or even fanciful, aspect of case-by-case reasoning sometimes confuses and frustrates people, because they cannot understand why purely fictitious examples should be of any importance in rational decision making. But the answer to their puzzlement is not so hard to find. The analogue must above all be a case toward which our attitude is clear: an obviously valid argument, invalid argument, right action, wrong action, legal action, illegal action, correct decision, incorrect decision, or whatever. We will make little progress by comparing one confusing case with another. The analogue must really be like the primary subject in those ways that are relevant to the case. Provided these conditions are met, we are pushed by consistency into taking the same stance on the primary subject as we do toward the analogue.

Our attitudes and our moral and logical beliefs are about a whole range of actions, events, and arguments—not just about those that have actually occurred, or existed up to the present moment of time. For instance, we do not know whether in fact any mother ever killed her newborn baby by boiling it to death in hot lead, but we do know that our attitude toward such an action should be one of extreme repugnance. Any action that can be shown to be relevantly similar to this hypothetical one is also to be condemned.

Because the analogue in this kind of consistency reasoning need not be something that actually happened, the analogy used is sometimes called an *a priori analogy*. As we have seen in Chapter 5, the words *a priori* in Latin mean "from the first" and are used by philosophers to refer to concepts and beliefs that are independent of sense experience. The analogies examined so far have been a priori analogies in the sense that it does not matter whether or not the analogue describes any real experienced events. What is at issue in these analogies is structure: something we have to reflect on. The analogy will be a good one insofar as the analogue and the primary case share all logically relevant features. Whether this is the case is something we can determine a priori, from reflective examination of the cases.

The point of classifying these analogies as a priori will become more obvious when we go on to look at *inductive analogies,* in which comparisons must be with actual cases. Inductive analogies, which are often used in history and science, form the basis for prediction, rather than decision.

To evaluate an argument from analogy, you can use the ARG conditions as you do for any argument. Suppose that the argument is based on an a priori analogy. The conclusion is about one case—the primary subject—and it is reached by comparing that case with another one—the analogue. The premises will describe the analogue and the primary subject. As in any argument, the premises are to be judged for their acceptability. When the analogy is a priori, the analogue may be something invented. Thus you cannot question the description of the analogue except on the grounds that it is internally inconsistent and hence contradictory. You can check to see that the primary subject—the case in question—is accurately and fairly described. If the premises assert that similarities exist between the two cases, then you must reflect to determine whether those similarities are genuine.

But what is really at issue in these analogies is relevance. In some loose sense, virtually any two things in the universe are alike in some ways. The issue is how relevant the similarities are to the merits of the case. The parallel that is being implicitly or explicitly drawn between the analogue and the primary subject must hold up for the important, essential, features of the two cases: those features that are relevant to the issue to be resolved in the conclusion. Think back to the Eastern Airlines case, for instance. Suppose someone were to defend Lorenzo on the ground that he isn't like an orphaned young man because his mother is still alive. Such a defense would be flawed, because whether Lorenzo is orphaned or not is irrelevant to the issue of whether he wrongly caused Eastern's financial problems. The analogy is argued to hold because in each case someone has caused his own problems by wrongdoing and then begs for mercy. If the cases are relevantly similar in these respects, and if there are no relevant differences (such as Lorenzo being forced into selling Eastern assets), then the analogy holds and the argument will make its point.

You have to look at what the conclusion asserts about the primary subject, based on the analogy, and reflect on the similarities that hold between the primary subject and the analogue. Ask yourself whether the features of the primary subject that are highlighted by the analogy are relevant to the point asserted in the conclusion. Do those features give reasons to suppose that the conclusion is true of the primary subject? If they seem to, then try to think of relevant differences. There are always differences between any two things, just as there are always similarities between them. For instance, someone might urge that there is an analogy between traveling and reading, because both provide a person with a chance to leave his ordinary everyday world for another world. No doubt there are many similarities between these activities (both require some education if one is to truly benefit, both cost some amount of money, both give access to other cultures and experiences). Clearly there are also many differences: traveling costs more than reading, typically, and provides a fuller, more experiential immersion in a new setting. The issue is: how relevant, or important, are those similarities and differences to the point at issue in the argument? If someone were trying to argue that because travel is similar to reading and the government subsidizes reading, through public libraries, it should subsidize travel too, we would find some similarities (cultural broadening) and differences (cost) *relevant* to assessing the analogy and others (level of physical exertion involved) *irrelevant*.

An analogy encourages you to think of two cases as similar and to reason from one to the other. The similarities between the cases should be real, and there should be a number of relevant similarities, if the analogy is to provide the basis for a plausible argument. It is natural to try to refute an argument by analogy by thinking of differences between the primary subject and the analogue, but you cannot refute the argument just by pointing out that the analogue and the primary subject are different in some respect or other. You have to find differences that are negatively relevant to the conclusion—that is, to find differences that indicate that the conclusion is false or unacceptable. If you can find decisively relevant differences that upset the analogy in this way, then you can show that the argument fails on the (G) condition. The difference or differences will reveal that the similarities highlighted in the analogy are not sufficient to give good grounds for the conclusion.

Your own reasoning, if this is the line of criticism, will be along the following lines: "The analogue and the primary subject both have features 1, 2, and 3, but the analogue is *x* and the primary subject may well be not-*x*. The reason is that the primary subject has feature 4, which the analogue lacks, and feature 4 may be just the one that indicates that the primary subject is not-*x*, because . . . "

◆——————————————————————————————————

EXERCISE SET

Exercise 1: Part A

Appraise the following refutations by logical analogy. Find the primary subject and the analogue, and check the refutation by logical analogy using the ARG conditions as they apply to a priori analogies.

*1. Some have concluded that Japanese corporations are more fairly run than American corporations, just because in Japanese corporations decisions are typically reached by teams of managers, and not just by one top manager, as is typically the case in American corporations. But this is a silly reason for attributing fairness to Japanese corporations. The South African judicial system would not become fair to blacks just because single judges were replaced by teams of judges. Fairness is a matter of the distribution

of advantages and disadvantages. It doesn't just depend on how many people are involved in making decisions.

2. In the early 1970s, some people claimed that using marijuana caused heroin addiction. They made this claim on the grounds that most people who use heroin first used marijuana. But isn't this a very silly argument? We could just as well argue that using milk causes a person to use cocaine. After all, most people who use cocaine began in life by using milk.

(Adapted from an exchange between Norman Podhoretz and several philosophers in *Commentary* in the late 1960s.)

3. My neighbor says that boys are more difficult to bring up than girls because her own two boys are always in trouble, whereas her girls are no problem for her. Now this argument is a very

weak one because a person who happens to have two nice boys and two troublesome girls could equally well use her own experience to prove that boys are easier to bring up than girls. If you can prove a general conclusion from just personal experience in the one case, surely you can equally well prove it in the other case. But the result of putting both arguments together is absurd.

*4. Some people say that if God had meant us to love persons of the same sex, then He would not have created two different sexes in the first place. But by the same token, if God had meant us to wear clothes, we wouldn't have been born naked. The argument from what God might have intended is ridiculous in this context.

*5. *Background:* In 1983, there was a movement to achieve nuclear disarmament by the technique of having a worldwide referendum on the issue and using the results to put pressure on politicians. Various arguments were put against this proposal, including the following one, which is described here and then contested by a logical analogy.

"Some have proposed a referendum on the question of worldwide disarmament. An argument often given against having such a referendum is that almost everyone would vote the same way: everyone would favor worldwide disarmament. So this argument is that we shouldn't have a vote if nearly everybody agrees. But if general agreement is a reason against voting on disarmament, there would equally well be a reason against an election for mayor if the candidate were likely to win by a very large majority. Nobody would accept that conclusion! Similarly, we should not oppose a referendum just because we expect that almost everyone would respond to it in the same way.

6. In the fall of 1986, a Canadian cabinet minister, John Crosbie, said that people in Canada's Atlantic provinces should not complain about the high level of unemployment in their region. After all, he said, they were well-off compared to people in Third World countries. Crosbie said that people in these areas should compare themselves, not with Canadians in central and western Canada, but rather with citizens in poorer

parts of Asia and Africa. Calgary *Herald* columnist Alan Connery satirized Crosbie's comments by saying it was as if someone defended the performance of Canadian Prime Minister Brian Mulroney by pointing out that he was better than Hitler and Idi Amin. (Amin was a former Ugandan ruler responsible for thousands of tortures and murders.)

Question: Does Connery's satire effectively constitute a refutation, by logical analogy, of Crosbie's original argument?

Exercise 1: Part B

Of the following passages, identify those that contain arguments based on analogy. Then assess the arguments. Identify the analogue and the primary subject. Check the argument according to the ARG conditions. See whether the primary subject is accurately described and is really similar to the analogue in the ways the arguer asserts or implies. See whether the analogue is consistently described. Determine whether similarities are relevant to the conclusion. Use the technique of checking for relevant differences to see whether any relevant differences that provide evidence against the conclusion exist. *Note:* You do not have to write out all of these stages in your final answer; these instructions are intended as a guide to clear thinking. Not all passages contain arguments: if the passage does not contain any argument, or if it contains an argument that is not based on analogy, simply say so, and proceed no further.

1. *Background:* This passage deals with the issue of whether old people should be cared for by families or housed in institutions:

"But, we say, old folks get difficult and senile. Children get difficult and act as if they were senile, but no one has sanctioned an institution we can send our children to when we no longer wish to be responsible for them and they are not yet adults. Turn them out and you will be charged by the legal system."
(*Informal Logic Newsletter,* June 1979)

2. "In 'Children and Other Political Naifs,' Joseph Adelson says, 'I'm against the feminist movement, not against women.' Feminism is a part of so many women today that I don't think the two can easily be separated. It's like saying 'I'm against the civil rights movement, not against blacks.' "

(Letter to the editor, *Psychology Today,* February 1981)

*3. *Background:* In December 1982, Pierre Trudeau was prime minister of Canada. His government was subjected to extensive criticism, especially because the Canadian economy was quite weak and unemployment was high. Some urged that Trudeau should resign so that his Liberal Party could select a new leader. Others said an election should be called. Trudeau replied:

"People don't change doctors just because they're sick. Particularly if the other doctor down the street is, you know, dropping his pills and breaking his thermometer and he doesn't know what to do."

Hint: Assume that Trudeau's conclusion was that the people should not change the prime minister just because the economy was poor.

(Reported in the Toronto *Globe and Mail,* December 21, 1982)

4. *Background:* The following passage is taken from David Hume's "Dialogues Concerning Natural Religion." In these dialogues many different analogies are explored as alternative devices for reasoning about gods and the supernatural realm:

"The Brahmins assert that the world arose from an infinite spider, who spun this whole complicated mass from his bowels, and annihilates afterwards the whole or any part of it, by absorbing it again and resolving it into his own essence. Here is a species of cosmogony which appears to us ridiculous because a spider is a little contemptible animal whose operations we are never likely to take for a model of the whole universe. But sill, here is a new species of analogy, even in our globe. And were there a planet wholly inhabited by spiders (which is very possible), this inference would there appear as natural and irrefragable as that which in our planet ascribes the origin of all things to design by an orderly system and intelligence. . . . Why an orderly system may not be spun from the belly as well as from the brain, it will be difficult for him to give a satisfactory reason."

Hint: Assume Hume is comparing reasoning about creation in a world inhabited dominantly by people with reasoning about creation in a world inhabited by spiders.

(David Hume, "Dialogues Concerning Natural Religion," in *The Empiricists* [New York: Anchor Press, 1974])

5. *Background:* In February 1982, the Canadian defense minister, Mr. Gilles Lamontagne, sought a basis for strengthening Canada's commitment to NATO, claiming that NATO had kept the peace for thirty years. His remarks were questioned by a writer from a peace research institute, who said:

"Mr. Lamontagne claims that 'it is a well-known fact that, for the last 30-odd years, NATO has been the most efficient peace-keeping movement in the world,' but he cannot prove that to be true. Because A happens before B does not mean that A causes B. Snapping one's fingers to keep the elephants out of Ottawa appears to work because there are no elephants there; but the absence of elephants is no proof that snapping one's fingers is the cause of their absence."

(Letter to the editor, Toronto *Globe and Mail,* February 8, 1982)

*6. "Voracious toads the size of dinner plates are hitchhiking across northern Australia gobbling up wildlife, and officials are appealing to motorists not to give them lifts. The Queensland cane toad, which locals say eats almost anything, even lighted cigarets, is moving west rapidly. Some have been found travelling on vegetable trucks.

"Northern Territory Conservation Minister Steve Hatton is sending 'wanted' posters to garages, motels, and pubs, depicting the ugly amphibian and warning drivers to check their vehicles for stowaways.

" 'It's very worrying,' local conservationist William Freeland said. 'Toads have appeared up to 90 kilometres ahead of the main toad frontier. The bloody things eat some sorts of native wildlife into extinction.'

"The toad, introduced into Queensland early this century to combat a sugar cane parasite, has become a major pest, protected from predators by its poisonous skin."

(Reported in the Toronto *Globe and Mail,* July 6, 1985)

*7. *Background:* In the spring of 1985, a controversy arose about placing an anti-Jewish book in the collection of the University of Calgary Library. The book, titled *The Hoax of the Twentieth Century,* claimed that the murder of 6 million Jews in World War II did not occur. The university administration claimed that even though the book contained a false view of history, it was important for the library to have it on file. A letter to an alumni magazine expressed a dissenting opinion:

"The director of the University Library defended placing *The Hoax of the Twentieth Century* in the stacks with this comment: 'Why not both sides of this issue as well?'

"The Holocaust is NOT an issue and there are NOT two sides. We have physical evidence, eyewitness accounts from guards, prisoners and liberators, and film evidence from both German and underground sources. This is more than we have for more historical facts and certainly more than we have for criminal trials. While a university library should present all points of view, this does NOT apply to a tract based neither on evidence nor on logical thought. If a student wishes to know what was of interest during a particular time, does the library offer an equal choice between microfilm of the *Times* of London and bound copies of the *National Enquirer?* For geography, is there a choice between a globe and the clever drawings put out by the Flat Earth Society?"

Hint: There are, in fact, two analogues here.

(Letter by A.T., *Calgary Alumni Magazine,* summer 1985)

8. *Background:* A young philosopher contended that job security for professors, which results in no job opportunities for younger people, is unjust as an institution. A senior professor of philosophy wrote to object to the view saying:

"But consider this 'injustice' as well. My home was purchased only a decade ago, at less than half what it would bring on the market now, and throughout that period interest charges on the mortgage have averaged a single-digit percentage. A much younger person would find it difficult, if not impossible, to purchase a comparable dwelling now. Yet no one would suggest that, because of this, I should give up ownership and compete with homeless individuals for the three or five year leasing of it. Had that ever been a foreseeable eventuality, I would obviously not have 'bought' it in the first place. And one can multiply examples of similar 'injustice.'"

(Bulletin of the Canadian Association of University Teachers, March 1982)

9. *Background:* This analogy was used by one of several panelists in a university discussion on arms control and disarmament:

"The difference between arms control and disarmament is that the arms control approach is a much more gradual one. You can think of it in this way. You can imagine all the nuclear weapons in the world as being a huge chunk of granite. The arms controllers are, in effect, trying to make the chunk smaller by chiseling away at it. But the disarmament advocates, on the other hand, want to get rid of the entire block at once. Rather than using the slow chisel approach, they would prefer to blast the whole thing away with dynamite."

10. Responding to violence with more violence is like trying to put out a fire by adding matches. Matches can set off a fire, and when added to a fire, they will only make it burn more intensely. To put out a fire, we need to smother it or pour water on it. That is, we need something different from what's making the fire burn in the first place. And in just the same way, we can't stop violence by replying with more violence. Thus the way to stop terrorism is not to launch attacks on countries such as Libya and Lebanon, but rather to inject a genuinely new element into the situation. That element is a real

desire to work out the underlying political problems that keep terrorism alive.

11. The human mind has different parts or aspects. Some of these are superior to others. For instance, we have biological drives for food, water, sleep, and sex. We have emotions of fear, anger, hatred, and love. And we have an intellect that can reason. It is the intellect that should dominate in the mind, for this is the superior part of humankind. And similarly, there are different sorts of people in a society. Just as a mind will be disturbed if it is ruled by biological drives, or by emotions unguided by intellect, so society will suffer if it is not controlled by its superior people.

(Adapted from Plato's *Republic*)

*12. *Background:* In 1983, the Cold War between the United States and the Soviet Union was quite intense. It was accompanied by nuclear weapons buildups on both sides. Critics of the nuclear arms race, within the United States, had called for a nuclear freeze by both sides—which would stop new manufacturing and deployment of nuclear weapons. Representative Paul Simon of Illinois had this to say about the dangers of the nuclear arms race and the proposal for a bilateral freeze on the development and deployment of nuclear weapons:

"The United States and the Soviet Union are like two powerful automobiles coming from opposite directions, destined for a spectacular head-on crash that will eliminate both, as well as all the spectators. In this debate, some of us are saying: 'As a first effort, let's agree to have both cars put on the brakes.' But our opponents in this debate argue that we should not put on the brakes; we should put the cars into reverse. All of us share that hope, but for cars headed toward each other at breakneck speed, putting on the brakes is an urgently needed first step and must precede going in reverse.

"'But look at all the power in the other car,' some say. They see the fancy gadgets, most of which are meaningless, as well as the horsepower that is meaningful. That horsepower includes about 8800 Soviet strategic warheads, compared to our car's 9500; greater accuracy

on our car but more megatonnage on theirs. So the argument that we should ask these two cars to apply their brakes as a first step toward sanity holds true, no matter who has the 8800 and no matter who has the 9500.

"It's infinitely easier to put both cars into reverse once they have come to a stop. And every minute that we argue and do not act those two cars come closer to a collision. I hope the driver of our car, President Reagan, understands the desperate folly of the present course."

(*New York Times*, April 25, 1983)

13. "Smokers should be allowed to smoke only in private where it does not offend anyone else. Would any smoker walk into a restaurant and start eating half-chewed food on someone's plate, or drink a glass of water that previously held someone's teeth? Probably not, yet they expect non-smokers to inhale smoke from the recesses of their lungs. My privilege and right is to choose a clean and healthy life without interference."

(P. T. B., *Cape Town Argus*, quoted in *World Press Review*, January 1988, p. 2)

14. "Smoking is no more a sin than wearing high heel spike type shoes. These also are dangerous to your health and they destroy the property of others. Have you seen hardwood floors after a woman has walked over them in spike heels?"

(*U.S. Catholic*, June 1973, quoted in John Hoagland, *Critical Thinking*, p. 38)

15. *Background:* This argument deals with the issue of rights over territory acquired by conquest. It was formulated by philosopher John Locke in the eighteenth century.

"That the aggressor, who puts himself into the state of war with another, and unjustly invades another man's right, can, by such an unjust war, never come to have a right over the conquered, will be easily agreed by all men, who will not think that robbers and pirates have a right of empire over whomsoever they have force enough to master, or that men are bound by promises which unlawful force extorts from them. Should a robber break into my house, and, with a dagger at my throat, make me seal a deed to convey my estate to him, would this give him any title? Just such a title by his sword has an unjust conqueror who forces me into submission."

(John Locke, *Of Civil Government,* quoted in S. F. Barker, *Elements of Logic*)

INDUCTIVE ANALOGIES

We have now examined a number of a priori analogies and arguments based on them. Such arguments support a decision to classify a case in one way or another, or treat an action or argument as good or as poor. But analogies are used as a basis for predictions as well as for decisions. An a priori analogy is used to support a decision to treat cases in the same way—logically, morally, legally, or administratively. An inductive analogy provides a basis for prediction: we know that the analogue has certain characteristics, and because the primary subject resembles it in these aspects, we estimate or predict that the primary subject will resemble it in a further related respect as well.

As we have seen in some of the examples considered, the analogue in an a priori analogy is often merely an imagined case. It need not be a real case. However, in an inductive analogy, the analogue must be something that now exists or previously did exist. The factual, empirical properties of the analogue and the primary subject are essential to the way the analogy works.

We often need to make estimations about things that we are not in a position to observe—because they are in the future or in the past, or because there are moral or practical reasons against examining them directly. In such contexts, inductive analogies are important and useful: if we cannot examine A, but we can examine B, and if A is like B in many respects, then, given that B has characteristic x, we estimate or predict that A will have characteristic x. This is reasoning by inductive analogy.

Inductive analogies would not be necessary if we had general laws covering the unknown phenomena. Suppose, for instance, that we need to know whether human beings are adversely affected by urea formaldehyde foam, a substance sometimes used to insulate homes. If we knew that all mammals are adversely affected by the substance, our problem would be easily solved by a syllogism:

1. All mammals are adversely affected by urea formaldehyde foam.
2. All humans are mammals.
   Therefore,
3. All humans are adversely affected by urea formaldehyde foam.

But we do *not* know the first premise in this argument to be true. Nor can we (ethically) experiment directly on humans to see how they react to living in houses insulated with this material. The standard approach in such cases is to reason by analogy: inductive analogy. We study the effects of the material on nonhuman animals, and then predict what it will be in the case of humans. We will then argue like this:

1. Rats (or some other nonhuman animals) are like humans in respects 1, 2, 3, ...
2. Rats suffer effects *x, y, z,* when exposed to doses at such-and-such levels of urea formaldehyde.
3. A dose at so-and-so level in humans is equivalent to a dose at such-and-such levels in rats.

Therefore,

4. Humans will suffer effects *x, y,* and *z* when exposed to a dose at so-and-so level of urea formaldehyde foam.

In this analogy the primary subject is human beings and the analogue is rats. The two are being compared with respect to their reactions to doses of urea formaldehyde. This inductive analogy differs from a priori analogies in a very significant respect: the analogue must describe an actual thing and give factual information about it. An inductive analogy is based on information gained from human experience. The conclusion in an inductive analogy cannot be known with complete certainty, but as a basis for prediction, close comparison with a similar case or cases[10] is much better than no information at all.

Here is an example of an inductive analogy. The passage quoted describes a *New York Times* reporter, Benedict Nightingale, who began to reflect on his evidence for believing in the United States' Apollo moon landing of 1969.

> One evening he was presenting a news item dealing with the Apollo program when the idea struck him: "I was thinking how easy it would be to manipulate an event in a television age. All right, you couldn't invent the Olympics, because there would be too many people watching. But there was one event of really enormous importance that had almost no witnesses. And the only verification we have that anyone reached the surface of the moon came from one camera."
>
> And was a fraudulent space-shot, he asked himself, really so very implausible? Didn't that long-unacknowledged part the United States played in the early days of the Vietnam War indicate that such an undertaking could easily be sanctioned and organized? Think of it—a country bombing another country for eight months without anyone knowing about it. Think of all the planes involved, all the barracks that had to be built, all the beds that had to be made, all the meals that had to be cooked. My idea was peanuts beside that, much smaller in scope and scale and probability.[11]

Nightingale reasoned that it had been possible to hide eight months of bombing from the public, that it would be far easier to hide a deception about the moon landing, and that, therefore, it was possible that the moon landing was a fictitious event. It is important to see that he is not claiming that the moon landing did not occur—merely that it would have been possible to fake the event. The possibility is supported by an inductive analogy.

Inductive analogies are important and they are a common way of reasoning about human affairs. We use them in simple, practical decision making. For instance, suppose you have twice bought a certain brand of bathing suit, finding that a particular size fits comfortably, that the material wears well, and that the suit is good for active swimming. When shopping again, you may look for the same brand name. You are, in effect, reasoning by inductive analogy: you know the first two suits were a good buy and you infer that the third will be similar to them in its fit, comfort, and so on. Here you are inclined to attribute the good qualities to the manufacturer, so there is a reason for linking the similarities together.

More controversially, inductive analogies are used in political policy debates. Often a past event comes to be a kind of model for a present or future one. When Saddam Hussein of Iraq invaded and then claimed to annex Kuwait in the summer of 1990, many people were reminded of Hitler's annexation of Austria in 1938. Hitler was not stopped right away, and he went on in the next several years to invade Czechoslovakia, Poland, Holland, Belgium, France, and the Soviet Union. Hussein seemed similar to Hitler in running a ruthless government that had engaged in brutality against its own citizens and in being willing to go against moral standards and agreements by the international community. The obvious conclusion of this inductive analogy seemed to be that Hussein should be stopped immediately. This conclusion formed the basis for a United Nations Security Council resolution and the deployment of more than 500,000 United States troops in Saudi Arabia and nearby areas.

In 1982 many people opposed U.S. government policy in El Salvador on the grounds of similarities between what was happening there and what happened in Vietnam in the early 1960s. For the Americans considering this analogy, the Vietnam saga was over and—in most people's opinion—American intervention in Vietnam had been a disastrous failure. By pointing out what they regarded as crucial similarities between the Vietnam situation and circumstances in El Salvador, critics predicted failure for the U.S. efforts there also, under the slogan "not another Vietnam." The events of Vietnam were known; those of El Salvador yet to come. Hence the need to use the analogy. Disputes about U.S. policy in El Salvador in the early to mid-80s were, to a surprising extent, disputes about the merits of this analogy.

We assess inductive analogies in basically the same way we assess other analogies—that is, by evaluating the significance of relevant similarities and differences between the primary subject and the analogue. We try to consider all the relevant similarities and see how they support the conclusion. We then consider all the relevant differences and consider the extent to which they may undermine the argument. In these respects, evaluating inductive analogies is similar to evaluating a priori analogies.

However, some aspects of inductive analogies make their evaluation different. The most obvious of these is that in the inductive analogy, the analogue must describe something real, and the facts cited must be genuine. Imaginary examples are fine for a priori analogies, but not for inductive ones. The similarities on which inductive analogies are based are between empirical aspects of the primary subject and the analogue. We cannot determine the extent of the similarity merely by reflecting on structural features, as we could for a priori analogies. What really happened is our basis for predicting what is likely to happen, so we need experience.

Also, similarities cumulate in an important way. In an a priori analogy, what is important is that the similarities relevant to the conclusion hold. If they do, it does not matter whether there are many further similarities or none at all. But in the inductive analogy, the sheer number of similarities does matter. The closer the two cases are, in detail, the more likely it is that the inferred conclusion will be true. This means that the evaluation of inductive analogies depends more on factual background knowledge than does the evaluation of a priori analogies. If you don't know the background facts about Hitler and Hussein or about Vietnam and El Salvador, you will have to do research before you can properly estimate the strength of these analogies.

It is also important that the features cited in the analogies are relevant to the feature predicted in the conclusion; there must be some general basis for thinking that these features and the feature specified in the conclusion are connected to each other. In the simple case of the bathing suits, for instance, the fit, fabric, and design are the responsibility of the manufacturer; hence it is reasonable to expect that a third suit, made by the same manufacturer, will be similar to the first two in these respects.

To evaluate arguments based on inductive analogy, we first identify the primary subject and the analogue, just as we did for a priori analogies. Then, as before, we apply the ARG conditions. At this stage, the difference between a priori analogy and inductive analogy becomes significant for our evaluation of arguments. In an inductive analogy, the analogue is a real thing—not a case simply imagined or hypothesized by the arguer. Thus, when we check the premises for acceptability, it is very important to see whether the analogue is accurately described. For example, if someone is using information about two bathing suits to reason to a conclusion about a further suit, it is important that her beliefs about the first suit are correct. (If she thought mistakenly that she had a size 10 and reasoned that since it fit, another 10 would fit, the analogy would likely give a false prediction.)

To determine the relevance of the similarities that exist between the primary subject and the analogue, we have to look closely at the conclusion asserted and reflect on how the features that are similar are related to that conclusion. For instance, suppose a student reasons by inductive analogy that because Smith was a good instructor in a junior philosophy course, he will also be a good instructor in a senior interdisciplinary course. A full evaluation of the relevance of the analogy will require critical thought that goes beyond what is explicitly stated in the premises. You have to ask yourself some questions. In what respects is the primary subject (the instructor's performance in the senior interdisciplinary course) similar to the analogue (his performance in the junior philosophy course)? How relevant are those respects to the conclusion—that is, how are they likely to be connected to the property predicted in the conclusion? Class size and subject matter are relevant because there is general reason to suppose that they have some effect on the quality of instruction. The location of the class on one side of the campus or the other is probably irrelevant (why should this affect instruction?), but the size and seating layout of the classroom might be relevant (some instructors who excel at conducting seminars and are only fair at straight lecturing may perform much better in a room with a seminar table or chairs in a circle).

In inductive analogies our judgments about the relevance of similarities and differences between cases are not made by pure reflection, as they are for a priori analogies. Rather, they are made with reference to our background knowledge about how the various properties of things are empirically connected.

If the similarities between the analogue and the primary case are relevant to the property predicted in the conclusion, we still need to see whether they are sufficient to provide good grounds for that conclusion. To determine whether they are sufficient, we reflect on differences that may exist between the primary subject and the analogue. There are bound to be some differences: here, as with a priori analogies, the issue is whether differences are negatively relevant to the conclusion. The inductive analogy, as explicitly stated in an argument, will typically not mention differences. Like other analogies, it urges us to think of the similarities between the cases compared. We have to think of these differences ourselves in order to appraise the analogy.

With inductive analogies, finding the differences and determining how relevant they are requires background knowledge. A senior interdisciplinary course is different from a junior philosophy course in that the former will require both a greater breadth of knowledge and a greater ability to respond to complex questions. These differences between the primary subject and the analogue are negatively relevant to the prediction that an instructor who is good in one course will be good in the other. The courses require different knowledge bases and different talents. Thus the differences between the courses tend to undermine the force of the inductive analogy.

When we make such judgments about the cogency of inductive analogies, it is important to note the degree of certainty with which the conclusion is asserted. A student who concluded "Smith is sure to be good in Interdisciplinary Studies 400 because he was terrific in Philosophy 100" has a different argument from one who asserts "There is reason to think Smith will lecture well in I. S. 400 because he lectured well in Phil. 100." The second student has a conclusion that is more tentative and that is restricted to one aspect of the professor's performance—his lecturing skill. Since his argument is already sensitive to the limitations of the inductive analogy, it does not succumb to criticism as easily.

◆───

EXERCISE SET

Exercise 2

Some of the following passages contain arguments based on inductive analogies. Identify these arguments, and specify the primary subject, the analogue, and relevant similarities and differences between them. Then assess the strength of the inductive analogy as a basis for the conclusion. If the passage does not contain an inductive analogy, comment briefly as to what sort of passage it is. Does it contain no argument at all? Or another kind of argument? Or an a priori analogy?

1. Studying French without ever speaking the language does not result in a good command of French. Latin is a language too, so studying Latin without ever speaking it will not result in a good command of Latin.

2. In the civil service, people are spending other people's money. Civil servants do not have to earn the money they spend; it is given to them by government, which raises it from tax dollars. That makes civil servants careless about their expenditures. Universities are like the civil service. Their administrations do not have to earn the money spent. It comes from the government. Therefore, we can expect university administrators to spend money carelessly.

3. A watch could not assemble itself. The complex arrangements of parts into a working watch is possible only because there is a craftsman who designs and constructs the watch. In just the same way, the complicated parts of the world could not arrange themselves into the natural order. So there must be a designer of the world, and that is God.

4. Hannibal is well-known for having arranged to get elephants across the Alps when he was fighting against the Romans. That was an unbelievable feat. Hannibal's arrival in Italy, with an army and equipment carried by elephants, must have been a great surprise to the Romans.

*5. "A majority taken collectively is only an individual whose opinions, and frequently whose interests, are opposed to those of another individual, who is styled a minority. If it be admitted that a man possessing absolute power may misuse that power by wronging his adversaries, why should not a majority be liable to the same reproach? Men do not change their characters by uniting with each other; nor does their patience in the presence of obstacles increase with their strength. For my own part, I cannot believe it; the power to do everything, which I should refuse to one of my equals, I will never grant to any number of them."

(Alexis de Tocqueville, *Democracy in America*, quoted in S. F. Barker, *The Elements of Logic*, 3rd ed. [New York: McGraw-Hill, 1980])

6. Slavery was a human institution that existed for thousands of years. Now, slavery is largely eliminated. Morally dedicated citizens in religious and public action groups brought about the end of slavery, even though it was taken for granted as a natural fact of human existence. War, similarly, is a human institution that is taken for granted and that has existed for thousands of years. Morally dedicated citizens in a wide variety of groups, including many that have a religious basis, are working for the elimination of war. And the example of slavery shows that they can succeed.

*7. *Background:* The following is the first part of an advertisement by Foster Parents Plan. The advertisement appeared in *Harper's Magazine* in May 1990.

"Here's your chance to achieve a small moral victory. What would you do if you saw a lost, frightened child? You'd probably stop, pick him up, brush away his tears, and help him find his way. Without even thinking about it. And there's a reason. You know what's right. And right now, you can do just that. You can act on instinct . . . by reaching out to one desperately poor child, thousands of miles away. With your personal caring and help. Through Foster Parents Plan, you'll be helping a child who almost never has enough to eat. A decent place to sleep. Medical care. The chance to learn. Or hope . . . If you saw a helpless child on the street, you wouldn't wait. You'd help that instant. Please don't wait now, either. Achieve a small moral victory!"

*8. *Background:* This argument was used by Bud Greenspan who sought to show that sports officials cannot be expected to be perfect in their judgment and that it is unrealistic and counterproductive to check their expertise against video replays of the actions they judge.

"Athletes are human. So are officials. If we cannot expect perfection from the performers, how can we expect more from those who officiate? The structure of sports is based on the premise that all one can ask of an athlete is that

he or she be dedicated, prepared, talented, and courageous. Can anyone doubt that these qualifications do not hold true for officials?"
(Quoted in Gary Gumpert, *Talking Tombstones and Other Tales of the Media Age* [New York: Oxford University Press, 1987], p. 63)

9. *Background:* The following passage is a quotation from the artist M. C. Escher. Escher is describing how he sometimes feels as though some kind of subsystem in his brain is taking over when he is creating drawings.

"While drawing I sometimes feel as if I were a spiritualist medium, controlled by the creatures which I am conjuring up. It is as if they themselves decide on the shape in which they choose to appear. They take little account of my critical opinion during their birth and I cannot exert much influence on the measure of their development. They are usually very difficult and obstinate creatures."
(Quoted in Douglas Hofstadter, *Godel, Escher, Bach: An Eternal Golden Braid* [New York: Basic Books, 1977], p. 387)

10. *Background:* The following was a letter on the topic of preserving rain forests.

"The one kind of argument I do not seem to be hearing is one that I believe deserves to be heard when forest policy is being made. That is: Some (a few) of our most ancient and least disturbed forests in North America are biological communities of living things that have been accumulating and developing almost since the period of our last glacial age, nearly 15,000 years ago. These most ancient communities of living and growing things have been residents of this continent for so much longer than any of us humans that we should consider it our duty to avoid wrecking and pillaging them, simply as the deference owed by very much younger things to those who have lived and sheltered other life and fed nature's multitudes for ages."

Hint: Is this an inductive analogy?
(P. H., San Francisco, printed in *World Press Review,* December 1989, p. 2)

*11. *Background:* This example from Arthur Schopenhauer's *The Art of Literature* advocates independent thinking.

"Everyone who really thinks for himself is like a monarch. His position is undelegated and supreme. His judgments, like royal decrees,

spring from his own sovereign power and proceed directly from himself. He acknowledges authority as little as a monarch admits a command. He subscribes to nothing but what he has himself authorized. The multitude of common minds, laboring under all sorts of current opinions, authorities, prejudices, is like the people, which silently obeys the law and accepts orders from above."
(Arthur Schopenhauer, *The Art of Literature,* trans. T. Bailey Saunders [Ann Arbor: University of Michigan Press, 1960])

12. *Background:* The nineteenth-century philosopher Jeremy Bentham wrote primarily about ethics and politics. However, he also wrote a work called *Handbook of Political Fallacies,* in which he set out a number of arguments common in political life and maintained they were fallacious. (Bentham is dealing with the argument—common in his day, apparently—that those who criticize dishonesty in a particular government are seeking to undermine government in general.) This passage is taken from that work:

"In producing a local or temporary debility in the action of the powers of the natural body, in many cases, the honest and skillful physician beholds the only means of curing it; and it would be as reasonable to infer a wish to see the patient perish, from the act of the physician in prescribing a drug, as to infer a wish to see the whole frame of government destroyed or rendered worse, from the act of a statesman who lowers the reputation of an official whom he regards as unfit."
(J. Bentham, *Handbook of Political Fallacies,* rev. and ed. Harold Larrabee [New York: Thomas Y. Crowell, 1971])

13. "The thought was three days and three nights growing. During the days he carried it like a ripening peach in his head. During the nights he let it take flesh and sustenance, hung out on the silent air, colored by the country moon and country stars. He walked around and around the thought in the silence before dawn. On the fourth morning he reached up an invisible hand, picked it, and swallowed it whole."
(Ray Bradbury, "The Time of Going Away," *The Day It Rained Forever* [Middlesex, England: Penguin Books, 1963])

FURTHER CRITICAL STRATEGIES

An interesting critical strategy that can be applied both to a priori analogies and to inductive analogies is that of working out a different analogy that suggests a conclusion contrary to the one in the argument you are examining. This is the technique of *counteranalogy*. When an analogy is drawn, you start to think of the primary subject in a specific way, using the analogue as a model. You begin to transfer concepts and beliefs from the analogue to the primary subject. This analogue will always be one of a number of different possible ones. Adopting an alternative and setting out to conceive the primary subject in terms of that alternative will almost always bring fresh insights and new conclusions.

For instance, one might undermine the comparison between travel and reading, mentioned earlier as a possible basis for urging governments to subsidize travel, by a counteranalogy, comparing travel with play. The counteranalogy will tend to support the conclusion that governments should not subsidize travel. If the conclusions are incompatible with those implied by the original analogy and yet the new analogy is just as good, you have undermined the original analogy with a counteranalogy.

This technique of counteranalogies was used to great effect by the philosopher David Hume in his famous *Dialogues Concerning Natural Religion*. The Dialogues offer a prolonged critical appraisal of an inductive analogy: the argument that because the world is made of organized interconnected parts, like a machine, it must, like a machine, have been designed by an intelligent being. Hume pointed out that the model of the world as a machine is only one of a great number of possible models, and that other models suggest radically different theological conclusions.[12] He did this by creating a number of alternative analogies.

Here is a passage in which Hume employed the technique of counteranalogy:

> Now if we survey the universe, so far as it falls under our knowledge, it bears a great resemblance to an animal or organized body, and seems actuated with a like principle of life and motion. A continual circulation of matter in it produces no disorder; a continual waste in every part is incessantly repaired; the closest sympathy is perceived throughout the entire system; and each part or member, in performing its proper offices, operates both to its own preservation and to that of the whole. The world, therefore, I infer, is an animal, and the Deity is the soul of the world, actuating it, and actuated by it.[13]

Hume is saying that you could prove a deity that is the soul of the world just as well as you could prove a deity who is the external creator of the world. In effect, neither of these incompatible conclusions is more plausibly supported by analogy than the other. Thus, Hume is criticizing the machine analogy that supports the *argument by design*. He does it by pointing out that an animal analogy seems equally appropriate, and the animal analogy does not yield the conclusion that the world was created by an intelligent mind. Actually, Hume is using the technique of refutation by logical analogy, but the primary subject (the argument he seeks to criticize) is itself an inductive analogy. Hume's argument can be set out as follows:

ANALOGUE

The world is like an animal and must have a soul like an animal. Therefore, there is a Deity who is the soul of the world.
    is a possible way of thinking of the world
    highlights some significant features of the world
    leads to a conclusion nobody takes seriously

PRIMARY SUBJECT

The world is like a machine and must have an inventory like a machine. Therefore, there is a Deity who is the inventory (creator) of the world.
    is a possible way of thinking of the world
    highlights some significant features of the world

CONCLUSION

The argument that because the world is like a machine it must have an intelligent inventor or creator has a conclusion that nobody should take seriously.

By showing that there are many different analogies that seem equally plausible when we try to think of the world as a whole, Hume was pointing out that our experience of the world does not indicate which one of these analogies is the most appropriate one. If we choose to think of the world only as a machine, then, because machines have intelligent designers. we will think that the world must have had an intelligent designer. On the other hand, if we think of the world as an organism, we will reach a different conclusion: it will have resulted from sexual generation by other organisms! Hume's point was that if we find this conclusion ridiculous—as most religious believers surely would—we should give no more credence to the conclusion that the world has a designer. The two arguments are structurally parallel, so if one is not cogent, the other isn't either.

An analogy might be thought of as a special sort of screen or filter. (Note the analogy!) Using an analogy, whether in an argument or an explanation, or merely as a literary device, encourages you to focus on certain aspects of the primary subject—those that are similar to the analogue. An analogy is often said to highlight these aspects. Analogies can be helpful in creative and critical thought when they highlight important features that we might not have attended to before. However, they can also be misleading, in that features not highlighted may also be significant as well. Using different analogies emphasizes different features. Thinking of alternatives can be a liberating and creative experience, especially when language and thought are dominated by one particular analogy.

Thought and language are often dominated by models that we take for granted to such an extent that we do not even realize they are models. We adapt a language from one sort of thing and use it to think and talk about another. In doing so, we may export beliefs and assumptions from one area of knowledge to another, often in an uncritical way. Using a new model may reveal that these assumptions need to be questioned. A new model will sometimes suggest fresh ideas and insights. Thus new analogies can be more than counteranalogies. They may suggest original ways of thinking and talking and new projects and strategies for research.

As a matter of fact, it has been pointed out that our culture and language employ a kind of deep metaphor or analogy that is about argument itself. Argument is assimilated in much of our language to battle or even war. Just as people may defend territory in a war, they are said to defend positions in an argument. They may ward off attacks, have opponents, stake out positions, make counterattacks, achieve victories, retreat from positions when attacked, win and lose in debates, and so on. Perhaps we would have a different understanding of argument if we thought of an alternative deep metaphor, or model. It is hard even to imagine what this metaphor would be because the terminology of attack and defense is very deeply ingrained in our language. But no doubt there are other models. We might think of persons arguing as negotiators trying to work out as resolution to a common problem, as dancers forming a pleasing pattern, or as quilters making a new design from many individual contributions.[14] If such alternative analogies were explored seriously, new questions about arguments would no doubt arise, and some things like *winning* an argument or having an *opponent* when you argue might cease to seem as important as they now do.

LOOSE AND MISLEADING ANALOGIES

As mentioned earlier, we have developed our treatment of analogy in such a way as to emphasize its serious cognitive uses. On the whole, the arguments from analogy used to illustrate points have been cogent ones. But this should not be taken as an indication that all arguments from analogy are cogent arguments. Many arguments from analogy are quite dreadful, and analogies can be seriously misleading. We'll explore some common misuses of analogy now that we have seen how analogies can be important, cogent, and useful.

The Fallacy of Faulty Analogy

Certainly many arguments by analogy are poor; in fact the special fallacy label, *faulty analogy,* was invented to describe such cases. Sometimes the analogies on which arguments are based are so loose and farfetched that it is impossible even to classify them as a priori or inductive. It seems as though a gross image of a primary subject is given by the analogue and the unwary audience is supposed to be lulled into a conclusion. Such loose uses of analogy are often discussed as instances of the fallacy of faulty analogy. They involve an appeal to similarities that are highly superficial and give no real support to the conclusion sought.

Here is an example of a grossly flawed argument by analogy. It is taken from a letter to the editor in which the writer urged that the city of Calgary not develop a new subdivision that was proposed in order to provide housing for 50,000 people:

> Once a pleasant and friendly lady of the foothills, Calgary has become an obese, 200 pound dame and naturally suffers from all the diseases inherent to the distended community: smog breath, body odors, high traffic blood pressure, glandular dollarities, and skin blemishes such as high rises, towers, skyscrapers, and malls. . . . It would be well to consider if this continual expansion of Alberta cities is really needed or just a competitive show-off.[15]

Here the writer uses the analogue of an obese dame to dispute the wisdom of extending the city. He draws out the image in some detail. But it would be hard to take it seriously, either as an a priori analogy or as an inductive one. There is no serious demand for consistency between our attitudes toward obesity in people and size in cities! There is no norm of healthy size for cities anyway. Nor is there any inductive basis for predicting that the poor health a person is likely to experience as a result of gross obesity will somehow emerge in parallel for a city that undergoes expansion. The notion of "health problems" would be quite dubious in its application to a city. The analogy thus provides no support for the author's stance on the proposed subdivision. It gives him an entertaining and vivid way of stating his point but provides no rational support for it. As far as careful reasoning about the subdivision is concerned, the analogy is simply a distraction.

Loose analogies can be particularly deceptive when the analogue is something toward which people have very strong or very settled attitudes. These attitudes carry over too easily to the primary subject, even though there is no significant similarity between it and the analogue. You can see this transfer happening in the following argument, which was put forward in the seventeenth century by essayist Francis Bacon:

> Nobody can be healthy without exercise, neither natural body nor politic; and certainly to a kingdom or estate, a just and honourable war is true exercise. A civil war, indeed, is like the heat of a fever, but a fever of war is like the heat of exercise, and serveth to keep the body in health; for in slothful peace, both courage will effeminate and manners corrupt.[16]

How is the analogue similar to the primary subject? What, precisely, do they have in common? Do these common features have anything to do with the conclusion reached about the primary subject? Do they give sufficient grounds to support that conclusion? Many analogies between the body and the state are so loose that they cannot support specific conclusions.

It is obvious and well-known that the healthy human body requires exercise. Bacon exploits this common knowledge to try to show that the political organism also needs exercise, and he then contends that war constitutes this exercise. However, there is at best a loose similarity between the primary subject and the analogue in this case; again there is no clear standard of health for the primary subject, the state. Furthermore, even if we were to grant that a state or kingdom does need exercise, it is surely not clear that war would be the only form such exercise could take. Internal campaigns to eliminate poverty or pollution might be just as energetic and unslothful as war! These critical remarks are really very obvious, but the danger is that due to the familiarity of the fact that human bodies do need exercise, and the difficulty of thinking about the state or kingdom as a whole without some analogy, it would be all too easy to believe that Bacon has really established his point. Asking how the similarity alleged would function to establish the conclusion can expose the superficiality of the resemblance.

In addition to this kind of suggestive and loose use of analogy there are several more specific fallacies of reasoning that involve the misuse of analogy.

The Fallacy of Two Wrongs Make a Right

We have seen that there is a legitimate way of using analogies to push for consistency between relevantly similar cases. But a rather common type of argument, easily confused with legitimate consistency arguments, amounts to a fallacy of reasoning. This is the fallacy of thinking that *two wrongs make a right*. It is committed when a person tries to defend one thing that is allegedly wrong by pointing out that another thing that really is wrong has been done or has been accepted. In doing so, he is in effect reasoning that since we have allowed some wrong, we should (to be consistent) permit more.

The following example shows this kind of misuse of analogy. The context is a discussion of a rock concert. A reviewer had criticized the performers for using the language of sex and drugs and for encouraging fantasies of sex and drug use in the audience. A young rock fan, writing to defend the concert, said:

> There's not a thing wrong with what Roth did in front of 15,000 people. After all, don't millions of people see worse stuff in front of the television every day?[17]

The arguer is drawing an analogy between Roth's performance at the rock show and things that are shown on television. She is trying to reply to the suggestion that the performance is immoral by saying that it is not wrong because it is not worse than something else that is tolerated.

This is a two-wrongs-make-a-right argument, and it is a fallacy. It is rather like the use of analogy in consistency arguments, and yet it differs from them in a subtle, but crucial, way. The writer says that on television there is "worse stuff," thereby granting that some material on television is bad. If Roth's performance is similar in the respect of being tasteless, as she says it is, the correct conclusion to draw would be that Roth's performance is also bad. Yet this conclusion is just the opposite of the conclusion drawn.

Two-wrongs arguments are common in areas where abuses are spread across many institutions, countries, persons, and contexts. If someone attacks one instance of the abuse, claiming it is wrong and that reform is necessary, he is often criticized by those who use two-wrongs arguments. For instance, when Greenpeace campaigned against the killing of baby seals for pelts, many people pointed out that the killing of baby seals is by no means the only instance when humans treat animals cruelly. Animals raised and slaughtered for food are often very cruelly treated, and this cruelty is tolerated. Critics in effect demanded consistency from Greenpeace, asking, "If you tolerate slaughter for food, why criticize killing animals for their pelts?" This demand for consistency is fair enough. But it is a mistake to infer from the social toleration of killing animals for food (which, it is implied, is wrong) that killing animals for pelts (which is similar) should not be criticized. If the one thing is wrong and the other is similar to it, a correct appeal to consistency will imply that the other is wrong too. Two wrongs make two wrongs; they do not make one right. There is no point in multiplying wrongs in the name of consistency.

Consider two proposed actions: (a) and (b). If both are wrong, and similarly wrong, then the best thing would be to prevent both from occurring. Ideally, then, such groups as Greenpeace would work against the slaughter of animals for meat and against the seal hunt—granting that both involve wrongful cruelty to animals. But for reasons of time, available volunteers, money, and other factors, this may not be possible. One of the two wrongs, therefore, must be selected as the target of action. Now when this selection happens, critics may allege that the choice of targets is inappropriate; for instance, they may want to accuse the group of unduly emphasizing a problem that is not as important as some others. This criticism is fair enough. But it is not appropriate to argue that because there is more than one wrong, nothing should be done about that wrong. After all, reform has to start somewhere, and it cannot usually start everywhere at once. Following through on two-wrongs thinking would commit us to perpetuating immoral practices in the name of consistency.

The two-wrongs fallacy is common when there is a set of attitudes or beliefs that are connected and that are all open to criticism. (Examples include sexism in many areas of life, abuses of human rights in many parts of the world, human behavior toward nonhuman animals in many aspects of our culture, and arms buildups in many countries.) In such cases, would-be reformers who attack any single manifestation of the evil may be asked, quite legitimately, why that one is the appropriate one to be worried about. (Why do feminists worry about the use of *he* as a generic word when many women are battered by their husbands, and women's conditions in prisons are so awful? Why do people criticize American attitudes toward human rights in El Salvador when there are so many abuses of rights in China and Iraq? And so on.) But the target may be selected because it is close to home, because it is one for which we are directly responsible, or because it is relatively easy to change. It is fallacious to infer that one wrong should be condoned because there are other similar ones. The existence of these other wrongs is no reason to accept another one, however similar it may be.

The Fallacy of Slippery Assimilation

Perhaps you have heard of the so-called proof that no one is bald. It goes like this: consider a person with 50,000 hairs on his head. If you take away one of these hairs, that will not make him into a bald person. Now suppose you keep pulling out hairs, one at a time. Suppose you get the poor fellow down to the point where he has only 200 hairs left. He won't look very hairy at this point. But is he bald? How can he be? All you do is pull out one hair at a time, and no *one* hair will make the difference between being hairy and being bald. You are sliding along evenly from a state of hairiness. With no obvious stop along the slide, how do you stop calling the man hairy? If the first hair doesn't make the difference, neither does the second, nor the third, nor the fourth. Each hair is just like the one before it, and it would surely be arbitrary to say that the 40,004th hair could make the difference when the first or the tenth could not. This argument seems to provide a proof that no one can be bald. Very consoling to older men, perhaps, but paradoxical for logicians.

In fact, logicians have been puzzled about this kind of argument for several thousand years. It is sometimes referred to as the paradox of the heap because an early form of the argument was that you could never get a heap of grain from an accumulation of individual grains: no one grain would make the difference between having just a few separate grains and having a heap. Clearly something has gone wrong with the argument. We indicate this fact by referring to arguments of this type as *fallacies of slippery assimilation*.

Let's take a more abstract look at this puzzling line of reasoning:

1. Case (a) differs from case (b) only by amount *x*.
2. Case (b) differs from case (c) only by amount *x*.
3. Case (c) differs from case (d) only by amount *x*.
4. There is a whole series of cases (a) to (a plus *n*).
5. Within the series (a) to (a plus *n*), each member differs from those preceding and following it only by amount *x*.
6. Amount *x* is a small, even trivial, amount.
7. Case (a) is a clear case of *W*.
Therefore,
8. All the other cases in the series, from (b) to (a plus *n*), are also clear cases of *W*.

For baldness, the series would be long indeed, and each member would have one less hair than the one before; the conclusion would be that all are hairy. (The absurdity of the argument can also be pointed out by the fact that you could use it in reverse to prove that everybody is bald. Start with a completely bald person and add one hair at a time. There will be no *one* hair that makes the difference between being bald and being nonbald. Hence, no matter how many more hairs a person has than the bald man, he will turn out to be bald!)

The argument urges us to *assimilate* all the members in the conceptual series to the first member. The reason for the assimilation is that the difference between a member and its successor is very slight; if the first case is *W* and the second one differs from it only slightly, the second one is *W*—and so on for all the further cases. The argument ignores the fact that differences that are *separately* insignificant can (and often do) *cumulate* to be significant. One hair at a time is not significant, but the *cumulative* effect of pulling out 40,000 will be. Gaining an ounce won't affect your appearance, but if you gain an ounce a day for 1000 days, the cumulative effect (more than 60 pounds) will certainly be noticeable.

Even if you were slim at the beginning of this process, by the end of it you would be plump. There is a difference between being hairy and being bald, and a difference between being slim and being plump, even though it is impossible to specify exactly the one hair or the one ounce that will make the difference.[18]

Probably you have heard logically similar arguments in debates about abortion. The strategy is to insist that fetal development is gradual and that each stage of development differs only slightly from those preceding and succeeding it. Thus to select any one time in the nine months of development and say that the moment marks the difference between the fetus and human person will look arbitrary. Many antiabortionists infer from these facts that the fetus is a human person from the moment of conception; since we cannot draw a line, all stages represent a person. (We could equally well infer that all represent a nonperson, since the change into a person occurs at no one point. But this inference is less common.) However, both inferences are mistaken: both involve the fallacy of slippery assimilation.

Often slippery assimilation arguments are suggested by the rhetorical question, "But where do you draw the line?" The implication behind this question is usually that since you can't specify the one precise point where a line should be drawn, such distinctions as bald/hairy or slim/plump should not be made at all. But something has clearly gone wrong here. The mistake in the fallacy of slippery assimilation is one of ignoring the fact that differences that are separately trivial can cumulate to be significant. The argument from slippery assimilation does show that it will be debatable where distinctions are made, and it shows that there will be borderline cases: people who are neither clearly hairy nor clearly bald, neither clearly slim nor clearly plump, and so on. But it does not show that all the items in a conceptual series must be classified in the same way due to considerations of consistency.

The Fallacy of Slippery Precedent

A related abuse of consistency reasoning comes when a specific case is considered in relation to a whole series of further cases, some of which are morally very different from the original one. It is sometimes allowed that a particular action would, when considered by itself, be a good one to perform. However, this good action would, nevertheless, set a dangerous precedent, since consistency would make us slide on allowing further actions that do not share the moral value of the original one. On such grounds it is often urged that even though the action in question is admitted to be good, it should not be taken because it is too closely related to further actions that are not so good. We shall call this type of argument the argument from *slippery precedent*. Like the slippery assimilation argument, it has some resemblance to the legitimate uses of an a priori analogy. Again, like that argument, it relies on a series of cases, using the existence of a related series to justify a conclusion about a member in the series. We slide easily from one case to others; the way is slippery.

Here is an example of this slippery use of precedent:

As a student whose parents are undergoing divorce, and who has suffered from mononucleosis this term, you clearly would deserve an extension on your deadline. However, even though it would be fine for me to allow you this extension, if I did that, I would be bound to give an extension to every student who asked for one. I would wind up giving extensions to students who were just disorganized or who had been out drinking at parties, and soon my deadline would be completely meaningless.

We can easily imagine the familiar scene in which a professor uses this argument to reply to a student's plea for an extension. It pays the compliment of granting the student that her own request, considered by itself, is legitimate and would merit the extension. But it then insists that this legitimate extension would set a bad precedent, because it would provide a basis for further illegitimate extensions, which, in consistency, would have to be allowed. The professor ignores the possibility of considering the case on its own merits.

See if you can detect the same kind of reasoning in this next example, which moves up one level in the university hierarchy. (This one was used by a dean commenting on an action taken by a professor in his faculty.)

A faculty member has launched an appeal concerning his salary. He says that he did not, in the past, receive all the special merit increments to which he was entitled. In fact, this professor is disliked by the chairman of his department, and that chairman has admitted that in the past not all deserved increments were given to the man. If you consider his appeal just by itself, you have to admit that he deserves to win it. But the problem is, if he can appeal his salary, all the other professors can do that too. To grant his appeal will set the precedent that faculty members can squeal and protest whenever they don't get just what they want from the salary committee, and if that precedent is set, we'll be granting every appeal, and the very point of having such a committee will be defeated. The system would be completely unworkable. Therefore, even though this single appeal is well-founded, it should not be granted because of the precedent it sets.

In these arguments, a case that is admitted to be legitimate is assimilated to further cases that are similar in some respects but obviously not legitimate. The initial case is then set in the context of these others, and the arguer insists that it would set a precedent for them. Since these further cases are not to be allowed, it is inferred that the initial case should not be allowed either on the grounds that it would set a bad precedent.

When we reflect on such arguments, we realize that something must be wrong with them. The problem is that the premises are implicitly inconsistent, and therefore they cannot all be acceptable. If case (a) is legitimate and cases (b), (c), and (d) are not legitimate, then these cases just cannot all be relevantly similar to each other. There must be something about the first that relevantly differentiates it from the others as far as the decisions to be taken are concerned. Given this relevant difference, the first case cannot be a precedent for the others.

Let's look back at the example of the student and her deadline. If she has serious family problems and has been ill during the term, her case differs significantly from another one in which a student is pressed for time just because he was disorganized. That she has been seriously handicapped by factors outside her control makes her deserving of special consideration; that line of reasoning does not apply to the other students whose cases are mentioned. To allow an extension in a hardship case is not a precedent for allowing it in every case, provided we are clear as to why the extension is being allowed.

Similar points can be made for our second example. A professor who, by general admission, was mistreated in the past is in a different position from others who just happen to want a higher salary. Precedent reasoning is quite legitimate in general, but it is misapplied in these arguments. The reason is simple: cases that are straightforwardly deserving must be relevantly different from other cases that are straightforwardly undeserving. The former cannot set a genuine precedent for the latter. That is the reason we call these arguments slippery; in them there is an unwarranted slide from one kind of case to another. Whenever someone urges that a good decision would set a bad precedent, you can be sure that something has gone wrong. Somewhere along the line, a relevant difference has been ignored.

There are more subtle appeals to precedent that do not involve appealing to premises that are implicitly inconsistent. These more complex arguments play tricks in another way with our sense of what is fair. They admit that the further cases to which the initial case is compared are also deserving, but then they go on to add that for various reasons (costs, administrative overload, or whatever), not all deserving cases can be fully recognized as such. It is then argued that because all the cases cannot be treated in the same way and because all are equally deserving and relevantly similar from an administrative point of view, none should be allowed. Here again we have a series of cases related by analogy and an inference made, based on consistency reasoning, about the series as a whole. An example would be the following:

> It is good for people to know languages other than their native language. It would be good to teach German, Chinese, Cree, French, Ojibway, Spanish, and Russian in public schools, if we could. Each one of these languages is important in the world, and each is allied to a culture with a valuable literature and history so that knowing it is a big intellectual advantage. But schools clearly cannot teach all these foreign languages because they just don't have the time or money. Now we have this request, from the German community in Milwaukee, to put German in public schools as a foreign language. Doing so would be a good thing in itself, but the problem is that so would the teaching of all these other foreign languages. We just cannot fit them all in. We will have to do too much if we accept German as a precedent for foreign language teaching in public schools. We cannot teach them all, so we had better not teach any. After all, you have to draw the line somewhere, and no place is clearer than the very beginning.

The theme here is that too much of a good thing is unattainable, so we'll have to settle for none of it! The problem with this argument is different from the problem in our other slippery precedent cases. Here, since it is admitted that all the cases compared are morally similar (good), there is no inconsistency in the premises. The problem in this case is that the premises, taken together, fail to provide adequate grounds for the conclusion. The (G) condition of the argument cogency is not satisfied. In effect, the argument is asking us to infer that we should allow none from premises that show that we cannot allow all. This is a hasty inference because it ignores the possibility of allowing some. Beware of administrative appeals to precedent!

We are not saying, of course, that appeals to precedent always involve mistakes. Quite the contrary: as we urged earlier, these appeals are basic in law, morality, administration, and even in logic itself. It is always important to see how relevantly similar cases would be resolved, or have been resolved in the past, when we are trying to deal with a problem. The slippery appeals to precedent that we have discussed here are abuses of what is basically a sound and important procedure. Cases should be settled in a way that is consistent with the proper resolution of relevantly similar cases. When an argument admits that a case under consideration is legitimate, but urges that this legitimate case would set a bad or unmanageable precedent, something has gone wrong. Relevant differences have been ignored or compromise solutions have gone unconsidered.

EXERCISE SET

Exercise 3

Of the following passages, first identify those that contain arguments by analogy. For each argument by analogy, identify the primary subject and the analogue, mention key relevant similarities and differences between the primary subject and the analogue, and comment on the merits of the argument. If any passage contains any fallacy as two-wrongs, slippery assimilation, or slippery precedent, point this out and explain just how the fallacy is committed in that particular case.

1. People say that because nuclear weapons have not been used since 1945, they are safe and will never be used. They think that we can accumulate these weapons and get a balance of nu-

clear power with the Soviets and still remain safe and secure. But with 50,000 nuclear weapons in the world, we aren't very secure at all. Thinking that because it's been all right so far it will be all right later on is like a chap falling off the Empire State Building. He comes falling down, and by the time he has passed 100 stories, he's still all right. So he calls out, "Hey folks, look. I'm OK. No need to worry."

2. The altos and tenors in a choir are like the filling in a sandwich. When you first see a sandwich you notice the bread. And, of course, the taste of a sandwich depends very much on the taste of the bread. But what would a sandwich be without a filling of delicious roast beef, cheese, or peanut butter? Just nothing at all. And in the same way, the altos and tenors make a choir's music meaningful. Maybe you don't notice these middle parts as much as you notice the sopranos and basses, but without them, the performance would be empty.

(Calgary choir director, Jim Munro, on the importance of alto and tenor parts in a choir)

*3. "It is of course quite true that the majority of women are kind to children and prefer their own to other people's. But exactly the same thing is true of the majority of men, who nevertheless do not consider that their proper sphere is the nursery. The case may be illustrated more grotesquely by the fact that the majority of women who have dogs are kind to them and prefer their own dogs to other people's. Yet it is not proposed that women should restrict their activities to the rearing of puppies."

Question: Here Shaw is alleging that other people use a faulty argument. Do you agree with him?

(G. B. Shaw, "The Womanly Woman," in *Masculine/Feminine,* ed. Betty Roszak and Theodore Roszak [New York: Harper & Row, 1969])

4. Obviously, very small organisms, such as algae, do not think. From algae, we progress by small degrees to small sea creatures, insects, birds, reptiles, mammals, and human beings. The behavior of all these creatures exhibits changes only by degrees. Therefore, if we deny mind to algae, we must deny it also to human beings. And if we grant mind to human beings, we must grant it also to algae.

5. "Handgun control doesn't necessarily mean taking the guns away from everybody. It can mean simply to license these weapons, making it unlawful to own one without proper registration. After all, what's the big deal? You need a license to get married. You need a license for your dog. You need one for your vehicle and your business. You need permits for nearly everything. Nobody seems to suffer too much. Drivers must meet certain standards in order to obtain a permit to drive. As a result, thousands of lives are saved every year. So why not similarly license handguns? It'll cost a little, be a little inconvenient, and maybe it'll save a few lives. It really is the least we can do."

(Letter to the editor, *Los Angeles Times,* January 23, 1981, which was cited in the *Informal Logic Newsletter,* Examples Supplement, November 1981)

6. "It's sort of like the Theory of Relativity. With relativity, it's like this: If you go fast enough, time slows down. With Enriched Flavor, it's like this: The taste stays just as rich as you like even though the tar goes down. What could be simpler? Enriched Flavor, low tar. A solution with Merit."

(Advertisement for Merit cigarettes, printed in *Harper's Magazine,* March 1990)

7. *Background:* A contentious issue in Toronto city politics in 1989 was whether to build a domed stadium. Some critics of the stadium had urged that opera was more worthwhile than football and baseball; in response to these comments, newspaper columnist Michael Shapcott had said that no one ever died from lack of opera—that is, opera is not really a necessity of life. The following letter on the issue appeared in a Toronto paper:

"Michael Shapcott is right. No one has ever died from lack of opera. Nor, might I add, have the morgues ever been overpopulated with guests suffering from terminal lack of a domed stadium. Opera is meant to be enjoyed by everyone. . . . Unfortunately, opera gets littered with snobberies, and some wonderful music gets lost in the shuffle. If children were exposed to as much opera as they are to baseball, hockey, and football, opera would rapidly lose its image of being esoteric and intimidating."

(A. C., letter to the Toronto *Star,* reprinted in *World Press Review,* December 1988, p. 8)

*8. *Background:* Here is a piece of advice from the Trent University Philosophy Department on the matter of footnotes:

"Footnotes, like other conventions of academic writing, have no essential connection with philosophical thinking. They are helpful for making written work easy on the eye and for showing that the writer has, so to speak, funds to support the cheques issued in the main text."

9. *Background:* The following argument appears in the *American Sociological Review* for October 1950.

"One of woman's most natural attributes is the care of children. Since the ill and infirm resemble children in being physically weak and helpless as well as psychologically dependent and narcissistically repressed, women are also especially qualified to care for the sick."

(Cited by Howard Kahane in *Logic and Contemporary Rhetoric*, 3rd ed. [Belmont, Calif.: Wadsworth, 1983], p. 70)

*10. *Background:* Here is a piece on the subject of the moral status of animals. It was written by Lewis Carroll, the author of *Alice in Wonderland*. Carroll was also a logician of very considerable accomplishments. This passage is taken from his essay, "Some Popular Fallacies about Vivisection":

"In discussing the rights of animals, I think I may pass by, as needing to remark, the so-called right of a race of animals to be perpetuated and the still more shadowy right of a non-existent animal to come into existence. The only question worth consideration is whether the killing of an animal is a real infringement of a right. Once grant this, and a *reductio ad absurdum* is imminent, unless we are illogical enough to assign rights to animals in proportion to their size. Never may we destroy, for our convenience, some of a litter of puppies, or open a score of oysters when nineteen would have sufficed, or light a candle in a summer evening for mere pleasure, less some hapless moth should rush to an untimely end! Nay, we must not even take a walk, with the certainty of crushing many an insect in our path, unless for really important business! Surely all this is childish. In the absolute hopelessness of drawing a line anywhere, I conclude (and I believe that many, on considering the point, will agree with me) that man has an absolute right to inflict death on animals, without assigning any reason provided that it be a painless death. But any infliction of pain needs its special justification."

(Lewis Carroll, "Some Popular Fallacies about Vivisection," *The Complete Works of Lewis Carroll* [New York: Random House, 1957])

11. *Background:* Author Edward DeBono is discussing whether thinking can be taught:

"If thinking is indeed a skill, how is it that we do not acquire this skill in the normal course of events? We develop skill in walking by practice. . . . We develop skill in talking by communication. . . . Surely we must develop skill in thinking by coping with the world around us? The answer is that we do. But we must distinguish between a 'full' skill and a two-finger skill.

"Many people who teach themselves to type early in life learn to type with two fingers. This is because they do not set out to learn typing as such but to use typing in their work. With two fingers they can more quickly acquire a more tolerable level of competence than if they tried to develop skill with all ten fingers. . . . They learn a two-finger skill. Yet a girl who trains to be a typist can, within a few weeks, develop a much higher degree of touch-typing skill, or what we call a 'full' skill. The two-finger journalist has acquired skill in the course of dealing with a limited situation and his skill is only just sufficient to cope with that situation.

". . . Similarly the academic idiom taught at schools and refined in universities is a sort of two-finger skill. It is excellent at coping with closed situations where all the information is supplied, but it is very inefficient in dealing with open-ended situations where only part of the information is given, yet a decision still has to be made."

(Edward DeBono, *Teaching Thinking* [Harmondsworth, England: Penguin Books, 1984], p. 47)

12. *Background:* The following appeared as a letter to the editor. The writer is objecting to a previous writer who had expressed a strongly antiabortion position.

"Andrea Keene's selective morality is once again showing through in her July 15 letter. This time she expresses her abhorrence of abortion. But how we see only what we choose to see! I wonder if any of the anti-abortionists have considered the widespread use of fertility drugs as the moral equivalent of abortion, and, if they have, why they haven't come out against them, too. The use of these drugs frequently results in multiple births, which leads to the death of one of the infants, often after an agonizing struggle for survival. According to the rules of the pro-lifers, isn't this murder?"

(Cited in Brooke Noel Moore and Richard Parker, *Critical Thinking: Evaluating Claims and Arguments in Everyday Life* [Palo Alto, Calif.: Mayfield, 1986], p. 122)

*13. *Background:* Author Donald Griffin is dis-cussing whether animals are conscious and what sorts of thought they might have, if they are:

"The content of much human consciousness does not conform to objective reality. Fear of ghosts and monsters is very basic and wide-spread in our species. Demons, spirits, miracles, and voices of departed ancestors are real and important to many people, as are religious beliefs.

". . . Yet when we speculate about animal thoughts, we usually assume that they would necessarily involve practical down-to-earth mat-ters, such as how to get food or escape preda-tors. . . . But there is really no reason to assume that animal thoughts are rigoristically realistic. Apes and porpoises often seem playful, mischie-vous, and fickle, and anything but businesslike, practical, and objective. Insofar as animals do think and feel, they may fear imaginary preda-tors, imagine unrealistically delicious foods, or think about objects and events that do not ac-tually occur in the real world around them."

(Donald Griffin, *Animal Thinking* [Cambridge, Mass.: Harvard University Press, 1984], pp. 202–203)

14. If a ten-year-old can get away with writing on a school fence, then an eleven-year-old can get away with breaking windows, a twelve-year-old can pull off an unpunished mugging, and a thirteen-year-old can get away with murder. Casual vandalism must be punished.

15. *Background:* In 1974 Canadian Agriculture Minister Eugene Whelan was criticized because 27 million eggs had been allowed to spoil. He replied to criticism as follows:

"I wouldn't call that a surplus. It was only two days consumption for the whole province of Ontario. They think that's a lot, but how many billions, and I mean billions, of potatoes were dumped in Prince Edward Island years ago. Nothing was said about that."

(As cited in Ralph H. Johnson and J. Anthony Blair, *Logical Self-Defense*, 2nd ed. [Toronto: McGraw-Hill-Ryerson, 1983], p. 105)

16. *Background:* Here is an excerpt from a letter on the abortion issue, taken from the Calgary *Herald,* January 25, 1983. It was written to ar-gue against the position of a previous writer, Ross, who had urged that a fertilized egg be-comes a person at the moment of conception.

". . . that single cell is not a baby; it is sim-ply a cell, which, if conditions permit, may be-come a baby. In other words, it is a 'potential baby' and it is the destruction of this potential baby that Ross calls infanticide. But as he him-self puts it, there can be no 'cut off' point in the development of a baby, so why not go one step further and consider the unfertilized ovum? The ovum is half a human cell which, if conditions permit, may become a baby—it too is a poten-tial baby. Following Ross's own logic, the de-struction of an ovum would entail infanticide. Does he then denounce the birth control pill (which interferes with the release of the ovum) as infanticide?"

17. *Background:* The following analogy was used to try to show that problems between the Soviet Union and the United States are not best addressed by experts on weaponry.

"If you had a husband and wife who'd been quarrelling, and they were collecting crockery to throw at each other—more and more plates, bowls, heavy pottery, mugs—one subject would be crockery control. Let's limit the weight of the mugs; let's substitute plastic dishes for the heavy plates, and that would be crockery con-trol. And on that I would welcome the advice of ceramic engineers as to how to design plates ad-equately without making them dangerous. But anyone realizes that the true problem is: what we need is family counselling. We need to deal with the differences that are bound to come up between husband and wife, or between neigh-bours, or between us and the Soviets—how to deal with those differences in such a way that nobody will reach for the crockery. And, on that subject, don't ask for a ceramic engineer or a pottery manufacturer. You don't ask for a mili-tary man to give us expert advice on how to deal with our differences. That's a subject for every human being who has kids with whom they quarrel, parents, neighbours, boss and secretary; we know more about how to deal with differences than a nuclear physicist who does nothing but study nuclear particles. The more he narrows his mind down to the hardware, the less he understands the problem."

(Roger Fisher, quoted in *Nuclear Peace* [Toronto: CBC Transcripts, 1982])

❖ CHAPTER SUMMARY

There are both legitimate and illegitimate uses of analogy. A priori and inductive analogies are fundamental in the construction of human knowledge. A priori analogies depend on an appeal to consistency, a demand that relevantly similar cases should be treated similarly. They are important in logic, ethics, law, and administration and may be used to resolve important conceptual disputes. A refutation by logical analogy can constitute a conclusive refutation of an argument. This technique is common in logic itself and was used to good effect by the philosopher David Hume in his famous work, "Dialogues on Natural Religion."

Inductive analogies are indispensable in enabling us to bring known cases to bear on the unknown, giving us a basis for estimates that cannot be based on universal or general statements because we do not have sufficient evidence to render those statements acceptable. Whereas an a priori analogy demands a decision made in consistency with that in an analogous case, an inductive analogy is used as the basis for a prediction. With inductive analogies, the merits of the argument cannot be determined by reflection alone but must be assessed with consideration for the actual features of the cases compared, using empirical background knowledge. Inductive analogies are used in ordinary life, in scientific reasoning, and in policy reasoning when historical cases are brought to bear on present problems.

Analogies can also be misused. Some arguments are based on analogies so loose and remote that it is hard even to classify them as either a priori or inductive. These analogies are deemed to be fallacious; in fact, a special fallacy category, "faulty analogy," is defined to include them. Other faulty uses of analogy, such as the two-wrongs fallacy and the slippery uses of assimilation and precedent, involve more subtle abuses of the inherently legitimate case-by-case technique.

❖ REVIEW OF TERMS INTRODUCED

Analogy A parallel or comparison between two cases. Analogies may be used as the basis for arguments when people reason from one case to a conclusion about another deemed to be similar to the first. In addition, analogies are used in explanations, or as illustrations, or in descriptions, purely for literary style and vividness.

Primary subject   In an argument by analogy, the topic that the conclusion is about.

Analogue   In an argument by analogy, the thing to which the primary subject is compared and on the basis of which the arguer reasons to the conclusion about the primary subject. Some arguments by analogy use several analogues.

Appeals to consistency   Arguments relying on analogy and urging that similar cases be treated similarly. If *A* is relevantly similar to *B*, and if *B* has been treated as *x*, then, as a matter of consistency, *A* should also be treated as *x*. Appeals to consistency are especially common in logic, law, ethics, and administration.

Refutation by logical analogy   The refutation of one argument by the construction of another that is parallel to it in reasoning and that is clearly flawed.

Precedent   A relevantly similar case that has already been resolved. Reasoning by precedent is particularly common and important in law.

Conceptual issue   An issue in which the question at stake is how a concept should be applied or how it should be articulated.

A priori analogy   An argument by analogy in which there is an appeal to consistency and in which the analogue may be entirely hypothetical or fictitious without undermining the logical force of the argument.

Inductive analogy   An argument by analogy in which the conclusion is predicted on the basis of experience. The analogue must be a real case, and the factual features of the analogue and the primary subject are essential for determining the strength of the argument.

Counteranalogy   An analogy different from the one on which an argument is based, and leading plausibly to a conclusion different from, or contrary to, that of the original argument. If the counteranalogy is as well-founded as the original one, and if it leads to a different conclusion, its construction constitutes a powerful criticism of the original argument.

Faulty analogy   Name for a fallacious argument in which the analogy is so loose and remote that there is virtually no support for the conclusion.

Fallacy of two wrongs make a right   Mistake of inferring that because two wrong things are similar and one is tolerated, the other should be tolerated as well. This sort of argument misuses the appeal to consistency.

Fallacy of slippery assimilation   Argument based on the logical error of assuming that because cases can be arranged in a series, where the difference between successive members of the series is small, the cases should all be assimilated. This is a mistaken appeal to consistency. It ignores the fact that small differences can accumulate to be significant.

Fallacy of slippery precedent   Argument based on claiming that an action, though good, should not be permitted because it will set a precedent for further similar actions that are bad. Such arguments are flawed in that they use implicitly inconsistent premises. A good action cannot be relevantly similar to a bad action; there must be some relevant difference between them.

Notes

1. C. S. Lewis, *Mere Christianity* (New York: Macmillan, 1952), p. 75.
2. Albert Einstein, as quoted by Jonathan Schell in *The Fate of the Earth* (New York: Knopf, 1982), p. 10.
3. A truth table construction can be used to show that any statement of the form "P· − P" is always false.
4. Alan Connery, Calgary *Herald,* July 6, 1979. Reprinted with permission of the Calgary *Herald.*
5. Brothers's advice was reprinted in the *Informal Logic Newsletter* in the Examples Supplement for 1979.
6. These events were described in the Toronto *Globe and Mail* for February 8, 1982.
7. *For instructors:* It may be misleading, from the theoretical point of view, to assume that the pertinent features of the analogy can be picked out as easily as this model would suggest. Cf. Trudy Govier, "Analogies and Missing Premises," *Informal Logic,* vol. XI, no. 3 (Fall 1989): 141–152, for a discussion of this point and others pertaining to a priori analogy. This volume contains several interesting theoretical papers on analogy; see especially those by John Woods and Stephen Barker.
8. Robert Nozick, *Anarchy State and Utopia* (New York: Basic Books, 1974), pp. 169–170.
9. Letter to *Time* magazine, April 10, 1989.
10. Often, in inductive analogies, several analogue cases are cited and, in fact, this strengthens the argument when the various analogue cases differ from each other (there is a greater variety of evidence for the conclusion). To avoid complications, inductive analogies considered in this chapter have only one analogue case.
11. Gary Gumpert, *Talking Tombstones and Other Tales of the Media Age* (New York: Oxford University Press, 1987), pp. 45–46.
12. The use of inductive and a priori analogies by Hume in the "Dialogues" is clearly and interestingly discussed by Stephen F. Barker in "Reasoning by Analogy in Hume's Dialogues," in *Informal Logic,* vol. XI, no. 3 (Fall 1989): 173–184.
13. David Hume, "Dialogues Concerning Natural Religion," in *The Empiricists* (New York: Anchor Press, 1974), p. 467.
14. This point is discussed in an interesting way by Maryann Ayim in "Violence and Domination as Metaphors in Academic Discourse," in Trudy Govier (ed.), *Selected Issues in Logic and Communication* (Belmont, Calif.: Wadsworth, 1988), pp. 184–195.
15. Letter to the Calgary *Herald,* March 12, 1976.
16. Francis Bacon, *The True Greatness of Kingdoms,* quoted by Susan Stebbing in *Thinking to Some Purpose* (London: Pelican Books, 1938), p. 123.
17. Letter to the Calgary *Herald,* May 7, 1984.
18. The fallacies of slippery assimilation and slippery precedent are sometimes referred to as the "slippery slope" fallacy. What is later called "causal slippery slope" (discussed in Chapter 10) is often similarly described; hence the use of *slippery* in each description. Slippery assimilation, slippery precedent, and causal slippery slope are distinguished in this book because they differ in important ways. Arguments for this view may be found in Trudy Govier, "What's Wrong with Slippery Slope Arguments?" *Canadian Journal of Philosophy,* 12 (1982).

CHAPTER 10

Conductive and Inductive Arguments

WE HAVE NOW LOOKED AT THE nature of argument, conditions of acceptability and relevance, and several distinct ways in which premises may provide adequate grounds for a conclusion. We have discussed some common forms of formal deductive validity, and we have seen that arguments may be deductively valid by virtue of meaning as well as form. Also, we have examined various kinds of argument by analogy. Now we look at two other ways in which premises provide grounds for conclusions: conduction and induction.

CONDUCTIVE ARGUMENTS

Think back to the convergent support pattern that we defined in Chapter 2. When the support is convergent, the premises count separately in favor of the conclusion; they need not be linked together. If one or more premises should be removed from the argument, the relevance to the conclusion of those remaining would be unaffected.[1] (As you may remember from Chapter 2, this is not the case for a linked argument.) In most deductively valid arguments and in analogies, the support provided by premises is linked, not convergent. There are exceptions, as when a person offers two separate premises, both of which deductively entail the conclusion, but this is quite rare.

There are arguments in which support is convergent and in which the premises do not entail the conclusion nor support it by analogy. For such arguments, we can evaluate the (A) condition as usual but when we come to assess (R) and (G), we can only determine whether the premises (considered one at a time) are positively relevant to the conclusion and whether, in the final analysis, they (considered together) provide grounds for it in virtue of the relevance they separately have. These arguments we call *conductive arguments*.

Here is a simple example:

(1) She never takes her eyes off him in a crowd, and (2) she is continually restless when he is out of town. (3) At any opportunity, she will introduce his name in a conversation. (4) And no other man has ever occupied her attention for so long. You can tell (5) she is in love with him.

The issue here is whether someone is in love. The person arguing has offered several pieces of evidence to support his hypothesis. Even if one piece were faulty, the others would still count in support of his conclusion. Each piece of information is relevant, and separately relevant, to establishing that conclusion. This argument proceeds by specifying a number of relevant factors and then by weighing these factors to provide a basis for the conclusion.

All conductive arguments employ the convergent support pattern as this one does.[2] The argument just described can be represented pictorially as follows:

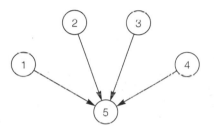

Some philosophers have referred to these arguments based on separately relevant factors as *good reasons arguments*. The relevant factors provide reasons for the conclusion, though they do not deductively entail it. But one problem with the "good reasons" label is that it suggests that all arguments of this type are based on good reasons. And they are not. Some may specify as relevant factors that are really irrelevant—as when straw man, ad hominem, and guilt-by-association fallacies are used. Others may provide premises that are genuinely relevant but do not add up to give enough support for the conclusion. To avoid the suggestion that all conductive arguments are good ones, we have avoided calling them good reasons arguments.

Conductive arguments are common in reasoning about practical affairs, where a number of separate factors seem to have a bearing on our decisions about what to do. Also, they are common when there are disputes about interpretation. Arguments about the correct interpretation of actions are often used in social theory and in history; these too frequently draw together several independently relevant factors because there are several distinct pieces of evidence that count for or against one interpretation or the other.

The recognition of *counterconsiderations* is especially common and natural when conductive arguments are being used. Counterconsiderations are reasons that count against the conclusion being put forward: statements of counterconsiderations are negatively relevant to the conclusion. If we want to represent arguments pictorially, we can include counterconsiderations by using wavy lines to indicate that they count *against* the conclusion rather than for it. (The counterconsideration could be regarded as a kind of antipremise!)

Thus, if we had three premises supporting a conclusion in a conductive argument and we came up with two counterconsiderations, we could represent the whole situation like this:

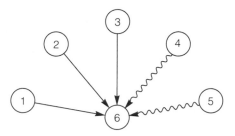

Statements (1), (2), and (3) are premises, (4) and (5) are counterconsiderations, and (6) is the conclusion.

Often counterconsiderations are put forward by someone who is still in the process of thinking an issue through, or by the critic of an argument. However, sometimes a person arguing for a position recognizes that there are factors counting against that conclusion. When this happens and the person nevertheless still wishes to support his conclusion on the basis of his premises, he is committed to the judgment that the supporting (positively relevant) premises outweigh the counterconsiderations that are negatively relevant to his conclusion.

It is difficult to give completely general guidelines about appraising conductive arguments. Our previous discussion of relevance will bear on this matter, and our understanding of relevance and irrelevance helps us to examine the relevance of premises in conductive arguments. Fundamentally, the evaluation of the (R) and (G) conditions in conductive arguments depends on how the reasons stated in the premises weigh up against counterconsiderations. In a conductive argument, there are nearly always counterconsiderations that are negatively relevant to the conclusion, even though they may not be explicitly acknowledged by the arguer. It is a creative task of evaluation to think what these counterconsiderations are and to determine how much they count against the conclusion and whether their import can be overcome by the evidence or reasons put forward in the premises.

We'll illustrate this point by considering an example:

(1) Voluntary euthanasia, where a terminally ill patient consciously chooses to die, should be made legal. (2) Responsible adult people should be able to choose whether to live or die. Also (3), voluntary euthanasia would save many patients from unbearable pain. (4) It would cut social costs. (5) It would save relatives the agony of watching people they love die an intolerable and undignified death. Even though (6) there is some danger of abuse, and even though

(7) we do not know for certain that a cure for the patient's disease will not be found, (1) voluntary euthanasia should be a legal option for the terminally ill patient.

This argument could be pictorially represented as follows:

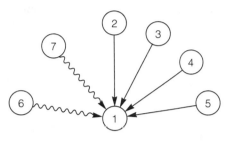

Four factors are cited as support for the normative conclusion that voluntary euthanasia should be legalized. The last statement acknowledges two counterconsiderations. Their role as counterconsiderations is made clear by the words *even though*. To accept the conclusion on the basis of the supporting premises, we must judge that they outweigh in significance both the stated counterconsiderations and any other counterconsiderations that are not stated in the argument. Clearly, a person who put forward the preceding argument would believe that the alleviation of pain and the recognition of the right to life are more important, on balance, than the risk that voluntary euthanasia might lead to abuses and the chance that a cure might be found so that the patient would not have had to die. To appraise the argument, we have to reflect on whether we agree with this judgment—given the acceptability of the premises and their relevance to the conclusion.

There is no simple logical formula for such judgments of the balance of considerations. Also, there can be counterconsiderations other than those acknowledged by the arguer. For instance, many religious groups oppose voluntary euthanasia, and that may be a reason against legalizing it. Also, patients undergoing severe pain may not be capable of making rational decisions about their lives, so that voluntary euthanasia would not really be voluntary after all. Other objections to the conclusion may be raised.

Obviously, evaluating this argument will involve making some sensitive judgments. We can set out a logical structure for raising questions about such arguments as this, and the structure is a useful guide for thought. Answers, however, especially for issues as profound as that of euthanasia, will emerge from individual judgment about the significance of the various factors.

The method for appraising conductive arguments is as follows:

1. Determine whether the premises offered to support the conclusion are acceptable.

2. Determine whether the premises offered to support the conclusion are positively relevant to it.

3. Determine whether any counterconsiderations acknowledged by the arguer are negatively relevant to the conclusion.

4. Think what additional counterconsiderations, not acknowledged by the arguer, are negatively relevant to the conclusion.

5. Reflect on whether the premises, taken together, outweigh the counterconsiderations, taken together, and make a judgment. Try to articulate good reasons for that judgment.

6. If you judge that the premises do outweigh the counterconsiderations, you have judged that the (R) and (G) conditions are satisfied. Provided that (A) is also satisfied, you deem the argument cogent. Otherwise, you deem it not to be cogent.

As with other cases of argument evaluation, following this procedure does not quite take you to the stage of determining whether the conclusion is true, or whether you have good reasons to accept it. It takes you only to the stage of determining whether the stated premises provide good reasons for accepting the conclusion. If you think the argument as stated is cogent, then you do think there are good reasons to accept the conclusion, so presumably you will accept it on the basis of the argument. But if you think the argument is not cogent, you may wish to proceed further to see whether the conclusion could be supported by other evidence or reasons not stated in the original argument.

To proceed, you have to reflect on whether there are further considerations, not stated in the argument, that would count in favor of the conclusion and would outweigh any counterconsiderations. Doing so takes you beyond appraising the stated argument and moves you ahead to a stage where you are amending or reconstructing that argument by adding more premises of your own. It is an important stage, of course, when your real interest is in whether you should accept the conclusion and not merely in whether the conclusion is well supported by the particular argument you are evaluating.

To say that the pro factors outweigh the con factors is to speak metaphorically, of course. The image brought to mind is that of an old-fashioned scale in which weights are placed on each side to balance the scale or to achieve a state of equilibrium. To say that we weigh the pros and cons, or see how the premises can provide grounds in the face of counterconsiderations, is to think of evidence and reasons as having significance that can be measured. This concept may sound obscure and difficult, but there is a sense in which people use it all the time, and they often seem to achieve reasonably reliable results.

Suppose a mother is trying to decide which of two babysitters to hire. Jane lives five minutes closer by car than Sue. But Jane has been convicted of theft, whereas Sue, whom the mother has personally known for some years, appears to be very reliable and trustworthy. Clearly the comparative closeness of Jane counts in favor of hiring her, whereas her unreliability counts against it and in favor of hiring Sue instead. A judgment of significance is very easy to make here; trustworthiness outweighs the rather trivial factor of five extra minutes driving time and a little more gas, where a babysitter is concerned. We could offer reasons for this judgment of significance in terms of the risk to children and property if an unreliable babysitter were hired. In fact, the weighing of factors here seems so obviously right that few people would question it or bother to support it with reasons.

Weighing pros and cons is nearly always a feature of practical decision making, and sometimes it is quite simple, as the preceding example illustrates. The fact that evaluating conductive arguments depends on our making such judgments of significance does not mean that the evaluation is an impossible task or that agreement will never be achieved. In fact, the notion of counterconsiderations can be used to good purpose when you are constructing arguments of your own. By thinking of counterconsiderations, points that count against your premises and conclusion, you can strengthen and qualify your position, thus improving the quality of your argument.

As we mentioned earlier, conductive arguments appear in many contexts. Moral reasoning is an especially important one, but we also find conductive arguments in history, science, literature, philosophy, and psychology. In fact, they are likely to occur anywhere we may have distinct factors that count in favor of a conclusion and other distinct factors that count against it. As with moral reasoning, making judgments about how these supporting and countervailing factors weigh up can be either quite difficult or relatively easy.

Suppose that a scientist had five experiments that tended to confirm a hypothesis and three that tended to disconfirm it. Suppose that he needed to make a practical decision as to whether he should continue to investigate this hypothesis, or whether, on the other hand, he should consider the three negative experiments sufficient to disconfirm it. He would almost certainly engage in conductive reasoning—trying to weigh the significance of the positive experiments against the significance of the negative ones, and trying to weigh all of this against the importance of the hypothesis for other scientific work and for human life in general. Judgments would be required. In some cases, reasons could be given for allowing some points to outweigh others. For instance, if the negative experiments were done in a lab in which the machinery had broken down shortly afterward, then the machinery's possible unreliability when the experiments were done would give the scientist a reason for not letting these negative experiments count very much—for letting the positive experiments outweigh them in significance.

You are likely to find yourself using conductive arguments when you are aware of several distinct reasons that count in favor of a decision or conclusion, especially one concerning what is to be done. The notion of counterconsideration is important to remember in such contexts; it can remind you to think in terms of cons or negatives, as well as pros or positives, and to be aware of the need for judgments as to the significance of the various factors. If you are quite convinced that the positives outweigh the negatives, it is worth stopping to reflect on your judgment to ask yourself why you think this, and to consider whether there are any additional factors you might have neglected to consider.

EXERCISE SET

Exercise 1

Evaluate the following conductive arguments. State any counterconsiderations on which your evaluation depends, and note whether these are your own contributions or whether they are explicitly acknowledged by the author of the argument. State whether the premises are positively relevant to the conclusion and whether, considered together, in light of counterconsiderations, they provide adequate grounds for the conclusion. If you believe that you lack the background knowledge necessary to evaluate the argument, state what sort of knowledge you would need and, if feasible, how you could go about finding it if there were a practical need to do so.

1. Susan must be angry with John because she persistently refuses to talk to him and she goes out of her way to avoid him. Even though she used to be his best friend, and even though she still spends a lot of time with his mother, I think she is really annoyed with him right now.

*2. There is no point in giving money to charity. The charitable organizations often waste it. Besides, when people are really needy, governments should support them and not rely on charity to do it. In addition, the advertisements put out by some of these charities are so emotional that they are positively manipulative.

3. You should return books to the library on time. When borrowing them, you in effect contract to do so. Also, other people may need them, and you can avoid expensive fines by being prompt.

4. Interdisciplinary courses, in which several different academic subjects are supposedly taught together, are not worth taking. They are hard for professors to teach. They are hard for students to understand. They demand so much extra research, for essays, that students do not have a hope of getting a good mark. Besides, many interdisciplinary courses try to combine so many different things that they wind up being a mishmash of unrelated theories and ideas.

5. *Background:* The following argument appeared in a letter to *China Daily,* reprinted in *World Press Review* (December 1989):

"We should smile sincerely at visitors from abroad. However, Chinese drivers, hotel clerks, and sellers should not distinguish between compatriots and foreigners. At present, some Chinese taxi drivers turn their backs if the clients approaching their cars are Chinese. Hotel guards quite rudely prevent Chinese people from entering. Some clerks in friendship stores turn up their noses at Chinese customers. I think, as a Chinese, that those who do such things are disgracing themselves.

"We may not be as wealthy as foreigners. But there are many kinds of wealth, and money is by no means the only representation of it. A person who looks down upon his compatriots will be cast aside by society and despised by the fair-minded foreigners as well."

Hint: Concentrate on the part after "we may not be as wealthy" and regard earlier sections as introduction.

*6. There is no free will. For the will to be free, it would have to be not caused by anything, and this is almost surely impossible. Besides, we all know people sometimes act out of control and can't fully choose what they do. Look at alcoholics, for instance. Religious people say God made us with free will. But there may not even be a god. And if there is, He would control the whole world and would control human actions so there wouldn't be any free will anyhow.

*7. The American Revolution was not a typical revolution. For one thing, the people in revolt were mainly middle class or upper class—not peasants. For another, the object of attack was something far away—a government in England—and not the close structure of the society in which the war occurred. In addition, the internal workings of the society did not change so very much after the revolution. Despite the fact that it is called a revolution, and despite its great importance for the history of the world, the American Revolution should not be thought of as a model for other revolutions. If we think this way, we will underestimate the importance of poor classes in the revolutionary process and we will fail to see the real potential for lasting violence after a revolution.

8. *Background:* The author is discussing the problem of rape and the question of whether rape is due to natural psychological impulses:

"Another canon in the apologetics of rape is that, if it were not for learned social controls, all men would rape. Rape is held to be natural behavior, and not to rape must be learned. But in truth, rape is not universal to the human species. Moreover, studies of rape in our culture reveal that, far from being impulsive behavior, most rape is planned. Professor Amir's study reveals that in cases of group rape (the 'gangbang' of masculine slang), 90 percent of the rapes were planned; in pair rapes, 83 percent were planned; and in single rapes, 58 percent were planned. These figures should significantly discredit the image of the rapist as a man who is suddenly overcome by sexual needs society does not allow him to fulfill."

Hint: There is a subargument here.

(Susan Griffin, "Rape: The All-American Crime," in M. Vetterling-Braggin, F. Elliston, and J. English, eds., *Feminism and Philosophy* [Totowa, N.J.: Littlefield Adams, 1977], p. 315)

9. There are many reasons to doubt whether teachers should be subjected to tests of competence after they have been teaching for some years. After all, teachers were tested at colleges and universities before they became teachers. Furthermore, other professions are not tested in midstream. Some teachers have been given legal and moral guarantees of continued positions, and the tests jeopardize them. In addition, tests for teachers are unreliable. Another problem is that if teachers fail, poor salary conditions may mean that the new teachers hired to replace them are just as ill-qualified as the fired ones.

(Adapted from "When Testing Teachers May Be Hoax," by Albert Shanker, *New York Times,* July 21, 1984)
(Shanker wrote about a teacher test given in Arkansas. Of 28,000 teachers given a three-part test in reading, writing, and math, 10 percent failed.)

10. *Background:* The issue here is whether a particular vaccine should be used against hoof-and-mouth disease, a serious and highly contagious disease that sometimes occurs among cattle. The author writes about the problem in Great Britain:

". . . in deciding whether to use vaccine there are several points to be considered which you were unable to detail in your article:

"—It is impossible to forecast which of the 60 known sub-types of virus will be the one to attack British cattle in the next outbreak. The cost of the vaccine rises steeply as each new sub-type is added to give the appropriate 'cocktail' of vaccine.

"—The price quoted is that of the manufacturer. It does not include the massive costs of administering a dose to each of the 5 million cloven-hoofed animals in Britain.

"—Immunity is short-lived, especially in younger stock, so that the vaccine would have to be given twice every year to ensure a good degree of immunity.

"—Pigs do not immunize well, and can become a source of virus for other species on the farm. This has been noted in Italy.

"—Strains of virus attenuated and made safe for one species of livestock may still be dangerous for other species.

"—Vaccinated cattle which happen to come into contact with field strains of virus may become symptomless carriers of the disease. Our livestock trade would vanish if such were the case, as no country will knowingly import this catastrophic disease.

". . . I am certain that if and when there is a safe, efficient, and cheap vaccine for this disease, we shall adopt it; nobody likes the thought of slaughtering herds as we have to do at present. The controversy about 'stamping out' versus vaccination is one which has gone on for years and certainly a vaccination programme would bring rich rewards to the manufacturers.

. . . But I doubt whether such a policy would be a scientific or an economic good for Britain."

(Letter by B. H., *The Economist,* April 11–17, 1981)

*11. The Bible is among the most trustworthy of ancient documents. We can see that this statement is true for a number of reasons. First, the New Testament was written only 20 to 70 years after the events it records. Second, the oldest manuscript of the New Testament is a copy of originals that were made about 250 years after these originals were written. It is closer to the time of the original than other ancient manuscripts, such as those of Aristotle's *Metaphysics,* for instance. Third, there are more than 13,000 surviving copies of various portions of the New Testament, which date from ancient and medieval times. This fact means that it is highly probable that the original documents are well represented. As far as the Old Testament is concerned, the recently discovered Dead Sea Scrolls are 700–1000 years closer in time to the original events than earlier manuscripts we used to rely on and yet their wording is very close to that of these other manuscripts. This is strong evidence that the text is accurately transmitted. In addition to all of these reasons, one of the world's outstanding archaeological experts says that archaeology confirms that the events described in the Old Testament did occur. Thus the Bible is among the most trustworthy of ancient documents.

(Based on a leaflet distributed by the Inter-Varsity Christian Fellowship)

12. *Background:* The following passage deals with economic and political integration in western Europe:

"We all have at least two strong reasons for wanting further, faster European integration, particularly in economic and security policy. These are the fear that the Americans will do less (militarily) and that the Japanese will do more (economically). But on top of these shared reasons, the French and the Germans continue to have their own reasons for wanting integration. Both have direct, traumatic experience of war and occupation. The French intention always was, by embracing the Germans, to contain them. It is less difficult for the French and the Germans to contemplate major changes in their political structures, for the simple reason that the continental states have had so many such changes already. The merely 30-year-old regime that President François Mitterand heads is, after all, France's Fifth Republic. Germany has had more regimes than Elizabeth Taylor has had husbands."

(Timothy Garton Ash, on Europe, *World Press Review,* January 1989; reprinted from the *Spectator*)

13. *Background:* The following appeared as a letter to the editor in the Calgary *Herald* for May 19, 1990.

"I, for one, enjoy living in a city where humidity is never mentioned in weather forecasts because it is always low. Calgary is a great city for book collectors, who do not have to worry about mildew or foxing. Our houses don't rot out from under us. The summer heat is far more bearable without high humidity, and the dry cold certainly is preferable to damp cold. Gardeners have fewer plant diseases to contend with than the more humid climes, and insects are not as serious a problem. Stamp collectors do not worry about the gum on their postage stamps automatically gluing the stamps to the album pages. Rust takes longer to work here than in the coastal cities. Running a humidifier in a Calgary house is no worse than running a dehumidifier elsewhere. People with breathing problems or allergies have an easier time in Calgary. Low humidity is no more of a curse than high humidity."

♦   ## INDUCTIVE ARGUMENTS

In *inductive arguments* both the premises and the conclusion are empirical: they are not a priori truths or evaluative propositions or propositions recommending what should be done. They describe the way the world has been or predict the way it will be. An inductive argument is based on some form of *inductive reasoning*. In the most general sense, inductive reasoning is that in which we extrapolate from experience to further experience. The assumption behind inductive reasoning is that cases we have examined can, if properly selected, tell us about further cases that we have not examined.

Even people who may not have heard of the terms *induction, inductive argument,* or *inductive reasoning* nevertheless do themselves reason inductively quite frequently. Induction is the way in which we learn from experience and it is indispensable for practical life. To realize this, we have only to ask ourselves the basis, in evidence, for our most obvious beliefs about the world. Why do we believe that January will be colder than August? That milkshakes are sweeter than carrots? That hurricanes are dangerous? The answer in every case is past experience.

Here is a very simple inductive argument that is famous in the history of philosophy because of the way it was discussed by the eighteenth-century philosopher David Hume.

1. Every day in known human history the sun has risen.
Therefore,
2. Tomorrow the sun will rise.

In this argument, the premise describes a great number of instances within human history, and the conclusion makes a statement about one instance that has not been experienced yet. It is an inductive argument based on extending past experience to the future.

No inductive argument is deductively valid. We cannot prove deductively that the unexamined cases will resemble the examined ones or, to put it in Hume's terms, that the future will resemble the past. There is always some possibility that unobserved cases will be different from observed ones. Distinctions can be made, however, between more and less cogent inductive arguments. Cogent inductive arguments are often called *strong,* whereas those that fail to be cogent because the inductive evidence cited is too slight to give adequate grounds for the conclusion are called *weak.*

Some Basic Types of Inductive Arguments

Inductive reasoning is a complex topic on which philosophers and scientists have not yet reached complete agreement. Here we offer a relatively simple introduction. We distinguish here between the following types of inductive argument:

1 Inductive Analogy In the inductive analogy the conclusion is about a single case and the premises describe an analogous case or cases.[3] Inductive analogies have already been discussed in Chapter 9. Formally, inductive analogies can be represented as follows, where case *A* is the analogue case, and case *N* is the primary subject.

1. Case *A* has feature *f*.
2. Case *N* is relevantly similar to case *A* in various ways.

So probably,

3.   Case *N* will have feature *f*.

2   Enumerative Inductive Generalization (Universal)   In these arguments, the premises describe a number of observed objects or events as having some particular feature, and the conclusion asserts, on the basis of this generalization, that all objects or events of the same type will have that feature. (Example: All the North American zoos I have ever visited cater to children; therefore, all zoos cater to children.)

This sort of inductive argument can be formally represented as follows:

1.   All observed *X*'s are *f*.
Therefore, probably,
2.   All *X*'s are *f*.

The conclusion of a universal inductive generalization is an *A* statement: a universal categorical statement. However, in recognition of the fact that inductive reasoning is not deductive reasoning and that the evidence does not deductively prove that the conclusion is true, the word *probably* is (or should be) included between the premises and the conclusion. *Probably* indicates that the premise is supposed to make it probable, or likely, that the universal conclusion is true. In an *enumerative inductive argument*—and indeed in all inductive arguments—there is no implicit or explicit claim that the conclusion is rendered absolutely certain by the evidence. The conclusion is universal in scope, but is asserted as probable—not certain.[4]

3   Restricted Enumerative Inductive Generalization   This sort of argument is like type (2) with the exception that the conclusion is restricted argument. The conclusion makes a claim about *most* items in the category rather than about *all*. The premise may be universal in form, or may be similarly qualified. Thus, if we said "all the department stores we are familiar with sell stockings; therefore probably most department stores sell stockings" or "most of the department stores we are familiar with sell stockings; therefore probably most department stores sell stockings" we would have given a qualified enumerative induction.

Formally, this type of argument can be represented as:

1.   All (or most) observed *X*'s are *f*.
Therefore, probably,
2.   Most *X*'s are *f*.

The conclusion is more restricted in scope than in the universal induction (type 2). This restriction in scope strengthens the argument, because a restricted conclusion requires less support.[5]

4   Inductive Argument to a Singular Conclusion   This kind of inductive argument can be thought of as a combination of type (3), the restricted enumerative induction, and type (1), the inductive analogy. It is similar to the inductive analogy in that the conclusion is about a single case. It is similar to the restricted enumerative induction in that a generalization, about many or most cases, is applied to that single case. Here is an example:

> Most Romanian orphans are in poor health; Sylvan is a Romanian orphan; therefore probably Sylvan is in poor health.

These sorts of inductive arguments, which are very common, can be formally represented as follows:

1. All, or most, observed *X*'s are *f*.
2. Case *A* is an *X*.

Therefore, probably,

3. Case *A* is *f*.

5 Statistical Inductive Argument In a *statistical inductive argument*, there is a generalization from past experience, but the past experience need not be uniform or nearly uniform as it is in the inductive arguments just mentioned. The premises describe a statistical relationship and the conclusion extrapolates that relationship from observed cases to unobserved ones. Here is an example:

> Thirty-five percent of the concert pianists in the 1990 Tchaikovsky competition in Moscow were left-handed; so probably about 35 percent of concert pianists are left-handed.

A statistical generalization is known for a number of cases and it is inferred that a larger group of cases will show the same statistical pattern.[6] Formally, statistical inductive arguments can be represented as follows:

1. *N* percent of observed *X*'s are *f*.

Therefore, probably,

2. Approximately *N* percent of unobserved and observed *X*'s are *f*

Note the qualification expressed in the word *approximately*. The inductive expectation is not that the statistical pattern observed will be exactly represented—rather, that it will be approximately represented.

6 Causal Inductive Arguments *Causal inductive arguments* are more complicated than any of the above types, which are all, in one way or another, based on the extrapolation (or extension) of observed features from known cases to unknown ones. In a causal argument, the conclusion is that one event, or one sort of event, is the cause of another. (The first event brings about, or produces, the second.) Typically, the premises of a causal inductive argument describe events that are associated or correlated in the sense that they occur together. Under certain conditions, these associations can provide evidence for a causal conclusion. Here is an example:

> Whenever he swims in chlorinated water he gets an unpleasant bumpy rash, and whenever he does not swim, or swims in natural water, he does not get the rash. So probably the chlorine in the water is the cause of his rash.

As we shall see, causal arguments present some challenging features. For the moment, we will keep the story simple and suggest that a causal argument be represented as follows:

1. *C* and *E* are regularly associated events.
2. *C* regularly occurs before *E*.
3. The claim that *C* is a cause of *E* is consistent with background knowledge about *C* and about *E*.

Therefore, probably,

4. *C* is a cause of *E*.[7]

Just what we mean by "background knowledge" and why it is so important for causal reasoning will be discussed and explained later in this chapter.

◆ ───

EXERCISE SET

Exercise 2

For each of the following arguments, indicate whether it is inductive. Then, if the argument is inductive, indicate whether it is: an *inductive analogy*, a *universal enumerative inductive generalization*, a *restricted enumerative inductive generalization*, an *inductive argument to a singular conclusion*, a *statistical inductive argument*, or a *causal inductive argument*.

Be prepared to justify your answer. If the argument is not inductive, or if the passage does not contain an argument, briefly explain why.

*1. Adults who are sleeping and who are found, by physiological tests, to be undergoing what is called REM (rapid eye movement) sleep regularly report dreams if they are awakened during that REM sleep. Cats exhibit brain activity closely similar to that adult human beings exhibit during REM sleep. Therefore, cats probably dream.

2. In October 1990, nationwide polls indicated that, of those surveyed, only 15 percent supported the Progressive Conservative party, which was the governing party in Canada at that time. Therefore, only 15 percent of Canadian voters were supporters of the government in October 1990.

3. "The governments, not only the military ones, but the governments in general, could be, I do not say useful, but harmless only in case they consisted of infallible, holy people. But the governments, by dint of their very activity, which consists in the practice of violence, are always composed of elements which are the very opposite of holy—of the most impudent, coarse, and corrupted men. For this reason every government . . . is a most dangerous institution."

(Leo Tolstoi, "Patriotism and Government," quoted in S. F. Barker, *The Elements of Logic,* 3rd ed. [New York: McGraw-Hill, 1980], p. 86)

*4. Most cocaine users have previously smoked marijuana. Therefore marijuana use causes cocaine use.

5. Usually when Mary wakes up before 6 o'clock in the morning, she is really tired by supper time. Susan was awake before 6 o'clock, so probably she will be exhausted by supper time.

6. Every magpie that has ever been measured is longer and heavier than the average robin. Therefore, magpies are larger than robins.

*7. In 1982, an American Roman Catholic organization called Applied Research in the Apostolate sponsored a poll of people across the world to determine their values, attitudes, and sources of satisfaction in life. Of the people polled, 1200 were Canadians, and of these Canadians, 95 percent reported being very happy or quite happy. In fact, Canadians were happier, according to this survey, than people in the United States or Europe. So probably, in the 1990s, Canadians are still happier than Americans and Europeans.

8. A study was made of gifted youth, where "gifted" was defined as testing with an IQ of 120 or more. The number of gifted students studied was 125, which included 67 males and 58 females. These students were asked which person impressed them most, and 44.8 percent named a family member. So probably near half of the gifted children and teenagers in a society are most influenced by family members.

9. People living alone are more likely to commit suicide than those living with others. Also, Catholics and adherents of religions stressing community are less likely to commit suicide than Protestants who emphasize the individual's responsibility for his or her relationship to God. These facts show that social support helps overcome anxiety, stress, and misery. It is social support that is responsible for these differential suicide rates.
(Adapted from Emile Durkheim's account of suicide)

*10. "For instance, the fact that Professor Smith is a stupid, maladjusted man of paranoid tendencies increases the probability that his views on economic theory are unsound, for we know from past experience that economic theory is a difficult subject and that intelligent men of balanced judgment are more likely to have sound views about it."
(S. F. Barker, *Elements of Logic*, 3rd ed., p. 204)

11. A study of convicted murderers in the United Kingdom and Canada shows that most of them have been convicted of the violent killings of family members or others with whom they have had intimate relationships and close connections. Such killings are the outcome of years of cumulated frustration in these relationships and of unique circumstances that are unlikely to recur. Therefore, most convicted murders in western industrialized countries are not likely to go out and kill members of the public at random.

12. Chimpanzees and other higher primates have techniques of reconciliation after violent episodes and are able to manage conflict so that they can continue to live in reasonably harmonious social groups. They have an instinctual base that provides for this conciliatory behavior. Human beings have a common evolutionary history with these primates. Therefore, they too have an instinctual base that provides for conflict resolution and reconciliation after quarrels.
(Adapted from Frans de Waal, *Peacemaking among Primates* [Cambridge, Mass.: Harvard University Press, 1989]

*13. The residence in London served food that caused food poisoning among students, and once even served a dish in which a student found a screw nearly an inch long. Stores in London sometimes sell meat that has not been properly refrigerated and is dangerous to eat. The hospitals in London are not very clean. The Underground (subway) is dirty and in poor repair. The railways are in poor repair. On the basis of these reports, we can conclude that most key social institutions in England are not functioning well.

14. A study of 98 divorced couples revealed that among those who had joint custody of their children, 30 percent were able to conduct respectful and friendly relations after the divorce, whereas among those in which the custody of the children had gone to the mother alone, only 20 percent were able to conduct amicable relations after the divorce. Based on this sample, we can conclude that for most divorcing couples, joint custody of children will be better than giving custody to the mother alone.

EVALUATING INDUCTIVE ARGUMENTS

We have distinguished, then, between the following types of inductive argument:

1. Inductive analogies
2. Categorical enumerative inductive generalizations
3. Restricted enumerative inductive generalizations
4. Inductive arguments to a singular conclusion
5. Statistical inductive arguments
6. Causal inductive arguments

We now explain some of the basics of evaluating inductive arguments, using these six categories as a reference point. We can omit category (1), inductive analogies, because these arguments have already been discussed in Chapter 9. As for the other types, categories (2), (3), and (4) and (5) have basic features in common and can, as we shall see, be discussed together. Causal arguments (6) are a special case.

Background Knowledge and Inductive Reasoning

Background knowledge plays an important role in the evaluation of inductive arguments. We'll use an illustration to show why this background knowledge has to enter the picture. Let's say you are examining robins' eggs for size. Suppose you examine six eggs and you find them all to be between one inch and one-and-one-quarter inches in diameter. Given what you already know about bird species in general and robins in particular, even this small sample of robins' eggs would be sufficient to give you a strong inductive basis for the conclusion that all robins' eggs are between three-quarters inch and one-and-one-half inches in diameter. We have good evidence that robins themselves fall within a fairly narrow size range and that eggs will have to be small enough for the robins to lay, and so on. Thus, in this case, an enumerative induction based on only six examined cases would be a fairly strong argument.

But now think of a different enumerative introduction based on evidence about six cases. Suppose that you were to go to France to examine six lakes. Suppose that all six turned out to be slightly contaminated with mercury and, on the basis of this evidence, you wanted to infer that all the lakes in France are slightly contaminated with mercury. This would be a very weak inductive inference. Lakes in France just aren't uniform enough. (For instance, some are near industrial areas; others are not.) The problem is they are not as similar to each other as are robins, and we do not have background knowledge that bears on their containing or not containing mercury in the same way that the size of robins bears on the size of robins' eggs.

The strength of inductive arguments that move from examined cases to unexamined cases depends on how likely the examined cases are to represent the unexamined ones. Generally speaking, having more cases and having a greater variety of cases in the sample increases the likelihood that the examined ones are representative of the unexamined ones. But we have to say "generally speaking," because the way in which these factors work varies enormously depending on what sorts of things we are talking about.

Background knowledge is needed when we try to estimate how well the sample (observed cases) represents the population (cases referred to in the conclusion) in an inductive argument. We cannot get along without this knowledge in inductive reasoning, and we need to appeal to it to back up judgments about stronger and weaker inductive arguments. Because background knowledge is necessary in this way, a purely formal approach to inductive reasoning is not possible. There are formal systems of inductive logic, but none are widely accepted in the way that formal systems of deductive logic are.

In this book we do not try to put forward a completely general formal set of rules that you can use to distinguish strong from weak inductive arguments. We believe that background knowledge is extremely important in the evaluation of inductive arguments. Relevant background knowledge varies a great deal from one example to another. We cannot easily detach any "form" of these arguments from their content. In this respect inductive arguments are similar to conductive arguments and analogies. Perhaps some of you will go on to study induction further in courses on probability theory, statistics, or the philosophy of science; if so you will have an opportunity to explore various formal and nonformal theories of induction that have been proposed by other writers. For now, we pursue a nonformal approach.

Points about Inductive Premises

As with any argument, the cogency of an inductive argument will depend upon the acceptability of its premises as well as on the merits of the reasoning from its premises to its conclusion. The premises of an inductive argument are based on someone's observation—either yours or someone else's. For the argument to have a solid base, those observations have to be *reliable*. There are circumstances and features that can make observations unreliable. It is easy to see this in your own case; if you are sleepy or ill or worried, you may easily make mistakes in observation, thinking you have seen or heard something that was not there, or forgetting important details, for instance. The same holds for observations by other people. In fact, we have already described such problems when we discussed testimony in Chapter 5. If the observations on which an inductive argument is based are unreliable in some way, then its premises are not acceptable, and the argument will lack cogency for that reason.

In addition to these features about observation itself, there are additional ways in which premises of inductive arguments may be subject to question. One important aspect is that of *classification*. The premise of an inductive argument alludes to observations under some description or classification. If we are to reason from the premise that all or most observed X's are f, we have tacitly accepted the classification of the items we have observed as being *X*'s and we have ascribed to them a particular feature, *f,* that *X* things can have. To accept such a premise is to assume that these items have really been observed, and that they are correctly and appropriately classified as being *X*'s.

Sometimes it's clear that we have observed something but not clear just how to classify it. For instance, we may be quite sure we hear sounds from a nearby building and yet not know whether these sounds are music. From what we hear, we may be unsure as to whether we are just hearing noise, or whether we are hearing notes in a melody.

The issue of classification is most apparent when what is observed gives rise to several alternate, or even disputed, classifications. In her book, anthropologist Riane Eisler describes ancient figurines of broad-hipped women. These were thought by some archaeologists to represent virgins in a fertility cult. Eisler argues that they represent women who have given birth and were goddesses in an ancient religion worshipping women as givers of life.[8] From premises about these goddess figurines and related evidence, she reasons that ancient social lives exhibited equality between the sexes. Archaeologists agree that the figurines have been observed, but there is still some disagreement as to how they are to be classified. Have archaeologists found ancient tokens of fertility? Or have they found figurines of goddesses? The different classifications would give premises as a basis for inductive arguments about life in ancient times—whether Eisler's claims about social life can be supported by archaeological evidence would depend on the correctness of the goddess classification and other related ones.

We are often not aware of the classificatory decisions that underlie premises in inductive arguments, because so many inductive arguments deal with familiar objects—robins and lakes, or chlorinated water and salt water, for instance. But the classificatory assumptions and judgments are always implicit in the premises. The premise that all or most observed *X*'s are *f* presupposes that what has been observed is correctly and appropriately classified as *X*. If the classification is mistaken or inappropriate, the premise is unacceptable and the argument is not cogent.

Here is an example that combines the matter of reliable observation with that of classification. Let us suppose that a young woman is feeling quite insecure and unhappy and that for this reason she frequently interprets other people's jokes and comments as being criticisms directed against her. She might, considering whether to go to a party, reason to herself as follows:

1. Many times in the recent past I have observed my fellow students laughing at me and making fun of me.
2. The people at the party are likely to be similar to my fellow students so far as their attitudes and behavior to me are concerned.
    Therefore, probably,
3. The people at the party will laugh at me and make fun of me.

On the basis of such an inductive argument, this unfortunate individual might decide not to attend the party. The first premise, though, could be unacceptable if she is unable to make reliable observations and classifications of other people's behavior. Often when we are upset and feel sensitive and vulnerable, we overreact to what others say, and misinterpret it. Strictly speaking we do not just observe others making fun of us or laughing at us. The unhappy woman imagined here has heard jokes and comments and has classified these as "laughing at me" and "making fun of me." If her interpretations are mistaken, her premise is unacceptable. Although the reasoning from behavior in other contexts to behavior at the party might be based on a correct inductive analogy, the argument will break down because it has an unacceptable premise.

A further more subtle problem can sometimes arise with classifications. Inductive arguments are based on regularities—patterns that are projected from some observed cases to others and (in causal arguments) patterns that are taken to require explanation. For a cogent inductive argument, we need a genuine regularity, not a *pseudo-regularity*. A pseudo-regularity is one that is founded upon a similarity that is too superficial to be the basis of an inductive argument. When a number of cases are classified and grouped together for the purposes of induction, the classification must not only be interpretively correct (as indicated in the example just discussed), it must be scientifically relevant. That is to say it must be based on some feature that is reasonable to extrapolate or (in the case of a causal argument) some feature for which it makes sense to look for a single explanation.

Suppose that we have five events that have one striking feature in common: they are all impossible to explain given present knowledge. We couldn't group them together just on this basis (classify them simply as "unexplained events"), and then, on the basis of the classification, look for a single explanation for all of them. There is no good reason to think the same thing has caused all of them.

A simple example follows, involving health and illness. Let us suppose that suddenly, on a Tuesday morning, you suffer from sore feet, a headache, a backache, and a runny nose. You can classify all of these things together: all are unpleasant minor health problems and all begin on Tuesday. You might say there is a pattern here: all these unpleasant symptoms came to you recently and at about the same time. Yet they do not belong together for the purpose of inductive or causal reasoning. (For instance, you might have sore feet from walking too far in new shoes; the appropriate regularity could be found by considering other cases of walking, other cases of new shoes, and other cases of sore feet. Your runny nose might be due to a minor case of hayfever; the appropriate regularity would include the season, the plants you've been exposed to, and other cases when you've had a runny nose. Your headache may be due to stress concerning an upcoming examination; the appropriate regularity would include other headaches and other stressful forthcoming events.)

A rather bizarre illustration of the phenomenon of pseudo-regularity can be found in Erich von Daniken's book, *Chariots of the Gods*.[9] Von Daniken cites a number of quite different unexplained events, including the building of the pyramids and what he regards as "landing strips" at various points around the earth. He argues that astronauts visited the earth from other planets, in ancient times—

on the grounds that this causal conclusion would explain all of these otherwise unexplained events. A major problem with the argument is that the events he groups together are too disparate. Given (and this itself is a highly questionable classification!) that there *are* "landing strips" around the earth, and that there are pyramids that could not have been built by unassisted human beings, there is still no good reason to group all these events together and seek one causal explanation for all of them.

In general, the premises of inductive arguments can be assessed for acceptability as can premises of other arguments. However, in virtue of their special dependence upon observation of regularities, we should check the following: reliability of observations, appropriateness of classification, and genuineness of regularity—no pseudo-regularity.

Evaluating Enumerative and Statistical Inductive Arguments

Inductive arguments—whether enumerative or statistical—are based on generalizing from a range of experience to a broader range. Features that have been observed in one range are projected to another; inductive reasoning is, in essence, an extrapolation. There are three features of inductive arguments that contribute positively to their strength. These are:

1. The *number* of cases already observed. That is to say, the number of cases described in the premises. Generally speaking, the more cases observed, the stronger the argument.

2. The *variety* of cases already observed. That is, the variety exhibited in the various cases described in the premises. For example, if the conclusion is about all birds or most birds, the argument will be stronger if the premises are based on observations about bird species of various sizes, geographical locations, and habits than if they are based only on observations of species all from the same geographical area and of about the same size. Generally speaking, the greater the variety of cases observed, the stronger the argument.

3. The *scope* of the conclusion. Generally speaking, an inductive argument is stronger insofar as its conclusion is restricted in scope. A qualified generalization is easier to support than a categorical one. An induction to a singular case is, other things being equal, more likely to be a strong argument than one in which the conclusion is universal or more general.

But we have to say "generally speaking" in these conditions because inductive arguments depend to a great extent on background knowledge. With certain kinds of background knowledge, we may be able to generate a strong inductive argument even from a small number of observed cases; with other background knowledge, even a large number of cases gives only a shaky basis for a conclusion.

Following contemporary practice in statistics, we can refer to the observed cases, those that are described in the premises, as the *sample* cases, and to the cases referred to in the conclusion as the *target population*. Consider the statistical induction

> Thirty-five percent of the pianists at the 1990 Tchaikovsky competition in Moscow were left-handed; so probably about 35 percent of concert pianists are left-handed.

The sample is "pianists at the 1990 Tchaikovsky Competition in Moscow" and the target population is "concert pianists."

The clue to reliable inductive generalizations is finding a sample that is *representative* of the population. To say that the sample is representative is to say that it is likely to be similar to the population in those ways relevant to the conclusion of the argument. If we choose a representative sample, then our inductive argument will be strong. If the sample is unrepresentative, it will be weak. For instance, suppose it were the case that a Russian piano instructor, left-handed himself and favoring left-handed students, had entered an unusually high number of candidates in the Moscow competition. If many of the pianists in the sample were from Moscow, left-handers would then be overrepresented in the sample, and the inductive argument would be unreliable.

Generally speaking, greater numbers of cases and a greater variety of cases observed and reported in the premises of an inductive argument strengthens the argument. There is a simple explanation for this strengthening: these factors tend to make the sample more *representative* of the target population. If we are trying to generalize from a sample of 200 cases to a target population of 2000 cases, our generalizing will be more reliable if the examined cases exhibit some variety. Ideally, they should exhibit just the sorts of variety that is in the target population. Of course, in practice, we cannot know that this is the case because we do not know all about the target population (if we did, we wouldn't need the inductive argument in the first place).

Having more variety in the sample increases the likelihood that any relevant variety in the target population will be reflected in the sample and thus increases the likelihood that the conclusion will be accurate. For instance, if we wanted to generalize about all concert pianists from a sample of 200 of them, we would have a stronger argument when our sample included many nationalities than if it included only Russians and Americans.

Similar comments can be made about sample size. The reason that size is important is that it increases the likelihood of representativeness. The essence of inductive reasoning is the projection of a property from a sample to a population; typically the population is substantially larger than the sample and cannot be studied in its own right. To study all Americans, all Canadians, all male adults, all birds, or whatever, is rarely possible. We have to rely on a sample.

Size of the population is not the only factor that makes sampling necessary. Sometimes the population includes events or situations in the past or future. These are not observable in the present, and if we wish to make estimations or predictions about them we have to rely on a sample of events or situations that we can observe. Often inductive reasoning is used in contexts of *prediction*, when we reason from known past and present cases to future cases. However, induction may also involve reasoning from the recent past and present to the distant past. Such reasoning is absolutely fundamental in archaeology and geology, for example. It is sometimes called *retrodiction*—we reason backward from present evidence to claims about the past—as opposed to prediction, where we reason forward from present or past evidence to claims about the future. (Reasoning from goddess figurines to the nature of social life in past ages—as in Riane Eisler's book—would be retrodictive.)

A sample is representative of a population if its members are typical of the members of the population. We can illustrate this statement more precisely with an example. Suppose that you are dealing with a population of 1000 people and that you sample that population by studying 100 of them. Now suppose that in your sample 30 people have blue eyes. This finding means that 30 percent of the sample have blue eyes. If it is also the case that 30 percent of the population have blue eyes, then the sample is perfectly representative of the population, with respect to eye color. We can define representativeness in a simple mathematical formula, as follows:

> A sample, *S*, is perfectly representative of a population, *P*, with respect to a characteristic, *x*, if the percentage of *S* that are *x* is exactly equal to the percentage of *P* that are *x*.

In practical terms, this definition is not terribly useful because typically we do not know the percentage of the population that are *x*; in fact, usually this is what we are trying to discover. The definition just tells us what *representativeness* means: it does not tell us how to get a sample that is representative when we are still in the position where we do not know all about the population. This is the practical problem of sampling.

It is often thought that the practical problem of sampling is a matter of mathematical statistics. Within statistics, you can prove that a generalization based on a certain number of cases (1000 to 2000) will, with extremely high probability, give reliable information about a population of many millions, provided the sample is taken *randomly*. A sample is taken randomly if every member of the population has an equal chance of getting into that sample.

The problem is that in many real situations, especially those in which studies are done on human populations, this strict technical sense of randomness is just about impossible to achieve. If you are a sociologist living in Philadelphia, and you look for 100 children to study, you just cannot honestly say that every child in North America has an equal chance of getting into your study—yet your target population may very well be North American children. The chances that the child of a sociology student in Philadelphia will be a subject in the study very greatly exceed the chances that a child from Alaska or Quebec will be a subject.

A sample of children from Philadelphia might be representative of American children with reference to some characteristic (for example, knee strength), but it would not be representative with respect to many others (for example, being a witness to or victim of street crime). As far as exposure to crime is concerned, a sample would have to include children from some rural areas, some small towns, some middle-sized cities, and a variety of large cities, to fully represent the population of North American children. In saying this, we are relying on our background knowledge and beliefs about what factors do, or are likely to, affect exposure to crime—illustrating the general dependence of inductive reasoning upon background knowledge. We make the sample as representative as we can by taking these factors into account in selecting it. This procedure does not mean that we have a fully random sample. The sample will be only as reliable as the background knowledge that we have used to construct it.

Sometimes the technique of *stratified sampling* is used. This technique also depends on background knowledge. Suppose that we have a large population, P, and we want to determine how many of this population are likely to do x. We may be able to divide P into relevant subgroups: A, B, and C. Now suppose that the composition of P is 10 percent A's, 30 percent B's, and 60 percent C's. We can then construct our sample so that it has this same composition. This will be a stratified sample. The stratified sample is more likely to represent the population because it perfectly reflects these significant subgroups within the population. The word *significant* indicates that we use background knowledge to construct the stratified sample: we have to determine which subgroups are significant with respect to the characteristic we are studying. Age, religion, and sex are known to be significant in voting patterns. But we would not expect religion to be significant, for instance, with regard to exercise habits. So which subgroups we look at depends on what we already know about the significance of possible subgroups—their relevance to the topic we are studying. If the beliefs we rely on to identify relevant subgroups are out of date or otherwise flawed, then stratified sampling can produce inaccurate results.

Stratified samples are used by polling centers such as the Gallup organization, and because these organizations have been studying such matters as voting habits for a very long time, they can obtain reasonably accurate results for populations of many millions from samples of 1000 to 2000 people. The stratification is based on past correlations: more southerners tend to vote Democratic, more blacks tend to vote Democratic, more older people tend to vote Republican, more women than men tend to oppose militaristic attitudes, and so on. But unfortunately this sort of background knowledge is very often not available. When it is not available, we are not able to use stratified sampling in a rigorous way to ensure sample representativeness. (We might be said to use an approximation of the technique, informally, when we try to include members of significant subgroups—as in the example of children and exposure to crime.)

Bearing all these points about sampling in mind, take a look at this report from a study on attitudes toward sex and competence:

WHEN A MAN TALKS, YOU LISTEN

When you want people to listen, it's what you say and how you say it that counts, right? Not always, report researchers Kenneth Gruber and Jacquelyn Gaebelein. When men and women give identical speeches, the men seem to have a significant edge in capturing an audience's attention.

These findings come from a study involving undergraduates at the University of North Carolina at Greensboro. Gruber, a graduate student, and Gaebelein, a psychologist, prepared videotaped speeches by two men and two women whom a panel of judges had selected for their speaking ability. Each speaker read from an identical script on chess (a topic that previous studies have shown people think of as masculine), interior decorating (thought of as feminine), and skiing(neutral).

Each of 60 student subjects viewed either a man or a women speaking on one of the topics. Afterward, students' ratings of how informative the speech they heard had been were nearly identical, regardless of the speaker's sex or topic. But both men and women who had seen male speakers recalled more information than those who had seen female speakers.

The researchers think the equal ratings of informativeness may be a by-product of the women's movement: students may have felt reluctant, consciously or unconsciously, to admit any bias against women. But previous studies have shown that whether their attitudes on the proper roles for men and women are "liberated" or not, people still expect men to be more competent, intelligent, and knowledgeable than women. If the subjects expected the male speakers to know more, the researchers say, they may well have paid them more careful attention.[10]

In the opening sentences, this report reads as though the findings were universal—about men and women generally. However, since it is obvious that people's attitudes toward competence and sex are likely to vary from one culture to another, we shall assume that the intended population is that of North American adults. This assumption adds some precision to the original. Obviously, this population is one of many millions—at least 100 million. The sample, on the other hand, is quite small: sixty people. If we knew that the population was uniform with respect to attitudes on gender roles and competence, this sample size might be adequate. But we do not know this; there is no reason to think that people of various ages, regions, political views, religions, and sexes are similar in their attitudes to gender roles; in fact, common sense and experience suggest quite the opposite.

Nor would the researchers, or anyone else, have the background knowledge needed to construct a stratified sample to address the sampling problem. If the researchers had built up a sample using so many Chinese-Americans, so many African-Americans, so many native Americans, so many Canadians, so many older and younger people, and so on, their sample would have been better than a group of sixty college students. But it would not be as firmly based as the polls that the Gallup organization and others use for voting predictions, for we do not know which subgroups within the larger population are significant as far as attitudes about sex roles are concerned.

In fact, the sample is seriously unrepresentative. Undergraduates are typically young, educated, less experienced in life, childless, and of a relatively high income bracket. These features differentiate them from other adults in North America, and it seems entirely likely that some or all of these features would be relevant to attitudes about sexual roles and male and female competence. (If students are more egalitarian about gender roles than others, the conclusion would, accidentally, be more likely to be true. The point is, however, that the student sample is so hopelessly unrepresentative that we have only slight evidence, in the study, for the conclusion drawn.)

The argument, as reported, seems to amount to the following:

1.   Of sixty undergraduates at the University of North Carolina (Greensboro), men and women recalled more information from male speakers than from female speakers.

So,

2.   Adult men and women in North America will recall more information from male speakers than they do from female speakers.

3.   A good explanation of adult men and women recalling more from male speakers than from female speakers would be that they expect male speakers to be more competent and listen to them more attentively.

Therefore,

4.   In North America, men and women expect male speakers to be more competent than female speakers and listen more attentively to male speakers than to female speakers.

It is worth reflecting on this example, for it is relatively common for research studies in the social sciences to be based on samples of undergraduate students. It is quite obvious, however, with respect to most social attitudes and capabilities that undergraduate students constitute a poor sample of the broader population. Serious researchers would not deny this. But a number of practical factors make undergraduates convenient subjects. Hard-pressed researchers are usually also college teachers, and they often have inadequate funds for research. Rather than going to the beer hall, the unemployment office, the hospital, or the daycare center to obtain a more representative group of adult subjects, they can make class announcements or post notices at a university and obtain subjects with a minimum investment of time, effort, and money. In cases where undergraduates are used to represent the general adult population, it is entirely clear that the sample has not been randomly selected.

Many subtle problems arise in connection with obtaining representative samples. Social scientists have to restrict their work to subjects whose cooperation they can obtain. If they send out a questionnaire, their sample will be of those who return the questionnaire, which will give the sample a certain bias in favor of people who are relatively well-organized and well-disposed to social science—and rich enough to afford a postage stamp. Similar points may be made for studies in which volunteers are used. People who volunteer for studies will have more time available, and be more favorably disposed to social science, than others who do not volunteer. If these traits turn out to be significantly related to the aspect being studied, the very fact of volunteers being used can work against the representativeness of the sample.

The Biased Sample

Occasionally sampling problems are worse than mere nonrepresentativeness. The sample may be selected in such a way that it demonstrably misrepresents the population. This is the *biased sample;* the sample is selected in such a way that it is bound either to underemphasize or to overemphasize the characteristic being studied. A simple example would be a sample composed entirely of students of literature, where the purpose was to study reading habits in the broad student population. The sample in such a case would be biased because literature students are a self-selected group so far as love of reading is concerned. The sample would be biased in favor of enthusiastic readers. Sometimes the bias in such a sample is a result of deliberate deception—as when advertisers test group after group of toothpaste users until they finally find one in which ten out of ten people have no cavities. Some biased samples are deliberately rigged; others are the product of honest mistakes.

An amusing instance of a biased sample occurred in an advertisement for Merit cigarettes. Advertisements are not based on serious scientific research, but they are often written so as to the authority of such research. (*Science* still functions as a kind of glamour word, and many advertisements seek to exploit it.) The Merit advertisement went like this:

> "Best-tasting low tar I've tried," report Merit smokers in latest survey. Taste Quest Ends. Latest research provides solid evidence that Merit is a satisfying long-term taste alternative to high tar cigarettes. Proof: The overwhelming majority of Merit smokers polled feel they didn't sacrifice taste in switching from high tar cigarettes. Proof: 9 out of 10 Merit smokers reported they continue to enjoy smoking, are glad they switched, and report Merit is the best-tasting low tar they've ever tried. Merit is the proven alternative to high tar smoking. And you can taste it.[11]

The intended population here is smokers. The sample is smokers of Merit cigarettes. We are not told how many were supposed to have been surveyed. We are supposed to make an enumerative induction, as follows:

1. Merit smokers enjoy Merit cigarettes and find them to be the best low-tar cigarettes.
Therefore,
2. Smokers in general will enjoy Merit cigarettes and find them to be the best low-tar cigarettes.

Here the sample is biased. It is not representative of the population, and the inductive argument is therefore a very weak one. With respect to their attitudes toward Merit cigarettes, smokers of Merit are a self-selected group. Obviously they would not smoke these cigarettes if they didn't like them. The reference to proofs and surveys is supposed to make you think that the merits of Merits have been successfully demonstrated. But since the sample was as biased as it could possibly be, nothing at all has been demonstrated.

It has come to light that an extremely influential study of moral reasoning was based on a biased sample. Educational psychologist Lawrence Kohlberg has long been famous for his studies of moral reasoning, from which he concluded that there is a natural progression in all human beings from self-centered concerns to appeals to universal standards of justice. Kohlberg identified six such stages. His work has been the basis for much theorizing in developmental psychology and for many programs of moral education for children. Carol Gilligan has brought to light the amazing fact that the studies on which Kohlberg's theories were based were of eighty-four boys. Despite this sampling bias, he and many researchers who followed him were willing to say that the theory applied to girls and women; they even concluded that many mature women were inferior in moral development because they did not go through the identified stages in the right way. Kohlberg's sample was clearly biased in leaving out girls. Also—a fact not emphasized by Gilligan—it failed to represent different cultural, language, and racial groups.[12]

When you are trying to determine whether a sample is large enough to be representative of the population, it will sometimes be helpful to do some elementary arithmetic. If you are told, for instance, that there are 30 male subjects, and that of these, 10 percent had such-and-such interest, stop and calculate 10 percent of 30. It works out to 3—a very small sample on which to base any inductive argument.

This simple strategy for criticism yields devastating results when applied to the following report, which describes a study in which 300 residents of Pasadena, California, were asked about their attitudes toward capital punishment: overall about 75 percent of the respondents in this conservative community favored capital punishment in some form. About half as many men as women were opposed to the death penalty under any circumstances.

> Among women who had undergone an abortion, only 6 percent were unqualifiedly against the death penalty; 11 percent thought it should be used more frequently; and the rest favored it for some crimes. Twenty-six percent of the women who had not had an abortion were against execution under any circumstances; 20 percent favored more frequent use; and the rest wanted it for heinous crimes. It was suggested that "two factors combine to produce this difference. Women who regard human life less highly are more apt to have abortions and endorse capital punishment; and the abortion itself led them to depreciate the value of life in general as a way of vindicating the abortion to themselves."[13]

Let us do some arithmetic and then analyze the argument. The researcher surveyed 300 people in Pasadena, California. He does not specify how many were female—not in this summary at least. Let us assume that 150 (half) were female. He wishes to contrast the attitudes of female subjects who have had abortions with those of female subjects who have not had abortions. However, we are not told in the report just how many of these (presumably) 150 subjects have had abortions, though we are told that of those who *had* abortions, "only 6 percent were unqualifiedly against the death penalty." The problem is: 6 percent of what? Abortion had been legal for only just over a decade, and numbers of abortions were probably somewhat less before it was legal. Presumably some women in the sample would have been in their childbearing years during a period when abortion was less common than it is now. Let us assume that 30 women out of 150 would have had abortions. (This is probably a very high estimate.) Now 6 percent of 30 is 1.8, or 2, women; 11 percent of 30 is 3.3 (3 women); the remaining 83 percent is 25 women. These are very small numbers on which to base any generalization that women who regard human life less highly are more likely to have abortions and endorse capital punishment. In all likelihood, the researcher's sample was far too small to imply any meaningful results, but you would miss this fact if you did not do the arithmetic.

One way in which researchers can improve sample adequacy is by combining results of several different studies. It might happen, for instance, that the same hypothesis had been confirmed in several different studies on different subjects. If the results are put together, the total sample is, of course, larger and more varied than the sample in any single study. For this cumulation of several studies to be feasible, it is important that the same hypothesis be addressed, and that, in methods used, there be no significant differences that could lead to misleading comparisons.

To strengthen inductive arguments, samples must be carefully chosen, using background knowledge and a variety of techniques to try to ensure that the sample is, as far as is practically possible, representative of the target population. In general, a larger more varied sample is more likely to be representative than a smaller less varied one.

EVALUATING CAUSAL INDUCTIVE ARGUMENTS

The nature of causation and the means of verifying causal claims are complex and controversial topics among philosophers, logicians, and social scientists. There are different things that can be meant by *cause,* which is one aspect of the problem. By *cause* we sometimes mean a necessary condition, sometimes a sufficient condition, sometimes a condition that is both necessary and sufficient, and sometimes something that is a contributory factor. Compare, for instance, the following claims:

   a. Arms races are a necessary condition, or necessary cause, of wars.

   b. Arms races are a sufficient condition, or sufficient cause, of wars.

   c. Arms races are a necessary and sufficient condition, or cause, of wars.

   d. Arms races are a contributory cause of (that is, help to bring about) wars.

Claim (a) asserts that we never have a war without an arms race preceding it. (As a matter of fact, this claim is historically false; there have been wars that have not been preceded by arms races between the countries involved.) Claim (b) asserts that we never have an arms race without a war following it. (This claim is also a historical falsehood; there have been arms races that have not been followed by wars.) Claim (c) asserts the conjunction of (a) and (b), so it too is false. Claim (d) is likely true; it says that arms races are a factor that contributes to the occurrence of wars. From a logical point of view, the important thing is to see that these claims are importantly different from each other; (a), (b), (c), and (d) make different assertions. Outside physical science, we are typically dealing with causation in the sense of contributory factors—as in (d). Rarely are we in a position to assert that one thing is either a necessary or a sufficient cause of another.

Something that is a cause contributes to the development or production or "bringing about" of an effect. One reason that causal claims are so difficult to verify is that this "bringing about" is not itself a directly observable thing; we have to infer it from the way in which events or phenomena are associated with each other. Background knowledge is needed to single out those associations, or correlations, of events that are relevant and significant in the establishment of causal claims from those that are not.

Correlations

Correlational claims are based on observations of two distinct objects or events. Researchers look at two aspects of each subject: they first determine whether it is *A* or non-*A*, and then whether it is *B* or non-*B*. The results of such a study may be of three different types:

(i) *Positive correlation:* if a higher proportion of *A*'s than non-*A*'s are *B*, then there is a positive correlation between being *A* and being *B*.

(ii) *Negative correlation:* if a smaller proportion of *A*'s than non-*A*'s are *B*, then there is a negative correlation between being *A* and being *B*.

(iii) *No correlation:* if the same proportion of *A*'s as non-*A*'s are *B*, then there is no correlation between being *A* and being *B*.

If a *correlation* is significant, then it indicates something of interest about the population, something that calls for further study and, eventually, explanation. When there is a significant positive correlation, we suppose there must be some explanation, whatever it is. When there is a significant negative correlation, the same point applies. But when a positive or negative correlation is very slight (as it would be, for instance, if 30 percent of men had a certain trait, and 31 percent of women had it), it is not said to be significant. Such a slight correlation as this could easily be due to accidental variations within the sample or to mere coincidence; thus it calls for no further explanation. As well as distinguishing between positive, negative, and no correlation, we have to distinguish between those positive or negative correlations that are significant and those that are not.

How do we know, in general, whether a positive or negative correlation is significant? That is a difficult question. Some statistics texts and some elementary texts on social science offer formulas that you are supposed to use in order to determine significance. The formulas include such factors as the size of the sample and the population, and the level of confidence that is sought. (Level of confidence refers to the chance of being right about the estimate of the population, based on the sample.) These formulas can be memorized and used; this way of handling correlations is standard in many elementary courses in psychology. We will not use it here, however. In many practical contexts, the assumptions on which such formulas have been devised simply do not hold up. They presuppose that the sample has been selected randomly from the population, and we have already seen that this is very often just not true. Since the mathematical formulas used to distinguish between significant and nonsignificant correlations depend for their validity on assumptions that very often do not apply to real cases, we do not use them in this book.

Distinguishing between significant and nonsignificant correlations is a complex matter. It depends on the size of the sample and the population and on the background knowledge that is relevant to the traits studied and their association or nonassociation. Generally correlations over .60 or so are regarded as quite significant. For example, if we found out that 70 percent of those who have heart disease had rheumatic fever as children, this would be an extremely significant correlation. We would certainly want to investigate further to discover why this correlation existed, and we might wish to warn people who had had rheumatic fever as children to beware of factors that might increase their vulnerability (overweight, smoking, or substantial alcohol use, for instance).

Sometimes we are interested not just in a correlation between two aspects (having heart disease and having had rheumatic fever), but in differential correlations. Here again, we have to look not just at the correlations but at their likely significance in light of other factors. Sample size is one. If we were to study 1 million women and 1 million men, and we were to find that 52 percent of the women and 49 percent of the men disapproved of the testing of nuclear weapons, the correlation between this attitude and gender would be extremely significant. On the other hand, if the sample size is small, this kind of correlation would not be significant at all. In a sample of only 30 people, small differences in percentages do not mean much. The difference between 10 percent of 30 and 50 percent of 30 is, after all, only 12 people, and it could happen that 12 out of 30 people might accidentally have some characteristic.

Also, as is nearly always the case with inductive arguments, background knowledge enters the picture. If there is very good reason, in terms of background knowledge, to expect that the *A*'s and the non-*A*'s in your sample will be similar with regard to *B,* then even a slight difference between them with regard to *B* may interest you enough to merit further study. Background knowledge and considerations of sample and population size have to be taken together. The crucial question with regard to the significance of a positive or negative correlation is: does the correlation that exists call for a further explanation?

Correlation and Cause

In this book we do not try to offer a complete theory of causation because the topic is too complicated and too logically controversial to be handled thoroughly in a few short pages. We only hope to give you some analytical tools so that you can look at causal arguments with a critical eye.

A major point, and one that can be easily understood, is that *correlation* is not the same as *causation*. Just because *A* is positively correlated with being *B*, that does not mean that *A* is the cause of *B*. This logical distinction between correlation and cause holds up no matter how strong the correlation is. Even granted that *A* and *B* are positively correlated and that this correlation is significant and calls for explanation, it does not follow that the explanation is that being *A* is the cause of being *B*. This is one possibility, but there are others as well.

If *A* is positively correlated with *B*, then one of the following will be true:

a. *A* causally contributes to *B*. That is to say, either *A* is the necessary or sufficient cause of *B*, or it is one of several contributory factors that combine to produce *B*. Or

b. *B* causally contributes to *A*. That is to say, either *B* is the necessary or sufficient cause of *A*, or it is one of several contributory factors that combine to produce *A*. Or

c. Some other factor, *C*, is the underlying cause of both *A* and *B*. Or

d. The correlation between *A* and *B* is an accident.

We cannot simply argue from a positive correlation between *A* and *B* to the conclusion that *A* is a cause of *B*; if we do, we infer (a) without giving any reason to exclude (b), (c), and (d). To make such an inference would be hasty because we have neglected three of the four alternative explanations without any compelling reason to do so. Since the data about correlation are compatible with all four of these hypotheses, we have to have some reason for taking any one of them to be the preferred explanation. There must be a basis for excluding the possibility that *B* causes *A*, that something else causes both, or that the correlation observed is a mere coincidence.

This means that arguments from premises about correlation to conclusions about causal relationships are very difficult to construct with accuracy. So many things might be underlying causes of both *A* and *B*, in most cases. Sometimes it is easy to exclude the possibility that *B* causes *A*; it may happen that *A* comes before *B* in time, or that we already have background knowledge that would rule out this possibility. But for some correlations, even this is not easy.

An example of a dispute about correlation and cause is the following: there is a positive correlation between being overweight and having high blood pressure. What is usually inferred from this correlation is that being overweight is one cause of having high blood pressure—that is, that it combines with other conditions to produce the high blood pressure. From this inference, medical doctors traditionally have made the further inference that high blood pressure patients can improve their condition by losing weight. However, some critics have urged that these inferences are too hasty, pointing out that those overweight people whose blood pressure has been observed have been dieting (due to being overweight) and have therefore been under stress. Also, they point out, our society makes life pretty difficult for people who are overweight. Perhaps the causal relationship holds between social attitudes to weight and high blood pressure, rather than simply to weight and high blood pressure. Being overweight in our society is quite stressful, and the stress that goes along with overweight might be the cause of high blood pressure.

That a correlation is mere coincidence is a possibility that science can never completely rule out. The best that can be done is to enlarge the sample: if a correlation persists, then it is a general regularity in the world and, according to the principles of scientific method, must have some explanation. Ruling out alternative explanations for a positive correlation between *A* and *B* is a difficult matter; it is far too hasty to simply infer from such a correlation that *A* is a cause of *B*.

An easy way to convince yourself that correlation is not the same as causation is to remember that correlation works both ways. If *A* is positively correlated with *B*, then it must also be true that *B* is positively correlated with *A*. But causation only works in one direction: if *A* is the cause of *B*, then *B* cannot be the cause of *A*! Suppose you found a positive correlation between being over 30 and being a successful parent. You might be tempted to argue that being over 30 is a cause of successful parenting. However, a logically parallel argument, using correlation only, would be that being a successful parent causes a person to be over 30. This inference is ridiculous; we know that age depends on birthday, not on parenting, successful or unsuccessful. Since both inferences have an equal basis, and since the second one leads us to a ridiculous conclusion, we know that both inferences are unsound. This is a refutation by logical analogy. (Compare the discussion of logical analogies in Chapter 9.) We cannot infer a cause straight from a correlation. We need considerable intermediate argumentation.

With these points in mind, consider the following report on teenagers' marijuana habits. The report is taken from a text in psychology, which seems at this point not to be taking the distinction between correlation and cause as seriously as it should:

A FRIEND IN WEED IS A FRIEND IN DEED

Among the factors responsible for adolescent students using drugs, one of the most potent is social conformity pressures. A large-scale 1971 survey of over 8000 secondary school students in New York State revealed that adolescents are much more likely to use marijuana if their friends do than if their friends do not.

To some extent initiation into the drug scene is a function of modelling parental drug use. . . . But the most striking finding was the role that peers played. Association with other drug-using adolescents was the most important correlate of adolescent marijuana use. "Only 7 percent of adolescents who perceive none of their friends to use marijuana use marijuana themselves, in contrast to 92 percent who perceive all their friends to be users." As can be seen, the influence of best friends overwhelms that of parents.[14]

According to this study, there is a positive correlation between perceiving friends to use marijuana and using it oneself: 92 percent of those who perceive all their friends to use it, use it; whereas only 7 percent who perceive none of their friends to use it, use it. Obviously, this is a significant correlation.

It is clear from the wording of this report that a causal relationship is claimed. The implication is evident in the phrases "among the factors *responsible* for adolescent students using drugs" and "as can be seen, the *influence* of best friends overwhelms that of parents." However, there is no evidence given for this causal relationship between friends smoking and a teenager smoking. There is only the data about the *perception* of friends smoking and smoking oneself. As described here, this research clearly involved a hasty inference from correlation to cause. There is no basis given for excluding such possibilities as that the use of marijuana influences one's selection of friends; the use of marijuana influences one's perception of one's friends; some underlying cause produces both the marijuana habit and the selection of a certain type of friend; and so on. This is an example of how *not* to reason from correlation to cause.

Before leaving the topic of correlation as such, we should say a few words about negative correlation. From the information that *A* is negatively correlated with *B*, we would not, of course, even be tempted to conclude that *A* is the cause of *B*. However, we might be tempted to infer that *A* *prevents* *B*. An example of negative correlation is the relationship between breast-feeding and breast cancer in women. Breast cancer occurs less frequently in women who breast-feed their babies than in women who do not breast-feed. On this basis it has been speculated that breast-feeding in some way prevents breast cancer, or at least inhibits its development. But this too is a causal claim, and like any other, needs more support than purely correlational data. Just as we need additional reasoning and evidence to argue from a positive correlation to cause, we need additional evidence to argue from negative correlation to prevention.

Finding the Cause

In order to move from a correlational claim to a causal claim without committing any logical errors, we have to eliminate alternative explanations of the correlation. Let us work this through by considering a specific example. (The example, by the way, is invented, not real.) Suppose that we observe 800 students, of whom 400 are highly skilled at playing the piano and the other 400 are less skilled. Now let us say that we study the handedness of students in each group. We are thereby dividing the group as to highly skilled or less skilled at piano playing, and into left-handed or right-handed. Let us suppose that of those less skilled at piano playing, 10 percent are left-handed and 90 percent right-handed, whereas of those highly skilled at piano playing, 25 percent are left-handed and 75 percent right-handed. There is in this sample of students a positive correlation between high skill at piano playing and being left-handed. The correlation is quite significant; the sample is fairly large, and the percentage difference between 10 percent and 25 percent is quite large also. Thus we expect there may be something to this relationship, and we start out to investigate it. For this case, the possibilities are:

a. Being left-handed causally contributes to developing high skill at playing the piano.

b. Playing the piano (frequently enough to become highly skilled) causally contributes to being left-handed.

c. Some underlying factor causally contributes to both left-handedness and high piano-playing skill, or causally contributes to both.

d. The relationship between handedness and piano-playing skill in this sample of students is purely accidental.

Now suppose that we want to reach the causal conclusion that being left-handed contributes to the development of high skill at playing the piano, and we wish to do so legitimately, without any leaps in logic. We have to give reasons for excluding (b), (c), and (d), and for maintaining (a). We can eliminate (b), for we know that handedness develops before people are old enough to be either skilled or unskilled at playing the piano. This leaves (c) and (d). As for (d), it is partly a matter of sampling. We have to check to see that the 800 students in our sample are representative so far as handedness, piano-playing skills, and related matters are concerned. But granting that the sample is representative, this is all we can do to rule out (d). It represents a kind of remote possibility. Scientific reasoning addresses such claims as (a), (b), and (c); the prospect of sheer utter coincidence as in (d) is something that the scientific method is not able to rule out.

For such a case, then, the real task in reaching a causal conclusion would be to eliminate (c) as an alternative hypothesis. If we want to conclude that handedness contributes to piano-playing skill, on the basis of our data, we will have to give grounds for rejecting the possibility that some other underlying cause is responsible for both.

How would this work if we were dealing with a real problem, not just an example in a textbook? It is not possible to give a complete answer, but background knowledge is certainly going to play a large role in our reasoning. We won't be trying to refute alternative hypotheses about any and every possible underlying cause. Some possibilities will be taken seriously; others will not. Consider, for instance, H1 and H2:

H1: Having a mother who eats carrots causes both left-handedness and piano-playing skill.

H2: Having the kind of brain in which hemisphere specialization is less than in normal individuals who are right-handed causes both left-handedness and piano-playing skill.

H2 is suggested by brain hemisphere research, which is confirmed for some other areas (for example, the treatment of some epilepsy patients and stroke victims). Our background beliefs regarding the significance of the brain in human abilities and behavior have a bearing on H2 too. On the other hand, H1 would not be taken seriously as an alternative hypothesis. No one is going to apply for a grant to survey the 800 mothers and try to determine their carrot-eating habits. The reason is that H1 just seems frivolous; we have no other knowledge that would make it likely as an explanation, and it is not worth investigating.

The point of all this is to show just how *background knowledge* enters into causal reasoning. Background knowledge yields the working distinction between serious and nonserious alternative hypotheses. To reach a causal conclusion, we have to have grounds for rejecting some alternative hypotheses, but we cannot possibly have grounds for rejecting every single one.

Experiments cannot be designed to rule out every imaginable alternative explanation. The best that can be done is to show that the serious alternatives are not probable. Thus causal conclusions always have a certain tentativeness about them. All arguments from correlation to cause will depend on background knowledge and beliefs at several stages. This factor causes difficulties because the background beliefs are often themselves rather insecure. Background knowledge tends to be more reliable in physical science than it is in social affairs, and thus causal conclusions tend to be more reliable in physics, chemistry, and biology than they are in history, political science, psychology, sociology, or anthropology. Sometimes it seems as though the background knowledge used to differentiate between significant and insignificant alternative hypotheses is just as questionable as the causal conclusion we are trying to confirm! This situation should remind us that conclusions about the causes, especially those about the causes of complex social events and problems, should be regarded as tentative and subject to revision.

EXERCISE SET

Exercise 3: Part A

Suppose that you have just landed on Mars and you begin to explore the planet. You encounter a number of creatures that appear to be gray, four-legged, and capable of emitting occasional high sounds. You tentatively conclude, on the basis of these initial observations, that Martian creatures are gray and four-legged and are capable of emitting high sounds for the purpose of intelligent communication. Consider, for each of the following factors, whether it would make your inductive argument stronger or weaker and explain the reason for your judgment in each case. *Note:* Consider the factors

one at a time; do *not* assume that items (1) to (10) are intended to tell a cumulating story.

1. You see more Martian creatures; these are eight-legged and are gray; so far as you can detect, they do not make any noise.

*2. All your initial observations were made in a kind of valley right near where your spaceship landed.

3. You count the creatures and realize that, although they made a striking impression, you have actually only seen twenty of them.

4. You are able to travel widely around Mars in a special vehicle designed for extraterrestrial exploration and, in doing this, you see many

more gray four-legged creatures, most of whom emit high sounds.

*5. You travel around on Mars and are able to make wider observations. You see some red eight-legged creatures who emit occasional high sounds, but no more gray creatures.

6. About 100 of the creatures group together, make many loud sounds, and then move, as a group, off in the direction of a large rock. They locate themselves behind the rock in such a way that your spaceship would be invisible to them—assuming that it makes sense to think of things being visible to them or invisible to them.

7. You continue to observe the creatures. You notice that they make sounds whenever it is dark and at no other time.

*8. You are feeling rather ill after the long voyage in space. You feel light-headed, and there is a ringing in your ears. You had a dream about your home back on earth, and after waking, you heard the noise from the creatures more intensely than ever. In fact, they seemed to be singing "Jingle Bells."

Hint: Apply these facts about your own condition to consider how acceptable your premises are, given that the basis for them is your own personal observations.

*9. You see creatures that are similar in shape and also have four legs but that are bluish-green in color. They make no noise whatever, as far as you can tell.

10. You see organisms on Mars that appear to be similar to cactus plants.

Exercise 3: Part B

Evaluate the following inductive arguments, by appraising the following features (as appropriate to the argument): sample size as compared to target population, variety in sample as compared to target population, apparent representativeness of sample, scope of conclusion (distinguish arguments with a singular conclusion from those with universal or restricted generalizations as conclusion), carefulness of causal reasoning, if any.

1. Of 500 Edmonton adults questioned about attitudes toward censorship, 160 were opposed, 240 were in favor, and 100 were uncertain. Respondents were asked, "Do you favor having police and customs officials restrict the display and distribution of violent pornographic materials?" Of those who answered "no," 84 said their opposition was due to the fact that such officials might make mistakes and censor material that wasn't really pornography, and 76 were opposed to all government censorship on principle. We can see from this poll that only a small minority of western Canadians object to censorship.

(Invented example)

*2. It has been found that out of 500 students in the midwestern United States who received a bilingual education in Spanish and English, only 120 were competently bilingual after age 25. The speculation was that you lose competence in a language that you do not regularly use, and that for many midwesterners there are few opportunities to use Spanish. This research shows that less than 30 percent of students given bilingual education will benefit from it as far as real adult competence in the second acquired language is concerned.

(Invented example)

*3. *Background:* A book entitled *Beyond the Male Myth* sought to explore male attitudes toward female personality, appearance, and sexual habits, and male desires about their own sexual experience. The authors tried to explore these attitudes through a questionnaire that contained both short questions and questions that required essay-type answers. The authors had these remarks to make about their sampling of male subjects:

"We wanted to survey at least 4000 men because, according to statistical principles, a sample that large is equivalent to an infinitely greater population. In other words, if we had gone on to survey 10,000 or 100,000 or 4,000,000 men, the percentages who responded in various ways would not be expected to differ significantly from the results obtained from 4000. This holds true, of course, only if the sample is a truly balanced one, representative of the entire nation."

Question: Do you think the authors are correct in their belief that their sample is representative? They obtained the 4000 responses by approaching men in shopping centers and malls, office buildings, tennis clubs, college campuses, airports, and bus depots. They say, "The communities in which the test sites were located varied in affluence, ensuring that our sample would include ample representation from all income groups."

(Anthony Pietropinto and Jacqueline Simenauer, *Beyond the Male Myth* [New York: Times Books], p. 18)

4. *Background:* (Use background information for question 3 in answering this question as well.) The authors of *Beyond the Male Myth* distributed a questionnaire on which one question was "What do you consider the ideal sex life for yourself?" To this question, respondents were to indicate one of the following answers:

marriage, wife being the only sexual partner
marriage, with outside sexual activity
living with one female partner, unmarried
a few regular partners
many casual partners
one female partner, but living separately

To this question, 50.5 percent of the men surveyed chose the first answer: marriage, with the wife being the only sexual partner. Suppose that we were to infer from this survey that half of American men prefer monogamous marriage as a sexual lifestyle. Would the survey by Pietropinto and Simenauer be an adequate basis for this inference? Why or why not?

*5. "A study by a Toronto psychologist suggests that young people between the ages of 12 and 17 are the primary consumers of pornography in Canada and that 37 percent of them watch sexually explicit videos at least once a month. Research by James Check . . . shows that 35 percent of youngsters 'expressed interest in watching sexually violent scenes,' whereas adults expressed very little interest in such scenes. Prof. Check also found that college students display an 'unbelievable acceptance of rape myths and violence against women.'"

(In the study more than a thousand Canadians were interviewed. Assume that the sample reflected the country's population in age and geographic distribution and that of that group, about 70 or 80 people would be in the age group between 12 and 17.)

(Toronto *Globe and Mail,* March 11, 1986)

6. Headline: *Three out of ten operations not needed: U.S. nurses*

Story: "New York: Nearly half the nurses surveyed in a nationwide poll claim 3 out of 10 operations are not needed, and many of them say about half of all hospital stays are unnecessary. Eighty-three percent of the nurses polled by the magazine *RN*, a journal for registered nurses and students, also favored informing patients of less extreme and sometimes less expensive therapeutic alternatives, even if the doctor won't. Based on a national poll of 12,500 nurses, the report provided evidence of a quiet mutiny—in the name of patients' rights—in the nation's hospital nurses."

Evaluate the enumerative inductive argument implicit in this story and, on the basis of your evaluation, state whether or not you believe the headline is misleading.

(Toronto *Star,* February 15, 1981)

*7. In Ireland disputes between contending Protestant and Catholic groups led to the partitioning of the country into Northern and Southern Ireland, and there is still fighting in Ireland today. In India disputes between Muslims and Hindus led to the partitioning of the country into India (primarily Hindu) and Pakistan (primarily Muslim), and there is much ill will and some fighting between India and Pakistan. In Vietnam, an attempt to divide the country between communist and noncommunist forces only led to continued fighting until the communist forces won a victory in 1975. In Korea, a similar division has led to much animosity, tremendous militarization on both sides of the divide, and occasional border disputes. On the basis of this evidence, we can see that partitioning countries experiencing religious or ideological conflict is generally a poor method of resolving conflicts within them and that, far from resolving conflicts, it is likely to inspire future ones.

(Based on historical arguments given in detail in Robert Schaeffer, *Warpaths* [New York: Basic Books, 1990]

8. Partitioning countries didn't provide a durable nonviolent solution to conflicts between contending groups in Ireland, Palestine, India, China, Korea, Vietnam, or Germany. So if Canada were to be divided between the French Canadians (or Quebecois) and other Canadians, it is unlikely that such a partition would provide a durable nonviolent solution to the tensions between French-speaking and English-speaking Canadians either.

9. There have been many famous Dutch artists and few famous Dutch composers or poets, whereas there have been many famous German composers and poets, but few famous German painters. So in the next few decades it is not to Germany that we should look for innovations in art; we should look to Holland.

10. The Catholic Church requires celibacy of its priests and the Catholic Church has recently been implicated in numerous charges of child abuse by priests and brothers who have contact with young boys in such contexts as choirs and orphanages. Clearly celibacy demands too much and is an unrealistic requirement. This policy should be changed to prevent, or at least reduce, child abuse by the clergy.

COMMON FALLACIES IN INDUCTIVE ARGUMENTATION

Hasty Inductive Generalization

A *hasty inductive generalization* is an argument in which the sample is hopelessly inadequate, so that the inference from the sample to the population is not reliable. Often the generalization is based on an exceedingly small sample of cases—sometimes only one or two. A person rather carelessly assumes that the case or cases that have come to her attention are more than just episodes or isolated events; she assumes, without sufficient warrant, that they indicate a general tendency or trend. Hasty generalization is an easy fallacy to lapse into because we are all interested in general knowledge and yet our own experience is limited and particular. What could be more natural than inferring a general trend from something we witnessed or experienced ourselves?

Consider, for instance, the following short argument.

> In 1974 I visited both Sweden and Denmark and found the Swedes to be gloomy and inhospitable, while the Danes were cheerful and friendly. Danes are a lot more agreeable than Swedes.

Unless we have some particular reason for regarding the arguer as unreliable, we can accept the premise as testimony; if someone says she had these experiences, we can believe her. Yet the limited sample of Swedes and Danes she would have encountered makes any inductive argument from that experience to a generalization about the attitudes of Danes and Swedes unreliable. As a tourist, one does not meet a representative sample of the population; the sample one encounters is selective (people in service occupations being overly represented) and usually quite small. In this, as in other hasty generalizations, the evidence may be acceptable, and it is relevant to the conclusion, but it does not provide adequate grounds for the conclusion. The (A) condition for argument cogency may be met; (R) is met; but (G) is not.

In arguments such as this one, the evidence is sometimes said to be *purely anecdotal,* meaning that it is based on anecdotes, or stories of what has happened to a person, as opposed to any systematic effort to obtain a representative sample from the population that the generalization is about.

The Post Hoc Fallacy

Perhaps you have heard of this one. Its name comes from the Latin expression *post hoc ergo propter hoc,* which means "after this, therefore because of this." Superstitions may have had their beginnings with post hoc inferences: a man walks under a ladder and then loses his wallet, so he infers that it is because he walked under a ladder that he lost his wallet. With all that we have said about the difficulties that arise when you try to prove a causal relationship, you can no doubt see that any inference of the type:

1. *A* came before *B.*
Therefore,
2. *A* caused *B.*

is inadequate. This is the basic form of the *post hoc fallacy.* It is even shakier than the inference from correlation to cause, for in post hoc there is only one anecdote or event, not a correlational pattern.

Here is an example of a post hoc argument prominent in some circles when Cold War debates about get-tough policies with the Soviet Union were common in North America.

1. Since the fall of 1980, the Americans have had a tough and bellicose president as far as Soviet-American relations are concerned.
2. After the autumn of 1980, the Soviets did not invade any country in the way that they invaded Afghanistan in December of 1979.
Therefore,
3. It is because the Americans have a tough, bellicose president that the Soviets did not launch further invasions since December of 1979.

From the fact that American presidential toughness came before the alteration in Soviet policy, it does not follow that the former caused the latter—for which there are many alternative causal explanations.

Objectionable Cause

The fallacy of *objectionable cause* occurs when someone argues for a causal interpretation on the basis of limited evidence and makes no attempt to rule out alternative explanations of the event. Sometimes logicians call this fallacy *questionable cause* or *false cause.* We have not used the label "false cause" because it suggests that the careless causal reasoning has led to a false causal conclusion. You might get a true conclusion—if only by good luck. The problem, in objectionable cause, is that the conclusion—even if true—has been reached too hastily.

The fallacy of objectionable cause goes like this:

1. *A* occurred.
2. *B* occurred.
3. We can plausibly connect *A* to *B* in a causal relationship.
Therefore,
4. *A* is the cause of *B*.

If you look at this pattern, you can see the problem. That *A* and *B* have occurred and can be plausibly connected is not sufficient to show that *A* caused *B*, because there is, in these premises, no basis for ruling out alternative explanations.

A particularly tempting variation on objectionable cause, prominent in political and moral discussions of society and its problems, is as follows:

1. *A* occurred.
2. *B* occurred.
3. Both *A* and *B* are bad things.
4. We can plausibly connect *A* to *B*.
Therefore,
5. *A* is the cause of *B*.

Here is a classic example of the sort of mistake that we are calling objectionable cause. It is taken from a letter to the editor of a Toronto paper. The letter was written at a time when there was a considerable public controversy in the city about some police raids on bathhouses frequented by homosexuals:

> We have one of the safest cities on the continent but it is changing. And who do you think is bringing this change about? Our institutions, including the courts, the schools, and the churches have failed us. Why? Because they have been infiltrated by the "lib-left" and their sympathizers.[15]

The author of this letter reveals extremely simplistic causal thinking. He suggests that institutions are not giving positive leadership. Let us assume he is correct, if only for the sake of argument. He believes that this phenomenon (which would be very complex, if it really is occurring) has one and only one cause: "infiltration" of key social institutions by the "lib-left" and their sympathizers. Even if there were such infiltration (a fact that would be very difficult to establish), and even if it came just prior to the alleged decline, that would not show that it caused the decline. There would still be a need for evidence to show that this causal explanation is more plausible than others. Other possible explanations such as public cynicism, economic hard times, professional burnout among teachers and the clergy, and so on have not been ruled out.

When you don't like *A* and you don't like *B* either, it is certainly tempting to think that *A* causes *B*. This way, you can perhaps link up the things you don't like into a causal chain, and you will be well on your way to a simple solution that will eliminate these bad things from the world all at once! A wonderful example of this normative approach to causation may be found in the following argument, which was used by a panelist on a television show shortly after the nuclear reactor accident at Three Mile Island in 1979:

> The responsibility for the near catastrophic nuclear accident at Three Mile Island rests squarely with the English teachers of America. For years now, they have been ignoring little flaws of language. They have emphasized self-expression above all else. They have told us that small faults and mistakes do not really matter as long as you communicate your true attitudes and feelings and creatively express your own identity. And the problem at Three Mile Island was, initially, just one of those supposedly little things. One valve was not in the right place. One might think: well, it's just one little thing; it doesn't really matter. But it did matter, and that was the problem. It is the teachers of English who have encouraged the attitude that small things don't count, and it is just that attitude which is the underlying cause of the nuclear accident.[16]

The panelist, who obviously had a low opinion of English teachers, didn't much like nuclear reactor accidents either. So he decided there was a causal connection between these two things. The hastiness of the causal inference here is so obvious that it doesn't need much comment. If there is a common attitude that "little things don't matter," then the existence of this attitude would be a complex social fact indeed, a widespread phenomenon, permeating many aspects of life. It would be amazing indeed if teachers of English had sufficient power to spread such an attitude all by themselves! If the general attitude existed, it would be likely that lax teaching of English would be its effect, not its cause. Needless to say, there are countless more plausible explanations of what happened at Three Mile Island that a careful causal argument would have to rule out.

We all have a craving for explanations for things that happen—and especially for simple, emotionally satisfying explanations of those phenomena we don't particularly like. But such explanations are logically and scientifically worthless unless there are good reasons to believe that they are more plausible than significant alternatives. This is an especially important point when we go beyond simple causal explanations to evaluating far-reaching scientific theories; if we can identify an alternative that is more plausible than the theory we are considering, then the existence of that alternative substantially undermines our reason for accepting the initial theory.

Causal Slippery Slope Arguments

So far we have concentrated on arguments in which the conclusion makes a causal claim. Of course causal claims may also serve as the premises of arguments. One example is the *causal slippery slope*. In this type of argument, it is alleged in the premises that a proposed action (one that by itself might seem good, or at least acceptable) would be wrong because it would set off a series of side effects, ending ultimately in general calamity. The idea behind the reasoning is that someone who embarks on the action has begun a tumble down a slope of effects, the last of which will be something terrible. Here is a familiar example:

> It sounds quite all right, letting people choose to die when they are suffering from painful and incurable diseases and when they are of sound mind. Certainly it would seem a responsible choice if someone in such circumstances chose to kill himself. In fact, the famous author Arthur Koestler recently did just that, and no one blamed him since he was an old man and was suffering terribly from several diseases. The problem is, though, once you allow voluntary euthanasia the forces are in play, and there will be pressure for assisted voluntary euthanasia. Once this is established, involuntary euthanasia will follow for patients who have incurable diseases but are comatose and cannot make their own decisions. The procedures that permit involuntary euthanasia for those with incurable diseases bring about euthanasia of the retarded and senile, and soon we will be in a state where an individual life just has no value at all.

In the premises of this argument it is alleged that allowing voluntary euthanasia for those patients who can make their own choices will bring about a state in which individual lives have no value. Underlying this claim is the assumption of a kind of causal chain; one reform causes a further change, which itself brings more changes. The idea is that the first action is a step down a slippery road to hell; the first step causes an inevitable slide to the bottom. The problem with the argument is that the causal claims in the premises are not supported by evidence and are not even very plausible if you think about it. The argument is based on a kind of scare tactic. Actually the series of dreadful effects is just invented as an objection to the initial action, which (as the argument admits) is quite desirable when considered on its own. The idea is to intimidate people with the suggested calamity, so that they won't think about the sweeping and implausible nature of the causal claims in the premises.

Unfortunately, these arguments can be very effective. One historically prominent example is the domino theory, which was so popular at the time of the Vietnam War. It went something like this:

> If Vietnam goes communist, then Laos, Cambodia, Burma, India, and all of southeast Asia will go communist. Then all Asia will be communist, and after that all Europe, and the whole world. So even though it might not seem to matter very much whether Vietnam as a single country is or is not communist, we have to stop this thing. It is now or never.

As the Vietnam War came under increased criticism, the domino theory lost credibility. A new version was constructed for Central America. William P. Clark, assistant to President Reagan for national security affairs, put it this way:

> If we lack the resolve and dedication the President asked for in Central America, can we not expect El Salvador to join Nicaragua in targeting other recruits for the Soviet brand of Communism? When, some ask, will Mexico and the

> United States become the immediate rather than the ultimate targets? President Reagan said: If we cannot defend ourselves (in El Salvador) we cannot expect to prevail elsewhere. Our credibility could collapse, our alliances would crumble, and the safety of our homeland would be put in jeopardy.[17]

Here is the key premise in a causal slippery slope argument from another period of history:

> Unbridled passion following the wake of birth control will create a useless and effeminate society, or worse, result in the complete extinction of the human race.[18]

This statement was a premise in an argument used decades ago to object to the legalization of birth control. It wouldn't fool anyone today. We've legalized birth control, and neither an effeminate society nor complete extinction has resulted. But contemporary slippery slopes can be more deceptive.

The slippery slope argument was brilliantly satirized by Thomas de Quincy in *Murder as One of the Fine Arts*. De Quincy wrote:

> If once a man indulges himself in murder,
> Very soon he comes to think little of robbing;
> And from robbing he next comes to drinking and Sabbath breaking.
> And from that to incivility and procrastination.[19]

De Quincy imagined a slide from serious offenses to trivial ones, instead of the other way around. He had obviously heard, and seen through, more typical causal slippery slope arguments.

EXERCISE SET

Exercise 4

For the following arguments, indicate any causal claims that appear either in the premises or in the conclusion. If causal claims are made in the conclusion, assess the reasoning offered to support them and say if you find examples of post hoc or objectionable cause. If causal claims are made in the premises, is the argument an example of causal slippery slope? Why or why not?

Note: Some arguments may contain no causal claims, and some passages may not contain arguments. If either of these is the case, simply note the fact and proceed to the next example.

1. "If the Christian churches wish to refuse ordination of gay people to the clergy, they have a right to their decision, however misguided it may be. But when the churches organize public referendums to repeal the civil rights of homosexual citizens, that's another matter. In Dade County, St. Paul, Wichita, and Eugene, Oregon, the churches openly ran petition drives, distributed the political literature, and raised the funds needed to bring out the public vote that revoked the rights of gays in those places. Unfortunately America is currently besieged by an army of religious zealots who see the Government and the ballot box as instruments for enforcing church dogmas. If the trend continues, we'll have Government-enforced religion and

the end of a 200-year-old democratic tradition."
(Letter to the editor, *Time*, June 1978)

2. Since 1945 we have had nuclear weapons, and since 1945 we have not had a world war. Therefore, nuclear weapons have served to prevent a world war.

3. "The statement by Archbishop John R. Quinn that Vatican strictures on birth control are being ignored by many U.S. Catholics reflects the misconception that the doctrines of faith and morals proclaimed by the church are changeable. Yet there has never been an about-face on any of these doctrines. The great secular breakthrough allowed by the promotion and acceptance of contraception has brought us the age of state-countenanced abortion, community-standardized pornography, and a more than embryonic euthanasia movement. This pro-pleasure, antichild mind-set won't intimidate the church of Peter ever to modify the doctrine that sees more to sex than orgasm and more to aging than diminished utilitarianism."
(Letter to the editor, *Time*, November 10, 1980)

4. Cutting out compulsory final examinations in grade six is a dangerous step. Sure, you can see why people would not want 11-year-old kids to have to go through the stress of studying for and writing competitive examinations. But the problem is, when will it stop? Laxity in grade six will lead to laxity in junior high schools. Soon exams will be eliminated there. Then there will be pressure to get compulsory finals out of the high schools. When universities and law and medical schools follow, we'll have such a non-competitive and no-stress educational system that we'll have no guarantee at all of professional competence.

*5. *Background:* The author is asserting that in the period between 1980 and 1986, the quality of the manpower enlisting in U.S. armed forces has improved.

"People can still argue about restoring the draft, but now the arguments are about principles: How should a democracy allot the burden of military service? Is it just and fair to leave the risk of dying to volunteers? The debates are no longer driven by concerns about the quality of people who have volunteered.

"But manpower, though historically the most important factor in military excellence, is not the only one—and certainly is not the principal force behind our increased spending. Pay has gone up—but not stupendously and certainly not by as much as the quality of the force. From 1980 to 1985 personnel costs rose by less than 20 percent, and as a share of overall defense spending, pay and benefits fell. The improvement in the force, hard to quantify but more like 200 percent than 20, has been due partly to the severe recession of 1982, partly to a sense that the military is 'de-civilizing' itself and restoring its standards and self-esteem, and partly to the general resurgence of nationalistic pride."
(James Fallows, "The Spend-up," *The Atlantic*, June 1986, p. 28)

*6. "On the one hand, although logic and common sense offer excellent solutions when they work, who has not had the frustrating experience of doing his very best in these terms, only to see things going from bad to worse? On the other hand, every once in a while we experience some 'illogical' and surprising but welcome change in a troublesome stalemate. Indeed, the theme of the puzzling, uncommonsensical solution is an archetypical one, reflected in folklore, fairy tales, humor, and many dreams—just as there are both popular and more erudite conceptions of the perversity of other people, the world, or the devil to explain the converse situation. Yet it seems that little serious and systematic inquiry has been focused on this whole matter, which has remained as puzzling and contradictory as ever."
(Paul Watzlawick, John H. Weakland, and Richard Fisch, *Change: Principles of Problem Formulation and Problem Resolution* [New York: Norton, 1974], p. xiii)

7. *Background:* The following appeared in a letter to the Calgary *Herald*, concerning the showing of Judy Chicago's controversial feminist artwork, *The Dinner Party*. The show included a number of plates with symbolic

depictions representing female genital organs. The letter was printed on December 10, 1982.

Hint: (Concentrate only on the causal reasoning here.)

"Re the rave reviews about Judy Chicago's *The Dinner Party.* Certainly the craftsmanship and skills represented deserve praise. I was involved in a campaign of a different nature—namely the Billy Graham crusade in 1981. I remember the begrudging remarks of our press about it—especially the cost involved and how that money could have been better spent. No such reference to this show's price tag of $393,483. An irrelevant comparison? They have in common the intention of not just entertaining, but of moving people to a spiritual commitment. May I weigh value by results? Two examples re the Billy Graham crusade, worth mentioning, are that the Calgary crime rate was down both before and after the crusade. In October '81, an article in the Edmonton *Journal* stated that the Social Services Department had an unusual drop in the number of caseloads last fall, from Red Deer and South, and attributed this to the effects of the crusade. I predict the afterwave of *The Dinner Party* will bring more destruction than healing. Yes, I believe in the equality of the sexes. This show is stirring up attention—but honor to great women? Frankly, it sounds more like Babylon revisited (genitalia were a common sight in the temple worship of Babylon). There has to be a better way."

8. *Background:* This item was part of an advertisement for numerology that appeared in the *Detroit Free Press:*

"We found that numerology is a very useful tool in producing good luck. For example, the letters in the alphabet have assigned numbers. Singer Dionne Warwicke took the advice of her numerologist and added an 'e' to the end of her name. She immediately skyrocketed to fame, a fact which she has revealed on the Johnny Carson show."

9. *Background:* This argument by Glenn T. Seaborg originally appeared in *Chemical Education News.* It was reprinted in the *Informal Logic Newsletter* Examples Supplement for June 1980:

"Let us say it's a few years hence and all nuclear power plants have been operating safely. But opponents of nuclear power succeed in enforcing a national moratorium on nuclear power. All nuclear power plants are shut down, pending complete re-evaluation in terms of public safety.

"First this moratorium causes a rush by electric utility companies to obtain more fossil fuels—particularly because oil and gas are in tight supply. Coal prices soar, and the government reacts by setting a price ceiling. Coal supplies dwindle, and power cutbacks are put into effect. Finally, restrictions on burning high-sulphur coal are relaxed somewhat, and air pollution rises. Miners, disgruntled over a wage freeze and laxness of employers regarding safety standards, go out on strike. Coal stockpiles diminish, and many power plants are forced to shut down; others, overloaded by power demands, begin to fail. Miners battle with federal troops who have been ordered to take over the mines. A chain of blackouts and brown-outs creeps across the nation. . . .

"Darkened stores are looted at night. At home, people burn candles and wash in cold water. Hospitals begin to use emergency generators, and deaths are reported in intensive care wards because of equipment failure. Ill or injured persons have difficulty getting to a doctor or hospital. Medical supplies begin to lag behind growing demand.

"Children who can get to school wear sweaters and coats in unheated classrooms. At night, there is no television, and people listen to battery powered radios where they hear hope of miners going back to work. But as time goes on, great doubt appears that things will ever be the same again. It's up to you to speculate whether they would be."

*10. "For the past thirty years, six-foot-four John Wayne has stalked through the American imagination as the embodiment of manhood. . . . He has left not only a trail of broken hearts and jaws everywhere, but millions of fractured male egos which could never quite measure up to the two-fisted, ramrod-backed character who conquered the Old West. The truth of the matter is

that no man could measure up to that myth in real life—not even John Wayne."
(Tim LaHaye, *Understanding the Male Temperament* [Charlotte, N.C.: Commission Press, 1977], p. 11)

*11. *Background:* This item appeared in the *Oakland Press* on April 6, 1974, and was reprinted in the *Informal Logic Newsletter* Examples Supplement for 1979:
"*A Good Way to Cure Colds*"

"University of Michigan medical researchers have discovered that highly educated people with low incomes catch cold more often than others, suggesting that susceptibility to colds might depend on one's frame of mind. Furthermore, more people come down with colds on Monday than any other day.

"Well, practically everybody thinks he is not being paid as much as his education calls for, and it's on Monday mornings when this feeling becomes most acute. So obviously, it's not a germ or virus that's causing all our colds but those cold-hearted people in the front office who never seem to realize how smart we are. A cure for colds? One way would be to give everybody a raise and tell them to take Monday off."

12. In 1986 incumbent mayor Ralph Klein was re-elected in Calgary with 90 percent of the popular vote, despite the fact that eight other candidates ran for election against him. Klein is a plump, relaxed unpretentious and amiable man whose personality would seem to fit the image Calgarians have of themselves as hospitable and informal people. Klein's success was created by his ability to personify the spirit of Calgary. Cities do have personalities, and successful city politicians are those who match in personality the cities they lead.

13. "Farmer John Coombs claims his cow Primrose is curing his baldness—by licking his head. Mr. Coombs, 56, who farms near Salisbury, in southwestern England, says he made the discovery after Primrose licked some cattle food dust off his pate as he was bending down. A few weeks later hair was growing in an area that had been bald for years. The farmer has the whole herd working on the problem now, the *Daily Telegraph* reported yesterday. Mr. Coombs encourages his cows to lick his head every day and believes he will soon have a full head of hair."
(Toronto *Globe and Mail,* March 6, 1987; cited by J. F. Little, L. A. Groarke, and C. Tindale, in *Good Reasoning Matters* [Toronto: McClelland and Stewart, 1989], p. 283)

DIFFERENT SENSES OF INDUCTIVE

Before closing this discussion we should deal with one further complication. You may have heard somewhere that all arguments are either deductive or inductive. In our sense of *inductive,* this statement is not true. A priori analogies and conductive arguments are not inductive in our sense, and they are not deductive either. People who say that all arguments are either inductive or deductive use the word *inductive* in a broader meaning than we use it in this book.

The most common broader sense of *inductive* is that in which it simply means "nondeductive." Obviously, if inductive arguments are by definition nondeductive, then, since all arguments must necessarily be either deductive or nondeductive, all arguments will necessarily be either deductive or inductive. (Since deductive and nondeductive express contradictory predicates, these terms will exhaust the possibilities.)

In this book we have given *inductive* its own definition, which is not formulated by contrast with *deductive.* In our sense, *inductive* and *deductive* are contrary predicates, not contradictory ones. We have made this choice because we find the definition of *inductive* as "nondeductive" too broad to be useful. According to that definition, every argument that is not deductive is an inductive argument. This situation would put conductive arguments, some ad hominem arguments, a priori analogies, enumerative inductions, cases of guilt by association, explanatory inductions, and many other arguments in the same category. These various arguments are quite different from each other in a number of ways, as you no doubt realize by now. Such a definition of *inductive* is too broad to be useful.

Historically, induction has been closely associated with empirical science. Influenced by this association, some modern theorists who have used the broad sense of *inductive* have then gone on to identify inductive arguments with those used in empirical science. The combination of the broad definition of inductive as "nondeductive" and a sensitivity to philosophical tradition has led them to forget the very existence of other arguments commonly used in law, history, ethics, and other fields. Thus the broad category can be quite misleading. We believe that we have excellent reasons not to adopt that system in this book. We have chosen to explain it briefly, however, as you will quite likely encounter it in other contexts.

In this book, then, *inductive* does not mean "nondeductive." There are deductive arguments, inductive arguments, and other arguments—conductive arguments and a priori analogies—that fit in neither category. In our sense, inductive arguments are arguments in which the premises and conclusion are all empirical propositions; the conclusion is not deductively entailed by the premises; the reasoning used to infer the conclusion from the premises is based on the assumption that the regularities described in the premises will persist; and the inference is either that unexamined cases will resemble examined ones or that a hypothesis is probably true because it has explanatory value. Given this narrower sense of *inductive*, the inductive-deductive split does not exhaust the possibilities for arguments. Many arguments in everyday life and in empirical science are inductive in our sense, and we have done our best to give you some helpful strategies for appraising them.

 ## CHAPTER SUMMARY

In this chapter we have described and discussed conductive arguments and several different types of inductive arguments. These arguments share the property that their evaluation depends greatly upon background knowledge and for this reason, no purely formal method exists for evaluating them.

In conductive arguments, several factors are drawn together to support the conclusion. They are put forward as relevant reasons, reasons making the conclusion plausible or sensible. Conductive arguments are common in many contexts;

they are especially prevalent in reasoning about practical decisions, policy issues, and problems of interpretation. Sometimes conductive arguments include reference to counterconsiderations, factors that are negatively relevant to the conclusion. To evaluate a conductive argument, we have to determine whether the premises are positively relevant to the conclusion (this is determined separately, for each premise) and how strongly they support the conclusion when counterconsiderations are taken into account (this is determined by considering the weight of the premises, together, in the light of counterconsiderations.) A challenge in evaluating conductive arguments is to consider counterconsiderations that the arguer did not mention and may not have been aware of.

Inductive arguments have empirical conclusions and empirical premises, and are based, ultimately, on the assumption that unobserved cases will be relevantly similar to observed ones. There are various types of inductive arguments ranging from inductive analogy to enumerative inductions of which the conclusion is a generalization (universal or restricted) or a conclusion about a singular case. In addition, some inductive arguments are statistical; a statistical pattern observed in a sample is projected onto a broader population. Others are causal arguments; the premises describe regularities among events and pertinent background knowledge, and the conclusion is that one sort of event causes another.

It is impossible to give completely general rules for the evaluation of inductive arguments, because the factor of background knowledge is so important. Generally, however, the argument is stronger insofar as the sample is larger and more varied and the conclusion is more restricted in scope.

For noncausal inductive arguments apart from inductive analogies (a special case treated already in Chapter 9), the main key to cogent argument is accurate observations about a representative sample. The sample should be sufficiently large and sufficiently varied that it can reasonably be expected to represent the target population. An exceedingly small sample leads to the fallacy of hasty generalization; here an attempt at an enumerative inductive generalization fails completely because the sample—which may be based only on a single experience—is just too tiny to give anything close to a reasonable amount of evidence for the conclusion. When the sample is selective in a way that will predictably distort the evidence in a direction favorable to the arguer's conclusion, it is said to be biased. To obtain representative samples, we have to aim for number and variety in a way that makes sense given what background knowledge we already have bearing on the sample and the population.

Inductive arguments to causal conclusions are especially important and complex. In a careful causal argument, the conclusion is derived from observed regularities or correlations between types of events and a causal conclusion is inferred as the explanation for those regularities. However, causation can never be correctly inferred from the mere fact of correlation, because a correlation can have alternative explanations. A reasonable basis must exist for ruling out important alternative explanations if the causal argument is to be justified. A number of interesting and important flaws in argument result when causal arguments are improperly constructed. These include mistaking correlation for cause, the post hoc fallacy, the fallacy of objectionable cause, and the fallacy of causal slippery slope.

The term *inductive* is sometimes used to mean "nondeductive." If it is given this meaning, then, by definition, all arguments are either inductive or deductive. However, in this book, the word *inductive* is not defined in this way; it is given its own definition (see Review of Terms Introduced). In our sense of *inductive* and *deductive* some arguments are neither deductive nor inductive. These include conductive arguments and a priori analogies.

❖   ## REVIEW OF TERMS INTRODUCED

Conductive argument   Argument in which the pattern of support is convergent (not linked; compare Chapter 2) and premises are put forward as separately being positively relevant to the conclusion. Counterconsiderations may be acknowledged by the arguer.

Counterconsideration   Claim that is negatively relevant to the conclusion of an argument. Counterconsiderations may be explicitly acknowledged by an arguer, as is reasonably common in conductive arguments. In this case, the arguer is committed to the claim that his stated premises outweigh the counterconsiderations in significance, so that the conclusion is reasonably supported by the premises. Often arguers fail to acknowledge or mention counterconsiderations, and critics have to discover them for themselves in order to fully evaluate an argument.

Inductive arguments   Arguments in which the premises and the conclusion are empirical—having to do with observation and experience—and in which the inference to the conclusion is based on an assumption that observed regularities will persist.

Inductive reasoning   Reasoning in which we extrapolate from experience to further experience.

Enumerative inductive argument   Inductive argument in which the premises describe a number of observed cases, or a statistical percentage of cases. These cases are implicitly enumerated in the premises. Enumerative inductive arguments may be either categorical in their conclusion or may have a restricted conclusion.

Statistical inductive argument   Inductive argument in which the premises describe a statistical relationship within a sample (of the type, N percent of observed X's are f) and the conclusion is that the same statistical relationship will probably hold for a broader population.

Causal inductive argument   Inductive argument in which the premise describes regularities or correlations between events of various types and the conclusion is that one event, or sort of event, is the cause of another.

Pseudo-regularity An apparent regularity founded on a similarity between cases that is too superficial or of too little scientific significance to be appropriate as the basis for an inductive argument. For example: All these symptoms came up on a Tuesday; so Tuesday is my bad day.

Sample A subset of cases chosen from an identified population and examined as the basis for an enumerative or statistical inductive argument. These cases are assumed to be more or less representative of a broader group of cases. For example, if we reach a conclusion about U.S. opinion by a television survey of 1000 people, these 1000 people are taken as a sample of the broader U.S. population.

Target population All of the cases within the scope of the conclusion of an inductive argument. The population is the broader group we are reasoning about, on the basis of our evidence about the sample. If we do a television survey of 1000 adult Canadians to reach a conclusion about Canadian public opinion on a certain matter, then the target population is Canadian adults.

Representativeness A sample, S, is perfectly representative of a population, P, with respect to a characteristic, x, if the percentage of S that have x is exactly equal to the percentage of P that have x. Obviously, we are rarely in a position to know that a sample is representative in this strict sense. We try to make samples representative by choosing them so that variety in the sample will reflect variety in the population. For example, if a university campus has a student population that is 70 percent white, 20 percent Chinese, and 10 percent African-American and that is 80 percent under 22 years of age and 10 percent over 30 years of age, we would try to reflect these proportions in our sample, so that the sample would represent the population.

Random sample A sample in which every member of the population has an equal chance of being included.

Stratified sample A sample selected in such a way that significant characteristics within the population are proportionately represented within it.

Biased sample A sample that demonstrably and obviously misrepresents the population. It is unrepresentative because its members are not typical of the population, and the way in which they fail to be typical is certain to affect the results of the survey or study. For example, if we sampled people making purchases at a liquor store in an attempt to find out what percentage of the adult population drinks more than one alcoholic drink per day, we would have a biased sample.

Correlation An association of two characteristics, A and B. If more A's than non-A's are B, there is a positive correlation between being A and being B. If fewer A's than non-A's are B, there is a negative correlation between being A and being B. *Note:* It is important not to confuse correlation with causation. Even when A and B are strongly correlated, this does not show us either that A is the cause of B or that B is the cause of A. It is possible that a third thing, X, causes both A and B. Alternatively, the correlation might be coincidental.

Hasty inductive generalization Inductive generalization in which the evidence in the premises is too slight to support the conclusion, usually because the sample is so small that it is extremely unlikely to be representative. The (G) condition will not be satisfied.

Anecdotal evidence Evidence that is about only a few episodes, usually something within the personal experience of the arguer. Such evidence is too slight to be the basis for a strong inductive argument. The (G) condition is not satisfied when evidence for a generalization is purely anecdotal.

Post hoc fallacy To infer, from the fact that *A* was followed by *B*, the conclusion that *A* caused *B*. Typically *A* and *B* are singular events. In effect, the post hoc is an argument that "after this, therefore because of this." Such arguments are not cogent because the (G) condition of argument cogency is not satisfied.

Objectionable cause fallacy The fallacy committed when someone argues to a causal conclusion on the basis of evidence that is too slight. It may be committed by inferring causation from correlation or by simply imposing one sort of explanatory interpretation upon events and failing to consider others.

Causal slippery slope fallacy Argument in which it is asserted that a particular action, often acceptable in itself, is unacceptable because it will set off a whole series of other actions, leading in the end to something very bad or even disastrous. The causal claim that such a series will be the result is not backed up by evidence and is typically implausible on close analysis. Such arguments are not cogent because the sweeping causal premise is not acceptable: the (Λ) condition is not satisfied.

Notes

1. I have benefited from studying a draft paper on the convergent/linked distinction by Mark Vorobej of McMaster University. Amendments of my earlier formulations of this distinction are attempts to address concerns he raised in this paper.

2. *For instructors:* The converse is not true. Not all arguments exemplifying the convergent support pattern are conductive. One might, for instance, have an argument with several distinct premises, each of which quite separately deductively entailed the conclusion. In such a case, the argument would be deductively valid and hence would not be a conductive argument, though it would exemplify convergent support. One might also insist that such a case represents several arguments all with the same conclusion; this issue has not, as far as I know, been confronted directly in the theoretical literature.

3. As was illustrated in Chapter 9, inductive analogies occasionally use several analogue cases as opposed to just one.

4. The word *probably* is not always explicit either. But the qualities of observed cases can never be guaranteed to be qualities of unobserved cases; thus the conclusion of an inductive argument should never be taken to be guaranteed by the premises.

5. If the conclusion asserts less, it takes less evidence to give good support for it. Given the same evidence, then, a more restricted conclusion will be more strongly supported.

6. Statistical generalizations can be based on more complex forms: for example, "35 percent of the pianists were left-handed and, of these, 80 percent came from the northern areas of the Soviet Union."

7. The analysis of causation here is intended to reflect educated common sense, as discussions by

logicians and others reflect disagreement and are too complex to be suitable as a basis for textbook treatment.

8. Riane Eisler, *The Chalice and the Blade* (New York: Harper & Row, 1987).

9. Erich von Daniken, *Chariots of the Gods? Unsolved Mysteries of the Past* (Translated by Michael Heron; paperback reprint of 1969 book; New York: Berkeley Publishing Group, 1984). I owe this example and my interest in the phenomenon of pseudo-regularity to Cary MacWilliams.

10. This item was taken from research resumes in Carol Austin Bridgewater, "When a Man Talks, You Listen," *Psychology Today.* Copyright 1980 Ziff-Davis Publishing Company.

11. This advertisement appeared in a variety of popular magazines in 1980 and 1981.

12. Carol Gilligan, *In a Different Voice* (Cambridge, Mass.: Harvard University Press, 1982). Recently Gilligan's own corrective work has been criticized because her samples of women (from which she seeks to generalize about a "female" style of moral reasoning) do not include any African-American women. Ideally an analysis of human moral reasoning would involve subjects from many times and places and various cultural and language groups, not just those that can be found in contemporary North America.

13. Cited in R. Giere, *Understanding Scientific Reasoning* (New York: Holt, Rinehart and Winston, 1979), p. 246.

14. The passage is taken from a commonly used first year textbook.

15. Letter to the Toronto *Star,* February 25, 1981.

16. Reported by Joanne Good, Department of Sociology, Trent University. Specific wording used is our own.

17. Cited by Theodore Draper, in "Falling Dominoes," *New York Review of Books,* vol. 15, no. 16, October 27, 1983.

18. This argument was used in the early days of birth control clinics, as reported in a review of a book on Dr. Stopes, an early birth control pioneer. Review by J. Finlayson in the Toronto *Globe and Mail,* January 13, 1979.

19. Thomas de Quincy, *On Murder Considered as One of the Fine Arts* (London: Philip Allan and Co., Quality Court, 1925). De Quincy's essay first appeared in *Blackwood*'s magazine in 1827. Thanks to David Hill for this example.

CHAPTER 11

Reflective Analysis of Longer Works

So far, our attention in this book has been concentrated on passages and arguments that are relatively short. In order to have examples of a manageable size and level of difficulty, we have selected illustrations of a few sentences or, at most, several paragraphs, in length. This policy is necessary in the interests of efficiency, and we hope that the many illustrations and exercises have made the distinctions and logical points come alive for you, in addition to giving a variety of material for you to analyze and evaluate. But in order to effectively use the knowledge and skills developed thus far in this book, you need to work on applying them to lengthier materials. The purpose of this chapter is to take some steps in this direction. We develop a number of points about the understanding and evaluation of essay-length works and then treat one essay length example using the method described. Several interesting essays are appended to the chapter to give you good material to work from.

INTRODUCTION

There are some ways in which appraising a lengthier essay is easier than working on a short passage. Most significantly there is the matter of context. It has probably not escaped your attention that when one or two paragraphs are excerpted from a book, editorial, or letter, it is often not clear just what point is at issue or why the author is attending to the subject at all. We have tried to address this problem by giving background information. The advantage with a longer selection is that claims and arguments you need to evaluate are located within a richer and more informative context. You do not have to guess at why the author or speaker is dealing with the topic or where he or she is going once a key argument has been given, because you have a lengthier, more substantial work to deal with. Often you have already developed background knowledge that bears on the issue discussed, because you are reading the longer piece as part of an ongoing interest in the topic.

There are, of course, features that make the analysis of longer pieces difficult as compared with that of shorter ones. You cannot work through a lengthy piece sentence by sentence or even paragraph by paragraph. You cannot even consider and carefully evaluate every argument in a longer piece. Typically there are too many distinct arguments; to locate every one, work out a standardized version, and appraise it using the ARG conditions would be too cumbersome a task. If you were to do this and write an essay describing the results, the result would probably be painfully boring for your readers! In order to reflectively and rationally evaluate an essay-length work, you have to be *selective* in what you address. You have to understand the essay well enough to identify the author's most important claims and arguments, and then concentrate your attention on them. Selectivity requires sensitive, accurate understanding and good judgment.

In this chapter we describe techniques for understanding and appraising essays, on the assumption that the immediate application of these skills will be in the task of writing an analytic evaluative essay of your own. Obviously there is no single recipe for getting a good result: we are offering guidelines that we hope will be helpful.

READING FOR UNDERSTANDING

In order to work out a reflective and well-reasoned response to an essay-length work, the first step is to read the work carefully and make sure that you understand it. For most substantive essays, genuine understanding requires more than one reading.

We often think of reading as a passive activity. In fact, there are various ways of reading actively. When you first read for understanding, just relax and try, as far as you can, to enter right into the thinking of the author. Try to go along with his or her point of view, to engage in it as though it were your own. We call this sort of reading *empathetic*. (Empathy is the identification with the feelings, beliefs, and point of view of another person; we empathize with someone when we understand, feel, and respond to something from his or her point of view.) Reading something empathetically does not imply that you are ultimately going to agree with it—after understanding, you may agree or disagree. What it means is going along, at least temporarily, with the thoughts and ideas of the writer, entering into his or her frame of reference and working through the flow of ideas and feelings. Doing this is an important device for understanding the work.

When you have read an essay using this empathetic approach, you should then try to state its main point *in your own words*. What is the author trying to say? What is his or her main idea? You should be able to state this *thesis* in your own words without looking back at the written work. A test of whether you have understood the essay is that you can state its main point without looking back at the original. If you find that you cannot do this, you need to read the essay again—perhaps several more times—until its point becomes clear to you.

Let's assume that you have identified the thesis of the essay and can state it in your own words.

Essentially, *X* says that *C.*

But in a good essay, there is not only a thesis, there are reasons given in its support. The author does not just pull a central claim out of nowhere; he or she develops and defends the point. If you understand the essay, on the basis of careful empathetic reading, you will be able to state the major reasons for this central claim. You should be able to put in your own words a statement of the following form:

Essentially, *X* says that *C,* because *R.*

In this formula, *X* represents the author, *C* represents the thesis, and *R* represents the reasons for it. The word *essentially* is present to indicate that you are trying to capture the main points of the author; you are not including every strand of supporting argument or every detail. You are attributing an argument to the author: *C* (conclusion) because *R* (premises). This argument is one you have stated in your own words; it represents your attempt to grasp the central point of the essay, so it will necessarily omit many details and qualifications. We'll refer to this construction as the *core thesis argument.*

When you have arrived at a version of the core thesis argument, reread the essay to check your statement against the original. As you read, keep asking yourself whether the author is really saying what you have understood him or her to be saying. This is a stage where you have to be careful not to commit the straw man fallacy. Especially if you are inclined to disagree with the author and have found empathy in reading difficult to achieve, you should cross-check your statement of the core thesis argument against the original to ensure you have not misrepresented him or her. Look for evidence that the author has indeed said what you have attributed to him or her.

There is a balancing act here—one requiring judgment and care on your part. You must use your own words and you must be selective; therefore your statement cannot represent every detail of support, every nuance, and every qualification in the original. On the other hand, you should not omit essential aspects of the core argument. You will be committing the straw man fallacy if you overstate the thesis or if you omit a central reason. If appropriate, revise your statement of the core thesis argument on the basis of rereading. You will use the core thesis argument for the next stages of analysis and appraisal, so it is important to get it right.

In this process there are several sorts of essays that pose special problems. You may find that you have great difficulty attributing a thesis statement to the author. Such difficulties can arise for various reasons. The essay may be inexplicit in its statement of a point of view; the author may make a point through satire or ridicule, for instance. Or, the essay may be confusingly written or even contradictory, so that you cannot identify a single clear thesis. Before going on, we take a brief detour to say something about these special cases.

The Inexplicit Essay   This type of essay has no obvious, directly stated central claim or supporting argument. Such an essay will often be written from a quite distinctive point of view but does not directly, explicitly state a central thesis claim or supporting argument. It may seem to be making a point, but not state that point directly in just so many words. We'll refer to such essays as *inexplicit*. They make a point but make it indirectly by using irony, ridicule, or satire. An essayist may implicitly criticize a policy or practice by drawing it out to extremes and making fun of it. You can, perhaps, get a better grasp of what is meant here by reading the following few paragraphs from one such essay.

These excerpts are taken from an essay called "Isn't Biotechnology Wonderful?" by Bob Bragg.[1] Bragg's essay begins as follows:

> Q: What do you get when you cross a tiger with a parrot?
> A: I don't know, but when it talks I listen.

After this provocative introduction, Bragg goes on to say that there is news from Italy to the effect that biogenetic scientists "using refined techniques of artificial fertilization" have crossed a chimpanzee with a human being. The experiments were interrupted at the embryo stage for ethical reasons, but were said in a report to be capable of creating a new breed of slaves, or a subhuman species to do boring chores for human beings. Bragg writes a lively set of witty comments on the situation, but he never comes right out and says directly that the biogeneticists were wrong. (Skepticism about their approach is indicated in the title of his own essay, which appears to be sarcastic.)

We cannot reprint the whole essay here, but the following passages will give you an idea:

> It seems like a real life case of Dr. Frankenstein. Another sorcerer's apprentice ignorantly toying with high technology yielding unforeseen consequences and a host of new, insoluble problems.
>
> But I wasn't shocked. As a matter of fact, I was encouraged. Biotechnology offers solutions to problems which have plagued mankind for millennia. Now the monkey's play looks like the helping hand. Science offers us the means to avoid the pain and turmoil so common in this vale of tears. . . .
>
> Take famine, for example. We no longer need to have millions of humans die off in Ethiopia and Mozambique. We simply cross humans with camels and produce a stubborn creature that can go for weeks without a drink.
>
> Will that be one hump or two?

The rest of the essay continues in the same vein. The final sentence is "Isn't science wonderful?"

After the author has mentioned camels crossed with Africans, politicians produced by crossing chameleons with parrots (they could change rapidly but also echo the voice of the people), and teenagers with army ants, the reader is going to suspect that the hopes of these scientists are being satirized as ridiculously unrealistic. As a reader, you will have to attribute both a central claim and (if appropriate) a supporting argument to such an entertaining author. As it stands, the essay explicitly states neither. Yet Bragg is clearly quite skeptical and cynical about the value of such scientific experiments. He seems to be implying some such thesis as:

> Experiments to genetically blend different species to produce some result useful to our own species are of dubious success and value.

If this is his thesis, then we have to read the essay to see whether there are any reasons for it given—directly or indirectly—in the satirical and witty remarks the author makes. In fact the author does not seem to give reasons: instead of arguing against the genetic experimentation, he ridicules it.

Another indirect approach, perhaps even more subtle than that of satire, is found in the essay that, in effect, makes a point by *redescription*. A commonly accepted practice is redescribed in terms and in a context designed to make readers see the phenomenon differently, setting it in a new light. Such redescription can make a familiar accepted practice seem unattractive, controversial, wrong, or just plain silly. Some such essays are brilliant and entertaining, though they contain no statement of a thesis and no direct argument on its behalf.

The strategy of essay evaluation described in this chapter has been designed primarily for direct argumentative essays. From our point of view, inexplicit essays are special cases; this book is primarily about arguments and these inexplicit essays are nonargumentative in form. But when you try to evaluate longer works you may find some of this type, so we will try to give a few helpful tips about them.

First of all, we recommend careful reading to see whether you can fairly attribute a central claim to the author, even though he or she does not state it in so many words. (It does seem possible to do this with Bragg's essay.) Reading carefully and imaginatively, you can often attribute a thesis to the author of a satirical or redescriptive essay, and sometimes you can attribute reasons for that thesis as well. If you can attribute a thesis, but no argument, then part of your appraisal of the essay will depend on your assessment of whether that thesis needs to be supported by an argument. If the claim does not seem acceptable without further reason and evidence, and you cannot plausibly attribute any argument to the author on the basis of his or her work, then the essay will be flawed due to its failure to give any rational support for its thesis. (In fact, this would be a criticism of Bragg's essay.) Other aspects of the methods described in this chapter can be fairly readily adapted to fit the inexplicit essay.

The Confused or Contradictory Essay   A second kind of problem essay is one that is *confusingly written or contradictory* in its content to such an extent that its thesis is just unclear. If you are unable to state the thesis of an essay and you suspect that your problems are actually the fault of the author, read the essay again with a critical eye. Leave the empathetic view behind and look carefully through the work with the specific goal of trying to identify a central thesis. If you cannot find a central claim, or if you find several that are inconsistent with each other, the essay fails to make a point—or at least fails to make it clearly—and your evaluation will be a negative one, pointing out confusion or contradictoriness in the original.

◆ READING FOR APPRAISAL

At this stage, you set aside empathy and read the essay from the point of view of a critic. You may find it useful to pretend that you are a teacher who has the task of marking the essay, or a reviewer for a newspaper who is going to write a piece evaluating it for prospective readers. You have a statement of the main claim and the core thesis argument, and you keep these in mind. On the assumption that this is the claim the author is putting forward, and these are the sorts of reasons he or she is giving for it, you want to look at the essay *critically* to get a sense of how well the argument is expressed. You want, tentatively, to reach an evaluation of the essay.

An essay is not evaluated solely on the basis of its logic and argument. Logic and argument are important aspects, but features such as organization, style, tone, interest, balance, and judgment also need to be considered. A good essay is one that makes a significant and important point in a plausible and interesting way, that engages the reader—perhaps even captivates him or her. If an essay is awkwardly written, or disorganized, or if it is boring, monotonous, or repetitious, these are flaws.

Other flaws closer to logic as such are the use of emotionally charged language in place of argument, explanation, or analysis; personal attacks upon or straw man misrepresentations of those with whom the author disagrees; or a pervasive failure even to consider plausible alternative interpretations and theories. Such topics have been discussed in this book, and we hope and expect that our discussions of language, of the ad hominem and straw man fallacies, and of causal reasoning will be helpful to you in appreciating these features of longer works.

We suggest the following *features list* as a guide for appraisal:

1. *Interest, importance, and plausibility of thesis.*
2. *Quality of core supporting argument.* Use ARG conditions.
3. *Apparent quality of further arguments.*
4. *Accuracy.* Plausibility of claims, acceptability of statements, documentation of claims (where appropriate).
5. *Clarity and organization.* Are points developed in an orderly way? Are background information, description, and explanatory material included where needed?

6. *Coherence and consistency.* Does the essay hold together? Explicit or implicit contradictions are a serious flaw.

7. *Balance.* Does the author consider objections to his or her position? Is the treatment of opposing views fair and accurate? Are counterarguments carefully developed, if appropriate?

Features 1 to 7 are, in a broad sense, logical: they have to do with the quality and reasonableness of statements, arguments, and reasons. In addition, essays can be evaluated for more literary aspects. These have not been emphasized in this text, because our main topic is logic and argument. However, as a careful and attentive reader of an essay, you are bound to be somewhat aware of its literary features—aspects having to do with word choice, imagery, grammatical structure, and general style. These are important dimensions of any essay. In recognition of this fact, we can add to our features list:

8. *Word choice.* Is the language well-chosen? Is the tone appropriate to the topic? (For instance, it would hardly be appropriate to discuss a Shakespearean play in the latest teenage slang, or a serious problem like capital punishment in humorous terms.) Is excessively emotional language avoided? Is the level of language appropriate for the intended readership? Is excessive repetition of key terms avoided?

9. *Grammatical structures.* Are sentences clearly constructed so as to be fairly easily understood? Is there sufficient variety (for instance between short sentences and longer ones) to avoid monotony and achieve interest? Are paragraphs about the right length? Do they flow naturally from each other?

10. *Impact.* Is there anything that demands and receives the reader's attention? (Impact can be achieved by stylistic strength, by vividness of imagery, by interest of the "voice" or person of the author, by originality of argument and topic, or in various other ways.)

As you read the essay critically, continue asking yourself the following question: given that *X* is trying to show that *C* because *R*, do the style, organization, and language of *X*'s essay contribute positively to the achievement of this goal? The features list given here is not intended to exhaust the possibilities; you may wish to add elements or features, if that seems appropriate for the particular essay you are analyzing. The features list, or an appropriate adaptation of it, is a useful guide for critical reading. You can use it to gain an overall impression of the quality of the essay. Make notes as you check the essay with regard to the features list; these can be used at a later stage of your work.

The features list directs your attention to different aspects of the essay. Obviously, an analysis using such a list can give various results. It is rather unlikely that all the aspects you note will point in the same direction, so you will have to examine your notes and reflect on them to reach an overall judgment. If an essay seems cogent in its argumentation and accurate in its claims, but is disorganized and worded in an awkward and uninteresting way, what is your overall judgment going to be? You have to weigh these factors in your mind and reflect on their respective significance with regard both to the topic and to the purpose for which the essay was written.

On the basis of your understanding of the core thesis argument and a careful critical reading of the essay, *tentatively* put the essay in one of the following three categories: *good, mixed,* or *poor.* This tentative evaluation gives you the basis to make an outline of your own essay, offering a reflective analysis and evaluation of the author's work.

DEVELOPING AN OUTLINE FOR YOUR ESSAY

You now work from the tentative evaluation of the essay toward an outline for an essay of your own. Evaluations you have made using the features list are tentative because you may wish to alter them on the basis of closer study. For example, you might have judged an essay to be of poor quality; you might later find, when you try to identify specific flawed claims and arguments, that the style and content were better than you had thought. You can then revise your assessment to "mixed"—or even "good" if the faults you thought you had identified turn out, on closer analysis, not to be there or not to be serious.

There are many ways in which essays can be set out. As you gain experience in writing reflective or critical essays, you may develop confidence and a sense of your own preferred organization and style. Here, we offer several alternate models, or pattern outlines, just to get you started. We think these models are quite useful; however, they should not be regarded as rigid patterns—just as suggestions intended to be helpful. We call these models *heuristic* because they are intended to give preliminary guidance, and we recognize that they can be amended and developed in various ways, as appropriate.

Our three heuristic models are based on the three evaluation categories of good, mixed, and poor. We suggest a different model for each category.

Appreciative Essay

When you have judged an essay to be good, you have found it to be well written and well organized, and to make a plausible central claim, based on what struck you, on reading, as convincing arguments and balanced considerations. In many cases you will be disposed to agree with the central claim; if you did not agree with it prior to studying the essay, you are likely to agree on reflection; the organized presentation and arguments in the essay are likely to have convinced you. In such circumstances, you might wonder what on earth you have to say. If the essay is just plain good—or even terrific—then what can you write about it?

This apparent problem, which occurs to many people when they are asked to respond to a very good essay or other piece of work, is actually not as difficult as it seems. In fact, we think it isn't really a problem at all! The problem seems to arise because people make a false assumption—the assumption that the only way to say something interesting and original about another person's work is to criticize it. Though we often tend to assume that commenting means criticizing and criticizing means negative criticism, actually we can comment positively— pointing out interesting, original, or important aspects of another's work and saying why we think they are significant, or going on from the author's claim to add further suggestions as to related points. A reflective essay can be *appreciative,* and that's the appropriate form if the work you are studying strikes you, on careful reflection, as good.

Like any essay, an appreciative essay reveals something about its author. It shows a generosity of spirit, a willingness to recognize and appreciate another's accomplishments, and an openness to the ideas and arguments of other people. An appreciative essay is not likely to display your penetrating critical intelligence or logical sharpness, but it does convey understanding, a sense of judgment, fairness, and accuracy, and—if carefully constructed—at least a modest amount of originality. Such an essay may not seem to you to be brilliant, but it is a worthy form, one that has been used to good effect by famous critics and social theorists. If you honestly find an essay to be good, and you tend to agree with the central thesis and the core argument on its behalf, then the appropriate response in your own essay is one of appreciation.

Here is a suggested plan for an appreciative essay:

OUTLINE PATTERN FOR THE APPRECIATIVE ESSAY

i. Introduction

Say whose essay you are evaluating, and state its title, where you found it, the context in which it was written, and the topic or problem it addresses. State the central claim and core argument, doing so in such a way that your reader will be able to achieve a good and accurate understanding of these points even if he or she has not read the essay you are commenting on. Briefly state that in your opinion the essay is excellent and does a good job of establishing its point. If appropriate, add a personal touch by describing why you found the essay of interest and how it helped you change your mind or come to a new understanding of an issue.

ii. Explanation for your judgment

Cite notable argumentative features that you think contribute to making the essay a good one. That is, mention any arguments that are essential to establishing the author's position or are striking in their originality, vividness, or form. Add any comment you may have on the strength of the arguments the author has given. Say why you think the central claim is interesting and important and, if appropriate, add clarification or emphasis. Cite any notable stylistic and organization features that, in your opinion, contribute to making the essay a good one.

iii. Any minor doubts or qualifications

Even in an essay you have judged to be good, you may have minor doubts about the claims or presentation made. Qualify your overall judgment, if appropriate. Cite details, specifically, to provide reasons for your minor doubts or qualifications.

iv. Additional reflections and suggestions
Try to provide additional evidence that would bear on the thesis, or interesting illustrations of the point made by the author.

v. Further implications of the work
Given that you have positively evaluated the author's contribution, after careful analysis, conclude by making some suggestions as to its practical or theoretical implications. How could the central claim be applied? Taken further? Related to other important or interesting issues?

On the basis of this outline, you should be able to write a reasonably good appreciative essay. The appreciative model is appropriate when your basic judgment about the essay you are analyzing is, simply, that it is a good one.

How might the ARG conditions of argument cogency be used in all this? As mentioned earlier, it is not possible to evaluate every argument in an essay; the task is just too long and cumbersome. But certainly you can use the ARG conditions in evaluating the core argument; if this argument is not cogent, the essay will not be deemed to be good, but rather to be of mixed or poor quality. In addition, you may use the ARG conditions when locating occasional details that are flawed—in the event that any of those details involved arguments used along the way. A further application for ARG is in the evaluation of your own work. When you have written a draft of your essay, try to read your own work from the point of view of a critic: look at your own arguments and ask yourself whether they are cogent according to the ARG criteria.

Mixed Reaction Essay

A *mixed reaction essay* is appropriate when you have judged the quality of the essay you are evaluating to be mixed; you have checked through the features list and have found both significant strengths and significant weaknesses. (In our experience, this is likely to be a common reaction; few essays are just plain good or just plain poor.) In the nature of the case, the "mixed" category can include considerable variety. Look at your features list and the notes you have made, and reflect on the thesis claim and the core argument. Ask yourself whether your overall sense of the quality of the essay tends more toward the positive or toward the negative. If you have a clear tendency in either direction, it is helpful to recognize it, as it can be relevant to the organization of your points and the emphasis you give them.

Here is a suggested model for the essay of mixed reaction.

OUTLINE PATTERN FOR THE MIXED REACTION ESSAY

i. Introduction
State whose essay you are evaluating, give its title, and explain the context in which it appeared and the problem or issue the author discusses.

Briefly state the thesis claim and core argument of the essay. Briefly state your judgment about the essay. This will be of the "it is good on the whole, but has such-and-such flaws" or of the "it is in many ways flawed, but has such-and-such virtues" variety. Or, if you cannot see a preponderance either way, you may say your reaction is just plain mixed due to a mixture of good features and flaws. (You do not need to justify these comments in your introduction; you will justify them later.)

ii. Detailing the essay's flaws

You probably cannot mention every single relevant detail here. Try to choose aspects that are significant and serious as far as the argument, style, and clarity of the essay are concerned. Back up your points with specific details, using brief quotations if this is feasible. If you are saying there are flaws in argument, defend your criticisms by showing (in effect) how arguments fail on the ARG conditions. (Don't use these terms, of course; you can't assume that all your readers will have read this textbook!)

iii. Detailing the essay's good features

These can be stylistic, organizational, or argumentative features, or they can have to do with the interest of its thesis claim and argument. You may deem an argument as lacking cogency but as interesting due to its original structure or challenging line of thought. You may deem an essay to be weak in argument and logical organization but to be vivid and attractive in style. Or you may deem the arguments of an essay to be cogent, but deem its style boring and its central claim obvious and not worth making. Say which aspects of the essay you appreciate and why you appreciate them. Back up your comments with specific details. (The notes you made using the features list should be helpful at this stage.)

iv. Summary statement, bringing (ii) and (iii) together

If appropriate, make a qualified judgment of the merits of the work, all things considered. Do you accept the thesis put forward by the author, despite the various flaws you have found? If so, why?

v. Further implications or suggestions

If you have criticized the arguments offered, have you any suggestions as to how they might be improved so that the central claim would be adequately supported? Would you recommend restricting or amending the central claim? Can you suggest (briefly) other arguments in its support? Do you have a counterclaim you wish to put forward? If your criticisms have not primarily been directed against the thesis of the essay, and if you have basically accepted it, then are there interesting applications or further ramifications of this thesis that might be mentioned?

The mixed reaction essay displays the balanced, careful, reasoned judgment of the author. A danger is that such an essay may turn out to be too wishy-washy and look as if it is saying nothing. You can avoid giving such an impression by being as specific as possible in your comments as to what is good and what is poor and by striving for some sort of overall response that accurately reflects both the original piece and your own comments about it.

Negatively Critical Essay

Sometimes an essay will strike you as just plain poor. When you are asked to write an appraisal of it, your evaluation in such a case will be mainly negative; it will consist of critical arguments from you, showing how and why the original essay is flawed. There are several risks, or dangers, in writing this sort of essay. One is that you might inadvertently commit the straw man fallacy; you have a negative view toward the central claim, or the argument, or style of the original, and you lapse into such a mood of rejection that you distort the position or miss essential qualifying details. It is important to check your features list and core central argument against the original essay to make sure that your allegations are fair. A second danger when your essay is primarily critical is that you might lapse into ad hominem attacks on the author, or into belligerent, exaggerated, emotionally loaded language. Make sure that you do not slide into attacking the author, as opposed to his or her work, and that your language remains polite and temperate.

Here is a suggested outline for a *negatively critical essay,* the sort you will write if your judgment of the overall quality of the essay you are appraising is poor.

OUTLINE PATTERN FOR THE NEGATIVELY CRITICAL ESSAY

i. Introduction
   Give the title, author, and context of the essay. State, in neutral terms, the problem or issue addressed and the central claim and core thesis argument. State that in your judgment the essay is of poor quality and does not succeed in accomplishing its purpose.

ii. Justification for your negative appraisal
   Here you can cite in more detail features that, in your opinion, show that the essay is flawed. Failures in argument should be mentioned: if it is your judgment that the author did not succeed in giving good reasons for the central thesis, then you should offer your critique of this argument. Why and how does it fail to be cogent? (Work out your critique using the ARG conditions, but do not state it in these terms; just point out problems of acceptability, relevance, or sufficiency of grounds by explaining, in nontechnical language, how they arise.) Other evidence that the essay merits negative evaluation should be given: check your features list and cite aspects of style, language, organization, tone, or additional argumentative flaws. For any objection that you raise, you should think through and describe why it is an objection. (Keep checking back against the original to make sure your evaluation is not too harsh.)

iii. Mention of any redeeming or positive features of the essay
Usually, even when an essay is quite poor, it has some redeeming features. It may be well written, though illogical in its argument. Or it may be entertaining, or have a novel illustration, despite flaws in other areas. If you can find any such features, identify them and express your appreciation.

iv. Suggestions as to how the essay might be improved
Are there ways in which the author could have strengthened his or her core argument? Are there other arguments, not mentioned by the author, that might support the thesis claim? Briefly mention any constructive suggestions you might have about the work. (Be careful to point out that these are your own amendments and say just why you think they would improve the argument or arguments offered by the author.)

v. Summary conclusion

We will illustrate our technique of essay appraisal with reference to a sample essay, set out in the following section. We do not offer a full example of an appraisal, but we do set out a representative outline. Several interesting recent essays are appended to this chapter as works for you to use to practice the techniques suggested here.

◆ A SAMPLE ESSAY

The following essay on morality and animals was written in 1978 by Rose Kemp of Peterborough, Ontario, and adapted for this volume.

MORALITY, ANIMALS, AND THE RIGHT TO LIFE

Traditionally it has been thought that moral relations are relations between people. We have our morally significant relationships with each other—with our friends, lovers, husbands, wives, and colleagues—that is to say with other fairly well-developed members of the human species. However, morality is not restricted only to others who are mature and relatively independent human beings. Morality extends to children, to helpless adults, and to seriously mentally handicapped adults. But what the exact boundaries of morality are is not entirely clear. Are human embryos and fetuses entities with whom we have moral relations? What about God, the Devil, and angels—if they exist? What about animals—individual animals and animal species? Or future people, who do not exist yet? Nation states? Or plants? Is it morally wrong to cut down a 1000-year-old tree and use the wood to make toilet paper? If this is wrong, is it because we wrong the tree itself?

Just what the boundaries of morality are is itself a moral question. This is obvious in the context of the abortion debate, where controversy rages, both in the popular press and amongst philosophers, as to whether a woman has a moral obligation to the fetus developing in her body and whether we condone murder if we condone abortion. Abortion is not the only controversy that involves an issue of moral boundaries. In current policy and politics, the status of future people, animals, animal species, and plants are also important—and in dispute. In this essay I shall not comment on the moral status of the embryo or fetus or of future people, God or angels, nation states or plants. My present topic is that of animals.

Our whole culture is based on the assumption that animals other than human beings lack the moral status that human beings have. We human beings treat other animals quite differently from the way we treat each other. We cultivate animals for food and clothing, raise them to be killed, keep them in confining and uncomfortable conditions on factory farms, use them experimentally for teaching and research, exhibit them in zoos, and keep them as pets. All these things would be unacceptable if we did them to people. Experimentation is a possible exception—but a controversial one. Ethical restrictions on experiments on people are quite strict and nearly always require that subjects of experiments give informed consent. Can animals consent to experiments done on them? Of course not—and some of these experiments impose terrible pain and suffering on their innocent victims.

We do not kill people in order to eat them, nor exhibit them in zoos, nor deprive them of material affection in order to satisfy our scientific curiosity as to what the effects of that deprivation might just happen to be. This difference is because of our own basic assumption about the moral status of animals. We don't think of animals as beings with an intrinsic worth, beings whom we should not hurt or wrong. There is something absurd in the idea that a squirrel or cat is a moral being. When one reads—as I did several years ago—that a dog was tried for murder, the story seems bizarre and incredible.

Yet this underlying assumption about animals is coming into the open, because some eloquent voices are speaking out against it. Many people are extremely upset and concerned when they see animals suffering or being cruelly treated. This kind of reaction isn't new; it's been going on for at least a century. In fact, humane societies for the protection of animals existed before the institutionalization of groups for the protection of human children.

The famous humanitarian Albert Schweitzer, who gave up a rewarding intellectual life in Europe to work with lepers in tropical Africa, believed that life itself, not just human life, was worthy of respect. He was unwilling to kill even the tropical insects whose presence hindered his medical work on behalf of leprous human beings. Peter Singer, an Australian philosopher and activist, wrote in his book *Animal Liberation* a fervent and dramatic appeal for attention to the prolonged and cruel suffering of animals in scientists' laboratories and on factory farms. Singer argued that our common assumption about animals is just plain wrong and convinced many of his readers that vegetarianism is a morally obligatory lifestyle. His vivid portrayals of the horrible conditions in which some animals lead their lives are unforgettable. Singer argued that animals can suffer, that they do suffer, that they merit moral consideration, and that we should act to end their suffering.

There are good reasons for these conclusions. Consider the basic human right: the right to life. There is no reasonable basis for giving this right to humans and denying it to animals. To say that all human beings have a right to life, a right that is a natural human right, is to say that it is wrong to take the life of a human being without some particularly compelling reason to do so, and that the wrongness of doing this does not depend on any particular legal system or social code. Certainly, to understand more fully what a natural right to life is, we would need to clarify what "particularly compelling reasons" might justify the taking of human life. And we need to explore why this right is natural or universal. But however problematic such aspects of a natural human right to life might be, many people do believe in it. It is enshrined in the United Nations Declaration of Human Rights, to which the United States and Canada are both signators. The right to life is important and basic. All other rights seem, in fact, to presuppose it. If one is not alive, one cannot exercise other rights such as the freedom of speech and worship, or the right to vote, or get an education and a job.

The right to life is commonly believed to belong to all human beings. Such a right is acknowledged in national and international law, and it is basic and minimal. Many of us do assume that all human beings have a right to life. But our way of life requires that non-human animals lack this right. If we thought they had a right to life, we wouldn't kill them for food and clothing, or in the course of experiments. Is this position about the moral status of human beings and animals a consistent one?

If human beings have a natural right to life, then all human beings have this right. And "all" really means all: the severely retarded, newborn infants, the very senile, the morally wicked, the grossly deformed . . . every last one of them. It may sometimes be justified to take human life, even given this natural right to life—if we had to kill another human being in self-defense, or to save him or her from an agonizingly prolonged and painful death, this might be morally permissible. But we can't reconcile killing humans as a source of food or of pleasure, or in the course of experiments, or because it's convenient or efficient, with our basic belief that human beings have a natural right to life. We do these things to animals, so obviously we think that animals do not have a natural right to life. Why not? What's the difference?

One common rationalization is that the difference is in the humans' capacity to reason. Another is that humans, unlike non-human animals, have the capacity to make moral decisions, to reflect on their actions, to take the needs of others into account—in short that human beings, unlike animals, are moral agents. But neither of these ideas stands up to analysis. The reason is simple: not all humans are rational and not all humans have moral capacity. (Infants and the severely retarded don't have these qualities; nor do those who are comatose, or extremely senile.) Yet *all* humans are believed to have the natural right to life. If this natural right to life is to apply to all of us, it must be founded on a feature that we all have, and since we do not all have either rationality or moral capacity, it cannot be exclusively founded on these features.

How can we possibly justify giving a right to life to a tiny human infant, or a seriously mentally retarded human being, and refusing it to a normal adult dog or chimpanzee? There is no general difference that would justify making such an enormously important moral distinction. The adult chimpanzee behaves in a more complex way than the human infant, he gives more evidence of desires and intentions, and his capacities for action and relationship are more fully developed. What feature could we possibly find that a human infant would have, and a chimpanzee lack, that could justify giving the human infant a right to life that the chimpanzee does not have? None: that's the answer.

There is no relevant difference that applies to all human beings and to no nonhuman animals and that would make us consistent in saying all human beings have a natural right to life, whereas no animals do. To be consistent, we should either admit that some human beings do not have a natural right to life or concede that some nonhuman animals do have this right.

If all human beings have a natural right to life, then non-human animals have that right too. People aren't going to like this position: they are going to find it radical and strange, and they are going to see that taking it seriously would require extreme changes in lifestyle. So they are going to resist it. What can be said on the other side? A common response is, "come on, human beings are human, and rats and chimpanzees are only animals. They can't have rights." But this statement expresses nothing more than chauvinistic mysticism. What's so special about being human, about being within one biological species rather than another?

Singer said that giving one species a privileged moral status was just the same thing as giving one race or sex a privileged status. He coined a term for the practice: speciesism. Downgrading animals, as less worthy of consideration than people, is speciesism—just like racism or sexism. And speciesism is a moral failing. Just being human is no more morally relevant than just being white or just being male.

If animals have a natural right to life, they are within the moral sphere, and it becomes a moral question whether we are justified in killing them in order to eat them. Unless it could be shown that animals provide a necessary element in human diet, the answer to this question should be a firm *no*. Even if meat were strictly necessary for the continuance of human life—it isn't, in fact—we would have a conflict of rights situation. To think that human interests always supercede those of animals is not only selfish, it's biased and arbitrary.

Save us, you will say, kind reader. Save us from this relentless and impractical logic? For the absence of a distinction between all humans on the one hand and all non-human animals on the other, we are going to change our eating habits, our farming habits, our whole way of life? Must we follow Singer into impractical and self-sacrificing idealism?

One who takes a different view is, by coincidence, another Australian, John Passmore. In a book called *Man's Responsibility to Nature,* Passmore said that moral obligations and responsibilities arise only within communities. If I am to have an obligation to you, you and I have to be connected, or related in some way; we must be members of the same community. There must be at least a chance of reciprocity. And, according to Passmore, "men, plants, animals, and soil do not form a community; bacteria and men do not recognise mutual obligations nor do they have common interests." If we treated plants and animals and landscapes as part of our community, Passmore says, we couldn't "civilise the world." This seems, incidentally, to be quite a revealing phrase. Strip mining, deforestation, the hole in the ozone layer, pollution, factory farming—these count as civilizing the world? God save us from civilization! Passmore argues that if we were to accept animals and plants as members of our moral community, we couldn't even go on living.

The implicit assumption underlying Passmore's idea that moral relationships must be within communities is that moral relationships must be reciprocal; they must be able to work both ways. According to this view, I have no duty to respect the right to life of a tiger, because a tiger is never going to have a duty to respect my right to life—and he's not going to respect it either. Tigers have no duties. Animals are not in moral communities with respect to one another, and they are certainly not in moral communities with respect to human beings. That's why we don't think a wolf is failing morally if it kills the lamb for food; the wolf is not a moral being and cannot have a duty to recognize any natural right to life that we think the lamb might have. And that's why it really would be ridiculous to try a dog for murder.

Those who want to go on enjoying steaks, leather coats, pets, and zoos would no doubt like to think that Passmore is right; his claim that morality requires reciprocity seems to give a compelling reason not to allow animals to count as moral beings. But the matter is not quite so simple. There is a striking and fatal counter-example to Passmore's assumption that moral relations require reciprocity. It's the case of children. Most parents love their children and want to care for them; we commonly believe that parents have duties toward their children and children have a right to nutrition, education, love, and basic care. Yet children cannot accept duties with respect to us. Nor can they rise to make moral claims; they are for many years not capable of proclaiming their moral status. And yet we do believe in obligations to children and we do think that they have rights. Children who are not full-fledged moral agents are nevertheless within our moral community.

It might seem that we have an argument, from Passmore, for keeping animals out of the moral sphere. But if we follow that argument, we are going to keep some human beings out of the moral sphere too. And this we are not going to countenance. So presuming that we do not wish to alter our beliefs about our obligations to infant humans, we are going to have to alter our beliefs about animals. This is just where the whole discussion started: how can we be consistent in keeping all humans within the bounds of morality while keeping all animals outside it?

Animals are not just like people; they are certainly importantly different from mature human beings, who can make moral choices and assume responsibilities, and deliberate on their actions. People's concepts are much more elaborate and sophisticated than those of animals, and their emotional range and the range of their interest is vastly greater. Only human beings can speculate about free will and the meaning of life; wolves and tigers and cows and pigs don't do this. Presumably this was the sort of thing the famous political philosopher John Stuart Mill had in mind when he made his famous remark that it would be better to be Socrates dissatisfied than a pig satisfied. Socrates wondered about the meaning of it all: pigs don't.

But that does not prove that pigs and other animals are right outside the moral order, that they are lower beings deserving no moral consideration. The problem about morality and animals is not that there are no differences between typical animals and typical people. It is, rather, that there are no differences that are relevant to our current practices with regard to animals— relevant in the sense of counting towards the justification of those practices— and that are also universally characteristic of human beings as contrasted with other animals. Why do these facts constitute a problem? Because we can't accept them and continue with our current practices towards animals. Because they are uncomfortable for us to think about. Because they make us uneasy. They show our need to reform our cruel practices, to revise our way of life with its inhumanity to non-humans.

There's no way to avoid this problem. If all human beings have moral status, then animals have moral status. All human beings do have moral status. Human beings have, among other things, the right to life. So, accordingly do non-human animals. The challenge we face is to change our thought and action to take these animal rights seriously. It won't be easy, but it has to be done.

WORKING THROUGH AN EXAMPLE

We shall now use the techniques described earlier in this chapter to analyze and evaluate Kemp's essay on morality and animals.

Finding and Stating the Main Thesis and Core Supporting Argument

Once we have read the essay empathetically several times, we try to state its main thesis. The main thesis of Kemp's essay is:

Animals have a moral right to life.

On the basis of this thesis, Kemp also states related ideas, such as the need for reform of social practices like scientific experimentation on animals and factory farming. But her main claim is for the moral status of animals. Kemp's main argument is essentially as follows:

1. It is a basic assumption in social and moral life that all human beings have moral status and have a right to life.
2. There is no difference between all human beings on the one hand and all non-human animals, on the other hand, that would support giving all humans a right to life and giving no animals a right to life.

So,

3. We cannot consistently maintain that all humans have a right to life and no animals have a right to life.

Therefore,

4. We should achieve consistency by acknowledging that animals have a right to life.

This statement of Kemp's thesis and core supporting argument seems accurate even after reading her essay again. Of course, such a core statement necessarily ignores aspects of the essay—the author's references to Singer, Schweitzer, and Passmore, and her counterargument against Passmore; her reference to specific social practices (zoos, use of leather, experimentation, eating meat) needing reform; and her reference to related problems of moral status (children, future people, angels, nation states, plants) mentioned in the introduction. Nevertheless, this core argument statement reflects the *main* point Kemp is trying to establish and the *main* line of argument for it.

Detailed Critical Scrutiny Using the Features List

We now move past the state of empathetic reading to more critical reading where we take notes and document aspects of the essay that strike us as especially good or especially bad or in some other way worthy of note. In doing this we can use the features list as a guide. For convenience, here it is again, in short form:

FEATURES LIST
1. Interest and plausibility of thesis
2. Quality of core supporting argument
3. Apparent quality of other arguments
4. Accuracy of claims and documentation
5. Clarity and organization
6. Coherence and consistency
7. Balance
8. Word choice
9. Grammatical structures
10. Impact

We read through Kemp's essay, noting details that are positively or negatively relevant to these features. There is, of course, something individual about the way this is done: different readers find different aspects interesting or important and will note different details. The matter depends on judgments about various details: which details we pick out can obviously vary. But just to give you an idea of how to go about it, here is a checklist for Kemp's essay. (When making up such a list you may wish also to include page numbers and specific phrases if your eventual essay is going to include documentation.)

1. *Interest and plausibility of thesis.* Interesting; somewhat plausible, given her argument. Should differentiate between some animals and others. (Insects, crabs, slugs surely aren't like pigs, tigers, cows, and cats.)

2. *Quality of core supporting argument.* Conclusion needs restriction to some animals, not all. Argument too indirect?

3. *Apparent quality of further arguments.* Consider: are Singer and Schweitzer erroneously appealed to as authorities? Singer—"speciesism"—only a label? Straw man in the "humans are human" view? Passmore refutation adequate? (Check out.)

4. *Accuracy.* No obvious inaccuracy. No documentation as to what exactly Singer, Schweitzer, and Passmore said and where (no references). Brutality toward animals on factory farms and in science labs? No specific abuse is described or documented.

5. *Clarity and organization.* Basically all right. A little long and repetitive, but clearly written.

6. *Coherence and consistency.* Good.

7. *Balance.* Important in light of the sweeping and radical claim Kemp defends. She does consider counterarguments to her position, but only two counterarguments are treated: "humans are special just because they are humans" and Passmore's argument about community. Other counterarguments? Especially practical considerations: consequences if we started to treat animals as moral beings.

8. *Word choice.* Not inspired but mostly unobjectionable. Slightly uneven; there are occasional rhetorical bits. The prose is quite emphatic and clear. The style is unpretentious.

9. *Grammatical structures.* Good.

10. *Impact.* Fairly strong, for readers to whom a defense of animal rights is new. Slightly derivative—relies a lot on Singer. Style adequate, not memorable. Needs more specific details, and documentation of what Kemp sees as immoral abuse of animals.

On the basis of this list, we can now reach an overall appraisal of Kemp's essay. It is relatively easy, given the points above, to see that the essay would go in the "mixed" category; it is neither strikingly good nor strikingly poor. So, to write a reflective evaluation of the essay, we will use the outline plan for the mixed reaction essay.

Preparing an Outline

Since we have judged Kemp's essay to be mixed in quality, we shall follow the model outline for the mixed reaction essay. (*Note:* this is an outline and only an outline; you would use it to write an essay in which all points were fully explained in clear sentences and in which you paid careful attention to your own literary style. Don't mistake our outline for a complete essay.)

We shall prepare an outline in five sections that, as indicated earlier in the chapter, will be:

i. Introduction

ii. Detailing of flaws

iii. Detailing of good features of the essay

iv. Summary statement, giving overall judgment based on (ii) and (iii)

v. Further implications

Of course, as we emphasized before, there are many possible strategies for responding to an essay such as Kemp's. Our approach here is only one possible one: it is recommended here not as a formula to use in all contexts, but rather as a reasonable way to get started if you are inexperienced.

Here is a sample outline, filled in with reference to specific details about Kemp's essay, as noted on the features list.

SAMPLE OUTLINE FOR RESPONSE TO "MORALITY, ANIMALS, AND THE RIGHT TO LIFE"

i. Introduction

Essay will respond to "Morality, Animals, and the Right to Life," by Rose Kemp. Kemp's essay (1978) was adapted for Govier's textbook, *A Practical Study of Argument* (1992). Kemp: animals have a moral right to life. Her argument: we assume that human beings have this moral right, and that there is no relevant difference between all non-human animals and all human beings to which we can appeal to make us consistent if we deny the right to non-human animals. Reaction to this essay: mixed. It's provocative, clearly written, and somewhat interesting; yet there are some basic flaws in argumentation, both regarding clarification of central thesis and argument for it, and regarding consideration of positions opposed to her own.

ii. Flaws

a. Central claim needs clarifying: all non-human animals or just some? Crucial problem: if it is all animals, the claim is implausible and intolerably impractical, whereas if it is some animals, we aren't told which ones and how to distinguish.

b. Defense of claim that all human beings have a moral right to life? We are only told that we all assume this. The argument is an appeal for consistency. We could become consistent by revising our beliefs about human beings' right to life. Why not? Kemp doesn't say.

c. Counterarguments. Only Passmore seems to be dealt with seriously. Are there no other serious counterarguments? Kemp should deal with allegation that it would be totally impractical for humans to respect a right to life on the part of all animals. Also, she should deal with claim that even though both animals and humans have a right to life, the right to life of humans outweighs that of animals. Not enough counterarguments are taken seriously.

d. Flaws in argument: Straw man re "humans are human": does anybody really say this? Kemp follows Singer, who only argues against this view by stipulating a negative name for it: "speciesism"; a kind of appeal to Singer's authority seems to be working here. Also reply to Passmore could be strengthened by using an example other than children. Children do grow up to be in reciprocal relation with the adults who have cared for them, so Passmore could fit the case of children into his theory by saying that they are potentially reciprocal members of a moral community. The case of the seriously mentally handicapped might be a more convincing example to argue against Passmore. They are typically seen as having moral status even though they do not reciprocate and never will.

    e. Minor flaw: no documentation regarding Schweitzer, Singer, Passmore. No direct quotations. No details regarding animal suffering in labs or factory farms. Detail and documentation would make essay more vivid and convincing.

iii. Good features

    a. Interesting, readable essay about an important subject.

    b. Challenging argument, gives lots to think about. If we are going to restrict conclusion to some animals, we sure have to think about which ones; also, we really do, as she says, believe in a human right to life. We have to think about that too.

    c. Gives knowledge of what some important other people have said about an important problem.

    d. Well organized, consistent, coherent, clearly written, grammatical. Style is unpretentious and interesting. Straightforward fair language, on the whole.

iv. Summary statement

Reaction is mixed: although the essay is enjoyable and teaches and challenges the reader, its arguments and, to a lesser extent, its presentation could have been strengthened in significant ways as described above: clearer more qualified conclusion, subargument for premise about human right to life, broader consideration of counterarguments, more accurate refutation of Passmore, and more documented, specific information about how animals are mistreated.

v. Further implications

Reader will remember and appreciate this essay: challenging. What is the human moral right to life and where does it come from? If only some humans or some animals have a moral right to life, which ones are they and why? How would we have to revise our lifestyle to properly acknowledge these rights and how practical would such revisions be? Don't know the answers to these questions, but Kemp's essay shows they are interesting and important.

We shall not go through the next stage of essay writing, where you fill in your outline with fuller, more complete sentences and arguments and with illustrations and other features designed to add interest and further evidence for the claims noted in point form in your outline. Obviously, this stage is something each writer will complete in his or her own way. Using a detailed outline makes it easier to write an essay that is logically ordered and touches on all the points you want to include from working with your features list.

Checking Your Work

Needless to say, when you have finished writing your essay, you have to check your own work—not only for spelling, grammar, style, and accuracy, but for readability, interest, accuracy of claims, and quality of argument. In fact, you can use the features list given here as a checklist for editing your own essay—in addition to reflecting on your own arguments using the ARG conditions.

It is often hard to read your own work in this way; as its author, you tend to be too close to it to be able to read it from a detached, critical point of view. Just *trying* to read your own work from the point of view of a critic is worthwhile and illuminating, however; you will probably find some errors that you are able to eliminate in preparing the final version of your work. You may do better as your own critic and editor if you allow a few days between writing a draft essay and editing it.

❖   ## CHAPTER SUMMARY

For the most part, this book has emphasized the analysis and evaluation of fairly short arguments—those of a few sentences or, at most, a few paragraphs in length. For the concepts and skills you have learned here to be useful in further work you will do—both inside and outside universities and colleges—you need to adapt these techniques so as to be able to apply them to longer works. We have tried, in this chapter, to assist you in beginning this process by describing a technique for appraising an essay-length work.

To use argument analysis and evaluation for a whole essay, you must be selective. You cannot carefully work through every single argument in the essay using the ARG conditions, because that would take too long and—if used as the basis for your own work—probably bore your readers unbearably. You read the essay several times, first empathetically, to gain a good understanding and determine what its central claim, or thesis, and core supporting argument are. You can then employ a list of salient features—we call it the features list—to look for details on the basis of which you will evaluate the essay. Checking through the features list, you note the good and bad aspects of logical argument and organization, and also some of the literary features of the work. Then you consider the list and make a tentative judgment as to whether you would classify the essay as good, mixed, or poor.

You prepare an outline in which you organize and (if necessary) further select which of the noted features you wish to discuss in your own responsive essay. On the basis of your outline, you write your response. When your own essay is done, you can use your understanding of the ARG conditions and the features list to check your own work. Before writing a final version of your essay, you should be your own editor—not just for spelling and grammar but for these other aspects as well.

The methods described in this chapter are guidelines that we think are useful for those who are beginning. Experienced writers will have their own personal approaches and strategies. The guidelines here are not meant to be rigid rules: we offer, for those who might need it, a way to begin.

❖ REVIEW OF TERMS INTRODUCED

Selective   Refers to the fact that only some claims and arguments can be treated when you write an essay responding to another essay or longer work.

Empathetic reading   Reading where the reader tries to enter into the thinking of the author, to enter into the author's point of view as though it were the reader's own. As described here, empathetic reading is used as a device for coming to understand just what it is that the author is trying to say.

Thesis   The main point or main conclusion of a longer work.

Core thesis argument   The main argument offered by an author for his or her central claim or thesis. The core thesis argument is stated in the form "Essentially, X says C because R" where X is the author, C is the central claim, and R are the reasons, or premises, put forward to support that central claim. The word *essentially* reflects the fact that you must be selective in stating the core thesis argument.

Inexplicit essay   Essay that makes its point indirectly, sometimes by satire or ridicule, or by redescription. The inexplicit essay has no explicitly, or directly, stated thesis or core supporting argument. Often, however, it is possible to attribute a thesis or supporting argument to the author.

Confused or contradictory essay   Essay that has no thesis because it is too unclear or contradictory to make any definite point.

Critical reading   Reading, after the first empathetic readings, in which the reader notes good and poor aspects of a work. A features list may be used to assist in this process.

Features list   Checklist of aspects to look for when reading critically. Features (1) to (7) are, in a broad sense, logical; features (8) to (10) are, in a broad sense, stylistic or literary. A reader may wish to add further aspects to this list. Features specified in the chapter are:

1. Interest, importance, and plausibility of thesis
2. Quality of core supporting argument
3. Apparent quality of further arguments
4. Accuracy

5. Clarity and organization
6. Coherence and consistency
7. Balance
8. Word choice
9. Grammatical structures
10. Impact

Heuristic device or strategy Device or technique adopted to give preliminary guidance. A heuristic device is not based on fixed and absolute rules. It can be adapted or even abandoned when it ceases to serve its purpose.

Appreciative essay Essay in response to another that you think is basically good.

Mixed reaction essay Essay in response to another to which you have a mixed response.

Negatively critical essay Essay in response to another that you think is basically poor.

Note

1. Bob Bragg, "Isn't Biotechnology Wonderful?"
Calgary *Herald,* May 17, 1987.

A Summary of Fallacies

MANY TEXTS ON PRACTICAL LOGIC HAVE a separate chapter on fallacies. Because we wished to explain the various fallacies against the background of the appropriate related standards of good reasoning, we have not treated fallacies in any single chapter. As a result, there is no one place where various fallacies are collected together. For your convenience, here is a list of the various fallacies treated in this text, together with a brief definition of each one, and a reference to the chapter in which it is explained in more detail. This set of brief explanations is provided only as a convenient summary and tool for remembering the fallacies; it is not a substitute for the more complete treatment given each fallacy in the appropriate section of the text.

Ad Hominem (Chapter 6) An ad hominem argument is an argument in which a premise or premises about a person's character or background are used to cast doubt on his argument or theory, and in which those premises are irrelevant to the merits of the position taken. Premises of such a type are irrelevant, except in the very special case where those theories and arguments happen to be about the person himself. But specific points about a person's background may bear on the reliability of his testimony or the legitimacy of his authority. In that case they may be relevant to our decision whether to accept claims on his testimony or authority, even though they are not directly relevant to the question of whether those claims are true or false. To reason from premises about the background, personality, or character of people to substantive conclusions about their arguments or theories is to commit the ad hominem fallacy, unless the premises are relevant to the conclusion in one of the ways just described. Abusive ad hominem arguments attack the character or background of an arguer; circumstantial ad hominem arguments attack the arguer's circumstances or actions.

Affirming the Consequent (Chapter 8) An argument having the form "$P \supset Q$; Q; therefore, P" is an instance of the fallacy of affirming the consequent. For example, "if you are overweight, you are unhealthy. You are unhealthy. Therefore, you are overweight." The mistake comes in affirming the consequent of a conditional and believing that from the conditional and the consequent one may infer the antecedent of the conditional. This is not a valid form of argument, as you can see from testing it on a truth table. Probably it seems valid due to its superficial similarity to "P; $P \supset Q$; therefore, Q" (*modus ponens*), which is valid.

Appeal to Popularity (Chapter 6) A fallacy that occurs when premises describing the popularity of a product or belief are used to justify a conclusion that states, or requires, that the product or belief has real merits. Such arguments are fallacious because popularity is irrelevant to real merits. This fallacy is sometimes called the *bandwagon appeal* or the *fallacy of jumping on a bandwagon*. It is also a fallacy to infer lack of merit from unpopularity.

Authority (Chapters 5 and 6) An appeal to authority is fallacious when any one of the following conditions is satisfied:

1. The claim, P, which the arguer is trying to justify, does not fall within a subject area that constitutes a recognized body of knowledge.

2. The person cited as an authority is not an expert within the particular subject area in which the claim, P, falls—even though he or she may be an expert about some other area of knowledge.

3. Even though the claim, P, falls within an area of knowledge and even though the person cited as an authority is an expert in that particular area, it so happens that the experts in that area disagree as to whether or not P is true.

4. The person cited as an authority has a vested interest in the issue of whether P is true—either because he or she is paid by another interested party or because he or she has some other personal stake in the matter.

Begging the Question (Chapter 5) Begging the question is a fallacy that occurs when the premise or premises either state the conclusion (usually in slightly different words) or logically presuppose that the conclusion is true. The conclusion cannot get any real support from the premise or premises because it needs to be accepted in order for those premises to be accepted. In a cogent argument, the premises have a greater initial acceptability than the conclusion—they should be more acceptable, to the intended audience, than the conclusion. When an argument begs the question, the logical relationship between the question-begging premise and the conclusion is so close that this greater acceptability is simply not possible. Example: The best jobs are those that pay the highest salaries, because the only good thing about a job is the money you can make from it.

Causal Slippery Slope (Chapter 10) In this type of argument it is alleged in the premises that a proposed action—which, considered in itself, might seem good—

would set off a series of further actions culminating in calamity. For this reason, it is concluded that the proposed action is wrong or should not be done. The idea behind the reasoning is that someone who undertakes the proposed action will unwittingly set off a series of effects, which will be disastrous. The proposed action is, therefore, the first step down a slippery slope to hell. The problem with such arguments occurs when the causal claim in the premises is not properly substantiated. Actually the argument amounts to a kind of scare tactic: the series of dreadful effects is invented by the arguer, who has no real foundation for his causal premise asserting that the proposed action will lead to these effects.

Confusing Correlation and Cause (Chapter 10) A correlational statement tells you that two things are associated. For instance, being a drinker is positively correlated with having high blood pressure if a higher proportion of drinkers than nondrinkers have high blood pressure. A causal statement tells you that one thing produces, or helps to produce, another. Since a positive correlation may exist for various reasons, you cannot simply infer a causal relationship from such a correlation. If there is a correlation between being A and being B, then there are four possible explanations for the correlation: either A causes B, or B causes A, or something else causes both A and B, or the correlation is an accident. Since three of these four possibilities do not involve A being the cause of B, it is a fallacy to infer that A causes B from the fact that A is positively correlated with B.

Denying the Antecedent (Chapter 8) An argument having the form "$P \supset Q; -P$; therefore $-Q$" is an instance of the formal fallacy of denying the antecedent. For example, "If machines can think, machines can correct some of their own mistakes. Machines cannot think; therefore, machines cannot correct some of their own mistakes." Someone who reasons this way thinks that by asserting a conditional and denying its antecedent, you can properly infer that the consequent is false also. This inference is a mistake, as a truth table analysis will reveal. Probably the inference seems plausible because it superficially resembles "$P \supset Q; -Q$; therefore $-P$" (*modus tollens*), which is a deductively valid inference.

Equivocation (Chapter 4) A fallacy of equivocation is committed when a key word in an argument is used in two or more senses and the premises appear to support the conclusion only because the senses are not distinguished. The argument is likely to seem cogent if the ambiguity is not noticed.

False Dichotomy (Chapters 7 and 8) A false dichotomy is not, all by itself, a fallacy; it is simply a false belief. Believing in false dichotomies may easily lead to faults in argument, however, because a false dichotomy can be a key premise in deductively valid arguments that are extremely convincing due to their logical validity. A false dichotomy is a statement of the type "it is either X or Y," where the two alternatives X and Y do not exhaust the possibilities. For instance, to say that a man must be either ugly or handsome is to construct a false dichotomy; people can be of average or moderate attractiveness. One common source of false dichotomies is mistaking contrary predicates (such as, for example, thin and fat) for contradictory predicates (such as, for example, thin and non-thin).

A dichotomy will always hold if it is based on the purely logical opposition of contradictory predicates: that is, a person will always be either X or non-X, for any predicate X. But a predicate Y that is in some general sense the opposite of X is often not its logical contradictory. For example, *unhappy* is the opposite, but not the logical contradictory of *happy; ugly* is the opposite, but not the logical contradictory of *beautiful* and so on. False dichotomies may be due to our tendency to oversimplify: we tend to see the world in black and white. The disjunctive statements that are the foundation of valid dilemma arguments are often false dichotomies due to this source. Consider, for example, "Either there will be a war in the Middle East or Israel will give full civil rights to its Arab population." This statement may be superficially plausible, but it is a false dichotomy since it ignores other possibilities—for instance, struggling along with the present situation.

Faulty Analogy (Chapter 9) A faulty analogy is an argument by analogy in which the similarities between the primary subject and the analogue (two things compared) are too superficial to support the conclusion. The two things have only a very loose and general similarity, and there are enough relevant differences between them that the comparison can lend no credibility to the conclusion. Analogies like this do no more than suggest an image in which we can think of a topic, and are often seriously misleading, especially when the analogue is something toward which we have very strong attitudes or feelings.

Guilt by Association (Chapter 6) The fallacy of guilt by association is committed when a person or her views are criticized on the basis of a supposed link between that person and a group or movement that is believed by the arguer and the audience to be disreputable. The poor reputation of any group is irrelevant to the substantive correctness either of its own views or of the views of any member of the group. Needless to say, it is certainly irrelevant to the substantive correctness of the views of those people or groups who are only very loosely associated with it.

Hasty Inductive Generalization (Chapter 10) A hasty inductive generalization occurs when a person generalizes from a single anecdote or experience, or from a sample that is too small or too unrepresentative to support his conclusion. Too narrow a range of human experience is taken as a basis for reaching a conclusion about all experiences of a given type. The fallacy occurs when we either forget the need to obtain a representative sample or too quickly assume that a small or biased sample is representative. For example, "boys are more temperamental than girls, because my two sons were far more difficult to bring up than my three daughters."

Ignorance (Chapter 6) Fallacious appeals to ignorance are arguments in which the premises describe our ignorance regarding a proposition, P, and the conclusion makes a substantive claim about the truth or falsity of *P*. Often, not-*P* is inferred from our ignorance of *P*, or *P* is inferred from our ignorance of not-*P*. For instance, people may infer from the fact that we don't know there are no ghosts that there are ghosts; or they may move from the fact that an event has no known natural cause to the conclusion that it has a supernatural cause. Such inferences are fallacious because our ignorance is irrelevant to the issue of the substantive truth, or even the substantive probability, of claims.

Objectionable Cause (Chapter 10) The fallacy of objectionable cause occurs when a reasoner imposes a causal interpretation on a set of events and makes no attempt to rule out alternative explanations of those events. Sometimes this fallacy is called *false cause*. We changed the name because you do not always get the cause wrong by this procedure. You may be right, but it will be by accident. In effect, reasoning to a cause too hastily, as in objectionable cause, goes like this: "*A* occurred; *B* occurred; *A* and *B* can plausibly be connected; therefore, *A* caused *B*." The pattern of argument is fallacious because there may be other explanations of the joint occurrence of *A* and *B*, and no basis is given in this kind of argument to rule out alternatives.

Post Hoc (Chapter 10) This is the fallacy of reasoning that simply because one thing precedes another, it must have caused it. Or, to put it differently, you reason that because *A* preceded *B*, then *A* must have caused *B*. The argument is a fallacy because it takes far more than mere succession in time to justify a causal conclusion. The conclusion states that *A* produced, or brought about, *B*; and the premise gives information only about sequence in time. To know that one thing causes another, you have to know that the sequence in time is typical and that the causal relation that you allege is the best explanation of the fact that the two elements occurred together. To know that the causal relation is the best explanation, you have to have a basis for ruling out other explanations.

Slippery Assimilation (Chapter 9) The fallacy of slippery assimilation occurs when someone reasons that because there is a series of cases differing only slightly from each other, all cases in the series are the same. For example, "Because there is a gradual progression, ounce by ounce, from weighing 100 pounds to weighing 300 pounds, there is no one spot where you can draw the line between being thin and being fat. Therefore, everyone is really fat." (Or, alternatively, everyone is really thin.) The fallacy here occurs because the argument proceeds as though differences that are separately insignificant could not cumulate to be significant. Obviously, as the weight example indicates, they can. The argument may show that there will be borderline cases, but it does not show that there is no distinction to be drawn. Cases are falsely assimilated in this argument.

Slippery Precedent (Chapter 9) In slippery precedent arguments a case that is acknowledged to be good, or deserving, when considered alone, is rejected on the grounds that it would set a precedent for permitting further cases that are not good or deserving. The premises compare the case in question to further cases, maintain that the cases in question would set a precedent for allowing those further cases, and claim that the further cases are bad. The conclusion rejects the case in question; what was initially deserving has become undeserving on the grounds that it would set a bad precedent. Slippery precedent arguments have inconsistent premises, because a case that is good cannot set a precedent for others that are bad. There must necessarily be a relevant difference between the cases that are compared, and this relevant difference is neglected in the premises of the argument, which slide from the initial case to the other ones as though there were no relevant difference between them.

Straw Man (Chapter 6) The straw man fallacy is committed when a person misrepresents the argument or theory of another person and then, on the basis of his misrepresentation, purports to refute the real argument or theory. The refutation is irrelevant to the merits of the real theory because the view in question has been misdescribed. The way to avoid straw man is to interpret the writings and sayings of other people carefully and accurately and to make sure that you take a strong and representative version of any general theory you criticize.

Two Wrongs Make a Right (Chapter 9) In this fallacious argument we see a misplaced appeal to consistency. A person is urged to accept, or condone, one thing that is wrong because another similar thing, also wrong, has occurred, or has been accepted and condoned. For example: "It is all right for the United States to support regimes that torture people because after all there is also torture in countries not supported by the United States." The line of argument is fallacious because it would have us perpetuate evil in order to be consistent. If one thing is bad and another thing is bad, then the conclusion to be reached is that both are bad. And ideally both should be prevented. If both cannot be prevented, then we must do what we can to prevent what we can control. The "two wrongs" argument seems to rely on the supposition that the world is a better place with sets of similar wrongs in it than it would be with some of these wrongs corrected and the others left in place. But there is no point in multiplying wrongs just to preserve consistency.

Undistributed Middle (Chapter 7) The fallacy of the undistributed middle is committed in a categorical syllogism in which the middle term is not distributed in at least one of the premises. The middle term is the term that appears in both premises of a syllogism, and it is distributed when it appears in such a way that it applies to all things within the category that the term designates. The subject term is distributed in *A* (universal affirmative) and *E* (universal negative) statements, and the predicate term is distributed in *E* (universal negative) and *O* (particular negative) statements. An example of the fallacy of the undistributed middle is "All teachers are prompt; all lawyers are prompt; therefore, all lawyers are teachers." Here the middle term, *prompt*, is not distributed in either premise. The syllogism is invalid.

Vagueness (Chapter 4) Vagueness arises when a word, as used, has a meaning that is insufficiently clear to convey the necessary information in that context of use. If a statement is expressed in vague language, and there is no clue in the context as to what it is supposed to mean, then we cannot tell whether the statement is true or false, because we will not have an adequate understanding of it. Vagueness as such is a fault when it goes to this point, but it is not as such a fallacy. Vagueness contributes to mistakes in reasoning when key terms are not precise enough in the context for us to judge whether the premises and conclusions are acceptable. As used in the argument, the terms are not sufficiently precise to enable us to understand the boundaries of their application. Arguments can trade on vagueness by using terms that cannot be pinned down sufficiently; meanings may become so indeterminate that we go along with the argument simply because we don't know exactly what is being said. At this point vagueness contributes to mistaken judgments about the merits of reasoning.

APPENDIX B

Selected Essays for Analysis

EDUCATION FOR SALE

J. M. McMurty

YOU DON'T HAVE to be a Platonist to know that the free market and education do not have the same methods—or goals. In the free market, you aim to maximize money profit. You do so by providing or producing whatever people want, at whatever price you can get, from whomever has the money to buy it. Education doesn't do any of these things. If it's any good, it challenges all of them. It opposes the sharing of knowledge to private profit, the development of understanding to the gratification of wants, and disinterested instruction to the sales pitch.

Yet the free market, we are told, is the way of the world, and the necessity of the future for all. Even the Evil Empire is submitting at last to its iron laws, and every other people and region from the Inuit to the world's rain forests are willingly or not being required to conform to its universal invisible hand.

So it should come as no surprise that education too is being brought into team-spirited dedication to the new Categorical Imperative of Life on Earth: "learning to compete in the tough new international marketplace."

Compete at what? Well, compete to produce and sell commodities cheaper and more profitably to those people in the world with enough money to buy and consume what multinationals sell.

That isn't the logic of learning, of thinking deeper than the idols of the marketplace. But if we are to believe what we now read and hear everywhere, it is. It's the new "new reality." Even University and faculty presidents now advocate the value of higher education itself on the grounds that it's . . . "required to compete in the international marketplace." The incantation is heard from Harvard to Hong Kong.

In other words, the academy's leadership now finally agrees with the captains of capital accumulation. Education is a *means,* and is to be valued as a means for a higher and overriding goal: more world-wide profit-making for one's country's multinational corporations. They now ring out this declaration of the one true faith of the corporate transculture from the ivory tower itself.

Of course, today's University administrations and faculty are over a barrel. If they are to carry on in this brave new world, they have to "adapt." They too must dedicate themselves to the annunciated creed of the bigger big business like everyone else—the politicians, the arts companies and museums, the Opus Dei, the third-world generals, the pay-as-you-pray religions, and the new East-bloc. If not, you can be sure that the mind-steering joint stock company of business investment and advertisement, the corporate mass-media, will trumpet their transgression from the global pulpit. "They're not facing the new reality," the promulgations of the new order will admonish. "They will continue to be underfunded until they do." Third-world debtor or philosopher scholar, it makes no difference. The free market will prevail.

The response of the universities to the advent of the new reality has, from the top down, been acquiescent. By and large they have run for cover. Remaining independent of the demands of commerce and the Furies of private profit was once a cherished duty and vocation. But now the universities and their researchers are climbing down. They're "establishing links with the business community," and jumping into the new game as players for sale. They are survivors. Take a look around. Who *isn't* trying to sell whatever idea or day's sweat or third-world country they have to the multinational market? These days you sell to the great takeover whatever you can to buy a life.

The New Totalitarianism

We of the modern world have long thought of the base-values of everything as its "capital," and of freedom as an "open marketplace" where, in the famous formula of Friedrich Hayek, "all are free to sell and buy at any price at which they can find a partner to the transaction . . . free to produce, buy and sell anything that can be produced or sold at all." In recent years, the language has become more explicitly corporate. It's "the bottom line" and being "internationally competitive" which rule. It's crept up on us. Now it's so deep in the mind-set that even the once critical "pointy-headed intellectuals" in the University presuppose the laws of international commodification as the ultimate framework of reality. They can't talk about what used to interrogate the status quo, higher learning, without translating it first into the going jargon of the corporate cul-

ture to ensure it makes sense to the Big Buyer out there. "Resource units" for what used to be subject disciplines and their professors. "Clients" and "customers" for what used to be students. "Uniform standards" for what used to be the search for quality, depth, originality. "Program packages" for what used to be education. "Products" for what used to be graduates. Corporate foundations, grants, and prizes trade-naming every academic recognition that's left. "Credibility" for what used to be "truth."

The unspeakable fact is: *The corporate culture has become totalitarian.* In the precise sense of the term. Its influence and control has been totalized so that all opposition is subsumed by it and reconstituted as one of its organs. There have been many fronts of movement in this reincorporation of the world. The military corporation takeover of social and government spending from the United States to Indonesia. The PACs' corporate takeover of electoral politics from developer-run city councils to multi-national controlled Presidents. The corporate media's takeover of all levels of public communication from the television screen to the University textbook. The corporate transformation of culture from sport to museums into marketing sites for big-business images.

Then, to forestall any resistance to these advances of corporate command, there's the political economy of cutback. The export of manufacture to cheap and obedient Asian labour and the deunionization of the working class. The transfer of tax burdens from the rich onto the middle and poorer classes. The breaking of the insurgent third world on the wheel of debt-interest payments. The underfunding of social and environmental agencies across the "newly competitive" world. And the "privatization" expropriation of the profitable public sector.

Together, these takeovers and cutbacks have formed an unmistakable pattern. For the regions of the globe still independent of the corporate economy, there has been a more open appeal to armed force. "Spending the Soviet Union broke" with threats of Armageddon and weapons build-up, and sending armies of goons called "freedom fighters" into newly socialist states. In this way, the political and economic base of a corporate totalization of power has been won which has transformed even official enemies and oppositions into yesteryear's losers. We have heard the pieces fall, but not seen the overall design.

As with 1930's fascism, only this time by the "discipline" of the multinational market rather than the nation-state jackboot, the Universities too have been made to jump into line. Sell to the multinational market or . . . you do not survive. Even here in Canada, (recently sold by the Free Trade Deal to the U.S. in exchange for unrestricted access by Canadian multinationals to the U.S. market), the country's leading religious philosopher is crowned a "Molson's Scholar." Universities in the country's largest province have negotiated to sell their library holdings to private corporations. Classroom textbooks have passed under the control of multinational conglomerates. Business schools and programs swagger into ever larger numbers and

facilities. And University administrators tubthump new corporate "links" as higher education's salvation.

The Real Meaning

The real meaning of Ronald Reagan's presidential election war-cry back in 1980 "to get government off our backs" is now clear. It meant: "No public-sector limit to the power of the corporations." As we know the ex-master of ceremonies for General Electric, number one producer of illegal toxic waste sites in America, fronted this liquidation of social limits well. His business regime's policies of systematic secrecy, ubiquitous deregulation, Supreme Court loading, social program decimation, and turnover of government decisions and finances to the weapons producing corporations, and any other bigbusiness interest his administration could get on side with, rode big holes through what few institutional constraints on total corporate power

CONTRADICTIONS IN PRINCIPLE BETWEEN THE MARKET AND EDUCATION MODELS

	Market Model	Education Model
Goal	To maximize private money profits	To advance and disseminate shared knowledge
Motivation	To satisfy the wants of whoever has the money to purchase the goods that are wanted	To develop the understanding of all who seek to learn.
Method	To buy or sell the goods it has to offer to anyone for whatever price one can get.	Never to sell the good it has to offer, but to require of all who would have it that they fulfill its requirements independently.
Standards of Excellence	(1) How well a product-line is made to sell against its competitors; (2) How problem-free the product is and remains for its buyer.	(1) How inclusive is the range of possibility that is comprehended; (2) How deep and broad the problems are to the one who has it.
Logics of Freedom	No bounds to what one is able to buy from others.	No bounds to what one is able to learn for oneself.

there were in the Republic. It is true, few burdens of public interest were left on the backs of big business. But as important to the reproductive cycle of a nation, the Reagan regime and the corporate media effectively teamed up to stampede all critical voices into a corner of public impotence. The press, ever more monopolized by the same multinational hands which Reagan mouthpieced and the Democrats, bankrolled or publicized by the same corporate culture, ceased to oppose anything that was going on. The only institutional place left in the feedback cycle of the nation's intelligence that might be counted on to pose a critical response to the swift, unpublicized totalization of big-business power over America's life, was the cross-country network of higher-learning establishments—the Universities. But their principal agents were too busy scrambling in the wake of the public sector cutback to get on board the nation's grand mission of selling to big business to sell to the world. Remember how it all started? With what Reagan's first Treasury Secretary David Stockman later revealed was a deliberate monetary crisis by high-interest rates to make the continued financing of the public sector a millstone around taxpayer's necks. Reagan's government "got off their backs" too, but by jumping two-footed on them first.

And so higher education too has adapted to the "new reality" as a willing research and training organ of the World Corporation Empire. University administrators, grant-benefactors and multinational text-producers anxious to gear their "services," "packages," and "products" to the new academic program of being competitively for sale in the multinational market.

It is an ecumenical mission.

But a point needs to be made about education before its absorption into the system of world product mandate is complete.

No-one, it seems, has dared to notice yet, in public, that the logic of education and of the corporate market are in fundamental contradiction. An education, unlike a commodity in the free market, cannot be bought or sold (despite the best-selling sycophancy of Alan Bloom in his aptly titled *The Closing of the American Mind* which approves of higher education only if it's for the rich). Education has an opposite logic to the free market. It is earned, not purchased; studied for by oneself, not produced by others; an internal development, not an external product; and a value in itself, not a medium for profit.

An education can never come, as every corporate commodity claims to, "problem free." The better it is, the deeper and tougher the problems it poses to the one who has it. Unlike any commercial product, an education cannot be "instant" or "ready-made" for its users. Nor can it be "guaranteed replacement" or "repaired cost-free." It cannot, in truth, be "produced" for, or "delivered to" or "reliably serviced" by another at all. As in learning how to think and write, it can only be achieved by one's own work, and it does not keep past the continuous demands it puts on its bearer. To say that it is consumed is a contradiction in terms, and if it is "sold on the open market," it's a fraud.

As for the principles of freedom governing education and the market, what is the best policy for selling a product—to offend no-one and no vested interest—is, as every definition of academic freedom recognizes, the worst possible policy for an institution seeking to advance and disseminate learning and truth.

The great irony of this greatest corporate takeover of all is that its imposition everywhere is sold as "*anti*-totalitarian," as "*freedom*" for all. The deepest signal of its success in stilling our capacity to think past it, is that we have come to assume this logic of the World Corporation Empire as an organizing principle of mind.

J. M. McMurty teaches in the Department of Philosophy, University of Guelph. Reprinted with permission of the author.

A RIGHT TO DISCRIMINATE?

Thomas Hurka

HALL THOMPSON'S LOOSE lips cost ABC-TV a lot of money. The founder of the Shoal Creek Golf Club in Birmingham, Ala., the site of the Professional Golfers Association Championship this month, told a reporter his club does not admit black members. In the ensuing uproar, several sponsors withdrew from ABC's tournament coverage, leaving a shortfall of more than $2-million.

Shoal Creek's practice is not unusual. A Philadelphia newspaper surveyed 34 leading golf clubs around that city and found that all 34 have no black members. Of the 21 clubs scheduled to play host to major championships in the United States over the next five years, 15 now admit no blacks and at least one admits no women.

Nor is this practice illegal, either in the United States or in most provinces of Canada. Most provincial human-rights laws forbid discrimination in the provision of goods and services "customarily available to the public." Under the current interpretation, the last phrase exempts private clubs. (The exception is Ontario, whose anti-discrimination law is not restricted to "public" services. But Ontario has a clause allowing recreational clubs to discriminate on the basis of sex.)

There are some areas where discrimination clearly must be illegal. It would be intolerable if government, or landlords and companies operating in the public economy, withheld services on the basis of race or sex. Normal accommodation and jobs must be equally available to all.

But there are also areas where discrimination, however distasteful, must be allowed. If someone uses racial criteria in deciding whom to marry or ask to dinner, the law should not interfere in this private choice. The same goes for some choices about accommodation and jobs. Provincial human-rights laws contain exemptions for people renting out rooms to boarders who will share their bathroom and kitchen, or hiring a private nurse to tend them at home. These, too, fall within a private sphere.

Where does a members-only golf club fit on the scale from public to private? Is it more like a company offering services to the public? Or a group of friends associating with people they find congenial?

The issue is complicated because there are different ways of defining privacy. One test looks at a club's admission procedures. If these are rigorous, checking new members seriously for compatibility with old ones, the club is private. A second looks at the club's functions or activities. Only if these are not commercial or business-related is the club private.

Those who think golf clubs shouldn't be allowed to discriminate use the second test. They note that a club isn't just a place to hit a little ball. It's where a city's elite congregate, where they make business contacts and deals. To be excluded from it is to be shut out from full participation in commercial life.

This argument is less compelling for a golf club than for a business one, such as the Petroleum Club in Calgary which, until recently, excluded women. Golf clubs do have a largely sporting function, but membership offers more than golfing privileges. Many people join these clubs, especially the exclusive ones, partly for the contacts they can make. Also, the privacy argument is weaker here. Sharing a fairway with someone you don't like is hardly as intimate as sharing your home.

When so much in business depends on whom you know, what looks private can in effect be public. Given this, the freedom of association that protects informal gatherings shouldn't be extended to formal clubs, where mere admission can confer status. A law committed to equality should require these clubs to be open to all.

Of course, legality isn't the only issue: things the law should allow can be immoral and worth fighting by other means. (If someone won't dine with blacks, you shouldn't dine with him.) Stung by the Shoal Creek controversy, the PGA will in future hold tournaments only at clubs committed to minority memberships. Let's hope the moral and financial pressure this applies will do as much good as a formal legal ban.

Thomas Hurka teaches philosophy at the University of Calgary. (Thomas Hurka, Globe and Mail, *1990. Reprinted with permission of the author.)*

WORD AND FLESH

Wendell Berry

TOWARD THE END of *As You Like It,* Orlando says: "I can live no longer by thinking." He is ready to marry Rosalind. It is time for incarnation. Having thought too much, he is at one of the limits of human experience, or of human sanity. If his love does put on flesh, we know he must sooner or later arrive at the opposite limit, at which he will say, "I can live no longer without thinking." Thought—even consciousness— seems to live between these limits: the abstract and the particular, the word and the flesh.

All public movements of thought quickly produce a language that works as a code, unless to the extent that it is abstract. It is readily evident, for example, that you can't conduct a relationship with another person in terms of the rhetoric of the civil rights movement or the women's movement—as useful as those rhetorics may initially have been to personal relationships.

The same is true of the environment movement. The favorite adjective of this movement now seems to be "planetary." This word is used, properly enough, to refer to the interdependence of places, and to the recognition, which is desirable and growing, that no place on the earth can be completely healthy until all places are.

But the word "planetary" also refers to an abstract anxiety or an abstract passion that is desperate and useless exactly to the extent that it is abstract. How, after all, can anybody—any particular body—do anything to heal a planet? The suggestion that anybody could do so is preposterous. The heroes of abstraction keep galloping in on their white horses to save the planet—and they keep falling off in front of the grandstand.

What we need, obviously, is a more intelligent—which is to say, a more accurate—description of the problem. The description of a problem as planetary arouses a motivation for which, of necessity, there is no employment. The adjective "planetary" describes a problem in such a way that it cannot be solved. In fact, though we now have serious problems nearly everywhere on the planet, we have no problem that can accurately be described as planetary. And, short of the total annihilation of the human race, there is no planetary solution.

There are also no national, state, or county problems, and no national, state, or county solutions. That will-o'-the-wisp, the large-scale solution to the large-scale problem, which is so dear to governments, universities, and corporations, serves mostly to distract people from the small, private problems that they may, in fact, have the power to solve.

The problems, if we describe them accurately, are all private and small. Or they are so initially.

The problems are our lives. In the "developed" countries, at least, the large problems occur because all of us are living either partly wrong or almost entirely wrong. It was not just the greed of corporate shareholders and the hubris of corporate executives that put the fate of Prince William Sound into one ship; it was also our demand that energy be cheap and plentiful.

The economies of our communities and households are wrong. The answers to the human problems of ecology are to be found in economy. And the answers to the problems of economy are to be found in culture and in character. To fail to see this is to go on dividing the world falsely between guilty producers and innocent consumers.

The planetary versions—the heroic versions—of our problems have attracted great intelligence. But these problems, as they are caused and suffered in our lives, our households, and our communities, have attracted very little intelligence.

There are some notable exceptions. A few people have learned to do a few things better. But it is discouraging to reflect that, though we have been talking about most of our problems for decades, we are still mainly *talking* about them. The civil rights movement has not given us better communities. The women's movement has not given us better marriages or better households. The environment movement has not changed our parasitic relationship to nature.

We have failed to produce new examples of good home and community economies, and we have nearly completed the destruction of the examples we once had. Without examples, we are left with theory and the bureaucracy and meddling that comes with theory. We change our principles, our thoughts, and our words, but these are changes made in the air. Our lives go on unchanged.

For the most part, the subcultures, the countercultures, the dissenters, and the opponents continue mindlessly—or perhaps just helplessly—to follow the pattern of the dominant society in its extravagance, its wastefulness, its dependencies, and its addictions. The old problem remains: How do you get intelligence *out* of an institution or an organization?

My small community in Kentucky has lived and dwindled for at least a century under the influence of four kinds of organizations: governments, corporations, schools, and churches—all of which are distant (either actually or in interest), centralized, and consequently abstract in their concerns.

Governments and corporations (except for employees) have no presence in our community at all, which is perhaps fortunate for us, but we nevertheless feel the indifference or the contempt of governments and corporations for communities such as ours.

We have had no school of our own for nearly thirty years. The school system takes our young people, prepares them for "the world of tomorrow"—which it does not expect to take place in any rural area—and gives back "expert" (that is, extremely generalized) ideas.

The church is present in the town. We have two churches. But both have been used by their denominations, for almost a century, to provide training and income for student ministers, who do not stay long enough even to become disillusioned.

For a long time, then, the minds that have most influenced our town have not been *of* the town and so have not tried even to perceive, much less to honor, the good possibilities that

are there. They have not wondered on what terms a good and conserving life might be lived there. In this my community is not unique but is like almost every other neighborhood in our country and in the "developed" world.

The question that *must* be addressed, therefore, is not how to care for the planet, but how to care for each of the planet's millions of human and natural neighborhoods, each of its millions of small pieces and parcels of land, each one of which is in some precious way different from all the others. Our understandable wish to preserve the planet must somehow be reduced to the scale of our competence—that is, to the wish to preserve all of its humble households and neighborhoods.

What can accomplish this reduction? I will say again, without overweening hope but with certainty nonetheless, that only love can do it. Only love can bring intelligence out of the institutions and organizations, where it aggrandizes itself, into the presence of the work that must be done.

Love is never abstract. It does not adhere to the universe or the planet or the nation or the institution or the profession, but to the singular sparrows of the street, the lilies of the field, "the least of these my brethren." Love is not, by its own desire, heroic. It is heroic only when compelled to be. It exists by its willingness to be anonymous, humble, and unrewarded.

The older love becomes, the more clearly it understands its involvement in partiality, imperfection, suffering, and mortality. Even so, it longs for incarnation. It can live no longer by thinking.

And yet to put on flesh and do the flesh's work, it must think.

In his essay on Kipling, George Orwell wrote: "All left-wing parties in the highly industrialized countries are at bottom a sham, because they make it their business to fight against something which they do not really wish to destroy. They have internationalist aims, and at the same time they struggle to keep up a standard of life with which those aims are incompatible. We all live by robbing Asiatic coolies, and those of us who are 'enlightened' all maintain that those coolies ought to be set free; but our standard of living, and hence our 'enlightenment,' demands that the robbery shall continue."

This statement of Orwell's is clearly applicable to our situation now; all we need to do is change a few nouns. The religion and the environmentalism of the highly industrialized countries are at bottom a sham, because they make it their business to fight against something that they do not really wish to destroy. We all live by robbing nature, but our standard of living demands that the robbery shall continue.

We must achieve the character and acquire the skills to live much poorer than we do. We must waste less. We must do more for ourselves and each other. It is either that or continue merely to think and talk about changes that we are inviting catastrophe to make.

The great obstacle is simply this: the conviction that we cannot change because we are dependent on what is wrong. But that is the addict's excuse, and we know that it will not do.

How dependent, in fact, are we? How dependent are our neighborhoods and communities? How might our dependencies be reduced? To answer these questions will require better thoughts and better deeds than we have been capable of so far.

We must have the sense and the courage, for example, to see that the ability to transport food for hundreds or thousands of miles does not necessarily mean that we are well off. It means that the food supply is more vulnerable and more costly than a local food supply would be. It means that consumers do not control or influence the healthfulness of their food supply and that they are at the mercy of the people who have the control and influence. It means that, in eating, people are using large quantities of petroleum that other people in another time are almost certain to need.

Our most serious problem, perhaps, is that we have become a nation of fantasists. We believe, apparently, in the infinite availability of finite resources. We persist in land-use methods that reduce the potentially infinite power of soil fertility to a finite quantity, which we then proceed to waste as if it were an infinite quantity. We have an economy that depends not on the quality and quantity of necessary goods and services but on the moods of a few stockbrokers. We believe that democratic freedom can be preserved by people ignorant of the history of democracy and indifferent to the responsibilities of freedom.

Our leaders have been for many years as oblivious to the realities and dangers of their time as were George III and Lord North. They believe that the difference between war and peace is still the overriding political difference—when, in fact, the difference has diminished to the point of insignificance. How would you describe the difference between modern war and modern industry—between, say, bombing and strip mining, or between chemical warfare and chemical manufacturing? The difference seems to be only that in war the victimization of humans is directly intentional and in industry it is "accepted" as a "trade-off."

Were the catastrophes of Love Canal, Bhopal, Chernobyl, and the *Exxon Valdez* episodes of war or of peace? They were, in fact, peacetime acts of aggression, intentional to the extent that the risks were known and ignored.

We are involved unremittingly in a war not against "foreign enemies," but against the world, against our freedom, and indeed against our existence. Our so-called industrial accidents should be looked upon as revenges of Nature. We forget that Nature is necessarily party to all our enterprises and that she imposes conditions of her own.

Now she is plainly saying to us: "If you put the fates of whole communities or cities or regions or ecosystems at risk in single ships or factories or power plants, then I will furnish the drunk or the fool or the imbecile who will make the necessary small mistake."

Wendell Berry, from What Are People For? *San Francisco: North Point Press, 1990). Copyright © 1990 by Wendell Berry. Reprinted with permission.*

THE WAR ON (SOME) DRUGS

Stephen Jay Gould

CATEGORIES OFTEN EXERT a tyranny over our perceptions and judgments. An old joke—perhaps it even happened—from the bad old days of McCarthyism tells of a leftist rally in Philadelphia, viciously broken up by the police. A passerby gets caught in the melee and, as the cops are beating him, he pleads, "Stop, stop, I'm an anticommunist." "I don't care what kind of communist you are," says the cop as he continues pummeling.

We seem driven to think in dichotomies. Protagoras, according to Diogenes, asserted that "there are two sides to every question, exactly opposite to each other." We set up our categories, often by arbitrary division based on tiny differences; then, mistaking names for moral principles, and using banners and slogans as substitutes for reason, we vow to live or die for one or the other side of a false dichotomy. The situation is lamentable enough when the boundaries are profound and natural; if cows declared war on chickens, we might deplore the barnyard carnage, but at least the divisions would be deep, and membership by birth could not be disputed. But when humans struggle with other humans, the boundaries are almost always fluid and largely arbitrary (or at least a curious result of very recent historical contingencies).

Our current drug crisis is a tragedy born of a phony system of classification. For reasons that are little more than accidents of history, we have divided a group of nonfood substances into two categories: items purchasable for supposed pleasure (such as alcohol) and illicit drugs. The categories were once reversed. Opiates were legal in America before the Harrison Narcotics Act of 1914; and members of the Women's Christian Temperance Union, who campaigned against alcohol during the day, drank their valued "women's tonics" at night, products laced with laudanum (tincture of opium).

I could abide—though I would still oppose—our current intransigence if we applied the principle of total interdiction to all harmful drugs. But how can we possibly defend our current policy based on a dichotomy that encourages us to view one class of substances as a preeminent scourge while the two most dangerous and life-destroying substances by far, alcohol and tobacco, form a second class advertised in neon on every street corner of urban America? And why, moreover, should heroin be viewed with horror while chemical cognates that are no different from heroin than lemonade is from iced tea perform work of enormous compassion by relieving the pain of terminal cancer patients in their last days?

Consider just a few recent items rooted in our false classification.

1. A *New York Times* editorial describes methadone as a drug that "blocks the craving for heroin." You might as well say that a Coke blocks the craving for a Pepsi. Methadone and heroin are both opiates, but methadone is legal as a controlled substance for heroin (fine by me; I think they both should be controlled and decriminalized). We permit methadone because some favorable features lead to easier control (oral administration, longer action, and a less intense high), but methadone is a chemical cousin to heroin.

2. Representative Charles Rangel (Dem., N.Y.), implacable foe of legalization, spurns all talk about this subject as the chatter of eggheads. In 1988, in a *New York Times* op-ed piece, he wrote, "Let's take this legalization issue and put it where it belongs—amid idle chit-chat as cocktail glasses knock together at social events." Don't you get it, Mr. Rangel? The stuff in the glasses is as bad as the stuff on the streets. But our classifications permit a majority of Americans to live well enough with one while forcing a minority to murder and die for the other.

3. Former surgeon general C. Everett Koop, who was hired by Reagan to be an ideologue and decided to be a doctor instead, accurately branded nicotine as no less addictive than heroin and cocaine. Representative Terry Bruce (Dem., Ill.) challenged this assertion by arguing that smokers are not "breaking into liquor stores late at night to get money to buy a pack of cigarettes." Koop properly replied that the only dif-

ference resides in social definition as legal or illegal: "You take cigarettes off the streets and people will be breaking into liquor stores. I think one of the things that many people confuse is the behavior of cocaine and heroin addicts when they are deprived of these drugs. That's the difference between a licit and an illicit drug. Tobacco is perfectly legal. You can get it whenever you want to satisfy the craving."

We do not ponder our methods of classification with sufficient scrutiny—and have never done so. Taxonomy, or the study of classification, occupies a low status among the sciences because most people view the activity as a kind of glorified bookkeeping dedicated to pasting objects into preassigned spaces in nature's stamp album. This judgment rests on the false premise that our categories are given by nature and ascertained by simple, direct observation. Nature is full of facts—and they are not distributed isotropically, so nature does provide some hints about divisions.

But our classifications are human impositions, or at least culturally based decisions on what to stress among a plethora of viable alternatives. Classifications are therefore theories of order, not simple records of nature. More important, since classifications are actively imposed, not passively imbibed, they shape our thoughts and deeds in ways that we scarcely perceive because we view our categories as "obvious" and "natural."

Some classifications channel our thinking into fruitful directions because they properly capture the causes of order; others lead us to tragic and vicious errors (the older taxonomies of human races, for example) because they sink their roots in prejudice and mayhem. Too rarely, in our political criticism, do we look to false taxonomies, particularly to improper dichotomies, as the basis for inadequate analysis.

Our drug crisis is largely the product of such a false dichotomy. At the moment, hundreds of thousands of drug users live in tortured limbo, driven to crime, exposed to AIDS, and doomed (at least statistically speaking) to early death. Millions of others suffer palpably from the deeds of the addicted—experiencing violence, robbery, or simple urban fear that steals the joy from life. Billions of dollars go down the rathole to enrich the entrepreneurs or to try to stem the plague by necessarily ineffective interdiction. The politics of several nations in our hemisphere are corrupted, the cultures of whole peoples severely compromised.

William Jennings Bryan once argued that we were about to crucify mankind on a cross of gold. Are we not now significantly lowering the quality of American life for everyone, and causing thousands of deaths directly, by basing our drug policy on something even worse—a false and senseless classification?

From "Taxonomy as Politics," by Stephen Jay Gould, in the Winter 1990 issue of Dissent. *Gould teaches paleontology at Harvard University. Reprinted with permission of the author.*

FEMINISM AND THE FORGOTTEN POWER OF SEX

Camille Paglia

SEX IS A far darker power than feminists have ever been willing to admit. Feminists grossly oversimplify the problem of sex when they reduce it to a matter of social convention; readjust society, they say, eliminate sexual inequality, purify sex roles, and happiness and harmony will reign. Here feminism, like all liberal movements of the past 200 years, is heir to Rousseau.

Rousseau's idea of man's innate goodness led to social environmentalism, now the dominant ethic of American human services, penal codes, and behaviorist therapies. It assumes that aggression, violence, and crime come from social deprivation—a poor neighborhood, a bad home.

Thus feminism blames rape on pornography and smugly interprets outbreaks of sadism as a backlash against itself. But rape and sadism have existed throughout history and in all cultures.

Aggression is innate. Society is not the criminal but the force that keeps crime in check. Feminists, whose goal is to remove power relations from sex, have set themselves against nature. For sex is a subset of nature. Sex is the natural in man.

From the beginning of time, woman has seemed an uncanny being. Man honored but feared her. She was the black maw that had spit him forth and would devour him anew. The identification of woman with nature is considered by many to be merely a myth. I think the identification is real, though most feminist readers will disagree. Nature's cycles are woman's cycles. Woman's sexual maturity means marriage to the moon. Moon, month, menses: same word, same world. The ancients knew that woman is bound to nature's calendar, an appointment she cannot refuse. Whether she desires motherhood or rejects it, nature yokes her into the brute inflexible rhythm of procreative law. The menstrual cycle is an alarming clock that cannot be stopped until nature wills it.

Woman's reproductive apparatus is vastly more complicated than man's and still poorly understood. The female body is a chthonic machine, indifferent to the spirit who inhabits it. Organically, it has one mission—pregnancy—which women may spend a lifetime staving off. Every pregnant woman has body and self taken over by a force beyond her control. In the welcome pregnancy, this is a happy sacrifice. But in the unwanted one, initiated by rape or misadventure, it is a horror.

Every month for woman is a new defeat of the will. Menstruation was once called "the curse," a reference to Eve's expulsion from the Garden of Eden. Most early cultures hemmed in menstruating women by ritual taboos. Even today, Orthodox Jewish women purify themselves of menstrual uncleanliness in the *mikveh*, a ritual bath. Menstrual blood is the birthmark of original sin, the stain that religion must wash from man. Is this identification merely phobic, merely misogynistic? I think it is not menstrual blood per se that disturbs the imagination—devastating and unstanchable as that red flood may be—but rather the albumen in the blood, the uterine shreds, placental jellyfish of the female sea. This is the matrix from which we rose. We have an evolutionary revulsion to slime, our site of biological origins.

Male bonding and patriarchy were the recourse to which man was forced by his terrible sense of woman's power. Feminism has been simplistic in arguing that female archetypes were politically motivated falsehoods created by men. By its techniques of demystification, feminism has painted itself into a corner. Sexuality is a murky realm of contradiction and ambivalence. It cannot always be understood by the social models that feminism constantly relies on.

What has nature given man to defend himself against woman? Here we come to the source of man's cultural achievements, which result from his singular anatomy. Man is sexually compartmentalized. Genitally, he is condemned to a perpetual pattern of linearity, focus, aim, directedness. Woman's eroticism is diffused throughout her body. Her desire for foreplay remains a notorious area of miscommunication between the sexes. Man is a victim of unruly ups and downs; male sexuality is inherently manic-depressive.

Men are in a constant state of sexual anxiety, living on the pins and needles of their hormones. The male genital metaphor is concentration and projection. Nature has given concentration to man to help him overcome his fear. Man approaches woman in bursts of spasmodic concentration. This gives him the illusion of temporary control of the archetypal mysteries that brought him forth. It gives him courage to return.

Sex is metaphysical for men, as it is not for women. Women have no problem to solve through sex. Physically and psychologically, they are serenely self-contained. Men are out of balance; they must quest, pursue, court, or seize. How often one spots a male pigeon making desperate, self-inflating sallies toward the female, as again and again she turns her back on him and nonchalantly marches away. But by concentration and insistence he may carry the day. Nature has blessed him with an obliviousness to his own absurdity. Man is driven toward sex as woman is not. He is driven into the very abyss from which he flees.

The male projection of erection and ejaculation is the paradigm for all cultural projection and conceptualization—from art and philosophy to fantasy, hallucination, and obsession. Women have conceptualized less throughout history—not because men have kept them from doing so but because women do not need to conceptualize in order to exist. The male orgasm is an act of imagination. It can be spurred or squelched by thought. The male has to prove his sexual efficacy before the woman, who is a shadow of his mother and of all women. Failure and humiliation wait in the wings. No woman has to prove herself a woman in the grim way that a man has to prove himself a man. He must perform, or the show does not go on. Ironically, sexual success always ends in sagging fortunes anyhow. Every male projection is transient and must be anxiously, endlessly renewed.

Concentration and projection are remarkably demonstrated by urination, one of the male anatomy's most efficient compartmentalizations. Freud thinks primitive man preened himself on his ability to put out a fire with a stream of urine. A strange thing to be proud of, but certainly beyond the scope of woman. Male urination really *is* a kind of accomplishment, an arc of transcendence. A woman merely waters the ground she stands on. Male urination is a form of commentary. It can be friendly when shared but is often aggressive, as in the defacement of public monuments by Sixties rock stars. To piss on is to criticize. John Wayne urinated on the shoes of a grouchy film director in full view of cast and crew. A male dog who marks every bush on the block is a graffiti artist, leaving his rude signature with each lift of his leg. Women, like female dogs, are earthbound squatters. There is no projection beyond the boundaries of the self.

The cumbersome, solipsistic character of female physiology is tediously evident at sports events and rock concerts, where fifty women wait in line for admission to the sequestered cells of the toilet. Meanwhile, their male friends zip in and out (in every sense) and stand around looking at their watches and rolling their eyes. This compartmentalization of male genitality has its dark side, however. It can lead to a dissociation of sex and emotion, to temptation, promiscuity, and disease. The modern male homosexual, for example, has sought ecstasy in the squalor of public toilets, for women perhaps the least erotic place on earth.

What is woman's basic physical metaphor? It is mystery, *the hidden*. Karen Horney, the psychoanalyst, speaks of a girl's inability to see her genitals and a boy's ability to see his as the source of female subjectivity and male objectivity. The female body's unbearable hiddenness applies to all aspects of men's dealings with women. What does it look like in there? Did she have an orgasm? Is it really my child? Who was my real father? Mystery shrouds woman's sexuality. This mystery is the main reason for the imprisonment man has imposed on woman. Woman is veiled. Violent tearing of this veil may be a motive in gang rapes and rape-murders, particularly ritualistic disemboweling of the Jack the Ripper type.

Rape is a mode of natural aggression that can be controlled only by the social contract. Modern feminism's most naive formulation is its assertion that rape is a crime of violence but not of sex, that it is merely power masquerading as sex. But sex *is* power, and all power is inherently aggressive. Rape is male power fighting female power. It is no more to be excused than is murder or any other assault on another's civil rights. Society is woman's protection against rape, not, as some feminists absurdly maintain, the cause of rape. The rapist is a man with too little socialization rather than too much. Strong evidence exists that whenever social controls are weakened, as in war or mob rule, even civilized men behave in uncivilized ways. Sex crimes are always male, never female, because such crimes are conceptualized assaults on the unreachable omnipotence of woman and nature.

From Sexual Personae: Art and Decadence from Nefertiti to Emily Dickenson, *by Camille Paglia. Paglia teaches humanities at the University of the Arts in Philadelphia. (Camile Paglia,* Sexual Personae *[New Haven, CT: Yale University Press, 1990].* This article appeared in Harper's Magazine, *March 1990, and is reprinted with permission of Yale University Press.)*

Answers to Selected Exercises

CHAPTER 1

Exercise 1: Part A

2. This passage does not contain an argument. It is a description of a physical environment, with the attribution of awareness of the environment to a subject.

4. This passage contains an argument. The conclusion is that any diet poses some problems. This conclusion is stated both at the beginning and (in slightly different words) at the end of the passage. The word *therefore* indicates the conclusion, where the specific problem is inferred from the alternatives considered.

6. This passage does not contain an argument. The first sentence identifies hockey as a winter game and says that it is popular in some northern countries. The second sentence mentions some requirements for players of the game. Neither sentence is offered as a reason for, or as evidence for, the other. Nor is there any evidence that someone is trying to justify or prove any claim about hockey or anything else.

10. This passage does not contain an argument. The first sentence tells how we can understand the relationship of a reactor to a steam generator and makes a comparison. The second sentence elaborates slightly on the comparison.

13. The passage contains an argument; a reason is given as to why the Soviet Union and eastern Europe should be assisted. The word *because* introduces the premise.

15. The passage does not contain an argument. It illustrates the possibility of getting a pattern without deliberately trying to. If the passage were set in a larger context in which this possibility were in doubt, it might be interpreted as an attempt to prove that not every resemblance is the result of an intentional depiction.

18. This passage does not contain an argument. It is part of a dramatic personal story.

Exercise 2: Part A

4. This passage does not contain an argument. It describes Sagan's message rather than trying to show that his message is either correct or incorrect. The author thinks that Sagan has something important to say, but he does not try to prove this.

5. There is an argument. The expression, "given this evidence," functions here as a logical indicator. The conclusion is "it is likely that men's brains are organized differently from women's brains."

10. The passage contains no argument. The word *because* is part of an explanation as to why she did not develop this independence.

12. This passage does contain an argument. The conclusion is that mountain climbers have accepted a risk of death. The indicator word *so* is a clue. The reasons are neatly set out: first some general conditions of accepting risk are announced; then it is stated that these conditions apply to mountain climbers; then the conclusion is drawn.

14. There is no argument. This is a descriptive passage, depicting the desperate character of peasant life.

15. The conclusion is that there should be freedom of expression of opinion. The reasons are that not to have this would be an evil that would rob us of opportunities to either discover error or to more fully appreciate the truth. (*Note:* This argument is an especially famous one that you are sure to encounter again if you go on to study the history of political theory.)

18. There is no argument here. The passage is a descriptive one, from a science fantasy.

19. There is no argument here. The passage tries to explain how these famous comic strip characters handle life and says they are all right because they set up safety valves for themselves. The word *because* is not a logical indicator, it is part of an explanation.

CHAPTER 2

Exercise 1: Part A

1. Standardization:
1. If a car has reliable brakes then its brakes work well in wet weather.
2. My car does not have brakes that work well in wet weather.
Therefore,
3. My car does not have reliable brakes.

3. Standardization:
1. When unemployment among youth goes up, hooliganism and gang violence go up too.

So,
2. Unemployment is probably a major cause of hooliganism and gang violence.
There is also an argument, from (2) to the conclusion that
3. Gang violence among youth is not caused by drugs.
Thus, there is a subargument from (1) to (2) and a main argument from (2) to (3).

5. Standardization:
1. Every logic book I have ever read was written by a woman.
Therefore,
2. All logicians are women.
This argument is obviously weak, but it is clearly an argument.

9. Standardization:
1. The main feathers of archaeopteryx show the asymmetric aerodynamic form typical of modern birds.
So,
2. The feathers of the archaeopteryx were used for flying.

10. Standardization:
1. People do science.
Therefore,
2. Science is a socially embedded activity.
The indicator word is *since*, which introduces the premise.

13. The passage does not contain an argument. It describes the San Andreas fault in California.

15. Standardization:
1. Genes in a lab plant called arabidosis are turned on when the plant's leaves are touched.
Therefore,
2. Plants may respond, at a genetic level, to stimuli.

18. Standardization:
1. The object of reasoning is to find out from a consideration of what we already know something we do not know.
So,
2. Reasoning is good if it gives us a true conclusion from true premises.
There is a second argument from premise (1) to:

3. Reasoning is not good if it does not give us a true conclusion from true premises.

Exercise 1: Part B

Note: These answers are partial due to the nature of the exercise. We have simply tried to indicate where we think a subargument is needed, and why.

2. In response to Peter's last question, Juan could use a subargument to support his claim that polls do not provide information needed to make a decision as to which candidate can best deal with important issues. Juan might say, for instance, that polls give information as to how popular a candidate is with voters, but they do not give information about substantive issues such as tax policy, environmental cleanup, foreign policy, and so on.

3. No subargument is needed. Nancy seems prepared to believe Catherine's story and the dialogue does not really contain arguments.

5. No argument is given, so no subargument is needed.

Exercise 2: Part A

1. Somewhat tentative, as indicated by the phrase "if the stories my daughter has to tell are anything to go by."

4. Somewhat tentative, as indicated by the word *probably*.

6. High certainty, as indicated by "no doubt" and "is murder." To make it absolutely clear that he does not want to qualify the judgment, the speaker includes "pure and simple."

10. Very tentative; "could be" indicates that this factor in allergies is being put forward as a possibility.

Exercise 2: Part B

3. There is an argument:
1. Logicians say "true" and "false" apply only to statements.
2. (Implicit) Logicians are right.
3. Pictures are not statements.

Therefore,
4. Pictures cannot be true or false.

4. The argument is:
1. Experiments cited show early immersion language teaching is effective in some circumstances.
2. Research has not yet shown the conditions that are required for the success of early immersion language teaching.
3. It is not known whether North York youngsters taught by early immersion will remain bilingual.
4. It is not yet known whether North York youngsters will pay too great a cost in knowledge of their primary language.
Therefore,
5. It is not yet proven that early immersion language teaching is the best way of teaching a second language.
The conclusion is not quite explicit but is indicated by the expressions "neither proves any such thing" and "it remains to be seen."

5. The premises are:
1. For those who govern, democracy implies permanent insecurity.
And,
2. Gorbachev governs.
The conclusion, which is added, is:
3. If Gorbachev abolishes monopoly of the Communist Party, he will be politically insecure.

7. The passage does not contain an argument. It sets forth a kind of thought exercise for the reader. The authors want the reader to do something (that is, repeat the word *chair* in their minds), and they offer a descriptive prediction as to what will happen when this is done.

8. The argument is:
1. CBS Cable lost $30 million when its chairman tried to produce high quality cultural programming.
2. The Entertainment Channel with BBC and Broadway material went out of business.
3. Tele-France USA had to give up its attempt to present French cultural programs on television.
Thus,
4. It is not likely that mass media will be able to produce more meaningful artistic products.

The conclusion is taken as indicated by the first two sentences, especially the phrase "economics still judges and strangles" and by our sense of the point of evidence cited about business failures.

Exercise 3

2. Argument:
1. Individuals are not reliable in their judgment.
2. Groups are made up of individuals.
So,
3. Probably groups are not reliable in their judgment.
The premises are linked to support the conclusion.

4. Argument:
1. The black hole concept is virtually impossible for nonexperts to comprehend.
2. The notion of antimatter is paradoxical.
3. In the context of elementary particles, it is impossible to understand what causation means.
Thus,
4. Modern physics is a mysterious subject.
The premises are convergent in their support.

7. Argument:
1. Law and force are the two methods of fighting.
2. Men fight by law.
3. Beasts fight by force.
4. Fighting by law is often insufficient.
Therefore,
5. One must often have recourse to fighting by force.
Premises link to support the conclusion.

10. Argument, with subarguments:
1. There could be no meaning if words could mean just anything.
So,
2. Language requires rules.
3. A single person could make anything he wanted right.
So,
4. A single person cannot follow a rule.
Thus,
5. Rules require more than one person.
Therefore,
6. A private language is impossible.

There is a subargument from (1) to (2) and another from (3) to (4); then a third from (4) to (5). In the main argument, (2) and (5) link to support (6), the main conclusion.

Exercise 4

2. 1. Butterflies need warm air and sunlight to breed.
<u>2.</u> (Implicit) The conservatory at the zoo has warm air and sunlight.
Therefore,
3. The conservatory at the zoo is the perfect place for butterflies to breed.

5. 1. If God had meant people to fly through the air they would have been born with wings.
<u>2.</u> (Implicit) People were not born with wings.
So,
3. People were not meant to fly through the air.

8. 1. Efficiency is necessary for competition.
2. Industries must compete.
<u>3.</u> (Implicit) Government-owned industry is not efficient.
Therefore,
4. Government-owned industry should be privatized.

10. 1. Understanding other people's ideas requires listening and trying to understand another world as another person experiences it.
2. Resolving conflicts requires understanding other people's ideas.
<u>3.</u> (Implicit) We are not good at listening to others and trying to experience the world as they experience it.
Thus,
4. It is unlikely that we will be able to work out, and fully resolve, conflicts.

Exercise 5

1. Like many ads, this one is very brief, but it seeks to establish a point and is best seen as an argument with unexpressed parts.
Standardization:
1. Bananas contain everything NutraSweet contains.
<u>2.</u> Bananas are not dangerous to eat. (inserted)
Therefore,

3. NutraSweet is not dangerous to eat. (inserted)
The missing premise is common knowledge. Also, we attribute it to the ad because it supplies the obvious rationale for comparing NutraSweet and bananas in the first place. The missing conclusion is attributed because we know ads are used to make people seek to consume the products, and we know that there has been some controversy about the safety of artificial sweeteners and other additives.

4. Standardization:
1. The teenage crime rate is going up.
2. Teenage theft is rising.
3. Teenage crime is connected to drug use. (inserted)
So,
4. Teenage drug use is not declining.
(2) is taken as a statement on the assumption that the last question is a rhetorical question assuming a negative answer. This also provides the interpretive basis for (3) and (4).

7. Some nonsmokers suffer headaches, runny noses, and itchy eyes as a result of exposure to secondhand smoke.
2. Secondhand smoke can cause minor health problems in nonsmokers.
3. Secondhand smoke can cause lung cancer in nonsmokers regularly exposed to smoke.
Therefore,
4. We have good reason to ban smoking in public places
(1) supports (2) in a subargument.

9. 1. Joyce Brothers thinks Weight Loss Clinic has what a weight loss clinic needs for success.
2. Joyce Brothers was impressed with Weight Loss Clinic.
So,
3. You too should be impressed by Weight Loss Clinic.
Since the passage is an advertisement, we might add a further missing conclusion that if you need to lose weight, you should go to Weight Loss Clinic.

10. 1. If man were born to be happy, he would not be born to die.
2. Man is doomed to die.
Therefore,
3. Man is not born to be happy.

12. 1. If dictionaries could settle all disputes about how words are to be used, then debates such as that on abortion could be solved by looking up words such as *human being* or *person* in the dictionary.
2. Debates such as that on abortion cannot be solved by looking up words in the dictionary. (inserted)
Therefore,
3. Dictionaries can't settle all questions about how words are to be used.
The extra premise is common knowledge, something the author would clearly accept, and is required to link the stated premise with the conclusion.

15. The passage does not contain an argument. Rushdie is describing human needs and questions to which he thinks religious beliefs have been a response.

CHAPTER 3

Exercise 1: Part A

1. Bob does not respond to Caroline's argument. He merely expresses his own dislike of mathematics and explains why he doesn't like it. In the last sentence, Bob hints at (but does not really express) an argument as to why mathematics should not be required.

3. Jan does not respond to Linda's argument. She expresses disagreement, calls the position shocking, one that a feminist should be ashamed of holding. She distorts the position. She never gives any objection to the premises or conclusion as Linda stated it.

5. Sam responds to Angelita's argument. He questions her premise that economic ties will help to prevent war, and he gives a reason for questioning that premise. Then, after responding to Angelita's position, he expresses another view.

7. Sheila does respond to Alexander's argument. She gives reasons for questioning his premise that anything that is good for a large company cannot be good for its employees.

Exercise 2

4. In the context, assume acceptability. The argument fails on (R); the information in (1) and (2) may show that the teacher is inexperienced as a teacher but it has no bearing at all on the issue of how much she knows about history. In (3) the information is entirely irrelevant to the issue of the instructor's competence in her subject. Because the argument fails on (R), it necessarily fails on (G) as well.

6. The premises are acceptable (A) and they are somewhat relevant (R), because all have to do with unexpected technological breakthroughs. But they do not give adequate grounds (G) because only three cases are described. Cases in which breakthroughs were sought but not obtained are not described, and AIDS may be different from the other problems in ways that make it less amenable to a breakthrough.

9. Assume acceptability (A)—it is an invented example. Premises are relevant (R). However, (G) is not satisfied because the people questioned in the poll may not believe, or may not have been aware when responding to the question asked in the poll, that doctors perform essential services.

10. The argument fails on all three conditions. (A) is not satisfied because we have no good reason to believe that all thinking is divided into only two types. No evidence is given for this and it is not something known by common experience or known a priori. The argument fails on (R) because the premises are about methods of thinking, whereas the conclusion is about the subject matter of thinking. And for the same reason, it fails on (G).

11. 1. In schools in Cuba, girls far outstrip boys in their achievements.
2. Cuba is a socialist state in which equality of the sexes is a matter of law.
3. In Cuba, men are legally required to do their share of the housework.
Therefore,
4. Under socialism and true equality of opportunity, women will show up as superior to men.
We cannot say whether the premises are acceptable unless we have more than just common knowledge regarding Cuba. However, we can accept them provisionally. Clearly they are relevant to the conclusion. However, they do not give adequate grounds: the argument fails on (G) because the premises are about only one socialist state, whereas the conclusion is about socialist states generally.

15. The argument passes on (A) and (R) but fails on (G) because other sorts of businesses (for example, multinationals) may not feel pressures in the same way. Other factors such as resource depletion, pollution, unemployment, and so on are not considered. Yet the argument reaches the conclusion that competition is valuable overall.

CHAPTER 4

Exercise 1

3. (d) The term would not be suitable for ostensive definition. It is too abstract, too subtle, and not something you can point to. Even if you were in the presence of a person who was wise, and acknowledged to be so, you could hardly define *wisdom* by pointing to him or her, because the person on whose behalf you were defining the word would not know which aspect you were pointing to.

3. (g) The word *freckles* would be quite easy to define ostensively. You could point to freckles on a real person, or in a picture.

3. (j) Defining this word ostensively would be hard, as it is somewhat abstract; also it functions both as a noun and as a verb, and you want the verb—a fact that would be hard to indicate ostensively.

4. (a) This definition is too broad because exchanges can be made using virtually anything as a medium—cattle or foodstuffs, for instance. Such things would not be regarded as money according to ordinary usage, since they would not be integrated into the functioning of an economy.

4. (e) This definition is too narrow. It requires that we concentrate very hard in order to be studying. But people can study provided they concentrate somewhat; in ordinary usage, this is still called studying. The definition also seems narrow in making memory the goal of studying.

Sometimes we study for other purposes—for example, to get a better understanding.

5. (c) The term *terrorism* is surely very difficult to define. A recent article on the subject reported discovering 109 different definitions! In this context, you want to avoid defining *terrorism* in terms of a particular religious or political party and to avoid defining it in terms of its having or not having government support. You want to use a definition according to which acts commonly called terrorist acts—bombings of cars, hostage takings, and so on—will count as terrorist acts no matter who commits them. *Suggestion:* Terrorism is the practice of using, or threatening to use, violence (typically unpredictable violence) against nonmilitary personnel in an attempt to bring about political change. (The point of this exercise is not so much to achieve a final definition as to appreciate the problems involved. Obviously *terrorism* has strong negative emotional implications and plays a key role in political rhetoric.)

5. (e) The new fruit could be called anything you like, but it would be natural to make up a name that reflects its origin and nature. You might call it a *prapple* or a *papple* or an *ap-pear,* for instance. Then you can stipulate a definition just by saying something like "A prapple is a fruit that is a cross between an apple and a pear." Your definition might also refer to properties the fruit has, by saying something like "a juicy green fruit that is a cross . . ."

6. (c) This statement is not a persuasive definition. It is probably not a definition at all, but just a statement about tea. If taken as a reportive definition, it could be criticized as too narrow because tea is consumed in places other than England and at times other than the afternoon.

6. (e) This statement is a persuasive definition that, in effect, seeks to evoke negative attitudes toward the police through emotionally negative terms such as *criminal* and *license to kill.* It ignores the social importance of having police, ignores the checks on police power, and may be inaccurate in its implication that police function only to implement their own personal judgments, and not to enforce the law.

6. (h) This statement is a disguised persuasive definition of *art.* Real or authentic art must be an artificial representation of reality; photography is not artificial, so it is not art. (*Note:* it is not at all clear how the word *artificial* is being used here.) The persuasive definition of *art* as something that requires artificial reproduction of reality is used to argue that photography is not art; no other reason is given. A clue to the presence of persuasive definition is *authentic.* The persuasive definition makes the premise unacceptable; hence the argument is not cogent.

6. (l) This statement is a persuasive definition that attempts to elicit a more favorable attitude toward insanity. The accurate mind is something good, and the suggestion that it is overtaxed when insane is intended to make us think reality is just too much for the really accurate mind, subtly suggesting that perhaps the fault for insanity is not in the mind of the insane person but in the world itself.

Exercise 2: Part A

3. The passage does not contain flaws in language.

4. This passage does not contain any argument to show flaws in Carl Sagan's show. The writer obviously believes that the show was cheap and poor, and he conveys this opinion with loaded language—"posture," "gimmicks," "schmaltz," "cheapens," "razzle-dazzle," and "bubble gum mentality." The emotional language hides the lack of argument.

5. There is an ambiguity. The word *equality* is used in two senses. First, it means sameness; then it means having equal standing. The argument depends on confusing these meanings, so it is an instance of the fallacy of equivocation.

6. Here we find two different uses of *natural* and *unnatural.* In the first sentence, *natural* is used to mean occurs in the natural world; in this sense, something natural is neither good nor bad as such. In the second sentence, a common belief about homosexuality being unnatural is alluded to. In that sense, *unnatural* means wrong. Obviously it cannot mean that homosexuality does not occur in nature; on this interpretation the

sentence would be an obvious falsehood. The final sentence exploits the confusion between the two senses.

7. This argument uses *oppression* in a vague way. The conclusion depends upon this vagueness. The argument is like the example about child abuse discussed in Chapter 3. It begins from a clear case of oppression where entitlement to a trial is violated. Then it moves to psychology, where any government causing fear in its people is called oppressive. Next, a routine government practice, needed virtually everywhere, is called oppressive. By this time, it would appear that any government that makes people do things (such as pay taxes) that they do not want to do will count as oppressive. The next two examples move even further, with schools and parents caring for children. These examples involve activities that may be laborious, but that many people want to do. The whole argument depends on using *oppression* in this vague way, and because the writer hasn't clearly told us what oppression amounts to in any given case, we can't tell whether *oppression* is being used consistently.

12. The letter is full of emotionally charged language such as "misguided," "ludicrous," "arrogant," "outrageous," "disgusting," and "deplorable." It asks what right Frum has to take the position he does—a rhetorical question implying he has no right. No reason at all is given for objecting to his position. The whole weight of the case is carried by the emotionally charged language and the rhetorical question.

14. The phrase "independent thinking" is ambiguous. As commonly understood, independent thinking means not believing everything one reads or is told but being willing to question some things and to search out evidence and arguments to arrive at one's own beliefs—at least when the issue is important and there is reason to question what one is told. As used in the premises, though, independent thinking is said to involve questioning everything one is told, so that one would have to start from scratch. This is, in effect, a stipulation that is unreasonable and that avoids the real topic of the argument.

Exercise 2: Part B

3. Negative emotionally charged language is present in "illiterate peewee critics."

6. No euphemism or emotionally charged language is present.

7. There is a euphemism in "passed away," used for "died." The expression "loved one" might in some contexts also be euphemistic; it is certainly abstract enough to hide the exact relationship between the man and the dead person. (Was this friend or relative genuinely loved?)

CHAPTER 5

Exercise 1: Part A

4. This statement is not a priori true. Legal responsibility is established by the state. Being a parent is biological. There is no fixed logical connection between a biological fact and a legal fact. For instance, a 12-year-old could be a biological parent but, due to her young age, not be a legal parent in some jurisdictions. Those who have adopted children are the legal parents of children of whom they are not the biological parents, which also illustrates that these two concepts are distinct.

7. This statement is a priori true. If a person fails to be happy, he is not happy.

10. The statement cannot be known a priori to be true. It is a common saying, to be sure, but that does not show it to be true; a moral evaluation that all is legitimate in love and war is being made. When you think about it, this moral judgment is certainly controversial, and quite probably false.

11. The statement is a priori true. It expresses the logical connection between cause and effect. If an action has a cause, it is the effect of that cause and it therefore must be the effect of something that precedes it, because a cause precedes its effect.

14. The statement is knowable a priori to be true. Girls are female, and mothers are female, by definition. Given this fact, and given that two creatures, both female, are of the same sex, it obviously follows that the female sex, girls, are brought up by parents of their same sex.

15. This statement is not knowable a priori; it makes a specific claim about what Houdini did.

Exercise 1: Part B

1. The premise is a matter of common knowledge and would be acceptable.

2. The claim is knowable a priori. If we consider a person now and a person in a previous life to be the same person, and we consider that these bodily existences are different ones, then for the same person to be present twice, his or her soul or personality would have to survive (in some sense) between the two bodily lives. At least enough of the person would have to survive for him or her to be capable of being reincarnated.

4. The claim is not acceptable a priori nor on the basis of common knowledge or authority; in the context there is no subargument. If it were defended by someone on the basis of testimony, it would not thereby become acceptable, because it goes far beyond testimony in its sweeping metaphysical implications. The only way the claim could be acceptable would be provisionally; but it is so sweeping and controversial that even provisional acceptance would not be reasonable.

6. This claim is acceptable as common knowledge.

Exercise 2: Part A

1. These statements are inconsistent. If they value virginity, they do not want young women to have sexual encounters before marriage; that is what virginity means.

4. There is no inconsistency in these statements. The expectation of improvement, and success of some African-Americans, is contrasted with the greater effect of unemployment on African-Americans.

7. There is an implicit inconsistency between the second statement and the third one. If God created all the goodness in the world, He would have had to create His own goodness, which would mean existing before He existed. (One could escape this contradiction if one assumed that God is not part of this world.) On the assumption that creation requires a creative act, the third sentence is inconsistent with the fourth one.

9. These statements are not implicitly inconsistent. They do, however, impose an impossible demand on knowledge.

10. There is no inconsistency. The passage merely describes the pros and cons of visiting earth from the point of view of an imagined civilization.

12. There is no inconsistency. Different aspects are manifested at different times.

13. These statements are inconsistent because capital punishment is taking a life and is granted to be morally permissible, whereas an earlier statement says that taking a life is never morally justifiable.

Exercise 2: Part B

3. The premises are "withholding information is just the same as lying" and "lying is wrong." If these are taken to be universal statements, covering all cases of withholding information and lying, they are both easily refutable and hence unacceptable.

8. The third premise is not acceptable, because sex has such great social importance that it is not reasonable to accept a ban on discussing it publicly. It is true sex is a private matter if by "private" we mean that it is done apart from public view; it is another thing to say that it is "private" in the sense of not being open to public discussion. Any temptation to accept the first and third premises probably comes from the exploitation of the ambiguity in "private."

11. Two premises are unacceptable: "No one knows why some persons of all strata of society become addicts" and "This slipping away from personal responsibility is unjust." The former is unacceptable because it presupposes that experts are incorrect, which is one of the points the author is trying to prove. The latter is unacceptable because it presupposes that people are individually responsible for their actions, which is one

of the things the experts deny. Neither of these claims can be taken as acceptable within the context of this argument. (*Note:* They might be true, nevertheless.)

12. The argument contains a subargument structure. The premise that in a democracy one has all the means needed to influence policy is used to derive the conclusion that hunger strikes are immoral in democracies. This premise is not knowable a priori, and is, in fact, refutable on the basis of experience; it is often extremely difficult to influence policy in democracies. The intermediate conclusion supports the main conclusion—that Jacques Hebert's hunger strike was wrong. In this stage of the argument the premise is not yet acceptable: it is not knowable a priori, by common knowledge, by testimony, or on the basis of a cogent subargument.

14. The premises are clearly acceptable on the basis of common knowledge. (The argument may be criticized on the (G) condition; other sports are not considered.)

CHAPTER 6

Exercise 1: Part A

1. Statement (a) is relevant to statement (b) because it gives some reason to suppose that (b) is true. The natural interpretation of the behavior described is that elephants are hiding others because the others are not living. If this interpretation is correct, then elephants have the concept "not living," which is, essentially, the concept, "dead."

5. (a) is irrelevant to (b). The unpronounceability of words for various ingredients has no bearing at all on the issue of whether these ingredients are dangerous.

6. Statement (a) is not relevant to statement (b) even though they both deal with the Holocaust. (a) is about a dispute among French historians, and (b) considers what would have happened without protective activities by some courageous people. These themes are different.

9. Statement (a) is clearly relevant to statement (b), because (a) claims agriculture is important,

which provides a general reason for (b), the claim that a weak agricultural system is an obstacle to economic advancement in the Soviet Union.

Exercise 1: Part B

1. The argument is:
1. A number of different religious denominations are represented within the public school system.
Therefore,
2. The public school system must be secular.
As stated, (1) is not relevant to (2) since having different religions is no reason for having no religion at all. We could make (1) relevant by reading in a missing premise to the effect that only a secular system will be tolerable by all the different denominations. This extra premise, however, would be easily refutable because some denominations feel very strongly about having some religion in education—so much so that they might prefer a religion other than their own to none at all.

5. The conclusion is that there is no single source or reason explaining all intractable conflicts. All other statements give relevant reasons to support this conclusion.

7. The main conclusion is that South African blacks are entitled to threaten violence. A subargument shows certain other countries are committed to threatening violence for their defense and are thus inconsistent if they deny such a right to South African blacks. The main argument is from the inconsistency of these countries to the legitimacy of threats of violence in South Africa. In this main argument, the premise is irrelevant to the conclusion; a failing in these other countries is no indication at all about what would be legitimate for South African blacks.

9. The premises are irrelevant because fish are an entirely different species from humans, not close in an evolutionary sense, and inhabiting an entirely different kind of environment.

10. The conclusion is that a complete proof of Christian beliefs would destroy the Christian religion. The fanciful story about thunderbolts is

relevant; it serves to establish that belief based on evidence that is too compelling would not be free belief.

14. Reagan's conclusion is that the Bible is divine in origin. His premises are:

1. The Bible is unique in having lasted thousands of years.

And,

2. The Bible is a best-seller.

Both (1) and (2) are irrelevant to the conclusion because neither indicates anything about the origin of the Bible, much less anything that would show its origin to be divine.

Exercise 2

1. This passage contains an argument with the missing conclusion that feminist philosophy should be opposed. Our justification for reading in this conclusion is the author's "I vigorously oppose . . ." and the terms she uses to describe feminism. The argument has irrelevant premises and is a case of the straw man fallacy because feminism does not advocate destroying traditions and democracy, nor does it advocate reducing traditional families to superfluity. (You may need background knowledge about what is involved in the feminist position to see this fallacy.)

3. There is no irrelevance in Jones's argument. Smith does not really address that argument. Instead, he himself offers several different arguments to contradict Jones's conclusion. There are numerous flaws of relevance. What animals do to each other is irrelevant to what people should do to animals, because animals do not have a sense of morality and cannot reason about what they ought and ought not to do. What people do naturally (being omnivores) is irrelevant to what they ought to do. There is also an argument from ignorance at the one point where Smith does tie his comments to Jones's argument. The fact that we don't know what sort of consciousness animals may have is not a reason for concluding that they have none or for concluding that they feel no pain.

6. Just as it stands, the quoted sentence is not an argument. If we assume that in a broader con-

text, it functions as part of an argument, we can see the fallacy of guilt by association. The statement seeks to link antiwar activists of the Vietnam era with the abuses of the North Vietnamese and the Cambodian regimes.

8. This passage contains the straw man fallacy and uses lots of loaded language to further discredit the absurd position attributed to Maude Barlow. Such opponents of pornography do not assume men are dimwits; rather, they assume that people will be affected by persistent portrayals of violence against women—subconsciously, if not consciously. There are hints of ad hominem in such expressions as "of her ilk" and "classed with purveyors of drivel." In addition, there are suggestions of guilt by association when Barlow is linked with others (Hefner and Guccione) who disseminate pornography. Apart from the straw man fallacy and suggestions of ad hominem and loaded language, no reason is given against the views Barlow holds.

13. Here the premise is relevant to the conclusion. If the only people who know art and art education are art professors or art instructors, that fact is a very good reason for concluding that art colleges should be administered by them.

15. The argument is based on an incorrect appeal to authority because the arguer asserts that one particular scientific view (the safeness of the spraying) is proven on the grounds that the judge pronounced in favor of it. The judge is not an authority on scientific issues and, in fact, the information in the letter implies that there were differing positions among scientific experts on the matter.

CHAPTER 7

Exercise 1

2. Some students are persons who came to the office asking to be excused from the final examination. (*I*)

5. All persons who can afford to stay at London's prestigious hotels are rich persons. (*A*)

6. Some evangelists are not poets. (*O*)

10. Some textbooks are not boring books. (O)

12. All mathematicians are persons who love abstraction. (A) This sentence is somewhat ambiguous as to scope; it might assert "Some mathematicians are persons who love abstraction." (I)

15. All women with jobs outside the home and no assistance with household work are persons burdened with at least two jobs. (A)

16. All persons who are enemies of my enemy are persons who are friends of mine. (A)

19. All things that are roses called by any name other than "rose" are things that are as sweet as roses. (A)

20. No communist countries are countries with consumer-oriented economies. (E)

Exercise 2: Part A

1. All pilgrims who came to Massachusetts are persons who left England of their own free will. (A)
Obverse: No pilgrims who came to Massachusetts are not persons who left England of their own free will.

3. Some things that are technical innovations are not things that are needed. (O)
Obverse: Some things that are technical innovations are things that are not needed. (I)

5. Some professors are not persons who are impractical. (O)
Obverse: Some professors are persons who are not impractical. (I)

7. All things that are art are things done in the pursuit of beauty and truth. (A)
Obverse: No things that are art are things that are not done in the pursuit of beauty and truth. (E)

8. All beliefs that are nationalistic are fervent beliefs concerning doubtful matters. (A)
Obverse: No beliefs that are nationalistic are beliefs that are not fervent concerning doubtful matters. (E)

10. Some feminists are not persons in favor of free choice regarding abortion. (O)
Obverse: Some persons are persons not in favor of free choice regarding abortion. (I)

Exercise 2: Part B

1. All T are E. (T represents those people who understand the new technology; E represents experts.) Converse: All E are T; not equivalent. Contrapositive: All non-E are non-T; equivalent to original. The original is an A statement; so too are the converse and the contrapositive.

4. All W are D. (W represents whales; D represents creatures in danger of extinction.) Converse: All D are W; not equivalent to original. Original is an A statement; so too are the converse and the contrapositive.

6. Some C are F. (C represents court proceedings; F represents things so complex as to be inefficient.) Converse: Some F are C; equivalent to original. Contrapositive: Some non-C are non-F; not equivalent to original. The original is an I statement; so too are the converse and the contrapositive.

7. Some S are not C. (S represents students; C represents competitive persons.) Converse: Some C are not S; equivalent to original. Contrapositive: Some non-C are not non-S; not equivalent to original. The original is an O statement; so too are the converse and the contrapositive.

8. No R are D, where R represents Russian authors and D represents those insensitive to nature.
Converse: No D are R.
Contrapositive: No non-D are non-R.
The converse is equivalent to the original and the contrapositive is not. All are E statements.

Exercise 2: Part C

1. All V are U. (V represents advice given to young parents by so-called experts; U represents things that are unreliable.)
This is an A statement.

The contradictory is an *O* statement.
Contradictory: Some *V* are not *U*.

3. Some *C* are *T*. (*C* represents crops; *T* represents things best grown on land that has been left fallow for one season.)
This is an *I* statement.
The contradictory is an *E* statement.
Contradictory: No *C* are *T*.

5. All *P* are *T*. (*P* represents persons who are productive and innovative scientists; *T* represents persons who enjoy freedom of thought and are not afraid to risk pursuing new ideas.)
This is an *A* statement.
The contradictory is an *O* statement.
Contradictory: Some *P* are not *T*.

Exercise 3

2. The argument in categorical form:
1. Some mothers are persons who find small children extremely irritating.
2. Some persons who find small children extremely irritating are persons who just cannot control themselves and suppress their rage.
Therefore,
3. Some mothers are persons who just cannot control themselves and suppress their rage.
Venn diagram of premises: *M* represents mothers; *C* represents persons who find small children extremely irritating; *J* represents persons who cannot control themselves and suppress their rage.

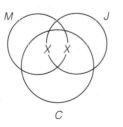

The argument is invalid. It would be possible for the premises to be true and the conclusion false because the *x*'s are on the line and there is no guarantee they will fall into the areas required for the truth of the conclusion.

7. The argument in categorical form:
1. All well-educated persons are persons who can read.
2. All persons who can read are persons who have heard of Hitler.
Therefore,
3. Some well-educated persons are persons who have heard of Hitler.
Venn diagram of premises: *W* represents well-educated persons; *R* represents persons who can read; *H* represents persons who have heard of Hitler.

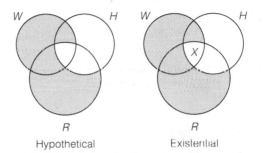

Hypothetical   Existential

The argument is valid only if we adopt the existential interpretation and assume that there are well-educated persons and there are persons who can read. With this interpretation, we can add *x* and the argument is valid.

9. All *V* are *T*; all *T* are *R*; therefore, all *V* are *R*. (*V* represents acts of sunbathing; *T* represents things that carry a risk of cancer; *R* represents things that are dangerous.)

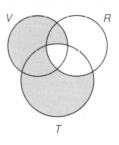

The argument is valid. Given the shading for the premises, we can see that all *V* are *R*. There is no area of the *V* circle left unshaded outside the *R* circle.

12. The argument in categorical form:

1. Some doctors are unhappy persons. (Some *D* are *U*.)

2. No unhappy persons are persons who find it easy to express sympathy for others. (No *U* are *E*.)

So,

3. Some doctors are not persons who find it easy to express sympathy for others. (Some *D* are not *E*.)

Venn diagram of premises: *D* represents doctors; *U* represents unhappy persons; *E* represents persons who find it easy to express sympathy for others.

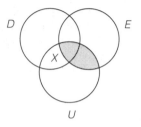

The argument is valid. The diagram of the premises shows an *x* in the area representing those who are doctors and who do not find it easy to express sympathy for others; the conclusion states there are persons in this area.

16. All positions involving power and influence in government are positions that should be allotted on the basis of elections (all *P* are *E*); all positions of being the spouse of the mayor are positions involving power and influence in government (all *O* are *P*); so, all positions of being the spouse of the mayor are positions that should be allotted on the basis of elections (all *O* are *E*).

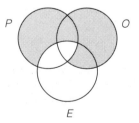

The argument is valid. To dispute the argument, one would dispute the second premise.

17. Some *R* are *D*; no *D* are *C*; therefore, some *R* are not *C*. (*R* represents religious people; *D* represents people who believe morality depends on religion; *C* represents people who have a true view of morality.)

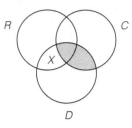

Valid.

Exercise 4

1. Some problems experienced by human beings are problems that result from climate (some *P* are *R*); no problems that result from climate are problems that result from abuses of human rights (no *R* are *A*); so, some *P* are not *A* ("Some problems experienced by human beings are not a result of abuses of human rights").

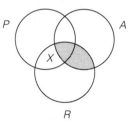

Valid.

2. All men who are other than I are men who die (all *M* are *D*); no men who are identical to I are men who are other than I (no *I* are *M*); therefore, no I are *D* ("I shall not die").

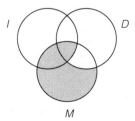

Invalid.

6. The argument in categorical form.
1. Some double letters are letters compounded of two vowels. (Some *D* are *C*)
2. No double letters are vowels. (No *D* are *V*)
Therefore,
3. Some letters compounded of two vowels are not vowels. (Some *C* are not *V*)
Venn diagram of premises; *D* represents double letters; *C* represents letters compounded of two vowels; *V* represents vowels.

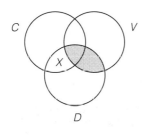

The argument is valid because this diagram shows an *x* in the area that is *C* and is not *V*, as is required for the conclusion to be true.

7. Stated premise: All *L* are *T* (where *L* represents leaders of our country and *T* represents persons who have not told the citizens where they want to lead us.)
Stated conclusion: All *L* are *C* (where *C* represents persons who are totally confused).
The argument can be turned into a valid syllogism by adding "all *T* are *C*" as a missing premise. The argument is then: all *L* are *T*; all *T* are *C*. Therefore, all *L* are *C*.
This syllogism is valid. We check this one with reference to the rules. The middle term is *T*; it is distributed in the second premise. The term *L* is distributed in the conclusion; it is also distributed in the first premise—thus satisfying the second rule. At least one premise is affirmative; the conclusion is not negative, so we do not need a negative premise. In addition, the syllogism does not have two universal premises and a particular conclusion; its conclusion is universal.

12. Stated premise: All persons who make it to the top of public life in Britain are persons who have educations appropriate for their roles at the top of public life. (All *T* are *A*)

Stated conclusion: All persons who make it to the top of public life in Britain are persons from expensive private schools. (All *T* are *E*)
By adding the missing premise that all *A* are *E*, the statements can be turned into a valid syllogism. To see why it is valid, compare the answer to question 7 above; the two arguments are formally identical.

13. With additions, this passage may be cast as two syllogisms. The context—namely that the author is writing about Canada—is used to supply them. *N* represents nations permitting the showing of violence night after night and not permitting the showing of love-making scenes. *C* represents nations that are Canada, *P* represents nations that are guilty of practicing obscenity and hypocrisy. *W* represents things without redeeming social value.
The first syllogism is: All *N* are *P*;
all *C* are *N* (inserted);
therefore,
all *C* are *P*.
(This is valid.)
The second syllogism is: All *C* are *P*;
all *P* are *W* (inserted);
therefore,
all *C* are *W*.
In this case, insertions are made due, first to the immediate inference made from the hypocrisy and obscenity to being without redeeming social value, and second to the strongly implied criticism of Canada, in the context. (The second syllogism is also valid.)
Whether these are cogent arguments will depend, then, entirely on our appraisal of the premises.

CHAPTER 8

Exercise 1: Part A

4. *F* represents "Fred will come." *S* represents "Susan will come." *O* represents "The outing will be a success." *J* represents "Joe will enjoy himself."
$F \lor S$
$F \supset O$
$S \supset J$

8. *E* represents "Extensive public relations efforts are being made on behalf of the nuclear industry"; *C* represents "Efforts being made on behalf of the nuclear industry are convincing the public."

$E \cdot -C$
$(E \vee C) \supset T$
So,
T

Exercise 1: Part B

2. *M* represents "You master calculus"; *D* represents "You have some difficulty with the mathematical aspects of first year university physics." The argument can then be represented as:

$M \supset -D$
M
Therefore,
$-D$

M	D	-D	M⊃-D
T	T	F	F
T	F	T	T
F	T	F	T
F	F	T	T

The argument is valid. There is no row where the conclusion is false and the premises are true.

8. *S* represents "You are a suitable student of philosophy of science"; *K* represents "You know philosophy"; *C* represents "You know science." The argument can then be represented as:

$S \supset (K \vee C)$
$-K \cdot -C$
Therefore,
$-S$

S	K	C	-S	-K	-C	-K·-C	K∨C	S⊃(K∨C)
T	T	T	F	F	F	F	T	T
T	T	F	F	F	T	F	T	T
T	F	T	F	T	F	F	T	T
T	F	F	F	T	T	T	F	F
F	T	T	T	F	F	F	T	T
F	T	F	T	F	T	F	T	T
F	F	T	T	T	F	F	T	T
F	F	F	T	T	T	T	F	T

The argument is valid. There is no row where the conclusion is false and the premises are true.

9. *E* represents "John exercises"; *G* represents "John is in good shape." The argument can then be represented as:

$E \supset G$
G
Therefore,
E

E	G	E⊃G	
T	T	T	
T	F	F	
(F)	(T)	(T)	Premises true. Conclusion false.
F	F	T	

The argument is invalid.

10. Let *N* represent "The negotiations will be successful," *C* represent "The problem will continue to be unresolved with the situation at a standoff," and *E* represent "The situation will escalate into violence." The argument is then represented as:

$(N \vee C) \vee E$
N
Therefore,
$-C$

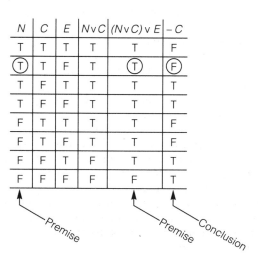

N	C	E	N∨C	(N∨C)∨E	-C
T	T	T	T	T	F
(T)	T	F	T	(T)	(F)
T	F	T	T	T	T
T	F	F	T	T	T
F	T	T	T	T	F
F	T	F	T	T	F
F	F	T	F	T	T
F	F	F	F	F	T

Premise   Premise   Conclusion

It is invalid, as is apparent from the second row of the truth table, where the premises are true and the conclusion is false.

Exercise 1: Part C

1. $S \supset L$; $L \supset B$; $B \supset H$; S; therefore, H.
This argument is valid. Set H as false. In order for the fourth premise to be true, S must be true. If S is true, L must be true in order for the first premise to be true. If L is true, B must be true in order for the second premise to be true. But if B is true, then H must be true in order for the third premise to be true. This stipulation is inconsistent with our assumption that H was false. There is no consistent assignment of truth values to the component statements that will make the premises true and the conclusion false.

3. $-(M \cdot H)$; therefore, $-M \vee -H$.
This argument is valid. For the conclusion to be false, both M and H have to be true. If M and H are both true, the premise is false. Thus the premise cannot be true while the conclusion is false.

5. $K \vee U$; $U \supset (L \vee N)$; $-N$; $L \supset (V \vee -W)$; $-L \cdot K$; therefore, $-W$.
K represents "The murderer used a kitchen knife"; U represents "The murderer carried an unusually large pocket knife"; L represents "The murderer was wearing loose clothes"; N represents "The murderer would have been noticed"; V represents "The murderer was very thin"; and W represents "The murderer was wearing clothes found at the scene of the crime."
To test by the shorter truth table technique, set the conclusion false; that is, W is true. Then, set N, L, and K false to make the premises $-N$, $-L$, and $-K$ come out as true. If K is false, U must be true to make the first premise true. If U is true then either L or N must be true, to make the second premise true. But both L and N have been set as false. Hence it is not possible to consistently assign truth values so that the premises come out true and the conclusion false. The argument is valid.

Exercise 2: Part A

5. $\{(P \cdot C) \vee (C \cdot B) \vee (B \cdot P)\} \supset -(F \cdot G)$
$\{(C \vee P) \cdot (C \vee B)\} \supset \{(F \vee G) \cdot -(F \cdot G)\}$
where P represents "you take physics"; C "you take chemistry"; B "you take biology"; F "you take French"; and G "you take German."

8. $(-R \cdot D) \supset (C \vee E)$
$(C \supset A) \cdot (T \supset S)$
$-G \supset (A \vee S)$
So,
$-R \supset -D$
Here R represents "land claims are resolved"; D represents "native leaders continue to distrust the government"; C represents "there will be continued nonviolent blockades"; E represents "there will be an escalation of the problem into terrorist action"; A represents "antagonism between whites and natives will increase"; S represents "the whole country will be adversely affected in a most serious way."

Exercise 2: Part B

3. O represents "The operation was painful"; L represents "The operation was pleasant." The argument is:
$-O$
$O \vee L$
Therefore,
L

O	L	$-O$	$O \vee L$
T	T	F	T
T	F	F	I
F	T	T	T
F	F	T	F

The argument is valid. There is no row where the conclusion is false and the premises are true. Note that you need two statement letters, because "The operation was pleasant" and "The operation was painful" are not contradictory statements. They could both be false.

8. $D \lor M$; $R \supset -M$; R; therefore, $-M \cdot D$.

Valid. For the conclusion to be false, either M must be true or D must be false. If M is true, the first premise is true. Then, for the second premise to be true, R must be false. Given these assignments, the third premise will be false. If D is false, then M must be true in order to make the first premise true. Then R must be false in order for the second premise to be true, and, as before, this case will result in the third premise being false. It is not possible to make the premises true and conclusions false; therefore, the argument is valid.

15. $(S \cdot I) \supset A$; $S \cdot I$; therefore, A.

Valid. For the conclusion to be false, either S or I will have to be false in order for the first premise to be true. But given this, you cannot make the second premise true.

17. $W \supset B$; $B \supset U$; $U \supset A$; therefore, $W \supset A$.

Valid. For the conclusion to be false, A must be false and W true. Then given W as true, B must be true for the first premise to be true. Given B true, U must be true for the second premise to be true. Given U true, A would have to be true for the third premise to be true. But A has been assigned as false. You can't make the premises true and the conclusion false.

19. $D \supset S$; $S \supset L$; $L \supset G$; therefore, $D \supset G$.

Second argument: $(D \supset G) \supset U$; $D \supset G$ (taken from first argument); therefore, U.

Both are valid. For the first argument, see the answer to question 17, where the argument is one of the same form. For the second argument, to make the conclusion false, U must be false. Then, to make the first premise true, $(D \supset G)$ must be false. But this assignment makes the second premise false.

Exercise 3

1. E represents "Elephants have been known to bury their dead"; C represents "Elephants have a concept of their own species"; U represents "Elephants understand what death means"; S represents "Elephants have a substantial capacity for abstraction."

The argument is:

E
$E \supset (C \cdot U)$
$U \supset S$
Therefore,
S

E	C	U	S	$C \cdot U$	$E \supset (C \cdot U)$	$U \supset S$
T	T	T	T	T	T	T
T	T	T	F	T	T	F
T	T	F	T	F	F	T
T	T	F	F	F	F	T
T	F	T	T	F	F	T
T	F	T	F	F	F	F
T	F	F	T	F	F	T
T	F	F	F	F	F	T
F	T	T	T	T	T	T
F	T	T	F	T	T	F
F	T	F	T	F	T	T
F	T	F	F	F	T	T
F	F	T	T	F	T	T
F	F	T	F	F	T	F
F	F	F	T	F	T	T
F	F	F	F	F	T	T

The argument is valid.

3. $J \supset M$; $-J$; therefore, $-M$.

Not valid. The conclusion is true if M is false. With M false, the first premise is true if J is false. If J is false, the second premise is true.

Alternate symbolization: $J \supset M$; $-J$; therefore, R.

This argument is not valid, obviously. The alternative results if we note that, strictly speaking, the stated conclusion is not the contradictory of M, where M is "Joe becomes more attractive to women." (The contradictory is that Joe does not become more attractive to women.)

5. $-R \supset -S$; $-R \supset A$; $A \supset -G$; therefore, $-R \supset -G$.

The argument can be shown valid by the shorter truth table technique. To make the conclusion false, − G must be false, and − R must be true. That means G must be true and R must be false. If G is true, for the third premise to be true, A must be false. If A is false, for the second premise to be true, − R must be false, which means R must be true. But we already stipulated R as false in order to make the conclusion false. Thus, there is no consistent assignment of true values that makes the conclusion false and the premises true. The argument is valid.

7. W represents "Workers agree not to strike within the next decade"; D represents "Prospects for the recovery of the plant are dim"; M represents "Management agrees to forego special parking and washroom privileges." In this context, "management does its part" is taken to mean that management agrees to forego special parking and washroom privileges and is thus represented by M. The argument is:

$-W \supset D$

$-M \supset -W$

Therefore,

$-D \supset M$

D	W	M	−D	−W	−M	−W⊃D	−M⊃−W	−D⊃M
T	T	T	F	F	F	I	T	T
T	T	F	F	F	I	T	F	T
T	F	I	F	T	F	T	T	T
T	F	F	F	T	T	T	T	T
F	I	I	I	F	F	T	T	T
F	T	F	T	F	T	T	F	F
F	F	T	T	T	F	F	T	T
F	F	F	T	T	T	F	T	F

The argument is valid.

12. M represents "Morality has a basis"; G represents "there is a god"; W represents "The world makes sense"; O represents "The world is ordered." The argument is:

$M \supset G$

$G \supset (W \cdot O)$

O

Therefore,

M

M	G	W	O	M⊃G	W·O	G⊃(W·O)
T	T	T	T	T	T	T
T	T	T	F	T	F	F
T	T	F	T	T	F	F
T	T	F	F	T	F	F
T	F	T	T	F	T	T
T	F	T	F	F	F	T
T	F	F	T	F	F	T
T	F	F	F	F	F	T
(F)	T	T	(T)	(T)	T	(T)
F	T	T	F	T	F	F
(F)	T	F	(T)	(T)	F	(T)
F	T	F	F	T	F	T
(F)	F	T	(T)	(T)	T	(T)
F	F	T	F	T	F	T
(F)	F	F	(T)	(T)	T	(T)
F	F	F	F	T	T	⊢

The argument is not valid.

13. Let I represent "Television programs improve in quality and appeal"; L represent "Large networks will lose their markets to video"; B represent "Programming budgeting increases"; and A "Advertisers are willing to pay more." The argument is then represented as:

$I \lor L$

$I \supset B$

$-A \supset -B$

$A \cdot (A \supset -B)$

$-I$

Therefore,

L

The argument is valid. We cannot make the premises all true and the conclusion false. For the conclusion to be false, L would have to be false. Then, for the first premise to be true, I must be true. If I is true, B must be true, in order for the second premise to be true. But the last premise requires that I, which has been assigned as true, must be false. Hence the argument is valid.

15. Let C represent "the comedian is funny"; L represent "people laugh at the comedian"; P represent "the comedian gets paid"; H represent "the comedian is happy." To formalize the argument requires a little ingenuity.

$F \supset L$
$-F \supset -L$
$(-F \supset P) \cdot (F \supset P) \cdot (L \supset P) \cdot (-L \supset P)$
P
$P \supset H$
Therefore,
$-L \supset H$

We can use the shorter truth table method to show the argument is valid. To make the conclusion false, set H false and $-L$ true—that is, L false. Then, for the first premise to be true, F must be false. The second premise then is true, because $-L$ is true; we must set P as true in order to make the fourth premise true. Given P as true, H must be true, due to the fifth premise. However, H has already been set as false. So the assignment cannot be made consistently. The argument is valid.

18. The passage does not express an argument.

Exercise 4: Part A

2. 1. $A \cdot -B$
2. $-B \supset C$ / (C is to be proven)
3. $-B$ from (1) by Simplification
4. C from (3) and (2) by *Modus Ponens*

5. 1. $(A \vee B) \supset D$
2. $-D$
3. $-B \supset (A \supset X)$
4. $(A \cdot B) \vee X$ / (X is to be proven)

You can struggle for quite a while and not manage to prove X from the given premises. (If you think you have done it, check your work. We'll bet you have made a mistake.)

In fact, this argument is invalid. If we assign X false, D false, A false, and B false, we can make all the premises true while the conclusion is false.

7. 1. $(D \cdot E) \supset (F \vee G)$
2. $-D \supset F$
3. $-(D \vee E)$ / ($F \vee G$ is to be proven)
4. $-D \cdot -E$ from (3) by De Morgan
5. $-D$ from (4) by Simplification
6. F from (2) and (5) by *Modus Ponens*
7. $F \vee G$ from (6) by Addition

9. 1. $A \supset B$
2. $C \supset D$
3. $(B \vee D) \supset E$
4. $-E$
(to be proven: $-A \vee C$)
5. $-(B \vee D)$ from (3) and (4) by *Modus Tollens*
6. $-B \cdot -D$ from (5) by De Morgan
7. $-B$ from (6) by Simplification
8. $-A$ from (7) and (1) by *Modus Tollens*
9. $-A \vee C$ from (8) by Addition

Exercise 4: Part B

4. 1. $O \supset I$
2. $-I$
Therefore,
$-O$

We can easily derive the stated conclusion $-O$ from premises (1) and (2). In fact, it takes one line:

3. $-O$ (1) and (2) by *Modus Tollens*

The only trick in this example is in formalizing; we have to see that the second premise negates the consequent of the first.

6. Let S represent "the food crisis is solved," R represent "the rich nations share their food," and P represent "the poor nations will force the world economy to provide them with more."

1. $S \supset (R \vee P)$
2. $-R$ / (to be proven, $S \supset P$)
3. S Assume
4. $R \vee P$ from (3) and (4) by *Modus Ponens*
5. P from (4) and (2) by Disjunctive Syllogism
6. $S \supset P$ from (2)–(5) by Conditional Proof

8. Let K represent "I know this pencil exists" and let H represent "Hume's principles are true."

1. K
2. $H \supset -K$ / (to be proven, $-H$)
3. $--K$ from (1) by Double Negation
4. $-H$ from (3) and (2) by *Modus Tollens*

12. S represents "The group will be successful"; W represents "All members of the group participate willingly"; M represents "Members of the group have a say in top-level decision making." The argument is:

1. $S \supset W$

2. $W \supset M$
3. M
Therefore,
4. S

S	W	M	$S \supset W$	$W \supset M$
T	T	T	T	T
T	T	F	T	F
T	F	T	F	T
T	F	F	F	T
(F)	T	(T)	(T)	(T)
F	T	F	T	F
(F)	F	(T)	(T)	(T)
F	F	F	T	T

The argument is not valid.

14. Let B represent "She can become a good mathematician"; S represent "She studies hard"; L represent "Her family life is happy"; H represent "Her general health is good"; E represent "She gets exercise"; and D represent "She gets decent food."

1. $B \supset S$
2. $S \supset (L \cdot H)$
3. $H \supset (E \cdot D)$
4. $E \cdot - D$ / (to be proven, $-B$)
5. $B \supset (L \cdot H)$ from (1) and (2) by Hypothetical Syllogism
6. B Assume
7. $L \cdot H$ from (5) and (6) by *Modus Ponens*
8. H from (7) by Simplification
9. $B \supset H$ from (6)–(8) by Conditional Proof
10. $B \supset (E \cdot D)$ from (9) and (3) by Hypothetical Syllogism
11. $- E$
12. $- E \lor - D$ from (11) by Addition
13. $-(E \cdot D)$ from (12) by De Morgan
14. $- B$ from (10) and (13) by *Modus Tollens*

CHAPTER 9

Exercise 1: Part A

1. The primary subject is the argument that Japanese corporations are more fairly run than American ones because decisions are typically reached by teams rather than by individuals. The analogue is the argument that a hypothetical South African judicial system might make decisions by teams, while still applying laws that are unfair to blacks. The premises of the primary argument are acceptable, and it is genuinely similar to the analogue argument in that the key feature of having groups, rather than individuals, make decisions is retained. The analogue shows that more than group procedure is needed for fairness. This is a successful refutation by logical analogy of the original argument.

4. The primary subject is the argument that we should not love people of the same sex because God did not intend us to, which, in turn, is inferred from the fact that God made two sexes. The analogue argument is that we should not wear clothes because God did not intend us to, which He presumably did not because He caused us to be born naked. The premises in both arguments are acceptable provided we grant that God exists. (If we disagree that God exists, we will not follow the primary subject argument through at all, so it will not need the refutation by logical analogy, which is aimed at the (R) and (G) conditions.) The arguments are similar in both making obvious statements about what God would have created, granted that He did create us at all. The analogue argument is relevant to the primary argument because the two are closely parallel in their inferences of God's intentions from the way things are in nature and in their inference about what people should do given God's intentions. There are no relevant differences undermining the logical analogy; hence the (G) condition is also met. The refutation is successful.

5. The primary subject is the argument that a disarmament referendum should not be held because nearly everyone would support disarmament. The analogue is the argument that a mayoralty election should not be held because nearly everyone would vote for the same candidate. The premise in the primary subject argument is not acceptable. In fact, results on such referenda have varied. Some people oppose disarmament for a variety of reasons, and they have indicated this on referenda, which (when held in Canada in 1982–84) gave results varying from

60 percent in favor to 97 percent in favor. Mayoralty elections are regular occurrences that are held as constitutionally required, regardless of the popularity of candidates. Referenda are special votes on issues that are especially important, divisive, or crucial in certain contexts. These differences undermine the parallel. The refutation by logical analogy does not work, but the original argument that it is intended to criticize can be seen to be poor because its premises are unacceptable.

Exercise 1: Part B

3. The primary subject is Trudeau's continuing as prime minister and liberal leader when Canada had a troubled economy and the opposition was said (by Trudeau) to be fumbling. The analogue is a doctor's continuing as a patient's doctor when that patient is sick and the doctor down the street is fumbling. Trudeau's point was that you wouldn't change doctors, so you shouldn't change prime ministers. Trudeau's argument is poor. In terms of acceptability of premises, we should not accept on his testimony or authority that the opposition is fumbling (conflict of interest). Also, his assumption, built into the analogue case, that a patient does not change his doctor when sick, may be questioned. A desperate patient might change doctors, even if the doctor down the street had given signs of fumbling. More fundamentally, however, the analogy can be challenged for its relevance. The two relationships (politician, country; patient, doctor) are too different for a convincing analogy. A doctor is a qualified trained professional in a one-on-one relationship with a patient. A politician is an elected person, rarely chosen mainly for competence. Furthermore, there are no clear standards for the health and management of an economy as there are for a sick person. There is no reason to trust a political leader as you would a doctor.

6. This passage does not contain an argument or an analogy. It is a report of problems with these toads.

7. This passage is a logical analogy. The primary subject is the argument that the anti-Holocaust book should be in the library because both sides of an issue should be represented there. There are two different analogues. One analogue is a choice of both the *National Enquirer* and the *Times* of London for two accounts of historical and current events. This case would be ridiculous, and seen so by library staff. Similarly (second analogue), there is the matter of having clever drawings by the Flat Earth Society to offer as an alternative to globes, for geography. This too would be ridiculous, and seen so by library staff. A buttressing argument, not based on analogy, is that there is very good testimony and documentation to show that the Holocaust occurred. This documentation is the basis (acceptability condition) for claiming that stocking anti-Holocaust books would be doing something as ridiculous as the two analogues. The primary subject and the two analogues all share the feature that what might seem to be "two sides" are not equally sensible "sides"; they differ vastly in credibility. The argument appeals successfully to consistency and shows that ideas of representing two sides are not sufficient reason for the library to stock anti-Holocaust books.

12. The primary subject is the nuclear arms race and the desirability of the nuclear freeze, especially the argument that the United States should continue the arms race because the Soviets are ahead in some categories. The analogue is the case of two powerful cars headed for a crash. The crash is compared to a nuclear war, the putting on of the brakes to a freeze, and cutbacks in weaponry to a reversal of the cars so that they move away from each other. Drawing the analogy presupposes that a nuclear war is an inevitable result if the nuclear arms race continues. This assumption may strike many of us as terrifyingly plausible, but it needs support because many experts and insiders would firmly deny it. If the assumption is not granted, the analogy will seem irrelevant because we won't believe there is any clash to be avoided. Barring this difficulty, the analogy is close enough to be relevant. But the analogy breaks down in that, with the cars, putting on the brakes is necessary and sufficient to avoid the clash, whereas in the nuclear scene,

just stopping the making of more weapons may not be necessary and is surely not sufficient to avoid a nuclear war. The analogy is a stronger argument if taken as a rebuttal against another common argument regarding the freeze, namely, that a freeze is not good enough because we need drastic cuts. The point would then be that you have to stop making more arms before cutting back, just as you have to stop a car (brake) before reversing.

Exercise 2

5. This passage contains an inductive analogy. The comparison is between an individual who may abuse power (the analogue) and a majority of a group of individuals (the primary subject) who, it is inferred, might abuse power. The point is that because (for the analogue) it would not be reasonable to give absolute power to an individual, neither would it be reasonable to give absolute power to a majority (the primary subject). This argument seems to be a strong one because the differences that do exist between groups and individuals do not undermine the basic similarity on which the argument depends: their capacity to abuse power.

7. This argument is not really an inductive analogy; it is an a priori analogy. The primary subject is giving your money to Foster Parents Plan, which the argument urges you to do. The analogue is helping, on the basis of emotion and instinct, a lost child who is in tears. You are urged to support Foster Parents Plan out of consistency with what would be your instinctive emotional response to a hurt child. Relevant differences between the cases are that you do not encounter the child Foster Parents Plan would direct you to; you have to depend on their organization to direct you to the right child and to administer the money you give. Though these tasks may in fact be well done by Foster Parents Plan, the fact that you depend on an institutional network in the primary case and not in the analogue case constitutes a difference that undermines the analogy; your instinctive emotional response to a lost child says nothing about the reliability of the institutions, which is crucial in

the rationality of giving money to Foster Parents Plan.

8. The analogue is athletes and the primary subject is officials in athletic competitions. The two are urged to be similar, as human beings who are not perfect; the conclusion is, in fact, quite modest, urging only that officials should not be expected to be perfect. The analogy does give adequate support for this conclusion.

11. This passage does contain an analogy, but it is not clear that the analogy is part of an argument. The analogue is a monarch who makes judgments and decrees all by himself. The primary subject is the person who thinks for himself, who makes judgments without attending to popular opinions and prejudices. Clearly, the tone of the passage and choice of analogue show that Schopenhauer is in favor of thinking for yourself. However, it does not appear that the analogy is put forward as a reason for this view; it seems more like a vivid way of stating the view.

13. This passage does not contain an argument. A vivid image is developed, in which the thought is regarded as a developing fruit.

Exercise 3

3. There are two analogues here as well as a primary subject. The primary subject is the argument that since the majority of women are kind to children and prefer their own children to other people's, women's proper sphere of activity is "the nursery" (taking care of their own children). The first analogue is as above, except that it substitutes men for women. When this substitution is made, the argument is one no one would accept. The second analogue is as above, except that it substitutes dogs for children. Again, nobody would take the analogue seriously. From the two analogue arguments and the fact that they are parallel in structure to the primary argument, it is inferred that the primary argument is a poor argument.

8. This passage contains an analogy between funds and supporting evidence but does not contain any argument based on this analogy.

10. This passage illustrates the fallacy of slippery assimilation. Because the destruction of a litter

of puppies is similar to the opening of a score of oysters, which in turn is similar to killing a moth, Carroll contends that we cannot draw a line between these three actions. Either all of these actions are morally permissible, or all are morally wrong. This conclusion is based on slippery assimilation. Carroll infers that all killings of animals by humans are morally permissible, provided the deaths are painless.

13. The conclusion is that animals may think about fictitious objects and events. Part of the support for this conclusion comes from a premise that is about animal behavior (the apparent playfulness of apes and porpoises) and does not depend on an analogy. However, part comes from an analogy with humans. In this part of the argument animals are the primary subject, and humans are the analogue. This appears to be an inductive analogy; however, it is flawed because of the immense differences between animals and humans with regard to such relevant features as culture, complexity of language, and sophistication of brain. Thus, part of the argument only appeals to an inductive analogy; the direct nonanalogous part of the argument is more cogent.

CHAPTER 10

Exercise 1

2. There are three supporting premises for the final statement, which is the conclusion. The first and third are qualified, with "some" and, as such, are acceptable as known on the basis of common experience. The second is more controversial, but even if acceptable, it is not relevant since in fact governments do not give full support to the needy and their need is a present fact, regardless of what governments ought to do. The third premise is not relevant to whether you should give to charity; it is about the quality of ads. There are many counterconsiderations not mentioned in the argument: how needy people are, the fact that their needs may go unmet if you do not give to charity, the fact that other uses you might have for your money are often trivial compared to people's needs, and the sense of social contribution and self-worth that you may

derive from giving to charity. The single relevant supporting conclusion is not enough to outweigh these. The argument falls down on (A), on (R), and on (G); it is a weak argument.

6. The conclusion is that there is no free will. There are two converging strands of argument: one about causation, the other about people acting out of control. Both are positively relevant to the conclusion. One counterconsideration, having to do with religious people holding that God has given people free will, is considered, but it is countered fairly successfully by the arguer. The argument is lacking in cogency because the (G) condition is not satisfied. We can see this in several ways. The conclusion is very categorical: there is *no* free will. Yet one line of argument holds that it is almost certain nothing is uncaused ("almost" is not enough for such a sweeping conclusion) and the other shows only, through the example of alcoholics, that people *sometimes* lack control over their actions. Taken together these are not sufficient, or adequate grounds: (G) is not met. And this problem becomes more clear when we consider that older counterconsiderations, not mentioned by the arguer, bear on the issue. For instance, the cause of many actions is not known, and physical science in its most modern form, does not assume that for every event there is a fully sufficient cause.

7. The conclusion is stated first and reiterated later in slightly different words. ("The American Revolution should not be thought of as a model for other revolutions.") The second, third, and fourth sentences give supporting premises. The next sentence contains two counterconsiderations. The sixth sentence adds two practical reasons for not taking the American Revolution as a model—underestimating the role of the poor and failing to see potential for violence. The first three supporting premises are acceptable and could be verified as such by checking standard sources on American history. The fourth supporting premise (requiring that the poor are very significant in revolutions) is plausible on the basis of common reports about revolutions around the world today, but they could be checked against accounts of revolution by historians and political scientists. The same may be said about

the fifth supporting premise (real potential for violence). The supporting premises are relevant to the conclusion provided we grant the assumption behind the argument: that a typical revolution involves moves, often violent, by the poorer classes to upset a social structure. Of the two stated counterconsiderations, the second (that the American Revolution is of great historical importance) is not negatively relevant to the conclusion: it is irrelevant. The first counterconsideration is obviously true and is relevant, but it is far too slight to outweigh the supporting considerations. As stated the argument satisfies (A) and (R) and seems to satisfy (G). Whether there are more counterconsiderations that outweigh the premises seems unlikely, but we could consult accounts of revolution by historians and political scientists to find out.

11. The conclusion is the first sentence, and it is also restated at the end. It is ambiguous; *trustworthy* may mean either that the document reliably transmits words and claims made in ancient texts, or it may mean (more ambitiously) that the claims made in the document (Bible) are true and really describe events that occurred. A number of premises are relevant to the conclusion only on the first interpretation and not on the second. The argument has two main converging branches: one gives reasoning pertaining to the New Testament, the other to the Old Testament. The evidence about the New Testament would show, if accepted, that the words are close to the words of documents written 20–70 years after Christ's life. To check the acceptability of the premises we would have to look up New Testament scholarship and classical scholarship. However, we note that all points made about the New Testament are relevant only to the conclusion in the less ambitious interpretation of its meaning, not to the other interpretation. As for the evidence about the Old Testament, the same comments apply, except for the claim about the expert. That claim embodies a faulty appeal to authority, in that experts differ on the matter; the expert may have a vested interest in converting people, and furthermore, the name of the expert is not mentioned so that the claim is too vague to verify. To find detailed counterevidence,

sources in classics and Old and New Testament scholarship would be needed. However, a major counterconsideration against the conclusion in the more ambitious sense is that people are strongly moved by emotion when in the presence of such figures as Jesus and may not be reliable observers of the nature and causes of events. The argument is weak if we interpret the conclusion in the ambitious sense. If we interpret the conclusion in the less ambitious sense, as being only about the reliable transmission of texts, the argument may be strong, but accuracy of the premises would have to be checked.

Exercise 2

1. There is an inductive argument based on an inductive analogy between people and cats; the conclusion is that cats probably dream.

4. There is a causal inductive argument; the conclusion is that smoking marijuana causes heroin use. (We will see later that this is a faulty causal argument.)

7. The argument is inductive; it is a restricted enumerative inductive generalization. On the basis of Canadians and others surveyed in 1982 there is a generalization about most people in these groups in 1982; then there is a further generalization to most people in these groups in 1990.

10. This is an inductive argument to a singular conclusion. The conclusion is that Smith's views on economics are probably unsound.

13. There is a restricted enumerative inductive generalization, from various cases of flaws (university residence, stores, hospital, subway) to a conclusion about most of the key institutions.

Exercise 3: Part A

2. This factor would make your argument weaker because you do not have variety in your sample. You have sampled one place only; perhaps the creatures you have seen are only in this valley and the other creatures on Mars are quite different.

5. These aspects weaken your inference that all Martian creatures are gray; in fact, that hypoth-

esis is conclusively refuted by your new observations. On the other hand, the hypothesis that Martian creatures can make high sounds is further confirmed; you now have better evidence for it, and a more varied sample on which you base that conclusion.

8. The argument is weakened; you have reason, in this case, to question your own observations. Your condition (light-headedness and ringing in the ears) makes you an unreliable observer in this case. These may be symptoms that you are unwell, or the ringing in your ears may affect the accuracy of your perception in this case. Furthermore, it is so implausible that any Martian creature would know how to sing the earthly tune of "Jingle Bells" that you should conclude, from what you seem to hear, that you were dreaming or hallucinating.

9. Your inferences with regard to both color and sound emission are weakened.

Exercise 3: Part B

2. The sample is 500 midwestern students who had a bilingual education in Spanish and English. The target population is all people given a bilingual education. The sample is insufficiently varied; those surveyed all studied the same two languages and were from the same part of the world. The argument is a statistical enumerative induction. Due to flaws in the sample, it is quite weak.

3. The statistical principles cited could not apply unless the sample were truly random. The authors appear, in their comments, to claim representativeness and randomness. This is not correct, theoretically speaking. The method of selecting subjects did not, in any event, guarantee representativeness, because the contexts chosen would overly represent employed, married, middle-class men, and the need for researchers to approach men would overly represent neat, unthreatening, cooperative men.

5. There is an enumerative induction. The population is young people in Canada between 12 and 17. The sample is those 70 or 80 young people between 12 and 17 who were questioned in the study. The sample is too small. The argument

is also infected by the vagueness in the term "expressing interest" and by possible reliability problems in responding to interviews on such sensitive topics.

7. The sample is four countries: Ireland, India, Vietnam, and Korea. The population is all countries with (serious) religious, ethnic, or ideological conflict—serious enough for partition to be a significant possibility. It is hard to say how large this population would be—at least twenty countries, perhaps more. Though the sample is small it is varied. The argument is a restricted enumerative inductive generalization. There are two conclusions: that partition is a poor method of resolving conflicts in these countries and that partition is likely to inspire future fighting in these countries. In view of the variety in the sample and the fact that the population is not huge, the argument could be regarded as based on a moderately strong inference.

Exercise 4

5. There are causal claims made about the improvement in manpower in the American armed forces. First the author makes a negative causal claim. The improvements don't result from increased spending. The reasons are that quality has gone up more than spending, which has gone up by less than 20 percent. (The premise is not acceptable because it involves implicit pseudoprecision: we cannot precisely quantify an increase in quality.) If acceptable, it would be relevant but it would show only that increased spending is not the sole cause of the improvement. A positive causal claim is made in the last sentence, where the author hypothesizes three factors—recession, de-civilianization, and nationalistic pride—as causally contributing to the improvement in the forces. No evidence is given for this conclusion. The whole argument assumes that the quality of manpower in the armed forces has improved very much, and this assumption is something for which evidence could surely have been given if, indeed, it is true at all.

6. This passage does not contain an argument. The authors describe a phenomenon that they say has been given little attention and is puz-

zling. They do not argue for any explanation of it; nor are there any inductive arguments of any other kind.

10. There is a causal claim implicit in "He has left." The passage says that the presence of John Wayne in the American imagination has resulted in broken hearts and jaws (presumably figuratively, in movies) and (more seriously) in millions of injured male egos. The only evidence given is that no real man could measure up to John Wayne's image. This evidence is relevant only if we assume that real men were trying to measure up to that image—something we do not know. The causal claim is not adequately supported.

11. The passage is jocular in tone and probably not meant seriously. Two correlational claims are made: that highly educated people with low incomes catch colds more frequently than others do, and that more people catch colds on Monday than on other days. The article makes a (probably nonserious) suggestion, on the basis of the correlational data, that colds are caused by dissatisfaction with one's job. The reasoning would not be adequate, but probably this passage does not contain serious reasoning from correlated data to a causal conclusion.

INDEX